MICROCOMPUTER SERVICING
Practical Systems and Troubleshooting
SECOND EDITION

Stuart Asser, PE

Queensborough Community College of the City University of New York

Vincent Stigliano, PE

Queensborough Community College of the City University of New York

Richard Bahrenburg

Grumman Data Systems Corporation

Merrill, an imprint of
Macmillan Publishing Company
New York

Maxwell Macmillan Canada
Toronto

Maxwell Macmillan International
New York   Oxford   Singapore   Sydney

Cover photo: Chip Jamison Photography
Editor: Dave Garza
Production Editor: Stephen C. Robb
Art Coordinator: Lorraine Woost
Cover Designer: Thomas Mack
Production Buyer: Patricia A. Tonneman

Photo credit: Page xviii (top photo). Courtesy of International
Business Machines Corporation.

This book was set in Times Roman and Univers Condensed by
Bi-Comp, Inc. and was printed and bound by Book Press, a Quebecor
America Book Group Company. The cover was printed by Lehigh
Press, Inc.

The Publisher offers discounts on this book when ordered in bulk
quantities. For more information, write to: Special Sales
Department, Macmillan Publishing Company, 445 Hutchinson Avenue,
Columbus, OH 43235, or call 1-800/228-7854.

Macmillan Publishing Company
866 Third Avenue
New York, NY 10022

Macmillan Publishing Company is part of the
Maxwell Communications Group of Companies.

Maxwell Macmillan Canada, Inc.
1200 Eglinton Avenue East, Suite 200
Don Mills, Ontario M3C 3N1

Library of Congress Cataloging-in-Publication Data
Asser, Stuart.
   Microcomputer servicing; practical systems and troubleshooting /
Stuart M. Asser, Vincent J. Stigliano, Richard F. Bahrenburg.—2nd ed.
      p.   cm.
   Includes index.
   ISBN 0-02-304241-9
   1. Microcomputers—Maintenance and repair.   I. Stigliano,
Vincent.   II. Bahrenburg, Richard.   III. Title.
TK7887.A878   1993
621.39′16—dc20
                                                    92-26681
                                                    CIP

Printing: 2 3 4 5 6 7 8 9   Year: 4 5 6

MERRILL'S INTERNATIONAL SERIES IN ENGINEERING TECHNOLOGY

Programming

Adamson, *Applied Pascal for Technology,*
0-675-20771-1
Adamson, *Structured BASIC Applied to Technology, 2nd
Edition,* 0-02-300827-X
Adamson, *Structured C for Technology,* 0-675-20993-5
Adamson, *Structured C for Technology (with disk),*
0-675-21289-8
Nashelsky & Boylestad, *BASIC Applied to Circuit
Analysis,* 0-675-20161-6

Instrumentation and Measurement

Berlin & Getz, *Principles of Electronic Instrumentation
and Measurement,* 0-675-20449-6
Buchla & McLachlan, *Applied Electronic Instrumentation
and Measurement,* 0-675-21162-X
Gillies, *Instrumentation and Measurements for Electronic
Technicians, 2nd Edition,* 0-02-343051-6

Transform Analysis

Kulathinal, *Transform Analysis and Electronic Networks
with Applications,* 0-675-20765-7

Biomedical Equipment Technology

Aston, *Principles of Biomedical Instrumentation and
Measurement,* 0-675-20943-9

Mathematics

Monaco, *Essential Mathematics for Electronics
Technicians,* 0-675-21172-7
Davis, *Technical Mathematics,* 0-675-20338-4
Davis, *Technical Mathematics with Calculus,*
0-675-20965-X

INDUSTRIAL ELECTRONICS/
INDUSTRIAL TECHNOLOGY

Bateson, *Introduction to Control System Technology, 4th
Edition,* 0-02-306463-3
Fuller, *Robotics: Introduction, Programming, and Projects,*
0-675-21078-X
Goetsch, *Industrial Safety and Health: In the Age of High
Technology,* 0-02-344207-7
Goetsch, *Industrial Supervision: In the Age of High
Technology,* 0-675-22137-4
Horath, *Computer Numerical Control Programming of
Machines,* 0-02-357201-9
Hubert, *Electric Machines: Theory, Operation, Applications,
Adjustment, and Control,* 0-675-20765-7
Humphries, *Motors and Controls,* 0-675-20235-3
Hutchins, *Introduction to Quality: Management, Assurance,
and Control,* 0-675-20896-3
Laviana, *Basic Computer Numerical Control Programming,*
0-675-21298-7

Reis, *Electronic Project Design and Fabrication, 2nd Edition,*
0-02-399230-1
Rosenblatt & Friedman, *Direct and Alternating Current
Machinery, 2nd Edition,* 0-675-20160-8
Smith, *Statistical Process Control and Quality Improvement,*
0-675-21160-3
Webb, *Programmable Logic Controllers: Principles and
Applications, 2nd Edition,* 0-02-424970-X
Webb & Greshock, *Industrial Control Electronics, 2nd Edition,*
0-02-424864-9

MECHANICAL/CIVIL TECHNOLOGY

Keyser, *Materials Science in Engineering, 4th Edition,*
0-675-20401-1
Kraut, *Fluid Mechanics for Technicians,* 0-675-21330-4
Mott, *Applied Fluid Mechanics, 3rd Edition,* 0-675-21026-7
Mott, *Machine Elements in Mechanical Design, 2nd Edition,*
0-675-22289-3
Rolle, *Thermodynamics and Heat Power, 3rd Edition,*
0-675-21016-X
Spiegel & Limbrunner, *Applied Statics and Strength of
Materials,* 0-675-21123-9
Wolansky & Akers, *Modern Hydraulics: The Basics at Work,*
0-675-20987-0
Wolf, *Statics and Strength of Materials: A Parallel Approach to
Understanding Structures,* 0-675-20622-7

DRAFTING TECHNOLOGY

Cooper, *Introduction to VersaCAD,* 0-675-21164-6
Goetsch & Rickman, *Computer-Aided Drafting with AutoCAD,*
0-675-20915-3
Kirkpatrick & Kirkpatrick, *AutoCAD for Interior Design and
Space Planning,* 0-02-364455-9
Kirkpatrick, *The AutoCAD Book: Drawing, Modeling, and
Applications, 2nd Edition,* 0-675-22288-5
Kirkpatrick, *The AutoCAD Book: Drawing, Modeling, and
Applications Including Version 12, 3rd Edition,*
0-02-364440-0
Lamit & Lloyd, *Drafting for Electronics, 2nd Edition,*
0-02-367342-7
Lamit & Paige, *Computer-Aided Design and Drafting,*
0-675-20475-5
Maruggi, *Technical Graphics: Electronics Worktext, 2nd
Edition,* 0-675-21378-9
Maruggi, *The Technology of Drafting,* 0-675-20762-2
Sell, *Basic Technical Drawing,* 0-675-21001-1

TECHNICAL WRITING

Croft, *Getting a Job: Resume Writing, Job Application Letters,
and Interview Strategies,* 0-675-20917-X
Panares, *A Handbook of English for Technical Students,*
0-675-20650-2
Pfeiffer, *Proposal Writing: The Art of Friendly Persuasion,*
0-675-20988-9
Pfeiffer, *Technical Writing: A Practical Approach,* 0-675-21221-9
Roze, *Technical Communications: The Practical Craft,*
0-675-20641-3
Weisman, *Basic Technical Writing, 6th Edition,* 0-675-21256-1

FOR OUR FAMILIES

Diane, Jason, Rebecca
Jeane, Joey, Robby
Maureen, Rachel, Daniel

I Tuoi Genitori E I Tuoi Maestri
Non Si Possono Mai Ringraziare Abbastanza

PREFACE

The computer service industry has been growing in geometric proportions for many years. That growth would not have been possible without the bright young minds that have emerged from our nation's schools. The next several years will place a great burden on our educational institutions as the need for computer specialists, engineers, technicians, programmers, service personnel, and sales people continues to grow.

Over the past 40 years, remarkable changes have taken place in digital computers. The amount of computational power that once required a roomful of vacuum tubes can now be found in small calculators. Complex calculations that would once have taken days to perform can now be done in seconds. Yet with all these changes, certain fundamental design concepts have remained unchanged. The basic organization and operating design of ENIAC (one of the first digital computer systems) is still used in the supercomputers of today. That is, data bits are retrieved from memory, brought to the central processing unit (CPU) to be operated on, and returned to memory for storage. What has changed is the size and speed of the modern-day computer system.

Not so long ago, computers were huge pieces of equipment. They were hidden away in antiseptic rooms and were operated by gurus who seemed to speak a different language. The advent of the microprocessor made computer systems available to everyone. Secretaries replaced their typewriters with computers and plastic disks containing word processing programs. Accountants put away their ledger pads in favor of more efficient electronic spreadsheets. Managers are relying less on "educated guesses"; instead, they are basing their decisions on information gained from the computer's ability to do hundreds of complex calculations almost instantly. On a more global note, bankers, merchandisers, police, fire, and defense and government personnel all use computers. We can't register our car at the motor vehicle bureau or land an airplane at an airport without a computer. Meanwhile, out of the arcades came the video game, introducing millions of American families to the computer as entertainment. Remarkably, today there are more microprocessors in the world than people.

Due to widespread use of computers, it has become a serious matter whenever one fails to work. Quick, efficient, reliable, and competent repair is necessary. Most people and businesses cannot afford to have their computers inoperative for extended periods of time. Thus, computer service has become one of the largest growing segments of the electronics industry today.

This textbook goes beyond the simple symptom fix association of repair manuals and of many prior texts. It addresses theory, practice, and professionalism in servicing the most practical computer ever built—the 8088-based PC. The authors are all seasoned computer-service professionals. The emphasis is on the *need-to-know* information, practical applications, and the fault symptoms and analysis required for computer repair. The text is organized into four sections to allow flexibility in application to different courses and/or different levels. Part I, *Review of Digital Logic,* revisits the fundamental concepts and real-world considerations of digital logic circuits. Part II, *Basics of Microprocessors,* introduces the student to the microprocessor and its support devices. The Intell 8088/8086 microprocessor family is used to present a balanced hardware/software approach to this subject. Part III, *Computer Systems and Peripherals,* exposes the student to the theory of operation and servicing of various components that together form the microcomputer system. The IBM PC/XT is used as a representative model of a modern computer system. Part IV, *Installation and Service,* describes the skills and tools necessary for the setup, installation, and servicing of a microcomputer system. Customer relations as well as diagnostics and troubleshooting are emphasized.

Each chapter contains a list of key terms, numerous illustrations, worked-out examples, and homework problems. An integrated glossary is built into the text with a crossword puzzle at the end of each chapter, which can be used as a formative measurement tool. Each chapter contains a special section entitled "Tech Tips and Troubleshooting—T^3," which presents practical insights to the art of servicing.

The text is intended for a one- or two-semester digital/microprocessor course in 2-year colleges and technical institutes. It can also be used for high school electronics programs or as a one-semester introductory course for BSEET or BSCET majors at 4-year colleges. The text can also be used in industry-based training programs and as a reference for practicing technicians and engineers. The prerequisite knowledge is an understanding of electrical circuit theory, electronic devices, and fundamentals of digital technology.

The development and production of a book of this nature requires the energy and dedication of many individuals. The authors feel fortunate to have had the opportunity to work with the talented professionals at Macmillan Publishing Company, particularly Dave Garza, electronics technology editor; Steve Robb, production editor; and Lorry Woost, art coordinator.

We would also like to acknowledge and thank the following reviewers for sharing their knowledge and expertise with us in this project.

Parley Applegate	Gateway Electronics Omaha, Nebraska
Russell Dallen	Control Data Institute Southfield, Michigan
John Hatch	ITT Technical Institute Buena Park, California
Robert Larson	Texas State Technical Institute Waco, Texas
Edward New	Central New England College of Technology Milford, Massachusetts
Mike Ratkiewicz	Keiser Institute of Technology Ft. Lauderdale, Florida
John Schoeffler	Total Technical Institute North Royalton, Ohio
Steve Tomsik	Keiser Institute of Technology Ft. Lauderdale, Florida
Bill Wood	Arizona State University Tempe, Arizona

We wish to thank James DiBlasi and Jerry Sitbon for their contributions and suggestions throughout the writing of this book. We are also indebted to Diane Asser for typing and reviewing the original manuscript and for her many helpful suggestions.

Every author and teacher must also learn his or her craft. Our learning began at Queensborough Community College of the City University of New York. We would like to express our deepest gratitude and respect to our colleagues and teachers at Queensborough, particularly, Professors Joseph B. Aidala, Robert L. Boylestad, Leon Katz, Gabriel Kousourou, Edward Leff, Louis Nashelsky, and Peter Stark, for teaching, guiding, and inspiring us.

Finally, the authors especially thank their wives, Diane Asser, Jeane Stigliano, and Maureen Bahrenburg, for their patience, encouragement, and love during the writing of this book.

Stuart M. Asser
Vincent J. Stigliano
Richard F. Bahrenburg

CONTENTS

Part 2 Basics of Microprocessors   94

MICROCOMPUTER SERVICING
Practical Systems and Troubleshooting
SECOND EDITION

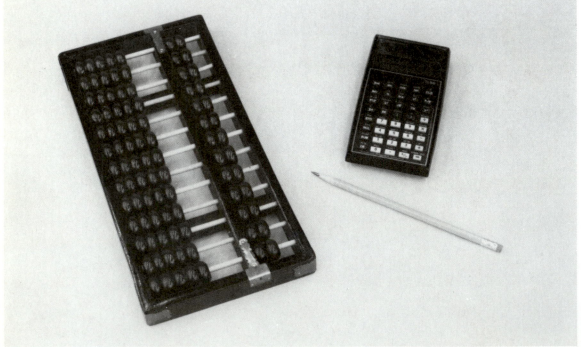

REVIEW OF DIGITAL LOGIC

The modern computer age dawned in 1946 with the completion of the Electronic Numerical Integrator Analyzer and Computer (ENIAC) by scientists and engineers at the University of Pennsylvania. The first electronic computer consisted of over 18,000 vacuum tubes and filled a very large room. Today the same processing power is available in a hand-held calculator.

While ENIAC is considered the grandparent of the modern computer, the history of computers actually began many years before ENIAC, with the invention of the abacus. The abacus was invented in Babylonia around 3000 B.C. It was made up of sliding beads on a frame and was used to perform arithmetic. Over 4000 years later, the next scientific milestone was the invention of a multiplication scheme by John Napier in 1617. Napier constructed a lattice of rods that could perform multiplication. Napier's ''bones,'' as they became known, were essentially a movable column of rods. Between 1623 and 1674 a number of mechanical calculators were invented. Among the more famous of these were the mechanical calculators invented by the French mathematician Blaise Pascal in 1645 and the slide rule, invented by William Oughtred and Richard Delamain in 1630.

Whether or not they actually worked, Charles Babbage's ideas and designs for a mechanical calculator, known as a differential engine and analytical engine, were the inspiration for the modern day computer. These designs were hampered by the limitations of technical machining of the early 1800s.

The next significant event in computer history was the publication by George Boole in 1847 of *The Mathematical Analysis of Logic*. Boole's work led to the mathematics of computers known as Boolean algebra.

In 1890 Herman Hollerith invented punch cards and tabulating equipment for the U.S. census. Later, Hollerith formed his own company called Computing-Tabulating-Recording Corporation (CTR). In 1914 Thomas Watson, Sr. joined CTR, which became IBM in 1924.

During the next 20 years, a great deal of research and development was done on various types of electromechanical calculators. Also during this time, Lee DeForrest developed the triode vacuum tube, W.H. Eccles and F.W. Jordan developed the flip-flop, and Claude Shannon showed the feasibility of switching circuits in electronic applications. These events culminated in the first fully functional electronic calculator, ENIAC, in 1946.

ENIAC was 8 ft high and 80 ft long and weighed 30 tons. Its 18,000 vacuum tubes, 70,000 resistors, 10,000 capacitors, 1500 relays, and 6000 manual switches consumed approximately 175 kW of power. This enormous machine was probably less powerful than your hand-held calculator. However, it demonstrated the feasibility of the electronic computer and led to the development of the modern computer.

Part 1, ''Essentials of Digital Logic,'' presents the fundamental concepts and skills of digital logic circuits, which are the basis of today's computers.

CHAPTER ONE

FUNDAMENTALS OF DIGITAL LOGIC

KEY TERMS

Alphanumeric Codes

AND

ASCII

Asynchronous Inputs

Binary Number System

Bistable

Bit

Boolean Algebra

Buffers

Complementary Metal-oxide Semiconductor (CMOS)

Decoupling

D Flip-flop

Dual-in-line Package (DIP)

Edge-triggered Flip-flop

Fan-out

Flip-flops

Float

Hexadecimal Number System

Integrated Circuit

JK Flip-flop

JK Master-Slave Flip-flop

Latch Flip-flop

Least Significant Bit (LSB)

Logic Families

Logic Gates

Most Significant Bit (MSB)

Multivibrator Circuits

Noise Immunity

NOT

OR

Power Dissipation

Propagation Delay Time

Race Condition

Schmitt Trigger

Setup Time

Three-state

Toggling

Transceiver

Truth table

Transistor-Transistor Logic (TTL)

Unit load

1.0 INTRODUCTION

Logic gates are essentially a combination of switches. These switches can be mechanical, electromechanical, or electronic in nature. The position or state of the switches can be used to represent information. Switches are inherently binary in nature. Thus they can be

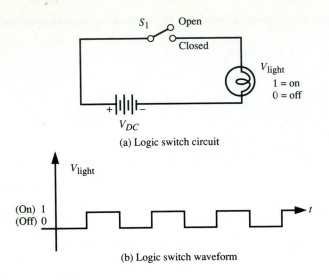

(a) Logic switch circuit

(b) Logic switch waveform

FIGURE 1.1
Logic switch circuit

either open or closed, so they can be used to represent the binary digits 0 and 1, as shown in Figure 1.1.

'Figure 1.1(a) shows a simple logic switch circuit. When switch S_1 is open, no current will flow through the circuit. Therefore, the light will be off. This can be represented as a logic level zero. When switch S_1 is closed, the circuit is complete, and current flows from the source V_{DC} to the light. The light is then on. This can be represented as a logic level 1. If the switch is repeatedly opened and closed, the light will blink on and off. This is illustrated by the waveform in Figure 1.1(b).

1.1 THE ONE/ZERO CONCEPT

The base 10, or decimal, number system is familiar to all of us. Most people never even question its use. For most of people's existence, this was the only number system known. It was based on the 10 fingers of the hands. We learn to use the decimal number system at a very early age. Therefore, it has become a natural method of counting for us. Why then must we use a different number system in today's computers? The first computing machines were mechanical and operated on the base 10 number system. For example, the abacus, Babbage's engine, and the many mechanical calculators that followed were all designed for the base 10 number system. The first electronic computing machines were an outgrowth of telephone switching circuits. Switches are inherently binary in nature. They are either open or closed. This led to the use of the binary number system to describe switching circuits.

The binary, or base 2, number system has only two digits, zero (0) and one (1). This number system is very easy to reproduce electrically. The on/off state of a switch can be represented by the binary digit 1 or the binary digit 0. A light can be on or off. Voltage can be high or low. Current can flow or not flow. Magnetism can be north or south. Questions can be answered yes or no. As you can see, these examples are all binary in nature.

1.2   THE BINARY NUMBER SYSTEM

The **binary number system,** or base 2 number system, has only two digits, 0 and 1. It is a *positional number system.* The value of any digit depends on its position. In this case the positions are weighted as powers of the base 2. Table 1.1 illustrates the positional values for the binary number system.

TABLE 1.1
Powers of two

	$2^0 = 1$
$2^1 = 2$	$2^{-1} = 1/2 = 0.5$
$2^2 = 4$	$2^{-2} = 1/4 = 0.25$
$2^3 = 8$	$2^{-3} = 1/8 = 0.125$
$2^4 = 16$	$2^{-4} = 1/16 = 0.0625$
$2^5 = 32$	$2^{-5} = 1/32 = 0.03125$
$2^6 = 64$	$2^{-6} = 1/64 = 0.015625$
$2^7 = 128$	$2^{-7} = 1/128 = 0.0078125$
$2^8 = 256$	$2^{-8} = 1/256 = 0.00390625$

The radix point is called the *binary point* in the base 2 number system. Each binary digit is called a **bit** (BInary digiT). The leftmost digit or bit is referred to as the **most significant bit (MSB),** and the rightmost digit or bit is called the **least significant bit (LSB),** as illustrated:

$$
\begin{array}{cccccccc}
 & 2^3 & 2^2 & 2^1 & 2^0 & & 2^{-1} & 2^{-2} & \\
\text{MSB} & 1 & 0 & 1 & 0 & . & 1 & 1 & \text{LSB}
\end{array}
$$

Binary point

For example, the binary number $(1010.11)_2$ can be represented as

$$
\begin{array}{ccccccc}
1 \times 2^3 & = & 1 \times 8 & = & (8)_{10} \\
0 \times 2^2 & = & 0 \times 4 & = & (0)_{10} \\
1 \times 2^1 & = & 1 \times 2 & = & (2)_{10} \\
0 \times 2^0 & = & 0 \times 1 & = & (0)_{10} \\
1 \times 2^{-1} & = & 1 \times 0.5 & = & (0.5)_{10} \\
1 \times 2^{-2} & = & 1 \times 0.25 & = & (0.25)_{10}
\end{array}
$$

The equivalent decimal value can be computed as follows:

$$
\begin{aligned}
&1 \times 2^3 + 0 \times 2^2 + 1 \times 2^1 + 0 \times 2^0 + 1 \times 2^{-1} + 1 \times 2^{-2} \\
=\; &1 \times 8 \;+ 0 \times 4 \;+ 1 \times 2 \;+ 0 \times 1 \;+ 1 \times 0.5 \;+ 1 \times 0.25 \\
=\; &\;\;8 \quad + \quad 0 \quad + \quad 2 \quad + \quad 0 \quad + \quad 0.5 \quad + \quad 0.25 \quad = (10.75)_{10}
\end{aligned}
$$

Note the use of the parentheses and subscript to signify the base system of the number.

1.3 BINARY TO DECIMAL CONVERSION

As we have just seen, numbers can be converted from binary to decimal by computing the sum of the products of each digit multiplied by its positional value. Consider the following examples.

EXAMPLE 1.1

Convert the binary number $(11001)_2$ to decimal.

Solution

Positional weight	2^4	2^3	2^2	2^1	2^0
Positional value	16	8	4	2	1
Binary number	1	1	0	0	1

$$
\begin{aligned}
&1 \times 2^4 \;+ 1 \times 2^3 \;+ 0 \times 2^2 \;+ 0 \times 2^1 \;+ 1 \times 2^0 \\
=\; &1 \times 16 \;+ 1 \times 8 \;+ 0 \times 4 \;+ 0 \times 2 \;+ 1 \times 1 \\
=\; &\;\;16 \quad + \quad 8 \quad + \quad 0 \quad + \quad 0 \quad + \quad 1 \quad = (25)_{10}
\end{aligned}
$$

EXAMPLE 1.2

Convert the binary number $(101.101)_2$ to decimal.

Solution

Positional weight	2^2	2^1	2^0	2^{-1}	2^{-2}	2^{-3}
Positional value	4	2	1	0.5	0.25	0.125
Binary number	1	0	1 .	1	0	1

$$
\begin{aligned}
&1 \times 2^2 + 0 \times 2^1 + 1 \times 2^0 + 1 \times 2^{-1} + 0 \times 2^{-2} + 1 \times 2^{-3} \\
=\; &1 \times 4 \;+ 0 \times 2 \;+ 1 \times 1 \;+ 1 \times 0.5 \;+ 0 \times 0.25 \;+ 1 \times 0.125 \\
=\; &\;\;4 \quad + \quad 0 \quad + \quad 1 \quad + \quad 0.5 \quad + \quad 0 \quad + \quad 0.125 \quad = (5.625)_{10}
\end{aligned}
$$

Notice that in the previous examples the process could have been simplified by leaving out all the zero terms. Furthermore, starting at the units position (2^0), each position to the left is multiplied by 2 (the base number) to obtain its positional value. Each position to the right is divided by two to obtain its positional value.

1.4 DECIMAL TO BINARY CONVERSION

The method of converting whole numbers from one base system to another is known as *repeated division*. The decimal number is divided by the base number to obtain a quotient plus a remainder. The remainder is then recorded as part of the binary number. The quotient is then divided by the base again to produce a second quotient and a second remainder. The second remainder becomes the second binary digit. The process is then continued until the quotient becomes zero. In the following example, since we are converting to binary we divide the decimal number by 2. Note that because we are dividing by 2, the remainder can be only a zero or a one. The binary result is obtained by writing the first remainder as the LSB and the last remainder as the MSB.

EXAMPLE 1.3

Convert the decimal number $(29)_{10}$ to binary.

Solution

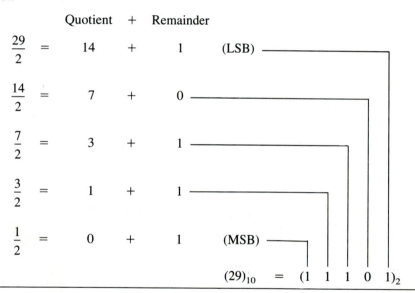

$$\frac{29}{2} = 14 + 1 \quad \text{(LSB)}$$

$$\frac{14}{2} = 7 + 0$$

$$\frac{7}{2} = 3 + 1$$

$$\frac{3}{2} = 1 + 1$$

$$\frac{1}{2} = 0 + 1 \quad \text{(MSB)}$$

$$(29)_{10} = (1\ 1\ 1\ 0\ 1)_2$$

The method of converting fractional decimal numbers to binary is known as repeated multiplication. The fraction is multiplied by the base, with the carry becoming the binary number. In this process, the first carry becomes the MSB, and the last carry becomes the LSB.

EXAMPLE 1.4

Convert the fractional decimal number $(0.625)_{10}$ to binary.

Solution

Carry ⌐

$0.625 \times 2 = 1.250$ MSB

$0.250 \times 2 = 0.500$

$0.500 \times 2 = 1.000$ LSB

$(0.625)_{10} = (0 . 1 0 1)_2$

In summary, to convert whole numbers from decimal to binary, the following relationship can be used:

$$\frac{\text{decimal number}}{\text{base number}} = \text{quotient} + \text{remainder}$$

The remainders become the binary number. To convert fractional numbers from decimal to binary the following relationship can be used:

$$\text{Fractional decimal number} \times \text{base number} = \text{carry} + \text{product}$$

The carries become the binary number.

1.5   THE HEXADECIMAL NUMBER SYSTEM

Modern computers use another number system called the **hexadecimal number system.** The hexadecimal number system is a positional base 16 system. It uses the digits 0 through 9 and the letters *A* through *F* as its symbols, as shown in Table 1.2.

TABLE 1.2
Hexadecimal number system

Hexadecimal	Decimal	Binary
0	0	0000
1	1	0001
2	2	0010
3	3	0011
4	4	0100
5	5	0101
6	6	0110
7	7	0111
8	8	1000
9	9	1001
A	10	1010
B	11	1011
C	12	1100
D	13	1101
E	14	1110
F	15	1111

As with other number systems, the value of a hexadecimal number is determined by the position of the digits. Table 1.3 illustrates the positional value of base 16 digits.

TABLE 1.3
Powers of 16

	$16^0 = 1$
$16^1 = 16$	$16^{-1} = 1/16 = 0.0625$
$16^2 = 256$	$16^{-2} = 1/256 = 0.00390625$
$16^3 = 4096$	$16^{-3} = 1/4096 = 0.000244140625$
$16^4 = 65536$	$16^{-4} = 1/65536 = 0.000015258789$

1.6 HEXADECIMAL CONVERSIONS

Hexadecimal to Decimal Conversion

Hexadecimal numbers can be converted to decimal by computing the *sum of the products of each digit times its positional value* as shown in the following examples.

EXAMPLE 1.5

Convert the following hexadecimal numbers to decimal.

a. $(5B)_{16}$ b. $(2AF)_{16}$ c. $(1C5)_{16}$

Solution

a.

Positional weight	16^1	16^0
Positional value	16	1
Hexadecimal number	5	B

$$5 \times 16^1 + B \times 16^0$$
$$= 5 \times 16 + 11 \times 1$$
$$= 80 + 11 = (91)_{10}$$

b.

Positional weight	16^2	16^1	16^0
Positional value	256	16	1
Hexadecimal number	2	A	F

$$2 \times 16^2 + A \times 16^1 + F \times 16^0$$
$$= 2 \times 256 + 10 \times 16 + 15 \times 1$$
$$= 512 + 160 + 15 = (687)_{10}$$

c.

Positional weight	16^2	16^1	16^0
Positional value	256	16	1
Hexadecimal number	1	C	5

$$1 \times 16^2 + C \times 16^1 + 5 \times 16^0$$
$$= 1 \times 256 + 12 \times 16 + 5 \times 1$$
$$= 256 + 192 + 5 = (453)_{10}$$

Decimal to Hexadecimal Conversion

To convert decimal numbers to hexadecimal numbers, simply apply the repeated division method, as shown in the following example.

EXAMPLE 1.6

Convert the following decimal numbers to hexadecimal.

a. $(93)_{10}$ b. $(142)_{10}$ c. $(1776)_{10}$

Solution

a.

Quotient + remainder

$$\frac{93}{16} = 5 + 13, \text{ or } D \quad \text{(LSB)}$$

$$\frac{5}{16} = 0 + 5 \quad \text{(MSB)}$$

$$(93)_{10} = (5 \ D)_{16}$$

b.

Quotient + remainder

$$\frac{142}{16} = 8 + 14, \text{ or } E \quad \text{(LSB)}$$

$$\frac{8}{16} = 0 + 8 \quad \text{(MSB)}$$

$$(142)_{10} = (8 \ E)_{16}$$

c.

Quotient + remainder

$$\frac{1776}{16} = 111 + 0 \quad \text{(LSB)}$$

$$\frac{111}{16} = 6 + 15, \text{ or } F$$

$$\frac{6}{16} = 0 + 6 \quad \text{(MSB)}$$

$$(1776)_{10} = (6 \ F \ 0)_{16}$$

Hexadecimal to Binary Conversion

Hexadecimal numbers are easily converted to binary numbers. In fact, hexadecimal numbers are also a convenient way of expressing binary numbers. Referring to Table 1.2, to convert hexadecimal numbers to binary numbers, simply *replace each hexadecimal digit with its 4-bit binary equivalent.*

EXAMPLE 1.7

Convert the following hexadecimal numbers to binary:

a. $(37)_{16}$ b. $(C4)_{16}$ c. $(DF6)_{16}$

Solution

a.

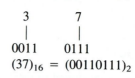

```
3       7
|       |
0011    0111
```
$(37)_{16} = (00110111)_2$

b.

```
C       4
|       |
1100    0100
```
$(C4)_{16} = (11000100)_2$

c.

```
D       F       6
|       |       |
1101    1111    0110
```
$(DF6)_{16} = (110111110110)_2$

Binary to Hexadecimal Conversion

To convert a binary number to its hexadecimal equivalent, simply *group the binary bits by four, starting at the radix point*. If necessary, you may have to add zeros to complete the groups.

EXAMPLE 1.8

Convert the following binary numbers to hexadecimal:

a. $(10101110)_2$ b. $(1110101)_2$ c. $(1111101000010000)_2$

Solution

a.

```
1010    1110
|       |
A       E
```
$(10101110)_2 = (AE)_{16}$

b.

```
0111    0101
|       |
7       5
```
$(1110101)_2 = (75)_{16}$

Note the leading zero that was added to complete the most significant group.

c.

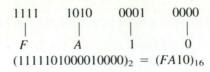

$$(1111101000010000)_2 = (FA10)_{16}$$

1.7 ALPHANUMERIC CODES

Codes have been developed to represent *letters* as well as *numbers* and *special symbols*. These codes are called **alphanumeric codes.** The *American Standard Code for Information Interchange* (**ASCII**) is a 7-bit code that is commonly used in today's computer systems. Since ASCII is a 7-bit code, there are 2^7, or 128, possible coding combinations. Each letter of the alphabet (upper- and lowercase) as well as the decimal digits 0 through 9 and special characters are represented by a unique code as shown in Table 1.4.

Conversion to ASCII and other alphanumeric codes is best accomplished by looking up the equivalent code in a table. For each alphanumeric character you wish to convert, an ASCII equivalent code can be found in Table 1.4. For example, the uppercase letter A is equivalent to 1000001, or 41H in ASCII code.

EXAMPLE 1.9

Convert the letters JOE to ASCII.

Solution

Alphanumeric	J	O	E
ASCII	1001010	1001111	1000101
Hex	4A	4F	45

1.8 BOOLEAN EXPRESSIONS AND TRUTH TABLES

In about the year 1850, George Boole, an English mathematician, developed the basic laws and theorems that became known as *Boolean algebra*. Boole's work was an outgrowth of a topic in philosophy known as logic. Logic can be used to break down complex problems into simple questions, which can be answered as either true or false. The binary nature of logic was recognized by Claude Shannon of MIT in 1938. Shannon applied Boolean algebra to relay logic switching circuits as a means to analyze these circuits.

From Boolean algebra comes the three basic logical functions that form the basis of all digital and computer circuits. These logical functions are called the **AND** function, the **OR** function, and the **NOT** function. These functions can be expressed mathematically using Boolean algebra or in tabular form using a **truth table.** The input and output variables are usually represented by letters such as *A*, *B*, and *C* or *X*, *Y*, and *Z*. The logic state of these variables is represented by the binary numbers 0 and 1.

Column bits

R O W (HEX)	B4	B3	B2	B1	000 / 0	001 / 1	010 / 2	011 / 3	100 / 4	101 / 5	110 / 6	111 / 7
0	0	0	0	0	NUL	DLE	SP	0	@	P	`	p
1	0	0	0	1	SOH	DC1	!	1	A	Q	a	q
2	0	0	1	0	STX	DC2	"	2	B	R	b	r
3	0	0	1	1	ETX	DC3	#	3	C	S	c	s
4	0	1	0	0	EOT	DC4	$	4	D	T	d	t
5	0	1	0	1	ENQ	NAK	%	5	E	U	e	u
6	0	1	1	0	ACK	SYN	&	6	F	V	f	v
7	0	1	1	1	BEL	ETB	'	7	G	W	g	w
8	1	0	0	0	BS	CAN	(	8	H	X	h	x
9	1	0	0	1	HT	EM	)	9	I	Y	i	y
A	1	0	1	0	LF	SUB	*	:	J	Z	j	z
B	1	0	1	1	VT	ESC	+	;	K	[	k	{
C	1	1	0	0	FF	FS	,	<	L	\	l	|
D	1	1	0	1	CR	GS	-	=	M	]	m	}
E	1	1	1	0	SO	RS	.	>	N	^	n	~
F	1	1	1	1	SI	US	/	?	O	_	o	DEL

Bits(row)

Column (HEX)

Control characters

NUL = Null
DLE = Data link escape
SOH = Start of heading
DC1 = Device control 1
STX = Start of text
DC2 = Device control 2
ETX = End of text
DC3 = Device control 3
EOT = End of transmission
DC4 = Device control 4
ENQ = Enquiry
NAK = Negative acknowledge
ACK = Acknowledge
SYN = Syn idle
BEL = Bell
ETB = End of transmission block
BS = Backspace
CAN = Cancel
HT = Horizontal tab
EM = End of medium
LF = Line feed
SUB = Substitute
VT = Vertical tab
ESC = Escape
FF = Form feed
FS = File separator
CR = Carriage return
GS = Group separator
SO = Shift out
RS = Record separator
SI = Shift in
US = Unit separator

Column bits $\{ B_5, B_6, B_7 \}$

ASCII
Code

Column bits $B_7 B_6 B_5 B_4 B_3 B_2 B_1$ Row bits

A = 1000001
or
A = 41(HEX)

(HEX)

TABLE 1.4
ASCII code

The AND Function

The AND function can be thought of as a series circuit containing two or more logic switches, as shown in Figure 1.2(a). The logic indicator L_1 will be on only when logic switch A *and* logic switch B are both closed. If we examine the circuit in Figure 1.2(a) further, we can see that logic switch A and logic switch B each have two possible logic states (open or closed). The logic states can be represented in binary form using 0 for *open* and 1 for *closed*. Furthermore, the logic indicator L_1 can also have two possible binary logic states, 0 for *off* and 1 for *on*. The truth table is used to illustrate all the possible combinations of input and output conditions that can exist in a logic circuit as shown in Figure 1.2(b). The Boolean expression used to represent *this* AND function is written as

$$A \cdot B = L_1$$

This expression can be read as "*A and B* equals L_1." It gives us a clear and precise mathematical method of describing the behavior of the circuit. It should be noted that the dot (·), or AND symbol, is often deleted. When this is done, the expression is written as $AB = L_1$.

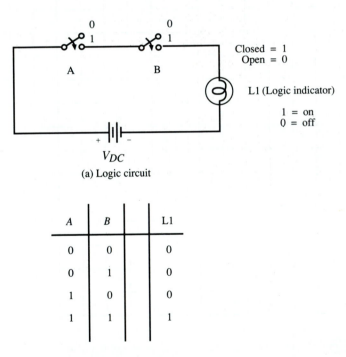

(a) Logic circuit

A	B	L1
0	0	0
0	1	0
1	0	0
1	1	1

(b) Truth table

$$A \cdot B = L1$$
(c) Boolean expression

FIGURE 1.2
AND function

The OR Function

The OR function can be thought of as a parallel circuit containing two or more logic switches, as shown in Figure 1.3(a). Here the logic indicator L_1 will be on whenever either logic switch *A or* logic switch *B or* both are closed. As previously described with the AND function, each logic switch can have two possible logic states (open and closed, which correspond to 0 and 1). The truth table shown in Figure 1.3(b) is again used to illustrate all the possible combinations of input and output conditions that can exist. It should be noted that the number of possible logic combinations is determined by the number of inputs. The number of logic combinations can be calculated as follows:

$$\text{Number of logic combinations} = 2^n$$

where *n* is the number of logic inputs. For example, if there are three inputs, *A, B,* and *C,* the number of possible logic combinations is calculated as follows:

$$\text{Number of logic combinations} = 2^n = 2^3 = 8$$

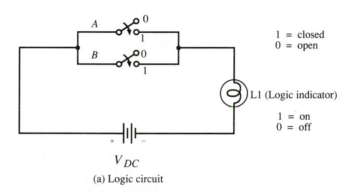

(a) Logic circuit

A	B	L1
0	0	0
0	1	1
1	0	1
1	1	1

(b) Truth table

(c) $A + B = L1$
Boolean expression

FIGURE 1.3
OR function

The Boolean expression used to represent the OR function in Figure 1.3 is written as

$$A + B = L_1$$

This expression can be read as "*A or B* equals L_1." It is used to describe the behavior of the circuit in Figure 1.3(a).

The NOT Function

The NOT function can be thought of as an *inverter,* or negation circuit, as shown in Figure 1.4(a). The logic indicator L_1 will be on whenever the logic switch *A* is open. If logic switch *A* is open, current will flow through the logic indicator L_1, which will cause the indicator to light. If logic switch *A* is closed, L_1 will be *shorted,* and the current will flow through the logic switch back to the power source. Remember, electricity will take the path of least resistance. Note that the resistor is shown here to protect the power source when logic switch *A* is closed. Once again the truth table of Figure 1.4(b) is used

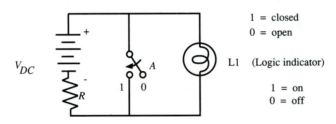

(a) Logic circuit

A	L1
0	1
1	0

(b) Truth table

$$\overline{A} = \text{L1}$$

(c) Boolean expression

FIGURE 1.4
NOT function

to describe the circuit operation. Unlike the AND and OR functions, the NOT function can have only one input. The Boolean expression used to represent *this* NOT function is written as

$$\overline{A} = L_1$$

This expression is read as *not A* equals L_1. That is, when logic switch A is open (0), the logic indicator L_1 is on (1). Conversely, it means that when logic switch A is closed (1), the logic indicator L_1 is off (0).

1.9 INTEGRATED CIRCUITS

The electronic circuits, or devices, that perform the Boolean logic functions, are called **logic gates.** The logic gates are made up of circuits containing transistors, diodes, resistors, and capacitors. These components are usually integrated onto a single device known as an **integrated circuit (IC),** or *chip.* The IC itself is rather small and fragile. In order to facilitate handling, ICs are usually packaged in various sizes, shapes, and styles. One of the most common styles is the **dual-in-line package,** or **DIP,** as shown in Figure 1.5. Notice that pin 1 is on the left-hand side of the end with the U-shaped notch, when looking down from the top of the DIP. Some DIP manufacturers use a dot instead of a notch to indicate the location of pin 1. Referring to Figure 1.5, the pin immediately to the right of pin 1 is pin 2. The pin numbers continue sequentially around the DIP, as shown in Figure 1.5.

Digital integrated circuit devices are manufactured using different techniques. These manufacturing techniques are classified by *logic families.* Integrated circuits contained within a logic family usually have similar electrical characteristics. For example, devices within a logic family will all operate at the same power supply voltages and are designed to be connected together. The two most popular logic families in use today are the TTL and CMOS families.

Transistor-transistor logic, or **TTL,** circuits are integrated circuits designed around the basic bipolar junction transistor (BJT). All TTL devices operate from a single $+5\ \mathrm{V_{DC}}$ power source. TTL devices are identified by a part number, which is composed of five segments:

S N	7 4	LS	0 8	N
manufacturer	series	subseries	device type	package

The first two letters, SN, indicate the manufacturer. In this case, SN stands for Semiconductor Network Program, which is manufactured by Texas Instruments. The next two numbers, 74, represent the series. 74 is the code for a standard TTL commercial device. 54 represents a high-reliability military version. The next letters, LS, define the subseries. In this case, LS represents a low-power Schottky device. The absence of a letter would represent a standard TTL device. The next digits, 08, define the number and

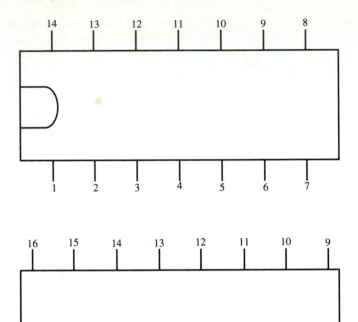

FIGURE 1.5
DIP

type of logic function to be performed. In this case, 08 defines a device containing four 2-input AND gates. The last letter, N, indicates the package type. Here the N describes a plastic DIP device.

Complementary metal-oxide semiconductor (CMOS) devices are integrated circuits designed around the field-effect transistor (FET). The power supply voltage for a digital CMOS device can range anywhere between $+3$ and $+18$ V_{DC}. CMOS devices consume much less power than comparable TTL devices. However, CMOS devices tend to be slower than comparable TTL devices. The identification process for a CMOS device is similar to that of the TTL device.

1.10 SUMMARY OF LOGIC GATES

It is important to understand thoroughly the operation of all the basic logic gates. Figure 1.6 summarizes the Boolean expressions, logic symbols, and truth tables of all of the basic logic gates. The information in Figure 1.6 should be memorized and completely understood. It forms the basis and foundation of all that is to follow.

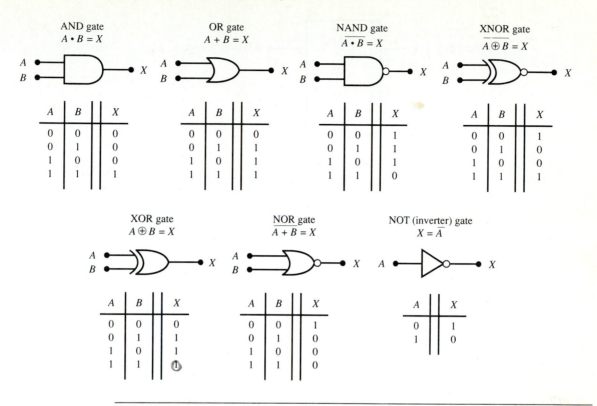

FIGURE 1.6
Summary of logic gates

1.11 SEQUENTIAL LOGIC

In the previous section we studied logic gates. These types of circuits exhibited no memory. The output was always dependent upon the input. We will now study a type of circuit which has memory and can store or hold its output state. These circuits are generally classified as **multivibrator circuits** and are often referred to as **flip-flops.** A flip-flop is a device that has two stable output states. That is, the output can be either a logic 1 or a logic 0. These output states are stored or stable even if the inputs are removed. Because of this feature, flip-flops are referred to as **bistable** (two states) devices which exhibit memory.

Flip-flops can be classified into two general types: **latch flip-flops** and **edge-triggered flip-flops.** In a latch flip-flop the output is controlled by the logic *level* of the input. In an edge-triggered flip-flop, the output is controlled by the leading or trailing *edge* of an input pulse.

1.12 LATCH FLIP-FLOPS

The basic flip-flop is shown in Figure 1.7(a). The inputs are commonly labeled *S* (**set**) and *R* (**reset**). Most flip-flops contain two outputs, which are generally called *Q* and

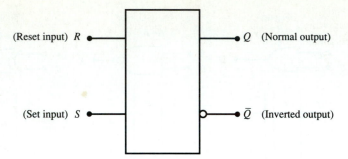

(a) Basic R-S latch flip-flop (NOR gates) symbol

R	S	Q	$\bar{Q}$	Action
0	0	Q	$\bar{Q}$	No change (Q, $\bar{Q}$ stay the same)
0	1	1	0	Set
1	0	0	1	Reset (clear)
1	1	-	-	Illegal

(b) Truth table

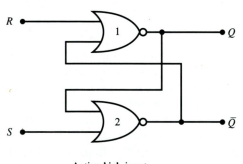

Active **high** input
(c) R-S latch flip-flop

FIGURE 1.7
RS latch flip-flop

$\bar{Q}$. $\bar{Q}$ is the inverted output of Q. $\bar{Q}$ is always at the state opposite that of the logic state of Q. Therefore, if Q is a logic 0, $\bar{Q}$ will be a logic 1. If Q is a logic 1, $\bar{Q}$ will be a logic 0. This can be thought of as a seesaw. That is, when one side is high the other side must be low.

Recall that with two input variables there are four possible combinations of input conditions which can exist. The input combinations and the resulting output states are described in the truth table of Figure 1.7(b).

To explain the operation of the flip-flop, consider the circuit of Figure 1.7(c). Two NOR gates are wired so that their outputs are fed back to the other's input. We begin by considering the first condition of the truth table. Both inputs S and R are at a logic 0, as shown in Figure 1.8(a). Under this condition, the outputs remain in whatever state they were in previously. The reason for this should become clear in a few moments. Assume for now that the Q output is at a logic level 0 and the $\overline{Q}$ output is a logic level 1. Next consider the condition where the S input goes to a logic level 1 and the R input remains at a logic level 0. Under this condition the inputs to NOR gate 2 are 1 and 0, as shown in Figure 1.8(b). This will force the output of NOR gate 2 to become a 0. The output of NOR gate 2 is fed back to the input of NOR gate 1. Thus the inputs to NOR gate 1 are 0 and 0, as shown in Figure 1.8(b). The output of NOR gate 1 will then be forced to a logic level 1 and fed back to the input of NOR gate 2. The inputs to NOR gate 2 are now 1 and 1. Therefore, the output of NOR gate 2 will remain at a logic level 0. Thus, the Q output becomes a logic level 1 and the $\overline{Q}$ output becomes a logic level 0. This is

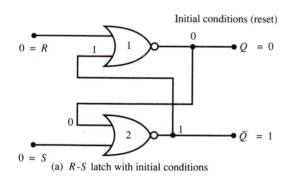

(a) *R-S* latch with initial conditions

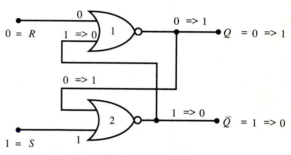

(b) Set input conditions, $S = 1, R = 0$
with Q feeding back to the input to gate 2
and the $\overline{Q}$ feeding back to the input to gate 1

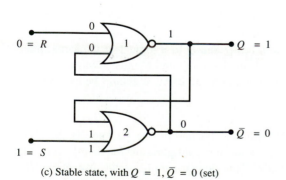

(c) Stable state, with $Q = 1, \overline{Q} = 0$ (set)

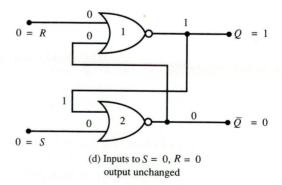

(d) Inputs to $S = 0, R = 0$
output unchanged

FIGURE 1.8
RS **latch flip-flop explained**

sometimes referred to as the SET condition ($Q = 1$), as shown in the stable state in Figure 1.8(c).

Notice that if the S input returns back to a logic level 0, causing both inputs S and R to be at a logic level 0, the output remains unchanged. The inputs to NOR gate 2 are now 0 and 1, as shown in Figure 1.8(d), so the output of NOR gate 2 remains at a logic 0. The inputs to NOR gate 1 are then 0 and 0, which causes the output to remain at a logic 1. Thus the SR input condition $0 = 0$ causes the outputs to remain the same as they previously were (no change).

All the possible output conditions can be summarized as follows:

1. $S = 0$, $R = 0$: Q and $\overline{Q}$ remain in whatever state they were in previously.
2. $S = 1$, $R = 0$: Q flips to a 1, $\overline{Q}$ flops to a 0. This is called the *SET* condition.
3. $S = 0$, $R = 1$: Q flips to a 0, $\overline{Q}$ flops to a 1. This is called the *RESET* condition.
4. $S = 1$, $R = 1$: This condition tries to force Q and $\overline{Q}$ to a logic 0 at the same time. This is an illegal condition, since in Boolean algebra Q and $\overline{Q}$ must always be in the opposite state. Therefore, although this condition can exist, it should be avoided.

NAND Gate RS Latch

Two NAND gates can be connected in the same manner as the NOR gates to create an active low input RS latch, as illustrated in Figure 1.9(a). The SET and RESET inputs are labeled $\overline{S}$ and $\overline{R}$, respectively. The outputs are labeled Q and $\overline{Q}$. All the possible input and output combinations are described in the truth table of Figure 1.9(b). Figure 1.9(c) shows the conventional and equivalent active state logic diagram representation of the NAND gate RS latch. Generally speaking, a low on the SET input $\overline{S}$ will force the Q output to a logic level 1 and the $\overline{Q}$ output to a logic level 0. A low on the RESET input $\overline{R}$ will force the $\overline{Q}$ output to a logic level 1 and the Q output to a logic level 0. To summarize:

1. $\overline{S} = 1$, $\overline{R} = 1$: Q and $\overline{Q}$ remain in whatever state they were in previously.
2. $\overline{S} = 0$, $\overline{R} = 1$: Q flips to a 1, $\overline{Q}$ flops to a 0. This is called the SET condition.
3. $\overline{S} = 1$, $\overline{R} = 0$: Q flips to a 0, $\overline{Q}$ flops to a 1. This is called the RESET condition.
4. $\overline{S} = 0$, $\overline{R} = 0$: This condition tries to force Q and $\overline{Q}$ to a logic 1 at the same time. This is an illegal condition, since in Boolean algebra Q and $\overline{Q}$ must always be in the opposite state. Therefore, although this condition can exist, it should be avoided.

A device that contains four RS NAND gate latches in one package is the TTL 74279 integrated circuit. Figure 1.9(d) shows the pin configuration for this device. All the integrated wiring is provided internally. This device simplifies the use of the RS NAND gate latch in digital logic circuits.

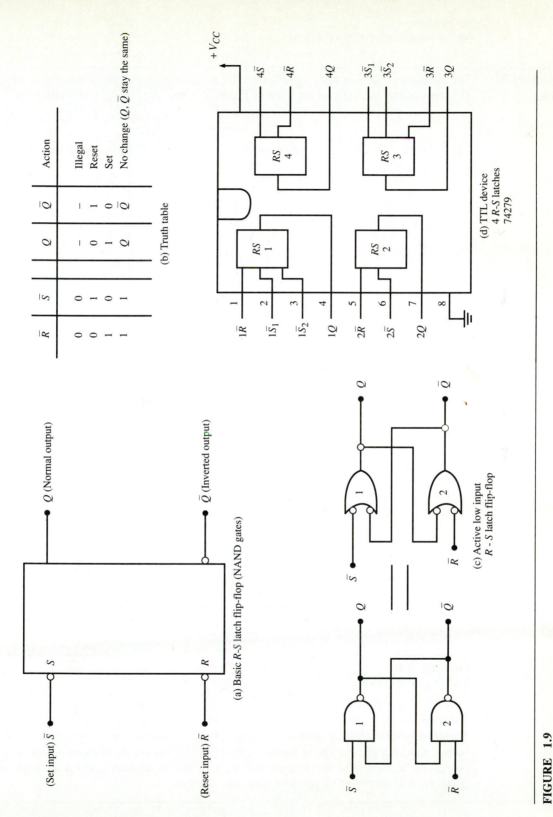

$\bar{R}$	$\bar{S}$	Q	$\bar{Q}$	Action
0	0	–	–	Illegal
0	1	0	1	Reset
1	0	1	0	Set
1	1	Q	$\bar{Q}$	No change ($Q, \bar{Q}$ stay the same)

(b) Truth table

(d) TTL device
4 R-S latches
74279

(a) Basic R-S latch flip-flop (NAND gates)

(c) Active low input
R - S latch flip-flop

FIGURE 1.9
RS latch using NAND gates

EXAMPLE
1.10

For the input conditions shown in Figure 1.10(b), determine the output waveform for the Q output of the NAND gate RS latch of Figure 1.10(a). Assume Q is initially high.

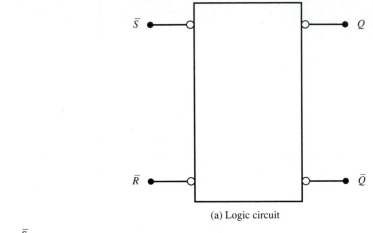

(a) Logic circuit

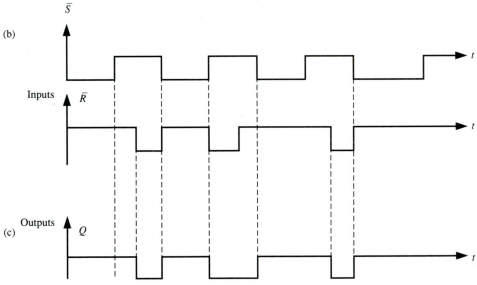

FIGURE 1.10
NAND gate RS latch

Solution

The Q output waveform is shown in Figure 1.10(c). Whenever the $\overline{S}$ input is low, the Q output will be high, and the $\overline{Q}$ output will be low. Whenever the $\overline{R}$ input is low, the $\overline{Q}$ output will be high, and the Q output will be low. Whenever both $\overline{S}$ and $\overline{R}$ are high, the Q output will remain in its previous state (no change).

1.13 EDGE-TRIGGERED FLIP-FLOPS

Edge-triggered flip-flops are flip-flops whose output is controlled by the leading or trailing edge of a gated clock pulse. That is, the output can change state only on an edge of a clock pulse. The output logic *(Q)* is still determined by the input logic levels. The two most popular types of edge-triggered flip-flops are the *D* flip-flop and the *JK* flip-flop.

D Flip-Flop

The ***D* flip-flop** is a single-input edge-triggered or edge-controlled flip-flop. On the positive-going, or leading, edge of a clock pulse, the input data *D* is transferred to the *Q* output, as shown in Figure 1.11(a). Note the use of the *chevron,* or small triangle, on the clock input to indicate an edge-triggered device. Functionally, the *D* flip-flop can be thought of as performing according to the circuit diagram of Figure 1.11(b). Note that although *D*-type flip-flops can be either positive-going edge-triggered or negative-going edge-triggered, most *D* flip-flops are positive-edge-triggered controlled.

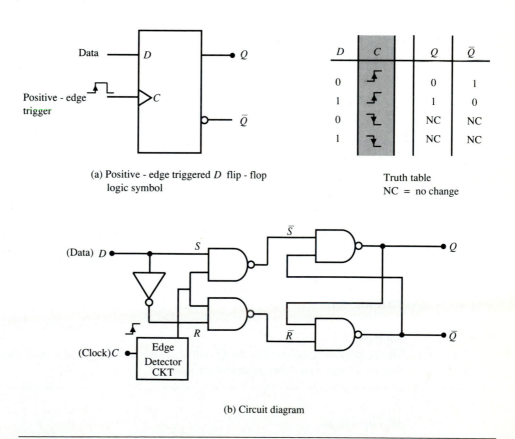

(a) Positive - edge triggered *D* flip - flop
logic symbol

D	*C*	*Q*	*Q̄*
0	⌐⌐	0	1
1	⌐⌐	1	0
0	⌐⌐	NC	NC
1	⌐⌐	NC	NC

Truth table
NC = no change

(b) Circuit diagram

FIGURE 1.11
Positive-edge-triggered *D* flip-flop

EXAMPLE 1.11

Determine the Q output waveform for the D flip-flop with the D and clock input waveforms shown in Figure 1.12. Assume Q is initially low.

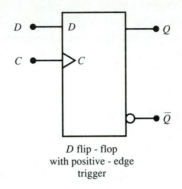

D flip - flop
with positive - edge
trigger

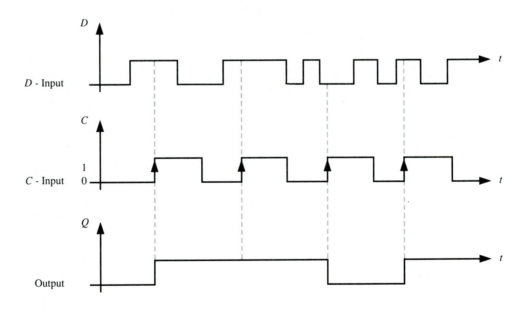

FIGURE 1.12

Solution

The D input is transferred to the Q output on the leading edge of each clock pulse. Note that no change can occur at any other time.

JK Flip-Flops

The **JK flip-flop** is a 2-input edge-triggered or edge-controlled flip-flop. *JK* flip-flops can be triggered on either the positive- or negative-going edge of a clock pulse.

However, negative-going edge-triggered *JK* flip-flops tend to be more commonly used in industry today. Since *JK* flip-flops have 2 inputs, there are four possible combinations of input conditions. The truth table of Figure 1.13 defines the output for each input combination. If both inputs are low, the output remains in its previous state (no change). When both inputs are different, the contents of the *J* input will be transferred to the *Q* output and the contents of the *K* input will be transferred to the $\overline{Q}$ output. When both inputs are high, the outputs will change to their opposite state. This is called **toggling.** The functional operation of a negative-edge-triggered *JK* flip-flop is shown in Figure 1.13b. Notice that it is a gated *RS* latch with the outputs fed back to the inputs in a cross-coupled manner. The *JK* flip-flop is probably the most widely used of all the different types of flip-flops.

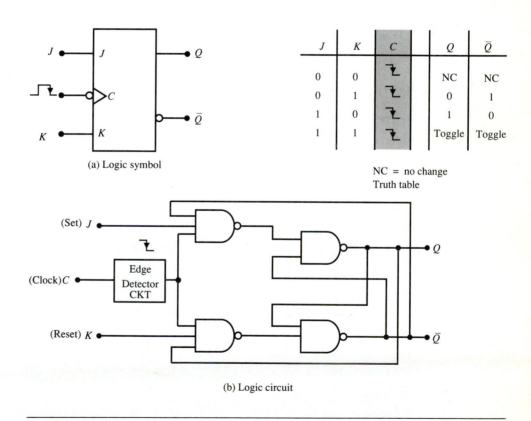

(a) Logic symbol

J	*K*	*C*	*Q*	$\overline{Q}$
0	0	⭨	NC	NC
0	1	⭨	0	1
1	0	⭨	1	0
1	1	⭨	Toggle	Toggle

NC = no change
Truth table

(b) Logic circuit

FIGURE 1.13
Basic *JK* flip-flop

EXAMPLE 1.12   Determine the *Q* output waveform for the *JK* flip-flop with the *J*, *K*, and clock inputs shown in Figure 1.14. Assume *Q* is initially high.

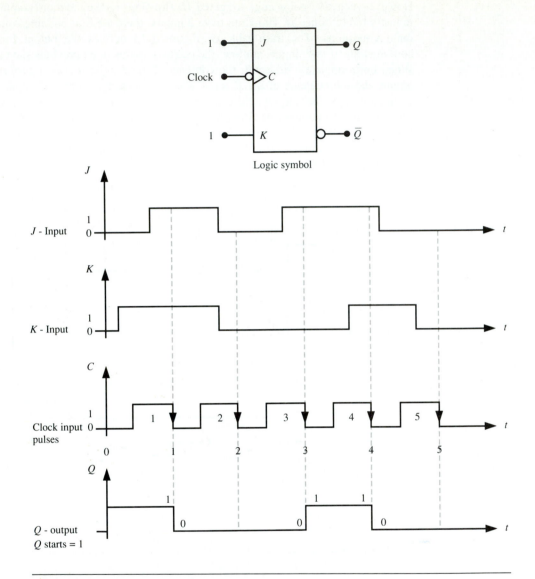

FIGURE 1.14

Solution

At the time of the first negative-going edge of the clock pulse, *J* is high and *K* is high. The *Q* output is therefore toggled to its opposite state. In this case it goes low. On the second negative-going edge of the clock pulse, *J* is low and *K* is low. Therefore, *Q* does not change. On the third clock pulse, *J* is high and *K* is low. Therefore, *Q* goes high. On the fourth clock pulse, *J* and *K* are both high. Therefore, *Q* toggles low. On the fifth clock pulse, *J* and *K* are both low, which results in no change of *Q*.

JK Master-Slave Flip-Flops

A practical problem with negative-edge-triggered flip-flops occurs when the input data changes at the same time that the clock trigger pulse occurs. This is because the inputs are not clearly defined, or stable, at the time of triggering, as shown in Figure 1.15. This is sometimes referred to as a **race condition.**

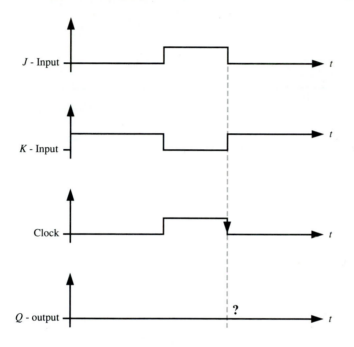

FIGURE 1.15
Race condition

The *JK* **master-slave flip-flop** of Figure 1.16 offers a solution for this type of situation. Consider the diagram of Figure 1.16. The *J* and *K* inputs are latched into the *master JK* flip-flop on the positive-going edge of the clock pulse. The *JK* inputs are then transferred to the output *slave JK* flip-flop on the negative-going edge of the clock pulse. The advantage here is that since the master has stored the inputs on the positive-going edge of the clock pulse, it is not necessary for the *J* and *K* inputs to remain stable once the negative-going edge of the clock pulse transitions.

The *JK* master-slave flip-flop is actually two *JK* flip-flops configured into one device. Figure 1.16(c) illustrates the operation of the *JK* master-slave flip-flop. When the clock is a low, the outputs of NAND gates 1 and 2 are forced high. This results in a no-change condition for the master *RS* latch. When the clock transitions to a high, the *J* and *K* inputs determine the state of the master *RS* latch. The slave *RS* latch is controlled, however, by the inverted clock signal. Therefore, when the clock C is high, $\overline{C}$ is low and the inputs to NAND gates 7 and 8 are forced high. This is the no-change condition for the slave flip-flop. When the clock C transitions from a high to a low, the slave clock $\overline{C}$ goes

(a)

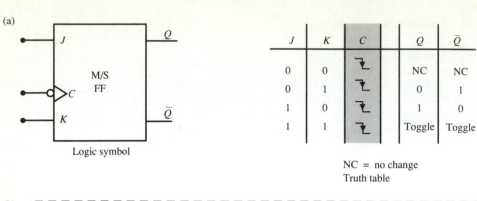

Logic symbol

J	K	C	Q	$\bar{Q}$
0	0	⌐⌐	NC	NC
0	1	⌐⌐	0	1
1	0	⌐⌐	1	0
1	1	⌐⌐	Toggle	Toggle

NC = no change
Truth table

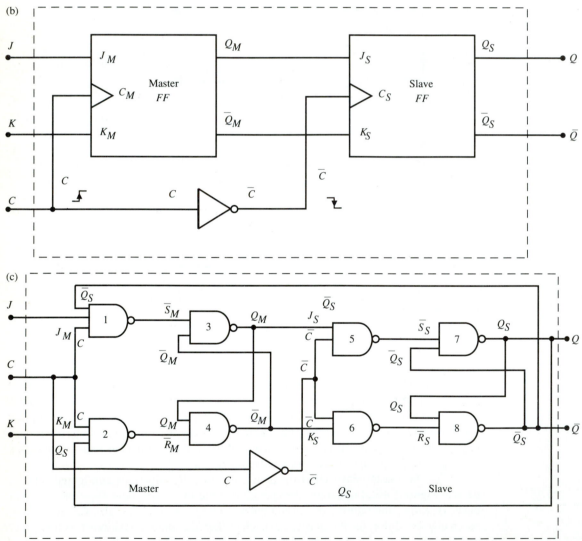

FIGURE 1.16
Master-slave *JK* flip-flop

high. The *JK* inputs to the slave J_S and K_S are then free to control the slave. Thus the data bits are transferred to the Q and $\overline{Q}$ outputs. The key control element is the clock inverter. It disables the slave when the master is enabled and vice versa. It is important to realize that the input data must remain stable during the time that the clock signal is high. This is because NAND gate 1 and NAND gate 2 are both enabled during this time.

Flip-Flop Timing

As we can see from our previous discussion, timing can be a very important consideration when dealing with flip-flops. Before using flip-flops, a technician must investigate a number of practical timing considerations, which can be obtained from the manufacturer's specifications or data sheet. The most important of these are setup time, hold time, and propagation delay, which are illustrated in Figure 1.17.

The **setup time** is the minimum time that the input data must be stable *before* the clock transition occurs. This is referred to as t_s on the manufacturer's data sheet. The setup time of a TTL flip-flop is typically 20 ns. It is typically 0 ns for a TTL master-slave flip-flop.

The *hold time* is the minimum time that the input must remain stable *after* the clock transition occurs. The hold time requirement for a TTL flip-flop is typically very short (5 ns). It is referred to as t_H on the data sheet.

The **propagation delay time** refers to the time required for the *output* of a flip-flop actually to change state. The propagation delay time from a low to a high transition may be different than the propagation delay from a high to a low. Typical TTL flip-flop propagation delays are 15 ns for a low to a high change (t_{PLH}) and 25 ns for a high to a low change (t_{PHL}).

It is important to note that setup time, hold time, and propagation delay time are all measured using the midpoint, or 50% point, of the pulse edge as a reference.

Asynchronous Inputs

Asynchronous means not synchronous or not clocked. **Asynchronous inputs** are inputs that act directly on a flip-flop regardless of the state of the clock and *JK* inputs (synchronous inputs). The asynchronous inputs of a flip-flop are labeled *preset* (PS) and *clear* (CL). The preset input *sets* the flip-flop, that is, the Q output is set to a 1 and the $\overline{Q}$ becomes a 0. The clear input *resets* the flip-flop and causes the Q output to become a 0 and the $\overline{Q}$ output to be a 1. Both asynchronous inputs are active low and therefore are usually referred to as $\overline{PS}$ and $\overline{CL}$. When both $\overline{PS}$ and $\overline{CL}$ are high, the flip-flop is ready for synchronous, or clocked, operation. This is referred to as the *armed* condition. The condition $\overline{PS} = 0$ and $\overline{CL} = 0$ should be avoided. This condition would force Q and $\overline{Q}$ to be a logic 1 at the same time. This is an illegal condition, since in Boolean algebra Q and $\overline{Q}$ must always be in the opposite state. Furthermore, since it is impossible for both $\overline{PS}$ and $\overline{CL}$ to go high (release) at exactly the same time, it is not possible to predict reliably the final new output state.

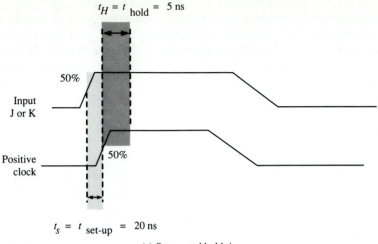

$t_H = t_{hold} = 5$ ns

50%

Input
J or K

Positive
clock

50%

$t_s = t_{set-up} = 20$ ns

(a) Set-up and hold times

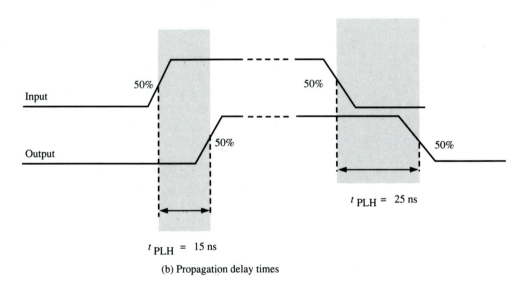

Input

50%

Output

50%

$t_{PLH} = 25$ ns

$t_{PLH} = 15$ ns

(b) Propagation delay times

FIGURE 1.17
Flip-flop timing

It is important to note that the asynchronous inputs *always* take precedence over the synchronous. Figure 1.18 shows the symbol for a flip-flop with asynchronous inputs, the truth table for these asynchronous inputs, and their functional operation.

Asynchronous inputs are often used to initialize flip-flops after the power to a circuit is first turned on. Asynchronous inputs are available on all types of flip-flops.

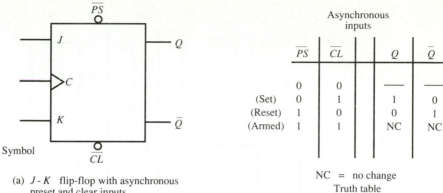

Symbol

(a) *J - K* flip-flop with asynchronous
preset and clear inputs

Asynchronous
inputs

	$\overline{PS}$	$\overline{CL}$		Q	$\overline{Q}$
	0	0		—	—
(Set)	0	1		1	0
(Reset)	1	0		0	1
(Armed)	1	1		NC	NC

NC = no change
Truth table

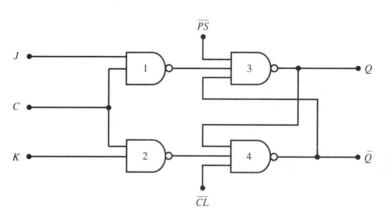

(b) *J - K* flip-flop with $\overline{PS}$ and $\overline{CL}$

FIGURE 1.18
Asynchronous inputs

1.14 THREE-STATE CONTROL DEVICES

In a computer system, there are often many subsystems that need to connect to, or
interface with, a bus or to another part of the system. Figure 1.19 illustrates a problem
where a memory subsystem, disk subsystem, and a tape subsystem are all connected to a
microprocessor's data bus. Obviously, all three subsystems cannot be allowed to put data
on the bus at the same time. For this reason, **three-state,** or *tristate,* logic devices were
developed. They are used to interface multiple devices onto a common bus.

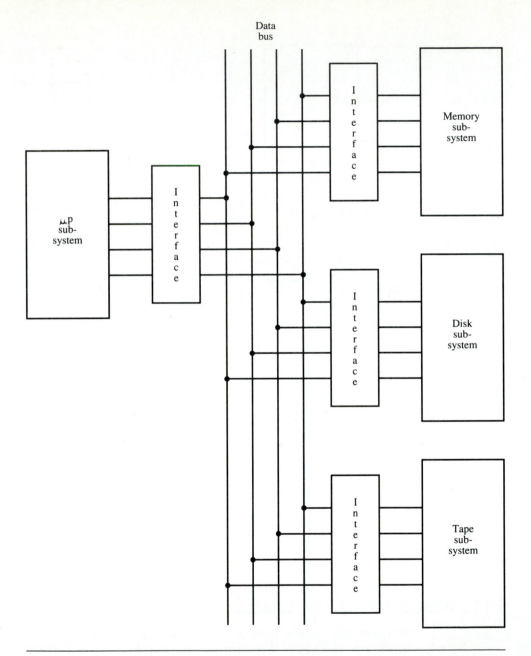

FIGURE 1.19
Microcomputer system

Three-state logic devices, unlike conventional logic devices, have three possible output logic states. These are:

Logic 0 state
Logic 1 state
Hi-Z state   (high-impedance state)

To explain the operation of a three-state device, we will consider the inverter of Figure 1.20. The enable control line can be considered like an extra input. When the enable line is active, the device functions normally. When the enable line is inactive, the device enters the high-impedance (Hi-Z), or disconnected, state. Thus the device looks like an open circuit to the common bus. Enable lines can be either active high or active low. Figure 1.20 illustrates the operation of an active high and an active low three-state inverter for all possible combinations of input conditions. Most types of TTL and CMOS devices are available in three-state and conventional form. A small inverted triangle (∇) added to the symbol is used to indicate a three-state device. Looking back at Figure 1.19, we can see the purpose and function of a three-state device. It is important to note that only one subsystem can be enabled to send data onto a bus at any given instant. Special control logic circuits must be designed to ensure that only one subsystem will be enabled at any time.

Buffers

Three-state **buffers** are devices that provide bus isolation and *driving power* in digital circuits. Buffers can be either inverting or noninverting. As their symbol implies, they can be thought of as *amplifiers*. Figure 1.21 illustrates the operation of the 74126 noninverting buffer.

Schmitt Trigger Devices

Many devices are available in **Schmitt trigger** versions. A Schmitt trigger is a circuit that switches states at threshold, or trigger, points. As soon as the input voltage reaches the trigger point, the output is caused to switch. The functional operation of a Schmitt trigger device is described in Figure 1.22 (p. 38). At the V_{TH} threshold level of the input signal, the output is switched high. At the V_{TL} threshold of the input signal, the output is switched low.

Most digital devices have specifications for pulse rise times. If the rise time is too long, the device will not operate properly. Schmitt trigger devices are often used as buffers to clean up distorted or slow-rising pulses. This is sometimes required when digital signals are transmitted long distances because the line capacitance tends to distort the signal. Schmitt triggers can be used to restore and correct distorted signals. Line lengths for TTL devices usually should not exceed 12 in. between devices.

The symbol used to indicate a Schmitt trigger type device is the hysteresis loop (⊓).

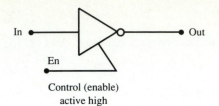
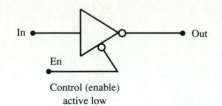

Control (enable)
active high

Control (enable)
active low

In	En	Out
0	0	Hi - Z
0	1	1
1	0	Hi - Z
1	1	0

Truth table
active high
enable

In	En	Out
0	0	1
0	1	Hi - Z
1	0	0
1	1	Hi - Z

Truth table
active low
enable

Hi - Z = High impedance or disconnected

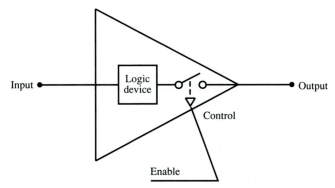

Block diagram of a three - state(tri - state)
device

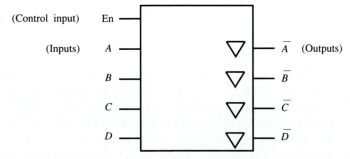

Four three - state inverters

FIGURE 1.20
Three-state logic

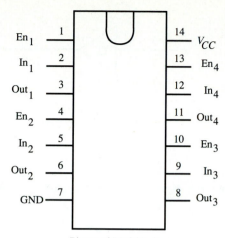

Pinout of 74126 buffer

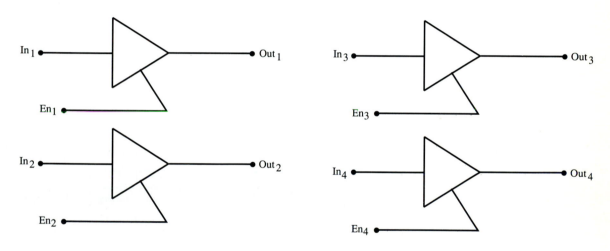

Logic circuit

In	En	Out
0	0	Hi - Z
0	1	0
1	0	Hi - Z
1	1	1

FIGURE 1.21
Four-bit noninverting buffer

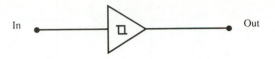

Logic symbol
Non - inverting Schmitt trigger

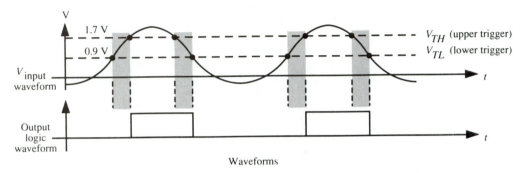

Waveforms

V_{TH} = upper trigger (threshold) level
V_{TL} = lower trigger (threshold) level

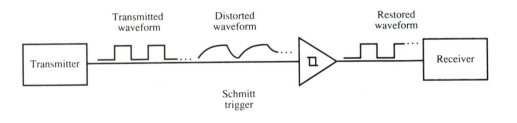

FIGURE 1.22
Schmitt trigger

Transceivers

When buffers are used to send data, they can be thought of as *transmitters*. When buffers are used to receive data they can be thought of as *receivers*. In either case, these devices are *unidirectional*. A **transceiver** is a *bidirectional* device that can transmit or receive data in *either direction* but not at the same time. Figure 1.23 describes the operation of a 74245 octal bus transceiver. This device has Schmitt trigger inputs and three-state outputs. The direction of data flow is controlled by pin 1. When pin 1 is low, data travel from *B* to *A*. When pin 1 is high, data travel from *A* to *B*. Three-state output enable is controlled by pin 19. When pin 19 is low, the device is enabled. When pin 19 is high, the device is disconnected (Hi-Z).

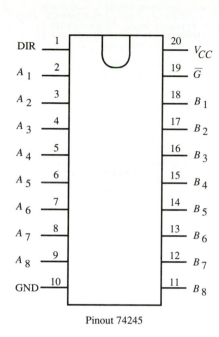

Pinout 74245

Enable	Direction Control	Operation
$\overline{G}$	DIR	
0	0	Data from B to A
0	1	Data from A to B
1	X	Isolation

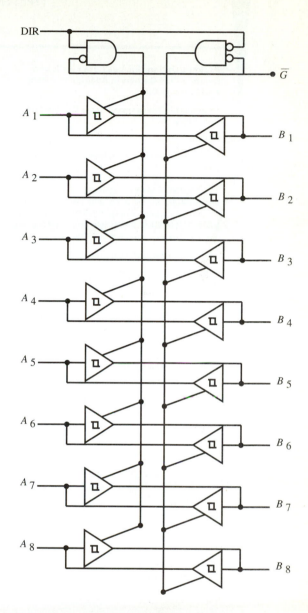

Logic circuit
74245

FIGURE 1.23
Octal bus transceiver with three-state output

1.15 IC SPECIFICATIONS

A typical IC data sheet, shown in Figure 1.24, can be broken down into three parts: (1) a summary, (2) a schematic diagram, and (3) electrical characteristics.

- Package Options Include Both Plastic and Ceramic Chip Carriers in Addition to Plastic and Ceramic DIPs

- Dependable Texas Instruments Quality and Reliability

description

These devices contain four independent 2-input NAND gates.

The SN5400, SN54H00, SN54L00, and SN54LS00, and SN54S00 are characterized for operation over the full military temperature range of $-55°C$ to $125°C$. The SN7400, SN74H00, SN74LS00, and SN74S00 are characterized for operation from $0°C$ to $70°C$.

FUNCTION TABLE (each gate)

INPUTS		OUTPUT
A	B	Y
H	H	L
L	X	H
X	L	H

logic diagram (each gate)

positive logic

$$Y = \overline{A \cdot B} \quad \text{or} \quad Y = \overline{A} + \overline{B}$$

SN5400, SN54H00, SN54L00 . . . J PACKAGE
SN54LS00, SN54S00 . . . J OR W PACKAGE
SN7400, SN74H00 . . . J OR N PACKAGE
SN74LS00, SN74S00 . . . D, J OR N PACKAGE
(TOP VIEW)

```
1A  [ 1    14 ]  VCC
1B  [ 2    13 ]  4B
1Y  [ 3    12 ]  4A
2A  [ 4    11 ]  4Y
2B  [ 5    10 ]  3B
2Y  [ 6     9 ]  3A
GND [ 7     8 ]  3Y
```

SN5400, SN54H00 . . . W PACKAGE
(TOP VIEW)

```
1A  [ 1    14 ]  4Y
1B  [ 2    13 ]  4B
1Y  [ 3    12 ]  4A
VCC [ 4    11 ]  GND
2Y  [ 5    10 ]  3B
2A  [ 6     9 ]  3A
2B  [ 7     8 ]  3Y
```

SN54LS00, SN54S00 . . . FK PACKAGE
SN74LS00, SN74S00 . . . FN PACKAGE
(TOP VIEW)

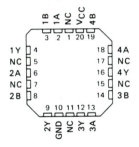

NC - No internal connection

TEXAS
INSTRUMENTS
POST OFFICE BOX 225012 • DALLAS, TEXAS 75265

3-3

3

TTL DEVICES

FIGURE 1.24a (pp. 40–42, reprinted by permission of Texas Instruments Inc.)
74LS00 data sheet

TYPES SN5400, SN54H00, SN54L00, SN54LS00, SN54S00, SN7400, SN74H00, SN74LS00, SN74S00
QUADRUPLE 2-INPUT POSITIVE-NAND GATES

schematics (each gate)

'00, 'L00

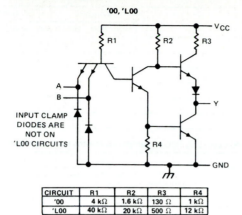

'H00

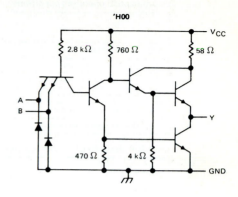

CIRCUIT	R1	R2	R3	R4
'00	4 kΩ	1.6 kΩ	130 Ω	1 kΩ
'L00	40 kΩ	20 kΩ	500 Ω	12 kΩ

'LS00

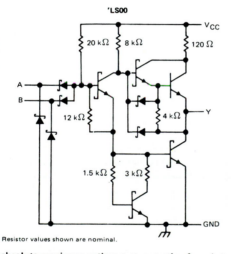

'S00

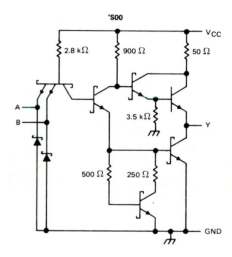

Resistor values shown are nominal.

absolute maximum ratings over operating free-air temperature range (unless otherwise noted)

Supply voltage, V_{CC} (see Note 1) '00, 'H00, 'LS00, 'S00 . . . . 7 V

'L00 . . . . 8 V

Input voltage: '00, 'H00, 'L00, 'S00 . . . . 5.5 V

'LS00 . . . . 7 V

Operating free-air temperature range: SN54' . . . . $-55°$C to 125°C

SN74' . . . . 0°C to 70°C

Storage temperature range . . . . $-65°$C to 150°C

NOTE 1: Voltage values are with respect to network ground terminal.

TEXAS
INSTRUMENTS

POST OFFICE BOX 225012 ● DALLAS, TEXAS 75265

FIGURE 1.24b
Continued

recommended operating conditions

		SN54LS00			SN74LS00			UNIT
		MIN	NOM	MAX	MIN	NOM	MAX	
V_{CC}	Supply voltage	4.5	5	5.5	4.75	5	5.25	V
V_{IH}	High-level input voltage	2			2			V
V_{IL}	Low-level input voltage			0.7			0.8	V
I_{OH}	High-level output current			−0.4			−0.4	mA
I_{OL}	Low-level output current			4			8	mA
T_A	Operating free-air temperature	−55		125	0		70	°C

electrical characteristics over recommended operating free-air temperature range (unless otherwise noted)

PARAMETER	TEST CONDITIONS †			SN54LS00			SN74LS00			UNIT
				MIN	TYP‡	MAX	MIN	TYP‡	MAX	
V_{IK}	V_{CC} = MIN,	I_I = −18 mA				−1.5			−1.5	V
V_{OH}	V_{CC} = MIN,	V_{IL} = MAX,	I_{OH} = −0.4 mA	2.5	3.4		2.7	3.4		V
V_{OL}	V_{CC} = MIN,	V_{IH} = 2 V,	I_{OL} = 4 mA		0.25	0.4		0.25	0.4	V
	V_{CC} = MIN,	V_{IH} = 2 V,	I_{OL} = 8 mA					0.35	0.5	
I_I	V_{CC} = MAX,	V_I = 7 V				0.1			0.1	mA
I_{IH}	V_{CC} = MAX,	V_I = 2.7 V				20			20	µA
I_{IL}	V_{CC} = MAX,	V_I = 0.4 V				−0.4			−0.4	mA
I_{OS} §	V_{CC} = MAX			−20		−100	−20		−100	mA
I_{CCH}	V_{CC} = MAX,	V_I = 0 V			0.8	1.6		0.8	1.6	mA
I_{CCL}	V_{CC} = MAX,	V_I = 4.5 V			2.4	4.4		2.4	4.4	mA

† For conditions shown as MIN or MAX, use the appropriate value specified under recommended operating conditions.
‡ All typical values are at V_{CC} = 5 V, T_A = 25°C
§ Not more than one output should be shorted at a time, and the duration of the short-circuit should not exceed one second.

switching characteristics, V_{CC} = 5 V, T_A = 25°C (see note 2)

PARAMETER	FROM (INPUT)	TO (OUTPUT)	TEST CONDITIONS		MIN	TYP	MAX	UNIT
t_{PLH}	A or B	Y	R_L = 2 kΩ,	C_L = 15 pF		9	15	ns
t_{PHL}						10	15	ns

NOTE 2: See General Information Section for load circuits and voltage waveforms.

3

TTL DEVICES

TEXAS
INSTRUMENTS
POST OFFICE BOX 225012 • DALLAS, TEXAS 75265

FIGURE 1.24c
Continued

The *summary part* contains information describing the functional type and part number of the device. It tells us the operating temperature range, the truth or function table, logic symbol or diagram, Boolean output equation, and packaging and pin configuration for the device. Figure 1.24(a) shows the summary part of a data sheet for a TTL quadruple 2-input positive logic NAND gate (74LS00). Referring to Figure 1.24(a), we note that the 74LS00 data sheets tell us the following:

1. The device contains four independent 2-input NAND gates.
2. The operating temperature is between 0°C and 70°C.
3. From the truth table, the output will be low *(L) only* when both inputs are high.
4. The logic diagram shows the symbol for a 2-input NAND gate with *A* and *B* as the input and *Y* as the output.
5. The Boolean expression is given as $Y = \overline{A \cdot B}$, or $Y = \overline{A} + \overline{B}$.
6. The pin configuration and packaging styles available from this manufacturer are shown.

The *schematic diagram part* of the data sheet shows the exact internal circuit diagram of the device. Figure 1.24(b) shows the 74LS00 schematic. Notice that four different schematics are shown, one for each available subseries of the device. For example, the first schematic is for the standard version, 00, and the low power version, L00. The second schematic is for the high-speed version, H00. The third is for the low-power Schottky version, LS00, and the fourth schematic is for the Schottky version, S00. Also given in the schematic diagram part of the data sheet are the absolute minimum ratings for V_{CC}, input voltage, operating temperature, and storage temperature.

The *electrical characteristics part* of the data sheet is divided into three subsections: recommended operating conditions, electrical characteristics, and switching characteristics. Figure 1.24(c) shows the electrical characteristics part of the 74LS00 data sheet. The most useful characteristics are as follows:

- V_{CC}—*supply voltage:* Typically the nominal value is $+5$ V_{DC} with a range of $+4.75$ V_{DC} to $+5.25$ V_{DC}.
- V_{IH}—*high-level input voltage:* The minimum input voltage needed to be recognized as a logic 1 by the device. Typically, $V_{IH} = 2.0$ V_{DC}.
- V_{IL}—*low-level input voltage:* The maximum input voltage allowed to be recognized as a logic 0 by the device. Typically, $V_{IL} = 0.8$ V_{DC}.
- I_{OH}—*high-level output current:* The maximum output current when the device is in the logic 1 output state. Typically, $I_{OH} = -0.4$ mA (minus sign indicates current is leaving the device).
- I_{OL}—*low-level output current:* The maximum output current when the device is in the logic 0 output state. Typically, $I_{OL} = 8$ ma.
- V_{OH}—*high-level output voltage:* The logic 1 output voltage. It defines the lowest voltage that the device will output in the logic 1 state. Typically, $V_{OH} = 3.4$ V_{DC}; minimum $V_{OH} = 2.7$ V_{DC}.
- V_{OL}—*low-level output voltage:* The logic 0 output voltage. It defines the highest voltage that the device will output in the logic 0 state. Typically $V_{OL} = 0.35$ V_{DC}; maximum $V_{OL} = 0.5$ V_{DC}.
- I_{IH}—*high-level input current:* The logic 1 input current that will flow into a device's input. Typically, $I_{IH} = 20$ μa maximum.

- I_{IL}—*low-level input current:* The logic 0 input current that will flow through a device's input. Typically, $I_{IL} = -0.4$ ma.
- I_{CCH}—*supply current high:* The supply current when the output is a logic 1 (high). The total current supplied to the device from V_{CC}. Typically, $I_{CCH} = 0.8$ ma; maximum $I_{CCH} = 1.6$ ma.
- I_{CCL}—*supply current low:* The supply current when the output is a logic 0 (low). The total current supplied to the device from V_{CC}. Typically, $I_{CCL} = 2.4$ ma; maximum $I_{CCL} = 4.4$ ma.
- t_{PLH}—*propagation low to high:* The time required for the device to switch or change its output state from a logic 0 to a logic 1 (low to high). Typically, $t_{PLH} = 9$ ns; maximum $t_{PLH} = 15$ ns.
- t_{PHL}—*propagation high to low:* The time required for the device to switch or change its output state from a logic 1 to a logic 0 (high to low). Typically, $t_{PHL} = 10$ ns; maximum $t_{PHL} = 15$ ns.

All the preceding typical, minimum, and maximum specifications are from the 74LS00 data sheet shown in Figure 1.24.

1.16 DATA SHEET ANALYSIS

Three useful electrical characteristics can be derived from the data sheet by calculation, power dissipation, noise immunity, and fan-out.

Power Dissipation

Power dissipation is the power consumed by the device. In general, power dissipation can be calculated by equation (1.1).

$$P_D = V_{CC} \times I_{CC} \tag{1.1}$$

where V_{CC} is the voltage applied to the power supply pin on the device and I_{CC} is the current flowing through that pin. Note that for TTL logic family devices the power pin is usually labeled V_{CC}, whereas for CMOS logic family devices, the power pin is usually labeled V_{DD}.

As previously described, I_{CC} varies depending on the logic state of the device (i.e., I_{CCH}, I_{CCL}). Therefore, it is often useful to consider the average power dissipation by calculating an average I_{CC} as follows:

$$I_{CC(avg)} = \frac{I_{CCH} + I_{CCL}}{2} \tag{1.2}$$

and

$$P_{D(avg)} = V_{CC} \times I_{CC(avg)} \tag{1.3}$$

Noise Immunity

Noise immunity is a measure of a circuit's ability to handle noise voltage on its inputs. Noise voltage is an unwanted electrical signal that can be picked up by circuit wiring leading into a device. The noise voltage can be added to or subtracted from the intended input voltage causing a false or incorrect logic signal state to be interpreted by the device as shown in Figure 1.25.

Noise immunity calculations are referred to as the *noise margin* of a device. Output voltages greater than $V_{OH \ min}$ will be interpreted by the device as logic 1. Input voltages greater than $V_{IH \ min}$ will be interpreted by the device as a logic 1. The high-state noise margin becomes

$$V_{NMH} = V_{OH \ min} - V_{IH \ min} \qquad \textbf{(1.4)}$$

For the 74LS00 of Figure 1.24, the high-state margin is calculated as follows:

$$\begin{aligned} V_{NMH} &= V_{OH \ min} - V_{IH \ min} \\ &= 2.4 - 2.0 \\ &= 0.4 \text{ V} \end{aligned}$$

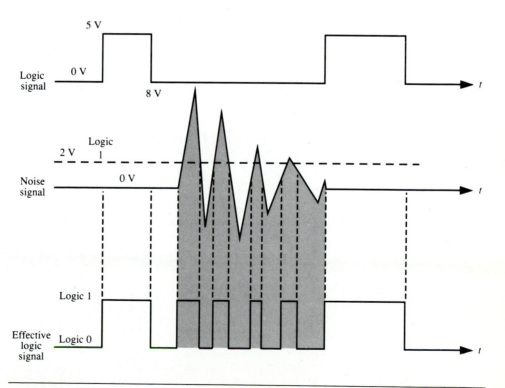

FIGURE 1.25
Noise immunity

Input voltages less than $V_{IL\ max}$ will be interpreted as a logic 0. Output voltages less than $V_{OL\ max}$ will be interpreted as a logic 0. Thus the low-state noise margin becomes

$$V_{NML} = V_{IL\ max} - V_{OL\ max} \qquad \textbf{(1.5)}$$

For the 74LS00 data sheet of Figure 1.24, the low-state noise margin is calculated as follows:

$$
\begin{aligned}
V_{NML} &= V_{IL\ max} - V_{OL\ max} \\
&= 0.8 - 0.4 \\
&= 0.4 \text{ V}
\end{aligned}
$$

Fan-out

Fan-out is defined as the maximum number of device inputs of the same logic family that a device output can drive in parallel. In Figure 1.26, the output of the 74LS00 (gate 0) is being used to drive 20 74LS00 (10 devices, gates 1–10) inputs. For most TTL logic family devices, this number is 10 inputs or more.

The calculation of fan-out requires analysis of two parameters—the current available from the output device and the current required by the device input. Recall that the output current available depends on the logic state of the device (I_{OH}, I_{OL}). This is also true for device input current requirements (I_{IH}, I_{IL}). Therefore, two calculations for fan-out are required, one for the high state and one for the low state. The actual device fan-out is said to be the worst case or lowest condition. Specifically,

$$\text{Fan-out}_{\text{high}} = \frac{I_{OH}}{I_{IH}} \qquad \textbf{(1.6)}$$

$$\text{Fan-out}_{\text{low}} = \frac{I_{OL}}{I_{IL}} \qquad \textbf{(1.7)}$$

For the 74LS00 data sheet of Figure 1.24, fan-out is calculated as follows:

$$
\begin{aligned}
\text{Fan-out}_{\text{high}} &= \frac{I_{OH}}{I_{IH}} \\[2mm]
&= \frac{0.4 \text{ ma}}{20 \text{ μa}} \\[2mm]
&= \frac{400 \text{ μa}}{20 \text{ μa}} \\[2mm]
&= 20
\end{aligned}
$$

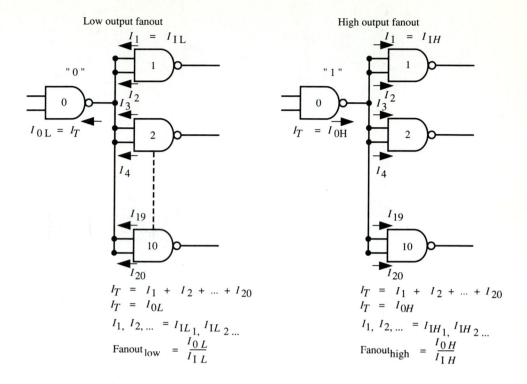

FIGURE 1.26
Fan-out

$$\text{Fan-out}_{\text{low}} = \frac{I_{OL}}{I_{IL}}$$

$$= \frac{8 \text{ ma}}{0.4 \text{ ma}}$$

$$= 20$$

Note that the fan-out for a device is the worst case, or lowest condition. In this case, for the 74LS00, fan-out$_{\text{high}}$ and fan-out$_{\text{low}}$ turn out to be the same value. This will not always be the case with other devices. It should also be noted that fan-out is sometimes referred to as **unit load** calculations.

Current Sourcing and Current Sinking

When the output of a gate is high and it is supplying current to the input of another gate or gates, this condition is known as *current sourcing*. Current sourcing can then be defined as I_{OH}, as shown in Figure 1.27(a). In Figure 1.27(a) the output of NAND gate

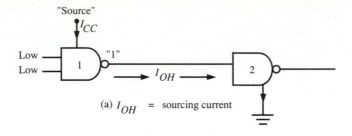

(a) I_{OH} = sourcing current

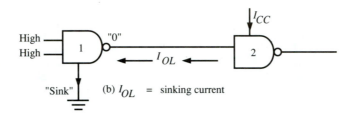

(b) I_{OL} = sinking current

FIGURE 1.27
Sourcing/sinking

1 is high and supplying current to the input of NAND gate 2, where ground is supplied externally.

When the output of a gate is low and current is flowing from the input of another gate or gates into the output, this condition is known as *current sinking*. Current sinking is then a measure of how much current can enter a device output when it is in the logic 0 state and not have the output rise above a specified limit. Current sinking can then be defined as I_{OL}, as shown in Figure 1.27(b). In Figure 1.27(b) the output of NAND gate 1 is low (providing ground internally) and NAND gate 1 must sink current from the input of NAND gate 2.

1.17 TECH TIPS AND TROUBLESHOOTING—T³

The logic probe is a tool that you will find extremely useful for troubleshooting digital circuits. Figure 1.28 shows an example of a typical logic probe. The logic probe is a very handy instrument for determining the logic state of a device. While logic probes may vary in their features and capabilities, they are all quite similar.

From our discussion on logic devices, we have seen that there are different types of logic families. Each logic family operates at different voltages and has different input and output characteristics. Because of these differences, logic probes are designed to operate with a particular logic family. Some logic probes have a switch that will enable operation with two or more logic families. Changing the position of the switch changes the logic family that can be tested.

Most logic probes are powered by the system under test. Power is obtained by connecting a cable from the logic probe to the system power supply (V_{CC}) and ground.

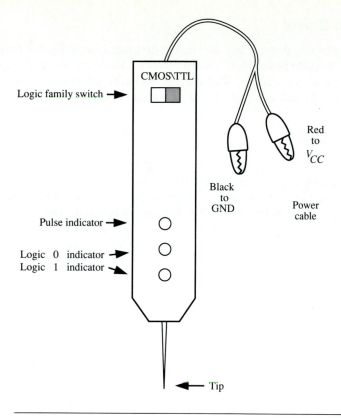

FIGURE 1.28
Logic probe

At the bottom of the logic probe is a naillike tip. The tip is used to *probe,* or test, the state of a logic device. When the tip is placed on an IC pin or test point in a circuit, the logic probe will indicate the current logic state of that point.

Most probes have visual indicators to signify a logic state. For example, a red light may indicate a logic 1 condition, and a green light may be used to indicate a logic 0 condition. If no light is lit, it usually indicates an open circuit, or tristate condition. This is sometimes referred to as a **float.** Some logic probes have a third light that pulses to indicate that a constant pulsing is occurring. Others have an internal 1-bit memory built in, which is very useful in determining transient pulses.

The logic probe can be used to verify proper circuit operation. The proper operation of a logic circuit can be determined by probing the input and output pins of a gate. In general there are four types of problems to look for:

1. No V_{CC} or ground
2. Defective gate
3. Open connections or wires
4. Shorted connections or wires

No V_{CC} or Ground

When troubleshooting any device, the first step is to verify that power is applied to the circuit. Without power an IC cannot function. Therefore, the first step is to check for V_{CC} and ground connections. This test can be easily performed using the logic probe. V_{CC} will be indicated as a logic 1 and ground as a logic 0.

Defective Gate

Figure 1.29(a) illustrates a method that can be used to detect a defective gate. Beginning at the output of gate 3, the logic probe is used to determine the logic state of Z. In this case, we find it is *always* a logic 0. Next we probe the 2-input pins of gate 3. The top pin is found to be pulsing. The bottom pin is found to be a logic 0. Since gate 3 is an OR gate, we realize that any 1 on an input pin should force the output to be high. Therefore, the output should be pulsing. Since the logic probe indicated that the output of gate 3 was always a 0, we should suspect that gate 3 is defective.

Open Connections or Wires

Referring to Figure 1.29(b), suppose that our logic probing indicates no pulses on the top input to gate 3. Furthermore, suppose that by moving the logic probe back to the output of gate 2, we detect a pulsing condition. This would indicate an open or broken connection between the output of gate 2 and the input of gate 3. It is important to note the logic probe indication at the top input to gate 3. No lights are lit; recall that this is referred to as a float. For TTL gates, floats are always interpreted *by a logic gate as a logic level 1*.

Shorted Connections or Wires

Referring to Figure 1.29(c), we note a logic level 0 on both inputs to gate 3. Probing the output of gate 2 also indicates a logic level 0. Probing the inputs to gate 2 indicates a logic level 1 on the top input and pulsing on the bottom input. This might cause one to think that gate 2 is defective. If the condition remains the same after replacing gate 2, the technician should look for another cause to the problem. One technique that may be tried is to lift the output pin of gate 2 out of the socket. If the output pin is lifted out of the socket, pulsing should now be noted on the logic probe, as shown in Figure 1.29(d). But what if probing the inputs to gate 3 still indicates logic level 0s on both input pins? This is an indication of a shorted connection at the input to gate 3, since the top pin to gate 3 has been forced to a float (logic 1).

It should be noted that ICs are not always socketed. Therefore, it may be necessary to cut a pin in order to force a float condition. While this is not a preferred procedure, it can be performed as a test. The IC can then be either repaired by soldering or replaced.

The unused inputs to a TTL or CMOS device should always be connected somewhere. This is especially important when dealing with CMOS devices. An unused input on a TTL device will be perceived by the device as though a logic 1 were applied

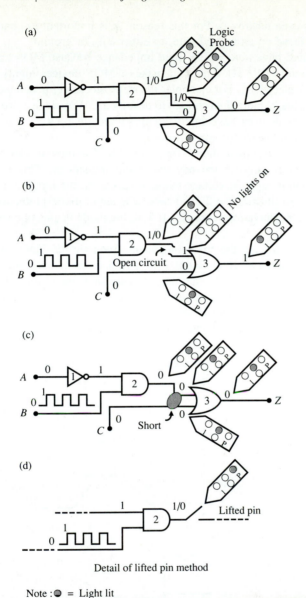

FIGURE 1.29
Logic probe troubleshooting

to its input. Although unused TTL inputs that are left open become more susceptible to EMI and stray electronic interference, they generally can provide reliable operation. When using CMOS devices, unused inputs should be connected to either V_{DD} or ground. Open inputs on CMOS devices can lead to unpredictable operation and even oscillation. Furthermore, the unused inputs on a CMOS device can increase the power consumption of the device and even destroy it. For this reason, it is important to connect all unused inputs, including those on an unused gate, to either V_{DD} or ground.

CMOS devices have a very high input impedance because MOS transistors are in effect an open circuit (10^{12} Ω). This fact makes CMOS devices highly susceptible to damage from static electricity. For example, the static electricity generated from walking across a carpet is usually more than enough to destroy a CMOS device. To help solve this problem, all CMOS devices have input circuit protection built in. This protection is accomplished through the use of input diodes.

TTL devices also use input diodes for protection. The input diodes on TTL devices are used to prevent ringing on the negative-going transitions. This is performed by limiting the maximum negative voltage that can appear on the input to a TTL device to -0.5 V. Figure 1.30 illustrates a TTL device with input diode protection. If the input voltage should ring negative in excess of -0.5 V, the diode begins to conduct, *clamping* the input.

Since input diodes are the first components seen by the input signals, they are prone to overload damage. If an input diode opens, the device may still function normally. If an input diode shorts, the device will not work at all. The problem that occurs is that often when an input diode is blown, it becomes a high-resistance short circuit. This is because the input diode is a small diode with a small junction. The silicon, which is a semiconductor, ends up shorting the junction, and the silicon creates

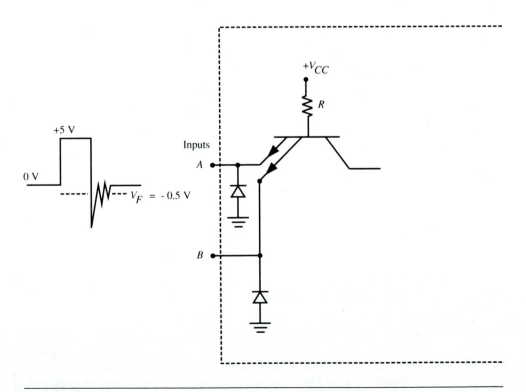

FIGURE 1.30
TTL input protection

a short of about 30 to 200 Ω. This can result in the device functioning unreliably. Depending on device threshold voltages and loading, enough current may be available for proper operation some of the time. This phenomena is sometimes known as the *input diode anomaly*. If the device is checked out statically, it will still appear to function properly, as defined by the truth table. However, dynamic operation in a circuit may be unreliable and cause intermittent errors. For this reason, it is important to check the input diodes in a device. Simply use a DMM with a diode scale and note the proper forward voltage drop. When the black lead of the DMM is placed on the input pin and the red lead to the ground, the DMM should indicate about 500mV. Reversing the leads will indicate an overload (OL) condition. It should be noted that analog meters usually do not have enough voltage to perform this test.

One final consideration when dealing with TTL devices is that of **decoupling.** Decoupling capacitors are used to eliminate unwanted *transients,* or *spikes,* on power supply lines. These spikes are created when the device output switches states. To remove these unwanted transients, decoupling capacitors are installed between V_{CC} and ground. Usually a large capacitor, 0.1 to 1 μF, is installed at the V_{CC} input pin of an edge connector on a printed circuit board. Also, smaller decoupling capacitors between 0.01 to 0.1 μF are installed between V_{CC} and ground for every one to three ICs. These capacitors are installed as close as possible to each IC with the lead length of the capacitors being as short as possible.

EXERCISES

1.1 Convert the following binary numbers to decimal:
  a. 01110001   b. 00010001
  c. 11110101   d. 00101111

1.2 Convert the following binary numbers to decimal:
  a. 1101.0101   b. 10111.0111
  c. 1000001.1111   d. 0101.11001

1.3 Convert the following decimal numbers to binary:
  a. 109   b. 128
  c. 250   d. 257

1.4 Convert the following hexadecimal numbers to decimal:
  a. *B5*   b. *FF*
  c. 10   d. 29

1.5 Convert the following decimal numbers to hexadecimal:
  a. 39   b. 78
  c. 256   d. 1000

1.6 Convert the following hexadecimal numbers to binary:
  a. *A4*   b. *FD*
  c. 11   d. 1*C*1

1.7 Convert the following hexadecimal numbers to binary:
  a. *ABCD*   b. *FE*15
  c. *F00E*   d. 04051

1.8   Convert the following binary numbers to hexadecimal:
        a. 001100110011   b. 1010.1111
        c. 100101101000   d. 001001111100

1.9   Convert the following binary numbers to hexadecimal:
        a. 1111110   b. 1000011101
        c. 00100001101   d. 111111011100100000111

1.10   Write the following characters or symbols in ASCII code:
        a. BECCA   b. ROBBY
        c. 1579   d. STOP

1.11   Decode the following from ASCII:
        a. 0110000   b. 1001111
        c. 1011010   d. 1000001

1.12   Decode the following from ASCII:
        a. 0000000 0001010   b. 0100100 0110101
        c. 1010011 1010100 1010101   d. 1010010 1001001 1000011
                                                                   1001011

1.13   Explain the term DIP. Draw one of the most common styles.

1.14   Identify the two most common logic families.

1.15   Which logic family can use a dc power supply voltage of $+3$ V to $+18$ V?

1.16   Give the logic symbol, truth table, and Boolean expression for a(n):
        a. AND gate   b. OR gate
        c. inverter

1.17   If four inverters are connected in series, determine the output of the last inverter when the input to the first inverter is a logic 1.

1.18   Give the logic symbol, truth table, and Boolean expression for a(n):
        a. NAND gate   b. NOR gate
        c. XOR gate   d. XNOR gate

1.19   Discuss the steps you would follow if you were to test a digital circuit using a logic probe.

1.20   How can you verify V_{CC} and ground with a logic probe?

1.21   How can you test for open connections in a digital circuit?

1.22   How can you test for shorted connections in a digital circuit?

1.23   Design an *RS* flip-flop using:
        a. NAND gates   b. NOR gates

1.24   Draw the diagram of a *JK* master-slave flip-flop.

1.25   Define the following terms for flip-flop devices:
        a. Setup time   b. Propagation delay time
        c. Asynchronous inputs   d. Race condition

1.26   Draw the logic diagram and truth table for an inverting, active low enable tristate device.

1.27   Draw the logic diagram and truth table for a 74126 buffer used to interface a 4-bit data bus to a 4-bit output device.

1.28   Draw the logic symbol and input/output waveforms for an inverting Schmitt trigger device.

1.29   Describe the package types and pin outs that are available for the 7400 device shown in Figure 1.24.

1.30   Referring to Figure 1.24, determine the operating temperature for:
       a. the 7400   b. the 5400

1.31   From the 74LS00 device specifications of Figure 1.24, determine the absolute maximum ratings for:
       a. V_{CC} b. Input voltage
       c. Storage temperature

1.32   From the 74LS00 device specifications of Figure 1.24, determine the maximum recommended operating conditions for:
       a. V_{CC} b. V_{IL}
       c. I_{OH} d. I_{OL}
       e. T_P (max)

1.33   From the 74LS00 device specifications of Figure 1.24, determine the minimum recommended operating conditions for:
       a. V_{CC} b. V_{IH}
       c. V_{OH}

1.34   What is the average power dissipated by a 74LS00 device?

1.35   Determine the noise margin V_{NMH} and V_{NML} for:
       a. 54LS00   b. 74LS76   (See the appendix.)

1.36   Determine the fan-out for the 54LS00 and the 74LS76 devices.

1.37   Explain what should be done with unused inputs on TTL devices and why.

1.38   How are the inputs to TTL and CMOS devices protected?

1.39   What is the input diode anomaly? Explain how input diodes can be tested.

1.40   Discuss the use of decoupling capacitors on TTL devices.

1.41 Crossword Puzzle

ACROSS

2. Base 2 number system.
6. IC.
10. Type of logic function.
11. Type of flip-flop.
12. Electronic circuit that performs Boolean functions.
13. Single binary digit.
14. Lowest positional binary digit weight.
16. Time required for a device to change logic state.
18. High logic state.
19. Base 16 number system.
20. Complimentary metal oxide semiconductor.
21. Transmitter/receiver IC.
22. Capacitor used to filter power line noise.
24. Minimum time that flip-flop data must be stable before the clock occurs.
27. When the output of a gate is high and it is supplying current to the input of another gate.

DOWN

1. Bistable circuit.
3. Alphanumeric code.
4. Inverter function.
5. Low logic state.
7. Preset and clear inputs on a flip-flop.
8. Flip-flop condition when $Q = 0$ and $\overline{Q} = 1$.
9. High-impedance logic state.
13. George Boole's math.
15. Threshold triggering circuit.
17. When the output of a gate is low and current is flowing from the input of another gate.
22. IC package style.
23. Type of logic family.
25. Most significant bit.
26. Logic gate that outputs a 1 only when all the inputs are 1.

CHAPTER TWO

MEMORY

KEY TERMS

Address

Address Decoding

Address Multiplexing

Application Specific
   Integrated Circuits (ASICs)

Bit Organized

Bit Parity

Blank PLD

Cell

Check Sums

Column-address Selector (CAS)

Combinational PALS

Cyclic Redundancy Check (CRC)

Dynamic RAM (DRAM)

Erasable PROM (EPROM)

Fuse Map

Maskable ROM

Memory Cell

Memory Location

Nonvolatile Memory

Product Line

Product Term

Programmable Array Logic (PAL)

Programmable Logic Array (PLA)

Programmable Logic Device (PLD)

Programmable ROM (PROM)

PROM Burner

Random Access

Random Access Memory (RAM)

Read Cycle

Read Only Memory (ROM)

Read Operation

Refreshed

Registered PALS

Row-address Selector (RAS)

Sequential PALS

Static RAM (SRAM)

Sum Line

Word Organized

Word Parity

Write Cycle

Write Operation

Volatile Memory

2.0 INTRODUCTION

Since the early 1970s, ICs or semiconductor memory have been the most widely used type of *primary memory* found in microcomputers. The simplest form of computer memory is the basic flip-flop. A flip-flop is called a **memory cell** when it represents a single storage bit (0 or 1). In most microcomputers 8 or 16 cells are connected together to form a memory byte or memory word. Each memory byte or word has a unique location in memory called an **address.** This address tells the computer where to find the memory cells and can be likened to the address of your house. Memory is a place, therefore, where data bits (0 or 1) can be stored and then later retrieved when the computer needs it. The process by which a computer stores data into memory is called *writing*. Therefore we say that a computer is in a **write cycle** or performing a **write operation** when it is storing data into memory. The process by which a computer retrieves data from memory is called a **read cycle** or **read operation** as illustrated in Figure 2.1.

FIGURE 2.1
Basic memory

2.1 MEMORY FUNDAMENTALS

Memory can be classified into two general types, **ROM** and **RAM.** ROM stands for **read-only memory,** and RAM stands for **random-access memory.** ROM generally contains permanently stored data that cannot be changed. It can be read but not written into. ROM is always available to the computer and is not lost when the power is turned off. For this reason, it is known as **nonvolatile memory.** RAM, on the other hand, is memory that can be read from or written to. Thus a computer can store or save data and later retrieve that data. The data can also be changed at any time. RAM memory is **volatile memory,** that is, it is lost or erased whenever the power is switched off. RAM memory can be compared with your notebook. You write notes in your notebook, read your notes, and sometimes even change your notes. On the other hand, ROM memory is like your textbook. Generally the information in your textbook may be read but not written or changed.

The term **random access** means that any memory location can be enabled or addressed in any sequence. That is, information does not have to be read or written to sequentially. Actually, both RAM and ROM memory are random access. The major

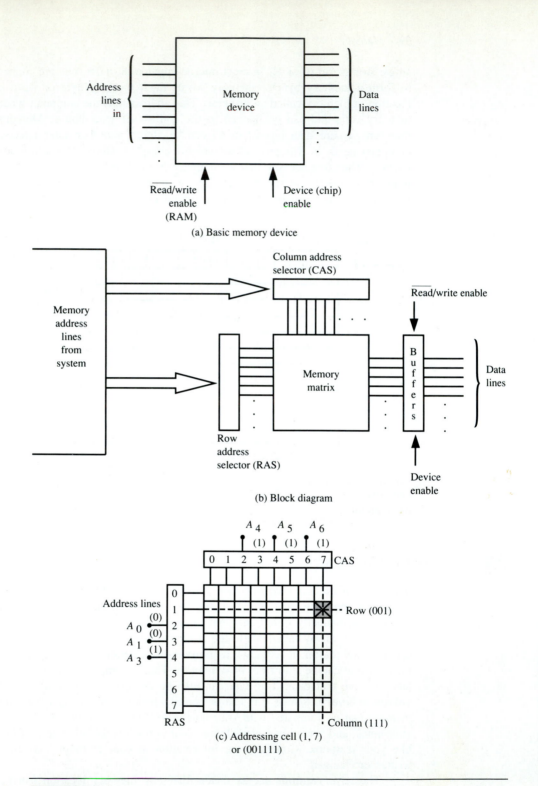

(a) Basic memory device

(b) Block diagram

(c) Addressing cell (1, 7)
or (001111)

FIGURE 2.2
Basic memory device

difference is that RAM is memory that can be read and written to. A better name for RAM might be read/write memory.

Memory Structure

Figure 2.2 illustrates a basic block diagram of a memory device. A memory device is connected to the rest of a microcomputer system through its address and data lines. It is controlled by its device-enable line and, in the case of RAM, its $\overline{\text{Read}}$/write control line.

Memory devices are generally organized in a matrix format. The matrix is organized into rows and columns to define an individual memory location or address as shown in Figure 2.2(c). This matrix can be thought of as a postal address scheme where the rows represent the street addresses and the columns represent the house numbers. Each box in the memory matrix is called a **cell,** or **memory location.** A memory cell or location is selected by the address selection or decode circuitry. This circuitry is broken up into two parts: the **row-address selector (RAS)** and the **column-address selector (CAS).** The memory address lines define the RAS and the CAS locations. The device-enable control line is used to turn on the memory output buffers from the tristate condition. The $\overline{\text{Read}}$/write control defines the type of operation or cycle being performed.

Memory is either **bit organized** or **word organized.** A bit-organized memory device can store a single bit for each address location. Thus for a bit-organized device, each box in the matrix of Figure 2.2(c) represents one binary digit. A word-organized memory device selects a group of memory cells at the same time for each address location. Thus for a word-organized device, each box in the matrix of Figure 2.2(c) represents a group of binary digits. Each group of cells is usually a byte (8 bits) or a word (16 bits) in length. Regardless of the type of organization being used, the maximum number of memory locations is determined by the number of address lines, using the following relationship:

$$\text{Maximum number of memory locations} = 2^N \tag{2.1}$$

where N represents the number of address lines.

Table 2.1 shows the relationship between the number of address lines and the number of memory locations. Note the use of the standard notation, which rounds the actual maximum number of memory locations. For example, 64K of memory actually has 65,536 memory locations.

2.2 ROM

As previously stated, ROMs are referred to as nonvolatile memory because the information stored in a ROM is not lost or destroyed when the power is turned off. ROMs can be classified into three general types. A **maskable ROM** is a ROM that is programmed with information or data by the manufacturer. Once programmed, these data bits cannot be altered or changed. A **programmable ROM,** or **PROM,** is a device that can be programmed by an individual user through the use of specialized equipment called a **PROM burner.** Once programmed, the data in a PROM, like a ROM, cannot be altered or changed. An **erasable PROM,** or **EPROM,** is a type of ROM that can be

TABLE 2.1
Address lines/memory locations

Address Lines	Memory Locations	Standard Notation
10	1024	1K
11	2048	2K
12	4096	4K
13	8192	8K
14	16,384	16K
15	32,768	32K
16	65,536	64K
17	131,072	128K
18	262,144	256K
19	524,288	512K
20	1,048,576	1M
24	16,777,216	16M
32	4,294,467,296	4G

programmed by an individual user but whose data may be erased or changed with the use of specialized equipment. Erasing is accomplished with ultraviolet light. ROMs are used in applications where the data bits are of a permanent nature—for example, code converters, character generators, fixed computer program instructions, fixed constants, and data tables like those used for the trigonometric functions of sine, cosine, and tangent.

Figure 2.3 illustrates a masked ROM configured from a diode array matrix. The ROM is programmed through the use of diodes. A diode is connected between an input address line and an output data line whenever a logic 1 is desired. For example, if a logic 1 ($+5$ V) is applied to one of the input address row lines, the corresponding diode, D_1, will be forward biased, resulting in a logic 1 output on the data line. If we wish the output to be a logic 0, we simply omit the diode. Therefore, if we apply a logic 1 to input address line A_0 and a logic 0 to all other input address lines, the output data on lines D_3, D_2, D_1, and D_0 will be 0101, respectively. The truth table of Figure 2.3 summarizes the output data patterns for various input addresses of the diode matrix ROM shown in Figure 2.3(a).

A PROM can be constructed using bipolar transistors (BJTs) or from enhancement field-effect transistors (MOSFETs) as shown in Figure 2.4 (p. 64). Programming is accomplished through fuses. If the fuse is connected, a logic 1 results. If the fuse is blown, a logic 0 results. To program the PROM, a device known as a PROM programmer or PROM burner is used. Once the desired address is selected, a large amount of current is used to blow out the desired fuses. This is why the data bits are permanently stored and cannot be changed or altered in this type of device.

The erasable PROM or EPROM uses enhancement MOSFET devices. Storage or nonstorage is accomplished by trapping charges at the gate of the enhancement MOSFET. Erasing is performed by exposing the MOSFET to intense ultraviolet light.

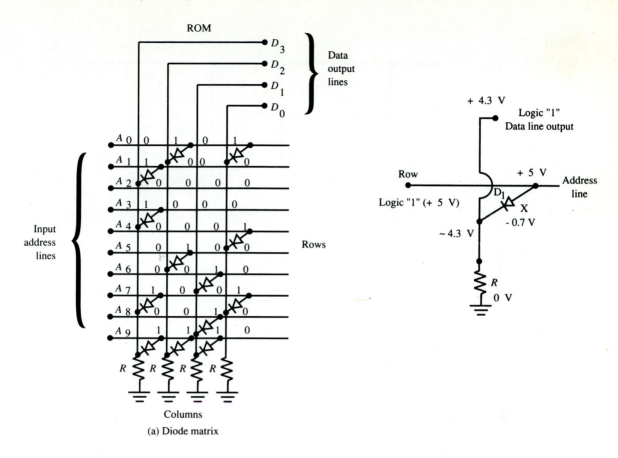

(a) Diode matrix

Input address										Output data			
A_9	A_8	A_7	A_6	A_5	A_4	A_3	A_2	A_1	A_0	D_3	D_2	D_1	D_0
0	0	0	0	0	0	0	0	0	1	0	1	0	1
0	0	0	0	0	0	0	0	1	0	1	0	0	0
0	0	0	0	0	0	0	1	0	0	0	0	0	0
0	0	0	0	0	0	1	0	0	0	1	0	0	0
0	0	0	0	0	1	0	0	0	0	0	0	0	1
0	0	0	0	1	0	0	0	0	0	0	1	0	0
0	0	0	1	0	0	0	0	0	0	0	0	1	0
0	0	1	0	0	0	0	0	0	0	1	0	0	1
0	1	0	0	0	0	0	0	0	0	0	0	1	0
1	0	0	0	0	0	0	0	0	0	1	1	1	0

(b) Truth table

FIGURE 2.3
Masked ROM from diode matrix

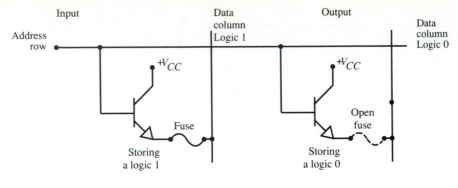

(a) Bipolar cells

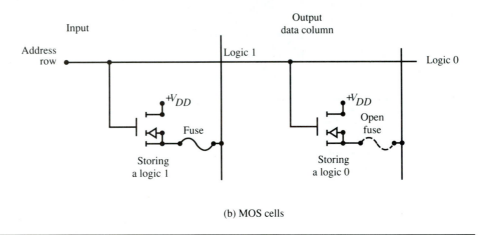

(b) MOS cells

FIGURE 2.4
PROM cells

Although ROMs may vary in size and shape, some terminology has become standard. ROMs may be classified by the number of storage locations and the number of output data bits. For example, a 256 × 4 ROM will have 256 storage locations of 4 bits each. A 1024 × 8 ROM has 1024 storage locations of 8 bits each. A 512 × 1 ROM has 512 single-bit storage locations, and so forth.

Figure 2.5 shows the block diagram and pin configuration for the Intel 2716, 2048 × 8 EPROM. The address lines are decoded to select the desired output data. Tristate output buffers are used to enable the device. Programming is accomplished by activating the $\overline{PD}$/PGM pin.

2.3 RAM

RAM, or read/write memory, is a type of volatile memory from which data can be read and into which it can be written. Any memory cell of RAM memory can be selected in any sequence, and the data contents, unlike ROM memory, can be changed at any time.

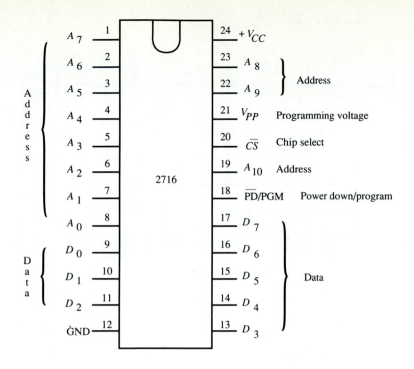

(a) 2716 Prom
pinout

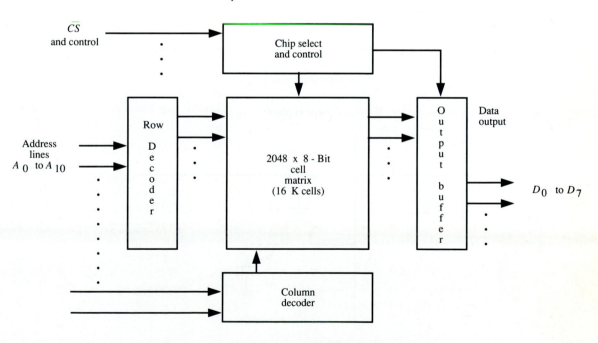

(b) 2716 prom block diagram

FIGURE 2.5
2716, 2048 × 8 EPROM

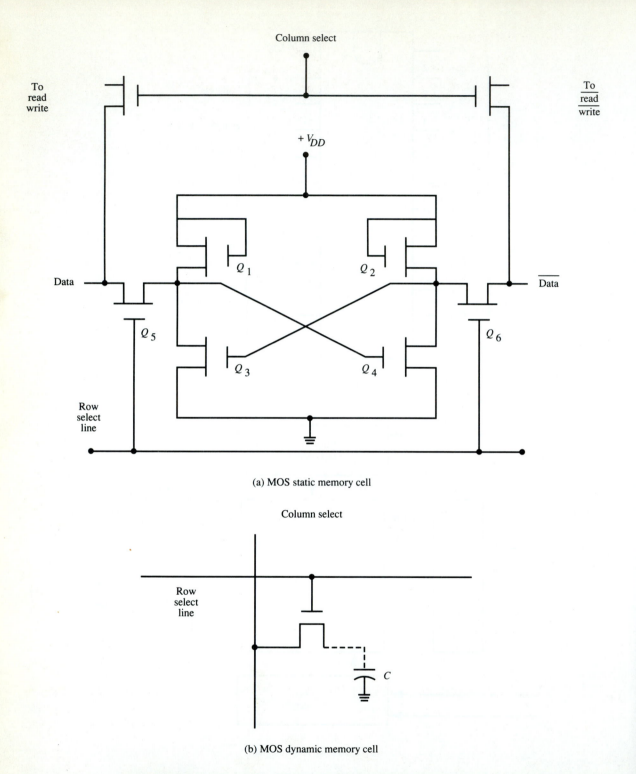

(a) MOS static memory cell

(b) MOS dynamic memory cell

FIGURE 2.6
RAM memory cells

RAMs can be classified as either static or dynamic. A **static RAM (SRAM)** holds data as long as the power is applied to the device. It is essentially an array of flip-flops in which each flip-flop represents 1 bit or one memory cell, as shown in Figure 2.6(a). A **dynamic RAM (DRAM)** is a type of RAM in which the data must be periodically recharged, or **refreshed.** Refreshing is accomplished by performing a repetitive read or write operation or a special refresh operation. The added cost and complexity of the DRAM are more than offset by the higher cell density, which lowers the per-bit cost of the device. DRAMs are made up from MOSFET devices, which appear to act like capacitors, as shown in Figure 2.6(b). If the capacitor is not recharged periodically, the data will be lost due to leakage. DRAMs require refreshing approximately every 2 to 4 ms. Refreshing is accompanied by reenergizing the capacitor to store a logic 1 and by maintaining the discharge of the capacitor to store a logic 0.

SRAM

Figure 2.7 illustrates the functional diagram, pin configurations, and truth table for a TMS 4016 SRAM. The TMS 4016 is a MOS device organized in a 2048×8-bit memory cell array. Pin 20, $\overline{G}$, controls the output buffer enable line. If $\overline{G}$ is high, the output is in the tristate. If $\overline{G}$ is low, the output is connected to the system. Pin 18, $\overline{S}$, controls the chip-select line. If $\overline{S}$ is high, the device is disabled and cannot read or write data. If $\overline{S}$ is low, the device is selected and can then be used to read or write data. Pin 21, $\overline{W}$, controls the read/write operation. If $\overline{W}$ is high, the device is in the read mode. If $\overline{W}$ is low, the device is in the write mode. A_0 through A_{10} are the address lines that define an individual memory cell in the array. D_1 through D_8 are the memory cell data input or output lines. The truth table illustrates the operation of the device. For example, to write or store data into the device, $\overline{W}$ must be low and $\overline{S}$ must be low. The data bits on the data lines are then written or stored in the address defined on the address lines. Note that during a write operation, the logic state of $\overline{G}$, the output control, is not important.

DRAM

Simplicity, cost, and high data density make the DRAM the most popular type of memory device used in microcomputer systems today. Since each memory cell is essentially a single MOSFET, large numbers of memory cells can be cheaply packaged into a single device. The drawbacks are generally slower speed and the need to refresh. Since the internal capacitance of the MOSFET is great enough to make it appear that a small capacitor (a few picofarads) exists in the MOSFET, data can be stored as charge or no charge in the capacitor. No charge or a logic 0 can be stored indefinitely. A logic 1 or a charged capacitor must be refreshed, or recharged, at least once every 2 ms, or the capacitor will lose its charge and the data.

Figure 2.8 shows the pin configuration for the TMS 4116 DRAM. The TMS 4116 is a MOS device organized in a $16K \times 1$-bit array. Recall from Table 2.1 that 16K of memory is actually 16,384 memory locations. This would require 14 address bits or 14 address lines, since 2^{14} equals 16,384. In order to save address lines and reduce the

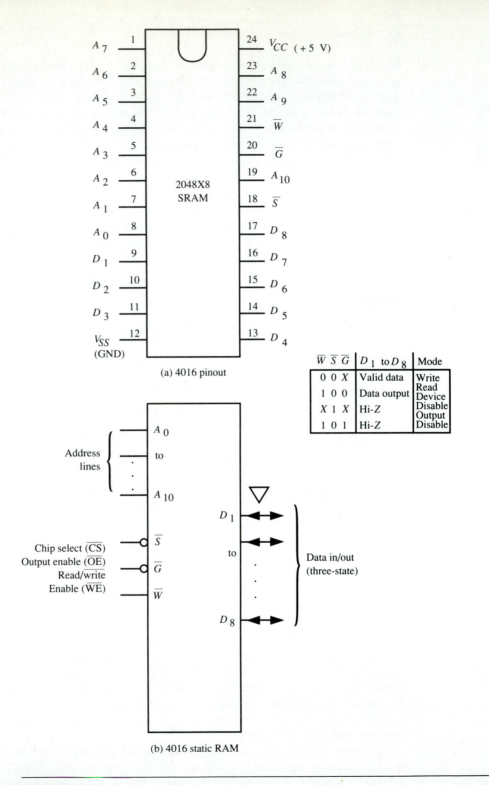

$\overline{W}$	$\overline{S}$	$\overline{G}$	D_1 to D_8	Mode
0	0	X	Valid data	Write
1	0	0	Data output	Read Device
X	1	X	Hi-Z	Disable Output
1	0	1	Hi-Z	Disable

(a) 4016 pinout

(b) 4016 static RAM

FIGURE 2.7
TMS 4016 static MOS RAM

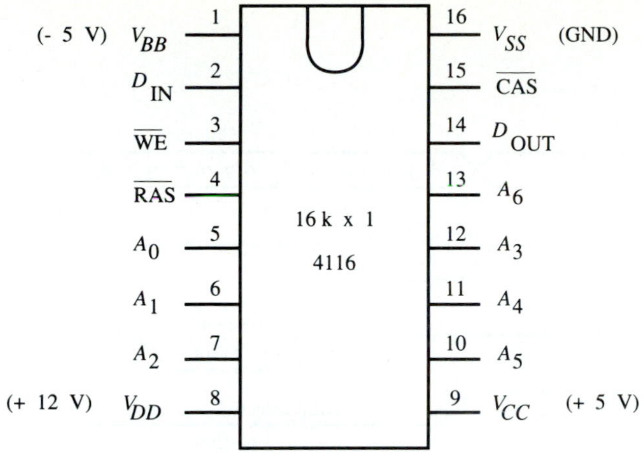

FIGURE 2.8
4116 DRAM pinout

number of pins required on the IC, most DRAMs employ a technique known as **address multiplexing.** Instead of 14 address lines, only 7 address lines are provided. During a read or write operation, the 7 address lines first contain the row information and then the column information. This is controlled by using the $\overline{\text{RAS}}$ and $\overline{\text{CAS}}$ control lines, as shown in Figure 2.9. Whenever the $\overline{\text{RAS}}$ line is low, the information on the address line will be held or latched in the *row-address latch*. Whenever the $\overline{\text{CAS}}$ line is low, the information on the address line will be held or latched in the *column-address latch*. The $\overline{\text{RAS}}$ and $\overline{\text{CAS}}$ control lines must never be allowed to both be low at the same time, or confusion within the device may result. The write enable line, $\overline{\text{WE}}$, determines the read/write mode. When $\overline{\text{WE}}$ is low, data on the D_{in} line will be written into the selected address. When the $\overline{\text{WE}}$ line is high, data from the selected address will appear on the D_{out} line.

Refreshing is accomplished by reading data, writing data, or by a separate refresh operation. Basically, the refresh control circuitry must sequentially select each row of memory cells, one row at a time, until all rows have been refreshed. This is called *burst mode refreshing*. During this time, data cannot be read from or written into the device until the entire refresh operation is complete. Another technique refreshes each row in discrete cycles. This is called *single-cycle refresh*. In Figure 2.10(a) the refresh control circuitry causes the multiplexer to switch from the address line to the refresh row address counter. Once the refresh row address counter is selected, the counter supplies the row address information (RA_0–RA_6) to step sequentially through each row of the memory array. When the refresh counter reaches its final count, which is the last row in the memory cell array, the refresh cycle is ended. The multiplexer is switched back to the address lines, and the memory cell array is then available to the system. Figure 2.10(b) illustrates the refresh cycle timing. The control signal initiates the refresh cycle by selecting the refresh row address counter. The $\overline{\text{RAS}}$ signal causes each selected row to be refreshed. The $\overline{\text{CAS}}$ signal is kept high in order to disable the output buffers.

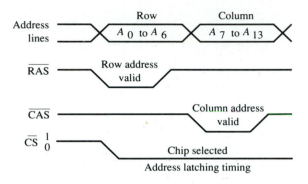

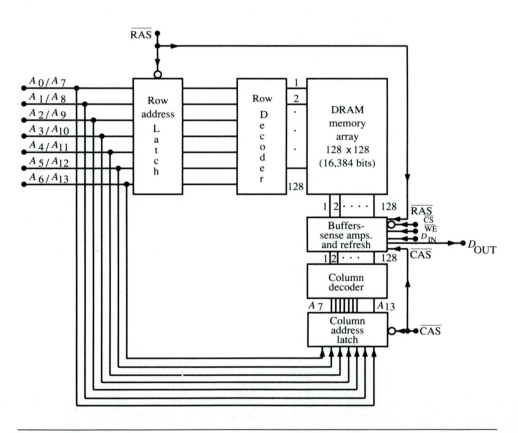

FIGURE 2.9
DRAM block diagram

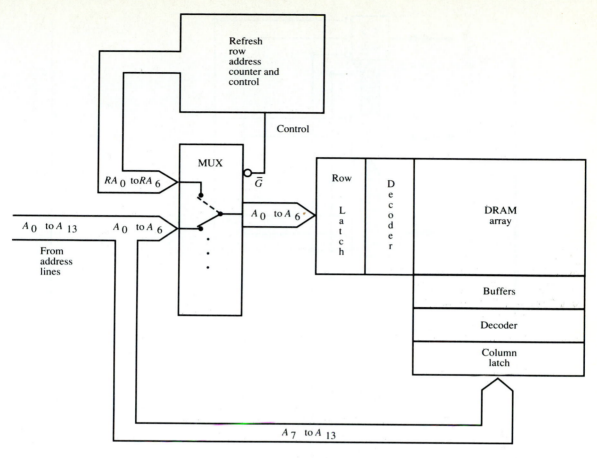

(a) DRAM with refresh control

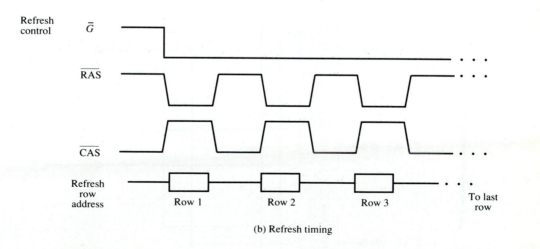

(b) Refresh timing

FIGURE 2.10
DRAM refresh

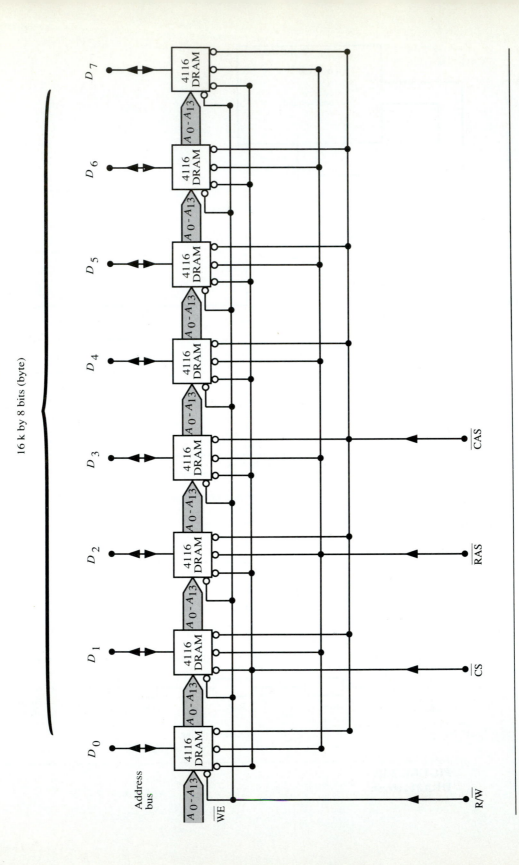

FIGURE 2.11
16K × 18-bit DRAM memory expansion using 4116 DRAMS (16K × 1 bit each)

2.4   MEMORY EXPANSION

We have seen that memory arrays can be organized in many ways, for example, 2048 $\times$ 8, 4096 $\times$ 4, and 16,384 $\times$ 1. Many microcomputer systems organize their data in 8-, 16-, and even 32-bit formats. A typical problem that arises is how to organize a certain size memory system. For example, suppose we want a 16K $\times$ 8-bit memory. We could use either eight 2048 $\times$ 8 memory chips or eight 16,384 $\times$ 1 memory chips. Let's first consider the case where we wish to make a 16K $\times$ 8-bit memory system out of eight 16,384 $\times$ 1-bit memory chips. The TMS 4116, which was previously discussed, is a 16,384 $\times$ 1-bit memory chip that can be used for this application. Essentially, all that is required for this type of memory expansion is to connect each memory chip in parallel, as illustrated in Figure 2.11. Notice that all the address lines and control lines are connected and parallel. If we are in the read mode, all eight memory chips will be in the read mode. If we are in the write mode, all eight memory chips will be in the write mode. The data lines are used to form the 8-bit-wide, or byte-wide, memory system.

To illustrate how to use eight 2048 $\times$ 8 memory chips to make a 16K $\times$ 8-bit memory system, we first consider a number of techniques that are commonly used to expand memory. We begin by expanding to a 4K $\times$ 8 system, then to an 8K $\times$ 8 system, and finally to a 16K $\times$ 8-bit memory system.

The 4K $\times$ 8-bit memory system is shown in Figure 2.12. It consists of two TMS 4016 static RAMs. Each 4016 is organized in a 2048 $\times$ 8-bit array. The 4016 has 11 address lines, A_0 through A_{10}. This is what you would expect for a 2K memory chip, since 2^{11} equals 2048 memory locations. To address 4K, or 4096, memory locations, an additional address line is required ($2^{12} = 4096$). This additional line is used to select which memory chip we wish to use. Therefore, A_{11} is connected to the chip-select pin. To distinguish between the lower 2048 memory locations (0–2047) and the upper 2048 memory locations (2048–4095), an inverter is used. For all memory addresses between 0 and 2047, A_{11} will be a logic 0, selecting the lower bank. For all memory addresses between 2048 and 4095, A_{11} will be a logic 1, selecting through the inverter the higher bank. As we can see, A_{11} is used as a bank selector. Using the higher-order address lines for bank selection is a common technique. It is sometimes referred to as **address decoding.**

The 8K $\times$ 8-bit memory expansion system is shown in Figure 2.13. It consists of four TMS 4016 2K $\times$ 8-bit static RAMS. To address 8K, or 8192, memory locations requires 13 address lines (A_0 through A_{12}), since 2^{13} equals 8192 memory locations. Each TMS 4016 has 11 address lines, A_0 through A_{10}. The additional address lines, A_{11} and A_{12}, are used to select the memory chip we wish to use as follows:

- U_1 defines memory locations $(0000-2047)_{10}$ or $(0000-07FF)_{16}$.
- U_2 defines memory locations $(2048-4095)_{10}$ or $(0800-0FFF)_{16}$.
- U_3 defines memory locations $(4096-6143)_{10}$ or $(1000-17FF)_{16}$.
- U_4 defines memory locations $(6144-8191)_{10}$ or $(1800-1FFF)_{16}$.

Chip selection is controlled by the gating arrangement illustrated in Figure 2.13. For all memory addresses between 0000 and 2047, both A_{11} and A_{12} will be low. Referring to Figure 2.13, we can see that if A_{11} and A_{12} are both low, the output of OR gate 1 will be

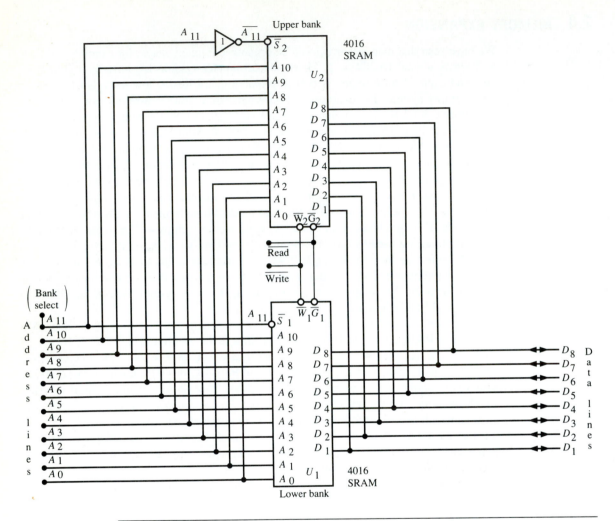

FIGURE 2.12
4K × 8-bit (byte) memory system using 4016 SRAMs of 2K × 8 bits

low, selecting only memory chip U_1. For all memory addresses between 2048 and 4095, A_{11} will be high, but A_{12} will be low. The combination of A_{11} high and A_{12} low will result in only memory chip U_2 being selected. For all memory addresses between 4096 and 6143, A_{11} will be low and A_{12} will be high, resulting in the selection of only U_3. Finally, for all memory addresses between 6144 and 8191, A_{11} and A_{12} will be high, resulting in the selection of only U_4.

The technique of using a gating arrangement to perform address decoding in memory-expansion systems would become cumbersome for larger memory systems. The 16K × 8-bit memory system of Figure 2.14 employs a slightly different technique. Eight TMS 4016 2K × 8-bit static RAMS are used to make the 16K × 8-bit memory system. Fourteen address lines, A_0 through A_{13}, are now required to define 16,384 memory

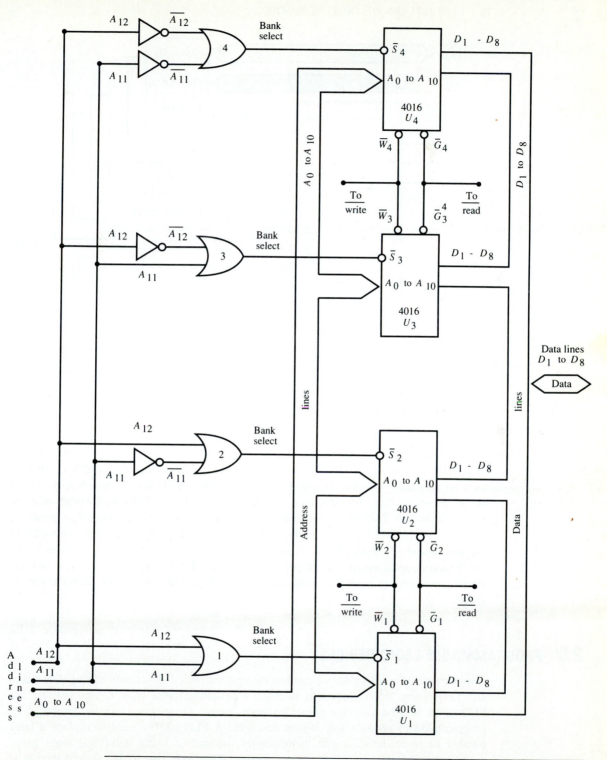

FIGURE 2.13
8K × 8-bit (byte) memory system

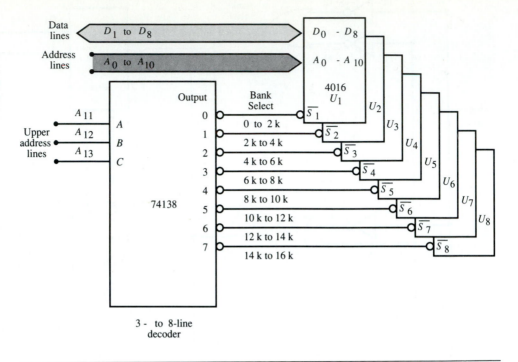

FIGURE 2.14
16K × 8-bit (byte) memory system

locations, since 2^{14} equals 16,384. The additional three lines, A_{11}, A_{12}, and A_{13}, are used for chip selection. Address decoding or memory chip selection is accomplished using a 74138, three- to eight-line decoder. In Figure 2.14 address lines A_0 through A_{10} are connected to each TMS 4016. Address lines A_{11}, A_{12}, and A_{13} are connected to inputs A, B, and C of the 74138, respectively. The 74138 outputs 0 through 7 are connected to memory banks U_1 through U_8, respectively. As memory addresses are defined, the 74138 decodes and selects the proper memory bank. For example, if A_{11}, A_{12}, and A_{13} are all low, memory bank U_1 is selected. For larger systems, additional decoders can be added.

2.5 PROGRAMMABLE LOGIC DEVICES

Another type of memory device that has the characteristics of not only storing data but of also performing logical functions is called a **programmable logic device (PLD).** The PLD is an IC that contains numerous logic gates. These gates can be combined by programming to produce any logical function. A PLD can be used to replace a large number of logic devices. The manufacturer, instead of using individual logic gates, programs a PLD to perform the same function. Thus only one IC is required instead of

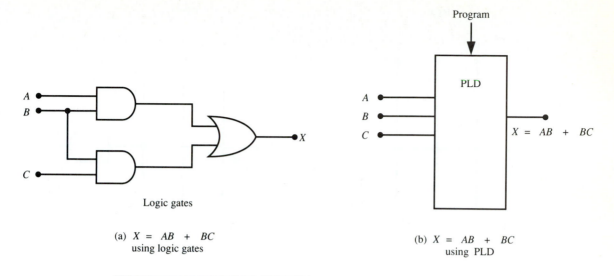

(a) $X = AB + BC$
using logic gates

(b) $X = AB + BC$
using PLD

FIGURE 2.15
PLD

many. This reduces cost and increases system reliability. For example, the circuit of Figure 2.15(a) can be replaced by the single PLD of Figure 2.15(b). Instead of wiring the circuit of Figure 2.15(a), the designer can program the PLD to perform the same function.

If you look at circuit boards used in recently manufactured computers, such as the IBM PS/2 series, and compare them with earlier ones, you will see that many of the individual gates have been replaced by PLDs. PLDs enable the manufacturer to save a lot of valuable PC board space and also provide more complex functions. This allows more features for the same given PC board area. For example, newer microcomputers have been able to provide all their graphic functions using PLDs. Design corrections or changes can be made by simply programming a new PLD and replacing the old one.

The most popular PLD is the PROM. Other PLDs are reprogrammable, such as the ultraviolet erasable (EPROM) and the electrically erasable (EEPROM) PLD. With these types of PLDs, the logic function can be erased and a new one programmed in, thus eliminating the need to replace the chip.

2.6 PLD INTERNAL STRUCTURE

A **product line** is an input line connected to an *AND gate*. The inputs to the PLD can be programmed such that they will be either connected or not connected to the product line. All the inputs that are connected are ANDed together. The result is called the **product term.** For example, if the product term $X \cdot Y$ is needed, lines X and Y remain connected, but line Z does not, as shown in Figure 2.16(a). If the term $X \cdot Z$ is desired, we connect lines X and Z only as shown in Figure 2.16(b).

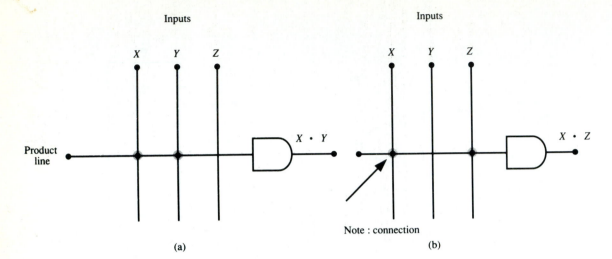

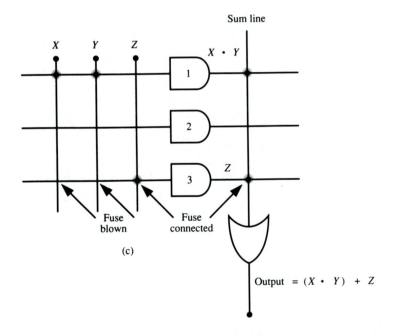

FIGURE 2.16
Fuse map

A **sum line** is a line connected by an *OR gate* to the output. For example, if the expression $(X \cdot Y) + Z$ is desired, the product line from AND gate 1 and the product line from AND gate 3 will be connected to the sum line, as shown in Figure 2.16(c). Note that the product line connections must also be made.

A PLD that is not programmed is referred to as a **blank PLD.** Each connection is made by a fuse. When the PLD is programmed, the fuses of the lines that are not to be connected are blown open. Internally, the PLD consists of a matrix of product lines and sum lines that is called a **fuse map.** The blowable fuses are used to connect the product and sum lines to the output. All the inputs to a PLD are connected through a buffer. This provides both inverted and noninverted inputs, as shown in Figure 2.17.

Some PLDs are completely programmable, whereas others have one level of gates fixed or permanently connected, which is the basic difference among different types of PLDs.

For example, a PROM is a PLD with fixed AND gates and programmable OR gates. The array of AND gates form the PROM address decoder, as shown in Figure 2.18. For a given address input, its product term from the AND gate will be high, whereas all the others will be low. For example, in Figure 2.18, if address inputs I_0, I_1, I_2, and I_3 are all high (logic 1), product line 15 through AND gate 15 will be high, and all others will be low. This will select or decode address 15. If we wish to store 1010 at this memory location, we must program the OR array to store this number. The number 1010 is stored by programming the OR array to blow the fuses of the sum lines A and C and leave connected the fuse connections of the sum lines B and D.

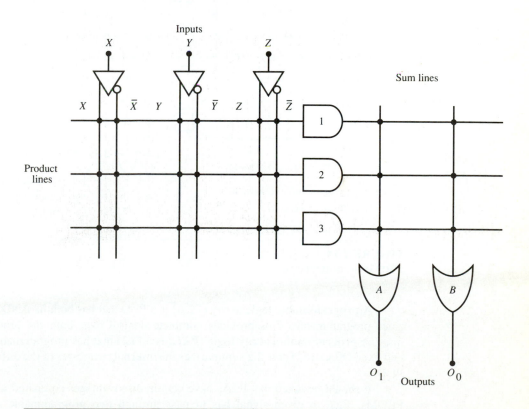

FIGURE 2.17
PLD with buffered inputs

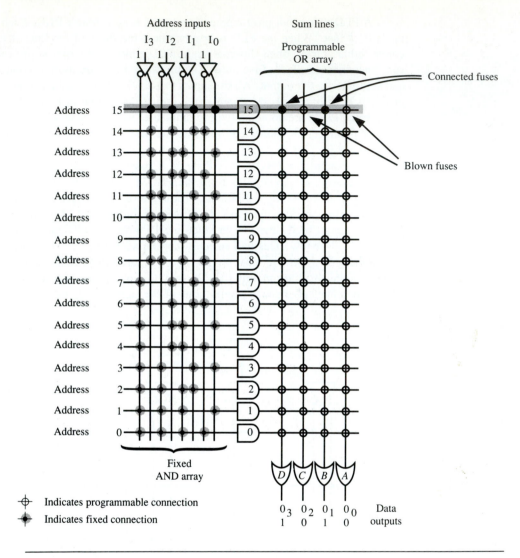

FIGURE 2.18
PROM array structure

A **programmable logic array (PLA)** is a PLD that has both its AND gates and OR gates programmable. This provides complete control over both the product and sum lines. A **programmable array logic (PAL)** is a PLD that has programmable AND gates and fixed OR gates. Table 2.2 summarizes the internal structures of the different types of PLDs.

It should be noted that PLAs have certain disadvantages compared with PALs and PROMs. First, a given signal has to pass through two programmable arrays, which increases propagation delays. Second, PLA programming equations are generally more cumbersome, making them more difficult to program. PROMs and PALs are generally very easy to program, thus making them more popular.

TABLE 2.2
PLD types

	PROM	PAL	PLA
AND	Fixed	Programmable	Programmable
OR	Programmable	Fixed	Programmable

2.7 PALs

PALs can be divided into two general types. **Combinational PALs** contain only logic gates; **sequential PALs** contain both logic gates and flip-flops.

Combinational PALs

Recall that in a PAL the AND gates are programmable, whereas the OR gates are fixed. Figure 2.19 illustrates the logic diagram of a PAL with three inputs, one output, and three product lines. The number of programmable fuses is then 3 inputs times 2 (inverted and noninverted) times 3 product lines, or 18 ($3 \times 2 \times 3$) fuses. The PAL shown in Figure 2.19 is programmed for the Boolean equation

$$O_1 = (I_1 \cdot I_2 \cdot \overline{I_3}) + (\overline{I_1} \cdot \overline{I_2})$$

Note that product line 3 will always result in a logic 0 output because all the fuses have been left connected, resulting in $I \cdot \overline{I} = 0$. If all the fuses were blown, the product term would result in a logic 1 output.

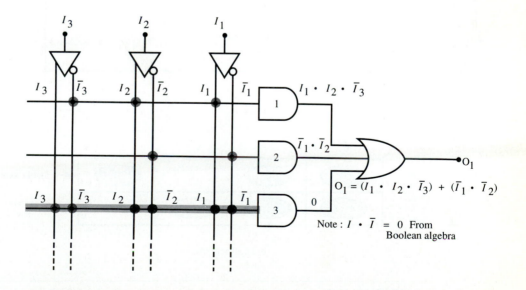

FIGURE 2.19
PAL

As you can see, PALs are easily programmed from Boolean equations in the sum-of-the-product (SOP) form. Each product term is made by one product line. All the product lines for a given output are then ORed to produce the SOP term.

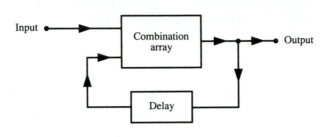

(a) Sequential logic

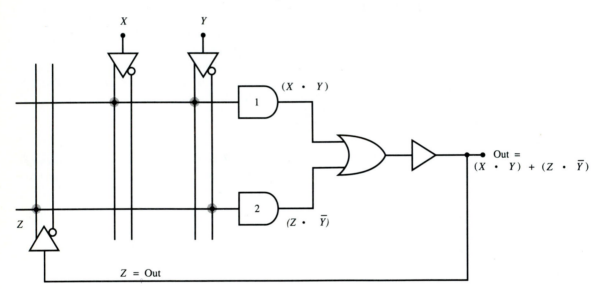

$Z = \text{Out}$

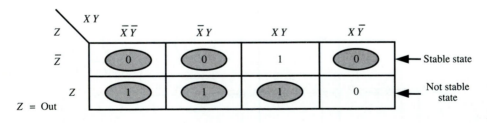

(b) Feedback PAL

FIGURE 2.20
Sequential PAL

The first step to be performed in programming a PAL is to write the Boolean equation in SOP form from the truth table. The number of product lines is limited, so the Boolean equation must be optimized. This can be done using the classical Karnaugh map method. Computer programs are now available to program the PAL and optimize the Boolean equation for you.

Sequential PALs

Sequential PALs employ feedback, as shown in Figure 2.20(a). That is, the output is fed back to the input, which can provide the ability to implement asynchronous sequential logic on a PAL. In this case the inputs plus the present state of the output are used to generate the next output state. The PAL becomes stable when the present state and the next state are the same. In Figure 2.20(b) we have programmed a PAL to implement the function

$$OUT = (X \cdot Y) + (\overline{Y} \cdot Z)$$

where Z represents the feedback output of the previous state. The Karnaugh map shows the resulting outputs, with the stable states circled.

Some PALs provide the ability to implement synchronous sequential logic. They are called **registered PALs.** In a registered PAL some of the outputs are terminated by D flip-flops. Once the product terms have been added, the sum is connected to the D input of the flip-flop. The Q output becomes the output of the PAL, and the $\overline{Q}$ output is used for the feedback path, as shown in Figure 2.21. The clock is the same for all flip-flops; it is usually on pin 1 of the chip. Here again, the outputs are a function not only of the inputs but also of the present state of the flip-flops.

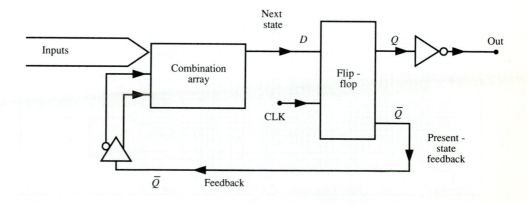

FIGURE 2.21
Registered PAL

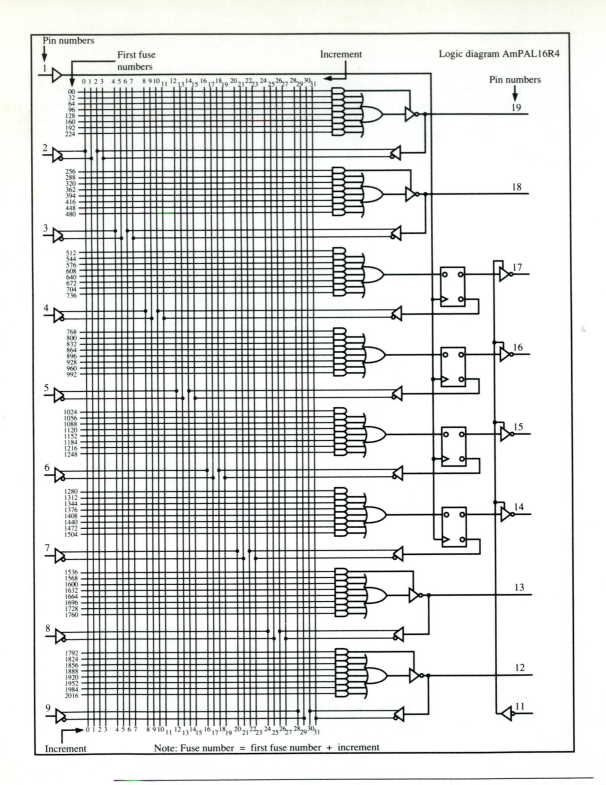

FIGURE 2.22
(Reprinted by permission of Advanced Micro Devices)

PAL Identification

PALs are identified by a numbering system that defines the number of input lines, the number of output lines, and the type of PAL. For example, a 14H4 PAL is a PAL with 14 inputs and 4 outputs and is active high. A 14L4 is similar except that it is active low. A 16R4 is a PAL with 16 inputs and 4 registered outputs (feedback paths). Figure 2.22 shows the logic diagram for a 16R4 PAL.

2.8   PAL DESIGN EXAMPLE

To illustrate the use of a PAL, we will design a 4-to-1 multiplexer using a PAL. Figure 2.23(a) illustrates the design problem. There are four input lines, I_0 to I_3. Since there are four inputs that we wish to switch to the output, two control lines ($2^2 = 4$) are required. The control lines are labeled S_0 and S_1. The control lines define which input will be switched to the output. The truth table defines the desired operation of the PAL. The Boolean equation for the output is then

$$OUT = (\overline{S_0} \cdot \overline{S_1} \cdot I_0) + (S_0 \cdot \overline{S_1} \cdot I_1) + (\overline{S_0} \cdot S_1 \cdot I_2) + (S_0 \cdot S_1 \cdot I_3)$$

The programmed PAL is shown in Figure 2.23(b).

2.9   APPLICATION SPECIFIC INTEGRATED CIRCUITS (ASICs)

Today, many microcomputers, such as the IBM PS/2 series and the Apple McIntosh II, have replaced many of the standard SSI and MSI integrated circuits with **application-specific integrated circuits (ASICs).** The ASIC can be thought of as a further advancement or enhancement of the PLD.

ASICs and ICs were designed for many of the same reasons, including increased reliability, smaller PC board area, less power consumption, simplified design, and improved speed. Designers are now using ASICs to replace hundreds of standard MSI chips. Furthermore, ASICs make it much more difficult to copy, or *clone,* circuits that utilize them. ASICs are designed using advanced *computer-aided engineering* (CAE) workstations. They represent one of the fastest growing segments of the IC industry today.

2.10   TECH TIPS AND TROUBLESHOOTING—T³

Most microcomputer memory systems use some method of *validating* the data bits that are stored in its memory. Validating means that the data bits in the memory system are checked and even corrected when they are received (written) or transmitted (read). Thus, *lost* or *stuck bits* will result in a system failure. Memory failures are one of the most common problems with microcomputer systems today. Many different techniques are used to detect memory errors, the most common being bit parity, word parity, check sums, and cyclic redundancy checks.

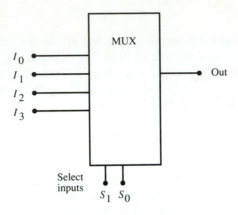

I	S_1	S_0	Output
I_0	0	0	I_0
I_1	0	1	I_1
I_2	1	0	I_2
I_3	1	1	I_3

$$\text{Out} = I_0 = (\overline{S_1} \cdot \overline{S_0} \cdot I_0)$$
$$\text{Out} = I_1 = (\overline{S_1} \cdot S_0 \cdot I_1)$$
$$\text{Out} = I_2 = (S_1 \cdot \overline{S_0} \cdot I_2)$$
$$\text{Out} = I_3 = (S_1 \cdot S_0 \cdot I_3)$$

(a) 4-1 Multiplexer

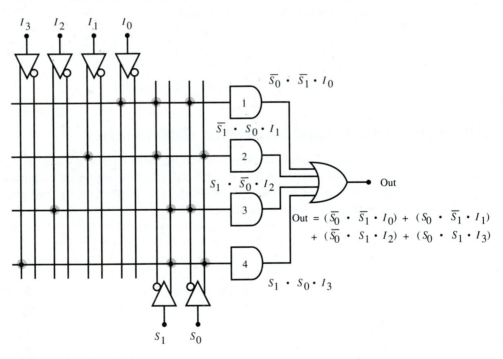

$$\text{Out} = (\overline{S_0} \cdot \overline{S_1} \cdot I_0) + (S_0 \cdot \overline{S_1} \cdot I_1)$$
$$+ (\overline{S_0} \cdot S_1 \cdot I_2) + (S_0 \cdot S_1 \cdot I_3)$$

(b) Circuit

FIGURE 2.23
PAL programmed for multiplexer

Bit Parity

There are two basic types of **bit parity** checks, *even parity* and *odd parity*. In both cases an extra bit is added to the data word. This bit is used to make the total number of 1s in the data word an even or an odd number. Thus in even parity, the added parity bit makes the total number of 1s an even number. In odd parity, the added parity bit makes the total number of 1s an odd number. For example,

Data Word
1100 0001
Even parity
1100 0001   1 ← Parity bit
Odd Parity
1100 0001   0 ← Parity bit

It should be noted that bit parity methods can detect only a single bit error. If two bits in a data word were to change at the same time, the parity bit *might not* detect the error.

Word Parity

A variation of the bit parity technique is **word parity.** In this technique a parity bit is added to each data word (row) and also for each vertical data position (column). For example, consider the following words using odd parity:

Data	Word	OP
1101	0001	1
1110	0100	1
1100	0101	1
1110	0010	1
1111	0000	1
1111	0010	0
1111	0011	1
1001	1100	1
1000	0000	0 ← Parity word

Eight data words are shown with an additional odd parity bit. The parity word is calculated by determining odd parity for each vertical position (column). If a single-bit error occurs, it can be detected and corrected automatically by the computer. For example, if during transmission word five develops an error in the fourth column from the left, the computer can detect and correct this problem, as illustrated.

Data	Word	OP	
110|1	0001	1	
111|0	0100	1	
110|0	0101	1	
111|0	0010	1	
111|0	0000	1	← Parity error detected
111|1	0010	0	
111|1	0011	1	
100|1	1100	1	
100|0	0000	0	← Parity word

└──── Parity error detected

Check Sums

Most ROMs and PROMs in microcomputer systems today employ a technique known as **check sums** for error detection. In this technique the last location of the ROM's or PROM's memory is reserved for a check sum word. The check sum word is a word that produces a sum of zero when added to the other data words in memory. For example, let's consider an 8-bit ROM with eight memory locations.

Location	Data Word	Hex Equivalent
0	1101 0101	D5
1	1100 0000	C0
2	1110 0010	E2
3	1100 1000	C8
4	1100 0101	C5
5	1101 0000	D0
6	1110 0010	E2
7	0100 1010	4A Check sum word
	110 0000 0000	6 00 Sum

Overflow

Memory location 7 contains the check sum word. Note that the sum of all the data words in memory including the check sum word is zero if we neglect the overflow bits. The check sum word is obtained by adding memory locations 0 through 6 and subtracting the result from the next higher order word (1 0000 0000B or 100H). The result becomes the check sum word.

Cyclic Redundancy Checks

The **cyclic redundancy check** (CRC) system can be used to detect double errors. This technique is commonly used in data communications such as those used in microcomputer disk drive subsystems. CRC calculations are performed using multisectional shift registers that are fed into EXCLUSIVE-OR gates, as shown in Figure 2.24(a). Data bits are fed into the multisectional shift register to produce *block check characters* (BCC). The BCC of the transmitting device is compared with the BCC of the receiving device using an EXCLUSIVE-OR gate, as shown in Figure 2.24(b). As long as the output of the EXCLUSIVE-OR gate is zero, no error exists. If the output of the EXCLUSIVE-OR gate is a 1, this signals the computer that an error has occurred. For a 16-bit system the CRC polynomial can be calculated using the algorithm

$$CRC_{16} = X^{16} + X^{15} + X^2 + 1$$

As each data bit is received through the data in line, it is cycled around through EXCLUSIVE-OR gate 1. The output of EXCLUSIVE-OR gate 1 is fed back into shift register A and is simultaneously fed back into shift registers B and C through EXCLUSIVE-OR gates 2 and 3, respectively, to produce a unique BCC word. This technique is duplicated at the transmitter and the receiver. The results are compared through another EXCLUSIVE-OR gate to perform the CRC. The algorithm is unique, so it is highly unlikely that a combination of errors will produce the same BCC at the receiver and transmitter CRC circuits. The most important property of CRC is that, due to the feedback elements in the circuit, the contents of the shift register depend upon the past manipulation of its states.

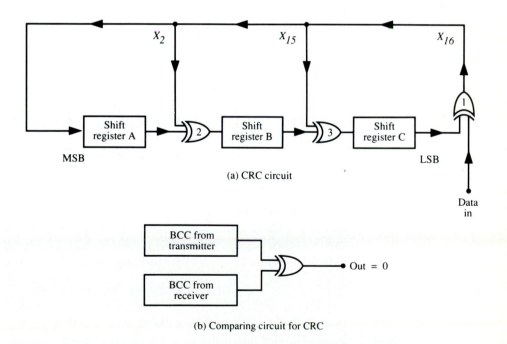

(a) CRC circuit

(b) Comparing circuit for CRC

FIGURE 2.24
Cyclic redundancy check

EXERCISES

2.1 Define the following terms:
a. Memory cell   b. Memory address
c. Memory read cycle   d. Memory write cycle

2.2 Explain how memory devices are generally organized or structured.

2.3 Compare volatile and nonvolatile memory.

2.4 Discuss the difference between bit-organized memory and word-organized memory.

2.5 The TTL 7489 RAM is a word-organized device with four address lines. Determine how many memory locations it contains.

2.6 List and describe the different classifications of ROMs.

2.7 List three applications of ROMs.

2.8 Redraw Figure 2.3(a) (for addresses A_0 to A_3 only). Use the following data: $A_0 = 1111$, $A_1 = 1100$, $A_2 = 0000$, $A_3 = 0101$.

2.9 Redraw Figure 2.4(a) so that the data 1100 will be stored in the BJT PROM.

2.10 Redraw Figure 2.4(b) so that the data 0101 will be stored in the MOSFET PROM.

2.11 Explain the differences between static and dynamic RAM.

2.12 Discuss how refreshing is accomplished.

2.13 a. Draw a diagram showing the wiring needed to write the data word 11111111 into a 4016 static RAM at memory address 0000000000.
b. How would the diagram change if the data just stored was to be read out?

2.14 List the advantages and disadvantages of DRAMs.

2.15 Explain how to address all 16K of memory in a 4116 DRAM with only seven address pins.

2.16 What is the function of the $\overline{\text{RAS}}$ and the $\overline{\text{CAS}}$ pins on a DRAM device?

2.17 Draw a diagram for a 16K $\times$ 4-bit memory using 4116 DRAMs.

2.18 In Figure 2.12 what logic levels should be applied to store the data word $(4)_{16}$ in memory location $(3)_{16}$?

2.19 In Figure 2.13 what logic levels should be applied to read the contents of memory location $(1FFF)_{16}$?

2.20 In Figure 2.14 what logic levels must be applied to select bank 1 (U_1)?

2.21 Explain the use of a PLD.

2.22 Referring to Figure 2.16, redraw the fuse map to implement the following Boolean expression: $\text{OUT} = (X \cdot Y) + (X \cdot Z)$

2.23 Referring to Figure 2.17, redraw the fuse map for the following Boolean expression:

$$\text{OUT} = (\overline{X} \cdot Z) + (\overline{Y} \cdot \overline{Z}) + (X \cdot Y \cdot Z)$$

2.24 Discuss the differences between a PROM, PAL, and PLA.

2.25 Redraw Figure 2.19 to obtain $O_1 = 1 + (\overline{I_1} \cdot I_2 \cdot \overline{I_3}) + 0$

2.26 Show how the PAL in Figure 2.22 can be used to implement the function $\text{OUT} = (X \cdot Y) + (Z \cdot \overline{Y})$ from Figure 2.20.

2.27   Design a 2 to 1 multiplexer using a PAL.

2.28   Add the correct parity bits to obtain odd and even parity for the following data words.
        a. 11001111   b. 01010100

2.29   Explain the meaning of the term parity word. Explain how it is used to detect and correct errors.

2.30   Explain the meaning of the terms:
        a. Check sum   b. CRC

2.31   Crossword Puzzle

ACROSS

1. Programmable logic array.
3. A check system that can be used to detect double errors.
5. PLD input line connected to an AND gate.
8. Type of PAL that contains both logic gate and flip-flops.
10. The use of higher-order address lines for memory bank selection.
15. Type of RAM that does not require refreshing.
17. Type of memory that loses its data when the power is turned off.
20. Programmable logic device.
21. Device used to program 19 Down.
23. PLD input connected by an OR gate to the output.
24. Type of parity.
25. Same as 17 Across.

DOWN

1. PLD with programmable AND gates and fixed OR gates.
2. Matrix of product lines and sum lines.
4. PALs that contain only logic gates.
6. Application specific integrated circuits.
7. A type of parity that is computed vertically.
9. Opposite of 24 Across.
11. DRAM operation.
12. Type of RAM.
13. Read-only memory.
14. Type of memory that is programmed with information by the manufacturer.
16. ROM and PROM error detection technique.
18. Method of validating memory data.
19. Programmable ROM.
22. Erased using ultraviolet light.

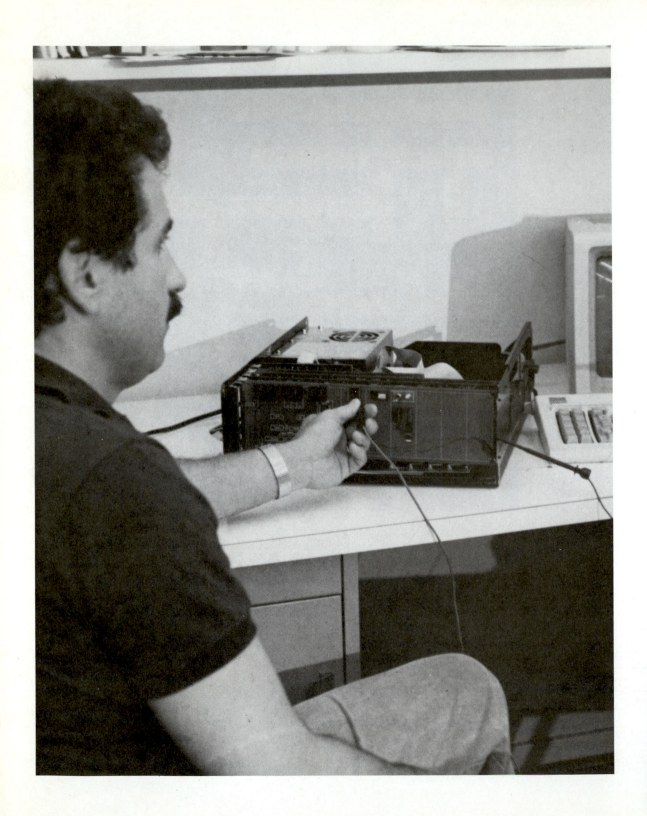

BASICS OF MICROPROCESSORS 2

In a world inundated with electronic gadgets, words like computer and microprocessor have become household words. Computer software and hardware terminology, jargon, and acronyms are heard every day. Words like bits, bytes, RAM, and ROM are becoming commonplace in our language. We have discussed the meaning of many of these terms in Part 1, but let's briefly review a few definitions before going on.

A **bit** is a single binary digit. A **nibble** is a collection of 4 binary digits or 4 bits. A **byte** is 8 binary digits, which is equal to 8 bits or 2 nibbles. A **word** equals 16 binary digits, 2 bytes, or 4 nibbles. A **bus** is a group of common wires in which signals travel. **RAM** stands for random access memory, which is memory that can be written to or read from. **ROM,** or read only memory, is similar to RAM but can only be read from. **I/O** stands for input or output, for example, keyboards and printers.

Since the beginning of digital computers, the basic architecture has not changed much. All digital computers can be considered to be made up of five parts as shown in Figure A (p. 250):

1. A central processing unit (CPU)
2. Memory unit or local storage (RAM and ROM)
3. Input units

4. Output units
5. Mass storage units such as disk drives and tape drives

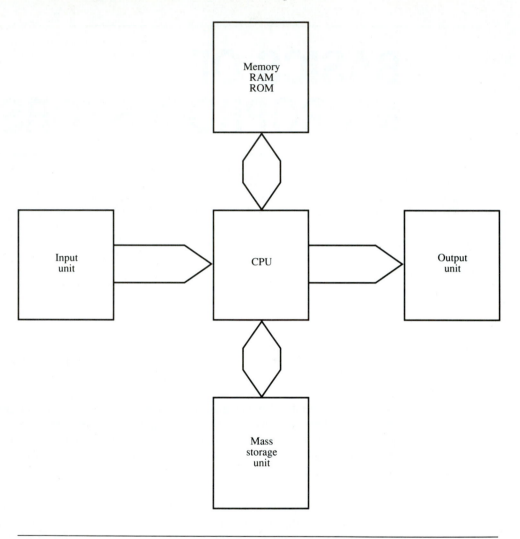

FIGURE A
Digital computer block diagram

The big difference in the evolution of computers has been their size and speed. As we have seen, computer systems are getting smaller and faster every year. Early computer systems of the 1950s, 1960s, and even the 1970s required air conditioned rooms and many kilowatts of electric power to operate them. Today, comparable computing power sits on a desk, plugged into a standard wall outlet.

There are two major contributors to this change in computing power. First are the advancements in IC design and technology. Low-power Schottky transistor-transistor logic (LSTTL), metal-oxide semiconductor (MOS), and, for very low power, complementary metal-oxide semiconductor (CMOS) as well as large-scale integration (LSI) and very large scale integration (VLSI) have all helped to reduce the size and power requirements as well as to increase the speed of digital computers.

The second major contributor is memory technology. Early computers used memories made up of arrays of magnetic cores that looked like tiny donuts. Today semiconductor memories have revolutionized the digital computer. Large amounts of memory are now available in a single IC. Semiconductor memory devices have also increased operating speeds and reduced size, power, and even cost requirements.

While these technological changes were taking place something unique happened: The concept of a microprocessor was introduced. A microprocessor is a large-scale IC that contains many of the logic circuits used in a computer—for example, the ALU, registers, and control circuits.

One of the first microprocessors was the INTEL 4004. The INTEL 4004 was a 4-bit, simple microprocessor designed for controller applications. Everything was fine until somebody decided to make it into a smart calculator; then the microcomputer revolution took place. Like everything else, the microcomputer has continued to evolve. The 4-bit microprocessor became 8 bits, and then 16 bits, and now some are 32 bits wide. The early, simple software, *instruction sets,* became very sophisticated and complex. Combine the new microprocessor with high-density memory and VLSI circuits and what was a supercomputer or mainframe computer can now be on your desk or your lap. Furthermore, it may even operate on batteries.

In this section we study the basic theory of microprocessors. Since complete textbooks are devoted to the study of microprocessors, our main objective will be to introduce only the principles that are required to be understood for the servicing of microprocessor-based systems. Although we concentrate only on what the technician needs to know for servicing, this section provides a solid foundation for future study in this area.

CHAPTER THREE

FUNDAMENTALS OF MICROPROCESSORS

KEY TERMS

Address Bus

Arithmetic Logic Unit (ALU)

Base Register

Bidirectional

Bus-Control Unit

Bus Cycle

Bus Interface Unit (BIU)

Code Segment (CS)

Control Bus

Data Bus

Data Registers

Data Segment (DS)

Execution Unit (EU)

Extra Segment (ES)

Fetch

FIFO

Flag Register

Index Registers

Instruction Pointer

Instruction Queue

Logical Address

Memory-mapped I/O

Multiplex

Peripheral Devices

Physical Address

Pointer Registers

Read Operation

Stack Segment (SS)

Write Operation

3.0 INTRODUCTION

The microprocessor, or microprocessor unit (MPU) as it is often known, is the brain of the computer system. The MPU is one of the most useful and flexible of all digital integrated circuits. It is found in an increasing number of practical applications, from digital clocks, microwave ovens, washing machines, and robots to temperature control devices in buildings, electronic fuel injection in automobiles, aerospace vehicles, and of course the general-purpose computer itself.

There are a number of microprocessors available today. In this text we use the Intel 8086/8088 series of microprocessors as a practical example. The Intel 8086/8088 microprocessor series is one of the most popular and powerful microprocessors in use today.

3.1 INTERNAL ARCHITECTURE

The term *architecture,* as used in microprocessor circuits, describes the functional components that make up the MPU and the interaction between them. These include the temporary storage devices known as registers, which are used to hold data, instructions, and status information. There are also devices to perform arithmetic, such as addition and subtraction, and the logic operations such as AND and OR. Control devices are used to control the flow of information through the MPU.

The basic 8086/8088 microprocessor consists of two sections known as the **execution unit (EU)** and the **bus interface unit (BIU),** as shown in Figure 3.1. The EU performs all the arithmetic and logic operations. The BIU obtains, or *fetches,* the instructions and/or data from memory. These instructions are used to control and operate the MPU.

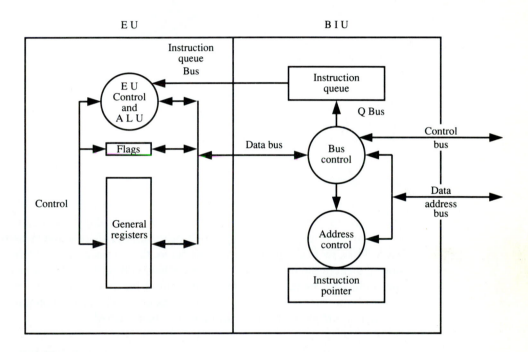

FIGURE 3.1
8088/8086 Microprocessor

Execution Unit (EU)

The EU is where the actual processing of data takes place inside the 8086/8088 MPU. It is here that the **arithmetic logic unit (ALU)** is located, along with the registers used to manipulate data and store intermediate results. The EU accepts instructions and data that have been fetched by the BIU and then processes the information. Data processed in the EU can be transmitted to memory or **peripheral devices** through the BIU. It should be noted that the EU has no direct connection to the outside world and relies solely on the BIU to feed it with instructions and data as indicated in Figure 3.2.

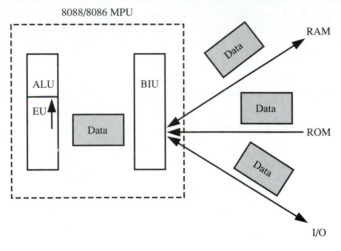

FIGURE 3.2
BIU/EU data feed

Bus Interface Unit (BIU)

The BIU is made up of the *address generation and bus-control unit, the instruction queue,* and the *instruction pointer.* It has the task of making sure that the bus is used to its fullest capacity in order to speed up operations. This function is carried out in two ways. First, by fetching the instructions before they are needed by the execution unit and storing them in the instruction queue, the 8086/8088 MPU is able to increase computing speed. Second, by taking care of all bus-control functions, the EU is free to concentrate on processing data and carrying out the instructions. The instruction pointer contains the location or address of the next instruction to be executed.

3.2 ADDRESS BUS

An address is a unique location in memory. It is like a mailbox in the post office, where each mailbox has its own unique number to identify its location. An address is necessary because there may be two people named Jones on the same street. An address gives a way of determining which person we want to contact.

In the Intel 8086/8088 the address is determined by a 20-bit number. This gives us 2^{20} possible address locations, or 1,048,576 bytes of memory.

An **address bus** is made up of 20 wires, or conductors, labeled A_0 through A_{19}, with A_0 as the LSB and A_{19} as the MSB, as shown in Figure 3.3. It is used to locate or find information in memory. It is also used to define a location in memory where information is to be stored. The address bus is sometimes used to identify which I/O port is used for input/output operations. For example, if the MPU were being used in an automobile to control the lights, power windows, and air conditioner vents, the address bus would define which light, power window, or air conditioner vent to control.

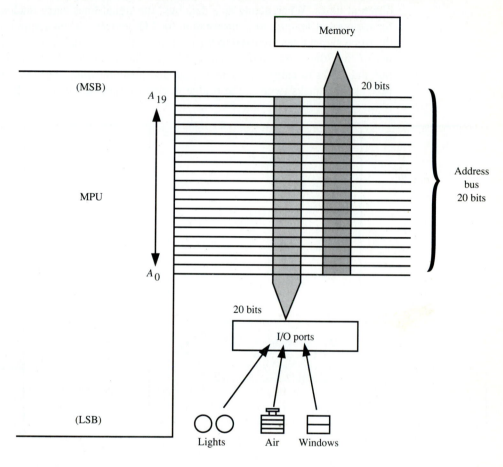

FIGURE 3.3
Address bus

3.3 DATA BUS

A **data bus** is used to move information (data and instructions) from the MPU to memory and other devices. This is sometimes referred to as a **write operation.** The data bus is also used to receive information into the MPU. This is called a **read operation.** Because the data bus receives and transmits information, it is known as a **bidirectional** bus. However, it cannot receive and transmit data at the same time.

The Intel 8086 has a 16-bit data bus labeled D_0 to D_{15}, where D_0 is the LSB and D_{15} is the MSB, as shown in Figure 3.4(a). The 8088 uses an 8-bit data bus labeled D_0

(LSB) to D_7 (MSB), as shown in Figure 3.4(b). This is the most significant difference between the 8088 MPU and the 8086 MPU.

Both the 8088 and 8086 microprocessors **multiplex** the address and data buses. Multiplexing is the process of using the same wires or pins to do different things at different times. When acting as a data bus, the signal lines carry read/write information for memory or input/output information for I/O devices. When acting as an address bus, the same signal lines are used to locate information. Figure 3.5 illustrates the multiplexing of the 8086/8088 address and data bus. This is analogous to using a single set of railroad tracks to carry a passenger train and a freight train over the same bridge. Both may use the tracks to cross the bridge in either direction but not at the same time.

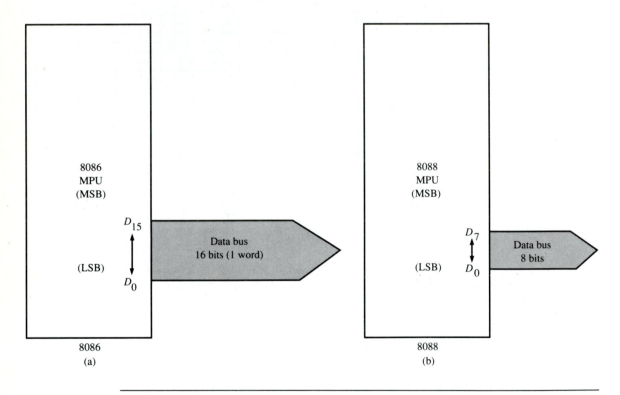

FIGURE 3.4
Data bus 8086/8088

3.4 CONTROL LINES

The 8086/8088 control lines determine how and when an operation is to be performed. For example, the control lines carry signals that determine whether the information on the bus is data or an address location. Figure 3.6 (p. 104) shows the pinout of the 8088 microprocessor with all its control lines. The control lines are sometimes referred to as

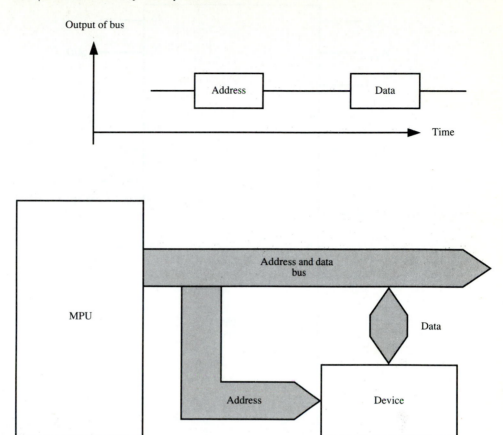

FIGURE 3.5
Multiplexed address and data bus

the **control bus.** The pin configuration for the 8088 MPU is summarized and can be grouped functionally as follows:

1. Power lines
2. Address/status lines
3. Data lines
4. Data/address control lines
5. Interrupt control lines
6. Operation control lines

1. *Power lines.* Pins 1 and 20 are used for power supply ground connections. Pin 40 is connected to $+5$ V, which is also called $+V_{CC}$.
2. *Address/status lines.* Pins 2 through 16 and pins 35 through 39 are used for the address bus. Pins 35 through 38 are also used by multiplexing to provide information or status about the MPU. These status signals are labeled S_3, S_4, S_5, and S_6, as shown.

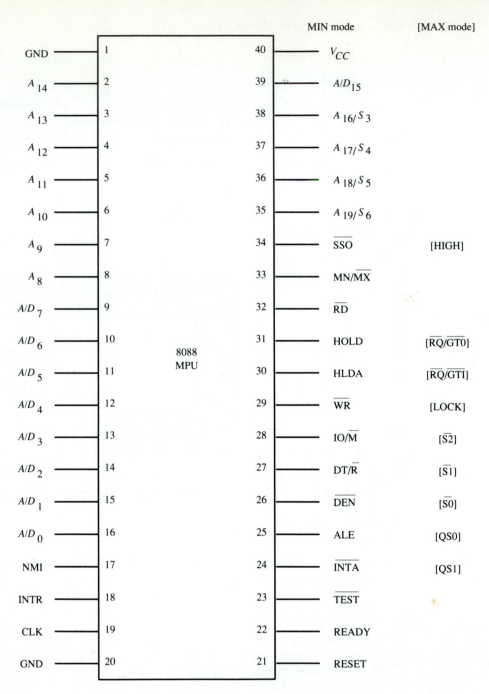

FIGURE 3.6
Pinout 8088 MPU

3. *Data lines*. Pins 9 through 16 are also used by multiplexing with the address signals for the data bus. These pins are labeled D_7 through D_0, respectively.
4. *Data/address-control lines*. Pins 25 through 29, and 32 and 34 provide control and status of the movement of information on the data and address buses.

- *Pin 25 ALE (address latch enable)*. An active-high output signal that indicates that a *valid* or stable address word is on the address bus.
- *Pin 26 $\overline{DEN}$ (data enable)*. A tristate active-low output signal that determines whether the data buffer is enabled or disabled. A logic level 0 turns on the data bus.
- *Pin 27 DT/$\overline{R}$ (data transmit receive)*. A tristate output signal used to control the direction of data flow. A logic level 1 indicates data bits are being transmitted *from* the MPU. A logic level 0 indicates that data bits are being received *into* the MPU.
- *Pin 28 IO/$\overline{M}$ (input/output/memory)*. This tristate output signal determines if the address bus is connected to memory or I/O. A logic level 1 indicates that the I/O is being addressed. A logic level 0 indicates that memory is being addressed, or *selected*.
- *Pin 29 $\overline{WR}$ (write)*. A tristate output signal that indicates that the MPU has put valid and stable data on the data bus. The active logic level 0 can be used as a latch pulse, or *strobe pulse*, to indicate that valid data bits are on the bus.
- *Pin 32 $\overline{RD}$ (read)*. A tristate active-low output signal that indicates that the MPU is ready to *read* data from the data bus.
- *Pin 34 $\overline{SSO}$ (status line 0)*. A tristate active-low output signal that when combined with IO/$\overline{M}$ and DT/$\overline{R}$ provides bus cycle information, as shown in Table 3.1.

TABLE 3.1
Bus cycle status

IO/$\overline{M}$	DT/$\overline{R}$	SSO	Bus Cycle Function
0	0	0	Instruction fetch
0	0	1	Read memory
0	1	0	Write memory
0	1	1	Passive
1	0	0	Interrupt acknowledge
1	0	1	Read I/O port
1	1	0	Write I/O port
1	1	1	Halt

5. *Interrupt-control lines*. Pins 17, 18, 21, 23, and 24 allow the software or devices in the system to stop or interrupt the MPU's operation.

- *Pin 17 NMI (Nonmaskable interrupt)*. An active-high input signal that interrupts MPU processing. This signal cannot be ignored, or *masked*, by the MPU.
- *Pin 18 INTR (Interrupt request)*. An active-high input signal that is used to interrupt MPU processing. This interrupt is maskable and can be made to be ignored by the MPU through software control.

- *Pin 24 $\overline{INTA}$ (Interrupt acknowledge).* An active-low output signal that indicates that an interrupt has been received and accepted by the MPU. This can be referred to as *servicing the interrupt.*
- *Pin 21 RESET (restart).* An active-high input signal used externally to start or reset MPU activity.
- *Pin 23 $\overline{TEST}$ (test interrupt).* An active-low input signal that is tested by the software WAIT instruction. If $\overline{TEST}$ is a logic level 1, the MPU will wait or interrupt the program execution until $\overline{TEST}$ is a logic level 0.

6. *Operation-control lines.* The remaining pins, 19, 22, 30, 31 and 33, as well as pins 21 and 23, are used to manage and run the execution of the MPU.

- *Pin 19 CLK (clock input).* The master timing signal for the MPU, which synchronizes all operations.
- *Pin 22 READY (data transfer ready).* An active-high input signal that provides a means for the memory and I/O devices to tell the MPU that they are ready for data transfer.
- *Pin 31 HOLD (hold request).* An active-high input signal that provides a way for a device to request access to the system data/address bus.
- *Pin 30 HLDA (hold acknowledge).* This active-high output signal indicates that the MPU has received or accepted a hold request. This causes the address, data, and control buses to go into the high-impedance tristate.
- *Pin 33 MN/$\overline{MX}$ (minimum/maximum mode).* An input signal that determines whether the MPU is in a single or multiprocessor mode. A logic level 1 selects a single MPU, or *minimum* system mode. A logic level 0 selects a multiprocessor, or *maximum* system mode.

Table 3.2 summarizes the 8088 I/O pin connections and includes a description of signal names with their associated functions.

3.5 INSIDE THE EU

The EU is made up of two parts known as the *ALU* and the *general registers*. It is here that instructions are received, decoded, and executed from the instruction queue portion of the BIU. The instructions are taken from the top of the instruction queue on a first-in, first-out, or FIFO, basis.

ALU

The *ALU* is the calculator part of the execution unit. It consists of electronic circuitry that performs arithmetic operations or logical operations on the binary-represented electrical signals. The control system for the execution unit can also be thought of as part of the ALU. It provides a path for the flow of instructions into the ALU, the general registers, and the flag register.

TABLE 3.2
8088 Input/output pin configuration

Label	Pins	Description	Function
GND	1,20	Power ground	Power
V_{CC}	40	$+5$ V$_{DC}$	Power
A/D_0–A/D_7	16–9	Address/data lines	Address/data
A_8–A_{14}	8–2	Address lines	Address
A_{15}	39	Address line	Address
A_{16}/S_3–A_{19}/S_6	38–35	Address/status lines	Address/status
ALE	25	Address latch enable	Address control
$\overline{\text{DEN}}$	26	Data enable	Data control
DT/$\overline{\text{R}}$	27	Data transmit/receive	Data control
IO/$\overline{\text{M}}$	28	Input output/memory	Address control
$\overline{\text{WR}}$	29	Write data	Data control
$\overline{\text{RD}}$	32	Read data	Data control
$\overline{\text{SSO}}$	34	Status line 0	Address/data control
NMI	17	Nonmaskable interrupt	Interrupt control
INTR	18	Interrupt request	Interrupt control
RESET	21	Restart	Interrupt/operation control
$\overline{\text{TEST}}$	23	Alternate form interrupt	Interrupt/operation control
$\overline{\text{INTA}}$	24	Interrupt acknowledge	Interrupt control
CLK	19	Clock input	Operation control
READY	22	Data transfer ready	Operation control
HLDA	30	Hold acknowledge	Operation control
HOLD	31	Hold request	Operation control
MN/$\overline{\text{MX}}$	33	Minimum/maximum mode	Operation control

The **flag register** is a special register associated with the ALU. The flag register is used to store information about the conditions of the operation of the ALU, as shown in Figure 3.7. For example, if two binary numbers are multiplied and the resulting product is too large to be stored in the assigned location, a flag is *set* in the flag register to tell the MPU of this condition.

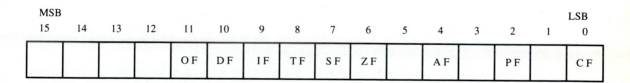

FIGURE 3.7
Flag register

The 8086/8088 has nine flags to record processor status information and control operations. Six flags are status flags—AF, CF, OF, SF, PF, and ZF. The remaining three flags are control flags—DF, IF, and TF. Table 8.3 presents a flag summary and highlights key concerns. Each flag is next discussed in detail.

TABLE 3.3
Flag summary

Status Flags	Description
AF (auxiliary flag)	Indicates if the instruction generated a carry out of the 4 LSBs.
CF (carry flag)	Indicates if the instruction generated a carry out of the MSB.
OF (overflow flag)	Indicates if the instruction generated a signed result that is out of range.
SF (sign flag)	Indicates if the instruction generated a negative result.
PF (parity flag)	Indicates if the instruction generated a result having an even number of 1s.
ZF (zero flag)	Indicates if the instruction generated a zero result.
DF (direction flag)	Controls the direction of the string manipulation instructions.
IF (interrupt-enable flag)	Enables or disables external interrupts.
TF (trap flag)	Puts the processor into a single-step mode for program debugging.

- *AF (auxiliary flag)*. If this flag is set, there has been a carry out or a borrow of the 4 least significant bits. This flag is used during decimal arithmetic instructions.
- *CF (carry flag)*. If this flag is set, there has been a carry out or overflow of the most significant bit. It is used by instructions that add and subtract multibyte numbers.
- *OF (overflow flag)*. If this flag is set, an arithmetic overflow has occurred; that is, a significant digit has been lost because the size of the result exceeded the capacity of its destination location.
- *SF (sign flag)*. Since negative binary numbers are represented in the 8086/8088 in standard 2s complement notation, SF indicates the sign of the result (0 = positive, 1 = negative).
- *PF (parity flag)*. If this flag is set, the result has even parity, an even number of 1s. This flag can be used to check for transmission errors.
- *ZF (zero flag)*. If this flag is set, the result of the operation is 0.
- *DF (direction flag)*. Setting DF causes string instructions to auto-decrement (count down); that is, to process strings from the high address to the low address, or from right to left. Clearing DF causes string instructions to auto-increment (count up), or process strings from left to right.
- *IF (interrupt-enable flag)*. Setting IF allows the MPU to recognize external (maskable) interrupt requests. Clearing IF disables these interrupts. IF has no effect on either nonmaskable external or internally generated interrupts.
- *TF (trap flag)*. Setting TF puts the the processor into single-step mode for debugging. In this mode the MPU automatically generates an internal interrupt after each instruction, allowing a program to be inspected as it executes instruction by instruction.

General Registers

The general registers consist of a set of data registers, which are used to hold intermediate results, and the pointer and index registers, which are used to locate information within a specified portion of memory.

The **data registers** are 16-bit registers labeled AX, BX, CX, and DX and are split into upper and lower halves of 8 bits, or 1 byte, each. The *H* represents the high-order or most-significant byte and the *L* represents the low-order or least-significant byte, as shown in Figure 3.8(a). The halves of each of these registers may be used separately as two 8-bit storage areas or combined to form one 16-bit (*one word*) storage area. The *H and L* group, as the general registers are sometimes called, can be used in most arithmetic and logic operations to hold or *accumulate* data.

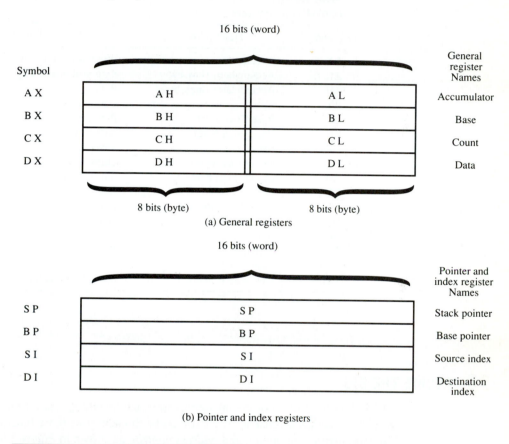

(a) General registers

(b) Pointer and index registers

FIGURE 3.8
General and pointer/index registers

Pointer and Index Registers

The **pointer registers** are labeled SP and BP, and the **index registers** are labeled SI and DI. These registers can also be used in most arithmetic and logic operations and can be considered under the general register heading (see Figure 3.8(b)); however, the pointer and index registers are usually used to point to or index to an address in memory. When used in this manner, these registers are address registers that designate a specific location in memory that may be frequently used by the program. The addresses contained in these registers can be combined with information from the BIU to physically locate the data in memory.

Table 3.4 summarizes all the registers that are part of the execution unit and includes some of their special functions and uses.

TABLE 3.4
Execution unit registers

Registers	Description	Special Functions
AX	Accumulator	Word arithmetic; I/O
AL	Accumulator (low byte)	Byte arithmetic; I/O
AH	Accumulator (high byte)	Byte arithmetic; I/O
BX	Base	Data transfer; memory address
BL	Base (low byte)	Byte transfer
BH	Base (high byte)	Byte transfer
CX	Count	String operations; loops
CL	Count (low byte)	Shifts; rotates
CH	Count (high byte)	Shifts; rotates
DX	Data	Indirect I/O
DL	Data (low byte)	Byte-wide I/O
DH	Data (high byte)	Byte-wide I/O
SP	Stack pointer	Stack operations
BP	Base pointer	Base register
SI	Source index	String source; index register
DI	Destination index	String destination; index register

3.6 INSIDE THE BIU

The BIU is the portion of the microprocessor that directly accesses or interfaces with the rest of the computer system. The BIU can be thought of as three functional blocks: *bus control, instruction queue,* and *address control,* as shown in Figure 3.9(a). The BIU is responsible for *prefetching* instructions to fill the instruction queue. It also sends and receives system control signals to and from other devices. Its final responsibility is to act as the interface to memory and the I/O ports.

Bus Control

The **bus-control unit** performs the bus operations for the MPU. It fetches and transmits instructions, data, and control signals between the MPU and the other devices of the system. For example, it is used to determine the direction that data is flowing on the data bus through the *data transmit/receive* control line (DT/$\overline{\text{R}}$).

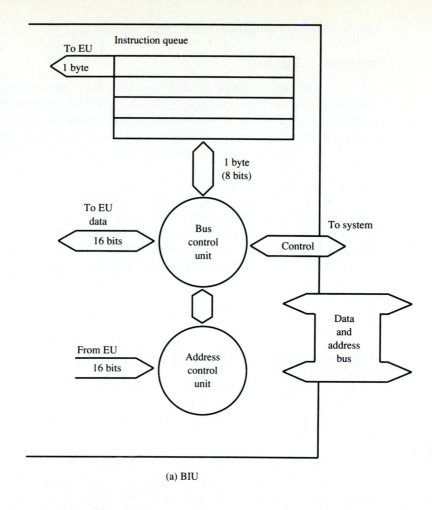

(a) BIU

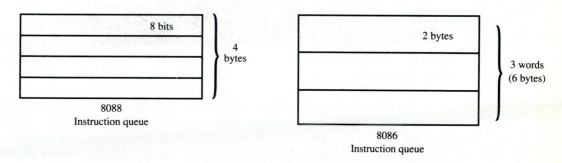

(b) Instruction queues

FIGURE 3.9
Inside the BIU

Instruction Queue

The **instruction queue** is used as a temporary memory storage area for data instructions that are to be executed by the EU. The BIU, through the bus-control unit, prefetches instructions and stores them in the instruction queue. This allows the execution unit to perform its calculations at maximum efficiency. Because the BIU and the EU essentially operate independently, the BIU concentrates on loading instructions into the instruction queue. This usually takes more time to do than the calculations performed by the execution unit. In effect, the BIU and the EU work in parallel.

The instruction queue is a *first-in, first-out* (**FIFO**) memory. This means that the first instruction loaded into the instruction queue by the bus control unit will be the first instruction to be used by the ALU. It should be noted that the 8088 MPU has a *4-byte-wide* instruction queue. Remember that the 8088 uses a byte-wide, or 8-bit, data bus. Therefore, there can be up to 4 bytes, or 2 words, of data in the instruction queue at any time. The 8086 MPU has a 3-word (16-bit) instruction queue. Its data bus is 16 bits wide; therefore, it brings in information 1 word at a time. This is another important difference between the two microprocessors, as shown in Figure 3.9(b).

Address Control

The address-control unit is used to generate the 20-bit memory address that gives the *physical* or actual location of the data or instruction in memory. This unit is composed of the *instruction pointer*, the *segment registers*, and the *address generator*, as shown in Figure 3.10.

Instruction Pointer   The **instruction pointer (IP)** is a 16-bit register that is used to *point* to, or tell the MPU, the instruction to execute next. Therefore, the instruction pointer is used to control the *sequence* in which the program is executed. Each time the execution unit accepts an instruction, the instruction pointer is *incremented* to point to the next instruction in the program.

Segment Registers   There are four segment registers. They are the **code segment (CS)**, the **data segment (DS)**, the **stack segment (SS)**, and the **extra segment (ES)**. These registers are used to define a *logical memory space*, or memory segment that is set aside for a particular function.

The CS register points to the current code segment. Instructions are fetched from this segment. The DS register points to the current data segment. Program variables and data are held in this area. The SS register points to the current stack segment. Stack operations are performed on locations in the SS segment. The ES register points to the current extra segment, which is also used for data storage. Each of the segment registers can be up to 64 kilobytes long. Each segment is made up of an uninterrupted section of memory locations. Each segment can be addressed separately using the *base address* that is contained in its segment register. The base address is the starting address for that segment. For example, if the code segment register has the address 200H in it, then the code segment instructions start at the *logical address* 200H. See Figure 3.11.

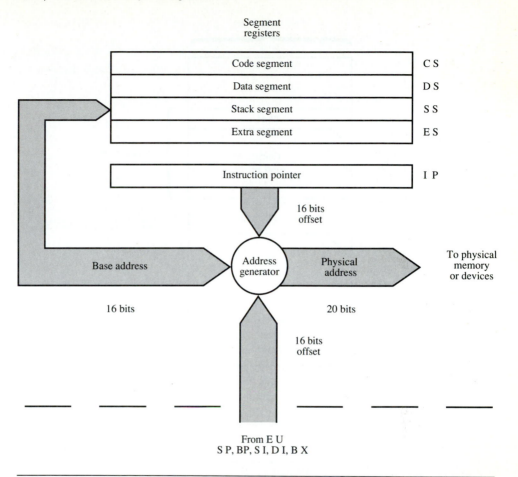

FIGURE 8.10
Address control

Address Generator   The address-generator unit is used with the segment registers to generate the 20-bit physical address required to identify all the possible memory addresses. The 20 address lines give a maximum *physical memory* size of 2^{20} address locations, or 1,048,576 bytes of memory. This creates a problem, since all the registers in the MPU are only 16 bits wide. Figure 3.12 shows how a 20-bit physical address is generated from a 16-bit segment register base address and a 16-bit segment register offset address. The physical address is obtained by shifting the segment base value four bit positions (one hex position) and adding the offset or logical address of the segment.

We have introduced some new terms here. The **base register** contains the starting address of a segment in memory. The **logical address** is the address of a piece of information within the 64-kilobyte block of the memory segment. This logical address is used to obtain the offset. This is done as shown in Figure 3.12. The segment base address is shifted left 4 bit positions (one hex position) to create a 20-bit address number. The

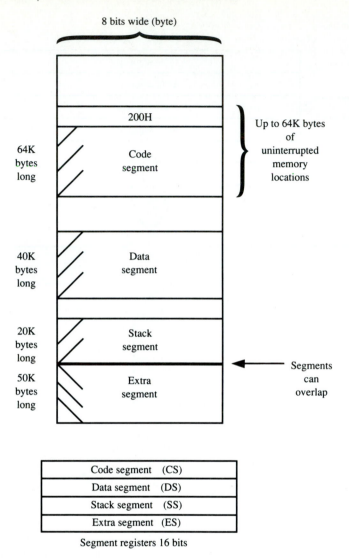

FIGURE 3.11
Segmentation of memory

logical address is used as an offset and is added to the shifted segment base address to obtain the **physical address,** which is a uniquely addressable memory location.

Since this idea tends to be somewhat confusing, we work through several examples.

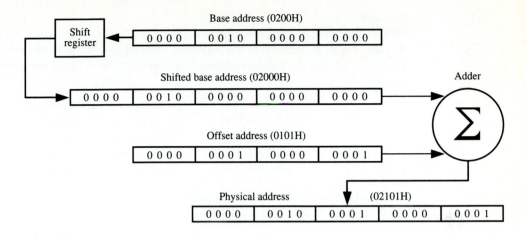

FIGURE 3.12
To produce a 20-bit physical address

EXAMPLE 3.1

The data segment base address is FF00H. The logical offset address is 0321H. Find the physical address of memory.

Solution

FF00H	Base address (DS)
0321H	Offset
FF000H	Shifted-left base address
+0321H	Added offset (logical)
FF321H	Physical address of memory

EXAMPLE 3.2

The stack segment base address is 1111H. The stack pointer register contains 0293H. Find the physical address of memory.

Solution

1111H	Stack segment base address
0293H	Offset (SP)
11110H	Shifted-left base address
+ 0293H	Added offset
113A3H	Physical address of memory

EXAMPLE 3.3

The instruction pointer points to 001FH. This is the next instruction to be executed. When we try to execute this instruction, we seem to have a memory problem. We suspect that there may be a problem in a memory device or circuit. Where do we look?

Solution

First we must obtain the base address from the active segment register. In this case, we find that the code segment is the register of interest and contains the value 0200H. We can now calculate the physical address and then examine the contents of that location in memory.

0200H	Code segment base address
001FH	Instruction pointer offset
02000H	Shifted-left base address
+ 001FH	Added offset
0201FH	Physical address of memory

We should examine the contents of memory location 0201FH.

Table 3.5 illustrates the segment registers, the offset source registers, and the type of operation being performed.

TABLE 3.5
Segment register operation

Segment	Offset Source	Operation
CS	IP	Instruction fetch
DS	BX, SI, DI	Data; string source
SS	SP	Stack
ES	DI	String destination

3.7 MEMORY

As we previously stated, memory can be thought of as a number of mailboxes, or storage locations. Each location must have its own unique address to identify it.

In a microcomputer system the memory locations are used to store data and instructions that tell the MPU what it is supposed to do. In order for the microprocessor to use the information stored in memory, it must **fetch,** or read, the information from memory. The information is read into the BIU of the microprocessor over the data bus. Once the data bits are processed, the results can be *stored* or written back into memory for use at a later time. This is called *writing to memory*. Again, the information flows back into memory on the data bus. Therefore, the data bus must be *bidirectional*. Figure 8.13 shows the relationship between the MPU and the memory subsystem. Notice that the address bus and the necessary control signals are also represented in Figure 3.13. Recall that the lower-order address signals are *multiplexed* with the data signals.

The operations of the memory control signals are as follows:

1. *ALE (address latch enable).* The falling edge of the ALE signal is used to latch or hold the memory address. The memory address is held, so that reading and writing operations can be performed, until the ALE signal returns high.

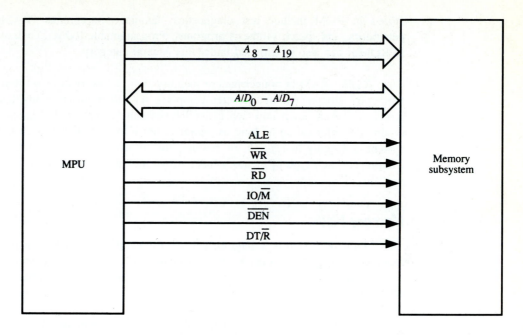

FIGURE 3.13
MPU's relationship memory subsystem

2. $\overline{WR}$ *(write)*/$\overline{RD}$ *(read)*. Once the address has been latched, the MPU activates either the $\overline{WR}$ or the $\overline{RD}$ signal. This activates a memory location or a device. These tristate signals are active low and cannot both be turned on simultaneously. Circuitry inside the MPU ensures that the $\overline{WR}$ and $\overline{RD}$ signals cannot be low at the same time.

3. *IO/$\overline{M}$ (input/ouput/memory)*. When this signal is low, a memory address is being selected. When this signal is high, an input or output port is being selected. This signal is necessary because the same address may be used for a memory location or for an I/O port.

4. $\overline{DEN}$ *(data enable)*. Due to bus timing problems most systems connect to the data bus through a buffer circuit. The $\overline{DEN}$ signal is a tristate active-low signal that is used to turn on or *enable* the buffer.

5. *DT/$\overline{R}$ (data transmit/receive)*. This tristate output signal is high when data bits are being transmitted by the MPU. It is low when the MPU is capable of receiving data.

RAM and ROM

Memory can be divided into two general types: ROM and RAM.

ROM ROM contains permanent information that can only be read. Start-up or *bootstrap* programs are stored in ROM. Other examples of information that may be stored in ROM include test diagnostics, language interpreters (BASIC), character generators, and speech synthesis programs. Programmable ROMs, such as PROMS and EPROMS, can also be grouped under this general category.

RAM RAM is nonpermanent memory that can be read or written to. It acts as temporary storage within the microcomputer for either program instructions or data. RAM is broken down into two general types called *static* and *dynamic*. Static RAM retains the information as long as power is not removed. Dynamic RAM requires the system constantly to *refresh,* or rewrite, the information. As previously discussed in Chapter 2, each type of memory has its own advantages and applications.

Memory Maps

A memory map is a diagram that represents all the occupied or used locations in memory. The memory map is used to identify the locations and their purposes. The memory map shows the locations or addresses, usually as a hexadecimal number, of ROM, RAM, port locations, interrupt vectors, program segments, and the like. Figure 3.14 shows an example of a memory map.

A method of treating a peripheral device as a memory location is known as **memory-mapped I/O.** For example, if a technician designs a microcomputer to be used as a fire alarm controller, the technician may physically connect the output of the fire sensors to specific memory addresses. These inputs are now memory mapped; this allows the programmer to access the data through these memory locations.

The memory map is used as an aid in partitioning the available memory. It shows the locations of all memory devices and segments, which is useful because some memory locations are dedicated for special purposes. For example, the bootstrap or start-up ROM may be located in memory addresses E6F2H through E728H. Some memory locations are reserved or set aside by the microprocessor manufacturer to allow for compatibility with future designs.

3.8 TIMING

All microprocessors use an oscillator to generate a master frequency to synchronize or time operations. For the 8086/8088 microprocessor the oscillator frequency, or *clock frequency,* is typically 5 MHz. The period of one clock cycle is then equal to

$$T = \frac{1}{F}$$

$$= \frac{1}{5 \times 10^6 \text{ H}}$$

$$= 0.2 \times 10^{-6} \text{ s}$$

$$= 200 \text{ ns}$$

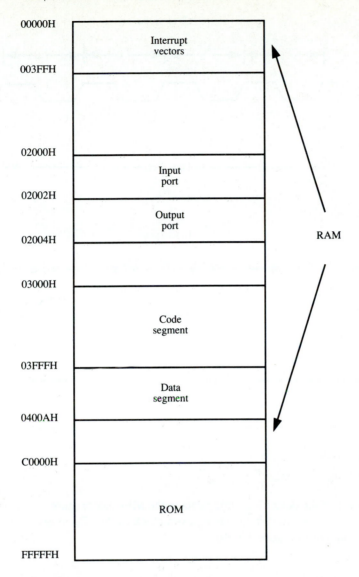

FIGURE 3.14
Memory map

The 8086/8088 operates in time periods called **bus cycles.** Each bus cycle requires *4 clock cycles* to complete. Therefore, in this example, the bus cycle is completed every 800 ns. A typical bus cycle is shown in Figure 3.15(a).

The two major bus cycles are the read bus cycle and the write bus cycle. The read bus cycle is activated when the MPU is *reading* information from memory or an I/O device. During the read bus cycle, there are normally four clock cycles. T_1, T_2, T_3, and

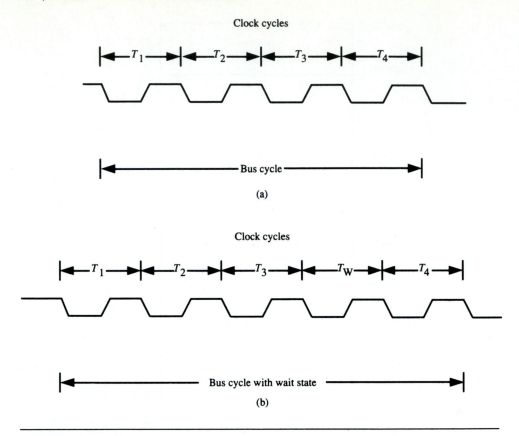

FIGURE 3.15
Timing-bus cycle

T_4. However, if the device outputting data to the MPU needs more time to send that data, a *wait state* (T_W) is initiated by placing extra clock cycles $(T_W$'s) between clock cycle T_3 and T_4 as shown in Figure 3.15(b).

Read Bus Cycle

Figure 3.16 shows an example of the typical read timing for the 8088 MPU.

T_1   During the first clock cycle the address/data bus is used to output the address of a memory or I/O location. Also outputted during the first clock cycle are control signals ALE, DT/$\overline{R}$, and IO/$\overline{M}$ by the 8088 MPU. At the end of T_1, ALE goes low and the address on the bus is latched.

T_2   At the beginning of clock cycle T_2 the multiplexed bus lines switch to their alternate function. The lower-order bus lines (A/D_0–A/D_7) go to their high-impedance state. The higher-order bus lines (A_{16}/S_3–A_{19}/S_6) go to their status output state. Bus lines

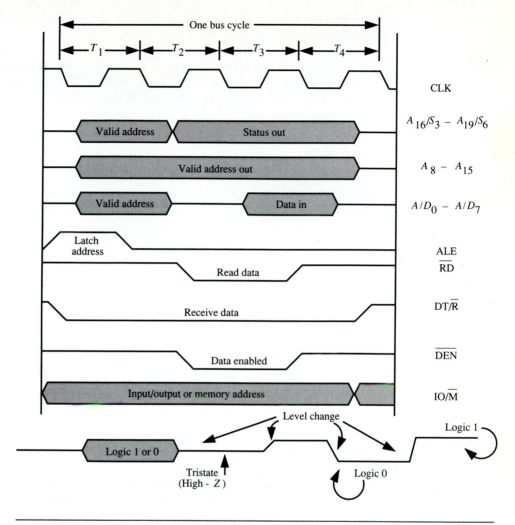

FIGURE 3.16
Read bus cycle

A_8–A_{15} do not change and are still outputting address information. Since A/D_0–A/D_7 and A_{16}/S_3–A_{19}/S_6 are no longer outputting address information, ALE is now low, indicating that the address is no longer valid on all the address lines. Note that A/D_0–A/D_7 stay in the high-impedance state for one clock cycle. This gives the data-sending device time to respond to the data request. During the read clock cycle T_2 the MPU outputs active-low signals for control lines $\overline{RD}$ and $\overline{DEN}$. The $\overline{RD}$ signal causes the memory or I/O device to output data. The $\overline{DEN}$ signal is used to activate the data bus buffers, allowing data to be sent onto the bus to the MPU.

T_3   During read clock cycle T_3 the memory or I/O device is putting data onto the bus. This cycle provides additional time for the data to become stable on the bus. The

MPU samples the READY pin during T_3. If READY is high, the next clock cycle is T_4. If READY is low, the next clock cycle is T_W, a wait state.

T_4 At the beginning of read clock cycle T_4, the MPU reads the data present on the data bus. At the end of T_4 all the tristate lines float to their high-impedance state in preparation for the next bus cycle. Control lines $\overline{RD}$ and $\overline{DEN}$ go high, signaling the end of the read bus cycle.

Write Bus Cycle

Figure 3.17 shows the timing diagram of the write bus cycle. This can be seen to be similar to the read bus cycle. The differences are that the one clock cycle delay on lines A/D_0–A/D_7 during the read cycle is no longer needed, since the microprocessor is

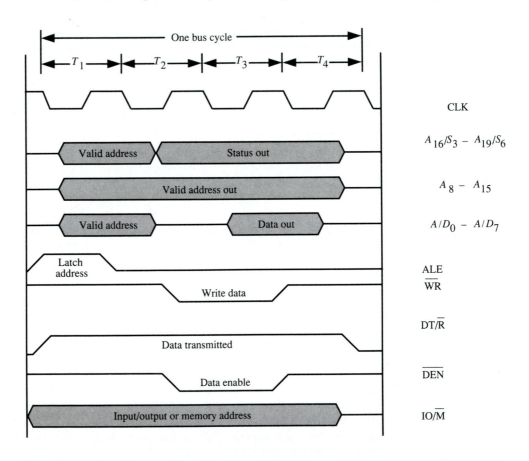

FIGURE 3.17
Write bus cycle

writing to memory or to an I/O device. Therefore, valid data bits are available after the beginning of clock cycle T_2. Note that just before the start of the write bus cycle the DT/$\overline{\text{R}}$ signal is latched high to signify that the MPU will be transmitting data. This signal remains high until the end of the write bus cycle. The $\overline{\text{WR}}$ line goes low after clock time T_2 to signal a write operation.

3.9 FETCH-EXECUTE CYCLE

We have looked at the read and write control timing. Now let's briefly investigate instruction timing. The microprocessor has two primary functions: fetch and execute. First it must fetch or read the program instruction or data. As we have seen, this can take one or more bus cycles. Once it has fetched the necessary program instructions and data through the BIU, the microprocessor's next step is to execute the instructions. The EU receives the instruction from the instruction queue and executes it. Some instructions may take 2 clock cycles to execute, whereas others may require as many as 100 clock cycles to execute. In older microprocessors this left the bus idle while the MPU was executing a long instruction, as shown in Figure 3.18. However, since the 8086/8088 MPU is broken up into two functional units, the BIU and the EU, it avoids much of the idle time required by older microprocessors. It does this by having the BIU prefetch instructions and place them into the instruction queue and data registers while the EU is executing the program instructions. Therefore, while the bus is busy during a read cycle, the EU can be executing a previous instruction. When the bus is busy during a write cycle, the EU can be executing another instruction. This greatly increases the effective speed of the entire system.

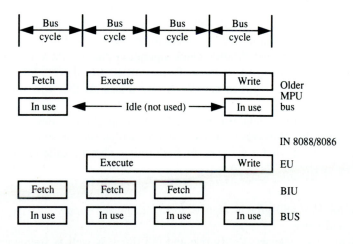

FIGURE 3.18
Fetch-execute cycle

3.10 TECH TIPS AND TROUBLESHOOTING—T³

MPU-related problems can be very difficult to troubleshoot. Due to the complex bus structure, the precise timing cycle relationships, and the software interactions and operation, the traditional types of test equipment will not be able to test the MPU adequately. Simple relationships between the software, hardware, and logic signals do not generally exist. Therefore, it is difficult to diagnose and localize MPU failures. Fortunately, MPU failures are rare. This is partially due to the fact that the MPU is in the center of the system. Other ICs that interface the control lines and bus signals to the rest of the system act as buffers to the MPU and provide the MPU with a certain amount of protection.

However, when an MPU failure is suspected, the first thing to do is visually inspect the IC. Look for burn marks on the top of the chip and on all the pins. Check for broken pins and connections. Clean away any dirt, grease, or corrosion. Touch the top of the MPU chip and feel its temperature. Although MPU chips will run hotter than other ICs, they should not be so hot that you cannot touch them.

If the visual inspection or operating temperature of the MPU leads you to believe that the MPU is defective, one technique is to *swap* the MPU, a shown in Figure 3.19. If the system works with the new MPU but does not work with the old one, then the old MPU is considered defective. Often MPU devices are installed in sockets for easy replacement. If this is the case, a swap will be very easy to do and can save a great deal of time and effort. However, a great deal of caution is required. MPU devices are very easily damaged by static electricity. Even if the MPU is not destroyed, static electricity can cause *intermittent* problems and shorten the life of the device. Therefore, always remember to ground yourself before you touch the MPU. If possible, use antistatic table mats and wrist straps. Also make certain that all the pins of the MPU are correctly inserted into the socket.

While the MPU chip rarely fails, there are several related items that can cause problems. MPU input control lines can *hang* the processor or stop its operation. Bus lines can be stuck high or low. Master clock operation can be incorrect. Bus *contention* conflicts can occur when two or more devices attempt to drive a bus line at the same time. The defective devices can cause constant interrupts that will slow or stop MPU operation.

Without the use of sophisticated test equipment, these types of problems can be difficult to identify. However, you can use an oscilloscope or logic probe to provide a general indication of what is going on by performing what are called *gross signal checks*.

1. Check for V_{CC} and ground signals from the power supply. Verify voltage levels, ripple, and noise.
2. Check for clock signals. Verify rise and fall times as well as frequency.
3. Check for the presence of signals on the address and data buses. There should be signal activity. Verify that these signals are not stuck high or low at all times. Remember that some lines may not show activity because the program does not call for any. For example, the high-order address lines may remain in the zero state because the program and the data reside in a lower part of memory. Therefore, you may have to run a special program that will exercise all the lines.

FIGURE 3.19

4. Check for control bus activity. Remember that the MPU outputs control and status information. Signals like ALE, $\overline{\text{DEN}}$, DT/$\overline{\text{R}}$, IO/$\overline{\text{M}}$, $\overline{\text{WR}}$, $\overline{\text{RD}}$, and $\overline{\text{SSO}}$ should be changing logic levels constantly during MPU operation.
5. Check the interrupt control lines. A constant interrupt can halt or drastically slow down MPU operation. Furthermore, a constant interrupt can cause address, data, and control lines to become inactive. For example, a constant high on the RESET line will cause the MPU to remain reset and stop it from beginning operation. A constant low on the $\overline{\text{TEST}}$ line will generate continual wait states.
6. If general activity is present, check for decoded outputs such as chip selects or output enables.

By understanding the operation and function of the different signal lines discussed earlier in the chapter, a technician can probe MPU pins to determine the health of the system. If signals are detectable and look good, the circuitry is probably good. If signals appear inactive or stuck high or low, then the possibility of a fault exists in this area.

Parts 3 and 4 of this text are specifically concerned with the theory, operation, and servicing of the microcomputer system. A more detailed explanation of servicing and troubleshooting procedures is found there.

EXERCISES

3.1   List six practical uses for a microprocessor.

3.2   Name the functional parts of the 8088 MPU.

3.3   Name the 16-bit data registers.

3.4   Identify the pointer and index registers.

3.5   Discuss the major differences between the 8088 MPU and the 8086 MPU.

3.6   Which functional unit is responsible for interfacing the 8088 MPU to the rest of the system?

3.7   What are the functional parts of the EU? the BIU?

3.8   Name the signal lines used to determine a memory location.

3.9   Which signal lines are multiplexed? What is their function?

3.10   Which microprocessor bus is bidirectional?

3.11   What is the addressable memory size of a microprocessor with:
   a. 8 address lines   b. 16 address lines
   c. 20 address lines

3.12   Following is a list of 8088 signal lines and functional groupings. For each signal line, choose the letter that identifies its functional grouping. (Letters may be used more than once.) Then, briefly, describe its use and operation.

Signal Lines	Functional Groups
1. ALE	A. Power-supply line
2. HLDA	B. Address/status line
3. NMI	C. Data line
5. $\overline{WR}$	D. Data/address control line
6. $\overline{INTA}$	E. Interrupt control line
7. $\overline{SSO}$	F. Operation control line
8. A_{15}	
9. V_{CC}	
10. DT/$\overline{R}$	

3.13   For each of the following, identify which signal or signals a technician should monitor.
   a. To determine if a memory write cycle is being performed.
   b. To determine the direction of data flow.
   c. To determine whether the output from a microprocessor is going to memory or an I/O port.
   d. To determine if a valid address is on the bus.
   e. To determine if the MPU is being interrupted.
   f. To determine if the MPU will accept the data transfer.
   g. To determine if the MPU is in multiprocessor mode.

3.14   Explain the function and operation of the instruction queue.

3.15   Describe the function of the flag register.

3.16   What flags are used to indicate the status of the MPU?

3.17   List the names and describe the functions of the general registers.

3.18   What is the use of the stack pointer? The instruction pointer?

3.19   Identify the segment register that is used to determine the starting location of a program's instructions.

3.20   What is the difference between a logical address and a physical address?

3.21   Explain the differences between static and dynamic RAM.

3.22   What is meant by memory-mapped I/O?

3.23   Draw a memory map that positions ROM at location E6F2H through E728H, interrupts at 0000H through 00FFH, RAM at 1000H through E000H.

3.24   Draw the timing diagram for a read bus cycle.

3.25   Draw the timing diagram for a read bus cycle with a wait state.

3.26   Determine whether each of the following statements is true or false.
a. A bootstrap program will usually be found in RAM.
b. An I/O device sends an active-high signal to the MPU to signify that it is ready for a data transfer.
c. The $\overline{RD}$ and $\overline{WR}$ control lines cannot be active at the same time.
d. During clock cycle T_2 the MPU outputs the address of a memory location.
e. During clock cycle T_3 the MPU reads the data on the data bus.

3.27   Explain the advantage of the 8088/8086 microprocessor over older microprocessors with relation to the fetch and execute cycles.

3.28   RMB associates designs a turbo microcomputer system that uses an 8-MHz clock frequency. Calculate the time for one clock cycle. Calculate the time for one bus cycle with two wait states.

3.29   The base address is F100H. The offset is 0200H. Determine the physical address of memory.

3.30   The instruction pointer contains 0777H. The code segment register contains 0200H. The data segment register contains 0900H. The stack segment register contains 1F00H. Determine the physical address for the first program instruction.

3.31   The physical address of a memory location is 421FH. The base address from the segment register is 0200H. Find the offset.

3.32   If it is suspected that the MPU may be faulty, what procedures and precautions should be taken to correct the problem?

3.33   Crossword Puzzle

<table>
<tr><td>

ACROSS

4. Sharing a bus.
5. Write.
6. Base register.
8. A term which describes the functional components of an integrated circuit.
10. 8088 queue width.
11. String destination.
12. Read.
15. Processing part of the 8088 MPU.
17. Count.
22. Connects to memory.
23. Five volts.
26. Wait state.
29. Valid address-control signal.
30. A signal used to stop the MPU.
31. Negate.
33. Computer chip.
37. Calculator part of the MPU.
38. MPU operational information.
40. 200 ns.
41. Indicates zero results.
42. Pin 22.

</td><td>

DOWN

1. Instruction storage prior to processing.
2. String source.
3. *AX, BX, CX, DX.*
5. Sixteen bits.
7. Next instruction to be executed.
8. Memory location.
9. Uses instruction pointer.
10. Four clock cycles.
13. Group of common signals or wires.
14. Four bits.
16. Interrupt enable.
18. Five megahertz.
19. Information.
20. Turns on a buffer.
21. 8086 data lines.
24. Name of a bus.
25. Binary digit.
27. EXTRA, CODE, DATA, STACK.
28. An instruction cycle.
29. Accumulator.
32. Address lines.
34. Overflow.
35. Register and segment.
36. Memory.
38. Indicates negative results.
39. Stack operations.

</td></tr>
</table>

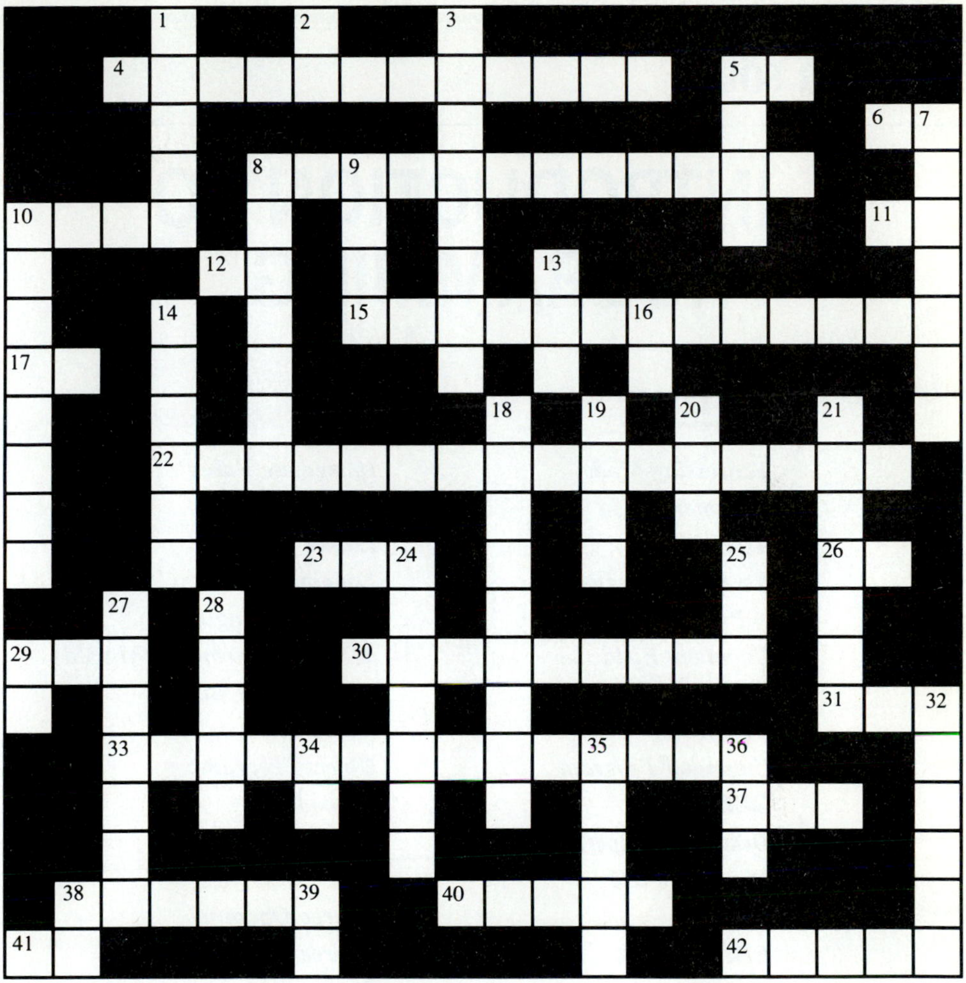
1
2
3
4
5
6
7
8
9
10
11
12
13
14
15
16
17
18
19
20
21
22
23
24
25
26
27
28
29
30
31
32
33
34
35
36
37
38
39
40
41
42

INTRODUCTION TO PROGRAMMING

KEY TERMS

Addressing Mode

Argument Field

Assembling

Assembly Language
  Programming

Comment Field

Comments

Compilers

Computer Program

DEBUG

Destination Operand

Directive Field

Editor

EDLIN

Flowcharting

Footer

Header

Immediate Value

Label Field

Linker Program

Looping

Machine Language

MACRO Assembler (MASM)

Masking Off Bits

Name Field

Object Program

Op-code

Operands

Poll

Source Operand

Source Program

Stack

Subroutine

4.0 INTRODUCTION

The microprocessor and the microcomputer system cannot be operated without a sequence of instructions known as a **computer program.** This program tells the computer what to do, how to do it, and when it should be done. The language that a computer can directly understand is called its **machine language.** Each microprocessor has its own machine language that is made up of a series of ones and zeros. These ones and zeros tell the system exactly what to do. For example, the machine language instruction to ADD a number may be written as

Function	Machine Language
ADD	00000011

Clearly, a program made up of many machine language instructions would be tedious and error prone. For this reason, so called *higher-level languages* such as Fortran, COBOL, Pascal, and BASIC were developed. These languages use English-like words for commands that make the programming task easier for people. Most high-level languages use **compilers** to translate instruction statements into machine language (1s and 0s) as shown in Figure 4.1. The compiler takes in instructions and turns them into machine language. The microprocessor can now understand these machine language instructions and execute them. However, the translation process increases processing time because of the added steps.

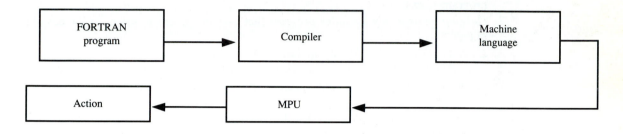

FIGURE 4.1
Converting a high-level language program

A compromise between the people-oriented, high-level languages and the computer-oriented, machine-level language is called **assembly language programming.** Assembly language does not require compiling, thus speeding up execution time and allowing faster access to peripherals. Instructions are assembled into machine code and executed directly by the CPU.

The assembly language program is also known as a **source program.** The act of converting the source program into the machine language that the computer understands is called **assembling** the program. This machine language output is also known as an **object program.** The entire process is summarized in Figure 4.2.

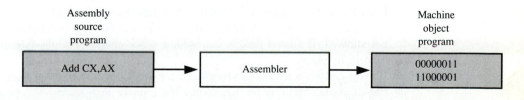

FIGURE 4.2
Assembling a program

It should be noted that compiling and assembling are very similar in nature. However, assembly language code is usually directly related to the resulting machine language code and therefore more efficient. Although compiled languages are easier to use, they usually require more machine language steps and are therefore less efficient.

4.1 ASSEMBLY LANGUAGE PROGRAMMING

Learning to write 8086/8088 assembly language programs is similar to learning to operate an electronic calculator. All data values must be entered and each operation, such as addition or subtraction, must be performed separately. Although assembly language programs and high-level language programs look different, the same procedures are used to develop each of them. These procedures are summarized as follows:

1. *Look and think:* What is the problem to be solved? What are the givens? What is to be found? This may require you to draw a flowchart or block diagram of how the program works.
2. *Develop an assembly language program* that uses the givens to solve for the desired output.
3. *Enter the program* into the computer.
4. *Assemble the program:* Use the assembler to translate the program into machine language. If the assembler finds errors, correct them and reassemble the program.
5. *Run the program.*
6. *Verify the results:* Check to see that the results are what you expected. If the results are incorrect, find the error and correct it.

Instruction Format

Each assembly language instruction in a source program is composed of up to four fields, as shown:

Label	Op-code	Operands	Comments
DATA:	MOV	CX,AX	;load CX with AX

1. The **label field** assigns a symbolic name to an assembly language instruction. This is sometimes called a *tag*. It lets other instructions reference the label by name rather than by a numeric location in memory. The first character in a label field must be a letter and the last character of a label field must be a colon. All letters A–Z, numerals 0–9, an underscore (__), and an at sign (@) can be used in label fields. Spaces are not allowed. If a label field is not used, a space character or tab (series of spaces) is used in its place.
2. The **op-code** is a mnemonic shorthand for an 8086/8088 microprocessor instruction. For example, MOV is the mnemonic for a move instruction. The beginning of the op-code field follows the colon of the label field or a space character. The end of the op-code field is determined by a space character or tab (series of spaces). See Appendix B for a complete listing of the 8086/8088 op-code instructions.
3. **Operands** tell the MPU where to find the data to be operated on. For example, in the instruction

```
MOV CX,AX
```

the operands are CX and AX. They tell the MPU to copy or move the contents of the AX register into the CX register. Some instructions use no operands, so the operand field is left blank. Other instructions use one or two operands. If there are two operands, they must be separated by a comma. When there are two operands, the first is called the **destination operand,** and the second is called the **source operand.**

```
MOV CX,AX
```

Destination operand = CX
Source operand = AX

The end of the operand field is determined by a semicolon if a comment is to be used. If *no* comment is to be used, the end of the operand field is determined by a carriage return.

4. **Comments** are used to describe a statement in the program to make a program easier to understand. Comments become very useful in longer programs. They will help you to remember why you did something a certain way. They will also help others to understand what you are doing. Comments must begin with a semicolon (;) and end with a carriage return. If a comment runs past the end of a line, it may be continued on the next line as long as the line begins with a semicolon.

Addressing Modes

The way in which the location of an operand is determined is called the **addressing mode.** How an operand is addressed in a program depends on the types and location of the data. There are three general types of addressing modes:

1. Immediate addressing modes
2. Register addressing modes
3. Memory addressing modes

Immediate Addressing Modes   The immediate addressing mode uses a number or a constant as its source operand. For example, in the instruction

```
MOV AX,0001H
```

the immediate value 0001H is moved into the AX register. The equivalent machine language instruction is written as

```
10111 000 0000000000000001
```

The first 5 bits, 10111, tells the MPU to perform an immediate word (16 bits) move. The next 3 bits, 000, define the destination operand as the AX register. The final 16 bits define the immediate value 0001H, which in binary is equal to 0000 0000 0000 0001B.

The immediate addressing mode can have a register or a memory location as its destination operand. If the destination is a register, the instruction will take approximately 4 clock cycles to execute. If the destination is a memory address, the instruction will take approximately 10 clock cycles to execute.

Register-addressing Modes   In the register-addressing mode both the source and destination operands of the instruction are in registers. Because this mode operates entirely within the MPU it is very fast. A typical instruction in this mode takes approximately 2 clock cycles to execute. For example, in the instruction

```
MOV AX,CX
```

the contents of the CX register are copied or moved into the AX register.

Memory-addressing Modes   The memory-addressing modes use either the source or destination operand as a memory address or label. There are two general types of memory addressing modes:

1. Direct addressing
2. Indirect addressing

Direct Addressing Mode   In the direct addressing mode, either the source or the destination operand is a specific memory location defined by the address number or a label. For example, in the instruction

```
MOV AX,MEM1
```

the contents of the memory address labeled MEM1 is copied or moved into the AX register.

Indirect Addressing Mode   In the indirect addressing mode, the memory address is not directly given. A register is used to indicate the address where the data can be found. Therefore, the register acts as an indirect address to locate the data. For example, in the instruction

```
MOV [BX],CX
```

the source of the data is the CX register. The destination, where the data are to be placed or copied to, is the *address* pointed to by the BX register. The brackets ([ ]) around BX indicate that the BX register contains an *address* and not a numeric value. There are many variations of indirect addressing modes that are available to the 8086/8088 assembly language programmer. However, the basic concept in all the indirect addressing modes remains the same.

4.2   ASSEMBLER DIRECTIVES

Assembler directives are instructions to the assembler program and are not executed by the MPU. The programs that you write will include assembler directives. However, the assembler directives are not translated into machine language. Assembler directives are used to pass information to the assembler such as where to begin the program (ORG), to reserve a space in memory for data (RS), or to indicate to the assembler that there are no more instructions to assemble (END). The assembler directives look very much like assembly language instructions. Each assembler directive consists of four fields.

Name	Directive	Argument	Comments
PI	EQU	3.14	;define value of PI

1. The **name field** is similar to the label field in the instruction statement. Some assembler directives require a name field, while others do not. The name field always begins with a letter and ends with a space.
2. The **directive field** is a mnemonic shorthand for the assembler directive operation. This is similar to the op-code in the instruction statement. It begins with a space and ends with a space or carriage return.
3. The **argument field** contains a memory address or a numeric value that is used with and determined by the directive. It also begins with a space and ends with a semicolon or carriage return.
4. The **comment field** is used exactly like the comment field in the instruction statement. It begins with a semicolon and ends with a carriage return.

Although there are many assembler directives, for our purposes we will limit our discussion to the directives shown in Table 4.1.

TABLE 4.1
Assembler directives summary

Directive	Description
ASSUME	Assume register segment
ORG	Originate
DB	Define byte
DW	Define word
DUP	Duplicate
EQU	Equate
PROC	Procedure
ENDP	End procedure
END	Program end

ASSUME   The assume assembler directive tells the assembler which segment registers the program is using. Otherwise, the assembler will not know the difference between the code segment and the data segment, and so forth—for example,

```
ASSUME CS:CODE, DS:DATA
```

ORG   The originate directive is used to set the instruction pointer to the starting address of the program in memory—for example,

```
ORG 0100H
```

This program begins at memory location 100H.

DB   The define byte directive can be used to allocate, define, and name a byte space in memory—for example,

```
DATA DB 90H
```

In this case the name DATA will be associated with a memory location that contains the value 90H.

DW   The define word directive is used to allocate, define, and name two consecutive locations in memory.

DUP   The duplicate directive is used as the operand of the defined byte or defined word directive to produce a block of data. It is often used to establish the stack—for example,

```
DB   100 DUP (0) ;100 bytes initially all 0
DB   100 DUP (?) ;100 bytes not initialized
```

EQU   The equate directive is used to associate a name with a value or another symbol—for example,

```
PI EQU 3.14
```

In this case the variable name PI is set equal to the value 3.14.

PROC   The procedure directive PROC is used to break up an assembly language program into blocks. It helps to modularize a program into smaller pieces. Only the simplest program and task can be written without being broken down into smaller blocks. The PROC directive is often used to define a *subroutine*, or portion of a program that is performed many times—for example,

```
DELAY PROC NEAR
DELAY PROC FAR
```

NEAR is used if the procedure is performed in one segment. FAR is used if the procedure extends into two or more segments.

ENDP   The end procedure directive ENDP is used to terminate a procedure in an assembly language program—for example,

```
DELAY    PROC    NEAR    ;   begin delay procedure
            .
            .
            .
DELAY    ENDP             ;   end of delay procedure
```

END   The end directive is used to tell the assembler that there are no more instructions left to assemble.

4.3   8086/8088 INSTRUCTION SET

The 8086/8088 instruction set is made up of over 100 basic assembly language instruction mnemonics that tell the MPU what to do. Each of the basic instructions can have many variations. For example, there are 28 different variations of the basic move instruction (MOV). The complete instruction set can be found in Appendix B. In this section we look at some of the more useful instructions from a technician's point of view. For clarity the instructions we examine in this section are classified into four groups:

1. Data-transfer instructions
2. Arithmetic instructions
3. Logical instructions
4. Program-control instructions

Data-Transfer Instructions

MOV   The fundamental data-transfer instruction is the move (MOV) instruction. This instruction can be used to transfer bytes (8 bits) or words (16 bits) of data. The general format of the MOV instruction is

MOV destination, source

The MOV instruction can be used to transfer data between two registers, as shown in Figure 4.3.

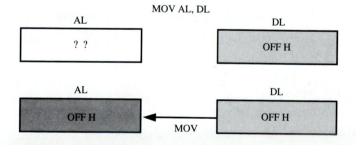

FIGURE 4.3
The MOV instruction register to register

Here the contents of the DL register (lower byte of the data register) contain the value of 0FFH. The AL register contains an unknown value or a value to be discarded. After the MOV instruction is executed, the contents of the DL register (0FFH) are also found in the AL register. Furthermore, the value 0FFH remains in the DL register after the move is completed. It should be noted that the leading zero is used here to differentiate or indicate that FFH is a constant value as opposed to a label. This is necessary to avoid confusion between interpreting hexadecimal numbers and label names. In assembly language programming a constant value is often referred to as an **immediate value.** Table 4.2 summarizes the various destinations and sources that are used with the move instruction.

TABLE 4.2
MOV instruction formats

	Destination	Source	Example
1	Memory	Register	MOV 100H,AX
2	Register	Memory	MOV AX,MEM1
3	Register	Register	MOV AX,BX
4	Register	Immediate (constant)	MOV AX,OFFFFH

The first example in Table 4.2 MOVes the contents of the AX register into memory location 100H. In the second example the contents of a memory location pointed to or named by the label MEM1 is loaded into the AX register. In the third example the contents of the BX register are loaded into the AX register. Finally, in the fourth example the constant value FFFFH is loaded into the AX register.

LEA   Load effective address (LEA) can be considered another type of move instruction. The LEA instruction is used to load a register with the *address* given. It is *not* used to move the contents of the given address. The general format of the LEA instruction is

LEA destination register, source label

The destination operand must be a register, and the source operand must be a label. For example, in the instruction

`LEA AX,MEM1`

the AX register is loaded with the *address* of MEM1 and *not* the data contained in MEM1.

Before introducing the next instructions, we examine the concept of a **stack.** Think of the image of a stack of cafeteria trays in a holding device. When a new tray is placed on top of the stack of trays, it *pushes* all the trays beneath it down one level. When the top tray is removed from the stack all the trays *pop* up one level. The last tray placed on the stack was the first tray removed. This is called a last-in, first-out (LIFO) operation and is illustrated in Figure 4.4.

PUSH/POP   The stack register is a convenient place to temporarily deposit data and memory operands from a program. For example, a program might want to save the contents of the AX register while it puts the AX register to some other use. The PUSH

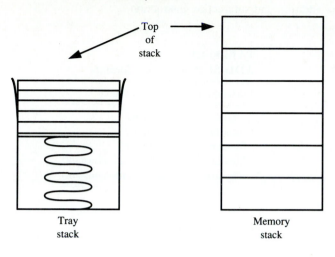

FIGURE 4.4
Stack operation

and POP instructions can be used to accomplish this task. The general formats of the PUSH and POP instructions are

PUSH source
POP destination

The source and destination operand can be a register or a memory address—for example,

```
PUSH AX    ;Save AX on top of the stack
POP AX     ;Retrieve AX from the top of the stack
```

PUSHF/POPF   The contents of the flag register may be stored or retrieved from the memory stack using the PUSHF and POPF instructions—for example,

```
PUSHF ;pushes contents of flag register onto the stack
POPF  ;retrieves contents of the flag register from the
      ;stack
```

Arithmetic Instructions

The arithmetic instructions cover the four basic mathematical operations of addition, subtraction, multiplication, and division.

ADD/SUB   The general formats of the add and subtract instructions are

ADD destination, source
SUB destination, source

Table 4.3 summarizes the various types of destination and source operands that may be used with the addition and subtraction instruction.

TABLE 4.3
ADD/SUB instruction formats

Destination	Source
Register	Register
Register	Memory
Memory	Register
Memory	Immediate (constant)
Register	Immediate (constant)

In all cases the result of an addition or subtraction will be found in the destination operand. For example, in the instruction

```
ADD AX,BX  ;add BX to AX
```

the contents of the BX register are added to the contents of the AX register. The results are stored in the AX register.

In the instruction

```
SUB CL,AL  ;subtract AL from CL
```

the contents of the AL register are subtracted from the contents of the CL register. The result is stored in the CL, or destination, register. Note that in this example we are subtracting the lower byte of the accumulator register from the lower byte of the count register. Thus there are many possible variations of the ADD and SUB instructions.

EXAMPLE 4.1

Write an assembly language program to add 5H plus 3H using the AL and BL registers.

Solution

```
MOV AL,05H      ;load 5H into AL register
MOV BL,03H      ;load 3H into BL register
ADD AL,BL       ;add BL to AL, result in AL = 8H
MOV 100H,AL     ;move result from AL into memory
                ;location 100H
```

EXAMPLE 4.2

Write an assembly language program to solve

$$\text{ANSWER} = 5H + 3H - 2H$$

Solution

```
MOV AL,05H          ;load 5H into AL register
MOV BL,03H          ;load 3H into BL register
ADD AL,BL           ;add BL to AL, results in AL = 8H
MOV BL,02H          ;move 2H into BL register
SUB AL,BL           ;subtract BL from AL
                    ;results in AL = 6H
MOV ANSWER,AL       ;move results to memory address
                    ;labeled ANSWER
```

Note that in the solutions to the previous examples the assembler directives have been omitted. This has been done for clarity. Complete programs that include assembler directives are shown later in this chapter.

MUL/DIV The general formats of the multiply (MUL) and divide (DIV) instructions are

> MUL source multiplier
> DIV source divisor

When the multiply command is used, the multiplicand must be moved into the AX or AL register. The source multiplier can be moved into any other register or memory location. Examples of multiply instructions are

```
MUL BX              ; multiplier in BX register
MUL MEM1            ; multiplier in memory address
                    ; labeled MEM1
```

When two bytes are multiplied together, the result, or product, is stored in the AX register. Note that in Figure 4.5 the multiplication of the two single-byte numbers results in a 16-bit, or 1-word, product in the AX register.

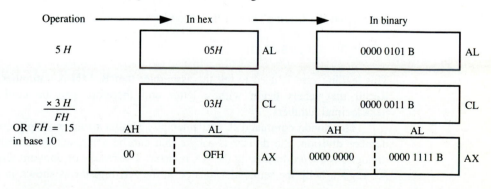

FIGURE 4.5
Using the MUL instruction

EXAMPLE 4.3

Write an assembly language program to multiply 5H by 3H using the CL register.

Solution

```
MOV AL,05H       ; move multiplicand 5H
                 ; into the AL register
MOV CL,03H       ; move multiplier 3H
                 ; into the CL register
MUL CL           ; multiply 3H by 5H
                 ; store product in AX register
MOV MEM1,AL      ; move product (0FH) from AL register
                 ; into memory location labeled
                 ; MEM1
```

When two 16-bit words are multiplied, the multiplicand must be moved into the AX register. The multiplier can be in any other register or 16-bit memory location. The results or product will be a 32-bit, or *double-word,* number and will be found in the DX and AX registers. The higher-order word will be in the DX register, and the lower-order word will be in the AX register.

EXAMPLE 4.4

Write an assembly language program to multiply 3A62H by 2B14H.

Solution

```
MOV AX,3A62H     ; move multiplicand 3A62H into AX register
MOV CX,0B214H    ; move multiplier B214H into CX register
MUL CX           ; multiply AX by CX, product = 289C63A8H
MOV MEM1,AX      ; move low-order word (63A8) into MEM1
MOV MEM2,DX      ; move high-order word (289C) into MEM2
```

Note again the leading zero in the second move instruction.

```
MOV CX,0B214H
```

This leading zero is used to tell the assembler that B214H is a number and not a label. Recall that labels begin with a letter and therefore can be confused with some hexadecimal numbers.

The divide command is fundamentally similar to the multiply command. In byte number division, the divisor is a byte that can be a register or memory location. The dividend is a word located in the AX register. The results or quotient will be found in the AL register with the remainder located in the AH register as shown in Figure 9.6.

$$\frac{6H}{3H} = 2H + 0 \text{ (Remainder)}$$

$$\frac{\text{Dividend}}{\text{Divisor}} = \text{Quotient} + \text{Remainder}$$

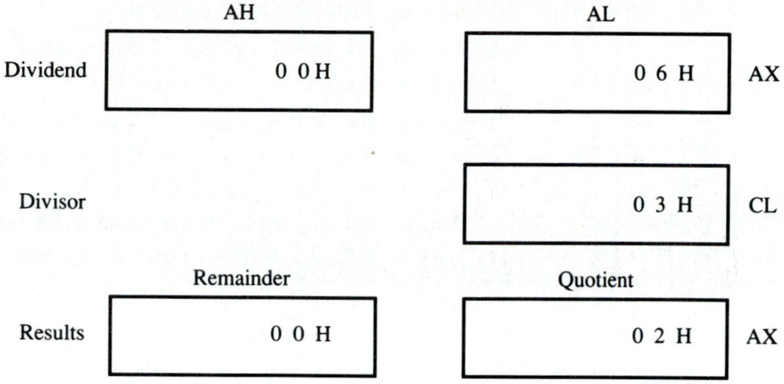

AH   AL

Dividend   0 0 H   0 6 H   AX

Divisor   0 3 H   CL

Remainder   Quotient

Results   0 0 H   0 2 H   AX

FIGURE 4.6
Divide operation

EXAMPLE 4.5

Write an assembly language program to divide 6H by 3H using the CL register.

Solution

```
MOV AX,0006H   ; move 6H into the AX register (dividend)
MOV CL,03H     ; move 3H into the CL register (divisor)
DIV CL         ; divide AX by CL
               ; quotient = 02H remainder = 00H
MOV MEM1,AL    ; move quotient into MEM1 (02H)
MOV MEM2,AH    ; move remainder into MEM2 (00H)
```

Note that 6H was entered as 0006H in order to fill the entire AX register. This was done to clear the high-order byte of the AX register of any erroneous data.

In word number division, the divisor is a word that can be a register or memory location. The dividend is a double word that is located in the DX and AX registers. The DX register will hold the high-order word, and the AX register will hold the low-order word. The result or quotient will be found in the AX register with the remainder located in the DX register.

EXAMPLE 4.6

Write an assembly language program to divide 1A034H by 1002H using the BX register.

Solution

```
MOV AX,0A034H    ; move low-order word
                 ; into AX register (dividend)
MOV DX,0001H     ; move high-order word
                 ; into DX register (dividend)
MOV BX,1002H     ; move divisor into BX register
DIV BX           ; divide DX AX by BX
MOV MEM1,AX      ; move quotient (1AH) from AX to MEM1
MOV MEM2,DX      ; move remainder (00H) from DX to MEM2
```

INC/DEC The increment (INC) command adds one to the operand. The decrement (DEC) command subtracts one from the operand. These commands are very useful for counting operations. The general format of the INC and DEC commands is

INC source
DEC source

The source operand may be a register or a memory address. The source operand may be a 16-bit word or an 8-bit byte—for example,

```
INC  AX       ; add one to AX register
INC  AL       ; add one to AL register
DEC  CX       ; subtract one from CX register
DEC  CL       ; subtract one from CL register
DEC  MEM1     ; subtract one from MEM1
```

EXAMPLE 4.7

Write an assembly language program to add 1 + 2 + 3 + 4 using the increment operand.

Solution

```
MOV AL,01H     ; move 1H into AL register
MOV BL,02H     ; move 2H into BL register
ADD AL,BL      ; add BL to AL (01H + 02H = 03H)
INC BL         ; add one to BL to obtain 03H
ADD AL,BL      ; add BL to AL (03H + 03H = 06H)
INC BL         ; add one to BL to obtain 04H
ADD AL,BL      ; add BL to AL (06H + 04H = 0AH)
MOV MEM1,AL    ; save sum in MEM1
```

Logical Instructions

Logical instructions include the Boolean operations NOT, AND, and OR. The NOT instruction inverts all the bits in a word or byte operand. The AND/OR instructions perform the Boolean AND/OR operations on each pair of bits in the source and destination operands. These instructions may be used with word or byte operands.

NOT   The general format of the NOT instruction is

NOT source

where the source operand may be a 16-bit word or an 8-bit byte. The source operand may be a register or a memory location: for example,

```
NOT AX
NOT BL
NOT MEM1
```

To illustrate the use of the NOT instruction, consider the following program:

```
MOV BL,00110011B       ; move binary number
                       ; into BL register
NOT BL                 ; negate BL
MOV MEM1,BL            ; save results in MEM1
```

The contents of the BL register were originally 00110011B. After the NOT operations are performed, the contents of the BL register are 11001100B.

$$BL = 00110011B$$
$$\overline{BL} = 11001100B$$

AND/OR   The general format of the AND/OR instruction is

AND destination, source
OR destination, source

AND/OR performs the Boolean operation between the source and destination operands. The results are stored in the destination operand. For example, in the instruction

```
AND AL,BL
```

the contents of the BL register are *ANDed* with the contents of the AL register. The results are stored in the AX register. If the number in the AL register is 00001101B and the number in the BL register is 00110011B, the result in the AL register after the AND operation is performed is:

	AL	00001101B
	BL	00110011B
Results	AL	00000001B

Table 4.4 summarizes the various types of destination and source operands that may be used with AND and OR instructions.

TABLE 4.4
AND/OR instruction formats

Destination	Source
Register	Register
Register	Memory
Memory	Register
Memory	Immediate (constant)
Register	Immediate (constant)

EXAMPLE 4.8   Write an assembly language program to implement the logic function of Figure 4.7 sixteen times.

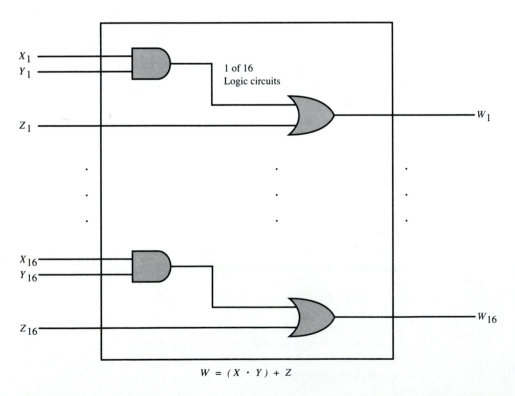

$$W = (X \cdot Y) + Z$$

FIGURE 4.7
Logic diagram

Solution

```
MOV AX,X        ; move X into AX
MOV BX,Y        ; move Y into BX
MOV CX,Z        ; move Z into CX
AND AX,BX       ; (X · Y)
OR  AX,CX       ; (X · Y) + Z
MOV W,AX        ; store results in W = (X · Y) + Z
```

Note that the label variables *X*, *Y*, and *Z* can represent 16 bits of information. Thus the program can perform the work of many logic AND and OR gates.

A technician wishes to use the program in Example 4.8 to solve for the output of W_3 only. By adding one additional AND instruction, the technician can set all the outputs except W_3 to zero. This process is known as **masking off bits** and is as follows:

```
MOV AX,X                       ; move X into AX
MOV BX,Y                       ; move Y into BX
MOV CX,Z                       ; move Z into CX
AND AX,BX                      ; (X · Y)
OR  AX,CX                      ; (X · Y) + Z
AND AX,0000000000000100B       ; mask off bits
MOV W3,AX
```

The results of the OR operation found in the AX register are:

	1010 1111 1001 1100B
Masked with (AND)	0000 0000 0000 0100B
Results in (W)	0000 0000 0000 0100B

Program-Control Instructions

Up to this point we have examined the instructions that perform a specific task once. From this we might conclude that if we need to perform a specific operation more than once in a program, we must duplicate the entire sequence of instructions each time we need to perform the operation. Duplicating a sequence of instructions many times in a program would be frustrating and time consuming. Program-control instructions help to eliminate this duplication.

JMP   When you read a set of instructions and reach a direction like "JUMP to STEP 10," you have come upon a jump instruction. The jump (JMP) instruction makes the MPU take its next instruction from someplace other than the next consecutive memory location. Jump instructions can be *unconditional* or *conditional*. An unconditional jump instruction is one that is always taken. Whenever it occurs in a program, it is executed immediately. A conditional jump requires the MPU to make a decision based on the contents of the flag register. The general format of the jump instruction is

JMP destination

The destination can be a label, memory address, or 16-bit register. A direct jump might be to a label. An indirect jump is to a register or memory location that *points* to the target destination. For example, consider the following:

```
         MOV BX,0001H    ; load BX with 1H
         SUB AX,AX       ; initialize AX to zero
REPEAT:  ADD AX,BX       ; add BX to AX
         JMP REPEAT      ; count by repeated addition
```

In this program the AX register will be incremented by 1 continuously until the computer is turned off. There is no condition to stop the program.

Conditional jump instructions can be used to control the program. They allow us to set a condition that causes the MPU to make a decision on whether to jump or not. For example, in the following program the JNZ (jump not zero) instruction is used to control the number of times a mathematical operation is performed.

```
         SUB AX,AX       ; initialize AX to zero
         MOV BX,0007H    ; load 7H in BX
         MOV CX,0003H    ; load 3H in CX
MULT:    ADD AX,BX       ; add BX to AX
         DEC CX          ; decrement CX by 1
         JNZ MULT        ; jump if not zero to MULT
         MOV PROD,AX     ; store results in PROD
```

This program can be used to do multiplication by repeated addition. We begin by initializing the AX register to zero. We could have used the instruction

```
MOV AX,0000H
```

to accomplish the same operation. Next we load the numbers we wish to multiply together into separate registers. The

```
ADD AX,BX
```

instruction will be performed until the contents of the CX register is zero. Each time the ADD instruction is performed, we will decrement the CX register by one (DEC CX) and test to see if the result is zero (JNZ). The JNZ instruction looks at the zero flag (ZF) in the flag register. If the ZF flag is reset (ZF = 0), we jump to the label MULT. If the ZF flag is set (ZF = 1), we skip to the next instruction, which in this case saves the answer. The zero flag will be set by the MPU anytime that an arithmetic operation results in a zero.

There are many types and variations of conditional and unconditional jump instructions. A complete list is located in Appendix B.

LOOP   The loop instruction (LOOP) is a special form of the jump instruction with a built-in count capability. Like the jump instruction, it is used to repeat an operation or a sequence of instructions. This is commonly referred to as **looping.** Loop instructions can be conditional or unconditional and are always used with the CX register. The general format of the loop instruction is

LOOP destination label

The LOOP instruction uses the CX or count register to determine the number of times the loop is to be performed. When the LOOP instruction is used, a value, or number, is first placed in the CX register. Every time the LOOP instruction is executed, the CX register is automatically decremented by 1. Next, the CX register is tested to see if it is zero. If it is zero, the loop is terminated and the next instruction performed. If it is not zero, the program will loop to the destination label.

There are also conditional LOOP instructions that use the count register and the flag register to determine when to loop. For example,

```
LOOPZ - loop while zero (ZF = 1 CX = 0)
LOOPNZ - loop while not zero (ZF = 0 CX = 0)
```

In order to illustrate the use of the LOOP instruction we will rewrite the previous program example (multiplication by repeated addition) using the LOOP instruction.

```
        SUB AX,AX        ; initialize AX to zero
        MOV BX,0007H     ; load 7H in BX
        MOV CX,0003H     ; load 3H in CX
MULT:   ADD AX,BX        ; add BX to AX
        LOOP MULT        ; repeat addition
        MOV PROD,AX      ; store results in PROD
```

4.4 PROGRAM STRUCTURE

As programs get longer and more complex, the need for organization becomes more important. One method of organization is to develop an outline. The outline can be used to break the problem down into smaller parts. These parts must be ordered or sequenced to allow the problem to be solved correctly. A method of outlining or mapping a problem is known as **flowcharting.** The flowchart is a block diagram that uses standard symbols to represent operations. Figure 4.8 shows some of the basic flowcharting symbols.

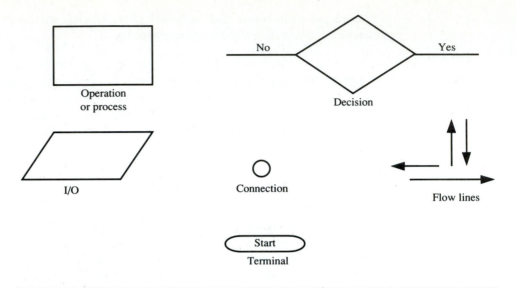

FIGURE 4.8
Flowchart symbols

Let's create a flowchart and an assembly language program to control an alarm in a truck weighing station. If a truck exceeds a certain weight, we wish to sound an alarm. If a truck is below the weight limit, we keep the alarm off and allow the truck to pass. Figure 4.9 describes a solution to this problem using a flowchart.

We begin by defining the data variables. The variable DATA_IN will be used to read in the truck weight. Note the use of the ''__'' in the variable name. This is done to separate the words DATA and IN without using a space. Remember that spaces are illegal in labels and variables. Programmers often use this technique when defining variables and label names for the purpose of clarity. The variable DATA_OUT will be used to control the alarm. An output code of 00H will keep the alarm off, and an output code of FFH will turn the alarm on. The output code could be sent to a digital-to-analog converter circuit to control an audible alarm. Finally, the variable MAX_WT will be used to define the maximum allowable truck weight, which has been set equal to 10 tons or 0AH in this problem.

The next box in our flowchart initializes the alarm output to be off. We then read in the weight of a truck (DATA_IN). If the truck's weight is *less than or equal to* the maximum allowable weight, we hold the alarm off and go on to read the next truck's weight. If the truck's weight *exceeds* the maximum allowable weight, we sound the alarm by outputting the FFH code. The program then returns to read in the next truck's weight. If the next truck's weight is less than or equal to the maximum allowable weight, the alarm will be turned off. Otherwise, the alarm will continue to sound.

Figure 4.10 illustrates an assembly language program that can be used to implement the solution to our truck weighing station problem. Note the use of the

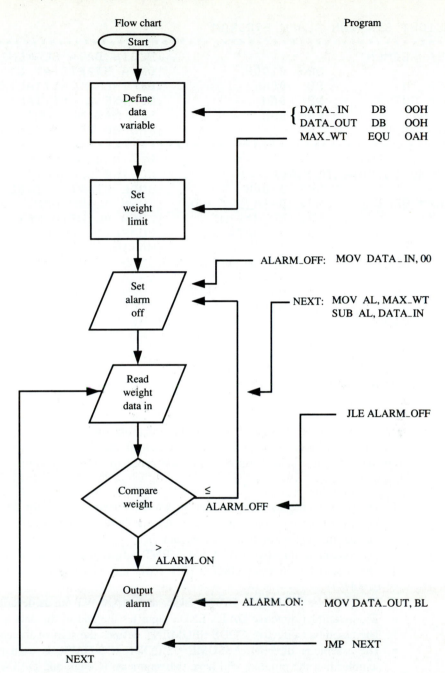

FIGURE 4.9
Flowchart—Weight station program

```
 1: ;WEIGHT STATION ALARM PROGRAM
 2: ;*************************************************************
 3: DATA SEGMENT                          ;BEGIN DATA SEGMENT
 4:                  ORG  0100H           ;DATA STARTS AT 0100H
 5: DATA_IN          DB   00H             ;DEFINE & INITIALIZE TO 00H
 6: DATA_OUT         DB   00H             ;DEFINE & INITIALIZE TO 00H
 7: MAX_WT           EQU  0AH             ;SET MAXIMUM WEIGHT LIMIT
 8: DATA ENDS                             ;END OF DATA SEGMENT
 9: ;*************************************************************
10: CODE SEGMENT                          ;BEGIN CODE SEGMENT
11: ASSUME CS:CODE,DS:DATA                ;DEFINE SEGMENTS
12:                  ORG  0200H           ;CODE STARTS AT 0200H
13: ALARM_OFF:       MOV  DATA_OUT,00H    ;TURN ALARM OFF, OUTPUT 00H
14: NEXT:            MOV  AL,MAX_WT       ;LOAD AL WITH MAX WGT LIMIT
15:                  SUB  AL,DATA_IN      ;COMPARE TRUCK WEIGHT TO
16:                                       ;MAXIMUM WEIGHT LIMIT
17:                  JLE  ALARM_OFF       ;JUMP TO ALARAM_OFF IF
18:                                       ;DATA_IN < MAX_WT
19: ALARM_ON:        MOV  DATA_OUT,0FFH   ;TURN ALARM ON, OUTPUT 0FFH
20:                  JMP  NEXT            ;READ NEXT TRUCK WEIGHT
21: CODE ENDS                             ;END OF CODE SEGMENT
22: END                                   ;END OF PROGRAM
```

FIGURE 4.10
Weight station alarm program

program segments to separate the data portion from the code portion of the program. Furthermore, in this example we have presented the use of assembler directives to illustrate their use in an assembly language program. The following points should be noted:

1. The program begins with a comment, which is used as a title for this program.
2. The use of the semicolon followed by the star border is purely aesthetic and is used for highlighting portions of the program.
3. The assembler directive DATA SEGMENT defines the start of the data segment.
4. The assembler directive ORG 0100H starts the data segment at logical address 0100H.
5. The variables DATA_IN, DATA_OUT, and MAX_WT are as described before.
6. The assembler directive DATA ENDS signifies the end of the data segment.
7. The assembler directive CODE SEGMENT defines the start of the code segment.
8. The assembler directive ASSUME CS:CODE, DS:DATA is used to tell the assembler that the program will have two segments (CODE and DATA).
9. The assembler directive ORG 0200H starts the code segment at logical address 0200H.
10. The code segment instructions were also described above.
11. The assembler directive CODE ENDS signifies the end of the code segment.
12. The assembler directive END signifies the end of the program.

4.5 SUBROUTINES

A **subroutine** is a portion of a program that is used to perform a particular task. Usually subroutines are used to perform a task that needs to be repeated many times in the program. For example, a program that computes the square root of a number can be used as a subroutine in another program. Any time we wish to calculate the square root of a number we can call upon our subroutine without having to rewrite the instructions each time, which is the advantage of a subroutine. This also saves memory space. Thus if we need to calculate the hypotenuse of a right triangle 1000 times, the square root subroutine will be very helpful.

The instruction that allows us to go to a subroutine is the CALL instruction. The instruction that allows us to return to the main program once the subroutine is completed is the RET (return) instruction. The general format of the CALL and RET instruction is

CALL destination
RET

The CALL destination can be a label, an address, or a 16-bit register. The RET instruction usually does not have an operand.

When the microprocessor executes a CALL instruction, the address of the next main program instruction must be saved. If this was not done, the MPU would not know where to return in the main program. This is performed in coordination with the stack. The CALL instruction pushes the current contents of the instruction pointer onto the stack. Next the MPU puts the memory address of the subroutine into the instruction pointer. Thus the stack is used to save the return address of the main program, and the instruction pointer is used to point to the beginning address of the subroutine. When the subroutine is completed, the return address is popped back out of the stack and into the instruction pointer, and the program is continued. To summarize:

1. The CALL instruction is read and decoded by the MPU.
2. The instruction pointer is now incremented to point to the *next* instruction in the main program.
3. The contents of the instruction pointer are now pushed onto the stack.
4. The instruction pointer is now loaded with the starting address of the subroutine.
5. The subroutine is executed.
6. The RET instruction, which must be the last instruction in the subroutine, pops the return address of the main program from the stack.
7. The return address is loaded into the instruction pointer, and the main program continues.

To demonstrate the use of the subroutine, let us now consider the previous weight station alarm program. Suppose our weight station actually has three scales. We wish to use our alarm program to **poll**, or check, the weight of each scale. Due to the speed of the microprocessor we can read the weight of the first scale and check to see if we should sound the alarm. Next, we read the weight of the second scale and check to see if we should sound the alarm. Finally, we read the weight of the third scale and again determine if we should sound the alarm. The entire process is repeated over and over again. Figure 4.11 illustrates the flowchart that will be used to create the assembly language program. Note that the original weight station alarm program has been modified to be used as a subroutine. Figure 4.12 shows an assembly language program that can be used to solve this problem.

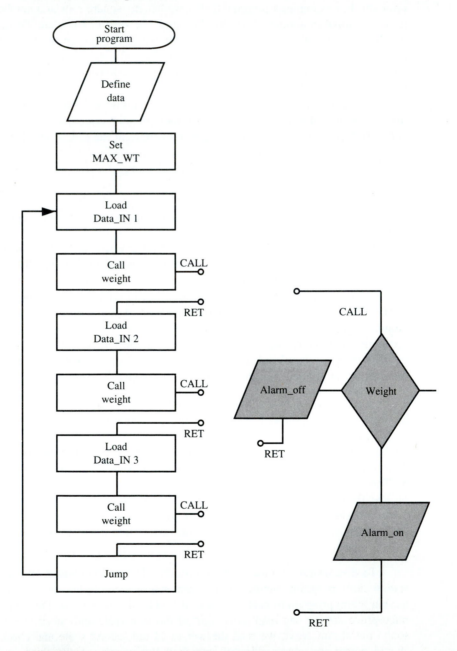

FIGURE 4.11
Flowchart—Three-scale weight station program

```
 1: ;THREE SCALE WEIGHT STATION ALARM PROGRAM
 2: ;****************************************************************
 3: STACK SEGMENT STACK                 ;BEGIN STACK SEGMENT
 4:                 DB     20 DUP (?)   ;STACK SIZE = 20 BYTES
 5: STACK ENDS                          ;END OF STACK SEGMENT
 6: ;****************************************************************
 7: DATA SEGMENT                        ;BEGIN DATA SEGMENT
 8:                 ORG    0100H        ;DATA STARTS AT 0100H
 9: DATA_IN1        DB     00H          ;DEFINE & INITIALIZE TO 00H
10: DATA_IN2        DB     00H          ;DEFINE & INITIALIZE TO 00H
11: DATA_IN3        DB     00H          ;DEFINE & INITIALIZE TO 00H
12: DATA_OUT        DB     00H          ;DEFINE & INITIALIZE TO 00H
13: MAX_WT          EQU    0AH          ;SET MAXIMUM WEIGHT LIMIT
14: DATA ENDS                           ;END OF DATA SEGMENT
15: ;****************************************************************
16: CODE SEGMENT                        ;BEGIN CODE SEGMENT
17: ASSUME CS:CODE,DS:DATA,SS:STACK     ;DEFINE SEGMENTS
18:                 ORG    0200H        ;CODE STARTS AT 0200H
19: START:          MOV    BL,DATA_IN1  ;READ SCALE 1
20:                 CALL   WEIGHT       ;WEIGHT ALARM SUBROUTINE
21:                 MOV    BL,DATA_IN2  ;READ SCALE 2
22:                 CALL   WEIGHT       ;WEIGHT ALARM SUBROUTINE
23:                 MOV    BL,DATA_IN3  ;READ SCALE 3
24:                 CALL   WEIGHT       ;WEIGHT ALARM SUBROUTINE
25:                 JMP    START        ;RESTART PROCESS
26: WEIGHT          PROC   NEAR         ;BEGIN SUBROUTINE
27: ALARM_OFF:      MOV    DATA_OUT,00H ;TURN ALARM OFF, OUTPUT 00H
28:                 MOV    AL,MAX_WT    ;LOAD AL WITH MAX WGT LIMIT
29:                 SUB    AL,BL        ;COMPARE TRUCK WEIGHT TO
30:                                     ;MAXIMUM WEIGHT LIMIT
31:                 JLE    RETURN       ;JUMP TO RETURN IF
32:                                     ;DATA_IN < MAX_WT
33: ALARM_ON:       MOV    DATA_OUT,0FFH ;TURN ALARM ON, OUTPUT 0FFH
34: RETURN:         RET                 ;READ NEXT TRUCK WEIGHT
35: WEIGHT          ENDP                ;END OF WEIGHT PROCEDURE
36:                                     ;SUBROUTINE
37: CODE ENDS                           ;END OF CODE SEGMENT
38: END                                 ;END OF PROGRAM
```

FIGURE 4.12
Three-scale weight station alarm program

Let's analyze the program in detail.

1. Since we will be using the CALL instruction, a stack will be required to save the contents of the instruction pointer when we jump into our subroutine. The stack segment instruction DB   20 DUP (?) establishes the stack area in memory.
2. The data segment defines the variables that are used in the program. Furthermore, it should be noted that the DATA_IN1, DATA_IN2, and DATA_IN3 are memory-

mapped I/O addresses, as shown in Figure 4.13, that connect the scales directly to memory addresses 0100H, 0101H, and 0102H, respectively.
3. DATA_OUT is also memory mapped and connects the alarm directly to memory address 0103H.
4. The instruction MAX_WT   EQU   0AH is used to set the maximum allowable truck weight equal to 10 tons.

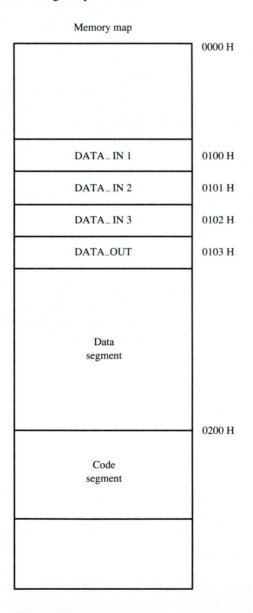

FIGURE 4.13
Memory map

5. The code segment of the program begins at 0200H (ORG   0200H).
6. The instruction MOV   BL,DATA_IN1 moves the truck weight at scale 1 into the BL register.
7. The next instruction, CALL   WEIGHT, causes the program to jump to the subroutine labeled WEIGHT.
8. The instruction WEIGHT   PROC   NEAR defines the beginning of a subroutine procedure within the code segment labeled WEIGHT.
9. The program continues as previously described to determine whether or not to sound the alarm until the RET instruction is reached.
10. The ENDP directive tells the assembler that the procedure is complete.
11. RET returns us to the main program, causing the second scale to be read (DATA_IN2).
12. This process repeats itself for DATA_IN3 (the third scale).
13. The JMP   START instruction restarts the entire process.

4.6   CREATING PROGRAMS

The assembler converts assembly language instructions into machine language instructions. Recall that it reads the *source code* instructions and outputs *object code* instructions. The final step is to *link,* or merge, this object code with the operating system of the computer in order to create a fully executable program. In the IBM PC a program called the **MACRO Assembler (MASM)** performs all these tasks for us.

Let's assume that we have created a flowchart and worked out the logic of an assembly language program. We have written the program down on paper and are ready to see if it works. The next step is to input our source code into the computer. This task is usually performed using a program called an **editor.**

The Editor

There are many screen editors that we may use to develop our source code file. We may even use a word processor providing that it outputs a standard ASCII file—most do. The text editor that comes with the IBM PC Disk Operating System (DOS) is called **EDLIN** for LINe EDitor program.

To begin, insert the DOS diskette in drive A and a second *formatted* diskette in drive B. At the DOS prompt, type

```
A>EDLIN B:PROGRAM.ASM <ENTER>
```

and then press the ENTER key. B: tells EDLIN to save your program on the diskette in drive B. PROGRAM is the name of the program we are going to write. The extension .ASM is used because we are going to create an assembly language program. Note that it is customary, but not necessary, to write source code in capital letters. Therefore, we may choose to press the CAPS LOCK key first.

The computer should respond with

```
A>EDLIN B:PROGRAM.ASM
New file
*
```

This signifies that the EDLIN program is ready. At the asterisk (*), type the command I for insert and press ENTER.

```
A>EDLIN B:PROGRAM.ASM
New file
*I<ENTER>
```

The computer should respond with

```
A>EDLIN B:PROGRAM.ASM
New file
*I
  1:*
```

We are now ready to enter our program. Try entering the following program. Note the columns for each of the fields. The TAB key will be helpful to create the columns. Don't worry about mistakes. We will learn how to correct them later.

```
 1:              STACK SEGMENT STACK
 2:              DB                        12 DUP (?)
 3:              STACK ENDS
 4:              CODE SEGMENT
 5:              ASSUME CS:CODE,SS:STACK
 6:    BEGIN     PROC                      FAR
 7:              PUSH                      DS
 8:              SUB                       AX,AX
 9:              PUSH                      AX
10:              MOV                       AL,45H
11:              MOV                       BL,03H
12:              ADD                       AL,BL
13:              MOV                       DL,AL
14:              MOV                       AH,02H
15:              INT                       21H
16:    DONE:     RET
17:    BEGIN     ENDP
18:              CODE ENDS
19:              END
```

Starting at line 1, type

```
  1:*  STACK SEGMENT STACK <ENTER>
```

Then press the ENTER key. The computer should respond with

```
1:    STACK SEGMENT STACK
2:*
```

Now type

```
1:    STACK SEGMENT STACK
2:* DB    12 DUP (?) <ENTER>
```

Continue typing, paying attention to the rules even if words exceed a TAB zone.

When the program is entered, hold down the Ctrl key and press Scroll Lock (BREAK key on some keyboards) to end the program.

```
20:*^C
```

Now type E for END and then press the ENTER key to save the program and exit to DOS.

```
*E <ENTER>
```

If we had typed Q and then pressed the ENTER key, we could have also QUIT the session but we would *not* have saved the program on the diskette. We would use Q only if we did not want to save the program or if we wanted to begin again.

Once we are in DOS again, use the DIR B: command to verify that our program is on the diskette. To see a *listing* of the program, we must first call up EDLIN again. Type

```
A>EDLIN B:PROGRAM.ASM <ENTER>
```

The computer should respond

```
A>EDLIN B:PROGRAM.ASM
End of input file
*
```

Type L for LIST and press the ENTER key. A complete listing of the program should appear on the screen. Typing 10L will list only the lines from line 10 to the remainder of your program. This is sometimes useful on longer programs.

Making Corrections

Let's suppose that line 8 has a mistake. It reads

```
8:    SAB   AX,AX
```

At the asterisk (*) type

```
*8 <ENTER>
```

The entire line will be reproduced on the screen. Now press the right cursor control key until the cursor is directly under the A.

```
8:        SAB       AX,AX
8:        S_
```

Type the letter U to make the correction. Then press the right cursor control key until the cursor reaches the end of the line. Now press the ENTER key. After the change is made, use the list command L to verify that the correction has been made. If characters are missing or if characters need to be erased, make these corrections in a similar manner using the INSERT and DELETE keys. After all the corrections have been made, return to DOS by ending the session using the Ctrl Scroll Lock and E command.

The Assembler

To assemble the program we find it convenient to set drive B as the default drive. Return to DOS and type B: to set drive B as the default drive. Insert the MACRO Assembler diskette into drive A and type

```
B>A:MASM <ENTER>
```

The computer should respond

```
Source filename [.ASM]: _
```

Type the name of the file, which in this case is PROGRAM, and then press the ENTER key.

```
Source filename [.ASM]: PROGRAM <ENTER>
```

MASM will respond with three more questions. Answer each of them by pressing the ENTER key.

```
Source filename [.ASM]: PROGRAM
Object filename [PROGRAM.OBJ]: <ENTER>
Source listing [NUL.LST]: <ENTER>
Cross reference [NUL.CRF]: <ENTER>
```

If there are no errors, MASM will assemble the program and respond

```
Warning Severe
Errors  Errors
0       0
```

MASM has now assembled the program and saved it on the diskette in drive B using the file name PROGRAM.OBJ. To watch the program being assembled, line by line, type CON for console monitor or PRN for printer listing after the second question:

```
Source listing [NUL.LST]: _
```

If there were any errors in the program, the program did not assemble. Correct them using EDLIN before going on.

The Linker

After we have obtained an error-free assembled program, we are ready to convert the object file into a PC DOS executable program file. The object file created must now be linked, or merged, with DOS to be executable. The **linker program** will do this for us. To call the linker, type

```
B>A:LINK <ENTER>
```

The linker will respond with the message

```
Object Modules [.OBJ]: _
```

Since the file name extension .OBJ was created by the assembler, type

```
Object Modules [.OBJ]: PROGRAM <ENTER>
```

The linker will respond with three more questions. Respond by pressing the ENTER key each time.

```
Object Modules [.OBJ]: PROGRAM <ENTER>
Run File [PROGRAM.EXE]: <ENTER>
List File [NUL.MAP]: <ENTER>
Libraries [.LIB]: <ENTER>
```

The linker has now created and saved the executable program file on drive B using the file name PROGRAM.EXE. You can verify this by typing DIR.

Running the Program

To execute the program, simply type the name of the program after the DOS prompt. In this case, type

```
B>PROGRAM <ENTER>
```

The program does not do very much. It simply prints the ASCII character H on the screen. It does, however, demonstrate all the steps necessary to create and execute an assembly language program. The first nine lines of the program are required for the linker to work with DOS. They will be required on most programs, so we refer to them as a **header.** Lines 10, 11, and 12 add two hex numbers to define and determine an ASCII character. Lines 13, 14, and 15 are used to display the character on the screen. When the INT 21H command is executed with 02H in the AH register, DOS will display the character in the DL register on the screen. Lines 16, 17, 18, and 19 are used to terminate the program. Since all programs need to be terminated, we refer to them as a **footer.** If you do not terminate a program, the 8088 will continue executing whatever else is in memory. Since most programs require a header section and a footer section for proper assembly and linkage, a general format for most programs is presented next.

```
STACK SEGMENT STACK
                  DB          256 DUP (?)
STACK ENDS
; ******************************************************************
DATA SEGMENT
        (ADD DATA DEFINITIONS HERE)
DATA ENDS
; ******************************************************************
CODE SEGMENT
ASSUME CS:CODE,DS:DATA,SS:STACK
MAIN               PROC      FAR
                   PUSH      DS
                   SUB       AX,AX
        (INSERT MAIN PROGRAM LOGIC HERE)
                   RET
        (INSERT SUBROUTINES HERE)
MAIN            ENDP
CODE ENDS
END
```

4.7   TECH TIPS AND TROUBLESHOOTING—T³

DEBUG is an essential *utility* program for assembly language programs. DEBUG comes with IBM PC DOS and allows us to examine internal registers to determine what is going on in a program. Rarely will programs work perfectly the first time they are executed. DEBUG will help clarify what is going on because:

1. It allows you to set break points and halt the program's execution.
2. It allows you to single step, or trace through the program one instruction at a time.

To use DEBUG, type the following at the DOS prompt:

```
A>DEBUG <ENTER>
```

The computer responds

```
A>DEBUG
-_
```

Now type in the following program

```
-A 0100 <ENTER>
101D:0100 MOV AL,22 <ENTER>
101D:0102 MOV BL,05 <ENTER>
101D:0104 ADD AL,BL <ENTER>
101D:0106 INT 20 <ENTER>
101D:0108 <ENTER>
```

When you are finished entering the program, press the ENTER key. Note that DEBUG expects everything to be in hex. It will not accept the H at the end of a number.

This program will simply add the two numbers 22H and 5H. The INT 20 command is a PC DOS command that is used to terminate a program. It is similar to END. The A 0100 command tells DEBUG to assemble the program starting at memory address 0100. Before executing this program, type U0100 0106 <ENTER> to list the program. The computer will respond with

```
-U0100  0106
101D:0100  B022      MOV      AL,22
101D:0102  B305      MOV      BL,05
101D:0104  00D8      ADD      AL,BL
101D:0106  CD20      INT      20
-
```

If you had just typed the command U, the computer would have listed the next 15 lines following the current position of the instruction pointer. Now type R <ENTER> to examine the registers. The computer will respond with

```
-R
AX=0000   BX=0000 CX=0000 DX=0000 SP=FFEE BR=0000 SI=0000 DI=0000
DS=101D   ES=101D SS=101D CS=101D IP=0100 NV UP EI PL NZ NA PO NC
101D:0100 B022     MOV AL,22
```

Next type T <ENTER> to trace through the program one instruction at a time. The computer will respond with

```
-T
AX=0022   BX=0000 CX=0000 DX=0000 SP=FFEE BP=0000 SI=0000 DI=0000
DS=101D   ES=101D SS=101D CS=101D IP=0102 NV UP EI PL NZ NA PO NC
101D:0102 B305     MOV BL,05
```

Type T< ENTER> two more times, and the computer will respond with

```
-T
AX=0022   BX=0005 CX=0000 DX=0000 SP=FEEE BP=0000 SI=0000 DI=0000
DS=101D   ES=101D SS=101D CS=101D IP=0104 NV UP EI PL NZ NA RO NC
101D:0104 00D8     ADD AL,BL
-T

AX=0027   BX=0005 CX=0000 DX=0000 SP=FFEE BP=0000 SI=0000 DI=0000
DS=101D   ES=101D SS=101D CS=101D IP=0106 NV UP EI PL NZ NA PE NC
101D:0106 CD20     INT 20
-
```

Note the contents of the registers each time you type the T command. Furthermore, notice that the instruction pointer is updated each time to point to the next instruction to be executed. Typing T one more time will execute the INT 20 instruction. If we do this, we will have to step through many lines of instructions that reside in DOS and perform the INT 20 command. This command terminates the program and returns us to DOS. Instead, we will type G <ENTER> for GO to execute the program. The computer responds

```
G
Program terminated normally
-
```

You can now examine the registers again to see the results.

DEBUG has many other commands, features, and uses. For example, you can examine and change the contents of any register by typing R followed by the register name (RAX). You can enter or change the data in any location using the E or ENTER command (E0101 55). To exit DEBUG type Q for QUIT. You will find that DEBUG is a valuable aid in troubleshooting your programs. You may want to consult the IBM DOS manual or some other text to learn more about DEBUG.

EXERCISES

4.1　Give an example of a high-level computer programming language.

4.2　High-level programming languages use _____ to translate instructions into machine language.

4.3　List the procedures used to develop an assembly language program.

4.4　The way in which the location of an operand is determined is called the _____.

4.5　Explain the meaning of MOV CX,DX.

4.6　List the three general types of addressing modes.

4.7　Explain the meaning of MOV AX,[BX].

4.8　What is the EQU directive used for?

4.9　What is the general format of a data-transfer instruction?

4.10　Give an example of a data-transfer instruction using
　　　a. Register-addressing mode　　b. Memory-addressing mode
　　　c. Immediate addressing mode

4.11　List four data-transfer instructions and give an example for each.

4.12　Give an example of an arithmetic instruction using
　　　a. Register-addressing mode　　b. Memory-addressing mode
　　　c. Immediate addressing mode

4.13　List four different types of arithmetic instructions and give an example for each.

4.14　What is the difference between an assembler directive and an instruction?

4.15　What will the results of the instruction NOT AX, be if the AX register contains FFFFH?

4.16　Define the term *masking*.

4.17　What is the general format of the OR instruction? Give an example of its use.

4.18　What is the difference between a conditional and an unconditional program control instruction? Give two examples of each.

4.19   What is the difference between a JUMP and a LOOP instruction? Give an example of each.

4.20   Define a subroutine.

4.21   Write a program to add 4H to 3H using the AX and BX registers. Load the results into a memory address labeled SUM.

4.22   Write a program to compute the equation $Z = (2X + 5Y)/W$ where $X = 4$, $Y = 3$, and $W = 2$.

4.23   Write a program to compute $Z = (A \cdot B) + \overline{C}$ using MEMA for the value of A, MEMB for the value of B, and MEMC for the value of C. Store the results of Z in the memory location labeled STORE.

4.24   Write a program using a subroutine to compute the value of X, $2X$, $3X$, and X^2 for integer values of X between 1 and 10. Draw a flowchart for the program and explain what the program is doing by using comments. Be sure to include required assembler directives.

4.25   Write a program to sound an alarm when the temperature of a refrigerator rises above 50°F. Draw a flowchart for the program and explain what the program is doing by using comments. Be sure to include the required assembler directives.

4.26   Crossword Puzzle

ACROSS

3. Translates into machine language.
5. A special form of the jump instruction with a built-in count capability.
7. Mnemonic field.
8. A logical instruction used to complement a binary number.
9. An instruction used to tell the MPU to copy the contents of a register or memory location.
12. A place where information is stored.
13. Also called a machine language program.
17. MOV.
18. Define byte directive.
19. A language that uses English-like words for commands.
21. Arithmetic instruction.
23. Immediate, register, and memory _____ modes.
24. The field used to contain a memory address or a numeric value used with the directive.
25. A procedure contained in one segment.
29. When a register is used to indicate the address where the data can be found.

30. MASM.
32. The last instruction in a procedure.
33. Creates an executable program.

DOWN

1. An type of move instruction used to load an effective address.
2. The instruction to remove data from the stack.
4. What the computer directly understands.
6. A list of instructions that tells the MPU what to do.
8. Field similar to label field.
10. A constant source value.
11. Also called an assembly language program.
14. A field used to describe an instruction in a program.
15. Tells MPU where the data are found.
16. Repeatedly checking status.
20. Field assigned symbolic name.
22. Assembler instruction.
26. Subroutine instruction.
27. Intersegment procedure instruction.
28. Procedure instruction.
29. Adds one to the operand.
31. The last instruction.

CHAPTER FIVE

THE BASIC MICROCOMPUTER SYSTEM

KEY TERMS

Address Decoder

Address Decoding

Byte High Enable

Command Register

Direct Memory Access (DMA)

Grant

Interrupt

Interrupt Service Routine

Maskable

Nonmaskable

Ports

Programmable Peripheral Interface (PPI)

Pushing

Request

Vectoring

5.0 INTRODUCTION

Microcomputer systems can control and perform many tasks. While design applications may vary, all basic microcomputer systems consist of four subsystems, as shown in Figure 5.1.

1. *Microprocessor (MPU) subsystem.* This is the *brain* and *heart* of any microcomputer system. It performs all the logical instructions, sequences, and arithmetic computations. It also includes all the basic system timing.
2. *Memory subsystem.* This area is used to store both instructions and data for the basic microcomputer system. It consists of two types of memories: memories that never forget or change (ROM) and memories that can be changed (RAM).
3. *Input/output subsystem.* This section handles the communication between *peripheral devices* such as CRT displays, keyboards, and disk drives. It allows us to talk to the outside world.
4. *Bus subsystem.* This network of paths routes information between the MPU, memory, and I/O subsystems. It provides a highway for data, address, and control signals to flow.

These components, in conjunction with various support devices, form the basis for a microcomputer system. Note that the 8086 or 8088 microprocessor by itself is not a

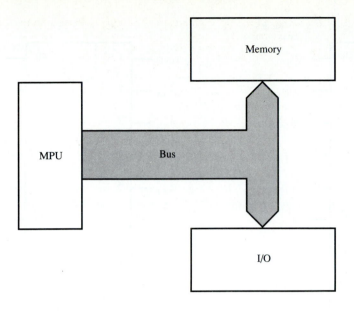

FIGURE 5.1
Microcomputer subsystems

microcomputer. The MPU does not contain any memory or I/O ports; therefore the MPU can think but by itself cannot remember or communicate.

5.1 THE MICROPROCESSOR (MPU) SUBSYSTEM

The microprocessor was introduced in Chapter 3 using the Intel 8088 microprocessor. In this chapter we study the microprocessor and how it works and interfaces with its support chips. We begin, however, by investigating the INTEL 8086 microprocessor. This is basically a more powerful version of the 8088 and is used in the IBM Series 2-Model 30 personal computer.

The 8086 Pinout

Recall that the major difference between the 8086 and the 8088 microprocessors is the size of the data bus. The 8086 has a 16-bit data bus, whereas the 8088 has an 8-bit data bus. Figure 5.2 illustrates the basic pin configuration of both microprocessors. From this diagram we can see that the 8086 pin configuration is almost the same as the 8088 in maximum mode. The major differences are:

1. A/D_0–A/D_{15} of the 8086 are the multiplexed address/data lines. This allows for a 16-bit or full-word data bus. The 8088 multiplexes only A/D_0–A/D_7 for an 8-bit or byte-wide data bus.

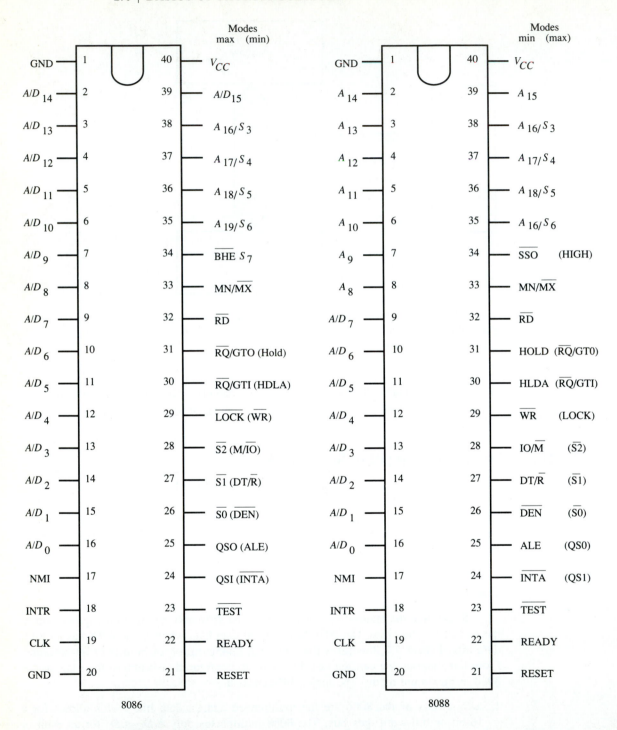

FIGURE 5.2
8088/8086 MPU pinout

2. M/$\overline{\text{IO}}$ (pin 28) of the 8086 functions opposite to that of the 8088. When memory is addressed, this signal is *active high*. When I/O information is on the address bus, this signal is *active low*. Recall that this is the opposite of the 8088's operation.

3. $\overline{\text{BHE}}/S_7$ (pin 34) is used on the 8086 to tell the memory circuits whether or not to access the 8 higher-order bits (D_{16}–D_8) on the data bus. This signal, **byte high enable,** is a tristate active low output signal. It is available during clock cycle T_1. During clock cycles T_2, T_3, and T_4, status information (S_7) is available on this pin. The $\overline{\text{BHE}}$ signal is not used on the 8088, since it has only an 8-bit bus. Instead, the 8088 uses this pin to provide the status information $\overline{\text{SSO}}$.

Maximum Mode Pins

For operation with a coprocessor both the 8086 and the 8088 MPU must operate in maximum mode. This is achieved by applying a logic level 0 to pin 33 MN/$\overline{\text{MX}}$. In maximum mode pins 24–31 take on an alternate function.

QS_1 (pin 24) and QS_0 (pin 25) tell us status information about the instruction queue. Recall that the instruction queue for the 8088 is 4 bytes long; for the 8086, it is 6 bytes long. Table 5.1 describes the function of the queue status pins.

TABLE 5.1
Queue status

QS_1	QS_0	Queue Status
0	0	No operation
0	1	Indicates first byte of op-code from queue
1	0	Indicates queue is empty
1	1	Indicates subsequent byte from queue

$\overline{S_0}$ (pin 26), $\overline{S_1}$ (pin 27) and $\overline{S_2}$ (pin 28) are used for bus-control status information. This status is used by the 8288 bus-controller chip to generate all memory and I/O control signals. Table 5.2 describes the bus control functions of status lines $\overline{S_0}$, $\overline{S_1}$, and $\overline{S_2}$.

TABLE 5.2
Bus-control functions

$\overline{S_2}$	$\overline{S_1}$	$\overline{S_0}$	Control Function
0	0	0	Interrupt acknowledge
0	0	1	Read I/O port
0	1	0	Write to I/O port
0	1	1	Halt
1	0	0	Code access
1	0	1	Read memory
1	1	0	Write to memory
1	1	1	Passive

$\overline{\text{LOCK}}$ (pin 29) is a tristate active low signal that prohibits coprocessors from gaining control of the bus. It remains active for instructions prefixed by LOCK.

$\overline{\text{RQ}}/\overline{\text{GT}}_1$ (pin 30) and $\overline{\text{RQ}}/\overline{\text{GT}}_0$ (pin 31) are used with coprocessors to **request** and **grant** bus control to the coprocessor. These are time-multiplexed bidirectional active low signals. Thus the coprocessor requests bus control during one clock cycle, and the master MPU grants bus control during another clock cycle.

MPU Timing

All microprocessors require timing signals to synchronize operations. The 8284A clock generator chip provides the basic timing requirements for the 8086/8088 microprocessor. Furthermore, it provides the basic timing for the entire microcomputer system, as shown in Figure 5.3.

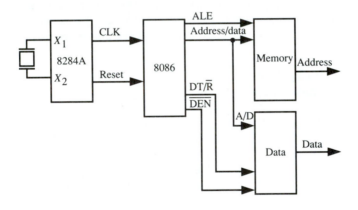

FIGURE 5.3
Basic timing circuit for system

The 8284A is an 18-pin integrated circuit and is illustrated in Figure 5.4. We now discuss the functions of each of the signal pins.

1. V_{CC} (pin 18). Power supply input pin, which is equal to $+5\ V_{DC}$.
2. GND (pin 9). Power supply ground.
3. X_1 (pin 17), X_2 (pin 16). External crystal input pins. These are used to provide the source input frequency for the clock generator. On the IBM PC this fundamental frequency is 14.31818 MHz.
4. OSC (pin 12). The oscillator output signal is a TTL level signal at the same frequency as the crystal. It is used as an input to other clock generator chips in the microcomputer system.
5. CLK (pin 8). The clock signal is the input timing signal for the MPU. Its frequency is one-third of the crystal frequency with a 33% duty cycle, as shown in Figure 5.4 (one-third on, two-thirds off).

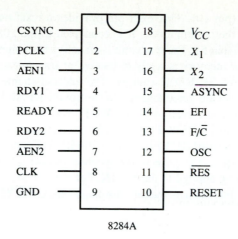

8284A

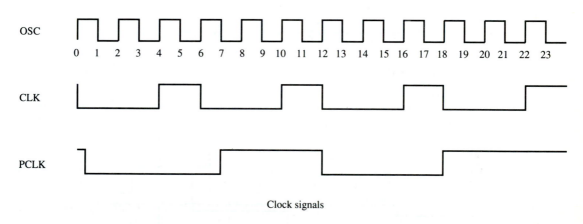

Clock signals

FIGURE 5.4
8284A clock generator and waveforms

6. PCLK (pin 2). The peripheral clock signal provides timing for various peripheral devices in the system. Its frequency is one-half of CLK, or one-sixth of the crystal, with a 50% duty cycle, as shown in Figure 5.4.

7. F/$\overline{C}$ (pin 13). The frequency/crystal input determines if the input signal is a crystal or an external clock frequency. A logic level 0 defines a crystal input to X_1 and X_2 (pins 17 and 16). A logic level 1 defines an external input to EFI (pin 14).

8. EFI (pin 14). The external frequency input pin is used as a timing input signal from a source other than a crystal (i.e., another 8284A).

9. CSYNC (pin 1). The clock synchronization pin is used to synchronize multiple 8284A chips to one clock frequency. When a crystal is used, this input pin is tied low.

10. $\overline{RES}$ (pin 11). The system reset pin is used to provide a power on reset pulse. An *RC* circuit is used to provide a pulse that lasts for at least four clock cycles.

11. RESET (pin 10). This reset pin provides a reset output that synchronizes the $\overline{\text{RES}}$ input to the system clock. It is connected to the 8086/8088 RESET input pin.
12. READY (pin 5). The ready pin is an active high signal that tells the MPU that an I/O device or memory is ready to receive or transmit data.
13. $\overline{\text{AEN1}}$ (pin 3), RDY1 (pin 4). The address enable 1 input signal and the ready 1 input signal are gated together to control the READY output line, as shown in Figure 10.5. They are used to create WAIT states.
14. $\overline{\text{AEN2}}$ (pin 7), RDY 2 (pin 6). This is a second set of ready inputs that are ORed with $\overline{\text{AEN1}}$ and RDY1 to control the READY output line, as shown in Figure 5.5.
15. $\overline{\text{ASYNC}}$ (pin 15). The ready synchronization select pin defines the type of ready input being applied to the 8284A. For devices that are normally not ready, ASYNC is high. For devices that are normally ready, $\overline{\text{ASYNC}}$ is kept low.

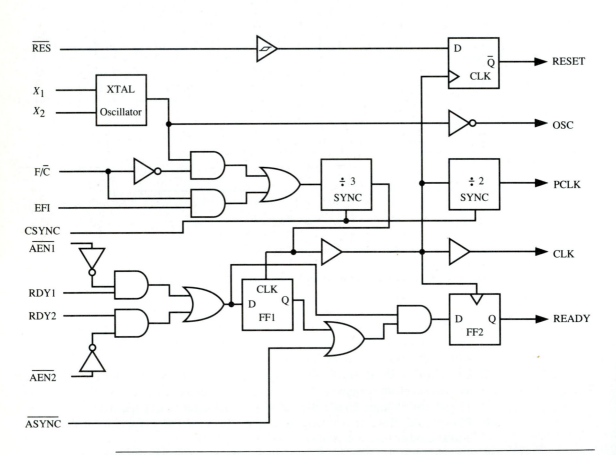

FIGURE 5.5
8284A block diagram

5.2 THE BUS SUBSYSTEM

The bus subsystem is centered around the 8288 bus-controller chip. The 8288 supplies I/O and memory read and write control lines to the other subsystems. Also included in the bus-control system are the address bus, latch/buffers (74LS373), and the data bus transceivers (74LS245). These devices buffer and interface the MPU subsystem to the memory and I/O subsystems, as shown in Figure 5.6.

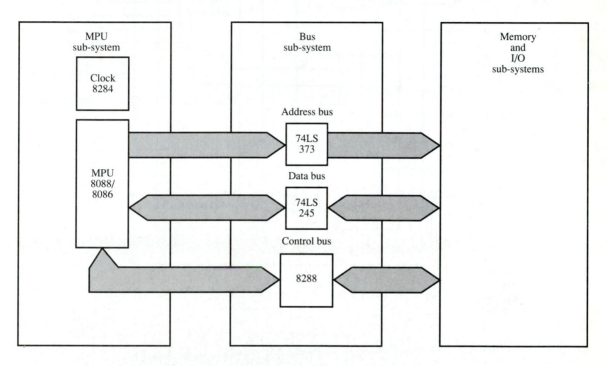

FIGURE 5.6
MAX mode bus subsystem

The 8288 Bus Controller

When the MPU subsystem is operated in maximum mode, the 8288 bus controller *must* be used to provide the control signals that were *eliminated* by setting the MPU in *maximum mode*. This was previously described in Figure 5.2. It should be noted that the IBM PC and compatibles are operated in maximum mode to allow for the use of an optional 8087 math coprocessor.

The block diagram and pin configuration for the 8288 bus controller are shown in Figure 5.7. The status decoder block is used to decode status lines $\overline{S_0}$, $\overline{S_1}$, and $\overline{S_2}$, as was

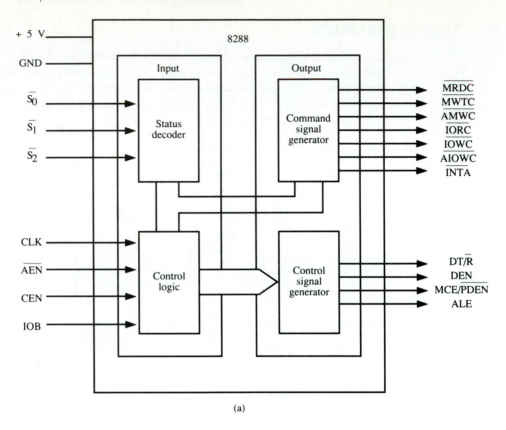

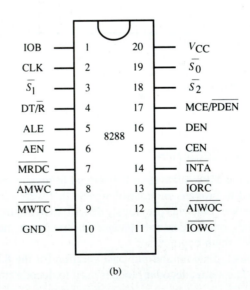

FIGURE 5.7

described previously in Table 5.2. The control logic block is used to determine what command the 8288 is to issue. The command signal generator block issues the output command. The output commands are as follows:

$\overline{\text{MRDC}}$	Memory read command
$\overline{\text{MWTC}}$	Memory write command
$\overline{\text{IORC}}$	I/O read command
$\overline{\text{IOWC}}$	I/O write command
$\overline{\text{AMWC}}$	Advanced memory write command
$\overline{\text{AIOWC}}$	Advanced I/O write command
$\overline{\text{INTA}}$	Interrupt acknowledge

The control signal generator block interfaces to the address latch/buffers, the data transceivers, and the interrupt-control signals. The output-control signals are as follows:

DT/$\overline{\text{R}}$	Data transmit/receive
DEN	Data enable
MCE/$\overline{\text{PDEN}}$	Master cascade enable/peripheral data enable
ALE	Address latch enable

The signal functions of the 8288 bus controller are as follows:

1. V_{CC} (pin 20). Power supply input voltage ($+5$ V_{DC})
2. GND (pin 10). Power supply ground
3. $\overline{S}_0$, $\overline{S}_1$, $\overline{S}_2$ (pins 19, 3, and 18, respectively). Status input signals from the MPU subsystem. These signals are decoded by the 8288 to generate the bus control signals as previously described in Table 5.2.
4. CLK (pin 2). Input clock from the 8284A. This signal provides bus-control timing.
5. $\overline{\text{AEN}}$ (pin 6). Address enable tells the 8288 to issue the memory-control signals.
6. CEN (pin 15). Command enable controls all the command outputs as well as control outputs DEN and $\overline{\text{PDEN}}$. When CEN is high, the appropriate command/control signals are activated. When CEN is low, these signals are disabled.
7. IOB (pin 1). Input/output bus mode signal. When this input signal is high, the 8288 is in the I/O bus mode. When it is low, the 8288 operates in the system bus mode. The I/O mode is used when separate buses are available for I/O and memory. The system bus mode is used when a single bus is shared for I/O and memory.
8. $\overline{\text{MRDC}}$ (pin 7). The memory read command signal is an active low output. It tells the memory to put data onto the data bus for the MPU to read. This is called a memory read operation.
9. $\overline{\text{MWTC}}$ (pin 9). The memory write command signal is an active low output. It tells the memory that the data on the data bus is to be written or recorded into memory. This is called a memory write operation.
10. $\overline{\text{AMWC}}$ (pin 8). The advance memory write command signal is an active low output. It is used to provide an early or advance notice to memory that a write operation is going to be performed.
11. $\overline{\text{IORC}}$ (pin 13). The I/O read command signal is similar to the $\overline{\text{MRDC}}$ signal except that it applies to an I/O device. It tells the I/O device that the MPU wants to read data from the device.

12. $\overline{\text{IOWC}}$ (pin 11). The I/O write command signal tells an I/O device that the MPU wants to write data to the I/O device. This is called an I/0 write operation.

13. $\overline{\text{AIOWC}}$ (pin 12). The advance I/O write command signal is similar to the AMWC signal except it applies to an I/O device. It provides an early, or advanced, notice to the I/O device that a write operation is going to be performed.

14. $\overline{\text{INTA}}$ (pin 14). The interrupt acknowledge signal is used to tell an interrupting device that the MPU has accepted or acknowledged the interrupt request.

15. DT/$\overline{\text{R}}$ (pin 4). The data transmit/receive signal is used to control the direction of data through a transceiver. A high indicates that the MPU is transmitting data. A low indicates that the MPU is receiving data.

16. DEN (pin 16). The data enable signal is an active high output signal. It is used to turn on or enable the data transceivers.

17. MCE/$\overline{\text{PDEN}}$ (pin 17). Master cascade enable (MCE), with IOB low during an interrupt operation, signals the interrupt controller that a cascaded address is to be read. It combines the interrupt address (vector) with the address bus to create the service address. *Peripheral* data enable ($\overline{\text{PDEN}}$), together with IOB, is used to enable the I/O bus transceivers.

18. ALE (pin 6). The address latch enable signal is an active high output. It is used to strobe an address into the address latch circuitry.

The 74LS373 Latch

The 74LS373 is a tristate output 8-bit latch. It is specifically designed for high-capacitance or low-impedance loads. It contains eight D-type latches in which the Q outputs will follow the data (D) inputs. Figure 5.8 shows the logic diagram, pin configuration, and truth table for the 74LS373.

The output control pin ($\overline{\text{OC}}$) determines whether the latches are in the high-impedance state or attached to the bus as indicated in the truth table (Figure 10.8). $\overline{\text{OC}}$ does not affect the internal operation of the latches. Data can be retained and new data entered even while the outputs are in the high-impedance or floating state.

The latch enable input pin (G), when high, allows the Q outputs to *follow* the data (D) inputs. When the latch enable goes low, the Q outputs will be latched to the state that the data (D) was set up to.

In an 8086 MPU microprocessor system the 74LS373 is often used to latch and buffer the address lines from the multiplexed buses. Recall that the address information is on the bus for only a short time. The latch, controlled by the ALE (address latch enable) signal, is used to capture the address information.

The 74LS245 Transceiver

The 74LS245 is an 8-bit bidirectional bus transceiver. This tristate device is used to buffer and control the direction of data flow on the data bus. Figure 5.9 shows the logic diagram, pin configuration, and truth table for this device.

When the enable pin $\overline{G}$ is high, the device enters the high impedance state. When the enable pin $\overline{G}$ is low, the data flows in the direction determined by the DIR pin. If DIR

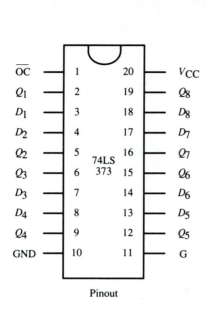

Pinout

$\overline{OC}$ Output control	G Enable Latch	D Input	Q Output
L	H	H	H
L	H	L	L
L	L	X	No change
H	X	X	Hi-Z

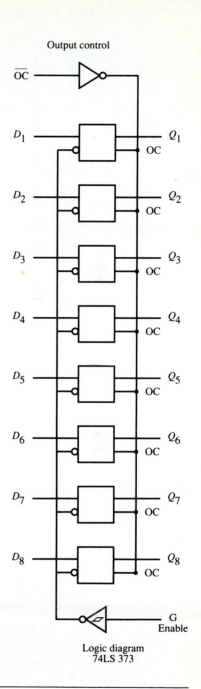

Logic diagram
74LS 373

FIGURE 5.8
74LS373 D-type latch (8-bit)

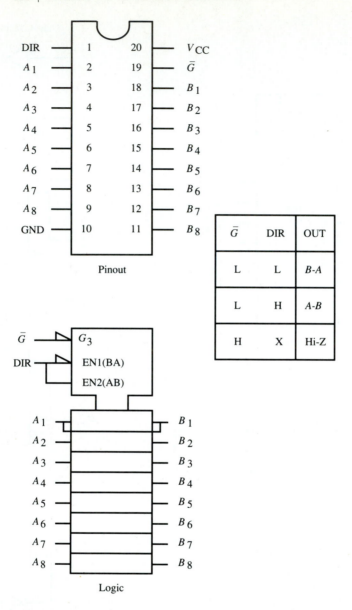

$\overline{G}$	DIR	OUT
L	L	B-A
L	H	A-B
H	X	Hi-Z

FIGURE 5.9
74LS245 bus transceiver (8-bit)

is low, data flows from the B inputs to the A outputs. If DIR is high, data flows from the A inputs to the B outputs.

In an 8086 MPU microcomputer system the 74LS245 is often used to control the direction of data flow on the data bus. When the DIR pin is tied to the DT/$\overline{R}$ (data transmit/receive) signal line, it is used to determine whether data is to be transmitted or received by the MPU. The enable input $\overline{G}$ is tied to the DEN (data enable) signal to control the output connection to the data bus.

5.3 THE MEMORY SUBSYSTEM

The memory subsystem is centered around the microcomputer system's RAM and ROM devices. Since the amount of addressable memory is large, a method of selecting the desired memory address is necessary. The selection method is known as **address decoding.** In more sophisticated systems it is desirable to have a method that allows direct and automatic access to the memory without utilizing the MPU. This frees up the MPU for other tasks, thereby speeding up the entire system operation. This process is called **direct memory access (DMA)** and requires a special, dedicated device like the 8237 DMA controller.

RAM and ROM

Memory devices were discussed in detail in Chapter 2. Recall that there are two basic types of memory devices. ROM is like a textbook. The information is preprinted and meant to be read only. The ROM is used to store information that the microcomputer system always needs to operate. ROMs are referred to as nonvolatile, since the information is not destroyed or lost when the power is turned off. RAM is like a notebook. The information is meant to be written to or read from. RAM is used in a microcomputer system for temporary storage of information. RAMs are volatile, that is, their information is lost or destroyed when the power is turned off. As was discussed in Chapter 2, there are several different types of RAM and ROM devices. RAM can be either static or dynamic. ROM can be preprogrammed by the manufacturer or field programmed by the user (i.e., PROMs, EROMs, and EEROMs).

Address Decoding

The **address decoder** is used to interface the MPU subsystem to the memory subsystem. The MPU address bus has 20 address lines, but most memory devices do not. Therefore, some circuitry is required to handle the mismatch in the number of address lines. This circuitry is called the address decoder. Address decoding facilitates memory expansion and efficiency.

The 74LS138, a one-of-eight line decoder, is a commonly used device for address decoding. This device is illustrated in Figure 5.10. Selection lines A, B, and C are used to decode the desired output. Since there are three select lines, there are 2^3 combinations, or eight possible outputs (0–7). E_1, E_2, and E_3 are chip enable inputs. E_1 and E_2 are active low, and E_3 is active high. When the device is disabled, the output pins are all high, as indicated in the truth table of Figure 5.10. When the device is enabled, only the selected output will go low.

Figure 5.11 illustrates a typical ROM decoding circuit. The ROM decoding circuit is controlled by the 74LS138 IC. Since ROM is usually located at the high end of

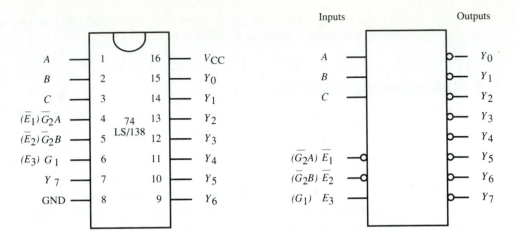

Select			Enable			Outputs							
C	B	A	$\overline{E_1}$	$\overline{E_2}$	E_3	$\overline{0}$	$\overline{1}$	$\overline{2}$	$\overline{3}$	$\overline{4}$	$\overline{5}$	$\overline{6}$	$\overline{7}$
0	0	0	0	0	1	0	1	1	1	1	1	1	1
0	0	1				1	0	1	1	1	1	1	1
0	1	0				1	1	0	1	1	1	1	1
0	1	1				1	1	1	0	1	1	1	1
1	0	0				1	1	1	1	0	1	1	1
1	0	1				1	1	1	1	1	0	1	1
1	1	0				1	1	1	1	1	1	0	1
1	1	1				1	1	1	1	1	1	1	0
X	X	X	1	X	X	1	1	1	1	1	1	1	1
			X	1	X								
			X	X	0								

Disabled

Note : X = don't care

FIGURE 5.10
74LS 138 8-output line decoder

the memory map, address lines A_{19}, A_{18}, A_{17}, and A_{16} (the highest-order lines) are used to enable the decoder device (74LS138). The 74LS138 is enabled for all addresses above F0000. This occurs when A_{19}, A_{18}, A_{17}, and A_{16} are all logic level ones (1111 = F). $M/\overline{IO}$ is gated with the high-order address lines to define a memory operation. This signal is high for memory operations and low for I/O operations. The next three address lines, A_{15}, A_{14}, and A_{13}, are used to determine which ROM device to select. Each of the

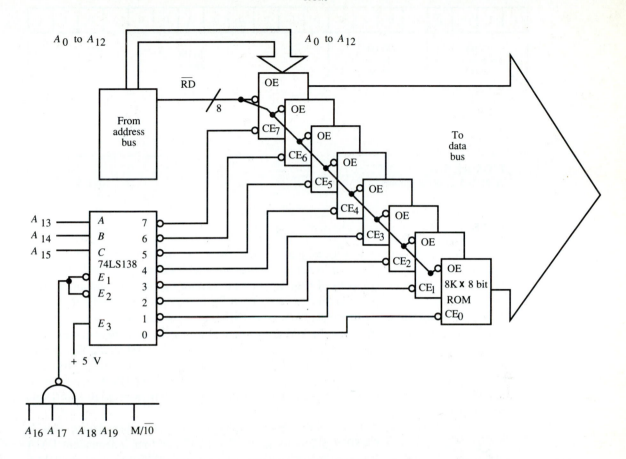

FIGURE 5.11
ROM decode circuit

74LS138 outputs is connected to only one ROM chip enable input (CE). Thus only one ROM device is enabled at any time. Address lines A_{12} through A_0 from the bus subsystem are connected to each individual ROM device. These lines determine a unique address in the selected ROM device. The data bits are outputted on the data lines when $\overline{RD}$ goes low. $\overline{RD}$ is connected to the output enable (OE) pin of each ROM device.

Figure 5.12 illustrates how the actual ROM decoding is performed. The 4 high-order bits (A_{19}, A_{18}, A_{17}, A_{16}) are a logic 1, which define a ROM memory select. The next 3 bits (A_{15}, A_{14}, A_{13}) define the ROM device to be selected. In this case, ROM1. The 13 low-order bits (A_{12}–A_0) define the unique address of interest on ROM1. Grouping the bits by four gives us the physical address of the memory in hexadecimal, in this case, F2003.

A_{19}	A_{18}	A_{17}	A_{16}	A_{15}	A_{14}	A_{13}	A_{12}	A_{11}	A_{10}	A_9	A_8	A_7	A_6	A_5	A_4	A_3	A_2	A_1	A_0
1	1	1	1	0	0	1	0	0	0	0	0	0	0	0	0	0	0	1	1

| ROM memory select | | | | ROM device select | | | | ROM address | | | | | | | | | | | |

ROM address in hex

F 2 0 0 3 H

FIGURE 5.12
A ROM address decode

DMA

DMA is a type of I/O technique in which data can be transferred between the microcomputer memory and an external device without utilizing the MPU. DMA is typically used to transfer blocks of data between the memory subsystem and an external device. A DMA read operation transfers data from the memory to an external device. A DMA write operation transfers data from an external device to memory.

Since the main purpose of the DMA operation is to transfer data between external devices and memory without involving the MPU, another device is required. This device is called a DMA controller. The DMA controller must be capable of performing read and write operations in the same manner as the MPU. Therefore, the DMA controller is actually a special-purpose microprocessor whose only task is to perform high-speed data transfers between memory and an external device.

The INTEL 8237 DMA controller is a 40-pin programmable device that is compatible with the 8086/8088 microprocessor. The 8237 has four independent DMA channels, as shown in Figure 5.13. This means that one 8237 can provide DMA transfers to several external devices—for example, a cassette recorder, a floppy disk drive, a Winchester disk drive, and some other external hardware circuitry. Data transfers begin with the DMA request lines $DREQ_0$–$DREQ_3$. $DREQ_0$ has the highest priority, and $DREQ_3$ has the lowest priority. Handshaking with the DREQ are the acknowledge lines $DACK_0$–$DACK_3$. As their names imply, these lines are used to *acknowledge* a DMA channel request. The 8237 uses the 8086/8088 HOLD signal to take over the system bus. After being initialized by the MPU, the 8237 takes control of the bus in order to perform the DMA operation. Data bits are then transferred between a peripheral or external device without involving the microprocessor. Before discussing the DMA operation in detail, let's look at the basic pin configuration of the 8237, as shown in Figure 5.14.

- CLK (pin 12). Clock input controls the interval operations of the 8237 and may be operated at frequencies up to 10 MHz.
- $\overline{CS}$ (pin 11). The chip select signal is an active low input used to select the 8237 as an I/O device. This allows the MPU to communicate on the data bus.

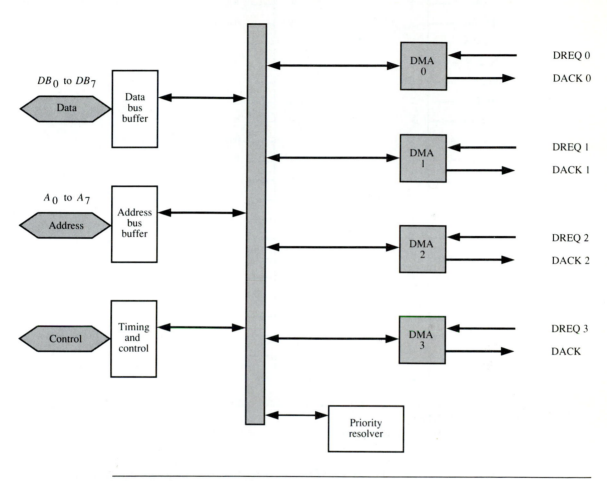

FIGURE 5.13
8237A DMA controller simplified block diagram

- RESET (pin 13). This is an active high input signal that clears command, status, request, and temporary registers.
- READY (pin 6). This is an active high input signal used to accommodate the read and write lines with slow memories or I/O peripheral devices.
- HLDA (pin 7). Hold acknowledge is an active high input signal from the MPU that indicates that the MPU has given up control of its buses.
- $DREQ_0$–$DREQ_3$ (pins 19–16). The DMA request lines are asynchronous channel inputs used by external devices to obtain DMA operations. These signals are programmable to be active high or active low. The RESET pin initializes $DREQ_0$–$DREQ_3$ as active high.

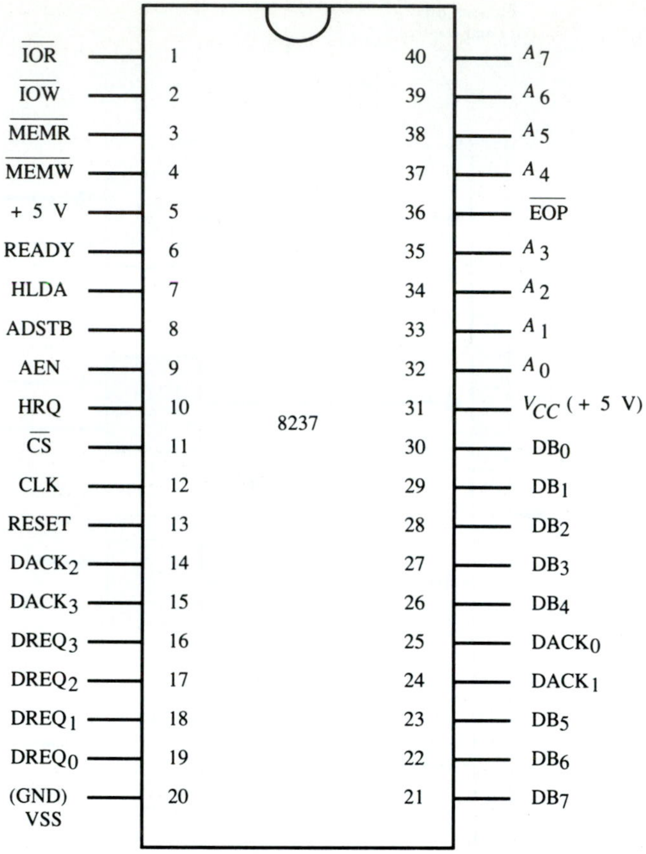

Left	Pin		Pin	Right
$\overline{\text{IOR}}$	1		40	A_7
$\overline{\text{IOW}}$	2		39	A_6
$\overline{\text{MEMR}}$	3		38	A_5
$\overline{\text{MEMW}}$	4		37	A_4
+ 5 V	5		36	$\overline{\text{EOP}}$
READY	6		35	A_3
HLDA	7		34	A_2
ADSTB	8		33	A_1
AEN	9		32	A_0
HRQ	10	8237	31	V_{CC} (+ 5 V)
$\overline{\text{CS}}$	11		30	DB_0
CLK	12		29	DB_1
RESET	13		28	DB_2
$DACK_2$	14		27	DB_3
$DACK_3$	15		26	DB_4
$DREQ_3$	16		25	$DACK_0$
$DREQ_2$	17		24	$DACK_1$
$DREQ_1$	18		23	DB_5
$DREQ_0$	19		22	DB_6
(GND) VSS	20		21	DB_7

FIGURE 5.14
8237A DMA controller pinout

- DB_0–DB_7 (pins 30–26 and 23–21). The data bus lines are tristate, bidirectional signals connected to the system data bus. During DMA operations these lines are multiplexed to output the most significant address bits A_{15}–A_8.
- $\overline{\text{IOR}}$ (pin 1). I/O read is an active low, bidirectional, tristate line used during the idle cycle when the MPU is waiting for a DMA request. It is used to read the control registers. In the DMA, or active, cycle, it lets the 8237 access data from external devices during a DMA write transfer.
- $\overline{\text{IOW}}$ (pin 2). I/O write is an active low, tristate, bidirectional line. In the idle cycle it is used by the MPU to load information into the 8237. In the DMA, or active, cycle, it is an output control signal used by the 8237 to load data to external devices during a DMA transfer.
- $\overline{\text{EOP}}$ (pin 36). End of process is an active low, bidirectional signal. Placing a low on this line terminates DMA service. When used as an output, this signal is used to interrupt the processor to signal the end of the DMA operation.

- A_0–A_3 (pins 32–35). The four least significant address lines are bidirectional, tristate signals. During the idle cycle they are used as inputs. During the DMA, or active, cycle, they are used as outputs.
- A_4–A_7 (pins 37–40). The four higher-order address lines are tristate outputs and provide 4 bits of address information. They are enabled only during a DMA service.
- HRQ (pin 10). Hold request asks the MPU for control of the system's buses.
- $DACK_0$–$DACK_3$ (pins 24, 25, 14, 15). DMA acknowledge is used to notify external devices that a DMA cycle has been granted to one of the devices.
- AEN (pin 9). Address enable is an active high output signal. It is used to enable an address latch that is connected to the data lines D_0–D_7. Recall that these lines are multiplexed to provide the most significant address byte A_{15}–A_8.
- ADSTB (pin 8). The active high address strobe signal is used to strobe the upper address byte into an external latch. AEN enables the latch. ADSTB strobes the address data into the latch.
- $\overline{MEMR}$ (pin 3). Memory read is an active low tristate output used during a DMA read operation. It is used to access data from a selected memory location.
- $\overline{MEMW}$ (pin 4). Memory write is an active low tristate output used to write data to a selected location during a DMA write operation.

The 8237 DMA controller is designed to operate in two major cycles, the idle and active cycles. When the 8237 is in the idle cycle, no external device is requesting a DMA transfer. In this cycle the 8237 samples the DREQ lines every clock cycle to determine if any of the four channels are requesting service. When one of the DMA request lines $DREQ_0$–$DREQ_3$ becomes active, the 8237 will enter the active cycle. When the 8237 is in the idle cycle and a channel requests a DMA transfer, the 8237 outputs a HRQ (hold request to the MPU and enters the active cycle, as shown in Figure 5.15. It is in this cycle that the DMA transfer actually takes place. When ready, the MPU responds to the 8237 with a HLDA (hold acknowledge), indicating that it has released control of the buses by entering the tristate. The 8237 then responds to the external device requesting the DMA with a DACK (DMA acknowledge), indicating the start of the active cycle. Figure 5.16 illustrates the basic block diagram of the DMA interface. The 8237 interfaces to all four subsystems to perform memory data transfers for the MPU.

When the 8086/8088 MPU is in the maximum mode it uses the $\overline{RQ}/\overline{GT}$ (request/ grant) signal line to interface with the 8237. These two signals come from a single bidirectional pin and function similar to the HOLD and HLDA in the minimum mode. The 8086/8088 contains two request/grant pins ($\overline{RQ_0}/\overline{GT_0}$, $RQ_1/\overline{GT_1}$), which allows interfacing for up to two DMA controllers or coprocessors, or a maximum of eight external devices. $\overline{RQ}$ (request) is like the HOLD signal. $\overline{GT}$ (grant) is like the HLDA (hold acknowledge) signal. The request/grant pin is used for the request/grant/release cycle.

First, the DMA controller requests a HOLD from the MPU in response to a DREQ (DMA request) from an external device. Next, when the MPU recognizes the request and is ready, it outputs a grant signal on the same signal line back to the DMA controller, as shown in Figure 5.17. The DMA controller can now use the buses to transfer data between memory and an external device. The DMA controller now signals the requesting external device with a DACK (DMA acknowledge) signal. This indicates the start of a

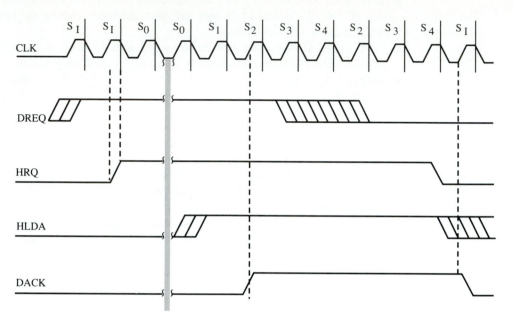

FIGURE 5.15
DMA timing diagram

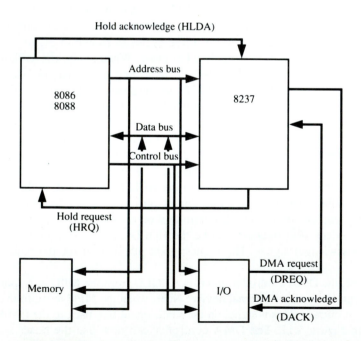

FIGURE 5.16
DMA interface basic block diagram

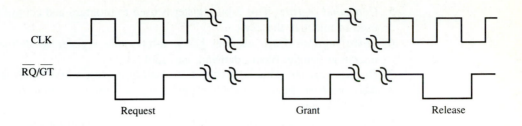

Request   Grant   Release

FIGURE 5.17
RQ/GT timing

DMA transfer. When the DMA controller completes the data transfer, it outputs an EOP (end of process), which indicates the completion of the DMA transfer. It now returns bus control to the MPU.

The 8237 in its active cycle can perform a DMA transfer in one of four modes, *single mode, block mode, demand mode,* and *cascade mode.*

1. *Single transfer mode.* In this mode the 8237 is programmed to transfer one byte of data each time the request is active.
2. *Block transfer mode.* In this mode the 8237, once activated by DREQ, continues to make transfers until a block of data is transferred. The 8237 is programmed with the starting address of the data and the number of bytes to be transferred. The transfers continue until the word count register in the 8237 reaches its final count or an EOP is received. The number of bytes transferred will always be one more than the initial number loaded into the word count register.
3. *Demand transfer mode.* In this mode the 8237 is programmed to continue making transfers until an EOP is received or until a DREQ from an external device goes inactive. In this mode one byte of data is transferred for each demand (DREQ) received.
4. *Cascade transfer mode.* This mode is used to cascade more than one 8237 together for system expansion.

The 8237 has a number of internal registers. These registers are used to control the DMA cycle operation.

1. *Current address register.* Each channel has a 16-bit current address register. This register holds the address of the data to be transferred. It is programmed to be *incremented* or *decremented* after each transfer.
2. *Current word register.* Each channel has a 16-bit word count register. This register determines the number of transfers to be performed. It is incremented after each byte transfer.
3. *Base address register.* This 16-bit register stores the original or starting address of the current address register.
4. *Base word register.* This 16-bit register stores the original value of the current word register.

5. *Command register*. This 8-bit register is used to program and control the 8237. It is used to initialize the device.
6. *Mode register*. Each channel has a 6-bit mode register to define its mode of operation (single, block, demand, cascade).
7. *Request register*. This 4-bit register is used to request a DMA transfer by software.
8. *Mask register*. Each channel has a mask register bit that is used to disable incoming DREQ signals.
9. *Temporary register*. This is an 8-bit register used to hold data during a memory-to-memory transfer.
10. *Status register*. This is an 8-bit register used for the microprocessor to read the present status of the 8237.

To use the DMA feature the programmer must first access the internal registers of the 8237. The **command register** must be loaded with a command word to define the initial conditions, mode of operation, and the type of operation. Next, depending on the mode and type of operation, the internal registers must be loaded with information defining the starting address of the data in memory, the number of bytes to transfer, where the data is to go, DMA channel number, and so forth. Finally, the DMA channel's request signal must be enabled. Initialization and programming of the 8237 is accomplished by writing control words to the 8237 using the I/O OUT instruction, which is discussed in Section 10.4 (I/O Instructions). The OUT instruction is used to send control words to the internal registers. Each bit in the control word defines the setup of an operation. The definition of each bit for each internal register can be found in the manufacturer's 8237 data sheet.

5.4 THE I/O SUBSYSTEM

The I/O subsystem is responsible for the movement of data between the basic microcomputer system and the peripheral or external devices connected to it. It performs the same functions as a seaport or airport for a city. Data bits are moved *in* or *out* of the I/O subsystem in the same way as people and goods are moved *in* and *out* of the seaport or airport. The I/O subsystem exchanges data with peripheral devices through interface circuitry known as **ports.** The peripheral device is physically connected to the port. The port is physically connected to the interface control circuitry, as shown in Figure 5.18.

Once the peripheral device is connected to the port, it needs a method of accessing the MPU. This method is called an **interrupt.** An interrupt is used to cause a temporary halt in the execution of a program. The MPU responds to the interrupt with an **interrupt service routine,** which is a short program or subroutine that instructs the MPU on how to handle the interrupt.

There are two basic types of interrupts, **maskable** and **nonmaskable** interrupts. A nonmaskable interrupt requires an immediate response by the MPU. It is usually used for serious circumstances such as power failure. A maskable interrupt is an interrupt that the MPU can ignore depending upon some predetermined condition defined by the status flag register. Interrupts can be generated by both hardware and software. Interrupts are also prioritized to allow for the case when more than one interrupt needs to be serviced at the same time. For example, a *power fail* interrupt has a higher priority than a *printer out-of-paper interrupt.*

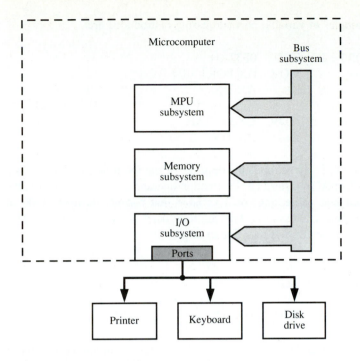

FIGURE 5.18
Microcomputer with I/O subsystem

I/O Instructions

Before discussing the I/O interface control devices, we need to study two additional 8086/8088 programming instructions, the IN instruction and the OUT instruction. The IN instruction is used to *input* data *to* the MPU *from* a peripheral or external device *through* the I/O port. The OUT instruction is used to *output* data *from* the MPU *to* a peripheral or external device *through* the I/O port. The general format of the IN and OUT instructions is

IN   destination, source
OUT   destination, source

The IN instruction operand *must be* the AX or AL register. The source operand can be a constant value between 0 and 255 (fixed port addressing) or a variable that can access up to 64K of port locations (variable port addressing). The address used in variable port addressing *must be* contained in the DX register. Two examples of fixed port addressing instructions are:

1.   IN   AH,0244H
2.   PORT_IN EQU 0F8H
            IN   AX,PORT_IN

Two examples of variable port addressing instructions are:

```
1.  PORT_IN  EQU   0F37AH
             MOV   DX,PORT_IN
             IN    AX,DX

2.           MOV   DX,0F37AH
             IN    AX,DX
```

The OUT instruction is the opposite of the IN instruction. The source operand *must be* the AX or AL register. The destination operand can be a constant value between 0 and 255 (fixed port addressing) or a variable that can access up to 64K of port locations (variable port addressing). The address used in variable port addressing *must be* contained in the DX register. For example,

```
1.            OUT   0F3H,AL
2. PORT_OUT  EQU   0FF7FH
             MOV   DX,PORT_OUT
             OUT   DX,AX
```

In the second example the data in the AX register is outputted through the port defined or pointed to by the DX register. In this case the DX register is pointing to port number FF7FH.

The 8255A Programmable Peripheral Interface (PPI)

The 8255A is a **programmable peripheral interface (PPI)** device that connects peripheral devices to the microcomputer system. It is compatible with the 8086/8088 microprocessor and is designed for the implementation of parallel I/O ports to the microcomputer system without the need for additional external circuitry in most cases. The 8255A provides a very flexible parallel interface that is software controlled.

Figure 5.19 gives the functional block diagram of the 8255A PPI. The MPU side of the 8255A PPI includes the 8-bit bidirectional data bus buffers (D_0–D_7) and the read/write control logic signals ($\overline{RD}$, $\overline{WR}$, A_1, A_0, RESET, $\overline{CS}$). The I/O side of the 8255A PPI is represented by port A (I/O signals PA_0–PA_7), port B (I/O signals PO_0–PB_7), and port C (I/O signals PC_0–PC_7). Ports A and B are 8-bit bidirectional ports. Port C is divided into two 4-bit (nibble) ports. The upper 4 bits are defined as PC_7–PC_4, and the lower 4 bits are defined as PC_3–PC_0. These signal lines are used to transfer data, commands, and status information between the MPU, the 8255A PPI, and the peripheral devices.

Timing of the data transfers to the PPI is controlled by the read ($\overline{RD}$) and write ($\overline{WR}$) control signals. These signals allow the MPU to read from the PPI or write to the PPI. When the read ($\overline{RD}$) signal is active low, the MPU reads data or status information from the PPI over the data bus. When the write ($\overline{WR}$) signal is active low, the MPU writes data or control words into the PPI over the data bus.

8255 Programmable peripheral interface (PPI)

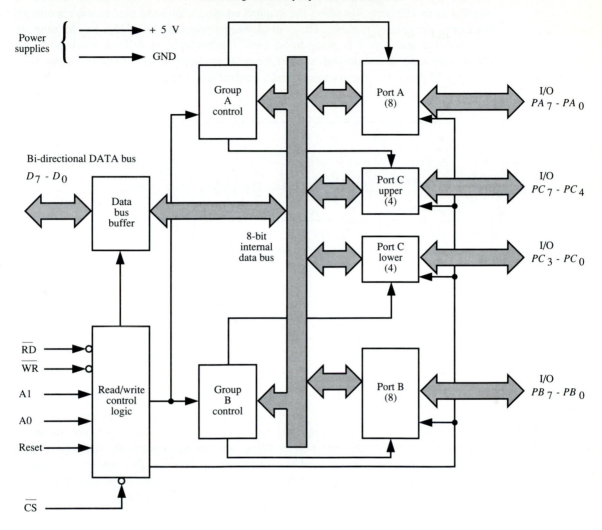

FIGURE 5.19
8255 PPI

The selection of ports is accomplished using input signal lines A_0 and A_1 as follows:

A_1	A_0	Port
0	0	A
0	1	B
1	0	C
1	1	Control

The 8255A is configured for operation by software control. The control register is mapped as an I/O port. Accessing the mapped address allows the user to write a control word into the control register. The control word *initializes* the 8255A by defining its configuration and how it is going to be used. For example, it defines which ports are going to be used. It also defines whether the ports are being used to input or output data. Figure 5.20 illustrates the meaning of the control word bits.

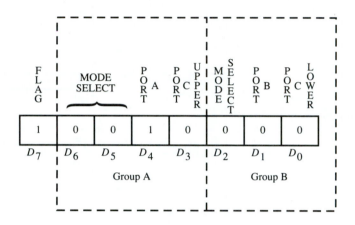

FIGURE 5.20
8255A control registers

Bit D_0 defines whether the port C lower nibble is being used as an input or an output. D_1 defines whether port B is being used as an input or an output, and so on. A logic level 1 indicates that the port is being used as an input port. A logic level 0 indicates that the port is being used as an output port. Bits D_2, D_5, and D_6 are used to define the mode of operation for the device. D_2 defines the mode of operation for port B and port C lower nibble. D_5 and D_6 define the mode of operation for port A and C upper nibble. Basically there are three modes of operation. They are

Mode 0: Basic I/O
Mode 1: Strobed I/O
Mode 2: Bidirectional operation

In mode 0 the 8255A functions as a latch—that is, the data once outputted by the MPU remains in the 8255A until it is changed. In mode 1 the data remains in the 8255A for a brief period of time. It must be strobed into an external latch if it needs to be saved. Mode 2 is an advanced mode that is used for bidirectional operation. Note that port B and port C lower nibble can be operated only in mode 0 or mode 1 because there is only one data bit to define the mode of operation. The last control word bit, D_7, is the mode-set flag bit. It must be set to a logic level 1 whenever the mode of operation is to be changed.

In Figure 5.20 the control word defines the operation of the 8255A. Bit D_7 is set, indicating that we are initializing the control register (mode flag set). D_6, D_5, and D_2 are a logic level 0, indicating that all ports are being used for basic I/O operations (mode 0). D_4 is set, defining port A as an input port. D_3, D_1, and D_0 are all logic level 0, defining ports B and C (upper and lower) as output ports. Note that in assembly language programming it is customary to write constants in hexadecimal. Grouping the bits by four, we convert the control word from a binary to a hexadecimal number. In this case, it is equal to 90H.

The following assembly language program illustrates how to initialize and use the 8255A PPI.

```
DATA SEGMENT
                ORG  100H
CTRLR           EQU  0FFFFH    ;CONTROL REGISTER ADDRESS
INIT            EQU  80H       ;CONTROL WORD
PA              EQU  0FFF8H    ;PORT A ADDRESS
DATA 1          EQU  AAH       ;1/0 PATTERN
DATA ENDS
CODE SEGMENT
ASSUME CS:CODE, DS:DATA
                MOV  AL,INIT   ;LOAD CONTROL WORD
                MOV  DX,CTRLR  ;LOAD CONTROL REGISTER ADDRESS
                OUT  DX,AL     ;OUTPUT CONTROL WORD
                MOV  AL,DATA1  ;LOAD 1/0 PATTERN
                MOV  DX,PA     ;LOAD PORT A ADDRESS
                OUT  DX,AL     ;OUTPUT DATA
CODE ENDS
END
```

The data segment defines the values that will be used to initialize and control the 8255A. OFFFFH is the mapped address of the control register. OFFF8H is the address of port A. 80H is used to initialize all ports as mode 0 operation output ports. Recall that 80H equals 10000000B and corresponds to D_7–D_0, respectively. The data to be outputted is a value AAH, which results in a pattern of alternating 1s and 0s. AAH equals 10101010B. The code segment begins by moving the initialization value 80H into the AL register. Next, the control register address 0FFFFH is moved into the DX register. The OUT instruction outputs the initialization value to the address pointed to by the DX register. In this case it is the address of the 8255A control register. We then move the data into the AL register and the address of port A into the DX register. The next OUT instruction sends the data to the address pointed to by the DX register. In this case the data bits are sent to the 8255A port A, which was initialized as a mode 0 output port.

Before completing our discussion of the 8255A, let's take a brief look at the 8255A signal lines. Figure 5.21 illustrates the 8255A pin configuration and defines the functions of each signal. Since these signals have all been discussed, we do not dwell on them any further.

Pin	Name	
34 to 27	$D_0 - D_7$,	Data bus
4 to 1	$PA_0 - PA_3$,	Port A
40 to 37	$PA_4 - PA_7$,	Port A
18 to 25	$PB_0 - PB_7$,	Port B
14 to 17	$PC_0 - PC_3$,	Port C (lower)
13 to 10	$PC_4 - PC_7$,	Port C (upper)
25	RESET,	Sets all ports to input
6	$\overline{CS}$,	Chip select
5	$\overline{RD}$,	Read input
36	$\overline{WR}$,	Write input
9,8	$A_0 - A_1$,	Port address select
26	V_{CC},	+ 5 Volts power in
7	GND,	0 Volts power in

(a)

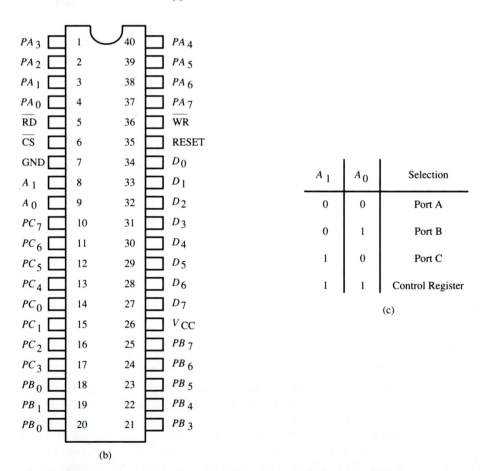

(b)

A_1	A_0	Selection
0	0	Port A
0	1	Port B
1	0	Port C
1	1	Control Register

(c)

FIGURE 5.21
8255A pin function

The 8259A Programmable Interrupt Controller (PIC)

In most microcomputer systems there is a method that allows an I/O device to gain the attention of the MPU. We have already seen that the 8086/8088 microprocessor has several signals that are dedicated to the *interrupt* function. When the MPU receives an interrupt request (INTR or NMI), it performs a sequence of steps that allow it to respond or service the interrupt request. It first completes the current process instruction and then determines if it is going to acknowledge the interrupt request. In the case of the nonmaskable interrupt (NMI) request, it *must* acknowledge and service the request. In the case of the interrupt request (INTR), the MPU first checks the flag register to see if the interrupt has been turned off or masked. It then services the interrupt if necessary. When the MPU services the interrupt, it first must save the contents of the instruction pointer and the affected registers. It does this by **pushing** the contents of the instruction pointer and the pertinent registers onto the memory stack. It then services the interrupt by looking up the location of the *interrupt service routine,* which is stored in ROM. This is called **vectoring.** The interrupt service routine is a program that defines the steps to be taken to service a particular type of interrupt.

The concept of interrupt is familiar to all of us. When a teacher is lecturing to a class and a student wishes to ask a question, the student must interrupt the teacher. The teacher must determine whether to acknowledge the question (interrupt) at the present time. If the question is to be answered, the teacher must first note where the interrupt occurred in order to return to that point to continue the lecture. The teacher can then answer the question or service the interrupt.

If two students were to ask a question at the same time, the teacher would have to determine which student to acknowledge first. Likewise, the microcomputer system must have a method of handling multiple interrupts. The 8259A Programmable Interrupt Controller (PIC) is a device designed for this purpose. It simplifies the implementation of the interrupt interfacing for the 8086/8088 microprocessor.

Figure 5.22 illustrates the basic block diagram and pin configuration for the 8259A PIC. The 8259A PIC is a software-controlled device that can be used to interface eight interrupt signals to the MPU. Eight additional 8259As may be *cascaded* or connected together to handle a maximum of 64 interrupts. The 8259A signals perform the following functions:

1. V_{CC} (pin 28). Power supply, $+5$ V_{DC}.
2. GND (pin 14). Power supply ground.
3. $\overline{CS}$ (pin 1). Chip select is an active low input signal. It is used to enable the 8259A.
4. $\overline{WR}$ (pin 2). Write is an active low input signal. This signal, in conjunction with $\overline{CS}$, enables the 8259A to accept command words from the MPU.
5. $\overline{RD}$ (pin 3). Read is an active low input signal. This signal in conjunction with $\overline{CS}$ enables the 8259A to release status information onto the data bus for the MPU.
6. CAS_0–CAS_2 (pins 12, 13, 15). The cascade lines form a control bus for use with multiple 8259A system designs. They are the outputs of the master 8259A and the inputs for the slave 8259A's.
7. $\overline{SP}/\overline{EN}$ (pin 16). Slave program enable buffer is a dual function pin. It is used as an output to control buffer transceivers in the buffer mode (EN). It is used as an input to designate cascading 8259A's in the SP mode.

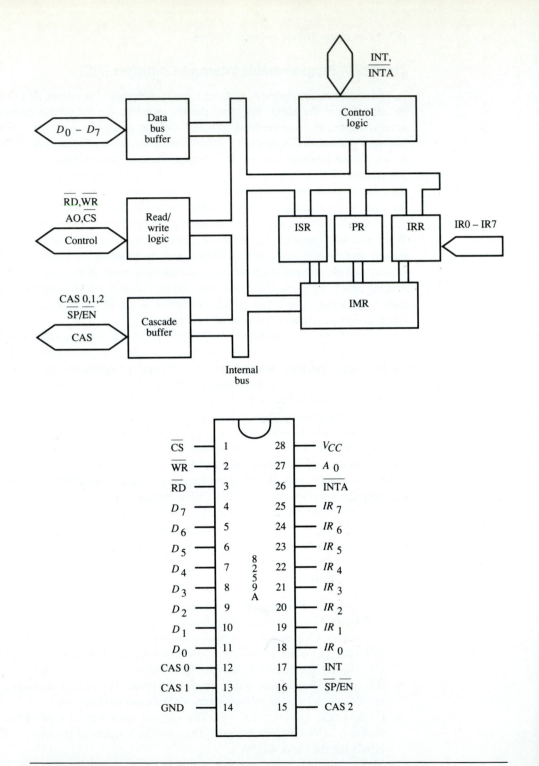

FIGURE 5.22
8259A Programmable Interrupt Controller

8. INT (pin 17). Interrupt is an active high output that is used to interrupt the MPU.
9. IR_0–IR_7 (pins 18–25). Interrupt requests are asynchronous active high inputs used to signal an interrupt request from a system device.
10. $\overline{INTA}$ (pin 26). Interrupt acknowledge is an active low input signal from the MPU that is used to acknowledge that the MPU is going to service the interrupt.
11. A_0 (pin 27). The A_0 address line in conjunction with the chip select, write, and read signals is used to select different command words for the 8259A.
12. D_7–D_0 (pins 4–11). The bidirectional data bus signals are used for transfer, control, status, and interrupt vector information.

The internal architecture of the 8259A is made up of eight basic functional blocks, as shown in Figure 5.22. The data bus buffers interface the data bus to the internal bus of the 8259A. This 8-bit bidirectional tristate buffer is enabled by the read/write logic block. The read/write logic block provides for direction, timing, and source or destination for the data transferred through the data bus buffer block. Control signals are provided by the $\overline{RD}$, $\overline{WR}$, A_0, and $\overline{CS}$ control input signals. The interrupt request register (IRR) stores the status of the interrupt request inputs. The inservice register (ISR) stores the interrupt level that is presently being serviced. The priority resolver (PR) determines which of the active interrupt inputs has the highest priority. The interrupt mask register (IMR) is used to enable or mask out individual interrupt request inputs. The control logic block uses the information provided by the IRR, ISR, and PR to control the INT (interrupt) output signal that requests an interrupt to the MPU. It also handles the $\overline{INTA}$ (interrupt acknowledge) input signal from the MPU. The cascade buffer/comparator block provides an interface for the master and slave 8259A's during cascaded operation.

The 8253 Programmable Interval Timer

The 8253 is a programmable interval timer/counter device. Its main use is to allow the programmer to create accurate time delays under software control. It can be used to perform *timing/counter* functions such as variable rate generation, real-time clock generation, digital one-shot control, event counting, frequency generation, and motor control.

The 8253 consists of three independent 16-bit programmable counters. Each 16-bit counter is a presetable digital down counter. They can operate in either binary or BCD count modes. The block diagram and pin configuration of the 8253 timer/counter is shown in Figure 5.23. The 8253 can be divided into three sections. The *input section* contains the data bus buffers, the read/write control logic, and the control word register. The *internal bus section* is used to transfer data and control signals between the input section and the output section. The *output section* consists of three independent 16-bit down counters.

The 8253 signal lines perform the following functions:

1. V_{CC} (pin 24). Power supply input $+5$ V_{DC}.
2. GND (pin 12). Power supply ground.

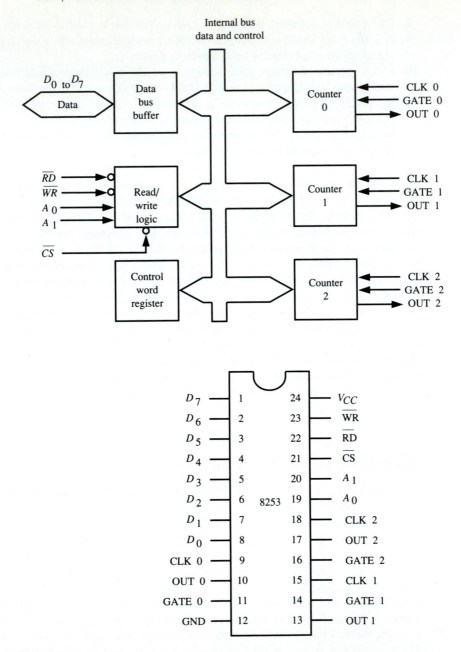

FIGURE 5.23
8253 programmable interval timer block diagram

3. D_7–D_0 (pins 1–8). Data bits D_7 to D_0 are tristate bidirectional signals that are connected to the data bus buffers. Data can be transmitted or received by the buffer by using the 8086/8088 OUT or IN instruction. These signal lines are used to set the 8253's mode of operation, set the initial value of the counters, and to read the data in the counters.
4. $\overline{RD}$ (pin 22). Read is an active low input signal that is used to tell the 8253 that the MPU is inputting data.
5. $\overline{WR}$ (pin 23). Write is an active low input signal that is used to tell the 8253 that the MPU is outputting data.
6. A_0/A_1 (pins 19, 20). These address bus signals are used to select one of the three counters or the control word register as shown next.

A_1	A_0	Function
0	0	Select counter 0
0	1	Select counter 1
1	0	Select counter 2
1	1	Select control word register

7. $\overline{CS}$ (pin 21). Chip select is an active low input signal that enables the read/write control logic section. Thus it activates the $\overline{RD}$, $\overline{WR}$, A_0, and A_1 input signals.
8. CLK0, CLK1, CLK2 (pins 9, 14, 18). The clock input signals are timing inputs to the respective counters.
9. OUT0, OUT1, OUT2 (pins 10, 13, 17). The OUT signals are the individual outputs of the respective counters.
10. GATE0, GATE1, GATE2 (pins 11, 14, 16). The GATE signals are active high inputs that are used to enable the respective counters.

The control word register is used to program and initialize the 8253. When A_0 and A_1 are both at logic level 1, the control register is selected. It is then able to receive information from the data bus buffers. This information is stored in the control register and is used to select the operational mode of each counter. Each counter of the 8253 is individually programmed by writing a control word into the control word register. The format of the control word is as follows:

D_7	D_6	D_5	D_4	D_3	D_2	D_1	D_0
SC_1	SC_0	RL_1	RL_0	M_2	M_1	M_0	BCD

The control word bits are defined as follows.

SC: SELECT COUNTER

D_7 SC_1	D_6 SC_0	Function
0	0	Select counter 0
0	1	Select counter 1
1	0	Select counter 2
1	1	Illegal

RL: READ/LOAD

D_5 RL_1	D_4 RL_0	Function
0	0	Counter latching operation
0	1	Read/load least significant byte only
1	0	Read/load most significant byte only
1	1	Read/load least significant byte first, then most significant byte

M: MODE

D_3 M_2	D_2 M_1	D_1 M_0	Function
0	0	0	Mode 0
0	0	1	Mode 1
X	1	0	Mode 2
X	1	1	Mode 3
1	0	0	Mode 4
1	0	1	Mode 5

Note: X indicates a don't-care state.
Mode 0: Interrupt on terminal count; output goes high when final count is reached.
Mode 1: Programmable one-shot
Mode 2: Rate generator
Mode 3: Square-wave rate generator
Mode 4: Software-triggered strobe
Mode 5: Hardware-triggered strobe

5.5 TECH TIPS AND TROUBLESHOOTING—T³

Troubleshooting the MPU support devices can be an involved process. Besides being highly complex, many of the support devices are software dependent. They have many different modes of operation, which can hinder fault isolation. The basic problem is that the output has no simple relationship to the input. In a logic gate, the technician can easily determine what the output should be for a given input condition. The MPU support devices, on the other hand, are somewhat *intelligent*. The output can depend on the input, the mode of operation, how it was initialized, how it was programmed, and its present state. Thus it is very difficult for the technician to determine what the output should be for a given input condition. Although troubleshooting with conventional tools can be difficult, there are numerous types of microprocessor system testers and analyzers that can be used to aid the technician in the troubleshooting process. These testers are discussed in Chapter 12. They can automatically exercise, test, and analyze all possible modes of operation for intelligent programmable devices, a process that may not be possible by manual means. For example, one defective transistor in an LSI device could result in only one of 64 modes of operation not working properly.

There are, however, things that the technician can do using conventional test equipment and common sense to localize failures. If the problem can be localized, component swapping can save a great deal of investigative time and effort. If the system works with the new component, the old component can be considered defective.

1. Always begin with a visual inspection. Check for loose and broken wires or connectors. Look for burned or discolored components. Check switch settings and jumpers for proper initialization.
2. With the power off, reseat PC boards and cables. Humidity can cause corrosion on gold-plated contacts. Reseating can clean corrosion and remake connections. Cleaning the connections is better. A soft pencil eraser can be very useful for cleaning gold-plated contacts.
3. Check all power supply voltages and grounds. Is V_{CC} and ground present on each device? Is V_{CC} within tolerance and free of excessive noise and ripple?
4. Use the test equipment you have, together with common sense, to localize problems. Perform gross signal checks as described in the Chapter 3 Tech Tips. Combining an understanding of the functions of the signal lines with gross signal checks can be a good clue as to whether or not a device is functioning properly. For example, a technician might use an oscilloscope to investigate the 8284A OSC, CLK, and PCK signals for proper operation. The 8288 bus controller's control, status, and bus signals can be checked for signal activity, and the like.
5. Sometimes it is possible to force a predictable output to occur. For example, placing a logic level 1 on an unused 8259A interrupt request line IR_0–IR_7 should force activity on the interrupt acknowledge ($\overline{INTA}$) line. Using a dual-channel oscilloscope, you can trigger on the interrupt request (IR_0–IR_7) and check for the interrupt (INT) and the interrupt acknowledge ($\overline{INTA}$) signals.
6. DEBUG can also be used as a diagnostic tool for the IBM PC. For example, the 8255A PPI can be checked by using DEBUG to output data to a port. The 8253 timer can be checked by using DEBUG to change a count register. In fact, many different types of checks can be performed using DEBUG. Let's see how. First install the DOS diskette containing   DEBUG into drive A. Now type

```
A>DEBUG
```

The computer responds

```
A>DEBUG
-
```

On the IBM PC the speaker is connected to port *B* of the 8255 PPI. Outputting a logic level 1 on the two least significant bits will enable the speaker. Port *B* of the 8255A is I/O mapped as address 61H. Therefore, the following instruction should sound the speaker. Type

```
0  61  6F
```

The 0 in DEBUG is similar to the 8086/8088 OUT instruction. 61 is the address of the 8255's port B. 6F is used to output a logic level 1 on the two least significant data bits. Recall that 6F in hexadecimal is equal to 01101111 in binary. 6F is used so as not to disturb the functions of the other higher-order bits. To turn off the speaker, type

```
0  61  68
```

68 is normally the initial value of the port *B* register. You can examine this register by using the DEBUG input instruction I. To do this, type

```
I  61
```

The computer will respond

```
I  61
68
```

Here we are asking the computer for the contents of memory address 61 (the 8255A port *B* address). The computer tells us the data (in hexadecimal) in this address.

The 8253 timer can also be investigated. On the IBM PC the 8253 timer's counter 2 is memory mapped to address 42H. This is also used to determine the speaker output frequency. To change the tone of the speaker's output, we must first enable the speaker as we did before. Next, we must output data to the 8253 timer's counter 2 to change the tone. Recall that the 8253 timer's registers are all 16-bit registers. Now type

```
0  61  6F
```

to enable the speaker and

```
0  42  FF
0  42  FF
```

to change that tone. Two output instructions are required to generate 16 bits of data. The pitch of the tone can be changed by changing the data.

Successful results indicate that the devices are functioning properly. Obviously we have not checked every mode or register so we do not know for sure that the entire device is functioning properly. However, these simple tests give us an idea of what is going on. Tests can be created to check many of the support devices. Performing these checks on a working system will validate the test and the results.

EXERCISES

5.1 List the four subsystems found in all basic microcomputer systems.

5.2 Draw the block diagram of a basic microcomputer system.

5.3 Which subsystem is used to communicate between peripheral devices and the microcomputer?

5.4 Explain the function of the bus subsystem.

5.5 Compare the 8088 MPU to the 8086 MPU. What are the major differences?

5.6 When is maximum mode used?

5.7 Describe the function of the QS_1 and QS_0 pins.

5.8 If a write-to-memory operation is being performed, what is the state of each of the bus control status information pins?

5.9 Describe the function and operation of the 8284A chip.

5.10 A microcomputer system uses an 8284A clock generator chip. If a 15-MHz external crystal is connected to pins X_1 and X_2, describe the clock signal CLK output.

5.11 Describe the function and operation of the 8288 bus controller.

5.12 Draw the block diagram and pin configuration of the 8288 bus controller chip.

5.13 Name the output control signals of the 8288 that interface to the address latch/buffers, data transceivers and interrupt control signals.

5.14 Explain how a 74LS373 8-bit latch might be used in an 8086 microcomputer system.

5.15 How is the 74LS245 8-bit transceiver used in an 8086 microcomputer system?

5.16 Explain how address decoding is used to interface the MPU and memory subsystems.

5.17 Draw a typical ROM decoding circuit using the 74LS138 decoder device.

5.18 What is DMA typically used for?

5.19 Draw the block diagram and pin configuration of the 8237 DMA controller chip.

5.20 Explain how a data transfer begins in a system that uses the 8237 DMA controller chip.

5.21 Describe the two major cycles of the 8237 DMA controller chip.

5.22 What is the function of the mode register in the 8237 DMA controller chip?

5.23 List the steps used to program the 8237 controller chip.

5.24 Design a microcomputer system using a DMA controller interfaced to all four subsystems.

5.25 What are the responsibilities of the I/O subsystem?

5.26 When the IN instruction uses a source operand with a constant value between 0 and 255, what type of addressing is being used?

5.27 The IN and OUT instructions must use the _____ or _____ registers.

5.28 To provide a very flexible parallel interface that is software controlled, _____ is used.

5.29 What signals control the timing of the data transfers to the 8255 PPI?

5.30 What signals are used by the MPU to receive interrupt requests?

5.31 What must be saved when the MPU services an interrupt?

5.32 Explain the meaning of the term vectoring.

5.33 What can be used as a method of handling multiple interrupts in a microcomputer system?

5.34 Draw the block diagram pin and configuration of the 8259 PICA.

5.35 Describe the function of the eight basic functional blocks of the 8259A PIC.

5.36 What is the main use of the 8253 PIT?

5.37 Draw the block diagram pin configuration of the 8253 PIT.

5.38 How are the three counters of the 8253 PIT selected?

5.39 List and explain the five modes of operation of the 8253 PIT.

5.40 Explain why it is difficult to troubleshoot MPU support devices.

5.41 Explain how DEBUG can be used as a diagnostic tool for the IBM PC.

5.42 How can the 8253 PIT be checked for proper operation?

5.43 Crossword Puzzle

ACROSS

7. An 8284A output signal with the same frequency as the crystal.
8. Power supply reference level.
10. 74LS373.
13. Subsystem used to store data.
14. Instructions to programmable devices to control their operation.
18. To send data.
19. When the 74LS245 _____ pin is high, the transceiver will enter the high impedance state.
22. See 24 Across.
24. Placing a low on this line (22 across) will _____ a DMA transfer.
25. Causes a temporary halt in the execution of a program.
27. Memory that does forget.
28. A software diagnostic utility program.
29. A _____ interrupt requires an immediate response by the MPU.
30. A 64K block of memory.
32. Multiple 8259A system design.
33. An I/O instruction.

DOWN

1. Memory that never forgets.

2. An 8284A signal that is one-third of the crystal frequency.
3. A signal used by the 8237 to indicate the start of a DMA transfer.
4. The 8253 consists of three independent 16-bit programmable _____.
5. Line used by the 8237 to ask the MPU for control of the system's buses.
6. The control word _____ the 8255A by defining how it is going to be used.
9. Subsystem used to route information between other subsystems.
11. Data enable.
12. To send data into memory.
15. To send information to an external device.
16. 8253 function.
17. Address _____.
20. Address latch enable.
21. Circuitry that connects an external device to the microcomputer.
23. Pin configuration.
26. Opposite of serial.
31. Subsystem that provides basic system timing.

COMPUTER SYSTEMS AND PERIPHERALS

Up to this point we have learned about the fundamentals of digital logic theory. We have also learned about the microprocessor and some of the related LSI devices. In this section we discuss all the elements of digital logic from a systems approach. Since all digital computers are similar in their basic designs, we will speak as generally as possible. However, in order to demonstrate principles on actual systems we use a specific system, the IBM PC, for all examples. We will discuss the IBM PC theory of operation in great detail. We also study in detail memory and display peripherals, magnetic recording theory, and digital video display theory. The topics are discussed from an analytical and service point of view rather than from a design viewpoint. This more detailed approach to the study of digital circuitry is necessary if a technician is expected to troubleshoot a complex computer system. Two levels of troubleshooting will be presented. The first level is the process of diagnosing and replacing defective PC boards and subassemblies. The second level involves the troubleshooting of PC boards and subassemblies to the component level. The second level is much more difficult and requires a more detailed knowledge of digital circuitry.

Before we begin let's briefly review a few terms. The digital computer *system* consists of a central processing unit, memory, and an input and output device. The central processing unit consists of the arithmetic unit and the control unit. Together they control the operation of the entire system. The memory section is used to store binary information. When information is stored in a computer's memory it is referred to as a **file.** Recently memory devices have become faster and smaller in size. The input and output devices are used to get information into and out of the computer. These are devices like keyboards, display terminals, card readers, magnetic tape systems, magnetic disk systems, printers, and analog-to-digital and digital-to-analog converters. These devices are referred to as the **peripherals.** The circuit that connects or interfaces these devices to the central processor is called a **peripheral controller.**

Understanding computer jargon or computer terminology is very important. Often, simple terms can be misleading and can cloud the understanding of concepts. Without an understanding of the language used in the computer industry it will be difficult to communicate with other persons in the field. Mastering the material in this book will allow the novice computer technician to gain the confidence necessary to begin the troubleshooting and repairing of microcomputers. Furthermore, since all computers are essentially the same, a competent technician can easily begin the troubleshooting and repair of larger computer systems. Serious troubleshooting on any type of computer system requires knowledge and skill.

CHAPTER SIX

THE MICROCOMPUTER SYSTEM

KEY TERMS

BIOS ROM	*Page RAM*
Bootstrap ROM	*Peripheral Controller*
Central Processing Unit	*Polled I/O*
Daisy-chained	*Power Supply*
Display	*Printer*
Disk Drives	*Prioritized Interrupt*
Duty Cycle	*Priority Encoder*
Flags	*Processor Bus*
Floppy Disk	*Pulse-width Modulation*
Foldback	*RGB Monitors*
Hard Disk Drives	*Segment RAM*
Internal I/O Bus	*Surge Protectors*
Interrupt-driven	*Switching Regulator Power Supply*
Interrupt Vector	*System Board*
IPL ROM	*System Bus*
Keyboard	*System Unit*
Linear Pass Power Supply	*Tick*
Line Conditioners	*Vectors*
Main PC Board	*Winchester Disk Drives*

6.0 INTRODUCTION

All computer systems, whether they be small personal computers or large business systems, are similar in nature. The variations occur in the size and number of peripherals connected to the system. The typical microcomputer system has a **central processing unit** (*CPU*), one or more **disk drives,** a **keyboard,** a **printer,** and a **display** device, as shown in Figure 6.1.

FIGURE 6.1
Microcomputer

6.1. SYSTEM CONFIGURATION

For a microcomputer system to be functional, there are several parts that must be connected, or configured, together. A minimum system configuration consists of a CPU, or system unit, an output device (display), and an input device (keyboard). Many microcomputer systems also have a mass memory storage device such as a disk drive or a tape drive. Other peripherals, such as printers, modems, acoustic couplers, and joysticks, are also found connected to the basic microcomputer system.

The System Unit

Most of today's microcomputer systems are built around a box called the **system unit,** or CPU. The system unit is usually made up of the **main PC board,** the **power supply,** and various **peripheral controller** boards plugged into the main PC board, as shown in Figure 6.2.

Displays

The display devices vary from one system to another. Less expensive systems use televisions or *composite color* video monitors. More expensive systems use direct red, green, blue, or **RGB monitors** for higher-resolution displays. The IBM PC uses a TTL level input RGB INTENSITY, or *RGBI, monitor.*

FIGURE 6.2
System unit

Keyboards

The keyboards also vary. Some systems use an *internal* keyboard—for example, the Tandy 1000 by Radio Shack—whereas the IBM PC uses a detachable keyboard. One thing to remember is that the key placement is not standardized from one keyboard to another. The letter keys usually follow the U.S. typewriter standard, but the carriage return, shift keys, and the symbol keys may not. This can be somewhat frustrating, especially if you are a typist.

Floppy Disk Drives

The **floppy,** or *flexible,* **disk** (Figures 6.3 and 6.4) has become a very common and economical means of data storage and data exchange. The floppy disk drive works very much like a tape recorder. Information is recorded on an oxide-coated mylar disk. However, the read/write head moves in or out to access different areas of the disk, whereas the head in a tape recorder remains fixed.

Most microcomputer systems come with at least one floppy disk drive for data and program storage. Many have them built into the system unit. The most common type of floppy disk drive is the 5.25-in. *double-sided, double-density* (DSDD) unit. Some, like the Apple Macintosh, the Commodore Amiga, and the IBM System 2 use 3.5-in disk drives instead of the 5.25-in. units.

FIGURE 6.3
Floppy disk drive and various-sized diskettes

Winchester Disk Drives

Winchester, or **hard disk, drives** (Figure 6.5) are similar to floppy disk drives with some major differences. First, the disk rotates approximately 10 times faster than the floppy disk, at a speed of 3600 rev/min as opposed to 300 rev/min. Second, the read/write head actually hovers, or *flies,* on a cushion of air over the disk surface at a height of approximately 20 microinches (Figure 6.6), similar to the puck in an air hockey game, which actually floats on the surface due to the air pressure under it. The third major difference is that the disk is made of rigid oxide-coated aluminum instead of flexible mylar.

The Winchester-type disk drive allows a much higher density storage and a faster access rate. These units store from 5 million to over 200 million bytes and transfer data at a rate of 5 million bits per second. Some of the more sophisticated systems have Winchester disk drives installed right in the system unit.

FIGURE 6.4
Floppy disk drive parts

Expansion Units

Almost all microcomputers have optional *expansion* units available, which allows the user to add more peripherals to the system than the system unit can handle. For example, the Radio Shack color computer allows only one peripheral controller at a time. If you want to use a disk drive and the graphics tablet at the same time, you must use the multipack expansion unit.

6.2 INSIDE THE IBM PC SYSTEM UNIT

As previously stated, the system unit contains the power supply, the system board, the floppy disk drives, and the adapter, or peripheral controller boards. For the remainder of this chapter we discuss the internal parts of the system unit, including the internal

FIGURE 6.5
Hard disk and parts

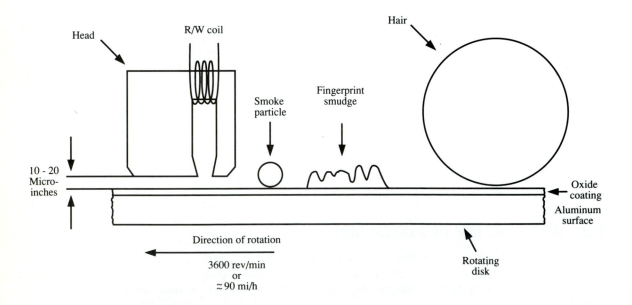

FIGURE 6.6
Hard disk head clearance

cabling. The peripheral adapter boards, the disk drives, and the external peripheral components are discussed in the next chapter.

The Power Supply and Fan

The power supply in almost all current systems is the **switching regulator** type, as opposed to the **linear pass** type (Figure 6.7). In many of the older microcomputers the power supply was the linear type, which required a large and heavy step-down transformer to convert 115 V AC to low-voltage AC for the rectifiers and regulators. One big disadvantage of the linear type is the amount of heat that it generates. The output pass transistor acts like a variable resistor controlling the output voltage. The excess voltage is not passed to the output but is dissipated as heat.

In the older S-100 microcomputer systems the power was stepped down, rectified, filtered, and sent down the bus as unregulated DC or what is called *raw* DC. The regulation was done *locally,* on the boards themselves. Each board had a small local regulator as opposed to one large regulator. One big advantage of the linear type is ease of servicing, since no hazardous voltages are present at the regulators.

The switching regulator is entirely different. It is a much smaller, lighter, and far more efficient power supply. Instead of wasting the unused power, it switches only the power needed to the output.

Think of a conventional home lamp dimmer; it works in much the same way as the switching power supply. When the knob is rotated to dim the lamp, the power is switched on and off at a high rate of speed. When the lamp is dim, the *on time* is shorter than the *off time*. As the knob is rotated to make the lamp brighter, the *on time* becomes longer in proportion to the *off time* (Figure 6.8). The lamp dimmer can carry as much as 600 W. Imagine the size of a 600-W rheostat; it would be about 12 in. in diameter and very heavy.

The big disadvantage of a switching supply is that it is a bit tricky to troubleshoot and repair. Basically the switching supply is a voltage-controlled switch (see Figure 6.9, pp. 220–21). The primary power (raw AC, right from the wall) is rectified and filtered as high-voltage DC (1). It is then switched to a high rate of speed, approximately 20 to 40 kHz, and fed to the primary side of a step-down transformer (2). The step-down transformer is only a fraction of the size of a comparable 60-Hz unit, thus relieving the size and weight problem. The secondary side of the transformer is rectified and filtered and then sent to the output of the power supply (3). A sample of this output is sent back to the switch to control the output voltage (4).

Most switching power supplies regulate their output using a method called **pulse-width modulation.** The power switch, which feeds the primary side of the step-down transformer, is driven by a pulse-width-modulated oscillator (5). In Figure 6.10 (p. 222), when the ratio of on time to off time, which is called the **duty cycle,** is at 50%, then the maximum amount of energy will be passed through the step-down transformer. As the on time or duty cycle is decreased, less energy will be passed through the transformer.

The width, or on time, of this oscillator is controlled by the voltage fed back from the secondary rectifier output, thus forming a closed-loop regulator. As we can see in Figure 6.10, the pulse width to the power switch is inversely proportional to the output

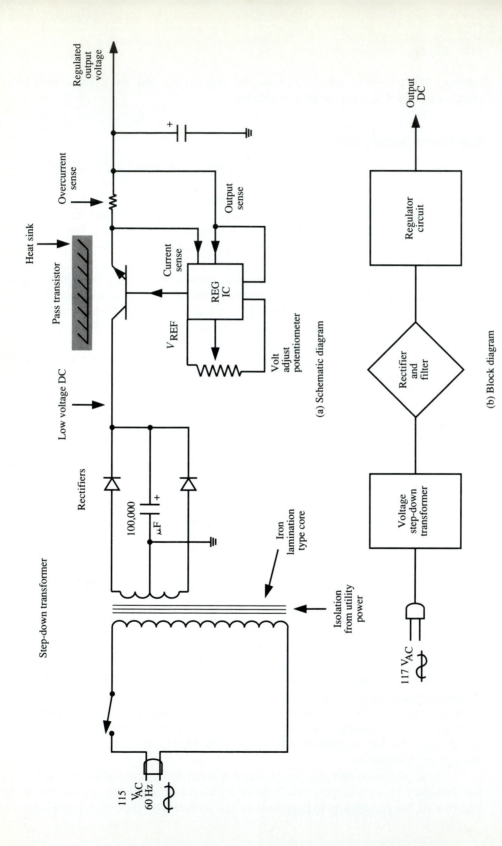

FIGURE 6.7
The linear power supply

Regulated output voltage

Overcurrent sense

Heat sink

Pass transistor

Current sense

REG IC

V REF

Volt adjust potentiometer

Output sense

Low voltage DC

Rectifiers

Step-down transformer

100,000 μF

Iron lamination type core

Isolation from utility power

115 VAC 60 Hz

(a) Schematic diagram

Output DC

Regulator circuit

Rectifier and filter

Voltage step-down transformer

117 V_{AC}

(b) Block diagram

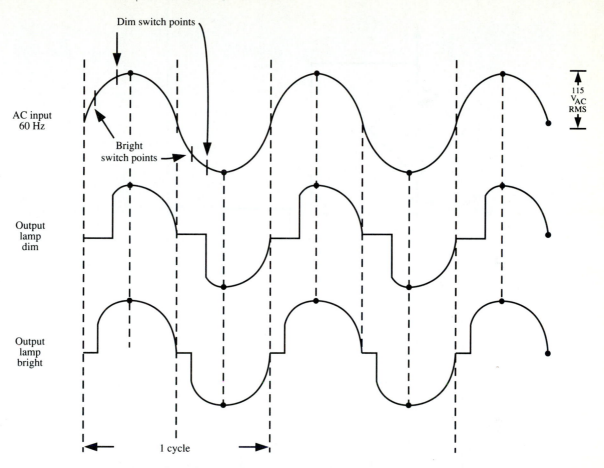

FIGURE 6.8
Lamp dimmer power output

voltage. When the output voltage drops, the switch is on longer, resulting in more energy delivered to the transformer and a higher output voltage. As the output voltage rises, the on time becomes shorter until the loop stabilizes.

Power supplies vary from one system unit to another, depending upon the number and type of peripherals mounted inside the system unit. The power rating is given as total power output in watts rather than the individual outputs in amps. Table 6.1 lists power supplies in the IBM PC family.

TABLE 6.1
IBM PC power supplies

Type	Power Rating
IBM PC Model 5150	65 W
IBM PCXT Model 5160	135 W
IBM PCAT Model 5170	200 W

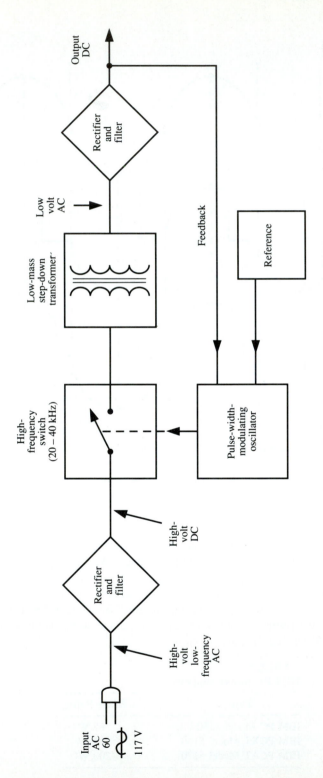

(a) Block diagram of a power switching supply

FIGURE 6.9
Switching power supply

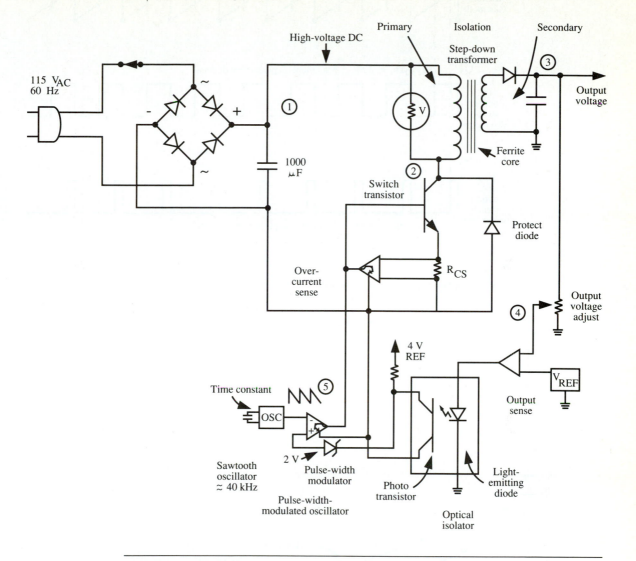

FIGURE 6.9 continued

The power supply rating is an important factor when configuring a new system or upgrading an old system. For example, some hard disk drives require 5 A peak on the +12-V line just to spin up or start, as shown in Figure 6.11. There have been cases where a hard disk was added to an older, floppy-based IBM PC with the original 65-W power supply. The result was intermittent power-on problems and premature power supply failures.

In Table 6.2. we must add the current draws of the system board, the display adapter, the floppy adapter, the floppy disk drives, and so forth to select the proper power supply. As a rule of thumb, always allow 25% to 50% margin of safety. For example, if 100 W of power is required, then use a 125- to 150-W power supply.

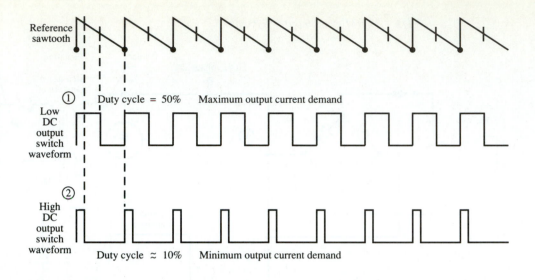

FIGURE 6.10
Switching power supply waveforms

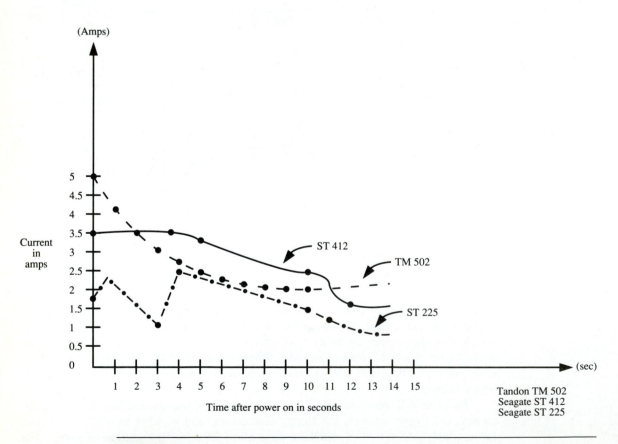

FIGURE 6.11
Hard disk power consumption

TABLE 6.2
IBM PC Board current usage

Component	Current Draw
System board	+5 V @ 2 A
Display controller	+5 V @ 1 A
Floppy controller	+5 V @ 0.5 A
Floppy drive	+5 V @ 0.5 A, + 12 V @ 1 A
Hard disk controller	+5 V @ 1 A
Hard disk drive	+5 V @ 0.75 A, +12 V @ 5 A Peak

Cabling and Connectors

The power supplies for the IBM PC and the PC/XT use four separate cable and connector assemblies, as shown in Figure 6.12. Two of the connectors are for the system board power. These are the long 6-pin connectors shown in Figure 6.13. IT IS VERY IMPORTANT THAT THESE CONNECTORS NOT BE REVERSED! Even though the connectors are keyed, the *keyways* can easily be broken off and the connectors reversed, which can result in severe damage to the system board and all controller boards.

FIGURE 6.12
IBM power supply

FIGURE 6.13
System board power connection

The other two connectors are 4-pin *molex-type* connectors that are used for the floppy disk drives and the hard disk drive power. These connectors are identical, so it does not matter which one is connected to which drive. Also, on the compatible "clones," the power supplies have two extra floppy/hard disk power connectors, thus allowing a total of four half-height disk drives.

The floppy disk and the hard disk drives are cabled up to the adapter boards by means of *flat ribbon* type cables crimped onto card edge connectors. The cable from IBM floppy disk to the controller is a little peculiar in that it has a twist in the middle, between the A drive and the B drive connectors, as shown in Figure 6.14. This is done to simplify the installation and servicing of the floppy disk drives in the system unit. All IBM PC floppy disk drives are set up in the same way because the actual unit is selected by the twist in the cable. The end with the twist in it or the last connector is drive A, and the middle connector is drive B. This simplifies field installation of a replacement floppy disk drive.

The speaker that is mounted on the front of the case is connected to a small set of pins on the front of the system board by means of a small 4-pin connector. The polarity of this connector does not matter; the speaker will work equally well in either direction.

FIGURE 6.14
The floppy disk interface cable showing twist in cable

The hard disk uses two flat ribbon cables. The first cable has 34 pins, like the floppy disk cable. The second cable has 20 pins and is for the data transfer and the select acknowledge signals. A separate data cable must be used for each hard disk drive installed.

Some of the multifunction controllers require additional connectors because they have many I/O devices on the board. Since only two or three connectors can fit on the small rear mounting plate, additional rear mounting plates have to be used.

The System Board

In earlier microcomputer systems the main board was just a common backplane with many connectors into which the microprocessor, memory, and the I/O controllers were plugged. Later microcomputers like the Apple II and the IBM PC put the microprocessor, memory, and control logic on the main board and called it the **system board.** The heart of the IBM system is the system board, which contains the microprocessor chip, base memory, bus decode logic, direct memory access (DMA) logic, interrupt logic, control logic, self test, and boot-up ROM. This is obviously the most complex part of the system and the most difficult to troubleshoot. The system board is discussed in greater detail in the next part of this chapter.

6.3 THE SYSTEM BOARD: A DETAILED THEORY OF OPERATION

In this part of the chapter we tie together all you have learned earlier in this book about logic and microprocessors. We refer to certain signal names from logic diagrams. Some of these signals are at a high level for a true state, whereas others are at a low level for a true state. We use an overbar to indicate a low true signal. For example, the signal CLK88 through an inverter becomes the signal $\overline{\text{CLK88}}$.

The IBM PC system board contains three buses. The first bus is the **processor bus,** which links the 8088 MPU, the 8087 math coprocessor, the 8259A interrupt controller, and the 8288 bus controller chips together. This processor bus is completely buffered from the system bus and acts as if it were a separate board, as shown in Figure 6.15(a).

The second bus is the **system bus,** which is the main bus and the one into which all the controller boards plug. This bus contains the address bus (signals A_0 through A_{19}), the data bus (signals D_0 through D_7), and the control bus (signals $\overline{\text{IOR}}$, $\overline{\text{IOW}}$, $\overline{\text{MEMR}}$, $\overline{\text{MEMW}}$, OSC, CLK, and AEN), as shown in Figure 6.15(b).

The third bus is the **internal I/O bus,** which contains the 8255 parallel port, 8237 DMA controller, 8253 triple timer, and the BIOS and BASIC ROM set. This bus is also completely buffered from the system bus with one exception—the DMA address drivers are connected directly to the system bus. The internal I/O bus contains an address bus (XA_0 through XA_{12}), a data bus (XD_0 through XD_7), and a control bus ($\overline{\text{XIOW}}$, $\overline{\text{XIOR}}$, $\overline{\text{XMEMW}}$, and $\overline{\text{XMEMR}}$), as shown in Figure 6.15(c).

Since the system board is very complex, we break it down into its major functions:

1. Main system timing. The system clocks, wait circuitry, and master system reset.
2. Central processing unit. The 8088, 8087, and the processor bus buffers.
3. BIOS and system ROMS. Including the decode and select circuit.
4. Main RAM. The memory chips, memory bus, refresh circuitry, and the memory parity circuitry.
5. DMA controller. The 8237 chip, the page RAM, and the DMA control logic.
6. Interrupts. The 8259A chip and control logic.
7. Internal I/O. The 8255A parallel port and the 8253 timer chip.

6.4 MAIN SYSTEM TIMING

The IBM PC system uses five main timing signals, OSC, CLK88, PCLK, RESET, and READY.

- OSC is the fundamental crystal frequency from the master oscillator.
- CLK88 is the basic timing for the microprocessor and the bus controller.
- PCLK is the peripheral clock, which is one-half the frequency of CLK88.
- RESET is the master system reset line.
- READY is used to synchronize the processor.

The entire system timing originates from the 8284 chip at location U_{11} (see Figure 6.16, p. 230). The main clock, OSC, operates at a frequency of 14.31818 MHz, which is generated by the crystal Y_1 and the trimmer capacitor P_1. This frequency was chosen for NTSC compatibility and is the U.S. color television standard.

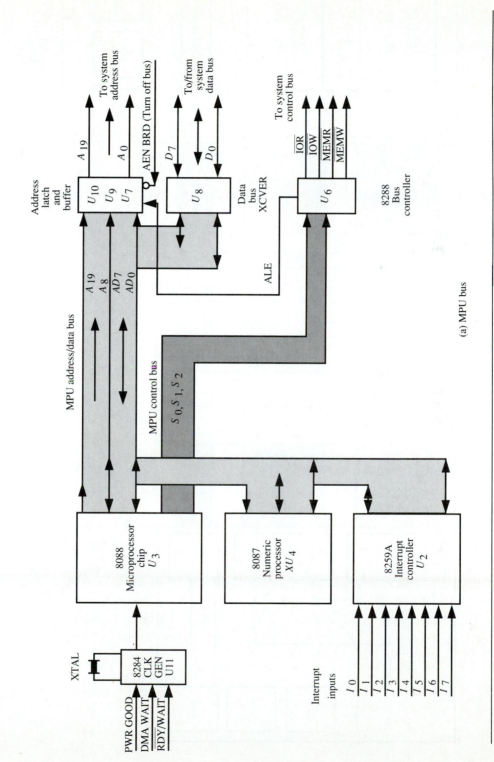

FIGURE 6.15a
IBM PC buses (pp. 227–29)

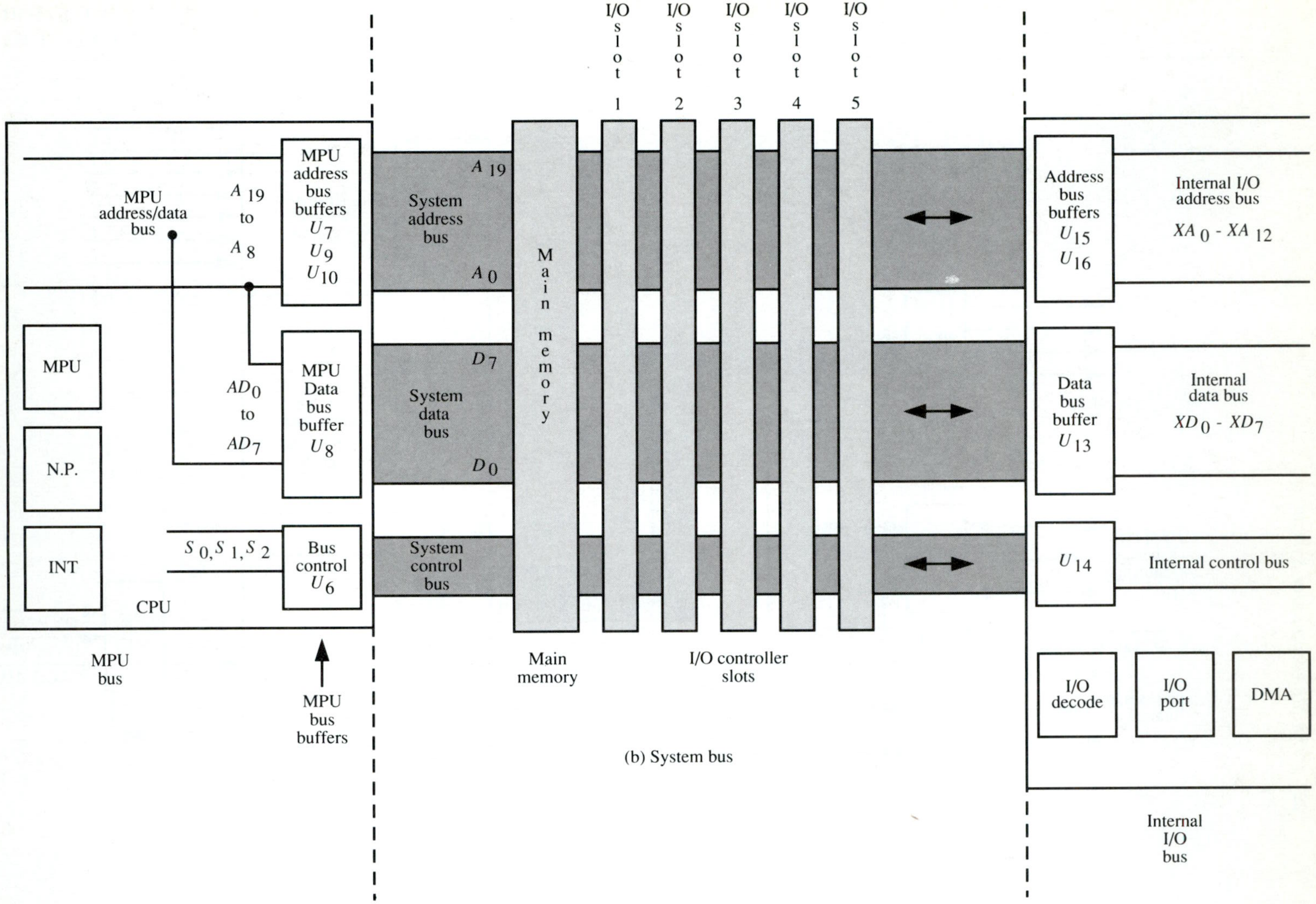

I/O slot 1
I/O slot 2
I/O slot 3
I/O slot 4
I/O slot 5
MPU address/data bus
A 19 to A 8
MPU address bus buffers U7 U9 U10
MPU
N.P.
INT
AD0 to AD7
MPU Data bus buffer U8
S 0, S 1, S 2
Bus control U6
CPU
MPU bus
MPU bus buffers
System address bus
A 19
A 0
System data bus
D 7
D 0
System control bus
Main memory
Main memory
I/O controller slots
(b) System bus
Address bus buffers U15 U16
Internal I/O address bus
XA 0 - XA 12
Data bus buffer U 13
Internal data bus
XD 0 - XD 7
U 14
Internal control bus
I/O decode
I/O port
DMA
Internal I/O bus

FIGURE 6.15b

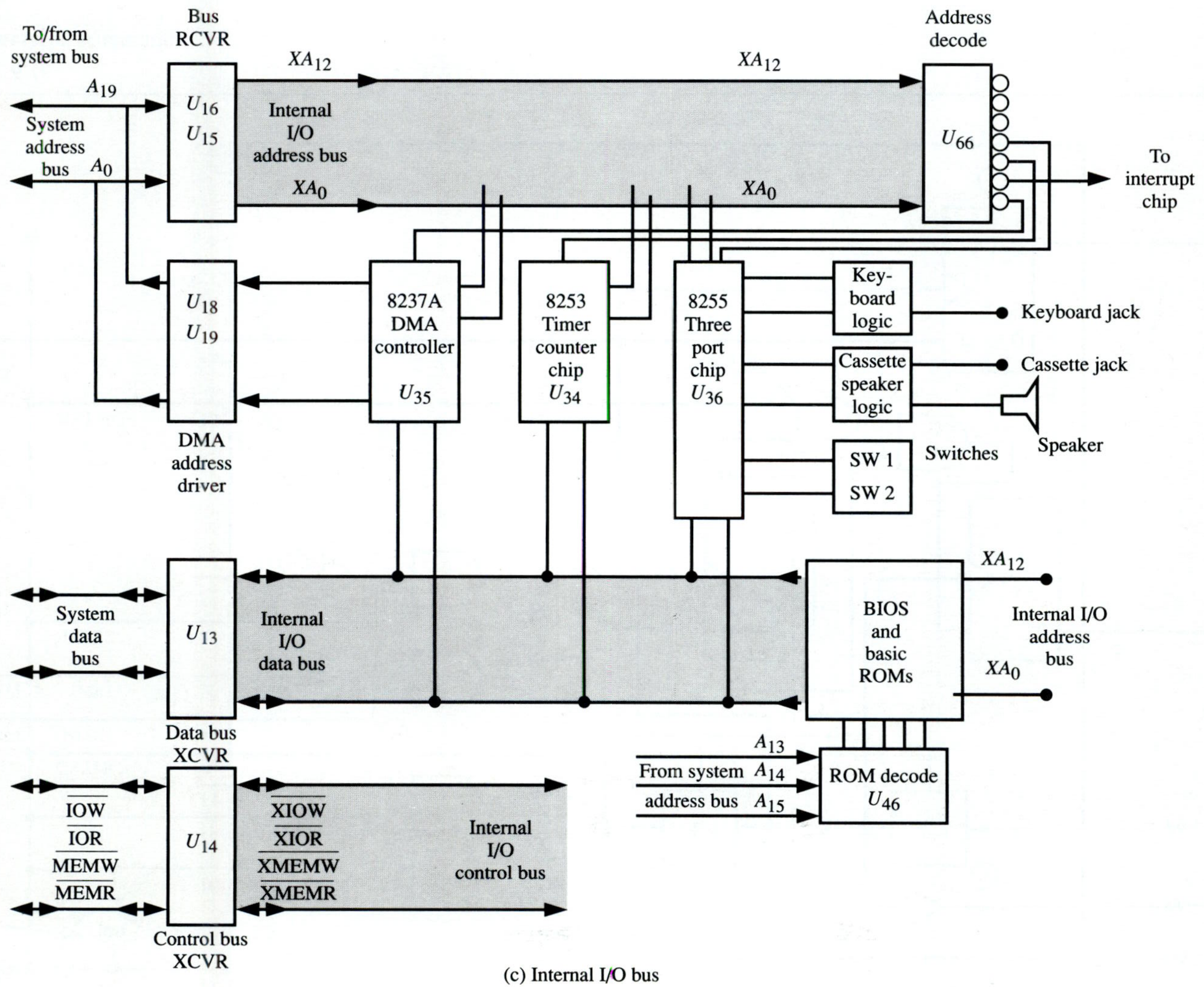

FIGURE 6.15c

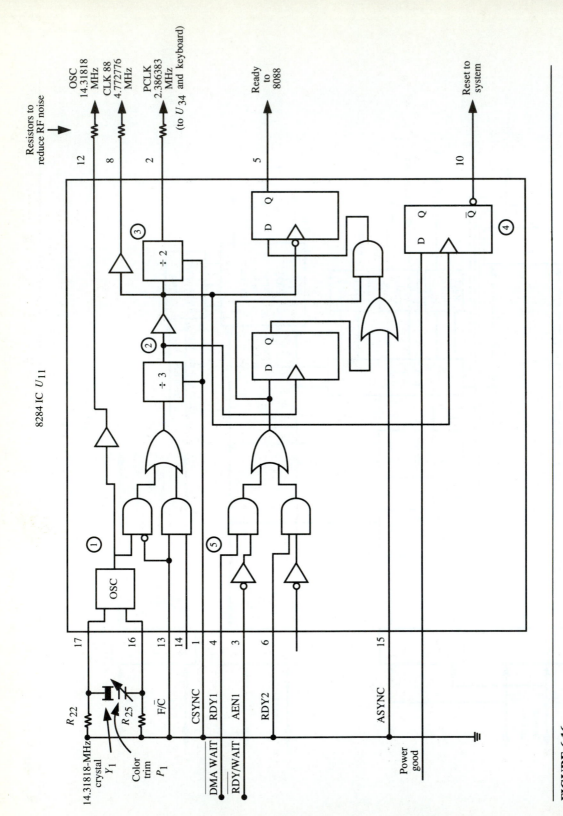

FIGURE 6.16
Clock generator schematic

The fundamental OSC frequency, 14.31818 MHz, is divided by 4 to yield 3.579545 MHz, which is the fundamental color-burst frequency of the NTSC standard. The OSC signal (14.31818 MHz) is used by the color graphics adapter to create the composite color video output, which is discussed in the display section.

The next timing signal is the processor clock, CLK88. This is used by the 8088 MPU chip for its internal timing. This clock is derived from the 14.31818-MHz OSC signal divided by 3, which yields a frequency of 4.7727266 MHz.

The third timing signal is the PCLK output from the 8284 chip. The PCLK timing is used by the triple timer chip at U_{34} and the keyboard circuit. This timing signal is derived from the CLK88 signal internally divided by two by the 8284 chip, which yields a frequency of 2.386383 MHz.

The system RESET signal is derived by using the PWR GOOD signal from the power supply, and internally synchronizing it with the CLK88 signal by the 8284 chip.

The READY signal output is derived from two different sources. The first signal is the RDY1 input to the 8284 chip. This signal is called $\overline{\text{DMA WAIT}}$ and is derived from the DMA circuitry. Remember that the processor is not needed for DMA transfers, so it must be told to stop accessing the bus and wait. This will be discussed in greater detail in the DMA section.

The second signal is the $\overline{\text{AEN1}}$ input to the 8284 chip. This signal is called $\overline{\text{RDY}}$/WAIT. It is used by slow I/O devices to tell the processor to wait until they are ready to transfer data. This signal is derived by U_{82}, U_{98}, U_{64}, U_{84}, U_{83}, and the DMA circuitry.

Refer to Figure 6.17. During normal I/O accesses the signals $\overline{\text{XIOR}}$ or $\overline{\text{XIOW}}$ (1) will cause the $\overline{\text{RDY}}$/WAIT line to go high, thus causing the processor to wait (2). On the next processor clock cycle the CLK signal, which is the CLK88 signal buffered by U_{15}, will release the wait condition, by clocking U_{98} (3), thus resulting in a one-cycle wait state.

If a slow device is installed into one of the bus slots, it must pull the line I/O CH RDY low, thus causing an indefinite wait state to occur. This happens because the I/O CH RDY line is tied directly to the preset input of U_{82} at pin 10(4). This will force the Q output at pin 9 of U_{82} to remain high, overriding all other inputs to that flip-flop. Once this line is released, by the slow external device, the MPU resumes its processing on the next processor clock cycle. One thing to note here is that if the I/O CH RDY line is low for longer than one clock cycle, the Q and Q outputs of flip-flop U_{82} will both be high because the $\overline{\text{PS}}$(4) and $\overline{\text{CL}}$(5) will be low. At first glance this condition looks wrong, but it is valid in a 7474 flip-flop. As soon as the slow external I/O device releases the wait condition, the $\overline{\text{RDY}}$/WAIT goes true first before the signal RDY TO DMA. The overall system timing is summarized in Figure 6.18.

6.5 THE CENTRAL PROCESSOR

The microprocessor in the IBM PC is the INTEL 8088 configured in the maximum mode. It uses the 8284 clock driver and the 8288 bus-controller chips to form the central processor.

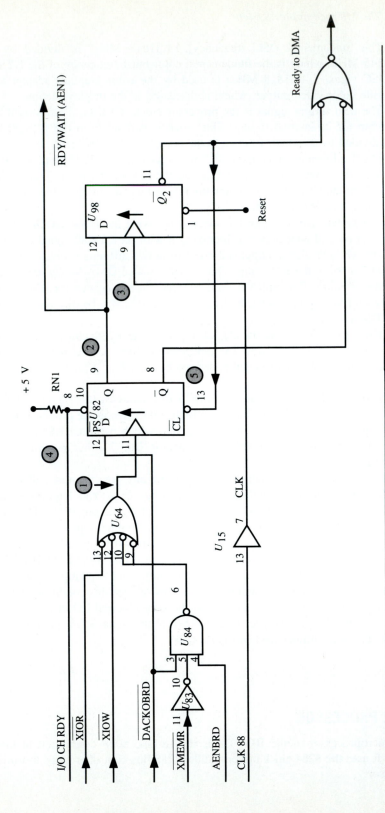

FIGURE 6.17
AEN1 schematic

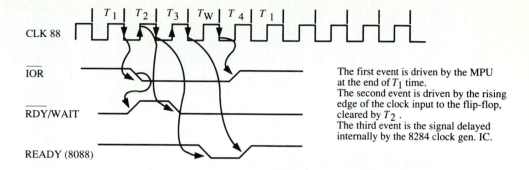

The first event is driven by the MPU at the end of T_1 time.

The second event is driven by the rising edge of the clock input to the flip-flop, cleared by T_2.

The third event is the signal delayed internally by the 8284 clock gen. IC.

(a) Maximum I/O transfer rate is 5 cycles or 1.05 ys per byte.

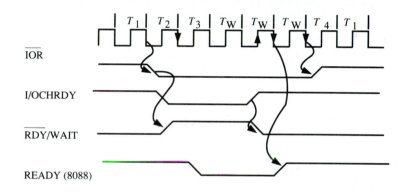

(b) System I/O timing, read cycle, externally generated wait state (I/O CHRDY)

FIGURE 6.18
System I/O timing, read cycle, internally generated wait state

As we see in Figure 6.19, the basic CPU consists of the 8088 MPU, 8087 coprocessor, 8259A interrupt controller, 8284 clock generator, and 8288 bus-controller chips.

The CPU block is buffered from the rest of the system by the 74LS373 tristate buffers in locations U_7, U_9, and U_{10} and the 74LS245 bus transceiver chip U_8. The 8288 supplies the I/O and memory read and write control lines. The 8284 supplies the timing clocks and the reset control lines and synchronizes the DMA timing. The 8259A catches the incoming interrupts, handles the priority of the interrupts, and sets the proper interrupt service address. The interrupt controller is discussed in detail later in this chapter.

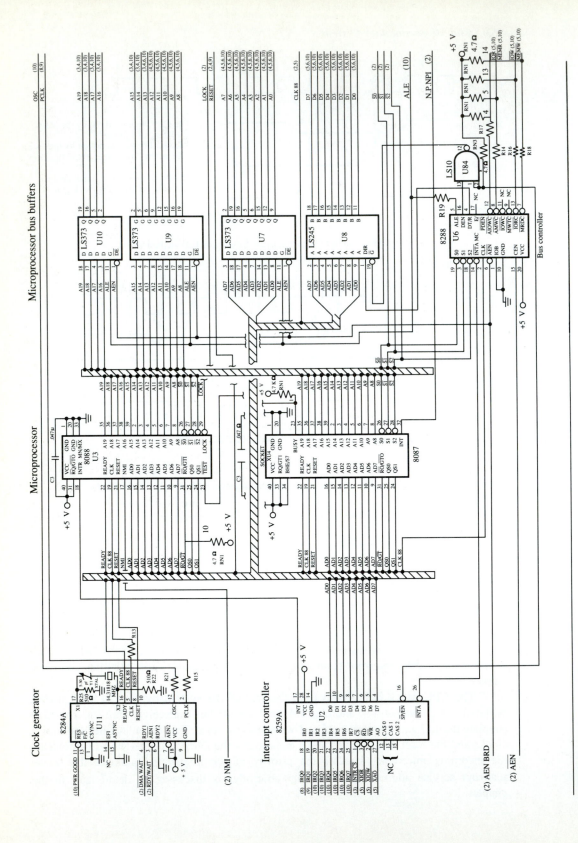

FIGURE 6.19
IBM PC system board (Courtesy of International Business Machines Corp.)

6.6 BIOS AND SYSTEM ROMS

Computers have no intelligence of their own, so they must be told what to do by means of programs. Since the RAM memory contains nothing but garbage at power up, how does the computer know what to do? Formerly, the operator manually had to toggle in the loader, or initialization, program. This program was a short and simple program to read in a bigger program from the disk or tape drive. This program would load and start the operating system and other related programs.

Eventually, the manual process of entering the loader was replaced by storing the loader program in ROM. This ROM is sometimes called the **bootstrap ROM** or the **IPL ROM,** but in the IBM PC it is known as the **BIOS ROM,** for *basic input/output system.* In addition to the loader program the BIOS ROM in the IBM PC contains the power-on self-test program (POST), which tests out the system upon power up, and also contains many of the low-level I/O device driver programs. Other ROMs in the IBM PC contain a BASIC language interpreter program. The BIOS ROM is installed in location U_{33} on the system board.

ROM Selection

The BIOS ROM is accessed by means of memory read instructions and responds to the addresses FE000H through FFFFFH. In the IBM PC the upper 65,536 bytes of memory are reserved for the system board ROMs. Address bits A_{16} through A_{19} are tied to the inputs of a 4-input NAND gate, U_{64} as shown in Figure 6.20. This gate generates the signal $\overline{\text{ROM ADDR SEL}}$ (1) when all four address lines, A_{16} through A_{19}, are high. The signal $\overline{\text{ROM ADDR SEL}}$ is true (low) for memory addresses F0000H through FFFFFH. Since the ROMs in the IBM PC are 8192 by 8-bit ROMs, the individual ROMs are selected by a one-of-eight decoder, U_{46}. Address bits A_{13}, A_{14}, and A_{15} (2) are tied to the binary inputs of the decoder. The decoder is enabled when the signals $\overline{\text{ROM ADDR SEL}}$ and $\overline{\text{XMEMR}}$ are true (low) (3) and the signal $\overline{\text{RESET DRV}}$ is false (high). At this point, one of the eight outputs of U_{46} (4) will be true (low), selecting one of the ROMs on the system board.

As an example of this, suppose the processor wants to read memory address FEC35H. As we can see, this address is one of the ROM addresses. First, let's write this address in binary. Starting from the most significant bit (A_{19}), FEC35 in binary is

$$A_{19} \quad \texttt{<1111/1110/1100/0011/0101>} \quad A_0$$

From this example we can see that $\overline{\text{ROM ADDR SEL}}$ is true (low) because A_{19}, A_{18}, A_{17}, and A_{16} are true (high). The signal $\overline{\text{XMEMR}}$ is true (low) because we are doing a memory read operation. The signal $\overline{\text{RESET DRV}}$ is false (high) because we are not in a reset state.

From the preceding conditions we can conclude that the signal $\overline{\text{CS}_7}$ is true (low), which is pin 7 of IC U_{46}. This is the signal that actually turns on the ROM in socket U_{33}, the BIOS ROM as shown in Figure 6.20.

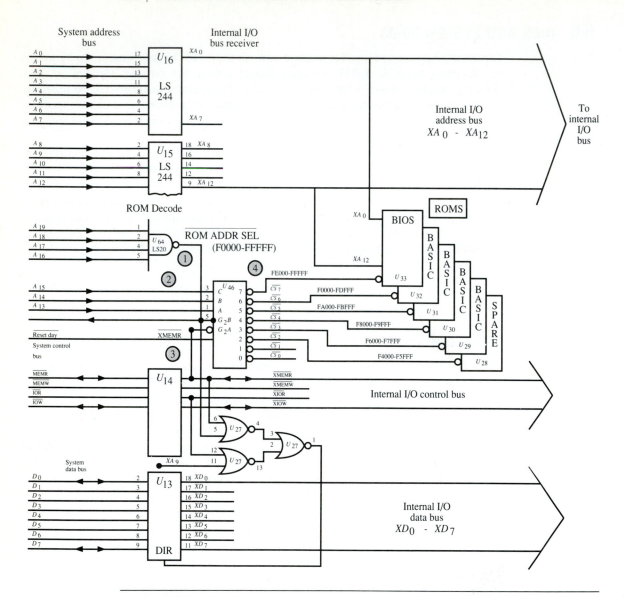

FIGURE 6.20
ROM decode and internal bus buffers

The ROM's address and data buses are buffered from the system buses by the ICs U_{13}, U_{14}, and U_{15}. They are actually treated as an external device and reside on the XA and the XD buses. IC U_{27} is used to control the direction of the data between the DATA bus and the XDATA bus through IC U_{13}.

The rest of the system board ROMs respond to the addresses F4000 through FDFFF hex, as shown in Table 6.3.

TABLE 6.3
ROM addresses

Location	Function	Low	High	Size
IC U_{33}	BIOS ROM	FE000	FFFFF	8K × 8
IC U_{32}	BASIC ROM	FC000	FDFFF	8K × 8
IC U_{31}	BASIC ROM	FA000	FBFFF	8K × 8
IC U_{30}	BASIC ROM	F8000	F9FFF	8K × 8
IC U_{29}	BASIC ROM	F6000	F7FFF	8K × 8
IC U_{28}	Spare ROM	F4000	F5FFF	User may insert ROM here
None	Not used	F2000	F3FFF	Decoded space not used
None	Not used	F0000	F1FFF	Decoded space not used

Main RAM

We treat the RAM memory as a separate part. The memory system is made up of the RAM chips, delay line TD1, and ICs U_{48}, U_{47}, U_{81}, U_{65}, U_{49}, U_{62}, U_{79}, U_{27}, U_{94}, and U_{96}, as shown in Figure 6.21. The main RAM on the system board is decoded to respond to memory addresses 00000H through 3FFFFH, which are the first 256K of memory addresses. The logic circuitry used here is a simple one-of-eight decoder, as shown in Figure 6.22. The A, B, and G_2A inputs of IC U_{48} are tied to ground. The C input is tied to address bit A_{18}, and the enable input is tied to address bit A_{19}. The G_1 enable input is tied to the $\overline{\text{DACKOBRD}}$ signal, which is the memory refresh acknowledge signal. From this we can see that the signal $\overline{\text{RAM ADDR SEL}}$ is low only when the signals A_{18} and A_{19} are low and $\overline{\text{DACKOBRD}}$ is high. The main RAM is selected only when the preceding conditions exist.

The RAM memory is built around the INTEL D4164 64K by 1-bit dynamic RAM chip, as illustrated in Figure 6.23 (p. 240). Note that addressing 65,536 addresses would require 16 lines. So how is this done in a 16-pin package? This type of RAM chip has both the low-order 8 bits and the high-order 8 bits on the same 8 lines. Recall that this arrangement is referred to as multiplexing, addressing by row first then column. To access the dynamic RAM chip, a sequence of events in a specified time period must be followed.

1. The row address 8 bits must be present on the address lines.
2. The $\overline{\text{RAS}}$ pin must be driven low, which strobes in the row address lines.
3. After the specified time the address lines must be changed to reflect the desired column address 8 bits.
4. After the specified time the $\overline{\text{CAS}}$ pin must be driven low.
5. After the specified time the data can be written to or read from the RAM chip.
6. After the desired action the $\overline{\text{RAS}}$ and the $\overline{\text{CAS}}$ pins must be driven high. The required timing for the RAM chips is shown in Figure 6.24 (p. 241).

Some new terms must be noted here. $\overline{\text{RAS}}$ is row address strobe not, active low. The $\overline{\text{RAS}}$ signal is to clock in the first set of address lines into the RAM chips. $\overline{\text{CAS}}$ is column address strobe not, active low. This signal is to clock in the next set of address lines and to complete the cycle.

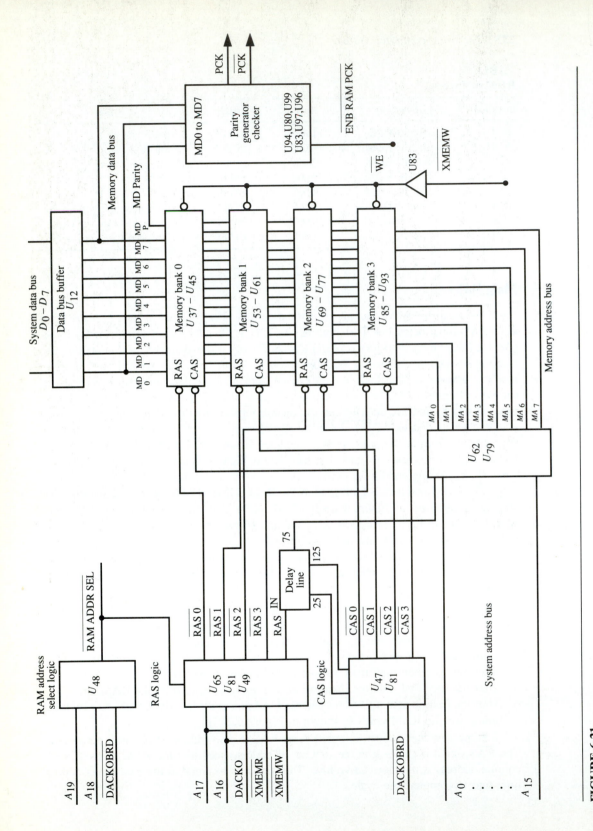

FIGURE 6.21
Main RAM block diagram

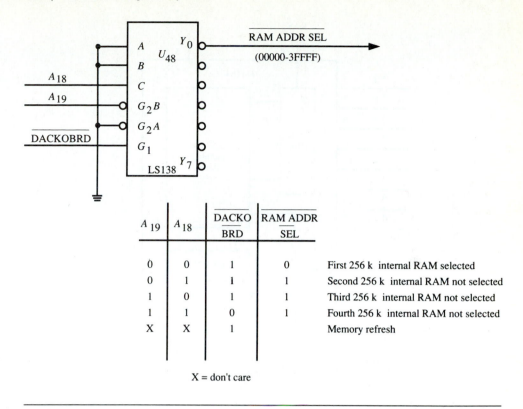

A_{19}	A_{18}	$\overline{\text{DACKO}}$ $\overline{\text{BRD}}$	$\overline{\text{RAM ADDR}}$ $\overline{\text{SEL}}$	
0	0	1	0	First 256 k internal RAM selected
0	1	1	1	Second 256 k internal RAM not selected
1	0	1	1	Third 256 k internal RAM not selected
1	1	0	1	Fourth 256 k internal RAM not selected
X	X	1		Memory refresh

X = don't care

FIGURE 6.22
Main RAM select logic

Main RAM Timing The basic RAM timing is done by using a TTL delay line, TD_1. The memory system is triggered by the signals $\overline{\text{XMEMR}}$ or $\overline{\text{XMEMW}}$ from the bus, which indicate that a read or write is requested, as shown in Figure 6.25. In Figures 6.25 (p. 242) and 6.26 (p. 243) signals $\overline{\text{XMEMR}}$ or $\overline{\text{XMEMW}}$ (1) generate the initial $\overline{\text{RAS}}$ signal (2). The bank selection comes from the address lines A_{16} and A_{17}. The address lines A_{16} and A_{17} drive a one-of-four decoder (U_{65}) to select one of the four RAM banks (3). During this time the low-order address lines are gated to the RAM address lines MA_0–MA_7 by U_{62} and U_{79} (quad 2-line to 1-line multiplexers) and are latched into the RAM chips, as shown in Figure 6.26.

Seventy-five nanoseconds later TD1 raises the line ADDR SEL to the multiplexers (4), thus switching from the low-order address bits to the high-order address bits. Fifty nanoseconds after ADDR SEL goes true, TD1 raises $\overline{\text{CAS}}$ through gate U_{81}, as shown in Figure 6.27 (5) (p. 244). This is then further decoded to select which, if any, internal RAM bank is selected by the one-of-four decoder (U_{47}) ANDed with the signal RAM ADDR SEL. This is true as long as the address is less than A_{18} or A_{19}, thus selecting one of the four $\overline{\text{CAS1}}$–$\overline{\text{CAS4}}$ lines to the RAM chips.

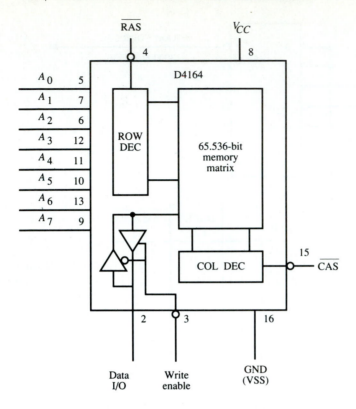

Note : V_{CC}, + 5 V and GND, 0 V
are reversed from a standard TTL-type chip.

FIGURE 6.23
64K by 1-bit dynamic RAM chip

The data bus (D_0–D_7) is buffered from RAM chips (MD_0–MD_7) by the bus transceiver U_{12}, which is enabled by $\overline{\text{RAM ADDR SEL}}$. The direction is controlled by the $\overline{\text{XMEMR}}$ line from the bus. The RAM chip write enable line is buffered from the bus by U_{83}.

Main RAM Parity   The memory system used in the IBM PC has 4 extra bits. These 4 bits are used for parity checking, 1 bit for each bank or byte. As was discussed earlier in this book, parity checking is a means of checking memory for correct data. The parity circuit consists of ICs U_{94}, U_{96}, U_{27}, U_{99}, U_{97}, U_{83}, U_{80}, and the pin 22 output of U_{36}. The heart of this circuit is a 74S280 9-bit odd/even parity generator/checker chip, U_{94}.

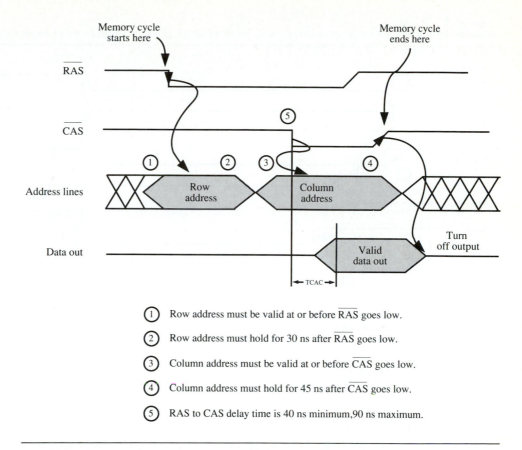

FIGURE 6.24
Dynamic RAM timing

As shown in Figure 6.28 (p. 244), during a memory write cycle, pin 4 of U_{94} is held low by gate U_{97} pin 6 (1). This causes the even output of U_{94} (2) to be high when the data bits are even. If the data bits are odd, the even output is low. This forces odd parity to be written into RAM. For example, when the bus data bits are even (i.e., 10001000), the even output of U_{97} is high. This is gated to the parity RAM chip input during the $\overline{WE}$ signal time, which is written into RAM. The actual pattern that is in RAM is 100010001, which is odd parity. If the state of the data bus is 11001000, then the even output is low. A zero is written into the RAM parity bit or a pattern 110010000, which is again odd parity. Correct parity must always be written into RAM even if it is not being checked so that future reads will not cause a parity error.

During a read cycle the parity RAM output is gated into the ninth input of U_{94} from U_{97} pin 6 (1) along with the 8 data bits from the data RAM, as shown in Figure 6.29 (p. 244). If this results in odd parity, then U_{94} pin 6 (odd) is high (2). If the result is even, indicating a parity error, then when the signal $\overline{RAM\ ADDR\ SEL}$ is low and ODD

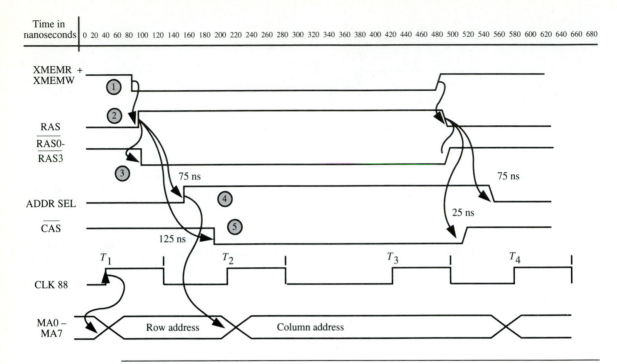

FIGURE 6.25
Main RAM timing, read cycle

is low, the D input of U_{96} is high through gate U_{27} (3). This causes the PCK flip-flop U_{96} to be set, creating a nonmaskable interrupt (NMI) to the processor (4). The PCK signal is also fed to U_{36}, the I/O port, so the MPU can tell if a parity error has caused the NMI to occur. This signals that an error has occurred in main RAM and some action should be taken by the software.

The parity checking circuit can be disabled and defaults that way on power up by $\overline{\text{ENB RAM PCK}}$ to IC U_{99} pin 5 (5). This signal originates from the I/O port chip U_{36} pin 22. The main RAM contains garbage on power up and must be initialized or written with good parity by the BIOS; then the parity circuit must be enabled to check it.

Main RAM Refresh Let's not forget that these RAM chips are dynamic RAM chips—that is, they will forget unless you refresh their memory at a rate of at least once every 2 ms. During sequential read cycles in RAM this is not needed, but during ROM read and wait cycles the RAM is not accessed. To perform this refresh you must access all 128 rows every 2 ms or sooner.

The circuitry used here is quite simple and depends entirely on the 8237A-5 DMA controller chip and the 8253 timer chip. At a rate set by the BIOS ROM, timer channel 1 generates a DMA request on the DREQ0 line once every 72 clocks (15 μs). The refresh cycle begins when timer channel 1 reaches the preset time count. The timer chip U_{34} pin 13 goes high, thus clocking the refresh request flip-flop U_{67} pin 11. On the rising

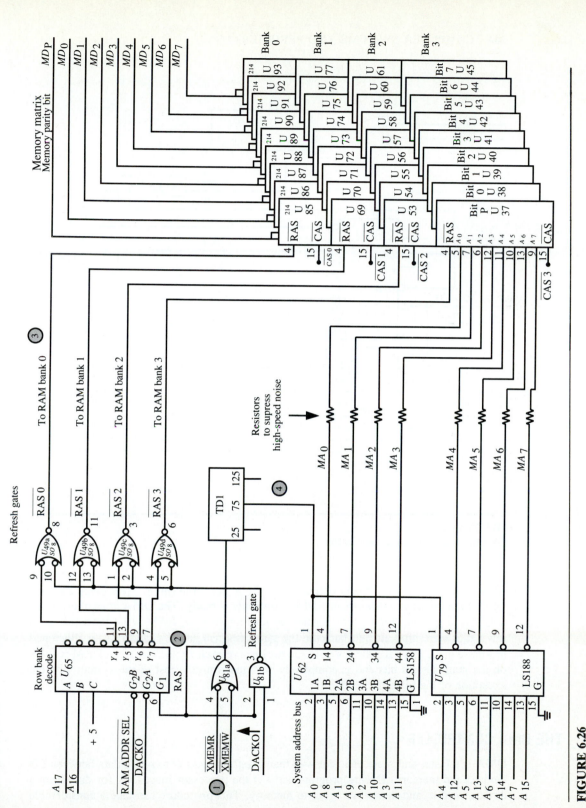

FIGURE 6.26
RAS lines and memory address multiplexers

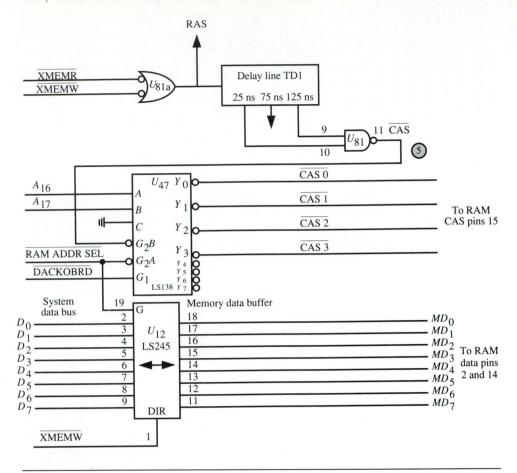

FIGURE 6.27
CAS lines and memory data buffer

edge of the timer output, the Q output pin 9 of U_{67} goes true (high). This event causes a DMA cycle to occur as soon as the DMA controller is ready. The DMA controller causes DACK0 to go true (high), which gates on all four rows of RAMs (the $\overline{RAS}$ line goes low), thus refreshing all four banks at the same time via gate U_{81} and U_{49}, as illustrated in Figure 6.30. The read data is not used during a refresh cycle. The main RAM resides on the main system bus and is completely buffered from the rest of the system with the exception of the refresh circuit.

6.7 THE DMA CONTROLLER

DMA is a faster and more efficient way than *programmed I/O* to move data between I/O devices and memory. During programmed I/O the processor must look for data from a device, read it, and then write it out to memory. This procedure can take a considerable

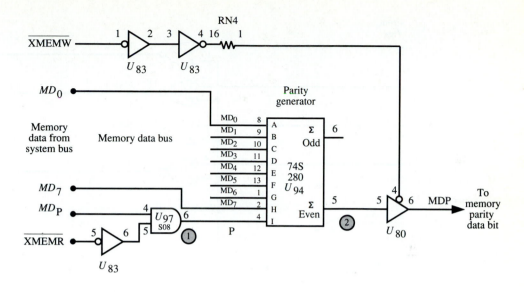

FIGURE 6.28
Parity generate logic

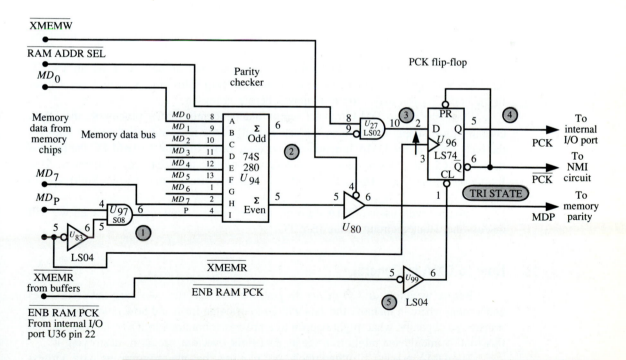

FIGURE 6.29
Parity check logic

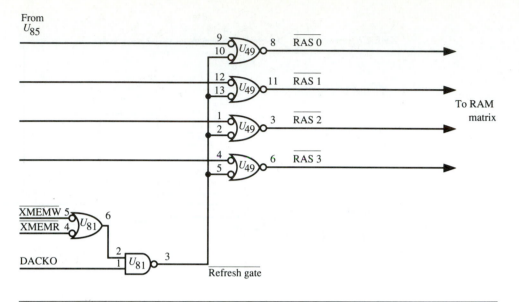

FIGURE 6.30
Memory refresh circuit

time to execute. DMA, on the other hand, links a device directly to memory without the use of the processor, thus freeing it up.

The DMA circuit is a bit complex. It is centered around IC U_{35}, an INTEL 8237A-5 advanced direct memory access controller chip. This chip was discussed earlier in the book, so you may want to review it before going on.

Since the actual DMA transfer works independently of the processor, the DMA circuitry must supply the memory address as well as the read and write control lines for the bus. Think of the DMA function as a separate processor. In the IBM PC the longest transfer is 65,536 bytes of data and cannot cross into the next segment of memory. This limitation is due to the 16-bit DMA address registers. Recall that 16-bits limits you to 65,536.

First we will discuss DMA transfers as they apply to any computer, then we will discuss the detailed circuit in the IBM PC.

How to DMA in General

Before we allow an I/O device to grab the bus and run, we must set some rules concerning where in memory the data will go to or come from and how much data can be transferred. Imagine what might happen to a program contained in RAM if we do not do this first. Some device might transfer its data right over our program, destroying it.

The DMA process is quite simple and requires that we program the base address and the base word count registers. We must also program the extended address register, if any. At this point we may tell the applicable I/O device that it is safe to perform DMA transfers by setting its DMA enable circuit. When the device has finished the transfer, it can inform the processor by causing an interrupt or setting a bit in its status register for the processor to poll or check.

The IBM PC DMA Circuit

The DMA circuit used here is made up of the 8237A IC U_{35}, U_{17}, U_{19}, U_{18}, U_{99}, U_{52}, TD$_1$, and U_{51}. As you know, the 8237A IC actually contains four DMA controllers in one package. The first channel, channel 0, is used exclusively for the main RAM refresh. This channel must never be altered unless you wish to destroy all the data in RAM. The other three channels, 1 through 3, may be used at any time. Before any DMA activity can take place, the 8237A chip must be initialized, or programmed, by the processor. This all happens during the power-up self-test in the BIOS ROM.

The DMA controller's internal registers are accessed by way of the I/O instructions. The addresses of the DMA controller are 00H through 0FH. Whenever one of these addresses is true, pin 11 of IC U_{35} will be low, activating the $\overline{\text{DMA CS}}$ line, as shown in Figure 6.31. When $\overline{\text{DMA CS}}$ is true along with $\overline{\text{XIOR}}$ or $\overline{\text{XIOW}}$, one of the internal registers will be accessed by the MPU.

For this next discussion please refer to Figures 6.31–6.33 (pp. 248–50). Upon receiving a DMA request, by one of the $\overline{\text{DRQ0–DRQ3}}$ lines (Figures 6.31, 6.33 (1)). the DMA controller begins a DMA cycle. The next event is the activation of HRQ DMA at U_{99} pin 2 and U_{52} pin 2 (2). This releases the clear input to the HOLDA (U_{67}) flip-flop (3), which arms the circuit to wait for the MPU to enter the passive state. As soon as the processor becomes passive, it raises $\overline{S_0}$, $\overline{S_1}$, and $\overline{S_2}$ along with $\overline{\text{LOCK}}$, which indicates the passive state. U_{98} pin 15 goes high on the next rising edge of the CLK signal (4). On the next falling edge of the clock cycle, U_{67} pin 5, the HOLDA flip-flop, is set (5). This signals the DMA controller that it is now free to grab the bus. On the next rising edge of the clock signal, the Q_0 output goes true (U_{98} pin 2), which is the AEN BRD signal (6). This turns off the processor bus buffers, thus freeing up the bus. On the next cycle, the $\overline{Q_1}$ output (U_{98} pin 6), which is the signal $\overline{\text{DMA WAIT}}$, goes true (low) (7). This causes the processor to wait one additional cycle before coming out of the passive state and also turns on the DMA bus buffers (U_{17}, U_{18}, and U_{19}). The DMA controller will signal the I/O device by raising the applicable DACK line on the bus (8). This causes the device to drop DREQ (9). At this point the DMA controller has total control of the bus. The DMA controller now drives the $\overline{\text{IOR}}$ line low (10). On the next DCLK cycle, the DMA controller drives the WRITE line low (11). At this point, 1 byte of data is transferred. On the next DCLK cycle the DMA controller executes one wait state. On the next DCLK cycle the DMA controller drives the $\overline{\text{MEMW}}$ line and the HRQ DMA line high (12). The DMA logic also begins to release the bus at this point. The next DCLK cycle is the last cycle, and the DMA controller drives the $\overline{\text{IOR}}$ line high (13).

Since the DMA controller used here is capable of controlling only a 16-bit address bus, a 4-bit by 4-word multiport RAM chip is also used here, as shown in Figure 6.34 (p. 251). This **page RAM,** or **segment RAM,** is a 74LS670 at location U_{19}, which is used for the upper 4 address bits. This must be preprogrammed by the processor to determine which 65,536-byte segment will be used for the DMA transfer.

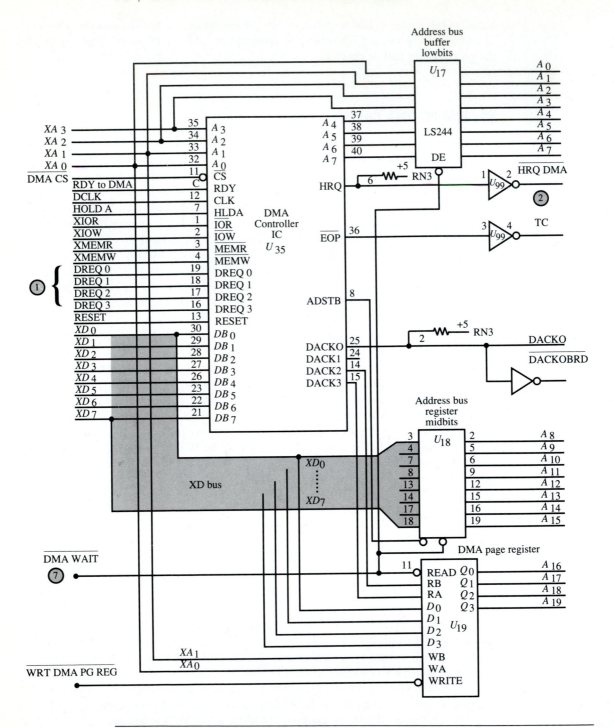

FIGURE 6.31
DMA controller and page register

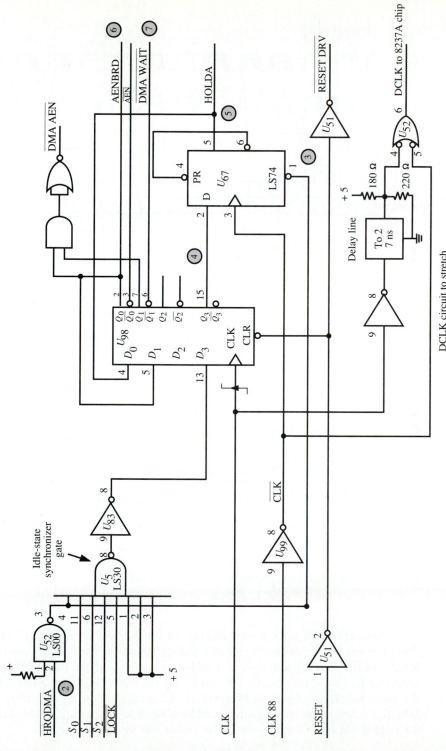

FIGURE 6.32
DMA timing circuit

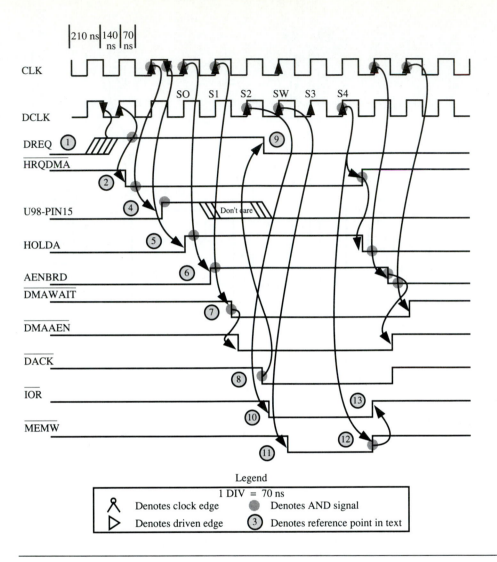

FIGURE 6.33
DMA timing diagram (one floppy to memory transfer)

Since channel 0 is for refresh and not for DMA transfers, we really have access to only three channels. That is why the read address inputs are not fully decoded to the page RAM. Both channel 0 and channel 1 address location 0 of the page RAM. Channel 2 addresses location 2 because DACK 2 is tied to the most significant address bit, RB, of the page RAM, as shown in Figure 6.31. Channel 3 addresses location 1 because DACK 3 is tied to the least significant address bit, RA, of the page RAM. Location 3 of the page RAM is not used by the DMA circuit and should be ignored.

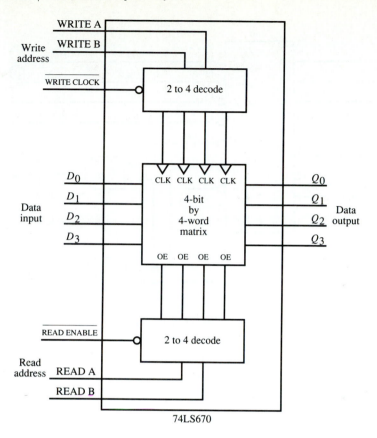

FIGURE 6.34
DMA page RAM illustration

The processor can program the DMA page RAM by writing to I/O locations 80H through 83H hex but it cannot read it back. This is accomplished when the processor performs an I/O write operation to addresses 80H through 83H. The one-of-eight decoder U_{66} output pin 11 ANDed with $\overline{\text{XIOW}}$ by U_{50} pins 12 and 13 will cause U_{51} pin 12 to go low, as shown in Figure 6.35 (1). This generates the signal $\overline{\text{WRT DMA PG REG}}$ to the page RAM. The signal $\overline{\text{DMA AEN}}$ will turn on the outputs of the page RAM. The 4 bits addressed by the applicable DMA channel will now be present on the A_{16} through A_{19} address bus bits. As we can see here, there is no way for the DMA circuit to alter the contents of this page RAM, which is why the DMA transfers are limited to 65,536 bytes and cannot cross a 65,536-byte segment, as we discussed earlier. The DMA circuitry resides on the internal I/O bus with the exception of the DMA address drivers, which reside on the main system bus.

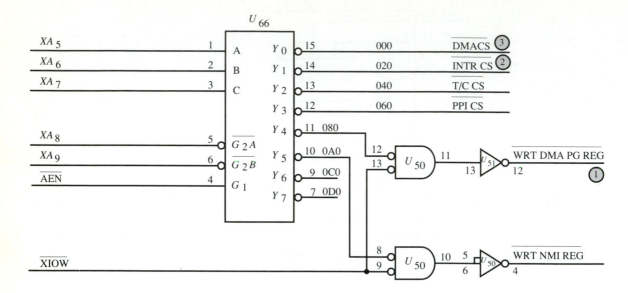

FIGURE 6.35
Internal I/O decode

6.8 THE INTERRUPT SECTION

Using an **interrupt-driven** I/O system is a faster and more efficient way of handling multiple I/O devices than polling. In a **polled I/O** system the processor must ask each I/O device that is on the system if it has any data to transfer. The processor must also ask each I/O device for its status. This process can waste considerable time. In an interrupt-driven system the I/O device **flags** the processor when it has a request for data or status to the processor.

Visualize an office of five workers and one boss. The boss gives all five workers a task to perform. In a polled system the boss must continuously ask all five workers about their status on the assigned task to see if they are done or having a problem. As we can see, this can tie up the boss' time. As an alternative and more efficient system, we assign the workers their tasks and instruct the workers to interrupt the boss only when they have a problem or are finished with the task. This frees up the boss' time and allows the boss to perform other tasks and get more tasks ready for the workers. In a **prioritized interrupt** system the workers who are performing critical tasks always get the boss' attention first.

Interrupt Systems in General

Most all modern computer systems use interrupt-driven I/O schemes. In addition to the address lines and I/O control lines they have interrupt request and interrupt acknowledge lines. Some systems use **daisy-chained** (in series) lines and some use separate lines. Others, like the PDP-11 minicomputers, use daisy-chained and separate interrupt lines together.

Since it may be possible for more than one I/O device to interrupt the processor at the same time, a priority system must be set up, using either hardware or software, or a combination of the two. In a daisy-chained system the I/O device electrically closest to the processor receives the interrupt acknowledge first. If that I/O device does not request the interrupt, then it passes the acknowledge signal to the next device on the bus. When the requesting device receives the acknowledge signal it then directs the processor to the program that can handle the request. When separate interrupt lines are used, the incoming interrupts are fed to a circuit known as a **priority encoder.** This circuit passes only the highest priority interrupt to the processor and blocks the rest until the priority interrupt has been completed.

In a software-prioritized system, the processor must first poll the I/O devices to ask which one has requested the interrupt. The first device polled gets serviced first, establishing the order of priority. The address of the program to service that interrupt is implied by the polling routine. As an alternative to polling, **vectors** are used. An **interrupt vector** is an address generated by the interrupt controller. These vectors direct the processor to the proper interrupt service routine rather than having the processor figure out the address first.

6.9 THE IBM PC INTERRUPT CIRCUIT

The interrupt scheme used in the IBM PC is a separate line prioritized and vectored system. The interrupt circuitry is built around the INTEL 8259A programmable interrupt controller chip. This chip was discussed in Chapter 5; you may want to review it before going on. In this circuit configuration there are eight levels of interrupts. Interrupt 0 is the highest-priority level, and interrupt 7 is the lowest. In the IBM PC the two highest interrupt levels are dedicated to internal functions. Interrupt level 0 is used for the real-time clock function and is tied to channel 0 of the timer chip. Interrupt level 1 is used for the keyboard and becomes true every time a key is pressed on the keyboard. The rest of the interrupts are for general I/O use by the controller boards. Upon power up the interrupt controller chip is programmed by the initialization program contained in the BIOS ROM. The interrupt controller chip responds to I/O addresses 20H through 3FH. The interrupt controller chip requires only two consecutive addresses, 20H and 21H. The rest of the addresses up to 3FH are not fully decoded and should be ignored.

The interrupt controller is accessed by the MPU when the $\overline{\text{INTR CS}}$ signal is true along with the signals $\overline{\text{XIOR}}$ or $\overline{\text{XIOW}}$, as shown in Figure 6.36 (1). The $\overline{\text{INTR CS}}$ select signal originates from IC U_{66} pin 14, which is the output of a one-of-eight decoder, as shown in Figure 6.35 (2). The A_0 line is tied to the address bus bit 0 to select the internal registers inside the interrupt controller chip as shown in Figure 6.36 (2).

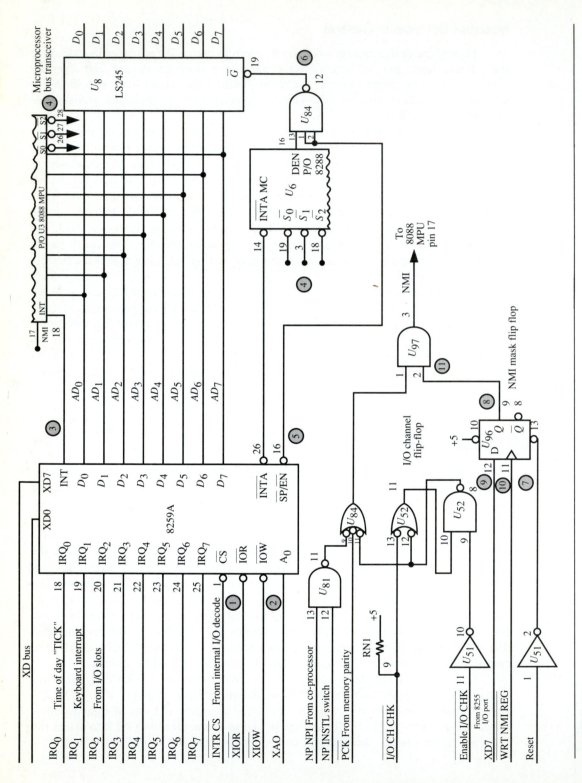

FIGURE 6.36
Interrupt circuit

When an interrupt occurs on one of the IRQ0 through IRQ7 lines, the interrupt controller raises the INT line to the MPU (3). When the MPU acknowledges the interrupt flag, it signals the bus controller chip, U_6, to generate the signal $\overline{\text{INTA}}$ by setting $\overline{S_2}$, $\overline{S_1}$, and $\overline{S_0}$ all low (4). The MPU performs this sequence twice. The second time the interrupt acknowledge is performed, the interrupt controller chip drives the $\overline{\text{SP/EN}}$ output low (5). This forces the pin 12 output of U_{84} high (6), which turns off the data bus transceiver chip U_8, thus freeing up the processor data bus. The interrupt controller chip then places the interrupt vector on the processor data bus, as shown in Figure 6.36. The MPU reads in this vector and formulates the address of the proper interrupt service routine. We must keep in mind that the interrupt input to the 8088 microprocessor is maskable by the processor. If the interrupt mask bit called IF is cleared, then the MPU will ignore the interrupt until this bit is set by the software.

The 8088 microprocessor also uses software interrupts. These interrupts are software generated instead of hardware generated. The BIOS program makes extensive use of this interrupt, and all BIOS calls must be made using software interrupts.

One additional hardware interrupt is the NMI to the microprocessor. This interrupt is dedicated for error detection and not for general I/O use. The NMI is of the *highest* priority and is not maskable by the microprocessor internally. This NMI signal is maskable externally to the microprocessor by a flip-flop, U_{96}, and a gate, U_{97}. The clear input at pin 13 of U_{96} is tied to the master reset line through inverter U_{51} pin 2 (7). This signal clears the NMI mask flip-flop, U_{96} pin 9 (8) upon power up. The D input to this flip-flop, pin 12, is tied to the internal I/O data bus bit XD_7 (9). The clock input, pin 11 of U_{96}, is tied to the signal $\overline{\text{WRT NMI REG}}$ (10), which is derived from the signals $\overline{\text{XIOW}}$ and address 0A0H.

As we can see here, any write to I/O address 0A0H with data bit 7 high will set the NMI mask flip-flop, which will allow the NMI. Conversely, if we write the address 0A0H with data bit 7 low, we clear this flip-flop and mask out any NMI due to the low on pin 2 of IC U_{97} (11). The interrupt signal can originate from three different sources, as follows:

1. The memory parity circuit, as discussed earlier in the memory section, asserts the signal PCK on pin 10 of U_{84}.
2. An externally generated I/O channel error sets the I/O channel error flip-flop, U_{52} pin 11, but only if the function is enabled by the software. This is so because the reset input to this *RS* flip-flop, U_{52} pin 9, is tied to the internal I/O port, U_{36}, through an inverter, U_{51} pin 10.
3. The 8087 math coprocessor generates an NMI signal if an error condition exists on it. This signal is maskable by gate U_{81} and the switch tied to pin 12 of that gate. If the 8087 coprocessor is not installed, the switch will be closed, thus grounding the input and preventing an erroneous interrupt, as shown in Figure 6.36.

Note that the interrupt controller resides on the processor bus with the exception of the select, read, and write lines, which reside on the internal I/O bus.

Internal I/O

In the IBM PC, some of the more essential I/O devices are mounted on the system board. These internal I/O devices are on the internal I/O bus, as discussed earlier. The internal I/O devices include the *triple timer*, the *triple I/O port*, the *keyboard interface*, and the *speaker driver*. Another function of this internal I/O section is the I/O address decode logic, upon which the other sections depend.

The internal I/O address decoding is centered around a 74LS138 one-of-eight decoder IC at location U_{66}, as shown in Figure 6.35. The binary decode inputs are tied to the address bus lines XA_5, XA_6, and XA_7. The decode enable lines are tied to the address bus lines XA_8, XA_9, and the address enable line $\overline{AEN}$. The range of the internal I/O decode circuitry is for 00H through 0FFH because both the G_2A and the G_2B must be low to enable the decoder. When either of those inputs is high, the decoder will be disabled. Each output of the decoder is a group of 32 (20H) addresses, as shown in Table 6.4.

TABLE 6.4
Internal device decode

Address	Output Pin	Internal I/O Use
000–01F	Y_0 pin 15	DMA controller chip select
020–03F	Y_1 pin 14	Interrupt controller chip select
040–05F	Y_2 pin 13	Triple timer chip select
060–07F	Y_3 pin 12	Internal I/O port chip select
080–09F	Y_4 pin 11	DMA page RAM access
0A0–0BF	Y_5 pin 10	NMI mask flip-flop access
0C0–0DF	Y_6 pin 9	Decoded but not used here
0E0–0FF	Y_7 pin 7	Decoded but not used here

Note that the I/O addresses are not fully decoded. Many of the internal I/O devices will respond to more than one set of addresses. Also it is not possible to take full advantage of the 65,536 I/O byte addressing range of the 8088 microprocessor. This is due to the lack of decode logic in the original design of the IBM PC. Any I/O address that has address bits A_8 and A_9 low enables the internal I/O address decoder. I/O address 400H decodes as if it were I/O address 00H, the DMA controller chip address. The next set of usable addresses is 500H through 7FFH. Again, address 800H responds as 00H.

The first set of decoded internal I/O addresses is for the DMA controller IC. Since the DMA controller must be initialized before it can function on its own, the microprocessor must have access to its internal registers. The microprocessor accesses the DMA controller registers at I/O addresses 00H through 1FH because output Y_0 of the decoder is tied to the DMA controller IC's chip select pin as shown in Figure 6.35 (3).

The next set of decoded internal I/O addresses is for the interrupt controller IC. Again, the interrupt controller IC must be initialized by the microprocessor. The microprocessor accesses the interrupt controller registers at I/O addresses 20H and 21H because output Y_1 of the decoder is tied to the interrupt controller IC's chip-select pin (2).

The next set of decoded internal I/O addresses is for the triple-timer chip. The internal timers used in the IBM PC are based on the INTEL 8253 programmable interval timer IC. This chip was discussed earlier, and you may wish to review it. The triple-timer chip is accessed by the microprocessor at I/O addresses 40H through 43H. All three timers are driven by a common clock of 1.19 MHz. This frequency is derived from the system PCLK divided by two by IC U_{26} pin 10, as shown in Figure 6.37 (1).

The timer output 0 section is used for the real-time clock function. This output drives the interrupt 0 line (2). Timer channel 0 is programmed to interrupt the microprocessor at a fixed rate of time called a **tick,** which is used by the software to update the time of day and the calendar. This timer should not be used or altered by the user software, or the internal timekeeping function will suffer.

The timer channel 1 output is used for the main RAM refresh (3). This function was discussed earlier in the main RAM section. The timer channel 2 output is the tone generator function of the IBM PC (4). This is where all that music comes from. This output is also used to drive the cassette tape recorder output from the PC. The pitch of the note is controlled by programming the timer register 2, and the duration is controlled by the gate input from the parallel port pin 18, as shown in Figure 6.38 (1). The speaker can also be turned off by the SPKR DATA signal from the parallel port pin 19 (2). This is important when using the cassette function so we do not hear the tone for the tape data. The speaker output comes from a driver IC at location U_{95}, as shown in Figure 6.37. This chip is driven from the speaker gate U_{63} pin 11 (5). The cassette data output comes from IC U_{63} pin 3 through a jumper setable attenuator (6).

The next set of decoded internal I/O addresses is for the internal parallel I/O ports. The IBM PC uses three 8-bit I/O ports that are based on an INTEL 8255 programmable peripheral interface IC at location U_{36}, as shown in Figure 6.38. This chip was discussed in detail in Chapter 4, so you may want to review it before going on. The internal I/O ports are accessed by the microprocessor through I/O addresses 60H through 62H, with 63H as the control register.

The A port is configured as an input port and has two sources of input. The first source is the hardware configuration switches, from which the microprocessor can determine the display type, the number of floppy disk drives, how much RAM, and whether or not the numeric coprocessor is installed. This source is a 74LS244 8-bit buffer at location U_{23}, as shown in Figure 6.38. The buffer is enabled when the microprocessor drives the bit 7 output of the B port high, which drives the enable inputs, pins 1 and 19 of IC U_{23}, low through inverter U_{99} pins 13 and 12. The second source of input to the A port is the keyboard data register. The microprocessor reads the keyboard data register by driving the B port bit 7 low, thus disabling the switch buffer and enabling the keyboard register on pin 8 of U_{24}.

The B port is configured as an output port and is used to control some of the internal I/O functions. Since the output bits are used for many different functions, we will discuss them one at a time.

Port B bit 0 is used to control the output of triple timer channel 2. The microprocessor starts timer channel 2 by driving port B bit 0 high and stops it by driving the bit low.

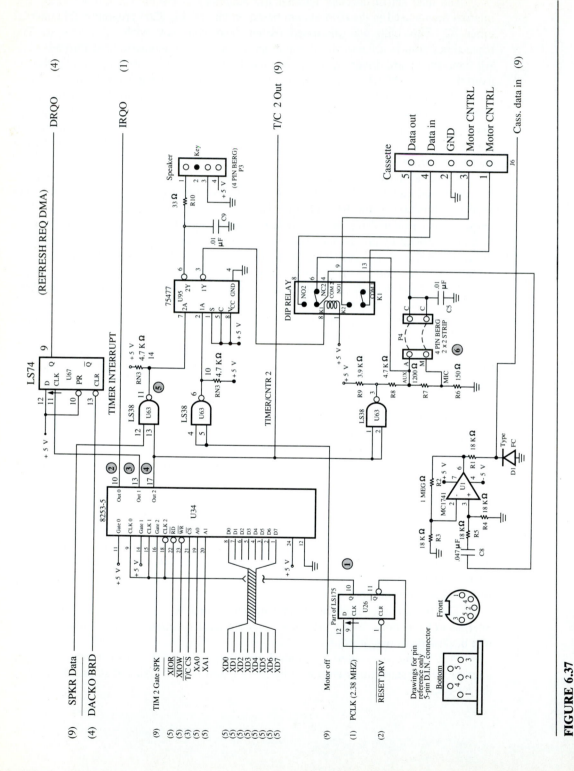

FIGURE 6.37
Triple timer and cassette logic (Courtesy of International Business Machines Corp.)

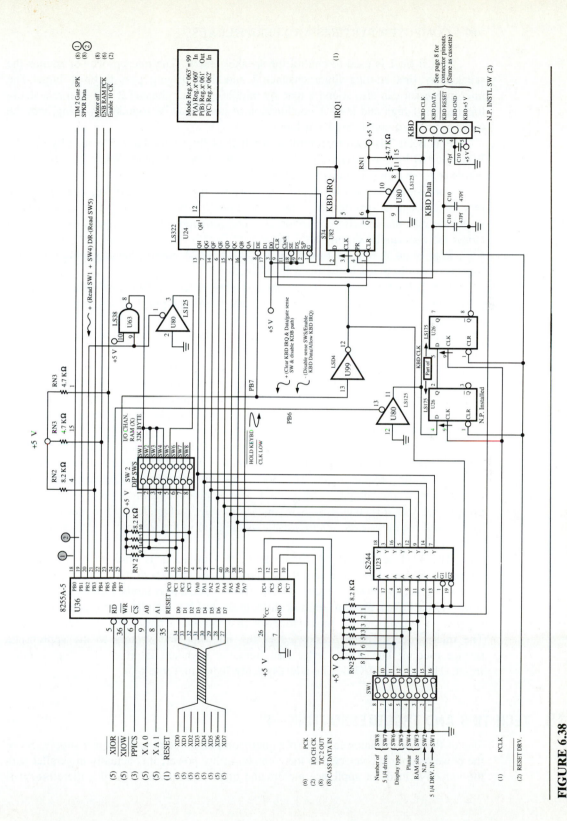

FIGURE 6.38
Internal I/O port logic (Courtesy of International Business Machines Corp.)

Port B bit 1 is used to control the speaker output. The microprocessor sounds the speaker by first starting timer channel 2 and then driving port B bit 1 high. The microprocessor can also sound a tone by inhibiting timer channel 2 and then repeatedly toggling bit 1 high and low. A combination of tones may be sounded by using both the timer output and port B bit 1 together.

Port B bit 2 is used to control which half of the switch bank 2 is read by port C. When port B bit 2 is driven high, switches 1 through 4 are read. When port B bit 2 is driven low, switches 5 through 8 are read.

Port B bit 3 is used to control the cassette tape motor by driving a relay coil on relay K_1 through an inverter, U_{63} pin 6, and a driver chip, U_{95} pin 5. The relay contacts go to the external cassette connector, J_6. The microprocessor energizes the relay and closes the contacts by driving bit 3 low.

Port B bit 4 is used to control the main RAM parity checking circuitry. This function was discussed in the main RAM section.

Port B bit 5 is used to control the I/O error detection flip-flop. When this bit is driven low, it allows an NMI interrupt to pass by driving pin 9 of U_{52} high through an inverter, U_{51} pin 10, which arms the flip-flop.

Port B bit 6 is used to inhibit the keyboard clock input. When the microprocessor drives this bit low, the keyboard is prevented from clocking in its data.

Port B bit 7 is used to control the port A data steering and was discussed earlier.

Port C of the internal I/O port is divided into two parts. The first half, bits 0 through 3, is used by the microprocessor to determine the cause of an NMI interrupt. The second half, bits 4 through 7, is used to read switch bank 2 to determine how much memory is plugged into the I/O slots.

The keyboard interface is made up of a dual D-type flip-flop, a gate, and an 8-bit serial in–parallel out shift register. The keyboard is designed to produce bit serial data to simplify the cable requirements. Therefore, only four conductors are required to connect the keyboard to the computer. Since the keyboard produces 8 bits of data when a key is pressed, we would need at least a 10-conductor cable if a parallel data format were used. This would require a large, clumsy cable as opposed to the flexible, coiled cable that is used.

The keyboard interface circuit is quite simple; it is just a serial-to-parallel converter. When a key is pressed, the keyboard sends the data to the shift register IC U_{24} 1 bit at a time, as shown in Figure 11.38. The keyboard also sends a timing clock to the shift register. When the shift register shifts in the last bit, the QH output goes high. This triggers an interrupt to the microprocessor that informs it that a key has been pressed. The microprocessor then acknowledges the interrupt and vectors to the appropriate service routine. The acknowledge also frees the keyboard interface to accept another input. The internal I/O device addresses are listed in Table 6.5.

6.10 TECH TIPS AND TROUBLESHOOTING—T³

One of the most common failures of a microcomputer system is the power supply. Since the power supply is connected to the common utility power, it is actually in parallel with the inductive loads of appliance motors and other unforeseen transients; therefore, it is

TABLE 6.5
Device Addresses

Hexadecimal Address	I/O Function
000	DMA channel 0 base and current address register
001	DMA channel 0 base and current word count register
002	DMA channel 1 base and current address register
003	DMA channel 1 base and current word count register
004	DMA channel 2 base and current address register
005	DMA channel 2 base and current word count register
006	DMA channel 3 base and current address register
007	DMA channel 3 base and current word count register
008	DMA command and status register (read-status)
009	DMA write request register (write only)
00A	DMA write single mask register bit (write only)
00B	DMA write mode register (write only)
00C	DMA clear byte pointer FF or read temp. register
00D	DMA master clear (write only)
00E	DMA clear mask register (write only)
00F	DMA write all mask register bits (write only)
010	Repeat of above I/O addresses through 01F
020	Interrupt controller OCW 1
021	Interrupt controller OCW 2 and OCW 3
024	Repeat of above sequence through 03F
040	Triple timer counter 0
041	Triple timer counter 1
042	Triple timer counter 2
043	Triple timer control word (write only)
044	Repeat of above sequence through 05F
060	Internal I/O port A
061	Internal I/O port B
062	Internal I/O port C
063	Internal I/O control register (write only)
064	Repeat of above sequence through 07F
080	DMA page register for channel 1 (write only)
081	DMA page register for channel 2 (write only)
082	DMA page register for channel 3 (write only)
083	DMA page register **not used** (write only)
084	Repeat of above sequence through 09F
0A0	NMI mask register access (write only)
0A1	Repeat of NMI mask register through 0BF
0C0	Not used through 0FF
0FF	End of internal I/O decoded space
100	Start of external I/O space
3FF	End of external I/O space
400	Do not use. This address will respond as 000
4FF	End of duplicate addresses
500	Next available external I/O address through 7FF

subject to an unstable environment. Furthermore, power supplies are usually designed to run at their rated maximum power output in order to keep their physical size and weight to a minimum. Thus power supplies naturally tend to run warm. While a warm operating temperature is normal and poses no danger to the unit, excessive heat buildup due to overloading or poor cooling or ventilation will cause electronic components to fail prematurely.

The problem of power line transients is easily solved by using commercial **line conditioners** or **surge protectors.** These devices are inexpensive and can protect the entire system. Heat buildup problems can usually be solved by using good common sense. Be sure that the air flow passages are clean and not blocked. If an air filter exists, replace it periodically. Consider the location of the system. Try not to place it near a hot appliance like an oven or near a radiator.

If a power supply failure is suspected, consider the following steps:

1. Check the condition of the line cord. Often the cord breaks from flexing at the ends.
2. Check the fuse if one exists. Sometimes fuses are hidden internally in power supplies.
3. Check the condition of the output connectors. Excessive humidity will cause corrosion to build up over time, causing an open circuit. This is a common problem and is solved by cleaning the connectors. Simply removing and reconnecting the connector a few times will clean it. A soft pencil eraser will also do a good job on edge connectors. Be careful not to rub too hard because it is possible to remove some of the gold plating.
4. Measure the output voltages. Remember that an overload or short on the system board will cause the power supply to shut down. This is known as **foldback** current limiting.
5. Check the output for ripple. Remember that a VOM will average excessive ripple, so an oscilliscope must be used.
6. When bench testing switching power supplies, be aware that some load is required, or no output will be available. A 5-Ω load across the +5-V output is usually sufficient.

EXERCISES

6.1   Name five parts of a computer system.

6.2   The system unit or CPU consists of _____, _____, and _____.

6.3   Name three types of video display devices used with a microcomputer.

6.4   What are the common types of floppy disk drives used on microcomputers?

6.5   Compare the Winchester disk with the floppy disk.

6.6   What are the advantages of the Winchester disk over the floppy disk?

6.7   What types of power supplies are found in microcomputers?

6.8   Draw the block diagram of a linear power supply.

6.9   Draw the block diagram of a switching power supply.

6.10   Compare the linear and switching power supplies.

6.11   If a hard disk is being added to a PC, should the 65-W power supply be replaced?

6.12   In an IBM PC which connector on the interface cable is used on the A drive?

6.13   In the IBM PC the system board contains _____, _____, _____, _____, and _____.

6.14   What does each bus contain or connect?

6.15   List the three buses used on the system board.

6.16   Draw the system board block diagram.

6.17   List the major functions on the system board.

6.18   What are the five main timing signals and what are they used for?

6.19   In the IBM PC what is the frequency of the processor clock?

6.20   How is this signal obtained?

6.21   What is the purpose of the $\overline{RDY}$/ WAIT signal?

6.22   What are the main functions of the 8284 chip?

6.23   Draw a block diagram of the CPU in the IBM PC.

6.24   How is the CPU block buffered from the system?

6.25   What does the 8259A chip do?

6.26   Define BIOS.

6.27   What does the BIOS do?

6.28   Which bus are the ROMs on?

6.29   Which chip contains the BIOS ROM?

6.30   How are the ROMs buffered from the system?

6.31   Referring to Figure 6.21, which two ICs are used for the RAM multiplexers?

6.32   How is the main RAM selected?

6.33   What memory addresses are for the main RAM on the system board?

6.34   What is the sequence of events to access the dynamic RAM chips on the IBM PC system board?

6.35   How are the RAM banks selected?

6.36   How is the data bus buffered from the RAM chips?

6.37   How many parity bits are on the system board?

6.38   What are they used for?

6.39   Draw and explain the parity generator circuit.

6.40   Draw and explain the parity check circuit.

6.41   What is RAM refresh and why use it?

6.42   Draw and explain the RAM refresh circuit.

6.43   What is DMA used for?

6.44   Explain how DMA works, in general.

6.45   Explain the IBM PC DMA circuit.

6.46   Compare an interrupt-driven system with a polled system.

6.47   Explain an interrupt-driven system, in general.

6.48   Explain the IBM PC interrupt circuit.

6.49   List the internal I/O devices in the IBM PC.

6.50 What is the internal I/O address decoding centered around?

6.51 How are the ports configured on the 8255 PPI chip?

6.52 What is the range of the internal I/O space?

6.53 List the internal I/O address major decodes.

6.54 Crossword Puzzle

ACROSS

4. An I/O device.

5. DMA is faster and more efficient than _____ I/O system.

8. The system unit is also known as _____.

10. One additional hardware interrupt that is not for general I/O use.

11. _____ unit allows the user to add more peripherals than the system unit can handle.

14. Group of wires.

15. Similar to a floppy disk, but ten times faster.

17. Disadvantage of linear power supply.

20. Signal applied to the input RDY1 on the 8284A chip in the PC.

21. Dynamic RAM requirement.

24. _____ checking is a means of checking memory for correct data.

26. The 8088 in the IBM PC is in the _____ mode.

27. The peripheral clock signal.

30. Some interrupt systems make use of series of _____ chained interrupt request lines.

31. 64K of memory.

DOWN

1. The big disadvantage of a switching power supply is that it is tricky to _____.

2. Column address strobe NOT, active low.

3. Input device.

4. The main RAM in the PC uses _____ RAM chips.

6. The hard disk uses two flat cables.

7. _____ bus links the MPU, coprocessor, interrupt controller and the bus controller.

9. A type of power supply.

12. IBM PC model.

13. Interrupt-driven system improves this method.

16. 8087 coprocessor function.

18. Memory chips, memory bus, memory parity, and refresh circuitry are all part of the _____.

19. Row-address strobe NOT, active low.

22. Most PCs today use a _____ regulator power supply.

23. System clocks, wait circuitry, and master system reset are all part of the main system _____.

25. The 8237 chip, page RAM, and control logic are part of the _____ controller.

28. Connectors are _____ to prevent being reversed.

29. Type of parity.

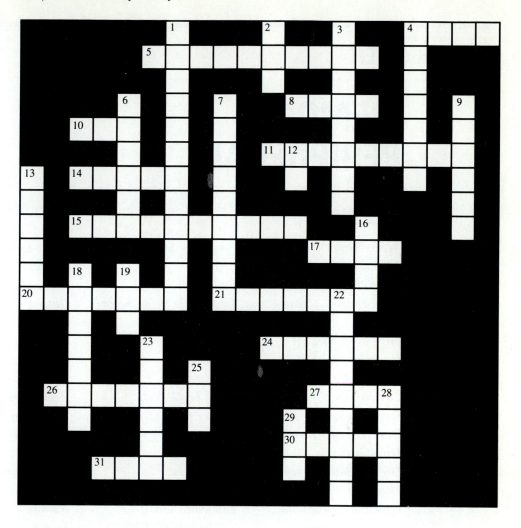

CHAPTER SEVEN

MEMORY PERIPHERALS

KEY TERMS

Access Time
Alignment Diskette
Azimuth Burst Sets
Band-Driven Actuator
Bit Cell
Cat's-eye Lobes
Centering Cone
Coercivity
Comparator
Data Field
Data Transfer Rate
Differentiator
Differentiator Droop
Directory
Disk Driver Exerciser
Door Open Sensor
Double Density
Encoding
Enhanced Small Device
  Interface (ESDI)
External Storage
Fields
File Allocation Table
  (FAT)
Floppy Disk
Formatting
Frequency Modulation
  (FM)

Frequency Shift Keying
  (FSK)
Full-height
Grooved Disk Actuator
Half-height
Head and Carriage
  Assembly
Header Field
Head Load Pad
Head Load Solenoid
High-Level Format
Hysteresis
Index Burst
Index Sensor
Integrated Drive
  Electronics (IDE)
Lead Screw–Driven
  Actuator
Low-Level Format
Magnetized
Magnetic Floppy Disks
Magnetic Flux Reversal
Magnetic Recording
  Tape
Modified Frequency
  Modulation (MFM)
Partition
Permeable
Phase Distortion

Phase-locked Loop
Postamble Field
Preamble Field
Quad Density
Radial Alignment
Read/Write Head
Read Amplifier
Read Chain
Recalibrate
Recording Head
Retentivity
Roll Off
Run Length Limited
  (RLL)
Runout
Sector
Seek Time
Single-density Recording
Small Computer
  Standard Interface
  (SCSI)
Spindle Assembly
Sync Bytes
Tone Encoding
Track
Track 00 Sensor
Wobble
Write-protect Notch
Write-protect Sensor

7.0 INTRODUCTION

One of the most important components of any computer system is **external storage.** An external storage device is required for initial program loading and for mass data storage and retrieval. In the early days of computing, programs were loaded from paper tapes. Paper tapes are long strips of paper in which holes are punched to represent the 1 state, as shown in Figure 7.1. The paper tapes were punched and then read by a *teletype*

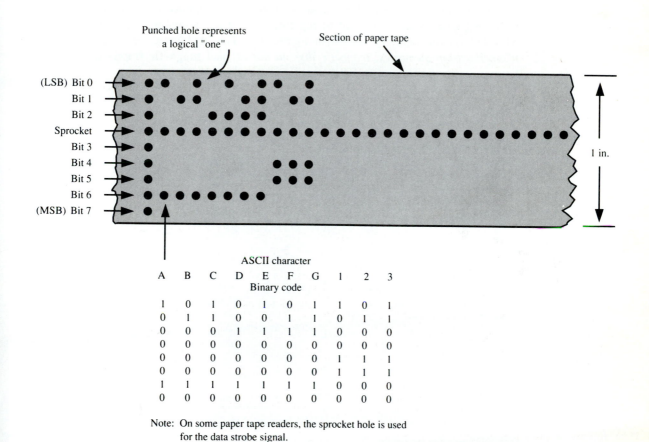

	A	B	C	D	E	F	G	1	2	3
	1	0	1	0	1	0	1	1	0	1
	0	1	1	0	0	1	1	0	1	1
	0	0	0	1	1	1	1	0	0	0
	0	0	0	0	0	0	0	0	0	0
	0	0	0	0	0	0	0	1	1	1
	0	0	0	0	0	0	0	1	1	1
	1	1	1	1	1	1	1	0	0	0
	0	0	0	0	0	0	0	0	0	0

Note: On some paper tape readers, the sprocket hole is used for the data strobe signal.

FIGURE 7.1
Eight-level paper tape

reader/printer device. The teletype also served as the local console terminal. One major drawback of paper tape is that it is somewhat clumsy to handle and represents a low-density storage. That is, the number of 1s and 0s or data per inch, is relatively small. Another disadvantage is that once the paper tape is punched, it cannot be reused. If an error is made, the paper tape must be discarded.

Some earlier computer system used *punched cards,* which are often referred to as IBM cards, instead of paper tapes for their mass storage. Punched cards are similar to paper tape in that a punched hole represents a 1 state, as shown in Figure 7.2.

As an alternative to the paper tape and punched cards, **magnetic recording tape,** which was already being used by the audio industry, was applied to recording computer data. Instead of a hole punched to represent a 1 state, a **magnetic flux reversal** is recorded on the tape, as shown in Figure 7.3. This technology was followed by *magnetic drum memories, magnetic disk memories,* and **magnetic floppy disks.** The latest innovation is the *optical disk memory,* or *compact disk.*

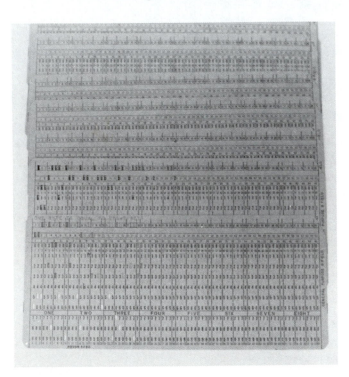

FIGURE 7.2
Punched card

7.1 MAGNETIC RECORDING FUNDAMENTALS

In magnetic recording a magnetic charge is stored on a permeable medium. This permeable medium must be a ferrous-type material that exhibits some magnetic retentivity. **Permeable** means that the applied magnetic flux is able to penetrate and flow through the medium easily, whereas **retentivity** means that the medium will hold the flux or become **magnetized** after the applied energy is removed. Different ferrous and ferrite materials exhibit varying levels of permeability and retentivity.

To demonstrate this effect, take a common household screwdriver and a permanent magnet. While holding the magnet in one hand, rap the end of the screwdriver blade onto one pole of the magnet. Repeat this several times on the same pole. The screwdriver will become magnetized. The end of the blade will be the opposite pole of the magnet you were using, as shown in Figure 7.4.

The screwdriver can be neutralized by placing the blade in an alternating magnetic field such as a standard tape head demagnetizer, illustrated in Figure 7.5.

The ease with which a material can become magnetized is known as its **coercivity.** A material that is known to have a high coercivity will not require as much flux density to become magnetized as will a material of low coercivity.

One of the most commonly used materials for magnetic recording is ferric oxide. This material was chosen because it demonstrates good permeability, high coercivity, and excellent retentivity. It is also low in cost and readily available.

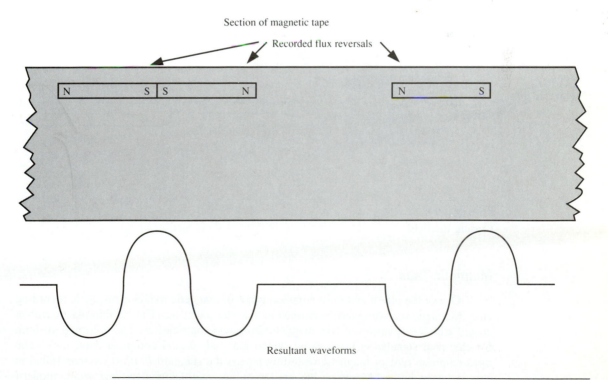

FIGURE 7.3
Recorded magnetic flux reversals

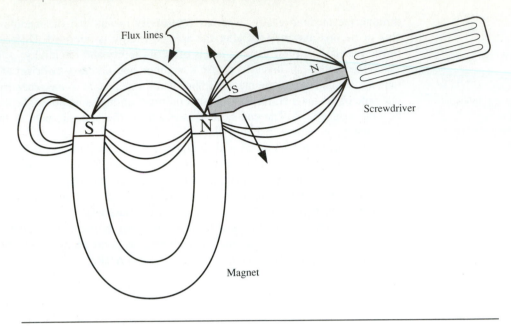

FIGURE 7.4
Magnetizing a screwdriver

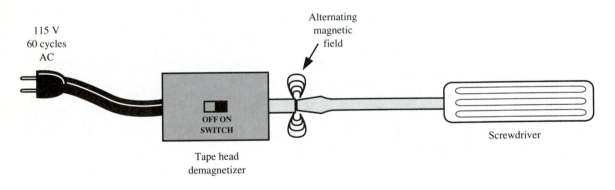

FIGURE 7.5
Erasing the field

Magnetic Tape

One of the oldest and most common types of magnetic media is magnetic recording tape. Magnetic recording tape is defined in Webster's dictionary as "a thin plastic ribbon coated with a suspension of ferromagnetic iron oxide particles used as a storage medium for electrical signals, as from sound, video material, digital computer data, etc." The most common type of magnetic recording tape is the standard *Phillips cassette* found in almost every home. Many of the earlier hobby microcomputers and some modern low-cost home computers use this cassette as their storage medium. Figure 7.6 illustrates the construction of magnetic tape.

Information is recorded on the magnetic tape by a **recording head.** As the tape is recording, it is pulled across the head by a *tape transport* mechanism, as shown in Figure 7.7.

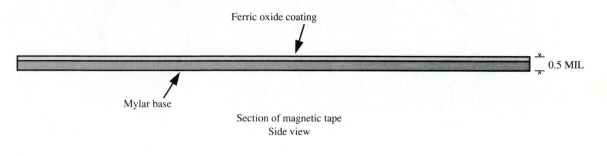

Ferric oxide coating

0.5 MIL

Mylar base

Section of magnetic tape
Side view

FIGURE 7.6
Magnetic tape construction

Read/Write Heads

The key component in magnetic recording is the recording head. In the digital world it is also known as the **read/write head.** The read/write head is basically an electromagnet in which the north and south poles are very close together. An electromagnet is simply a core of soft iron with a coil of wire wrapped around it. When an electric current is applied to the coil, the core becomes magnetized as shown in Figure 7.8. The core remains magnetized only as long as the electric current is applied. The magnetic field will collapse when the current is removed. In fact, if an external magnetic field is applied and then removed, an electrical field will be induced in the coil, thus forming a small generator. Thus the same head that is used to record the information can be used to read the information back. Recall that to generate a voltage, we need only a magnetic field, motion, and a conductor.

If the core is made up of hard iron or hard steel, as was the screwdriver, some of the magnetic field remains due to retentivity.

The read/write head is simply a modified version of the electromagnet, as shown in Figure 7.9 (p. 274).

In the magnetic recording process, the tape is pulled across the read/write head. As the tape is moving, magnetic flux reversals can be recorded by switching an electrical current across the coil in the head, as shown in Figure 7.10 (p. 274). When the tape is rewound and pulled across the head again, without current applied to the coil, small voltage changes will be present at the coil when the previously recorded flux reversals pass under the gap between the poles of the head. Because these voltages are so small, they must be amplified before they can be used. This is done by electronic circuitry known as the **read amplifier.**

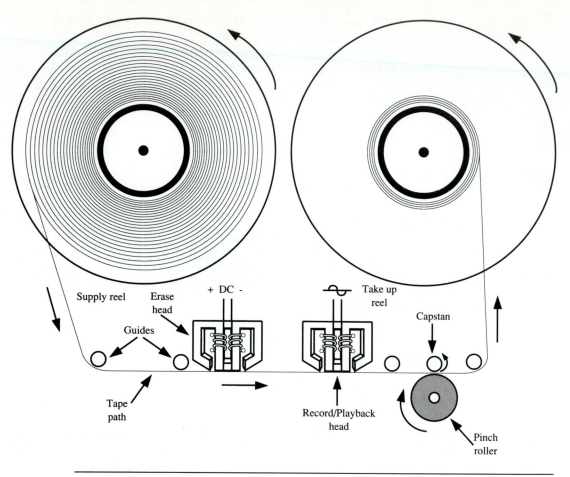

FIGURE 7.7
Tape transport

Read Amplifier Circuits

The read amplifier circuitry, which may also be called the **read chain,** differs greatly between analog and digital recording systems. In the analog system the head is connected to a high-gain preamplifier, which is followed by an equalizer circuit to boost the high-frequency and cut the low-frequency signals. This is necessary because high-frequency loss is characteristic of magnetic tape. The equalizer is followed by more stages of amplification and fed to the output of the tape deck, as shown in Figure 7.11.

When magnetic recording is used in digital applications, it is not possible to record and then play back DC levels on magnetic tape. It is not possible for the same reason that

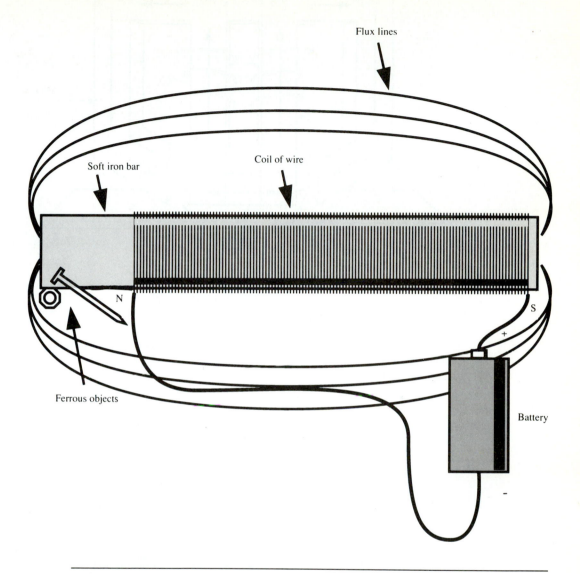

Flux lines

Soft iron bar

Coil of wire

N

S

+

Ferrous objects

Battery

−

FIGURE 7.8
The electromagnet

DC cannot pass through a transformer; an *alternating* field must be set up. The flux reversal is recorded on the medium. When a DC current is present on the head coil, the oxide particles are all magnetized in the same direction. This has the effect of *erasing* the tape. When the tape is rewound and played back, there is no voltage present at the head coil.

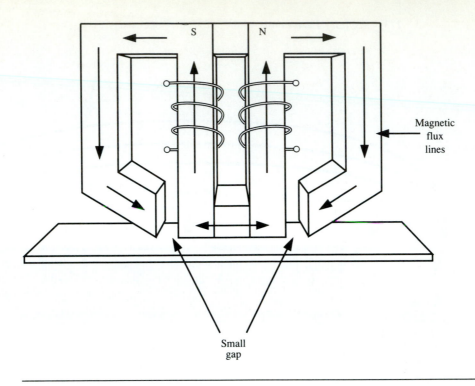

FIGURE 7.9
The read/write head

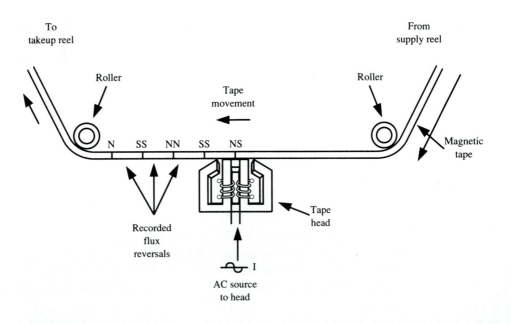

FIGURE 7.10
Magnetic tape recording

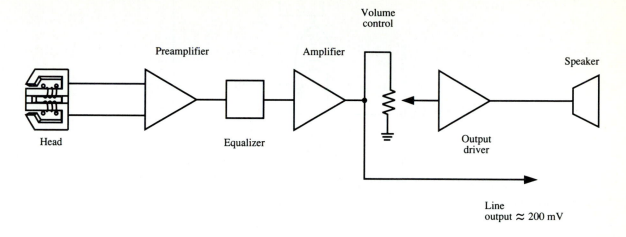

FIGURE 7.11
The analog read chain

The digital read chain is designed to operate at a fixed set of frequencies; therefore, no equalization is required. A **differentiator** circuit is used instead, as shown in Figure 7.12. The differentiator is required to restore the square waveform of the original digital signal, as shown in Figure 7.13.

Remember that the DC level will not record, and the playback signal will **roll off** until another flux reversal is recorded, as shown in Figure 7.14 (p. 278).

At high frequencies, when the flux reversals are at or near the high-frequency saturation of the medium, the roll-off is almost gone, and the playback signal resembles a sine wave. The problem of roll-off causes **phase distortion** and noise to be introduced into the playback signal. With the addition of the differentiator circuit, these problems are reduced because the circuit restores the recorded DC levels. As we can see in Figure 7.15 (p. 279), the output of the differentiator begins to droop as the input voltage begins to roll off. This is known as **differentiator droop.** The problem of differentiator droop is virtually eliminated with the addition of a **comparator** at the output of the differentiator, as shown in Figure 7.16 (p. 279). As long as the droop is not excessive and does not come close to the comparator threshold, the output will be immune to the droop and any noise that may be present on the signal.

The output of the comparator is followed by a noise-filtering circuit. Some comparators use a digital filter and a bidirectional one-shot. The one-shot triggers on both the positive and negative transitions of the recovered signal. The output is a pulse for every flux reversal read back. This output is referred to as *raw data.*

The Write Amplifier

The *write amplifier* in the digital recording system is essentially a current switch, as shown in Figure 7.17 (p. 280). When the write enable signal goes true, the write current is turned on to the write driver transistors. When a data bit is present at the input, the current across the head switches polarity. In digital recording, most systems drive the medium into saturation, so no erase head is required.

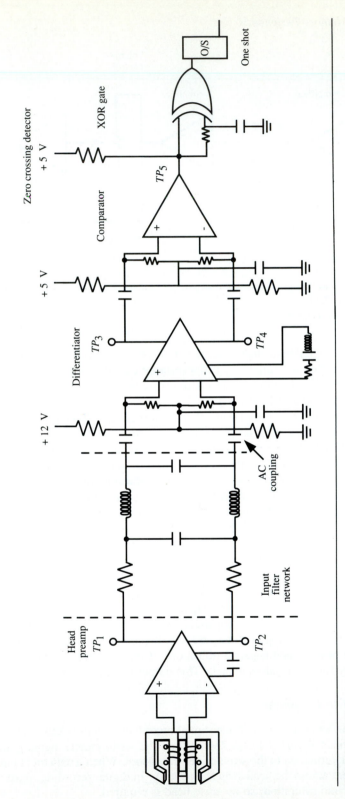

FIGURE 7.12
The digital read chain

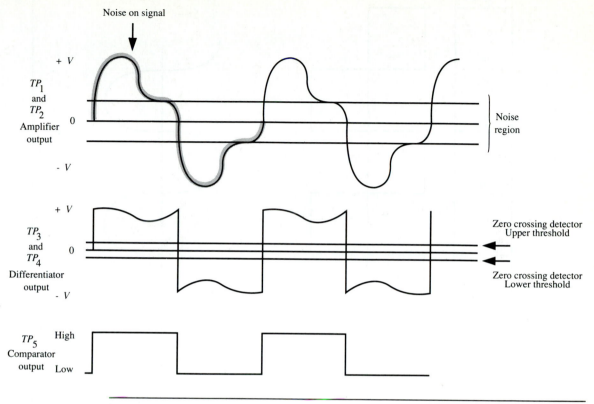

FIGURE 7.13
Read waveforms

7.2 DIGITAL MAGNETIC RECORDING

Before going on, let's stop and recall what we have just learned about magnetics and the magnetic recording process and apply it to the digital world. Is it possible to record digital data bits directly onto the medium? Recall that it is not possible to record DC onto the medium. As long as the bits are changing states, we can record the pattern. If the data stream is 1 1 1 1 or 0 0 0 0 . . . , the tape will become DC erased where the bits did not change states. For this reason we must change the data stream into an alternating pattern. This is known as **encoding** the data, and numerous encoding methods are used today. The simplest is **tone encoding,** which is used with voice-grade equipment. The most common encoding methods used in microcomputers are frequency modulation, modified frequency modulation, group code recording, and frequency shift keying.

Encoding/Decoding Techniques

Frequency shift keying (FSK) is used primarily for voice-grade devices such as audio cassette recorders. It is also used for telephone modems. This method encodes the data stream into a series of audio tones, as shown in Figure 7.18 (p. 281).

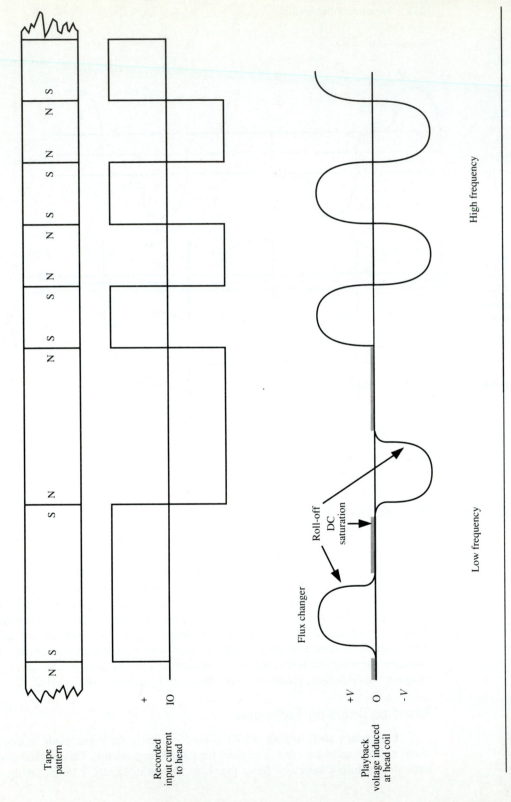

Tape pattern

Recorded input current to head

Flux changer

Playback voltage induced at head coil

Roll-off
DC saturation

Low frequency

High frequency

FIGURE 7.14
Recorded roll-off

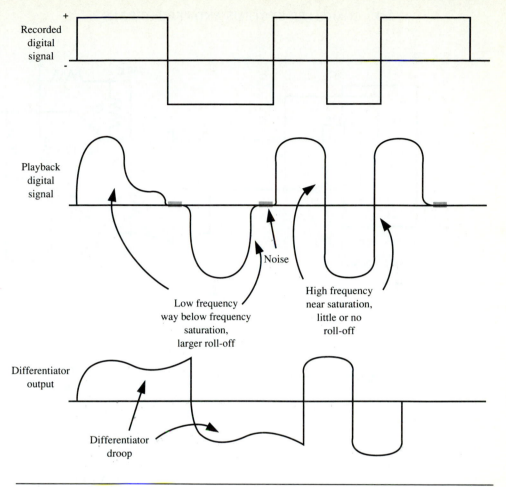

Recorded digital signal

Playback digital signal

Noise

Low frequency way below frequency saturation, larger roll-off

High frequency near saturation, little or no roll-off

Differentiator output

Differentiator droop

FIGURE 7.15
Differentiator droop

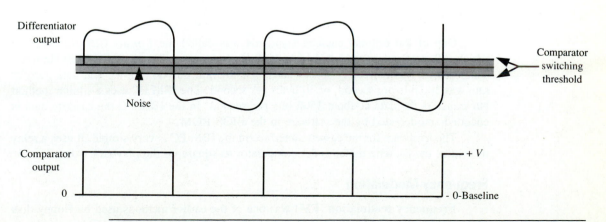

Differentiator output

Noise

Comparator switching threshold

Comparator output

+ V

0

- 0-Baseline

FIGURE 7.16
DC restoration

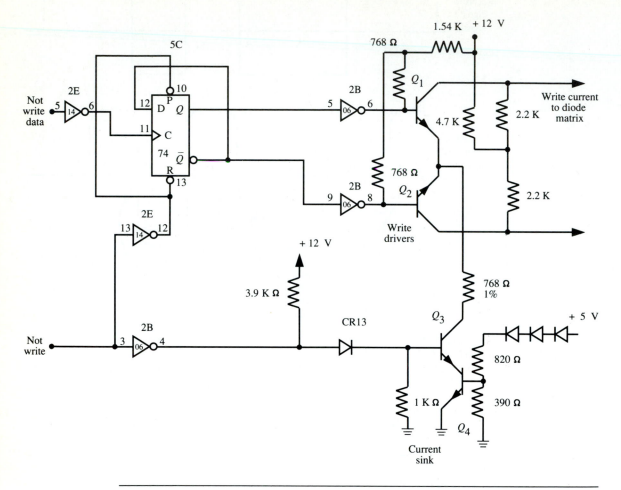

FIGURE 7.17
Write current circuit

One of the original cassette standards was called the *Kansas City standard*, in which a 0 state was represented by a 2400-Hz tone and a 1 state was a 1200-Hz tone. This method was extremely speed- and noise-tolerant but very slow. The data-transfer rate was 300 bits per second, or 30 bytes per second. The IBM PC uses a similar method but transfers the data at about 1500 bits per second. In the IBM PC the cassette data is encoded and decoded by the software in the BIOS ROM.

The hardware for the cassette interface in the IBM PC is very simple. It uses a relay to control the cassette motor and a comparator to square up the playback data.

Frequency Modulation

Frequency modulation (FM) was one of the earlier methods used by floppy disk systems. This method is also referred to as **single-density recording.** FM is similar to

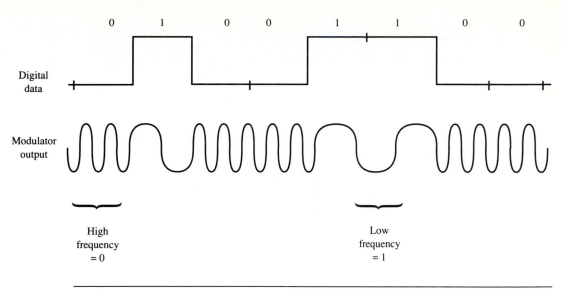

FIGURE 7.18
Frequency shift keying

frequency shift keying in that the frequency is shifted to represent the state of the data bits. It differs in that the flux reversals are used to decode the data instead of a frequency discriminator.

Frequency modulation follows two basic rules:

Rule 1 A flux transition is recorded at the beginning of every bit cell.

Rule 2 A flux transition is recorded in the middle of a bit cell if the current data bit is a 1 state.

This means that 1s are recorded at *twice* the frequency of 0s. The term **bit cell** is used to define the time allotted for 1 bit. Figure 7.19 shows that when 1s are recorded, two flux reversals are recorded per bit. When 0s are recorded, one flux reversal is recorded.

Decoding this method is simple and requires only timing circuitry. This method can also be decoded by software timing loops if the processor is fast enough. This method of encoding is known as *self-clocking,* since there is always one flux reversal per bit. Since the rules state that there must be a flux reversal at the beginning of a bit cell, we refer to the first reversal as the *clock*. If within a specified period of time another flux reversal is encountered, the bit must be a 1.

Modified Frequency Modulation

Modified frequency modulation (MFM) is a revised version of FM and is the most common encoding method used today. The major difference from FM encoding is that only *one* flux reversal is required for each bit cell regardless if the bit is a 1 or a 0. Recall that FM requires *two* flux reversals for a 1 state. For this reason, *twice* as many

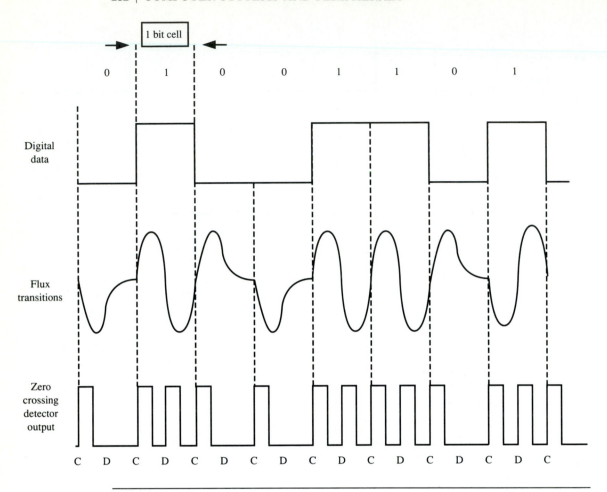

FIGURE 7.19
(FM) frequency modulation encoding/decoding

bits can be recorded using the MFM method than the FM method. Hence the term **double density** is used.

Modified frequency modulation follows two basic rules:

Rule 1   A flux reversal is written in the *middle* of the bit cell if the current bit is at a logic 1 state.

Rule 2   A flux reversal is recorded at the *beginning* of the bit cell if the current bit *and* the preceding bits are at a logic 0 state.

There is one important factor to consider when using MFM. If the preceding bit was at a logic 1 state *and* the current bit is at a logic 0 state, *no* flux reversal is recorded for this bit cell. For this reason, the MFM method *is not* self-clocking; therefore, an external clock generator circuit must be used. The external clock generator circuit usually contains a **phase-locked loop** that is synchronized during a steady data stream of all 0s. MFM is illustrated in Figure 7.20.

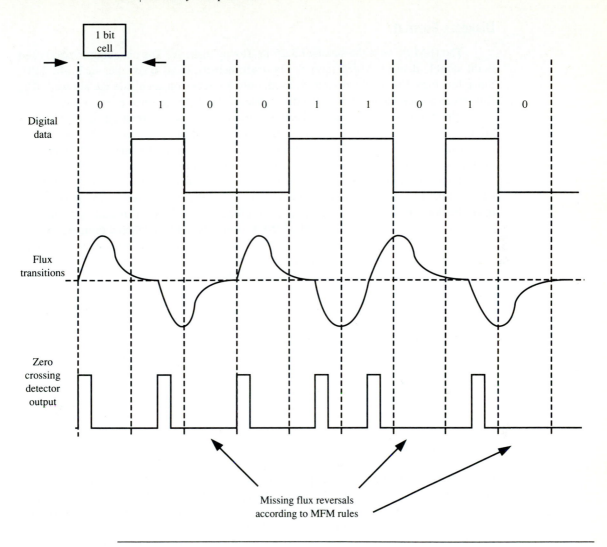

FIGURE 7.20
Modified frequency modulation

7.3 THE FLOPPY DISK SUBSYSTEM

The major disadvantage of magnetic tape storage is that the data must be recorded *sequentially* and read back *sequentially*. The task of reading random blocks is difficult and time consuming because the tape must be rewound, searched, read, and rewound again. The **floppy disk** is a more efficient way of recording and retrieving data because individual tracks of the floppy disk can be accessed at random. As was discussed earlier, the floppy diskette is a thin plastic disk coated with ferromagnetic particles. The read/write head is mounted on a slide mechanism and records circumferential tracks on the diskette as it rotates.

Diskette Format

The IBM PC uses the standard 5.25-in. floppy diskette. The encoding method used is the double-density, MFM format. The track density is 48 tracks per inch (48 TPI). Since less than 1 in. of the diskette is used, only 40 tracks on each side are allowed. The flux reversals are recorded at a maximum rate of 250 kHz, or once every 4 µs.

When a diskette is used for the first time, there is no information on it. The first thing we must do is to organize the diskette so we will know where to store data. We must also keep a record of where the data is stored so we can find it later on. This process of organizing the diskette is known as **formatting** the diskette.

To illustrate this concept more clearly, think of a file cabinet with many drawers in it. When the file cabinet is new, all the drawers are empty. If we start storing information in all the drawers, finding a specific piece of information will be a difficult task. Instead, we organize the file cabinet by labeling the drawers and putting labeled dividers in each drawer. In the front of the file cabinet we keep an index of all the information we have stored in the cabinet. Now the task of finding a specific piece of information is a simple one. All that is required is to look at the index, open the specified drawer, and go to the specified divider.

The diskette is organized in very much the same way. Think of each **track** as a drawer in the cabinet, and think of each **sector** as a divider in the drawer. A formatted diskette also contains a **directory,** which is like our index. The directory contains the name of the file and a pointer to the track and sector where the file begins. The diskette also contains a **file allocation table (FAT)** which keeps a record of which sectors are free for storing information and which are in use by existing files.

There are actually *two* levels of formatting involved here. The first is the physical track and sector format, which is like the physical file cabinet. The second level is the logical format, where the FAT and the root directory are written. Sometimes the actual operating system is also written on the disk at this time.

The IBM PC disk operating system (DOS) formats each track of the diskette into nine sectors containing 512 bytes per sector. This allows 9×512, or 4608, bytes to fit on each track. Since there are 40 tracks, we can store 184,320 bytes of information on each side. If we use both sides, then we can store a maximum of 368,640 bytes on one diskette. This is true only for DOS 2.0 and higher. The older versions, DOS 1.0 and 1.1, used 8 sectors, which limited the storage to 327,680 bytes for a double-sided diskette. In either case, 12 sectors are reserved for directory and FAT information. The 12×512, or 6,144 bytes are not available to the user. The maximum amount of user storage is $368,640 - 6144$, or 362,496, bytes. For convenience the IBM PC diskette drives used today are often referred to as 360 Kb drives. The physical diskette format is illustrated in Figure 7.21.

As we stated before, each track is divided into sectors. Each sector is divided into **fields,** known as the **preamble, header, data,** and **postamble fields.** The preamble consists of **sync bytes,** which are used by the floppy controller for data synchronization. The header contains the ID bytes, which are the track, side, sector, and sector size numbers that the floppy disk controller uses to find where to store or read data. The data field is where the actual data is written to or read from. The postamble is a small gap at the end of the sector, as shown in Figure 7.22.

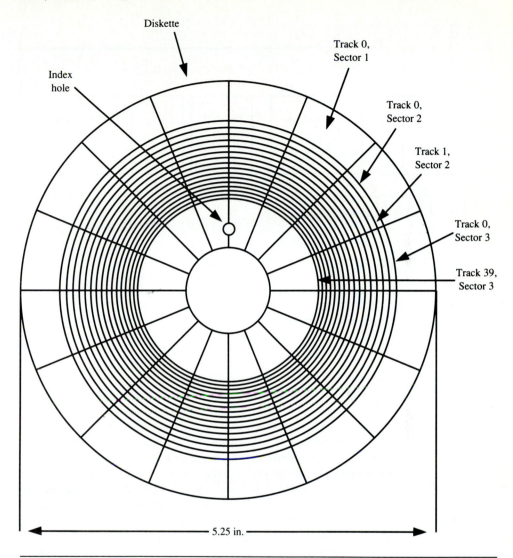

FIGURE 7.21
The formatted diskette

The Floppy Disk Adapter

The floppy disk adapter used in the IBM PC contains all the electronics required to interface a standard floppy disk drive to the system. The floppy disk adapter can be broken down into four basic parts: the floppy disk controller IC, a phase-locked loop data separator, a write precompensation circuit, and the drive-control register.

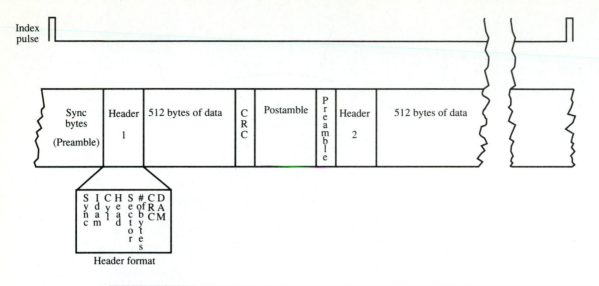

FIGURE 7.22
Typical track format

The heart of the floppy disk system is the floppy disk controller IC. The floppy disk controller used in the IBM PC is the NEC UPD 765 at location U_6 on the floppy disk adapter. This IC is itself a small computer and completely controls the floppy disk drive. The main system processor issues a list of instructions to the floppy disk controller by way of I/O instructions to I/O addresses 3F4H and 3F5H. The floppy disk controller then takes over and performs the requested operation. Data bits are transferred by using the DMA channel. No processor intervention is required unless there is an error or the operation is complete. When the requested operation is complete, or an unrecoverable error occurs, the floppy disk controller signals the system processor by raising one of the interrupt lines. Further information on the floppy disk controller IC can be found in the NEC UPD 765 data sheet or the INTEL 8272 data sheet.

The data separator and clock recovery circuit consist of a digital one-shot (ICs U_{22} and U_{23}), a phase-locked-loop clock generator (ICs U_{19}, U_{20}, U_{21}, and U_{24}), and a standard data generator (ICs U_{25} and U_{26}), as shown in Figure 7.23. When the floppy disk controller IC is not reading data from the disk, it drives the + VCO SYNC line low, which causes the phase-locked loop to synchronize to the 500-kHz write clock reference frequency. When the floppy disk controller IC receives a read command from the processor, it holds the line + VCO SYNC low for a specified time after the index hole. The + VCO SYNC line is then raised during the all-zero sync byte portion on the diskette, which causes the phase-locked loop to synchronize itself to the received flux reversals. Recall that one of the rules of MFM is that a flux reversal is recorded at the beginning of the bit cell if the current and preceding bits are at a 0 state. The circuit remains in synchronization with the incoming data stream until the read operation is complete.

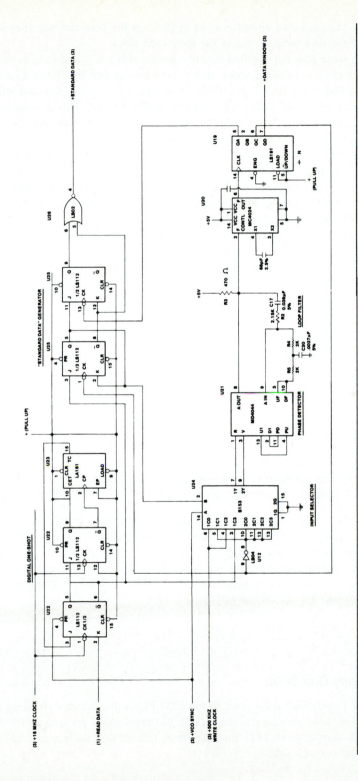

FIGURE 7.23
Phase-locked-loop data separator (Courtesy of International Business Machines Corp.)

The standard data circuit is used to position the received one flux reversal in the middle of the data window that is the recovered clock.

The write precompensation circuit consists of ICs U_{10} and U_{11}, as shown in Figure 7.24. This circuit shifts the write data pulse *early* or *late* by 250 ns as commanded by the floppy disk controller. This circuitry was added to improve the data reliability due to the high degree of peak shift common to the MFM method. This is more apparent on the inner tracks because of the tight bit density, where the frequency is at or near the maximum frequency response of the medium.

The drive-control register is an *8-bit write only* port consisting of ICs U_{12}, U_{15}, U_{16}, U_{17}, and U_{29}. The address of this port is I/O address 3F2H. This register is used to select *one* of *four* drives and to control the motors in all four drives. This register is also used to control the DMA and interrupt enables from the adapter. A breakdown of these bits is given next.

Bits 0 and 1 are the drive-select bits, decoded as follows:

Bit	1	0	Drive Select
	0	0	0, drive A
	0	1	1, drive B
	1	0	2, drive C
	1	1	3, drive D

1. Bit 2 resets the floppy disk controller IC when clear. This bit *must* be set for the floppy disk controller to operate.
2. Bit 3 is the DMA and interrupt enable bit. This bit *must* be set to the 1 state to allow the DMA and interrupts to pass.
3. Bits 4, 5, 6, and 7 are the drive motor control bits.

   - Bit 4 turns on the drive A motor if set.
   - Bit 5 turns on the drive B motor if set.
   - Bit 6 turns on the drive C motor if set.
   - Bit 7 turns on the drive D motor if set.

A schematic of the drive control register is shown in Figure 7.25.

The floppy disk adapter is completely buffered from the system bus by IC U_{30}, which is an *8-bit bus transceiver*.

The internal I/O addresses are decoded by ICs U_{13}, U_{28}, and U_{29}.

The internal timing is generated by a 16-MHz crystal oscillator and divided down by ICs U_2 and U_3, as shown in Figure 7.24.

The Floppy Disk Drive

The floppy disk drive used in the IBM PC is the industry standard 5.25-in. type. This type of disk drive rotates the disk at 300 revolutions per minute (300 rev/min) and has a track density of 48 TPI. Since less than 1 in. of disk surface is used, only 40 tracks are allowed on each side.

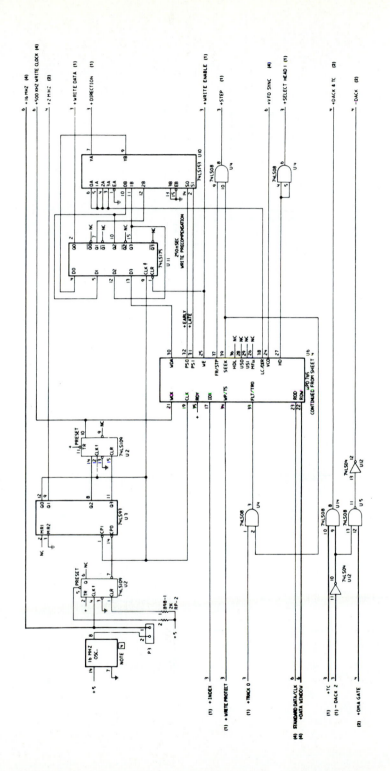

FIGURE 7.24
Write precompensation and timing (Courtesy of International Business Machines Corp.)

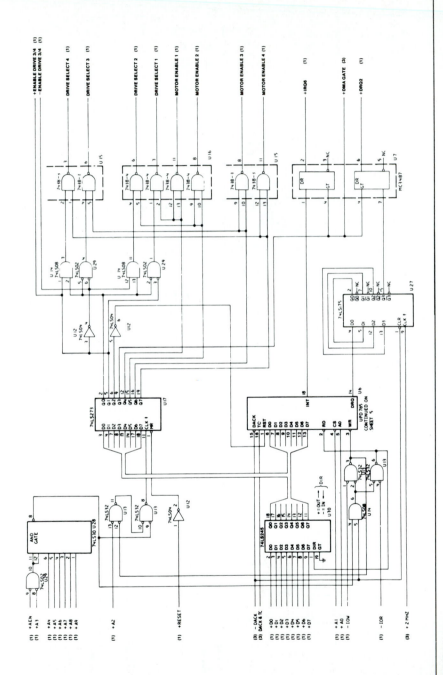

FIGURE 7.25
Drive-control register (Courtesy of International Business Machines Corp.)

A popular variation of this type of drive is known as **quad density.** The quad-density disk drive uses a track density of 96 TPI, which allows twice the storage of the double-density disk drive. Every other aspect of the drive is the same as the double-density drive. Do not confuse the 96-TPI quad-density diskettes with the new 1.2-megabyte "AT" style used in the IBM PCAT. The IBM PCAT high-density diskettes are recorded at *twice* the data rate and *are not* compatible with the units discussed herein.

The recording rate is 250,000 flux reversals per second, which is 250,000 bits per second in MFM format. If FM is used, the data rate is 125,000 bits per second.

The disk drive may have one or two sides, which are referred to as single-sided or double-sided, respectively.

The floppy disk drive consists of the following major assemblies:

- The **spindle assembly** clamps the diskette on center and rotates it at 300 rev/min.
- The **head and carriage assembly** positions the read/write head over the desired track for reading or writing the data.
- The **index sensor** assembly reports the presence of the index hole in the diskette.
- The **track 00 sensor** reports when the head is over track zero.
- The **write-protect sensor** reports the presence of a write-protected diskette.

Some drive manufacturers offer two additional options. An optional **door open sensor** signals the control electronics when the diskette door is open. An optional **head load solenoid** is used to reduce diskette wear. This allows the read/write head to contact the diskette only during read or write operations.

The *electronics board* contains the electromechanical interface for the floppy disk controller and can be broken down into the following sections: the read amplifier, write driver, spindle motor control, carriage motor control, and the sensor amplifiers.

Figure 7.26 shows a functional block diagram of the floppy disk drive.

Since there are so many manufacturers of the industry standard 5.25-in., 48-TPI unit, it is difficult to be specific about all of them. If you have a good understanding of the basics of the unit, you should not have a problem working with any manufacturer's drive. For this reason we will be as general as possible.

The Spindle Assembly   The spindle assembly is driven by a servo-controlled DC motor. The older **full-height** floppy drives used a separate motor coupled by a belt to the spindle assembly. The motor also contained a small generator, which provided the feedback to the motor control circuit, as shown in Figure 7.27. The output of the internal generator, which was often referred to as the *tachometer,* was compared with a reference voltage and fed to the motor driver circuit, which regulated the speed to the desired value.

The newer **half-height** disk drives use a "pancake" brushless-type motor that is directly coupled to the spindle shaft. These drives are often referred to as *direct-drive* units. This new design relieves two major problems found on the older units. The first problem was *belt slippage,* which caused the spindle speed to vary. The second problem was *brush wear,* which resulted in poor contact to the commutator. This introduced noise in the electronic circuitry and also caused motor speed variation.

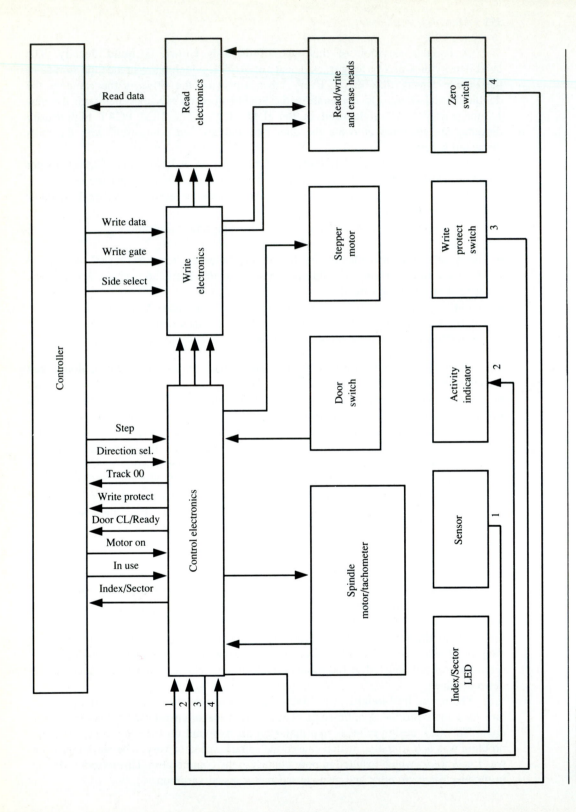

FIGURE 7.26
The floppy disk drive block diagram

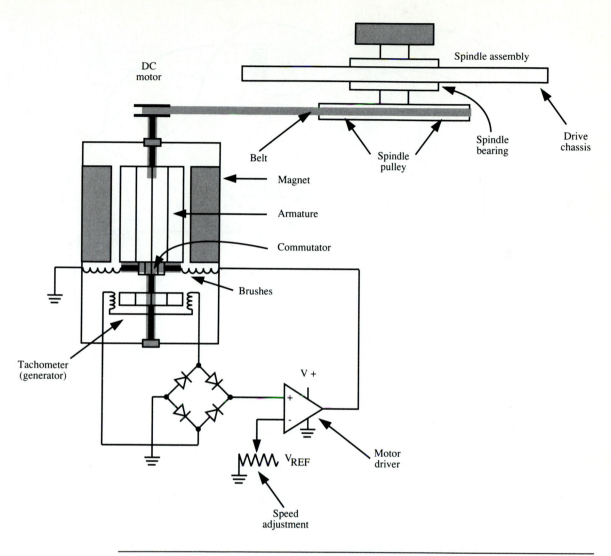

FIGURE 7.27
Belt-driven DC spindle motor

The new motor is a multiphase synchronous type requiring no brushes. The armature (rotor) is a permanent magnet that rotates in an alternating magnetic field (stator) as shown in Figure 7.28.

The direct-drive method has proven to be a more reliable design and has better speed regulation accuracy.

The diskette is mechanically coupled to the spindle by means of the *spindle clamp assembly*. This assembly also centers the diskette onto the spindle by the means of a flexible plastic cone known as the **centering cone.** The centering cone fits snugly into the inside diameter of the diskette and then into the inside diameter of the spindle as shown in Figure 7.29.

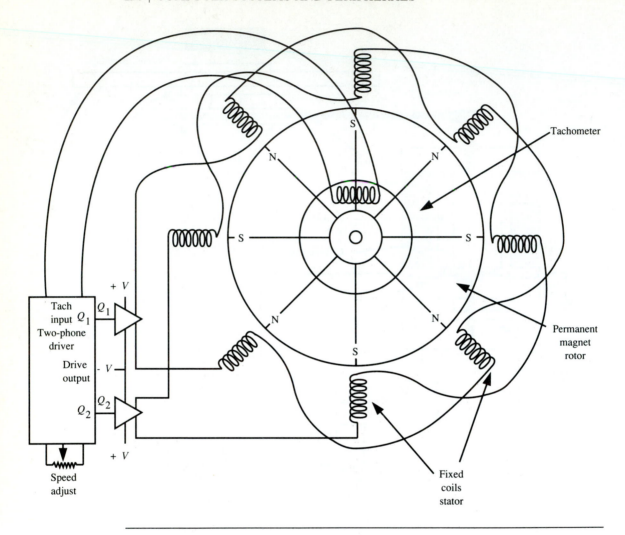

FIGURE 7.28
The direct-drive brushless motor

The speed and the centering of the diskette are *very critical* to the reliability of the read data. Recall that we are using FM techniques to encode the data, so any variation in speed causes a shift in frequency. If the diskette is not correctly centered on the spindle, the diskette will **wobble** as it rotates, which is called **runout.** This causes amplitude variations in the read signal and may also cause *cross talk* from adjacent tracks due to the alignment error. This will distort the read signal and cause read errors during playback.

The Head and Carriage Assembly The head and carriage assembly is the most *critical* part of the floppy disk drive and requires the most attention. This assembly is made up of the read/write head mounted on a sliding carriage. The carriage is driven by an electromechanical actuator, which is a multiphase stepper motor.

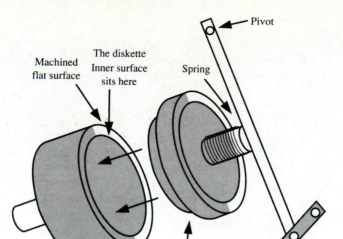

FIGURE 7.29
Centering and clamping cone

The read/write heads used on the 5.25-in. floppy drives are similar from one manufacturer to another. These heads are very much like the earlier example with *one* difference. The heads also contain *erase windings* and *pole pieces*. The pole pieces are mounted alongside both ends of the read/write gap, as shown in Figure 7.30. This design is known as *tunnel erase*. It trims the top and bottom *fringes* of the recorded flux reversals. It is *not* meant to be used as an erase head to erase the data fields. The resultant recorded pattern is shown in Figure 7.31. The tunnel erase head reduces the effect of track-to-track cross talk and minimizes the errors induced by minor **runout** problems on the diskette or diskette drive.

Head 0 is the lower head, which is mounted *rigidly* onto the carriage assembly. Head 1 (in double-sided drives) is mounted onto a *spring-loaded flexure* assembly. This allows the upper head to conform to the lower head and places even pressure on the diskette. Like the tape recorder, the diskette must be in physical contact with the read/write head during operation. In the case of single-sided drives, a spring-loaded pressure pad known as the **head load pad** keeps the diskette in contact with the head.

The actuator that drives the head and carriage is a stepper motor. The types of actuators vary greatly among different manufacturers, but there are basically three types used today: the lead screw, band drive, and the grooved disk types.

The **lead screw–driven actuator** works just like a screw and nut. The stepper motor shaft is coupled directly to the lead screw, which threads into the carriage

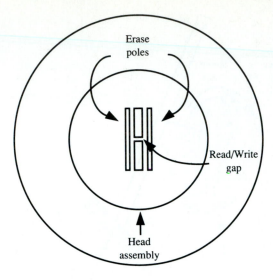

FIGURE 7.30
Erase poles in head

assembly. As the stepper motor rotates, the carriage assembly is pulled toward or pushed away from the stepper motor, as shown in Figure 7.32.

The **band-driven actuator** works like a belt and pulley. The band is pinned to one end of the carriage assembly and then wrapped *one turn* around the motor pulley and pinned to the opposite end of the carriage. The band is also pinned to the pulley to prevent any slippage. As the motor rotates, the carriage assembly is pulled in or out by the band winding on the pulley, as shown in Figure 7.33.

The **grooved disk actuator** works like a phonograph record. The stepper motor shaft is coupled to the grooved disk, which has a spiral groove cut into it. The carriage assembly has an indexing pin, which is usually a small ball bearing that fits into the groove on the grooved disk. As the grooved disk rotates, the carriage assembly follows the indexing pin in the groove, thus causing the carriage to slide in or out, as shown in Figure 7.34 (p. 300).

The Index Sensor   Recall that the floppy diskette used in the IBM PC has a single index hole punched into it. The control electronics uses this index hole to tell where to start to write the sectors and when to start to look for sectors. The control electronics also uses this index to tell when *one* revolution has elapsed.

The index sensor is made up of a phototransistor and a light-emitting diode (LED). The LED is mounted below the *index hole* in the diskette. The phototransistor is mounted above the index hole, as shown in Figure 7.35 (p. 301). As the diskette rotates, the index hole passes between the sensor elements. As the index hole passes, light from the LED passes through the hole to the phototransistor, causing the phototransistor to turn on and generate the index pulse. The timing of the index pulse is critical and may be adjusted by moving the phototransistor. This procedure will be discussed in the next part of this chapter.

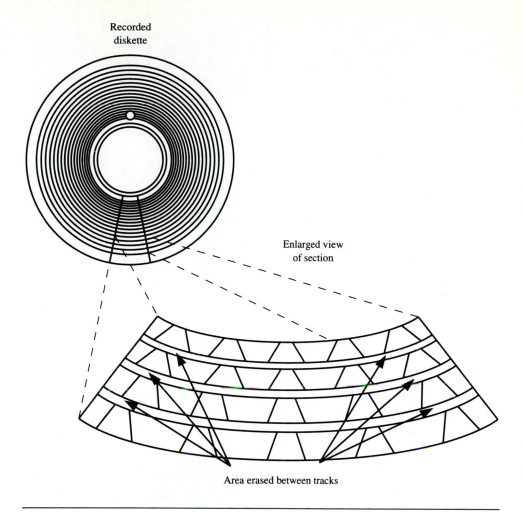

Recorded
diskette

Enlarged view
of section

Area erased between tracks

FIGURE 7.31
Tunnel erease (between tracks)

The Track 00 Sensor The floppy diskette drive used in the IBM PC uses a sensor to indicate when the read/write head is over track 0. This sensor is called the **track 00** sensor. The control electronics uses the output from this sensor when a **recalibrate** operation is performed. When the system is first turned on, the controller does not know what track the disk drive is on, so a recalibrate command is issued to the controller. The controller issues step pulses to the disk drive until the disk drive reaches track 0.

Two types of sensors are used in the disk drive, depending on the manufacturer. Most use the LED and phototransistor arrangement. This type has a small flag mounted at the rear of the carriage assembly. The track 00 sensor is mounted on the rear chassis of the disk drive. When the read/write head reaches track zero, the flag passes between the sensor elements, as shown in Figure 7.36 (p. 302). This signals the controller that the disk drive head is at track 0.

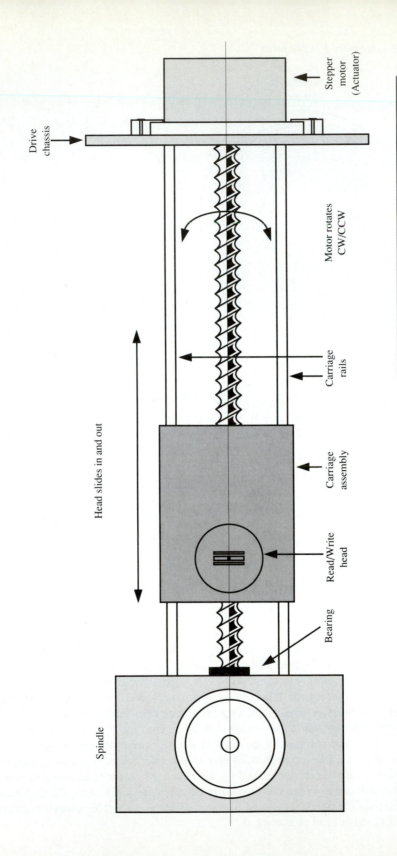

FIGURE 7.32
Lead screw—driven actuator

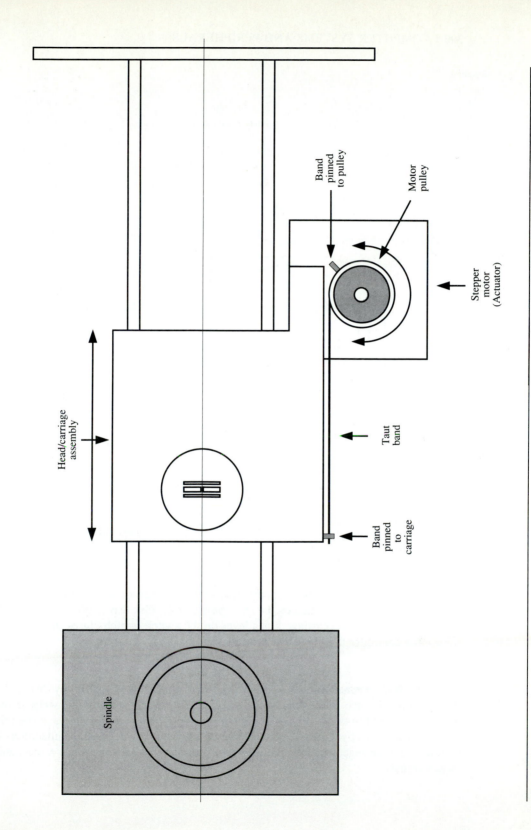

FIGURE 7.33
Band-driven actuator

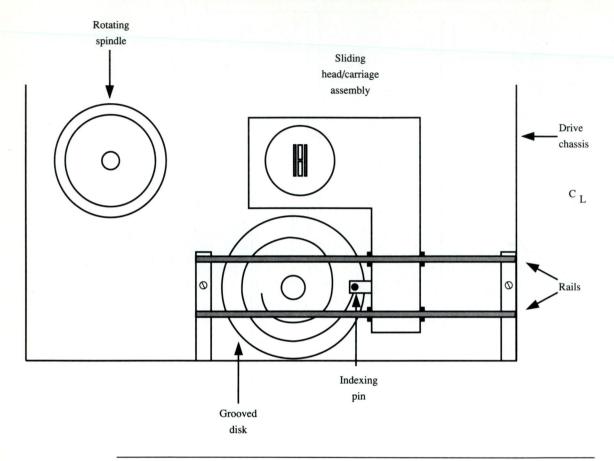

FIGURE 7.34
Grooved disk actuator

Some manufacturers use a mechanical switch instead of the photosensor. In this case, a small switch is mounted on the rear chassis of the disk drive. When the read/write head is over track 0, the carriage hits a lever on the switch, which closes the switch and signals the controller that the drive is at track 0.

The Write Protect Sensor   Recall from our discussion of the floppy diskette that there is a small notch in the side of the diskette. This notch is called the **write-protect notch** and is used to signal the controller when a write-protected diskette is in the drive. The notch is sensed by the write-protect sensor on the disk drive. Most manufacturers use a photosensor arrangement just like the index sensor, whereas others use a mechanical switch instead.

FIGURE 7.35
The index sensor

The Electronics Board   The electronics board contains the circuitry to interface the outputs of the various sensors to the controller. The motor drivers and the read/write amplifier circuitry are also contained on the electronics board. Some manufacturers put the spindle motor electronics on a separate board.

The read amplifier was discussed earlier and applies to every disk drive with which we are familiar. Some designs put the differentiator first and the amplifier second, but the function is basically the same. The double-sided drives also have a diode head-switching matrix in front of the read amplifier, as shown in Figure 7.37.

Figure 7.37 shows the schematic of the head-switching circuit for the IBM diskette drive type 1. The side-select signal comes from the control electronics into pin 9 of IC 2E. The output of IC 2E is fed to two open collector buffers, one inverting and one noninverting, which are ICs 2B pin 1 and 3E pin 13, respectively. The outputs of the buffers are fed to the head-switching transistors Q_6 and Q_7 through 750-Ω resistors. The output of the head switching transistors feeds the bias voltage to the head coil center tap. When head 0 is selected, a logical 1 is presented to IC 2E pin 9. This causes transistor Q_7 to turn on and transistor Q_6 to turn off. Diodes CR_2 and CR_3 become forward biased, and diodes CR_7 and CR_8 become reversed biased. The read signal from head 0 reaches the read amplifier through forward-biased diodes CR_{11} and CR_{12}. The read signal from head 1 is blocked because diodes CR_7 and CR_8 are reversed biased. A similar situation holds true during writing except that the bias voltage is raised to $+12$ V by transistor Q_5.

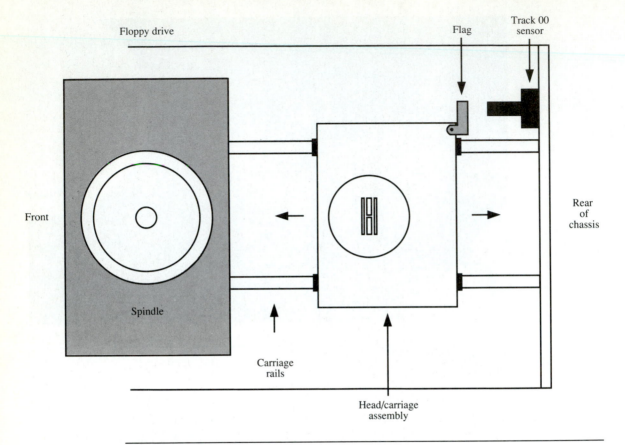

FIGURE 7.36
Track 00 sensor and flag

The design of the switching matrix differs from one manufacturer to another, but their function is basically the same.

The carriage stepper motor driver is contained on the electronics board and uses the step and direction signal from the controller to drive the carriage motor. The circuitry used is basically a bidirectional shift register with power drivers on the outputs. Since the designs vary greatly, we will not go into detail here.

7.4. FLOPPY DISK DRIVE ADJUSTMENTS AND ALIGNMENT

The floppy diskette drive is a delicate electromechanical device that requires periodic maintenance. The floppy diskette drive has proven to be one of the highest-failure items in a microcomputer system due to environmental contamination, user abuse, and mechanical wear. Many floppy disk drive problems can be solved by a cleaning and minor adjustments. In this section we cover the procedures required for the alignment and test of the floppy disk drive. Caution: The floppy diskette drive is a *delicate*

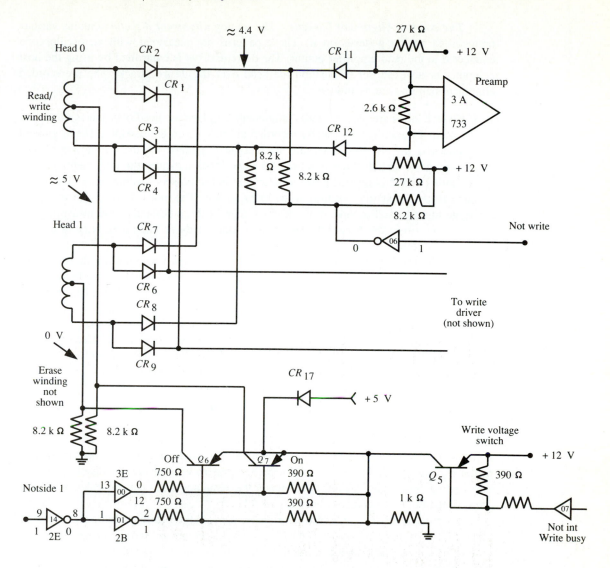

FIGURE 7.37
Head-switching diode matrix

instrument and must be handled *with care. Do not* overtighten or pry any parts when making adjustments.

Alignment Diskette

The **alignment diskette** is an essential tool for making any adjustment to the floppy diskette drive. This alignment diskette is a prerecorded standard to which all adjustments are made. There are two types of alignment diskettes, analog alignment and digital alignment diskettes.

The Analog Alignment Diskette The *analog alignment diskette* contains various prerecorded analog patterns on it. These patterns are measured with an oscilloscope connected to the read amplifier output. The diskette drive is controlled by using the host computer or an exerciser to position the head over the desired track. The prerecorded alignment patterns are as follows:

1. **Cat's-eye lobes** are used for radial alignment, to place the head over the centerline of the desired track. This is usually recorded at track 16 on the diskette. The alignment is checked by visually observing the cat's-eye pattern on the oscilloscope. The percentage of size difference between the two lobes indicates the alignment error.
2. An **index burst** is recorded 200 μs after the index pulse's leading edge. The index burst is used to set the position of the index sensor. The index timing is measured by triggering the oscilloscope on the leading edge of the index pulse and measuring the time delay from the trigger to the burst, or start of data. The index burst is usually located on tracks 1 and 34 of the diskette.
3. **Azimuth burst sets** are recorded on one of the inside tracks of the diskette. The azimuth bursts are used to measure the amount of rotational angular error between the head gap and the prerecorded track. The bursts are usually recorded at ±12, ±15, and ±18′ angles. The measurement is made in a similar manner as the index measurement, with the oscilloscope sweep speed set to display the desired burst.
4. **Constant amplitude and frequency carrier waveforms** of 1f and 2f are recorded to measure the head frequency response characteristics. These tracks are also useful for checking the presence of diskette runout and speed variation problems.

The Digital Alignment Diskette The *digital alignment diskette* is a recent development that in some cases eliminates the need for any test equipment. Like the analog diskette, it contains special prerecorded patterns. The patterns are actual data patterns recorded *intentionally* out of alignment at fixed intervals. A measurement is made by reading successive sectors of a desired pattern until an error is encountered. By determining how many sectors were read, the resultant error can be calculated. The prerecorded digital alignment tracks are as follows:

Progressive offset sectors are recorded to measure the **radial alignment,** or how far the head is off the track centerline. On this track the sectors are written progressively off center. The even sectors are written progressively offset toward the outside edge, whereas the odd sectors are written progressively offset toward the spindle, or inside edge. A measurement is made by sequentially reading all the sectors on the track and then comparing how many good even sectors against how many good odd sectors were read.

Alternate offset sectors are recorded on several tracks to measure the presence of runout of the diskette. All the odd sectors are recorded at a fixed amount toward the spindle, whereas the even sectors are recorded away from the spindle. The measurement is made by reading every sector on the track. If an error is encountered, it is an indication of runout.

The index mark is a special format recorded using filler bytes in the header area. The measurement is made by counting how many filler bytes are read after the index pulse.

The azimuth rotation pattern is recorded in a manner similar to that of the progressive offset track, except that the sectors are recorded progressively off angle. The measurement is made the same way as the progressive offset track.

Disk Drive Exercisers

The **disk drive exerciser** is a piece of test equipment that eliminates the need for the host computer system to make tests and adjustments of the floppy disk drive. Exercisers range in price and performance from cheap manual units to fully automatic units that make sophisticated analog measurements as well. Some units use the analog diskette, and some require a special digital diskette. Since there are so many different types, you will have to refer to the manufacturer's manual for the operation.

Removal and Installation

The removal and installation of the floppy diskette drive in the IBM PC is quite simple but must be done *carefully*. Follow the procedure, being careful to avoid static discharge to any internal components. This is usually done using a grounded wrist strap and working over an antistatic mat.

1. Remove the five cover screws on the rear of the system unit cover. Carefully slide off the cover.
2. If the A disk drive is to be removed, *carefully* mark and remove *all* the adapter boards. This is necessary to get access to the mounting screws of the A drive.
3. Remove the *two* side mounting screws holding the floppy disk drive.
4. Remove the *one* screw on the *bottom* of the case inside the *hole* under the floppy disk drive.
5. Slide the floppy disk drive *partially* out and remove the 34-pin ribbon cable and the 4-pin power cable from the disk drive. Remove the ground wire if one exists.
6. Carefully slide the floppy disk drive all the way out.

Visual Inspection

The *first* thing you should do after removing the diskette drive is to inspect it visually. The problem may be as simple as a write-protect tab that has fallen off a diskette and become lodged somewhere in the mechanism. A careful inspection should be made of the head assembly for oxide buildup or foreign objects or debris. Check that the head and carriage moves freely in and out without *binding*. Foreign objects on the carriage rails may cause binding. Check for bent or broken sensors if they are of the mechanical type. Check for loose or broken sensor brackets, especially if the brackets are made of plastic. Do not forget to check for loose or broken wires. Good common sense and a careful inspection may save you hours of work.

Spindle Speed Adjustment

As was discussed earlier in this text, the rotational speed of the floppy disk is very critical for both reliability of the data and for compatibility with other disk drives. Most floppy disk drives with which we are familiar have an adjustment to regulate the spindle speed. The spindle speed adjustment is usually a variable resistor mounted on the spindle motor control board. Some manufacturers do not use a separate motor control board; therefore, the adjustment will be on the main electronics board near the motor control circuitry.

The spindle speed for the 5.25-in. 48-TPI floppy disk drive is set for 300 rev/min. The speed must be regulated to 1% of the set value by the disk drive. The specification is 300 rev/min ± 3 rev/min.

The spindle speed is measured electronically by timing the occurrence of the index pulses. The index pulses are generated by the index sensor every time the index hole in the diskette passes between the index sensor elements. Since the diskette rotates at a speed of 300 rev/min, there will be *five* pulses every second. Using the formula 1 divided by frequency equals time ($1/F = T$) to convert frequency to time gives $1 \div 5 = 0.200$, or one pulse every 200 ms. The measurement is made by connecting an oscilloscope or electronic counter to the index test point on the electronics board of the floppy disk drive. The speed is set by turning the adjustment while the disk drive motor is running and monitoring the index rate. The speed may also be measured by using the host computer and a diagnostic program. Since the index sensor output is fed to the controller, the computer can read the status of the index output and time the occurrence of the index hole. Many programs are available on the market for this purpose.

Many drive manufacturers put strobe marks on the spindle pulley, as shown in Figure 7.38. The strobe marks allow the spindle speed to be set visually by using a flickering light source such as a fluorescent light. The adjustment is made by observing the spindle pulley while turning the adjustment until the strobe marks appear to stand still.

Once the spindle speed is set to the specified value, we test for the presence of any instantaneous speed variation (ISV). Small rapid variations of the spindle speed may be averaged out during the speed adjustment procedures, so they may go unnoticed. These rapid changes can be caused by a bad motor, belt slippage, diskette slippage, or mechanical binding. As was discussed earlier, speed variation is not allowed and must be checked and corrected. The ISV measurement is best made using an analog alignment diskette. The measurement is made by starting the disk drive and seeking the track with the 2f constant carrier frequency waveform on it, which is usually on track 00. Connect the oscilloscope to the read amplifier output test point and set the sweep speed, internally triggered, to display three or four sine waves, as shown in Figure 7.39. The waveform should appear steady, without jitter, after the trigger cycle. While slight jitter is acceptable, excessive jitter is an indication of ISV and *must* be corrected, as shown in Figure 7.40.

If the waveform is unavailable, the drive may be unable to seek the desired track or the head and/or the read amplifier may be dead.

Disk drive bottom view

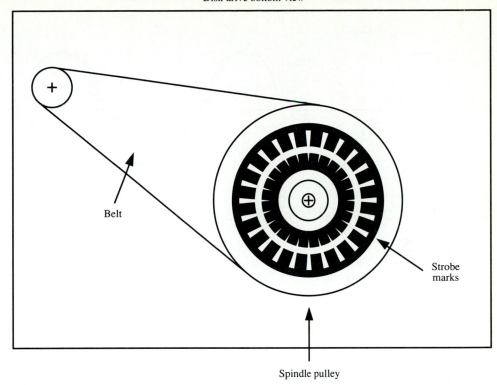

Belt

Strobe marks

Spindle pulley

FIGURE 7.38
Spindle pulley strobe marks

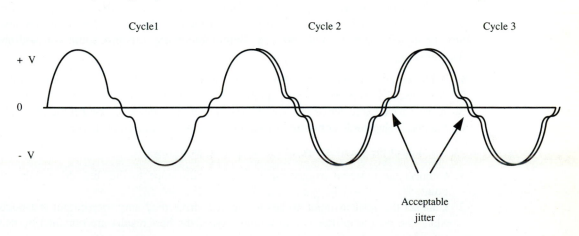

Cycle1   Cycle 2   Cycle 3

+ V

0

- V

Acceptable
jitter

FIGURE 7.39
Acceptable ISV

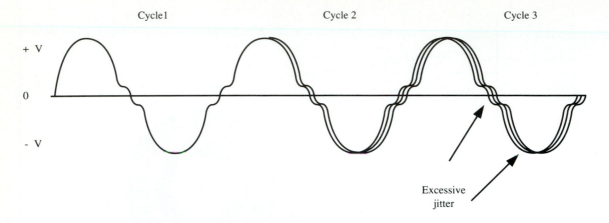

Cycle1   Cycle 2   Cycle 3

+ V

0

- V

Excessive
jitter

FIGURE 7.40
Unacceptable ISV

Disk Head Radial Alignment

The term *radial alignment* means adjustment of the read/write head directly over the track centerline. This alignment is very critical where floppy diskettes must be transferred to other computers. There are two methods, analog and digital, for checking and setting the radial alignment, depending on which test setup and alignment diskette you are using.

The Analog Radial Alignment Method   You must follow the analog procedure if you are using an analog alignment diskette or if the disk drive is so far out of alignment that the digital diskette cannot be read. Before attempting this procedure you will need the following:

1. A known good analog alignment diskette, such as the DYSAN 224/2A or equivalent.
2. A triggered-sweep oscilloscope, preferably a dual-trace type.
3. A disk drive exerciser or the host computer with a program to control the disk drive.
4. Standard hand tools consisting of various screwdrivers and nut drivers.

Connect the oscilloscope to the disk drive as follows:

1. Connect the external trigger input of the oscilloscope to the disk drive index test point.
2. Connect the vertical input probes to the disk drive read amplifier output test points. Since the read amplifier is a differential type, the best results are obtained by using two channels added with one channel inverted.
3. Connect the probe ground wires and the oscilloscope ground to the electronics board ground test point.

Command the disk drive to run and step to track 00, as indicated by the track 00 sensor. This command is known as recalibrate. Adjust the oscilloscope sweep to trigger on the leading edge of the index pulse and to display *one* complete index cycle. The read amplifier output should display a constant-amplitude carrier waveform. If the waveform is uneven or modulated, it is an indication of runout and *must* be corrected before going on. This is explained in the section on centering.

Command the disk drive to seek (step) to the radial alignment track, which is usually track 16. The oscilloscope should display a two-lobed cat's-eye pattern. The amplitude of the lobes should be within 70% of each other, which indicates that the radial alignment is within specified limits. If both lobes are of *equal* amplitude the alignment is perfect or ideal, as shown in Figure 7.41. If a double-sided drive is being tested, command the drive to switch sides and repeat the preceding procedure.

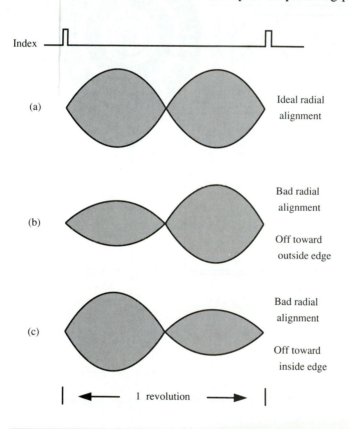

FIGURE 7.41
Cat's-eye lobes

If the amplitude difference is excessive, the head/carriage must be repositioned to bring the lobes to equal amplitude. The exact procedure to perform the radial alignment will differ from one manufacturer to another, so if possible, follow the manufacturer's procedure. In most cases all that is required is to loosen the stepper motor hold-down screws. Once the screws are loose, *carefully and slowly* rotate the stepper motor to make the lobes as equal as possible, as shown in Figure 7.42.

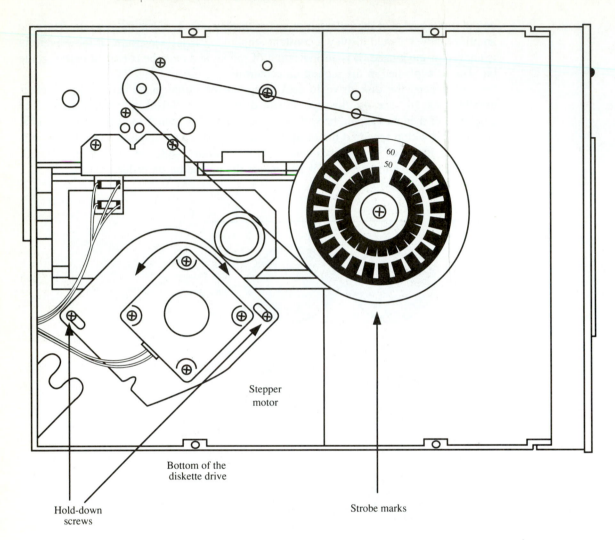

FIGURE 7.42
Radial alignment (Courtesy of International Business Machines Corp.)

On some types of disk drives, the entire carriage assembly may be moved in or out from the spindle to facilitate this adjustment. In this case, loosen the screws that hold the carriage assembly, and reposition the assembly until the lobes are equal by using the eccentric screw at the rear of the carriage, if provided.

Command the disk drive to switch heads to check the other side. If the lobes are unequal, repeat the alignment procedure to try to average the difference between the two heads. If the desired alignment cannot be achieved, the head/carriage assembly must be replaced.

Once the desired alignment has been achieved, you must check that there is not a **hysteresis** problem with the head position. Command the disk drive to step in 10 tracks. Command the disk drive to step back to the alignment track and check the radial alignment again. Repeat this sequence but step *out* and back 10 tracks. If the lobes are not within the desired limits, **hysteresis** exists, that is, the head lands in a different place on a step out than on a step in. The problem could be a binding carriage assembly or a bad stepper motor.

The Digital Radial Alignment Method   The digital method requires that a special digital diagnostic diskette be used. If a host computer is to be used, then a diagnostic program written specifically for that computer and diskette is also required. If an exerciser is to be used, then the exerciser must be designed for that purpose. The digital method eliminates the need for any other test equipment. The procedure is basically the same as the analog method except that you monitor the computer or exerciser display for the results. The output is a series of positive and negative numbers that indicate the number of even and odd sectors read. A reading like $+12$ -12 indicates ideal, or perfect, alignment. If the positive value is greater than the negative value, the alignment error is toward the inside edge. If the negative value is greater than the positive value, the alignment error is toward the outside edge.

Index to Sector Burst

As was discussed earlier, the index pulse signals the disk controller when to begin to look for sectors of data. The index timing is critical and should be checked periodically. As with the radial alignment, there are two methods for checking the timing, the analog and the digital.

The Analog Index to Sector Alignment   The test setup is the same as for the analog radial alignment procedure. Command the disk drive to seek the index burst track, usually tracks 01 and 34. Set the oscilloscope sweep speed to 50 μs per division. The index burst should occur 200 μs after the leading edge of the index pulse. The typical specification is 200 ± 100 μs. Command the disk drive to switch sides and check the timing again. If the index timing is not within the specified value, an adjustment of the index sensor is necessary.

1. Locate the index sensor bracket and loosen the locking screw.
2. *Slowly* move the index sensor until the desired reading is obtained, as shown in Figure 12.43.
3. Tighten the locking screw while watching the timing to make sure the timing has not slipped.
4. Command the disk drive to switch sides and repeat this procedure. Some compromise may be necessary due to variation between the two heads. If the variation is excessive, the head/carriage assembly must be replaced.

The digital method is the same as the analog method except that the oscilloscope is not required.

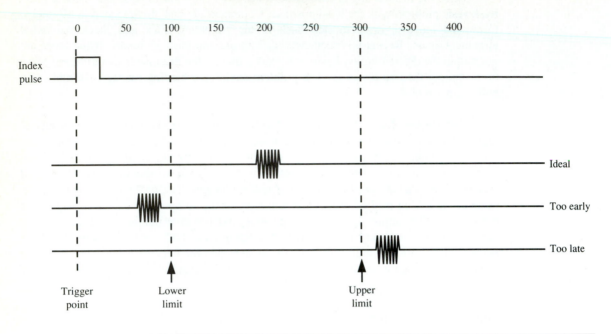

FIGURE 7.43
Index timing

Azimuth Alignment Check

Recall that the term *azimuth* means the rotational error of the read/write head gap. The azimuth is measured in minutes, which are fractions of a degree. The azimuth will usually *not* be out of tolerance, but should *always* be checked whenever the carriage assembly has been disassembled or the disk drive has been dropped. The azimuth should also be checked after the radial alignment has been made on the disk drive with the adjustable carriage assembly. Again there are two methods of measuring azimuth.

The analog azimuth check requires the same setup as the analog radial alignment. Command the disk drive to seek the azimuth track, usually track 34. Adjust the oscilloscope sweep speed to display a set of bursts, as shown in Figure 7.44. Three sets of bursts are recorded at different azimuth angles, usually 12′, 15′, and 18′, respectively. Most disk drives must be within the 15′ range. To measure this, observe the second burst set. If the two outside bursts are smaller than the inside bursts, the azimuth error is within the specification. If either outside burst is larger than the adjacent inside burst, the azimuth error is out of specification. Since the heads are not adjustable, the cause may be the carriage assembly rails, which may be *cocked,* or off center. In the worst case the chassis may be bent due to dropping of the disk drive.

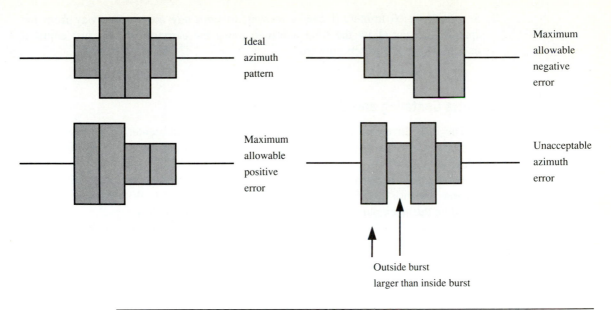

FIGURE 7.44
Azimuth error-indication patterns

The digital azimuth alignment check is similar to the digital radial alignment check. When the diagnostic program is running, a series of numbers is displayed. If the positive and negative numbers are equal, the azimuth alignment is ideal. The numbers $+42$ -42 indicate the drive is capable of reading an azimuth error of $42'$ clockwise and $42'$ counterclockwise.

The Track 00 Detector Adjustment

The track 00 detector adjustment is usually not necessary unless the track 00 sensor has failed or the carriage assembly has been disassembled. The sensor is adjusted by using the same setup as for the analog radial alignment.

1. Adjust the track 00 sensor to the maximum position away from the spindle.
2. Command the disk drive to seek the outermost track.
3. While observing the oscilloscope, command the controller to step one track inward at a time, until a constant 2f carrier frequency waveform is observed.
4. Adjust the track 00 sensor until the sensor indicates track 00.
5. Command the controller to step in one track.
6. The track 00 sensor should indicate the absence of the track 00 signal.
7. Command the disk drive to step out one track.
8. The track 00 sensor should indicate the presence of track 00, and the oscilloscope should display the 2f carrier frequency waveform.

9. Set the track 00 limiter, if one is present, to limit any movement away from the spindle. *Do not* allow the limit adjust to move the carriage inward, just adjust it enough to prevent a step outward.

Diskette Centering and Centering Cone Check

The disk drive should be checked for proper diskette centering for the reasons discussed earlier. Again, there are two methods for checking the centering, the analog and the digital methods.

The analog centering check requires the same setup as the radial alignment. Command the disk drive to seek or recalibrate to track 00. With the oscilloscope triggered on the index pulse, observe the read output waveform. The waveform should be the constant 2f carrier frequency waveform pattern and *must* be *even* in amplitude for the entire diskette revolution, as shown in Figure 7.45(a). Remove and reclamp the diskette a few times while observing the oscilloscope. Any deviation in amplitude is an indication of poor centering. While minor variations of 10% are acceptable, excessive deviation as shown in Figure 7.45(b) and (c) must be corrected, and the entire alignment must be repeated.

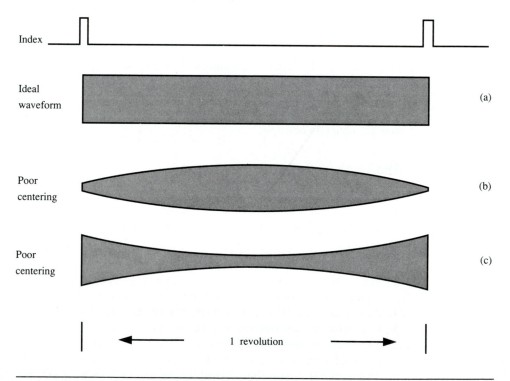

FIGURE 7.45
Centering waveforms

The digital centering check requires that the *entire* alternate offset track be read *without error*. If any sector cannot be read, it is an indication of poor centering and *must* be corrected.

Diskette centering problems are usually due to the centering cone. The centering cone, which is attached to the disk drive door or clamping lever, should be removed and disassembled. It should be inspected for any signs of cracks or distortion and must be replaced if these are evident. Other causes could be a worn spindle bearing or bent spindle shaft.

Read Resolution Check

The read/write head should be checked for the playback frequency response. The setup is the same as for the analog radial alignment. Most analog alignment diskettes have a 1f and a 2f carrier frequency waveform pattern close to each other, usually tracks 32 and 33. Command the disk drive to seek the 1f track. Measure and record the amplitude of the read amplifier output. Command the disk drive to seek the 2f track. Measure and record the amplitude again. The amplitudes of the 1f and the 2f tracks should be close. If they differ greatly, by more than 20%, the head should be replaced. Repeat this procedure on the other side of the diskette by commanding the disk drive to switch sides.

7.5 CLEANING AND PREVENTIVE MAINTENANCE

The read/write head requires periodic cleaning due to oxide buildup from the diskette and outside contaminates such as dust. When the computer system is heavily used, we recommend cleaning the head once a week. When the head is lightly used, cleaning it once a month is sufficient. Cleaning of the read/write head is accomplished by using a commercially available head-cleaning diskette by the system user. Follow the instructions on the cleaning diskette *carefully* and do not *overuse* the cleaning diskette. When the diskette drive is removed from the system for service, it should be thoroughly cleaned. Blow out any dust with *light* compressed air, like a camera lens duster. If the disk drive uses a lead screw positioner, clean the lead screw with alcohol and regrease it. Many manufacturers *do not* recommend lubricating the carriage rails. In any case *do not overgrease anything*. If grease gets on the diskette, *the diskette will be ruined*.

If the disk drive is the single-sided type, there will be a head load pad above the head. This head load pad should be replaced periodically, according to the drive manufacturer's recommendations.

Always exercise extreme caution when working on the carriage and head assembly. If the upper head is pulled up too far, the spring will be weakened. This will reduce the head load force and result in read errors. The head load force should be somewhere between 15 and 30 g as measured with a spring gauge.

If the spindle is the belt-driven type, check the belt for signs of wear. Check to see if the belt will slip too easily by holding the motor pulley and trying to rotate the spindle pulley. Use common sense here; the belt will slip when *forced* but should not slip too easily.

An alignment check should always be performed after any work is done on the disk drive.

7.6 THE WINCHESTER DISK SUBSYSTEM

The hard disk used in the IBM PC uses the flying head Winchester technology. The hard disk drive is quite similar to the floppy disk drive except that the medium is a rigid aluminum disk. The disk rotates at a speed of 3600 rev/min as opposed to 300 rev/min for the floppy diskette. The read/write head actually flies over the disk surface on a cushion of air. Since the head flies very close to the surface, *absolutely no airborne contamination* is allowed inside the head and disk assembly. The head and disk assembly is *sealed* from the outside environment with the exception of a pressure-equalizing filter. There is an air-scrubbing filter inside the head and disk assembly to capture any internal contamination. If contamination is present, it will build up on the leading edge of the head. This will disturb the flight attitude and may cause a loss of pressure or create a vacuum under the head. The loss of pressure will cause the head to crash on the surface and will destroy the disk and head.

When the disk drive is shut off, the head lands on the surface and rests there. For this reason it is *very important not* to rotate the head positioner stepper motor while the disk is not spinning. Since the head is resting on the surface, it is important not to subject the disk drive to mechanical shock. If the disk drive is dropped, the head will bounce on the surface and may chip off some of the oxide coating. The result will be a bad spot on the disk, which may result in a head crash.

Whenever a hard disk drive is removed for service or shipping, the head should be parked on the innermost track in case of shock. Since the inner track is rarely used, damage there will usually not be a problem.

The hard disk drive communicates with the rest of the PC through the adaptor or controller board. Basically, the controller directs the drive's physical operations and performs functions such as telling the drive where to position its heads. There are five commonly used types of hard disk controllers. They are: Modified Frequency Modulation (MFM), Run Length Limited (RLL), Enhanced Small Computer System Interface (ESDI), Small Computer System Interface (SCSI), and Integrated Drive Electronics (IDE) Interface.

The MFM, ESDI, and SCSI each use their own language to control the drive's heads and other operations. The controller translates the PC's commands to the particular language that the drive understands. IDE drives are unique in that they are designed to directly understand the PC's commands. Thus, translation is not necessary. As a result, the controller card for an IDE drive contains far less electronics than the controller card for an MFM, ESDI, or SCSI interface. Sometimes, the IDE controller is incorporated into the motherboard, eliminating the need for a physical controller board.

MFM and RLL

The original technology to encode data onto a hard disk's magnetic surface was plain Frequency Modulation or FM. FM was quickly replaced by a variation called **Modified Frequency Modulation** or **MFM.** As hard disk manufacturing matured and became more reliable, a more efficient encoding system that was originally used on mainframe computers came to the PC. It was called **Run Length Limited** or **RLL.** Actually, MFM and RLL hard disk drives are nearly physically identical. The only difference is in the method used to encode and store data. MFM drives use a 17 sectors-per-track data encoding format and transfer data at a rate of 5 megabits per second. RLL drives use a 26 sectors-per-track format and transfer data at 7.5 megabits per second. As a result, RLL drives are 50% faster and can hold 50% more data than MFM drives.

For example, the Seagate ST251 hard drive can store 40 Mb of data using MFM encoding. The Seagate ST251 hard drive could store 60 Mb of data using RLL encoding. This is not recommended because the ST251 is not RLL certified and may be unreliable with a RLL controller. Furthermore, it will void the manufacturer's warranty. If RLL encoding is used, a drive certified for RLL encoding should be used. The Seagate ST277R is the certified equivalent RLL drive for the ST251.

MFM and RLL drives are quickly becoming obsolete. Most manufacturers have stopped producing MFM and RLL drives. One advantage of the MFM and RLL standard is that they have become mature technologies. That is, they are the most reliable and least expensive of all the different types of interfaces available today. MFM encoding techniques are discussed in detail in section 7.2.

ESDI

The next high-performance standard for the PC is the **Enhanced Small Device Interface (ESDI).** ESDI drives currently offer the highest data transfer rate of any of the popular interfaces. Almost all ESDI disks use RLL data encoding but with a more efficient, high-level interface command language. ESDI drives translate commands on the controller but execute the commands and encode and decode the data on the disk drive electronics. MFM and RLL drives require the controller to translate commands, execute the commands, and encode and decode the data, thus slowing down the data transfer rate. Figure 7.46 illustrates a comparison of the principles of operation of all five types of interfaces.

ESDI data transfer rates typically run about 10 megabits per second. However, many manufacturers offer drives with transfer rates as high as 20 megabits per second. The controller and the disk *must* be certified for the same transfer rate. Because of a more precise control over the head movement, ESDI drives can store more data than the largest MFM or RLL drives can. Thus, ESDI drives offer high reliability and high speed, and permit very large capacity drives to be used. However, they are more costly.

ESDI drives use the same type of cables as MFM or RLL drives, which makes it difficult to tell the drives apart. This can create problems when upgrading or replacing a drive. Even if the cables and controller match physically, there is no guarantee that a drive and controller will support the same interface.

IDE

The **Integrated Drive Electronics (IDE)** interface is the latest controller for the PC. IDE drives are unique because the controller is built directly into the disk. In this

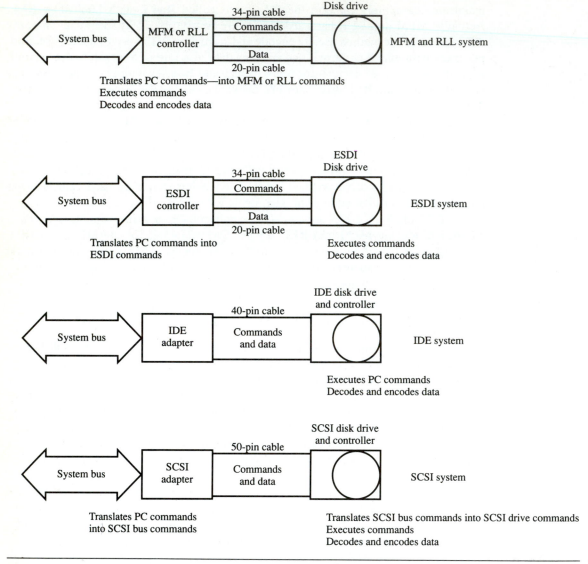

FIGURE 7.46
Hard disk system operation

way, IDE drives can accept commands directly from the computer. Thus, the interface requires very little electronics and is sometimes incorporated directly into the motherboard. Because IDE drives are made to understand PC commands, there is no need for the controller to translate the commands. As a result, IDE drives are surpassing ESDI drives in overall performance.

Improved technology has resulted in greater reliability, higher speed, and larger disk capacities. IDE drives connect to their adapters with a single 40-pin cable that incorporates both control signals and data signals.

IDE technology has some compatibility problems. While the physical interface of all IDE drives is the same, the electronics and method of processing commands may differ among different manufacturers. Thus, the user might be unable to connect an IDE drive from one manufacturer to a system that has an IDE drive from another manufacturer. Almost all IDE drives use RLL encoding. Data transfer rates are typically 12 megabits per second. Thus, IDE offers a simple and economical disk interface with excellent performance.

SCSI

The **Small Computer Standard Interface (SCSI)** has been available on Apple and Commodore computer systems for some time. All of the control circuitry is located on the controller or interface board, thus making SCSI disk drives totally independent. One SCSI controller or adapter card can support a maximum of eight SCSI devices. Many SCSI devices such as disks, printers, mice, modems, CD ROMs, tape drives, etc., are available. Thus, one SCSI controller can be used to control many different devices. Furthermore, daisy chaining up to 64 SCSI devices is possible.

Like IDE, most SCSI drives employ RLL data encoding techniques. Data transfer rates are also about 12 megabits per second. SCSI drives employ one 50-pin cable for both data and control signals. Since one controller operates many devices, SCSI devices can achieve greater speed performance when communicating to each other through the common SCSI controller. For this reason, SCSI has become very popular on network systems. However, non-network users may find the SCSI interface a bit slower. This is because the command language is far more complex than that of the other interfaces. This complexity results in longer times to translate commands. SCSI complexity has also resulted in compatibility problems. Not all SCSI devices will work with every SCSI controller. The new SCSI-II interface addresses this problem. Figure 7.47 illustrates several typical hard disk interface connections.

Hard Disk Specifications

Disk drives are classified according to the interface, speed, and capacity. There are several ways to measure speed: data transfer rate, access time, and seek time. The **seek time** is the amount of time it takes to position the head over a track. The **access time** is the seek time plus the average amount of time it takes to move a sector of data under the head. Since most hard disk drives rotate at 3600 RPM, one complete rotation takes 16.67 ms. Using one-half of 16.7 ms as an average time for the data to rotate under the head results in an additional 8.33 ms. Thus, the access time is equal to the seek time plus approximately 8 ms. Older disk drives have access times around 65 ms. Today, access times below 15 ms are common.

Data transfer rate is a measure of how fast the disk drive can transfer data to the computer under ideal conditions. Capacity is a measure of how much data a formatted disk can hold. Some disk drive manufacturers rate disk drives in unformatted capacity. Thus, you must be careful when comparing or choosing a replacement disk drive.

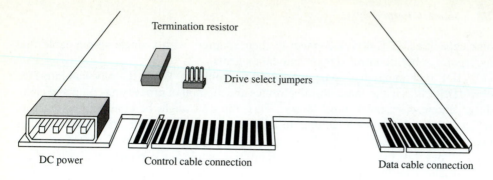

Termination resistor

Drive select jumpers

DC power   Control cable connection   Data cable connection

(a) MFM, RLL, ESDI

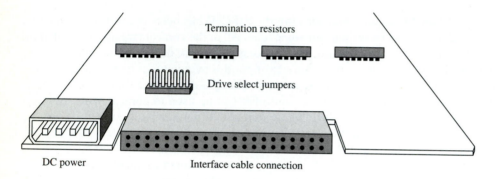

Termination resistors

Drive select jumpers

DC power   Interface cable connection

(b) SCSI

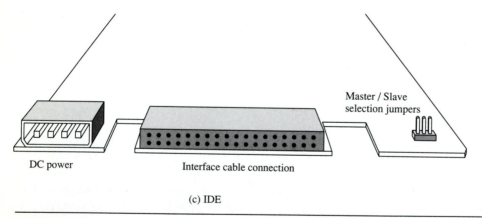

Master / Slave
selection jumpers

DC power   Interface cable connection

(c) IDE

FIGURE 7.47
Hard drive interface connections

Hard Disk Setup

There are three basic steps to setting up or initializing a hard disk drive. These include low-level formatting, partitioning, and high-level formatting of the drive. **Low-level formatting** is where the actual information that defines the tracks and sectors is outlined and written onto the disk platters. IDE drives all come from the manufacturer already low-level formatted. IDE drives should not be low-level formatted. Many IDE drive manufacturers will change the actual number of sectors on a track as the heads move from the outer tracks (larger circumference) to the inner tracks (smaller circumference). **Partitioning** involves the dividing of a physical drive into a number of logical drives. For example, one physical hard disk drive can be divided into logical partitions that are referred to as drive C, drive D, drive E, etc. The final step is the high-level formatting. **High-level formatting** creates the file allocation table (FAT) and the root directory.

Low-level formatting requires that you know the number of tracks, number of heads, and number of sectors per track on a disk. The first step is to record the information in the CMOS setup memory for your system. If you have a standard drive, this information is defined by the drive type number. Simply select the type number in the CMOS setup when prompted to do so. If you do not know the type number for your drive or if you have a nonstandard drive, you can select type 47, which is referred to as the user-defined setup. You will then have to enter the tracks, sectors, and heads information manually. Note that not all CMOS setup programs allow for user-defined setups.

Many disk controllers have the low-level format utility built into ROM on the disk controller card. A popular equivalent is ONTRACK'S Disk Manager program. Disk Manager allows you to mark any bad spots on the disk so that DOS will not try to write data in these locations. This is called a defect list and is generally supplied when you purchase a new drive. Disk partitioning should only be performed using the DOS FDISK program. Experience has shown that other partitioning programs create problems. High-level formatting is accomplished with the DOS format program. The following procedure outlines how to low-level format a hard disk using Disk Manager, set up a single partition using FDISK, and high-level format a disk drive using FORMAT.

1. Insert the ONTRACK Disk Manager program into drive A. At the A> DOS prompt, type DM/M and press the enter key.
2. From the menu, select I to obtain the initialization menu.
3. From the initialization menu, select D to enter the defect list.
4. From the menu, select A to add the first defect. Enter the cylinder number and press the enter key. Enter the head number and press the enter key. Continue in the same manner until all the defects are entered. When all of the defects are entered, press the escape key.
5. Press R to return to the initialization menu. At the question "Do You Want To Write These Changes To The Defect List File (Y/N)?", type N for no and press the enter key.
6. Select I from the menu and press the enter key to begin the initialization. Note the

defect list that is written on the screen and compare it against the list that you typed.

7. Type Y and press the enter key to confirm that the list is correct, or type N and press the enter key if the defect list is incorrect. Disk Manager will then allow you to make the appropriate changes.

8. Select D from the menu and press the enter key to initialize the entire disk.

9. Enter the correct interleave number that is determined from your controller and press enter. A warning message will appear on the screen. Type Y for yes and press the enter key to begin the low-level format. Low-level formatting will take several minutes to complete.

10. When completed, type R and press the enter key to return to the main menu.

11. Type R again and press the enter key to return to DOS.

12. To partition the disk drive, type FDISK at the DOS prompt and press the enter key.

13. At the menu, select 1 and press enter to create a single DOS partition.

14. Select 1, primary DOS partition, and press the enter key. At the message, press the enter key again.

15. Press the escape key to exit FDISK and return to DOS.

16. To high-level format the drive, type FORMAT C:/S at the DOS prompt. The /S option will add the system files for booting to the drive. Confirm by typing Y and press the enter key.

17. Enter the volume label name for the disk drive and press enter.

Note: Minor variations in the above procedure may exist due to the version of Disk Manager, FDISK, and FORMAT you are using.

7.7 TECH TIPS AND TROUBLESHOOTING—T³

Disk drives have one of the highest failure rates of the computer system. This is because disk drives are precision electromechanical devices. The following points are applicable to all types and sizes of disk drives:

1. The read/write head should always be cleaned when a problem arises with playback. Sometimes the head will become magnetized and may have to be demagnetized. If the read signal is dead, the head should be checked for continuity with an ohmmeter.

2. The spindle drive motor has proven to be a high-failure-rate item. The motor should be checked for dead spots and binding. The condition of the drive belt, if it exists, should also be checked. The speed of the motor should be monitored to make sure that no fluctuations exist.

3. The condition of the spindle clamp should be checked for cracks and proper operation. Any problems with the spindle clamp will result in problems with compatibility.

4. The head and carriage assembly should be checked for binding or signs of damage. The actuator components should be checked also. If the actuator is the lead screw type, it should be cleaned and greased.

5. The index sensor elements should be checked for any foreign objects or debris that will obstruct the light path. The brackets should be checked for cracks or looseness.

6. The track 00 sensor should be checked for proper operation. If the sensor is the mechanical switch type, the lever should be checked for bending or cracks.

7. The write-protect sensor should be checked for proper operation. Sometimes objects will lodge in the sensor, preventing it from detecting a protected diskette.

8. Whenever compatibility problems are evident, the radial and index timing alignment should be checked. These are the most critical when switching diskettes from one computer to another.

9. Whenever the disk drive fails, a good visual inspection may save hours of time. The problem may be a write-protect tab or other foreign object lodged in the mechanism.

10. If an alignment is indicated, perform all work carefully. Make all adjustments slowly. Never use force on any part because you may distort the part or mounting bracket. Be careful not to overtighten the locking screws.

11. Never record on the alignment diskette or apply power to the drive while the alignment diskette is clamped in the drive. Any recording on the alignment diskette will ruin it for alignment purposes.

EXERCISES

7.1 Name the low-density storage media made up of a long strip of paper.

7.2 A material that will allow magnetic flux lines to penetrate and pass through easily is a _____ _____ material.

7.3 What is the term used to describe how well a material will hold a magnetic charge?

7.4 If a material can become magnetized and demagnetized easily, it is said to have a high _____.

7.5 What is the most common material used for magnetic recording?

7.6 What is the key component for magnetic recording?

7.7 Name the device that will become magnetized only while an electric current is applied.

7.8 What is actually recorded on the magnetic media?

7.9 Is it possible to record DC onto magnetic media?

7.10 The digital read chain will use a _____ circuit to help restore the digital waveform.

7.11 When the playback signal begins to roll off, the differentiator will begin to _____.

7.12 The process of converting digital data into a recordable pattern is known as _____ the data.

7.13 For what does FSK stand?

7.14 Explain the two rules for frequency modulation.

7.15 Explain the advantage of modified frequency modulation.

7.16 Explain the two rules for modified frequency modulation.

7.17 True or false: There will be a flux reversal for every bit cell in modified frequency modulation.

7.18 How many tracks per inch are on the 5.25-in. double-density diskette?

7.19 One recorded circle on the diskette is known as a _____.

7.20 One track is divided into many _____.

7.21 The part of the diskette that contains the names of the recorded files is the _____.

7.22 The part of the diskette that keeps track of the free sectors is known as the _____ _____ _____.

7.23 How many bytes are contained in one sector?

7.24 Briefly describe the header of a sector.

7.25 When is the VCO synchronized?

7.26 What is the write precompensation for?

7.27 What is the address of the drive-control register?

7.28 At what speed does the 5.25-in. double-density diskette rotate?

7.29 Name three sensor assemblies used on the floppy disk drive.

7.30 Describe the function of the spindle assembly.

7.31 True or false: The direct-drive spindle motor is more reliable.

7.32 Why is proper centering of the diskette important?

7.33   Describe the purpose of tunnel erase.

7.34   The carriage assembly is driven by a _____ motor.

7.35   Name the three types of carriage actuators.

7.36   What does the index sensor sense?

7.37   Describe how the heads are switched.

7.38   What signals from the controller control the carriage stepper motor?

7.39   What is an alignment diskette?

7.40   Name the two types of alignment diskettes.

7.41   When using an oscilloscope to check radial alignment, what pattern is used?

7.42   Is the oscilloscope required when using the digital alignment diskette?

7.43   Describe the indication of correct radial alignment for both analog and digital methods.

7.44   Is it required to check both sides of a disk for correct alignment?

7.45   What is the specification of the index to sector burst?

7.46   Explain azimuth alignment.

7.47   Explain the indication of poor centering.

7.48   What should be checked when poor centering is evident?

7.49   Explain read resolution.

7.50   What should be cleaned periodically by the user?

7.51   What might be the result if the upper head is pulled up too far by the technician?

7.52   Describe the difference between the floppy disk drive and the hard disk drive.

7.53   During use, does the read/write head contact the disk on the hard disk drive?

7.54   What might be the result if contamination were to enter the head and disk assembly?

7.55   Is the hard disk drive sensitive to shock?

7.56   Where should the heads be during shipping of the hard disk drive?

7.57   Crossword Puzzle

ACROSS

4. The first thing that is done to a new diskette.
6. The motor that moves the head from track to track.
8. One recorded circle on the diskette.
10. One millionth of 1 s.
12. A measurement of speed.
13. MFM records in _____.
14. The alignment used to place the head over the track center.
15. A device that lets current flow in one direction only.
17. The notch on the side of the diskette.
19. The ID portion of a sector.
22. Modified frequency modulation.
23. The ability to hold a magnetic charge.
24. Stored data can be called _____.
27. The speed sensor in the motor.
28. Another word for wobble.

DOWN

1. File allocation table.
2. Instantaneous speed variation.
3. A diode that produces light.
4. A type of magnetic material.
5. The last part of a sector.
7. The first part of a sector.
9. A device that senses light.
11. Information on a diskette.
15. Where the file names are stored.
16. The ease in which magnetic flux lines will pass through a material.
18. Part of one track.
20. Frequency modulation.
21. The reference hole on the diskette.
25. Part of a disk drive that centers the diskette.
26. The part of a disk drive that reads and writes data.

CHAPTER EIGHT

PERIPHERAL DEVICES

KEY TERMS

Anode

Asynchronous Serial
   Data

Baud Rate

Cathode

Cathode-ray Tube
   (CRT)

Character Generator

Color Graphics
   Adapter (CGA)

Composite Video

Convergence Yoke

Daisy Wheel Printer

Data Circuit
   Terminating
   Equipment (DCTE)

Data Terminating
   Equipment (DTE)

Deflection Yoke

Dot Clock

Dot-matrix Printer

Dot Pitch

Electrostatic Deflection

Enhanced Graphics
   Adapter (EGA)

Filament

Frame

Framing Error

Full Duplex

Grids

Handshaking

Hard Copy

Half-Duplex

Impact Printers

Interlaced Scanning

Ink Jet Printer

Keyboard Encoder

Laser Printer

Magnetic Deflection

Modem

Modulator-demodulator

Nonimpact Printers

Null Modem

Pixels

Raster

Reactance Scanning

Retrace

RS-232C

Start Bit

Stop Bit

Super VGA (SVGA)

Thermal Dot-matrix
   Printer

Tracking Error

Triads

Video Graphics
   Array (VGA)

8.0 INTRODUCTION

A computer is useless without input and output devices. These devices, also known as peripherals, include keyboards, displays, modems, and printers. In this chapter we discuss the theory of operation of keyboards and video displays. We also review modems and printers.

8.1 KEYBOARDS

The keyboard is the simplest input device on a computer system; it is merely a collection of momentary switches. The outputs of the key switches are fed to electronic circuitry known as the **keyboard encoder,** which converts them into binary-coded values. These values are then fed into the computer, which interprets the key pressed.

The design of computer keyboards has evolved over time and differs among manufacturers. On some of the earlier computers the keyboard output was many parallel wires connected from the key switches into the computer, as shown in Figure 8.1.

To reduce the number of wires required to interface the keyboard, the key switches can be arranged into a *matrix,* as shown in Figure 8.2.

In the matrixed configuration the key switches are arranged as 4 columns by 4 rows of switches. The interface reads the keys by selecting one column at a time and then reading the row outputs. In Figure 8.2, a 16-key keypad was shown for simplicity. The matrixed configuration reduced the wire count from 16 to 8. If we apply the matrixed configuration to the typewriter-style keyboard consisting of 64 keys, the wire count can be reduced from 64 to only 16 by arranging the keys into 8 rows of 8 columns (Figure 8.3, p. 332). Virtually all modern keyboards are set up this way.

Keyboard Encoding Methods

Most modern computers have the keyboard encoding circuitry built into the keyboard assembly. Some exceptions are low-cost home computers, which use the system processor to scan and encode the key switches. Some earlier encoding designs used a large diode matrix to encode the key switches, as shown in Figure 8.4 (p. 333).

Encoding the output of the matrixed keyboard requires more logic circuitry than the parallel keyboard because the key switches must be scanned by using a counter, as shown in Figure 8.5 (p. 334). Each column must be scanned for a pressed key. If a key is pressed, the counter stops when the column with the pressed key is selected. The value that is in the counter reflects the binary value of the key pressed.

With changing technology, many manufacturers put the keyboard encoding circuitry on a single large-scale IC. The method used by many manufacturers today is a single-chip microcomputer, which scans the key switches and encodes the output, as shown in Figure 8.6 (p. 334). The operation of the single-chip microcomputer is quite simple: All the column wires are connected to one port of the microcomputer, and the row wires are connected to a second port. A program simulates the hardware model to scan the keys and encode the key pressed to a binary value. Changing the encoded value for a key or keys requires only a program change and not a hardware change. At first glance this may seem like overkill, but the economy and flexibility of using a standard microcomputer for this application is very attractive. The encoded data may then be converted to bit-serial format by the single-chip microcomputer, which further reduces the number of conductors to just three or four wires, allowing a thin, flexible cable to be used.

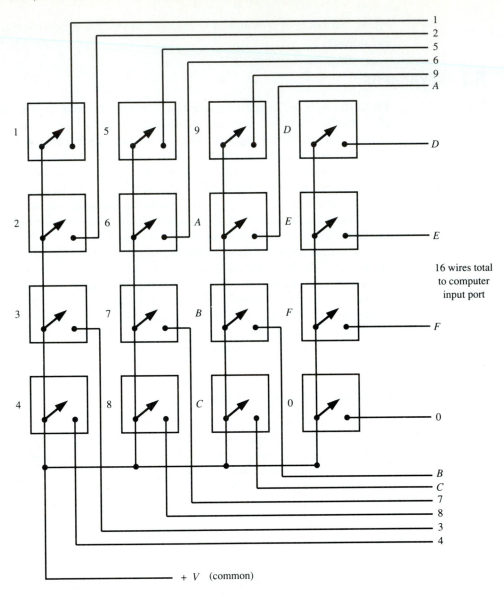

FIGURE 8.1
Simple output keypad

The keyboard used on the IBM PC is controlled by an INTEL 8048 single-chip microcomputer, as shown in Figure 8.7 (p. 335). The key switches used in the IBM keyboard are not contact switches but capacitive switches. When a key is pressed, a conductive plastic plate falls down on the etched plates on the PC board, which changes the capacitance of the etched plates. The capacitance change is detected by the sense amplifier, chip Z_1.

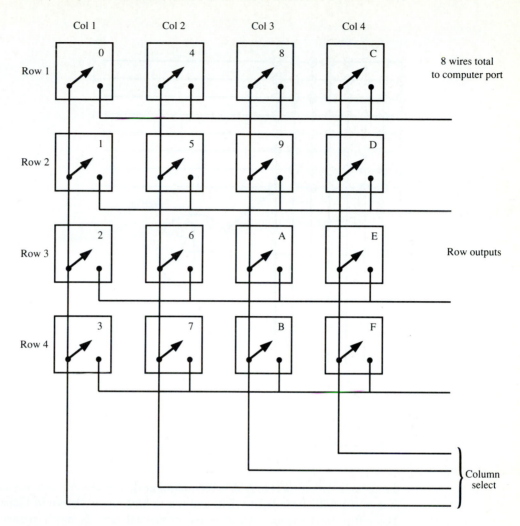

Col 1   Col 2   Col 3   Col 4

Row 1   0   4   8   C   8 wires total
                                 to computer port

Row 2   1   5   9   D

Row 3   2   6   A   E   Row outputs

Row 4   3   7   B   F

Column
select

FIGURE 8.2
Matrix output keyboard

8.2 VIDEO DISPLAYS

Most modern computer systems use *raster scan video displays* as the primary user output
device. The raster scan video display is very much like a conventional home television
receiver. In fact, many low-cost home computers use a television as their output device.
The major drawback of using a television is the lack of resolution or fine detail, which is
discussed later in this chapter.

The video display is a **cathode-ray tube (CRT).** An electron beam, which
originates at the **cathode,** is scanned across the phosphor-coated face of the CRT by the
deflection circuit. The intensity of the electron beam is controlled by voltage changes on

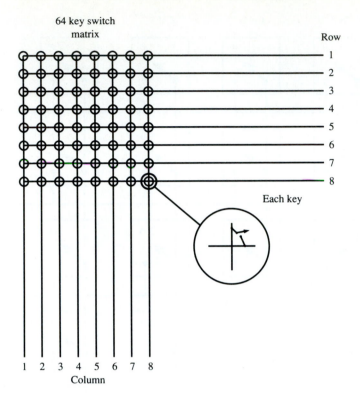

FIGURE 8.3
64-key keyboard

the cathode with respect to grid 1, the control grid. The electron beam is pulled across the face of the CRT from left to right and top to bottom, as shown in Figure 8.8 (p. 336). The left-to-right motion, which is the horizontal rate, is much greater than the top-to-bottom motion, which is the vertical rate. The period of time during which the electron beam is returning to the top or left of the screen is known as the **retrace** time. During this time, the electron beam is cut off, or blanked. The two rates for the horizontal and vertical deflection form a series of horizontal lines on the face of the CRT. This series of horizontal lines is known as the **raster.** The formula for obtaining the maximum number of lines in the raster is

$$\text{Max scan lines} = \frac{\text{horizontal rate}}{\text{vertical rate}}$$

The standard television scan rates are 15,750 Hz for the horizontal rate and 60 Hz for the vertical rate. When we divide the horizontal rate by the vertical rate, the result is 262.5:

$$\text{Scan lines} = \frac{15,750}{60} = 262.5$$

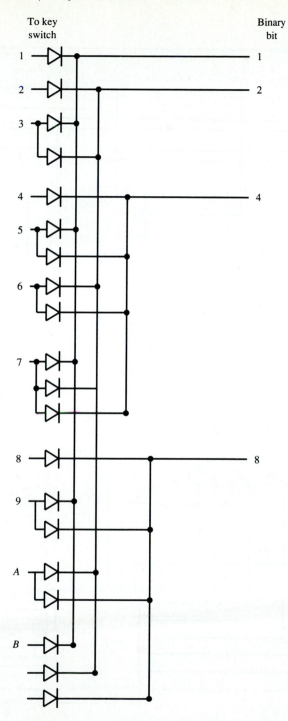

FIGURE 8.4
Diode encoder

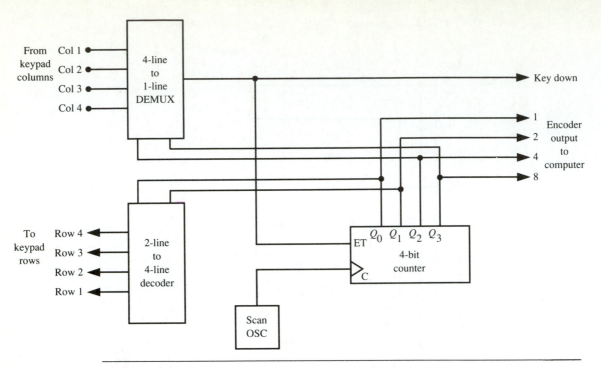

FIGURE 8.5
Scanning matrix decoder

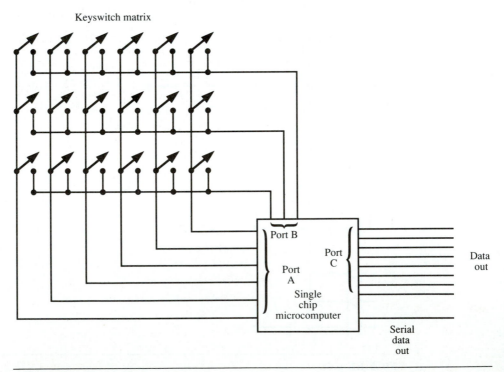

FIGURE 8.6
Microcomputer keyboard encoder

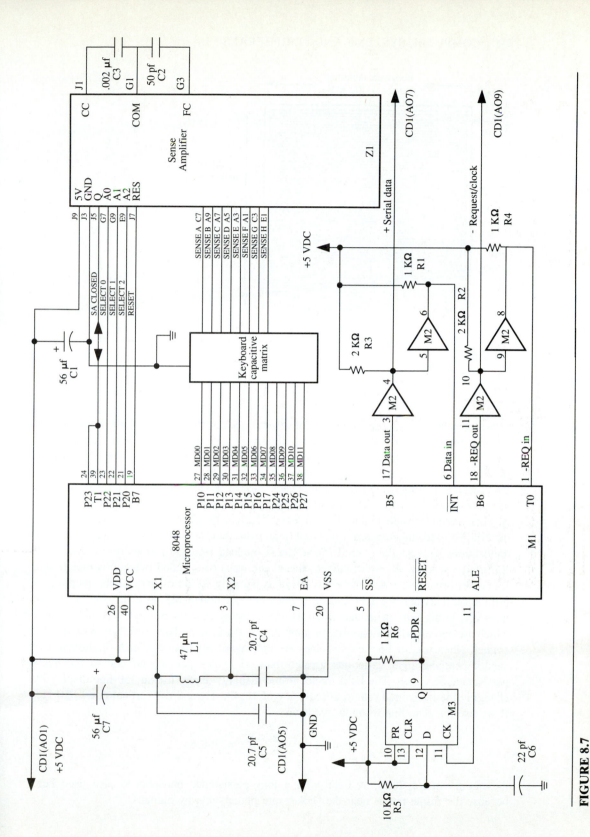

FIGURE 8.7
IBM keyboard (Courtesy of International Business Machines Corp.)

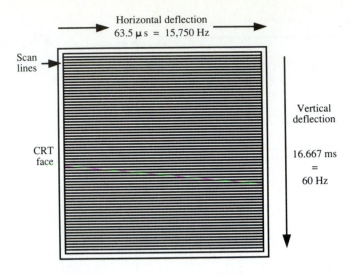

FIGURE 8.8
The raster display

This means that the *maximum* number of vertical lines is 262.5. Since some lines must be allowed for overscan and retrace time, slightly fewer are available. For example, the IBM color graphics adapter uses the standard scan rates and allows 200 vertical dots, or **pixels.** It is possible to double the number of vertical lines by using a method known as **interlaced scanning,** in which the odd raster starts at the top left edge and the even raster at the top middle of the CRT, as shown in Figure 8.9. The even lines fall between the odd lines, which results in a maximum total of 525 vertical lines. The interlaced scanning method is used in standard broadcast television but not in most computer display applications because the overall frame rate is reduced from 60 frames per second to 30 frames per second. As we discussed, the screen must be scanned *twice* to complete one frame. In broadcast video there are infinitely varying levels of gray in the picture, so differences between the odd and even lines are not noticeable on a line-by-line basis; however, in digitally generated video there are abrupt changes in the levels of intensity, which are perceived as flickering, or jumping, on the screen. This flickering is especially evident when text or fine graphic lines are displayed. Studies show that the human eye cannot perceive light variations greater than 45 cycles per second due to the eye's persistence of vision. The IBM monochrome display adapter uses a 350-line display by changing the horizontal rate to a frequency of 18,432 Hz and the vertical rate to 50 Hz. If we use the scan-line formula, we have

$$\text{Scan lines} = \frac{18,432}{50} = 368.64$$

maximum vertical lines. A CRT with a long-persistence phosphor is also used here because the frame rate is near the flicker rate perceivable by humans.

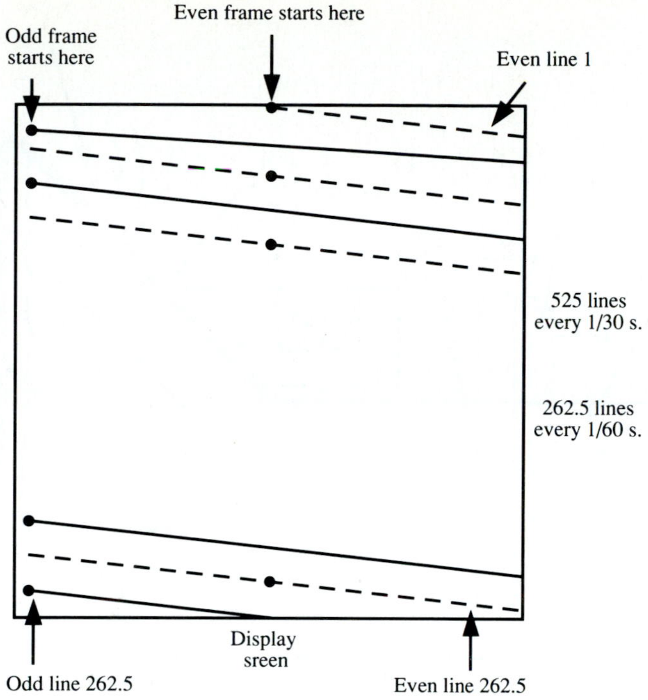

Even frame starts here

Odd frame
starts here

Even line 1

525 lines
every 1/30 s.

262.5 lines
every 1/60 s.

Display
sreen

Odd line 262.5

Even line 262.5

FIGURE 8.9
Interlaced scanning

8.3 THE CRT

The CRT, which is commonly known as the **picture tube,** is a large glass envelope containing an electron gun. All air must be evacuated from the CRT in order to create a nearly perfect vacuum. A vacuum in the CRT is necessary for three reasons. First, if air molecules are present in the CRT, the electron beam scatters when it strikes them. Second, gases ionize when subjected to high voltage. Ionized gases are conductive and effectively short out the electron beam. Third, the filament burns up in the presence of oxygen. The basic elements of the conventional CRT are the filament, cathode, grids, and the anode, as shown in Figure 8.10.

When heated the cathode begins to emit electrons. It is heated by the **filament,** which is sometimes called the heater. The **grids** control the flow of the electrons from the cathode to the **anode,** which is the most positively charged element. Since electrons are negatively charged particles, they are attracted toward a positive potential and repelled away from a negative potential.

Electron beams are also affected by magnetic fields. Since current is flowing through the electron beam, a circular magnetic field is associated with it. When a magnetic field is placed through an electron beam, the beam is deflected within the externally induced magnetic field in the same way that two magnets attract or repel each other. This phenomenon is known as **magnetic deflection.**

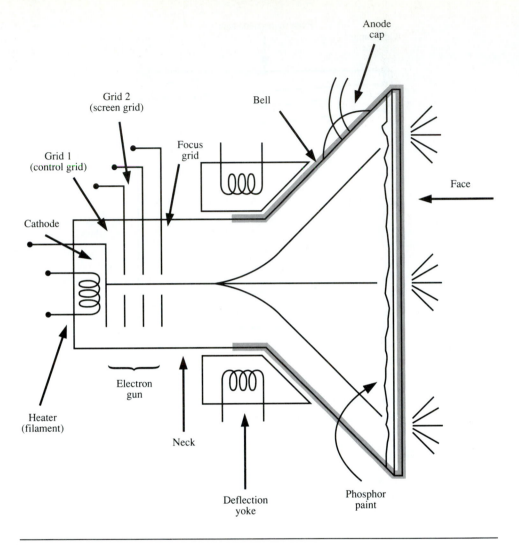

FIGURE 8.10
The CRT

The *inside* face of the CRT is coated with phosphor, which is a material that exhibits luminescence (it glows) when excited by electrons (beta radiation) or other sources of radiation. When the electron beam from the cathode strikes the phosphor, it produces a bright dot of light, which is known as cathodeluminescence. The intensity of the dot of light is directly proportional to the intensity of the electron beam, which can be controlled by varying the voltage differential between the cathode and the control grid. When the control grid becomes more negative than the cathode, somewhat greater than −60 V, the electron beam is cut off. As the voltage at the control grid becomes less negative, some of the electrons begin to pass through the control grid and strike the phosphor. The intensity may also be controlled by holding the control grid at a fixed voltage and by varying the voltage at the cathode. Most video display designs apply the video information to the cathode to create the image and control the overall brightness by varying the voltage at the control grid. The screen grid, or grid 2, is used to pull the electron beam toward the anode. Voltage changes at the screen grid also affect the brightness of the picture, but the voltage is usually set to a fixed value, at least $+400$ V for a monochrome CRT. The last grid is the focus grid, which focuses the electron beam to a pinpoint. The voltage present on the focus grid is usually adjustable from about -100 to $+1000$ V, depending on the design and type of CRT.

The last element is the anode. The inside surface of the "bell" is coated with conductive paint to form the anode. Since the electrons must travel a great distance from the cathode to the anode, high voltage must be present on the anode. The high voltage is usually 1000 V per inch of the face, or 12,000 V on a 12-in. CRT. Most color CRTs require 25,000 V regardless of the size of the face. A color CRT is similar to a monochrome CRT except that three electron guns are used, one for red, one for green, and one for blue, the primary colors of light. By mixing the three colors, any color is possible. The other main difference from the monochrome CRT is that a *shadow mask,* a metal plate with many tiny holes in it, is placed just before the face of the CRT. The face of the CRT is painted with many groups of red, green, and blue phosphor dots called **triads,** as shown in Figure 8.11. The shadow mask is set up in such a way that only the red electron beam hits the red dots, only the green beam hits the green dots, and only the blue beam hits the blue dots. Since the three electron beams do not originate from the same point, an additional set of deflection magnets, called the **convergence yoke,** is required. This type of color CRT is called a delta gun CRT because the electron guns are arranged in a delta form.

Many of the newer color CRT designs put all three electron beams into one common electron gun. Another difference in the new CRT design is that the phosphor is painted as groups of vertical stripes instead of dots. Directly behind the stripes is a slotted shadow mask instead of holes. One example of this design is the Sony Trinitron™ CRT. This single-gun design greatly reduces the number of convergence components required on the CRT and in some cases eliminates the need for the convergence yoke. Almost all the newer color monitors are designed this way and do not require periodic convergence adjustments.

High Voltage

Most video displays use the horizontal sweep circuit to generate the high voltage through a flyback transformer. In rare cases, on some very expensive monitors, a separate high-voltage power supply is used. As shown in Figure 8.12, the high-voltage circuit is a simple half-wave rectifier off the secondary of the flyback transformer.

No filter capacitor is required because the conductive coatings on the CRT act as a capacitor. It is for this reason that you must discharge the anode-to-chassis ground *before* removing or working around the CRT or high-voltage section. Discharging the anode to chassis ground is extremely dangerous and should be performed only by a qualified and experienced technician. *Failure to follow this precaution could result in a shock.* The high-voltage rectifier in the color display is a bit more complex because a tripler circuit is used to step the high voltage up to 25,000 V, as shown in Figure 8.13 (p. 342).

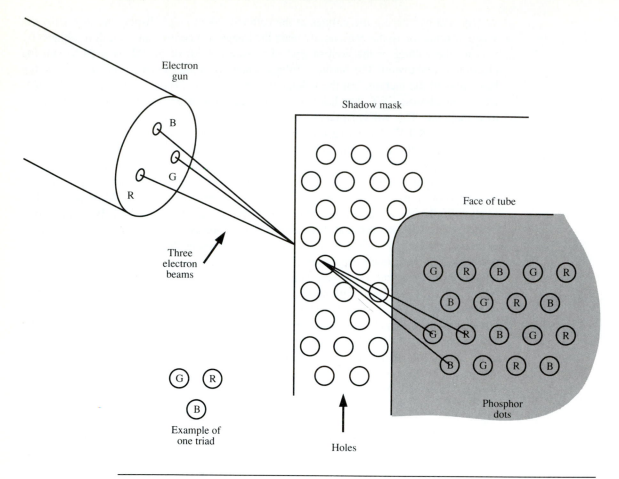

FIGURE 8.11
The color CRT

Another popular variation of the tripler is the multiple secondary flyback with integral diodes. In this configuration the secondaries are wired in series with diodes coupling the windings, as shown in Figure 8.14. This type of flyback is used in the IBM color monitor.

High-voltage failures are usually due to the absence of horizontal sweep or excessive loads on the flyback transformer. An additional winding is usually provided on the flyback to generate the grid biasing voltages, as shown in Figure 8.12. Diode D505 rectifies the 450-V screen grid voltage. Diode D504 rectifies the +55-V cathode bias voltage. Diode D503 rectifies the −170-V brightness control voltage, which is sent to the control grid from the brightness control circuit as shown in Figure 8.15 (p. 344).

Some monitor designs use the flyback output to generate *all* the low-voltage power supplies, as shown in Figure 8.14. This design puts additional loads on the horizontal scan circuit but has the advantage of reducing the cost of the monitor.

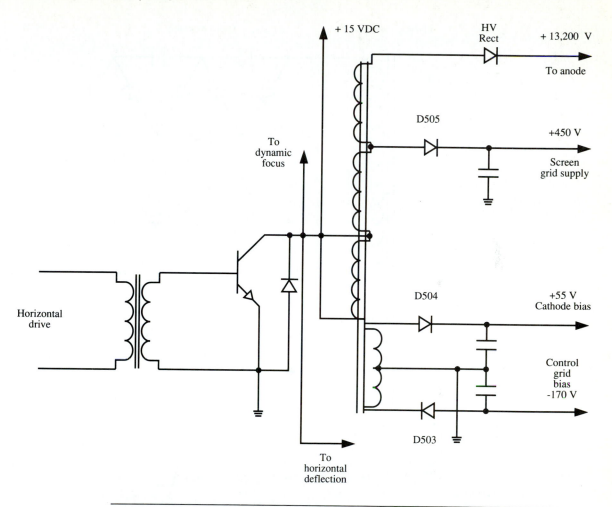

FIGURE 8.12
IBM monochrome display high voltage

Dynamic Focus

Many video display monitors employ dynamic focus circuits in their design to correct *focus nonlinearity,* a problem that is most prevalent in the newer wide-deflection-angle CRTs. Since the face of the CRT is relatively flat, the distance from the electron gun to all points on the face is not constant. To correct for this, the focus voltage must be varied relative to the electron beam position on the face of the CRT. If the correction is not made, the image will appear a bit fuzzy on the edges of the CRT. The addition of the inductor and capacitor circuits on the horizontal output generates a parabolic waveform, as shown in Figure 8.16 (p. 345). This waveform is fed into the focus circuit to change the voltage "on the fly." The focus voltage on the edges is different from the

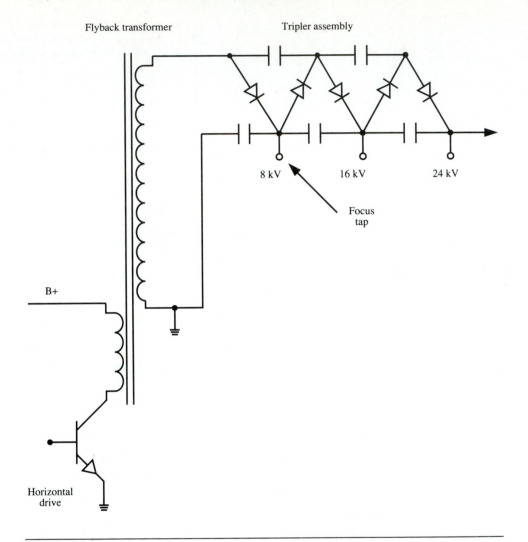

FIGURE 8.13
High-voltage tripler

voltage when the beam is in the center. These voltage changes cause the electron beam to remain in focus across the entire face of the CRT.

8.4 DEFLECTION

As was discussed earlier, the electron beam must be pulled across the face of the CRT in order to create a raster of horizontal lines. The position of the electron beam is controlled by the deflection yoke and the deflection circuits. There are in fact two types of deflection methods used in modern CRTs. The first is **electrostatic deflection,** which is used primarily in oscilloscopes. Since electrostatic deflection is rarely used in video

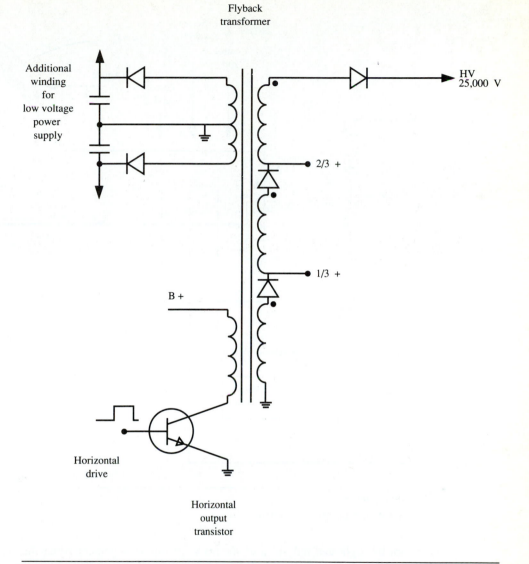

FIGURE 8.14
Multiple secondary flyback with integral diodes

display applications, it will not be discussed here. The second type is **magnetic deflection,** which is used in most video display applications. The main components of magnetic deflection are two sets of opposed electromagnets known as the **deflection yoke.** The deflection yoke is made up of four coils of wire mounted at 90° increments. The deflection yoke is slid over the neck and up against the bell of the CRT as shown in Figure 8.17 (p. 346).

Since the magnetic flux from a coil is at a right angle to it, the horizontal deflection coils are mounted above and below the neck. The vertical deflection coils are mounted

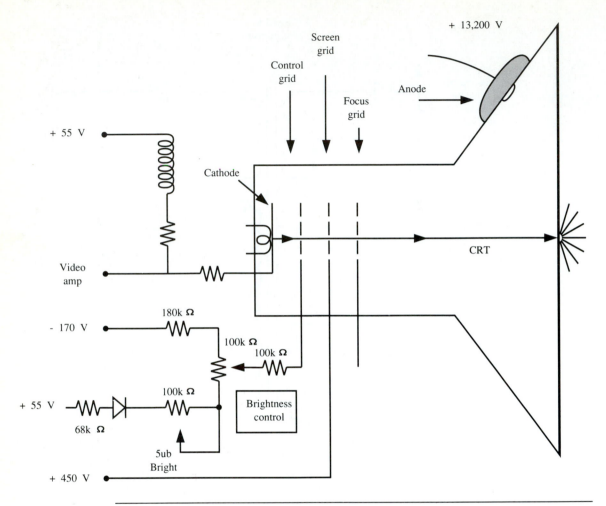

FIGURE 8.15
CRT and brightness control

on the right and left sides of the neck. In this arrangement when the vertical coils are energized, they pull the electron beam up or down. When the horizontal coils are energized, they pull the electron beam right or left. The deflection yoke coils are driven by the horizontal and vertical deflection circuits, which generate a current ramp waveform. The ramp pulls the electron beam at an even rate across the face and then back as fast as possible. When the waveform is viewed on an oscilloscope, it resembles a sawtooth, as shown in Figure 8.18.

Horizontal Deflection

The horizontal deflection section is typically made up of the horizontal oscillator, the horizontal output, the flyback transformer, and the deflection yoke. In most video

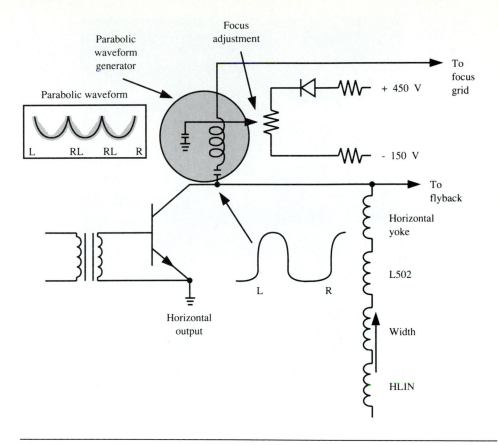

FIGURE 8.16
Dynamic focus circuit

display applications the output of the horizontal oscillator is a square wave and not a ramp. The square wave is then fed to the horizontal output, which is simply a switch. The combination of the flyback transformer, yoke coils, diodes, and capacitors forms the ramp for the deflection while also generating the high voltage through the flyback transformer. It is important to remember that the entire horizontal section is precisely tuned by the combination of *all* the components involved. *Any* component failure in the horizontal section may result in the loss of sweep and/or high voltage.

The horizontal deflection circuit used in the IBM monochrome display does not implement a free-running horizontal oscillator. The display adapter provides the horizontal drive signal directly to the horizontal driver circuit, so the IBM monochrome display screen is dark when the computer is not powered on. The entire horizontal deflection section consists of only three transistors, the flyback transformer, a coupling transformer, five capacitors, a diode, the deflection yoke, and three coils, as shown in Figure 8.19 (p. 348).

The horizontal drive signal is fed to the base of transistor TR22, which is configured as a saturated switch. The output of transistor TR22 is coupled through

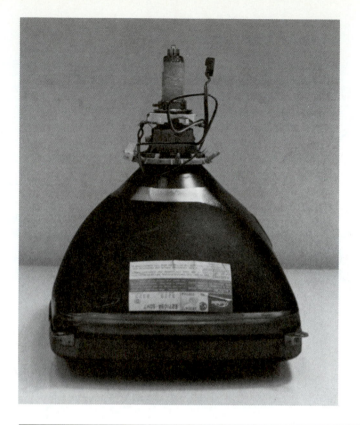

FIGURE 8.17
Picture of CRT and yoke

transformer T501 to the base of the horizontal output transistor TR23. The actual horizontal ramp is formed by the yoke inductance and the capacitor C505 while being controlled by the horizontal output transistor TR23 and damper diode D502. The operation of this circuit is illustrated in Figure 8.20. When the horizontal output transistor is first turned on, energy is stored in the flyback transformer primary. The moment that TR23 turns off, the energy is transferred to the secondary, creating the flyback pulse and the high voltage. At this same time energy is stored in the yoke, creating the **retrace** interval. A short time later the yoke current reaches the peak level, and diode D502 begins to conduct, creating the first half of the trace. As the current reverses polarity, transistor TR23 begins conducting, completing the trace until retrace time, when the cycle repeats. Components D502 and C504 protect the output transistor from excessive voltage transients. Coils L502, L503, and L504 are used to tune the resonance of the yoke and control the shape of the current ramp waveform. Transistor TR21 and associated components are used to cut off the horizontal drive signal if the power supply voltage becomes excessive due to a failure of the power supply. If this

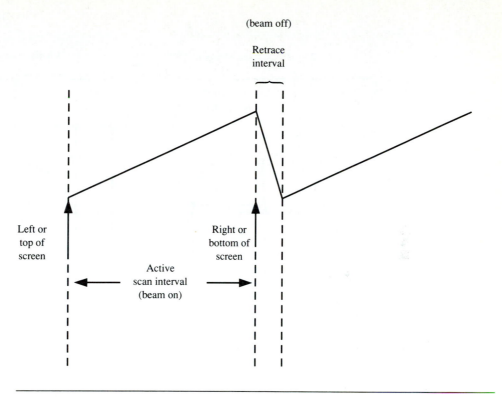

FIGURE 8.18
Sawtooth waveform

protection were not provided, the high voltage could possibly become high enough to allow some electron radiation to pass through the CRT, causing a radiation hazard to the user.

The scan method described is known as **reactance scanning** and is designed to operate at a fixed frequency. More sophisticated monitors that support variable scan rates employ more circuitry and usually have a separate yoke driver circuit. The IBM EGA and the NEC MULTISYNC are such monitors, and they are far more expensive.

Vertical Deflection

The vertical deflection circuit is more complex than the horizontal deflection circuit because of the lower frequency used. Recall from the previous section that the scan frequency of the horizontal deflection is 15,750 Hz. However, the frequency of the vertical scan is 60 Hz, so the reactance scan method is not possible. A *linear* current ramp must be generated and applied to the vertical deflection yoke coils. A typical vertical deflection circuit is shown in Figure 8.21 (p. 350).

The exact design of the vertical deflection circuits used by different manufacturers

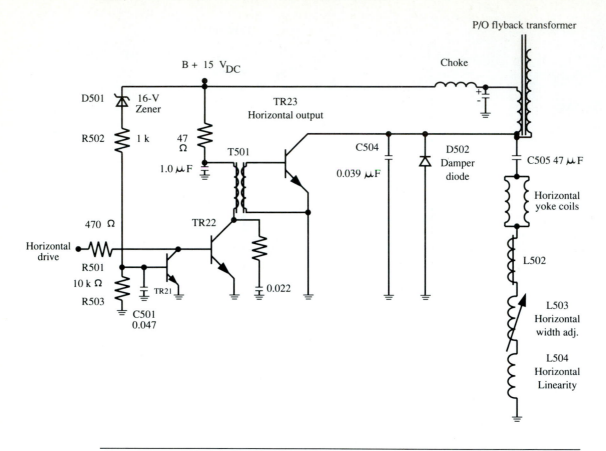

FIGURE 8.19
IBM monochrome monitor horizontal deflection

varies greatly, but their basic operation is the same. As shown in Figure 8.21, the vertical deflection circuit consists of various stages, each with a specific function. The first stage is the vertical oscillator, which has a free-running frequency of 50 or 60 Hz. The vertical oscillator is synchronized to the incoming vertical sync signal from the video controller board. The next stage is the vertical driver, which forms a linear ramp from the output of the oscillator. The shape of the ramp may be changed by adjusting the vertical linearity control. The final stage is the vertical output, which provides the required current to drive the yoke coils directly. Most solid-state monitors use a two-transistor push-pull design similar to an audio amplifier. Failures in the vertical deflection circuit can easily be diagnosed by observing the picture. A single horizontal line in the middle of the screen is an indication of total vertical failure, also known as *vertical collapse*. In most cases this is caused by a failure of the vertical oscillator. Loss of the top or bottom of the picture is usually caused by a failure of the output stage transistors. Distorted or elongated pictures are caused by wave-shape problems, as shown in Figure 8.22. Many

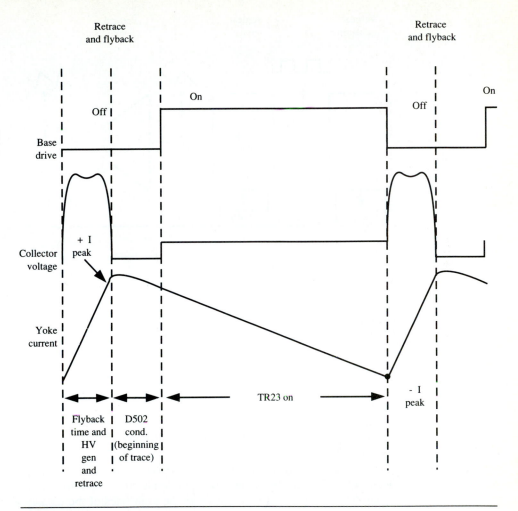

FIGURE 8.20
Horizontal sweep waveforms

new monitors use a single IC for the vertical deflection circuit. The IBM monochrome monitor uses the TDA1170 IC for the vertical deflection circuit, as shown in Figure 8.23 (p. 352).

Synchronization Circuits

In order to create a usable picture on a raster scan video display, the vertical and horizontal scan circuits must be precisely synchronized to the incoming video signal. In the case of the composite monitor, the sync signal must be stripped from the video and then separated into the vertical and horizontal sync signals. This stripping of the sync from the video is done by circuitry known as the *sync separator*. The sync separator is discussed in the composite video section. Most video displays used on IBM and compatible computers require that the vertical and horizontal sync signals be supplied

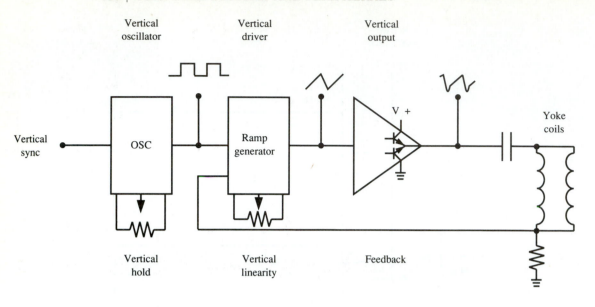

FIGURE 8.21
Vertical deflection circuit

separately. Recall that the IBM monochrome display requires a horizontal drive signal, which differs from a conventional horizontal sync signal, as shown in Figure 8.24. It is for this reason that the IBM monochrome display *should not* be connected to a color graphics adapter.

It is a well-known fact that when an external signal is applied to an oscillator near the oscillator's frequency, the oscillator tends to synchronize itself with the induced signal. This can be used to synchronize the scan rates of the display with the incoming video signal. This method is used in the vertical scan system by passing the signal through an integrator or low-pass filter into the vertical oscillator circuit. The integrator circuit is used to remove any noise or variations and to improve stability. In the case of the composite display the integrator also removes horizontal sync pulses.

The synchronization circuit required for the horizontal scan oscillator is more complex due to drift, phase, and noise problems. A phase-locked loop circuit is used here, which is often referred to as the horizontal automatic frequency control circuit. A typical horizontal oscillator is shown in Figure 8.25 (p. 354). As shown in Figure 8.25, the incoming sync pulse is split up into positive and negative pulses by transistor Q_1. A sample of the flyback pulse, which is the retrace time, is integrated into a ramp and fed to diodes D_1 and D_2. If the oscillator is running too slowly, the sync pulse arrives late and causes a negative voltage change at the junction of resistors R_4 and R_5. This negative change should cause the oscillator to speed up. If the oscillator is running too fast, the voltage change is positive and should cause the oscillator to slow down. An *antihunt* circuit is placed between the phase comparator and the voltage-controlled oscillator to prevent the loop from hunting or oscillating.

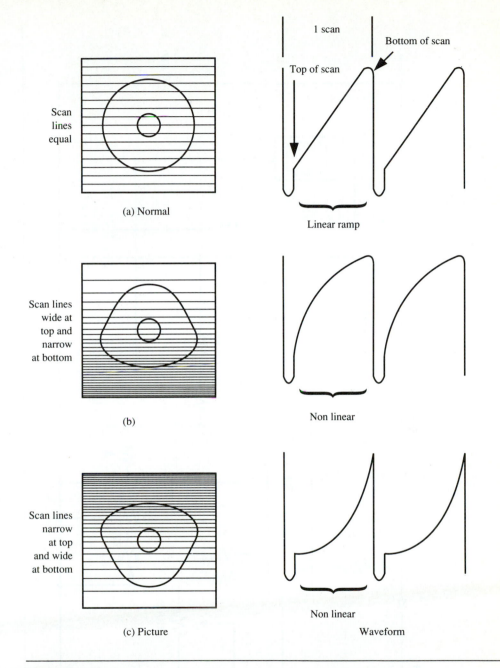

FIGURE 8.22
Distorted wave shapes

Many of the newer monitors are replacing the discrete components of the oscillator and synchronization circuits with IC chips. The IBM color monitor employs one IC with built in synchronization circuitry for both the vertical and horizontal oscillators.

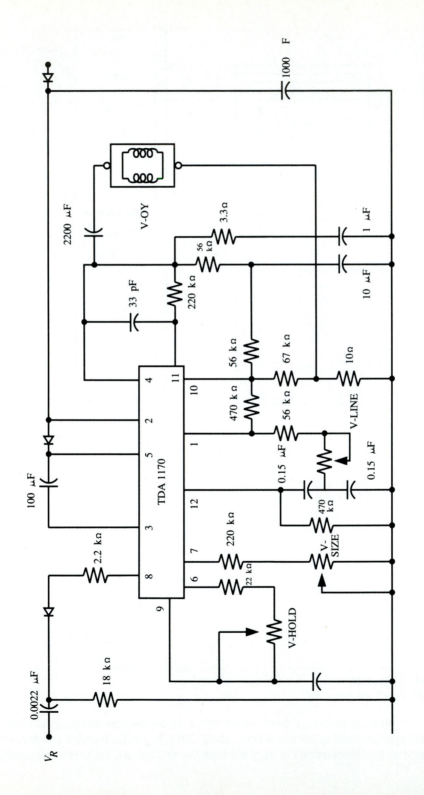

FIGURE 8.23
Vertical deflection

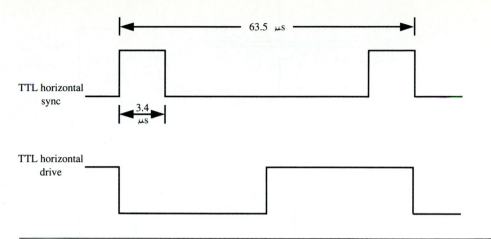

FIGURE 8.24
Horizontal sync and drive signals

8.5 VIDEO AMPLIFIER

Recall the operation of the CRT and how the intensity of the beam is controlled. The brightness of the phosphor is controlled by voltage changes between the cathode and the control grid. Once a raster is achieved and is in synchronization with the video source, an image can be reproduced by applying video information to the cathode or control grid. In most video display applications the video information is applied to the cathode. A useful tip to remember is that the cathode wire on the CRT socket is *almost always yellow*. In the case of the color CRT there are three cathode wires, *yellow with a red or green or blue stripe* (one for each gun color). The required voltage swing to go from black (beam cutoff) to maximum brightness (beam near saturation) is around 45 V for a monochrome CRT and as high as 150 V for a color CRT. It is for this reason that the video signal must be amplified before it is sent to the cathode of the CRT. The circuitry used here is called the video amplifier and must have a *bandwidth* from DC to more than 15 MHz for good resolution. The video amplifier design is a simple one- or two-transistor design. It must have an external gain adjustment, which serves as the contrast control. Varying the gain of the video amplifier changes the sensitivity between white and black images and thus changes the overall contrast of the picture. This gain control is usually in the emitter circuit of a common-emitter amplifier, as shown in Figure 8.26. As can be seen in Figure 8.26, varying the contrast control changes the amount of bypass in the emitter circuit, thus changing the amount of gain of the amplifier.

Many computers supply the video information as TTL logic levels and also supply a separate intensity bit for video attributes. In the case of the TTL logic levels, a modified video circuit is used, as shown in Figure 8.27 (p. 356).

The video signal is buffered and sent directly into the video amplifier through a resistor divider. A second video signal called dual, which is the intensity bit, is buffered,

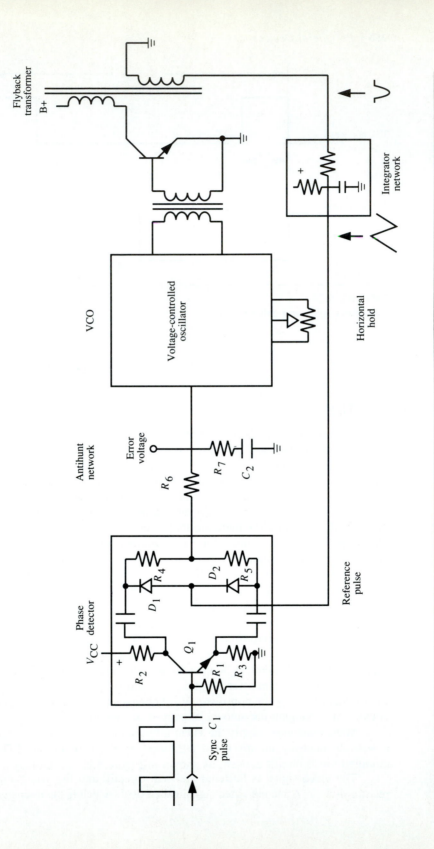

FIGURE 8.25
Typical horizontal phase-locked loop

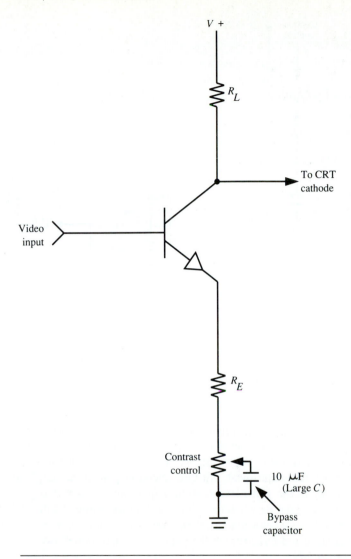

FIGURE 8.26
Typical video amplifier

and its amplitude is adjustable by the contrast control. This signal attenuates the supply voltage to the output of the video buffer, which adjusts the brightness of the intensified video.

8.6 COLOR VIDEO

The color video display monitor is actually *three* monitors in one package. The power supply, deflection, and high voltage are all shared in common, but there are three separate video channels. The three video channels are required to drive the three separate

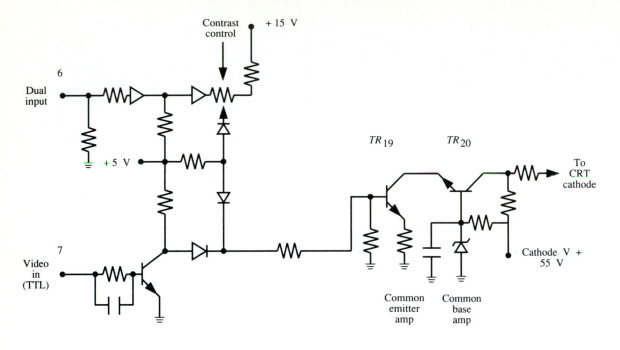

FIGURE 8.27
IBM monochrome video amplifier

CRT cathodes, as shown in Figure 8.28. Figure 8.28 is a block diagram of the IBM color display. Each video amplifier operates very much the same as those in the monochrome video display. One important difference is that each video amplifier must have a separate gain adjustment. All three electron guns in the CRT may not exhibit the same sensitivity to the video levels, so they may not produce true gray across the entire brightness range. That is, when the CRT is set up for white at full brightness, dark gray may appear to have a color tint like dark blue. This is known as a **tracking error** in the CRT and is corrected by changing the gains of the individual video amplifiers to match the CRT sensitivity.

Composite Video

Composite video is the term used when the synchronization, video information, and color subcarrier are all mixed on the same line. A typical waveform for an NTSC (National Television Standards Committee) video signal for one horizontal line is shown in Figure 8.29(a).

All voltages below the *black level* are considered synchronization information and are separated out and sent to the deflection circuits. These levels are also known as "blacker than black." The last portion of the horizontal sync pulse is called the **back porch** and is the location of the color burst signal. The color burst is the color subcarrier reference frequency that is used by the color demodulator circuitry. Figure 8.29(b)

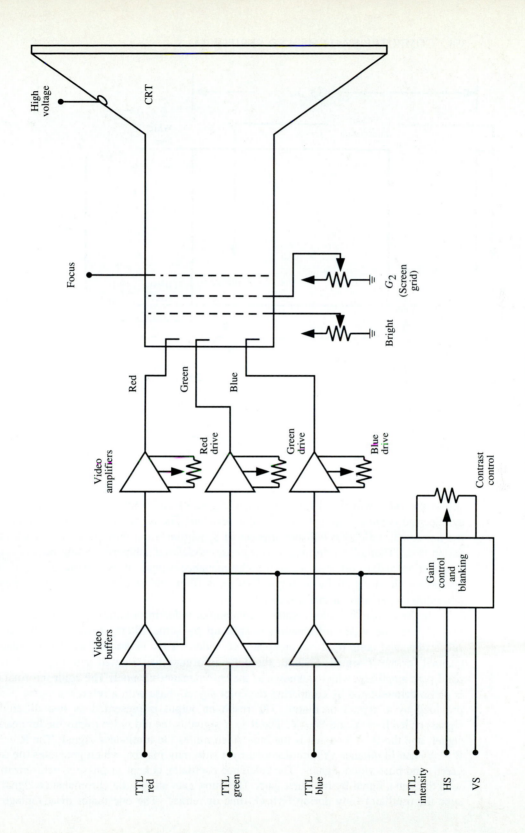

FIGURE 8.28
Color video amplifiers

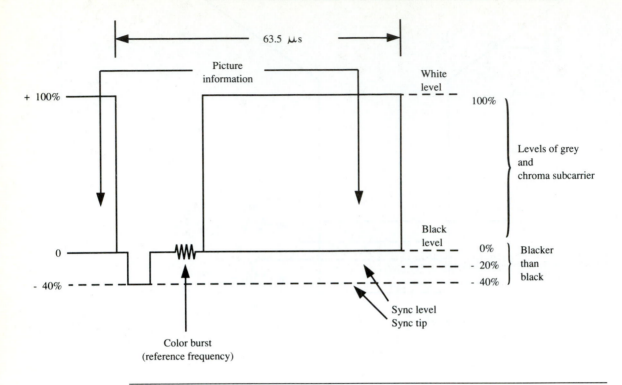

FIGURE 8.29a

shows the video waveform for one complete field of 262.5 lines. Note that the vertical sync period *is not* a solid sync level but is serrated. The serrations are necessary so that the horizontal deflection will not slip out of synchronization during vertical synchronization time. The color information is a *phase-modulated* subcarrier riding on the video information and is referred to as the chromanance signal. It is separated out of the composite video signal by a simple band-pass filter and sent to a three-output phase demodulator, as shown in Figure 8.30.

In the composite color display the incoming video information is processed in two ways. First, the video information is split up by some filters, stripped of the color subcarrier, and amplified as monochrome video. This is known as the luminance channel, or the Y signal. Second, the color information is filtered and amplified by a band-pass amplifier, which is known as the chromanance channel. The color information is phase demodulated by comparing the color signal phase with a reference signal phase provided by a crystal oscillator. The resultant output is presented as two difference signals called R − Y and B − Y. The R − Y signal is the red video minus the luminance signal, and the B − Y signal is the blue video minus the luminance signal. The R − Y, B − Y, and luminance (Y) are decoded by a summing matrix, which generates the red, green, and blue video signals. The reference oscillator is kept in phase synchronization with the burst signal by the burst gate. The burst gate allows the chromanance signal to sync the oscillator only during flyback time or retrace. The one major disadvantage of

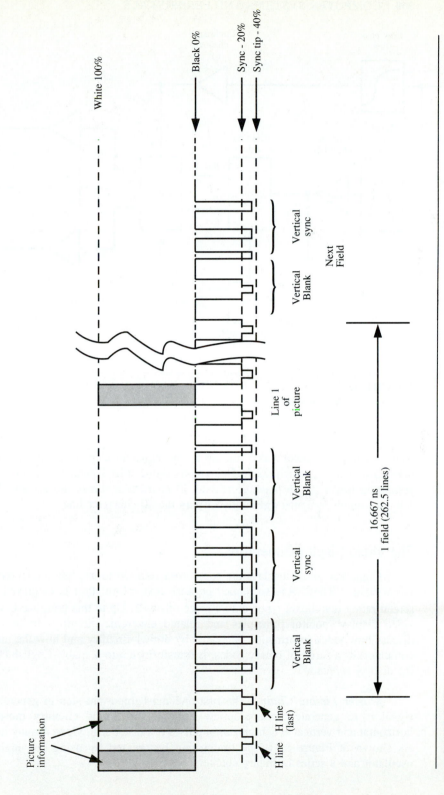

FIGURE 8.29b

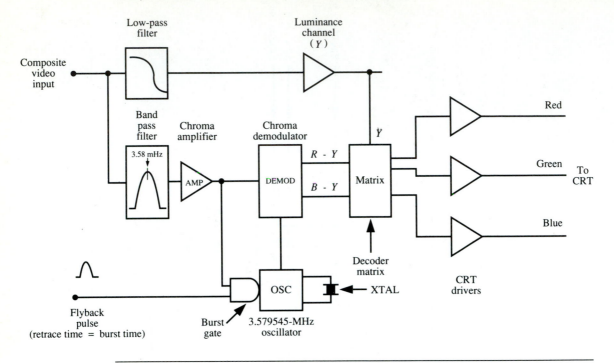

FIGURE 8.30
Composite color decoder

using a composite color video display is the reduced video bandwidth imposed by the chroma subcarrier, which results in a greatly reduced horizontal resolution. The reduced resolution limits the displayable text to 40 characters across the screen. This is why low-cost home computers generally display the 40-character line.

The Video Display Generator

Computer video displays are sometimes referred to as "glass teletypes" or "TV typewriters." They were so named because text information is displayed on a video screen rather than being typed onto a piece of paper. Up to this point we have discussed video display monitor principles and related electronic circuitry. In this section we discuss how video information is created by digital circuitry and how the output from a computer, as a series of binary codes, is transformed into readable English characters on the display screen.

Master Timing Chain   The first and most important step in generating a video signal is to generate the appropriate timing. The timing circuitry must create the horizontal and vertical synchronization pulses if a raster scan video display is to be used. As shown in Figure 8.31, the timing can be created by using one high-frequency oscillator and a series of binary counters.

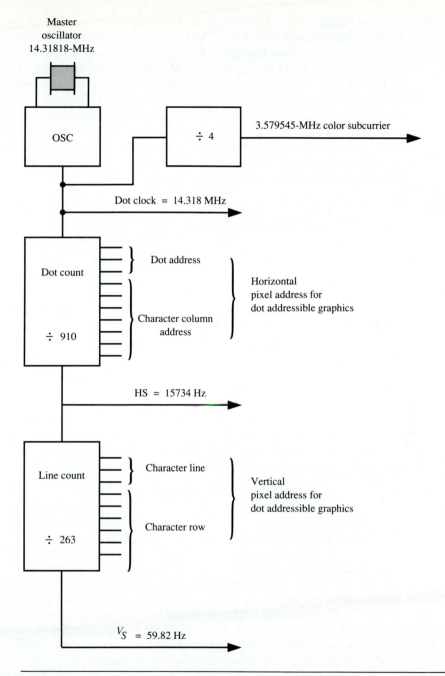

FIGURE 8.31
Example of a digital video timing chain

In Figure 8.31 a 14.318181-MHz clock frequency was used to accommodate the NTSC color subcarrier of 3.579545-MHz, which is the clock frequency divided by four. The horizontal sync time is obtained by using a counter that divides by 910, which yields a frequency of 15,734 Hz. In the case of color TV, the horizontal scan frequency is shifted slightly to accommodate the even divisor. The vertical sync is obtained by dividing the horizontal sync by 263, which yields a frequency of 59.82 Hz. The intermediate counter outputs can be used to generate the video memory addresses, which contain the picture element, or pixel, information. The maximum number of horizontal pixels is the maximum clock frequency, or **dot clock,** divided by the horizontal scan rate. The IBM color graphics adapter uses a dot clock rate of 14.318181 MHz. If we apply the following formula to the standard scan rate of 15,734 Hz,

$$\text{Max. hor. pixels} = \frac{\text{dot clock}}{f_{\text{HOR}}}$$

$$= \frac{14,318181 \text{ MHz}}{15,734 \text{ Hz}} = 910$$

Remember that we must allow some time for retrace and overscan. This is why the IBM color graphics adapter allows for only 640 maximum horizontal pixels. The maximum number of vertical pixels is limited only by the number of displayable scan lines, as discussed earlier.

Recently the counter and timing logic have been implemented on LSI ICs by many different manufacturers. Some manufacturers offer the entire video generator with the exception of the video RAM (pixel memory) on a single IC. Both the IBM monochrome display adapter and the IBM color graphics adapter use the Motorola MC6845 CRT controller chip, as shown in Figure 8.32. The implementation of this chip not only reduces the component count of the adapter but greatly increases the flexibility of the adapter by allowing for software modification of the display format.

Creating an Image   Once the appropriate timing has been generated and the display is scanning in synchronization, how is the image created? Recall that an image is created on the CRT by changing the intensity of the electron beam while the electron beam is scanning the face of the CRT. If we then connect a digital signal to the video input of the display, we can turn the beam on or off at will. When we apply a pattern like alternating 1s and 0s in time with the sync pulses, the resultant pattern should resemble a series of horizontal lines. The width and total number of lines will depend upon the rate, or dot clock, in which we are sending the alternating patterns, as shown in Figure 8.33. Of course, this simple bit pattern is useless except as a test pattern to adjust the display. A programmable pattern generator is necessary.

The programmable pattern area is known as the ref sh buffer or video RAM and is simply a random access memory matrix. The video RA M data outputs are fed into a shift register, clocked by the dot clock, which converts the parallel RAM data into bit serial data (the pixels) one bit at a time. A bit counter must be provided to load the next group of pixels after the last pixel is shifted out. In the case of an 8-bit RAM, an 8-bit shift register is used and must be reloaded after each group of 8 pixels is shifted out to the

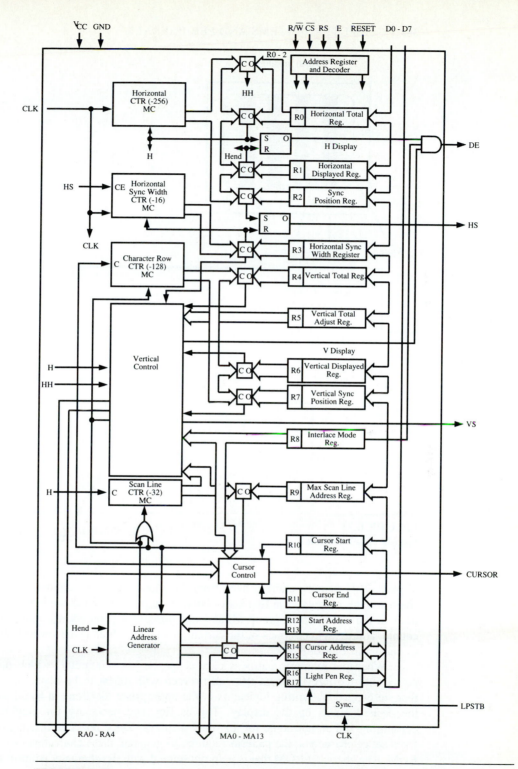

FIGURE 8.32
CRTC block diagram (Reprinted with permission of Motorola Inc.)

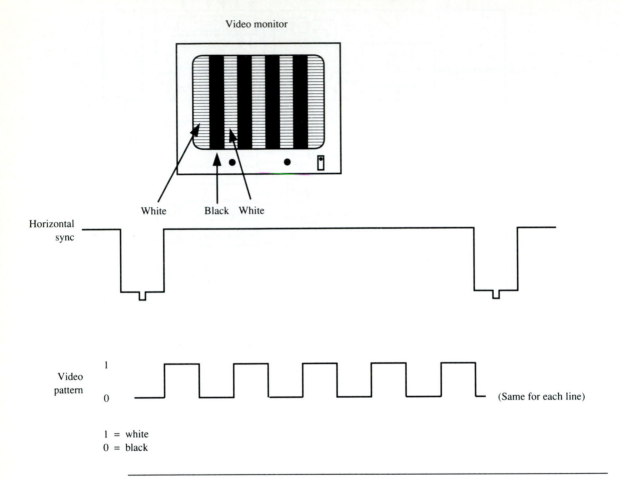

FIGURE 8.33
Simple video pattern

display. The memory address lines from the video RAM are connected to the timing chain counter outputs. The first set of counter outputs, which is the byte counter, keeps track of the current pixel group which is the horizontal pixel address. The second set of counter addresses keeps track of the current pixel line, which is the vertical pixel address, as shown in Figure 8.34.

When the memory matrix is cleared by the host computer, which must be dual ported into the RAM matrix, the video screen will appear to be blank. An image may then be created by writing logical 1s at the appropriate locations in RAM to illuminate the desired pixels on the display. This is fine and necessary for graphics but time consuming and cumbersome for text-only displays. Since readable text is made up of a fixed set of characters, the patterns required to generate these characters can be stored in ROM. The character ROM that is preprogrammed with the character patterns is known as the **character generator.** It is placed between the video RAM output and the video shift register, as shown in Figure 8.35.

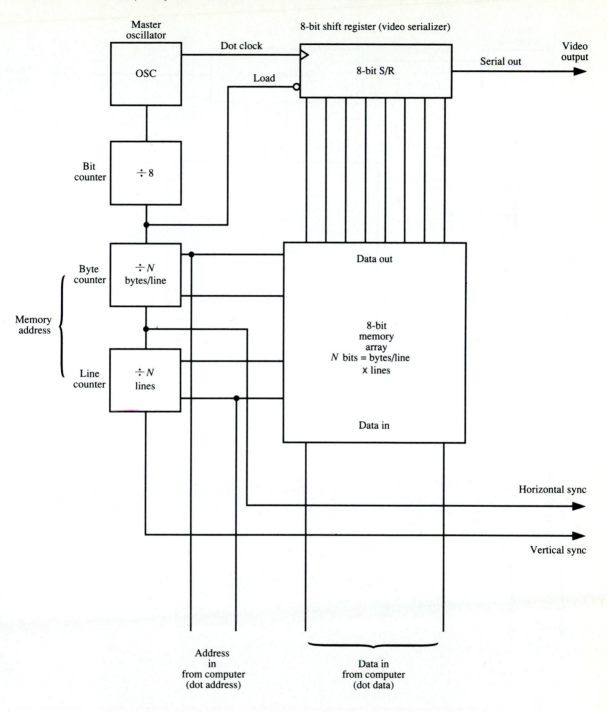

FIGURE 8.34
Memory-mapped video generator

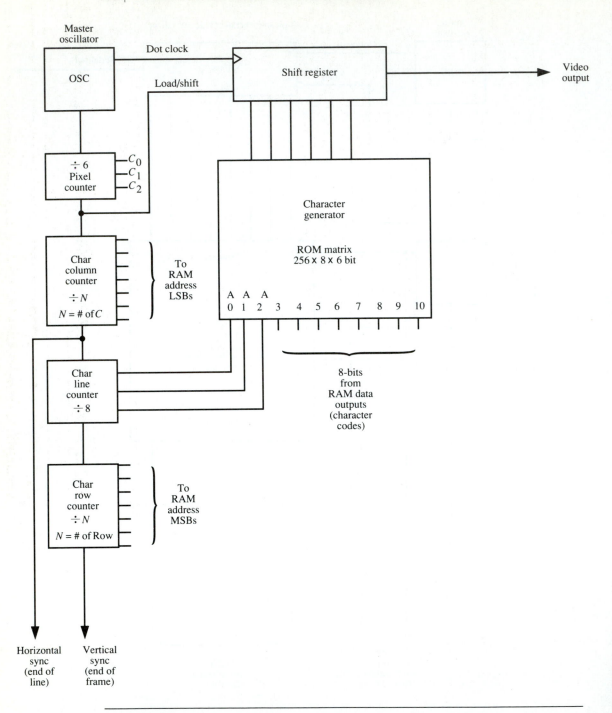

Figure 8.35
Character generator implementation

The character generator implementation shown here uses a 256- by 8- by 6-bit ROM, which is really a 2048- by 6-bit ROM. The system shown allows a 5-by-7 character mapped within a 6-by-8 box, as shown in Figure 8.36. We must allow for at least one dot space between the sides and bottoms of the characters so that they will not blend together. Also, the memory addresses are rearranged slightly. The pixel counter counts to six and reloads the shift register after the sixth pixel is shifted out. The character column counter keeps track of the current displayed character column and supplies the current horizontal character address to the video RAM. The character line counter keeps track of which line within the character box is currently displayed and supplies a 3-bit address to the character generator ROM. The final counter is the character row counter, which keeps track of the current row of characters displayed and also supplies the character row address to the video RAM. The final output of this counter generates the vertical synchronization, since it indicates the end of the frame. Figure 8.37 is an illustration of how the counter outputs and the displayed pixels are related.

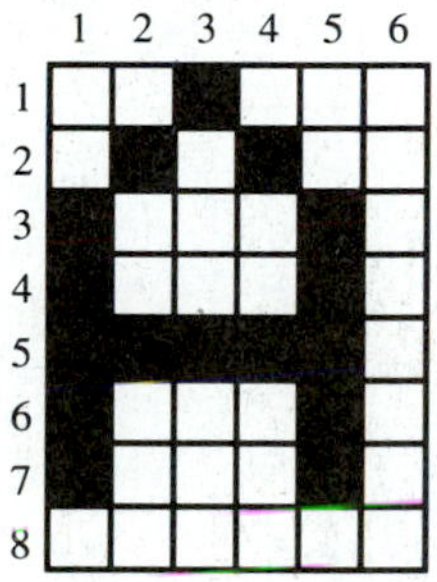

		ROM address							ROM data				
X	X	X	0	0	0		0	0	1	0	0	0
			0	0	1		0	1	0	1	0	0
			0	1	0		1	0	0	0	1	0
			0	1	1		1	0	0	0	1	0
			1	0	0		1	1	1	1	1	0
			1	0	1		1	0	0	0	1	0
			1	1	0		1	0	0	0	1	0
			1	1	1		0	0	0	0	0	0

Character spacing

FIGURE 8.36
One ROM character

8.7 IBM PC DISPLAY ADAPTERS

The IBM PC system offers a choice of video display adapters to accommodate the user. By using more than one type of adapter, it is possible to have multiple displays on a single system. For example, the user may wish to present a graphic drawing on one display while listing a set of instructions on the second display.

The IBM Monochrome Display Adapter

The IBM monochrome display adapter is designed for a text-only display. The text is displayed as 80 characters across by 25 rows down. The character format is presented in a 9-pixel-wide by 14-pixel-deep character box, which allows for a finely shaped and

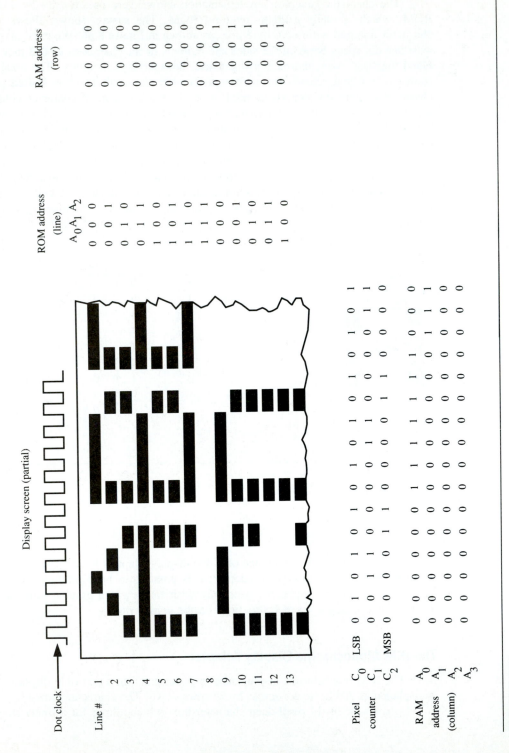

FIGURE 8.37
Character generator patterns and addresses

detailed character. The display adapter also supports three character attributes: inverse video, underline, and intensified video. This display adapter has 4096 bytes of video RAM and is memory mapped in the main system address from hex B000:0000 through hex B000:0FFF. Address hex B000:0000 is the upper-left character position, with hex B000:0001 as the attribute byte for that character. The adapter control registers are I/O mapped at I/O addresses hex 03B0 to hex 03BF. This display adapter *must* be used with a TTL-level direct-drive monitor. Also, the monitor *must* support a horizontal scan rate of 18 kHz. The IBM monochrome display adapter also contains a centronics parallel printer port. A block diagram for the monochrome display adapter is shown in Figure 8.38.

The IBM Color Graphics Adapter

The IBM **color graphics adapter** is designed to support both text and color graphics display formats. The text mode displays the characters inside an 8-pixel wide by 8-pixel-deep box and has two available modes. The first text mode is an 80-character by 25-line mode for direct-drive high-resolution display monitors, and the second mode is the 40-character by 25-line mode for television-type display monitors. The text attributes may be any one of 16 colors with any one of 8 background colors, blinking characters, and inverse characters on a character-by-character basis. This display adapter supports three graphics modes, as follows:

Mode 1: Low-resolution color graphics of 160 horizontal pixels by 100 vertical pixels in 16 colors. This mode is not supported in the IBM BIOS ROM and must be programmed without the use of ROM BIOS calls.

Mode 2: Medium-resolution color graphics of 320 horizontal pixels by 200 vertical pixels in two sets of 4 colors each. Only one color set may be used at a time, but the border may be any one of 16 colors. In this mode, *two* bits are required for *one* pixel. The combination of bits determines what color the pixel will appear, as follows:

Color Set 1		*Color Set* 2
Bits		
0 0	Pixel is background color	Same
0 1	Pixel is green	Pixel is cyan
1 0	Pixel is red	Pixel is magenta
1 1	Pixel is brown	Pixel is white

Mode 3: High-resolution black-and-white graphics of 640 horizontal pixels by 200 vertical pixels. In this mode 1 bit per byte represents 1 pixel on the screen.

The color graphics adapter has 16,384 bytes of video RAM, which is memory mapped in the main system at addresses hex B800:0000 through hex B800:3FFF. In the 40-character text mode eight text pages are available. Four text pages are allowed in the 80-character mode. Since all three graphics modes require the entire memory range, only one graphics page is allowed. The control registers are I/O mapped at I/O addresses hex 03D0 through hex 03DB. The color graphics adapter has three video outputs, which are for an RGB direct-drive monitor, a composite video color monitor, and an RF modulator for use with a standard color television set. A separate light pen port is also provided to allow the use of a light pen.

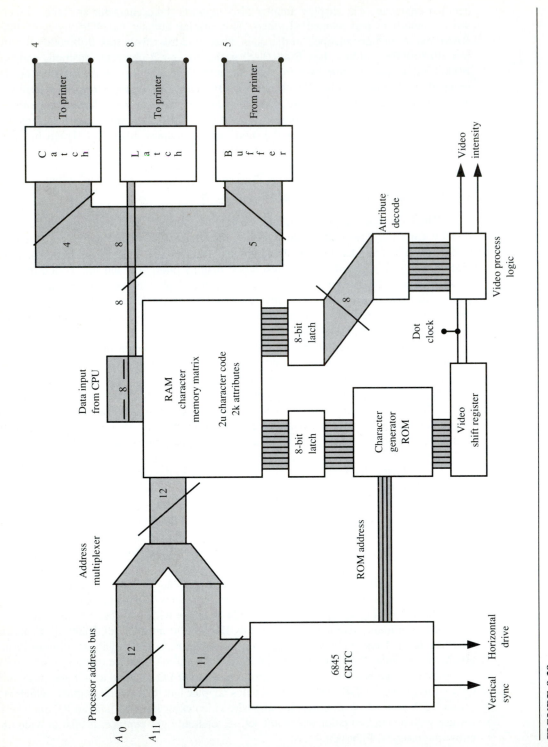

FIGURE 8.38
IBM monochrome display adapter

Enhanced Graphics Adapter

The **Enhanced Graphics Adapter (EGA)** was introduced with the original IBM PC AT in 1984. It was the first high-resolution color display standard for the IBM PC and compatibles. Basically, it provides the same text modes as CGA but uses a greater number of pixels for a clearer, more readable display. It also provides a selection of extended video modes with resolutions to 640 horizontal pixels by 350 vertical pixels. Graphics can be displayed in any of 16 colors from a palette of 64 colors or in any of two colors (monochrome mode). Most EGA adapters can support all of the CGA modes. Today, EGA has been replaced with the VGA standard.

Video Graphics Array Adapter

The **Video Graphics Array (VGA)** adapter is a higher resolution standard with a greater number of colors. VGA has many different modes of operation with resolutions to 640 horizontal pixels by 480 vertical pixels. Graphics can be displayed in any of 256 colors from a palette of 262,144 (256K) colors. VGA is much more technically sophisticated than EGA in that it allows very flexible control over the displayed image. The brightness of the screen can easily be scaled up or down and the relative color balance can be accurately adjusted. All of the colors and adjustments can be correctly controlled by the software.

An important difference between VGA and EGA or CGA monitors is the video format used. VGA adapters produce an analog or continuously variable signal for the monitor. EGA and CGA systems use the digital RGB method. It is this analog signal with its greater capacity for information content that permits the vast increase in the number of colors available to VGA. VGA adapters can also be made to interface with a 16-bit bus. This basically doubles the video speed over the 8-bit EGA or CGA system.

Super VGA Adapter

Super VGA or **SVGA** is still a higher resolution standard. For example, modes as high as 1024 horizontal pixels by 768 vertical pixels with 256 colors from a palette of 262,144 (256K) colors are available. Some manufacturers offer modes with 32,768 colors from a palette of 256 K colors. Today, many VGA adapters can be upgraded to Super VGA modes by adding additional memory. Standard VGA adapters generally have 256 K of video memory. Super VGA adapters require 512K and in many cases 1 Mb of video RAM.

Beyond Super VGA are DTP and XGA with still higher resolutions and more colors. All of the high-performance standards find their greatest use in professional desktop publishing, computer-aided design (CAD), and other graphic applications.

Dot Pitch

The spacing and number of dots or pixels on a screen will determine the degree of image detail or resolution. This spacing is called the **dot pitch** of the monitor. Dot pitch is usually measured in millimeters. There are four general classifications of monitors according to dot pitch.

Monitor Type	Dot Pitch
1. Standard television	0.62 mm or larger
2. Low resolution	0.41 to 0.61 mm
3. Medium resolution	0.30 to 0.40 mm
4. High resolution	0.29 mm or smaller

The smaller and closer the dots are, the greater the image detail that is possible. For example, a 12-in. diagonal monitor will typically have a horizontal display of 9.5 in. or approximately 240 mm. Characters are usually displayed in a 7 by 9 matrix (7 horizontal by 9 vertical) configuration within a 9 by 14 box as shown in Figure 8.39. The unused rows and columns of dots provide good separation between the characters.

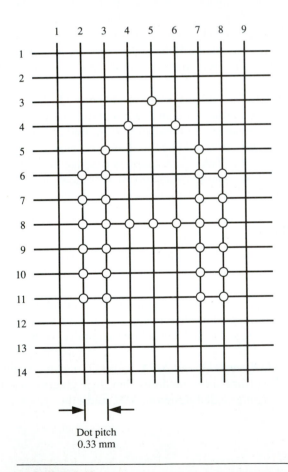

FIGURE 8.39
Dot pitch

If each character requires 9 dots and 80 characters must be displayed in each horizontal line, a total of 720 dots are required for a 240-mm line. The required dot pitch can be calculated as follows:

$$\text{Dot pitch} = \frac{240 \text{ mm}}{720 \text{ dots}}$$
$$= 0.33 \text{ mm/dot}$$

8.8 PRINTERS

So far in this chapter we have discussed the primary input and output devices, which are the keyboard and the CRT display, respectively. Sometimes it is necessary to produce the processed data as **hard copy,** or printed on a piece of paper. Since most modern computer systems use a CRT instead of a teletypewriter device, an additional peripheral device, a **printer,** is required. The printer is an electromechanical device that receives data in the form of binary-coded characters and prints the characters onto a piece of paper. New technology has had a tremendous effect on the evolution of the printer. Electronic and mechanical technological advances have transformed the huge mechanical machines into compact desktop units. There are many different types of printers available today. The type of printer chosen depends upon the user's specific needs, such as print speed, print quality, and economy. There are two major categories of printers: **impact printers** and **nonimpact printers.**

The impact printer forms the printed character by a mechanical contact with an ink-impregnated ribbon onto the paper. The many types of impact printers include dot-matrix, daisy wheel, drum, chain, and band printers. Impact printers have an electromagnet, known as a hammer, that supplies the mechanical energy to print the character.

A nonimpact printer forms the character without physically hitting an inked ribbon on the paper. The many forms of nonimpact printing include thermal transfer, ink jet, electrostatic, and laser printers. Nonimpact printers have the unique advantage of being extremely quiet.

Dot-Matrix Printers

The **dot-matrix printer** is the most widely used printer on microcomputers today. The characters are formed by printing a series of dots on the paper, similar to the method used by the display adapter, as shown in Figure 8.40.

Dot matrix printers are usually fast, but since the characters are made up of dots, the characters tend to be somewhat choppy. Some dot-matrix printers offer a "near-letter-quality" mode by printing more dots per character, but this slows down the print speed. The most widely used impact dot-matrix printers use a group of needles, or wires, connected to electromagnets. The needle-and-electromagnet assembly is known as the printhead. The needles are arranged in a group of 7 to 24 vertical dots, depending on the printer. The needles are often staggered to allow for the dots to overlap, which causes the dots to blend together for a smoother image, as shown in Figure 8.41.

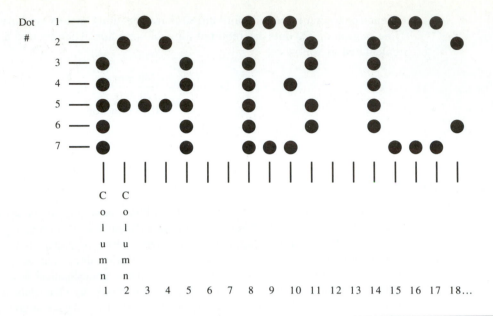

FIGURE 8.40
Dot-matrix characters

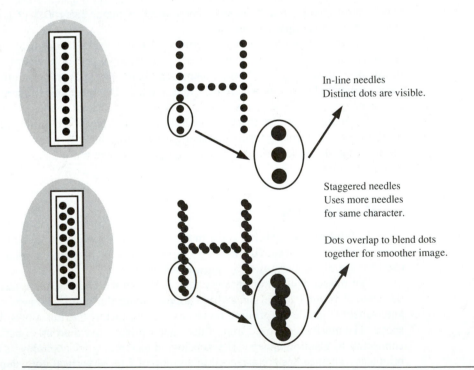

FIGURE 8.41
The dot-matrix impact printhead

The printhead is mounted on a motor-driven sliding carriage assembly. The older printer carriage drives were fixed-speed motors. The dot timing, which is the spacing between the dot groupings, was generated by an optical timing fence, which is a transparent strip containing a series of vertical stripes. Mounted below the printhead is a photosensor that senses these stripes and determines when the next group of dots are to be printed.

One variation of this design is the use of a slotted disk on the carriage motor shaft instead of the timing fence. In the newer printers the carriage drive system has been simplified with the use of a stepper motor. This allows for precise head positioning, so the head position sensor is not required. The paper feed mechanism is also stepper motor driven, which allows for precise paper positioning. Most newer printers have the ability to print graphics as well as text due to the precise positioning mechanisms.

Two variations of the dot-matrix printer are a single reciprocating hammer printer and the reciprocating "comb" printer. In the single reciprocating hammer printer the printhead consists of a single dot and electromagnet. The printhead reciprocates up and down the length of one character to form the vertical dot matrix while also sliding sideways on the carriage assembly. This is a simple and economical means of printing but has the disadvantage of being slow.

In the second variation a series of hammers is mounted on a comb of dots. The comb is mounted on a reciprocating shuttle assembly. The characters are formed by printing an entire line of dots at a time by firing the hammers while the shuttle is reciprocating horizontally. The paper is advanced a fraction of one character after each line is printed until all the lines have been printed to form the entire character.

The **thermal dot matrix printer** functions similarly, but the printhead is entirely different. Instead of electromechanical hammers and an inked ribbon to print dots on the paper, a group of heaters is used. The earlier thermal printers required the use of treated thermal paper, which changed color when heated. While these printers are usually less expensive than impact printers, the paper is far more expensive. If the paper is accidentally heated or left out in the sunlight, it turns dark, making the printed copy unreadable. As a solution to this problem the newer printers use a thermal ribbon. When the ribbon is heated against plain paper, the heated pigment transfers to the paper, forming an image on regular untreated paper.

Daisy Wheel Printers

Daisy wheel printers are impact printers. The entire printable character set is contained on a plastic wheel that resembles a daisy. Each petal of the flower has a different character on it. This method produces the best type quality, since the entire character is typed just as on a typewriter. Since the daisy wheel must start, spin, stop, and settle at the desired spot, these printers are much slower than dot matrix printers. A motor rotates the daisy wheel to position the desired character between the hammer and the inked ribbon, as shown in Figure 8.42. The hammer is then fired, which drives the character type onto the ribbon and the paper, thus forming an image of that character on the paper. The daisy wheel and hammer assembly is mounted on a sliding carriage similar to the dot-matrix printer. The one major disadvantage is that it is not possible to produce graphics on this type of printer.

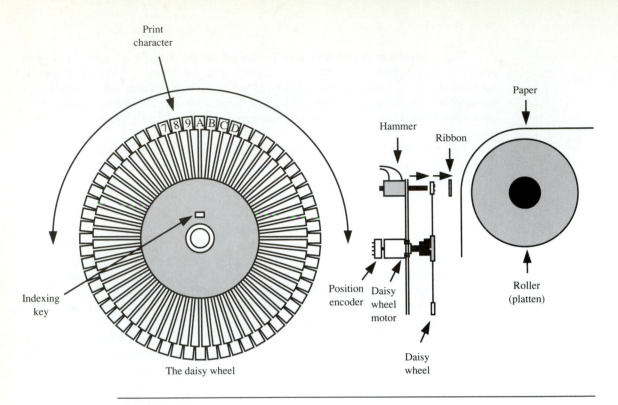

FIGURE 8.42
The daisy-wheel printer

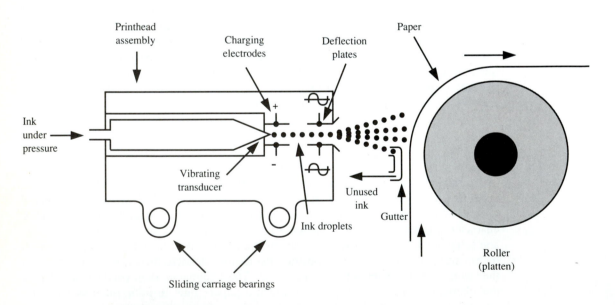

FIGURE 8.43
The ink jet printer

Ink Jet Printers

The **ink jet printer** is another form of nonimpact matrix printer. The characters or images are formed by firing ink droplets at a high velocity onto the paper. The ink droplets are formed by pumping liquid ink into a vibrating chamber with a small orifice at the opposite end. The ink droplets are electrically charged as they pass through an electrostatic field generated by charging plates. The droplets are then deflected up or down by the deflection plates to create the vertical matrix while the printhead is sliding sideways to create the horizontal matrix, as shown in Figure 8.43.

A variation of this method uses several orifices and impulse fires the ink droplets without using a deflection system, similar to the impact matrix system. The carriage and paper feed mechanisms for the ink jet printer are similar to those used for the impact matrix printer.

The Laser Printer

The **laser printer** is another form of nonimpact printer that uses the transfer electrophotography method of imaging, with a laser as the primary light source. The laser printer is really an expansion of the conventional office photocopier. The original lamps and glass faceplate of the office photocopier are replaced with a modulated scanning laser beam.

As shown in Figure 8.44, a laser light source is modulated with an acousto-optical shutter, which turns the beam on and off by electronic control. The modulated light beam is then channeled to a rotating polygon-shaped mirror. The rotating mirror causes the light beam, focused by a lens, to scan across the surface of a photoreceptor drum, which is a conductive drum that is coated with a photoconductive material such as cadmium sulfide (CdS) or a selenium-based substance. When the photoreceptor drum is charged by an electrostatic field and then parts of it are exposed to light, the electrostatic charge directly below the light beam bleeds down to the drum potential by photoconduction. This has the effect of leaving an image of charges on the surface of the photoreceptor drum. The polygonal mirror rotates continuously, creating repeated scans, while the photoreceptor drum rotates at a much slower rate, creating a raster of lines, similar to a video display. A charged, fine granular toner is then applied to the photoreceptor drum. The toner sticks only to the opposite charge on the drum. Plain paper is then charged opposite to the toner charge and fed under the photoreceptor drum at the same speed in which the drum is rotating. The image formed by the toner transfers to the paper due to the higher opposite charge on the paper. The paper is then sent to a fuser drum, which is heated and melts, or fuses, the toner image onto the paper, making the image permanent. The electronic circuitry required to generate the image is similar to the video display controller discussed previously.

8.9 INTERFACE STANDARDS

Since there are many different manufacturers of computers and computer peripherals, some form of standards is necessary. If interface standards were not used, it would be

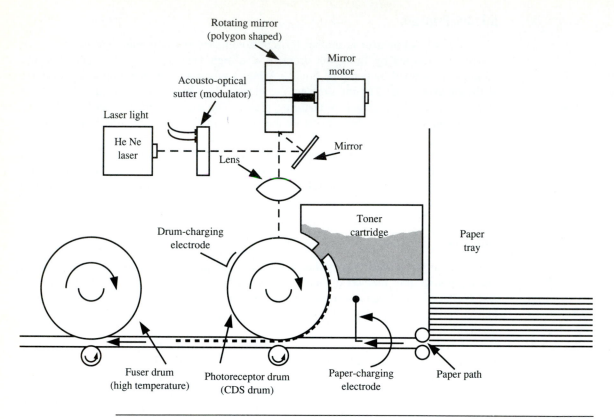

FIGURE 8.44
The laser printer

difficult to connect a printer from one manufacturer to a computer from another manufacturer. Most microcomputer systems support two types of peripheral interfaces, the centronics parallel interface and the asynchronous serial interface standards. There is another parallel printer standard known as the data products interface, but it is rarely used on microcomputers.

The Centronics Printer Interface

The centronics printer interface standard is used by the IBM PC and many other computers as well. This interface is an 8-bit parallel data interface with handshaking. The term **handshaking** means some form of status communication between devices. For example, when the printer is out of paper or it is off line, it must be able to tell the computer of this condition. The logic levels are defined as TTL logic levels, typically 0.80 V for a 0 state and 2.4 V for the 1 state. Not all printers use all the available status lines supplied by the IBM printer interface, but the strobe and busy lines must be used. The strobe line signals the printer that a character of data to be printed is currently on the data lines. The busy line is used to signal the computer when the printer is busy and cannot accept any data. The acknowledge line can be used when sending a stream of characters to accomplish the handshaking while filling the printer's internal buffer, if it exists. The rest of the status lines may or may not be used, depending on the printer. The IBM printer adapter card provides 12 output and 5 input lines. The first 8 bits are the character data and are decoded to I/O address 378 hex. The second group of 4 bits is used for printer control and are decoded to I/O address 37A hex.

The connector printouts are defined in Table 8.1.

TABLE 8.1
Centronics/IBM printer interface pinouts

Pin	Signal Name	Direction	Address	Data Bit
1	Strobe	To printer	37A	0
2	Data bit 0 (LSB)	To printer	378	0
3	Data bit 1	To printer	378	1
4	Data bit 2	To printer	378	2
5	Data bit 3	To printer	378	3
6	Data bit 4	To printer	378	4
7	Data bit 5	To printer	378	5
8	Data bit 6	To printer	378	6
9	Data bit 7 (MSB)	To printer	378	7
10	Acknowledge	From printer	379	6
11	Busy	From printer	379	7
12	PE (out of paper)	From printer	379	5
13	Select	From printer	379	4
14	Auto linefeed	To printer	37A	1
15	Error	From printer	379	3
16	Initialize printer	To printer	37A	2
17	Select input	To printer	37A	3
18	Ground	To pin 25 all grounds		
25	Ground			

The Asynchronous Serial Interface

Most computers provide at least one general-purpose communications port. This communications port may be used for almost any external peripheral device or as a link to another computer. The most universal and widely used method for data communications is known as the **asynchronous serial data** method. The term *serial data* means that the data bits are sent down the line one bit at a time, usually by loading a data byte into a shift register and clocking the data out in bit serial format. The term asynchronous means that no external clock or timing signals are required to accompany the data. The data is sent as a group of bits known as a **frame.** Each frame of data is preceded by one **start bit,** which is the first mark-to-space transition. The mark state is the TTL high state, and the space state is the TTL low state, *before any level conversion.* The start bit must be held for 1 bit time. Next, the data bits are sent, starting with the LSB. The data bits are followed with an optional parity bit. After the last bit is sent out, the line *must* return to the mark state for at least 1 bit time, which is known as the **stop bit(s).** A typical frame of data for an ASCII "A" with even parity is shown in Figure 8.45. Since the data is not synchronous, the stop bit may be any length as long as it is *at least* 1 bit time long. One exception is if the receiving equipment is expecting two stop bits, then two must be sent or a timing error known as a **framing error** will occur. The data bit field may be any length but is usually 7 or 8 bits long. Again, the sending and receiving equipment must be set to the same data length, or a framing error will occur.

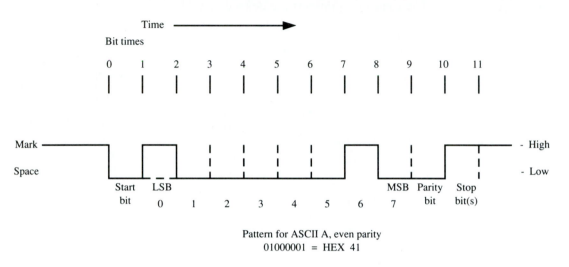

Pattern for ASCII A, even parity
01000001 = HEX 41

FIGURE 8.45
Asynchronous data frame

The rate at which the data bits are sent is known as the **baud rate.** A speed of 9600 baud means that 9600 bits per second are being transmitted. If the serial format is set for 8 bits, no parity, then 10 bit times are required for each character. This means that 960 characters are sent per second. There are many LSI IC chips on the market for serial data formatting, transmitting, and receiving. These ICs are often referred to as UARTs, which stands for universal asynchronous receiver transmitter. The latest chips are designed for microprocessor bus compatibility, and some contain built-in programmable baud rate generators. The IBM asynchronous communications adapter uses the INS8250 LSI chip and is completely programmable regarding speed, bits per character, parity, and stop bits.

Serial data is rarely interfaced at the TTL level but is usually converted to current loop or line driver levels. Most all serial interface lines today conform to the **RS-232C** standard. The logic levels are converted to the following values:

- *Marking level*. Logical true = -3 to -15 V, typically -12 V.
- *Spacing level*. Logical false = $+3$ to $+15$ V, typically $+12$ V.

Several status and modem control lines also accompany the transmit and receive data lines and are defined as follows:

- *Received data* (pin 2). Serial data into the computer or peripheral device.
- *Transmit data* (pin 3). Serial data from the computer or peripheral device.
- *Request to send* (pin 4). A status line from the computer that signals that the computer is ready to send data.
- *Clear to send* (pin 5). A status line to the computer that informs the computer when to stop or start sending data.
- *Data set ready* (pin 6). A status line, usually from a **modem** (a serial data transmission and receiving device), that signals the computer that the modem is ready to operate.
- *Carrier detect* (pin 8). A status line, usually from a modem, that signals the computer that a connection to a remote modem is established.
- *Data terminal ready* (pin 20). A status line from the computer or peripheral device that indicates that the device is on line or ready.
- *Ring indicator* (pin 22). A status line from a modem that indicates that the telephone line is ringing.

Two popular terms that are used in describing the connections on an RS-232 link are **DTE** and **DCE.** Without trying to confuse the issue, we will describe them briefly. DTE stands for **data terminating equipment,** and DCE stands for **data circuit terminating equipment.** The DTE is the computer or peripheral device, and the DCE is the modem or modem eliminator (crossover box) for direct connections without the use of modems. Most RS-232 interfaces use a 25-pin connector known as a DB-25-P or a DB-25-S connector. The P means pins (for male) and the S means sockets (for female). The printouts for most DTEs are shown in Table 8.2.

The interface and connections just discussed were originally designed to connect DTE, such as computers and peripheral devices, together through DCE, which are modems. There seems to be much confusion when connecting serial devices together, such as one computer to another computer or a serial printer to a computer through the serial port. It is obvious that it is not possible to wire the serial DTE devices together pin for pin. We must cross some of the pins or use a device called a *null modem,* which simply crosses pins 2–3, 3–2, 4–5, 5–4, 6–8–20, 20–8–6. In some applications—for example, the serial printer—the ready/busy status line from the printer must be wired to clear to send on the IBM PC for proper handshaking. In the worst case the receive data is simply wired to transmit data and signal ground is wired to signal ground. The rest of the status inputs are wired to the data terminal ready line (forced true always). This usually works if all else fails.

Some serial devices use the X-ON/X-OFF protocol for handshaking, which eliminates the need for status line wiring. The X-ON/X-OFF protocol is accomplished by sending control codes back to the host computer. The X-OFF control character tells the computer to stop sending data while the printer or other device is busy. The X-ON code tells the computer to resume sending data.

TABLE 8.2
RS-232 DTE printout chart

Pin	Signal Name
1	Safety ground (chassis)
2	Received data
3	Transmit data
4	Request to send
5	Clear to send
6	Data set ready
7	Signal ground (common)
8	Data carrier detect
19	Reverse channel
20	Data terminal ready
22	Ring indicator

Additional Nonstandard Pin Usage

9	+ Transmit current loop data
11	− Transmit current loop data
11	Ready/busy used by some printers
18	+ Receive current loop data
25	− Receive current loop data

Note: Be extremely careful when using nonstandard pins.

A Word About Current Loop   The current-loop communication method dates back to the days of the telegraph. This method was widely used in the 1960s and early 1970s when the teletype was commonly used as a computer terminal. In some cases the current-loop interface is still used today. There seems to be much confusion when connecting current-loop peripherals to computers. This confusion is easily eliminated when you understand how to connect to the interface. In the current-loop system there are two loops, one for the receiver and one for the transmitter. In the case of the printer in which no status is returned, only one loop is required. Each loop must have an active end and a passive end. The active end supplies the current for the loop. There is no standard that determines which end of the loop is active or passive. The teletype, for example, has an active printer and a passive keyboard, as shown in Figure 8.46. The keyboard circuit is a simple rotary switch. The printer circuit contains the current source and the print mechanism solenoid. The IBM asynchronous adapter will support current-loop devices. The receive circuit at the adapter card is a passive circuit and is simply an input to an optical isolator. The transmit circuit at the adapter card is active and supplies approximately 30 mA of current.

8.10   MODEMS AND ACOUSTIC COUPLERS

A modem is an electronic device that converts digital data into a series of audio tones for transmission on a voice-grade communication channel and also converts audio tones back into digital data. The word *modem* is an acronym for **modulator-demodulator.** The

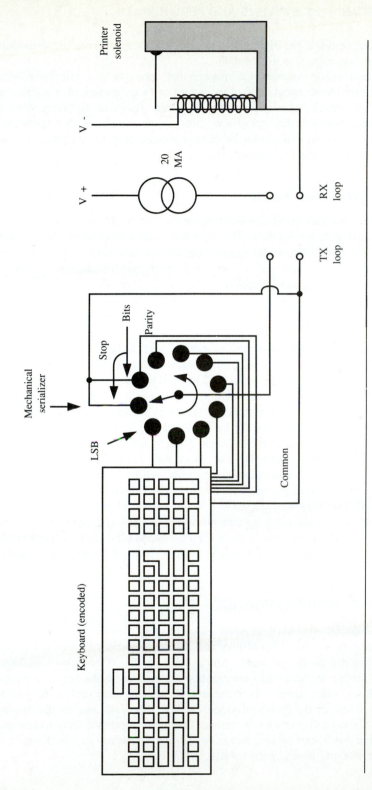

FIGURE 8.46
The teletype current loop

modulator converts the digital data into audio tones, whereas the demodulator converts the audio tones back to digital data.

An *acoustic coupler* is a modem that connects to a telephone without a direct connection. The connection is done acoustically by means of a speaker and a microphone, into which the telephone handset is laid. This was necessary years ago when the telephone company did not allow direct connections to its equipment. Currently, communication equipment may be directly connected to the telephone line *as long as the equipment meets the FCC standards.*

Full Duplex—Half Duplex

The term **full duplex** means that the modem is capable of sending data at the same time that it is receiving data. This is usually accomplished by using two sets of audio tones. The term **half-duplex** means that the modem may only send or receive at one time. It is not capable of sending and receiving simultaneously due to bandwidth restrictions or some other problem.

Modem Operation

There are two popular modem standards in use on microcomputers today, the Bell 103, 300 baud and the Bell 212, 1200 baud systems. The BELL 103 modem uses simple frequency shift keying. The BELL 212 modem uses a special grouped-bit phase encoding method. Lately modem manufacturers have begun adding microcomputers into the modem designs, making the modems "smart." These modems are capable of answering the telephone and automatically switching to the baud rate of the incoming call. One company set the standard for the smart modem communication protocol by creating the Hayes Smartmodem Instruction Set. Since then many have copied this instruction set. Among the many communication programs written for the instruction set, there are simple telephone dialers, multiterminal emulators, and automatic stock price–acquisition programs. The command set starts with the letters AT for attention. For example, ATD 777-1234 means dial the telephone number 777-1234 and connect if a carrier is sensed. Since the modem must conform to the FCC standards, it is recommended that modem repair be left to a *qualified* repair shop that can make measurements to verify compliance.

8.11 TECH TIPS AND TROUBLESHOOTING—T³

In this chapter we have covered video display theory in great detail. A thorough understanding of the video display and display generator is required if economical and timely repairs are to be made. Since the circuitry is complex—analog, digital, and critical timing are involved—troubleshooting even with the best test equipment will be difficult in some cases. As complex as this all may seem, if you have a good understanding of the theory of video display, the symptoms on the display screen will almost always tell you what is wrong. The most important thing to remember is: *Don't panic* and *don't start turning things or changing parts at random.* Keep in mind that you may be working around *high voltage, so be careful.*

At first the screen may not make any sense to you, so try to break the symptoms down to the related circuitry. For example, is it a sweep failure, or is the problem in the video circuit or the display generator card? First check for a raster by turning the contrast all the way down and the brightness up, which should result in an evenly lighted screen. In the following sections we present some tips and clues to make the job of repairing computer peripheral devices a little easier.

Troubleshooting Keyboards

Most keyboard failures are due to stuck keys or debris lodged in the contacts. Check that *every* key has a "good feel" and returns up rapidly. If multiple characters show up when only one key is pushed, that indicates key bounce, which is a bad contact on that key. The contacts must be cleaned or the keyswitch replaced. If a group of keys are dead, one wire to the keyswitch matrix may be broken, or the keyboard scanner may have a dead line. This can be checked with an oscilloscope. Using the schematics and some common sense should get you to the problem fast.

Troubleshooting the Video Display

The most common failures in video monitors are in the deflection circuitry (sweep). Horizontal sweep failures usually result in no brightness on the screen because the high voltage is generated by the horizontal deflection circuitry. In some cases all the low-voltage DC power is generated by the horizontal deflection circuitry. The first thing to do when troubleshooting a "dead," or dark, screen is to check for the presence of high voltage. The recommended procedure is to use a high-voltage probe on the anode lead of the CRT. If the probe is not available, then simply hold an NE-2 neon bulb near the anode lead. If the bulb glows, some high voltage is present. If no high voltage exists, check the horizontal output for the flyback pulse using an oscilloscope. The flyback pulse should be a large pulse with a "dimple" in the top and have a smooth rise and fall. Any deformation of the pulse indicates an excessive load due to a faulty flyback transformer or component on the secondary of the flyback.

The most common failures here are usually the horizontal output transistor or the damper diode. These failures usually blow the power supply fuse. If no flyback pulse exists, check the base drive to the output transistor. Failure of the base drive indicates that the horizontal oscillator or driver is failing. Some monitors, like the IBM monochrome, have X-ray protection built in if the power supply voltage becomes too high. The protection works by grounding the input to the driver circuit, thus killing the high voltage.

A gassy CRT or shorted high-voltage rectifier will kill the high voltage. To check for this, remove the anode cap from the CRT. Power on the monitor and check for high voltage at the anode wire. Using an insulated-handle screwdriver, try to draw an arc off the anode wire. Here is a little tip: *high-voltage AC will arc to floating metal, but high-voltage DC will not arc to floating metal*. A heavy arc indicates a shorted high-voltage rectifier. Carefully replace the anode cap onto the CRT. If the high voltage is present but the screen is dark, check the bias voltages on the CRT socket. Recall that if the cathode is more positive than grid 1 by about 70 V or more, the beam will be cut off. If the bias voltages are within specification and the screen is still dark, a bad CRT is indicated. Conversely, if the screen is too bright, check the bias voltages on the CRT socket. An open pin inside the CRT will sometimes cause the brightness to run away.

Many solid-state monitors AC couple the horizontal yoke coil through a nonpolarized electrolytic capacitor. A failure of this capacitor is indicated by a single vertical line in the middle of the screen. Since the yoke requires approximately a 15-A peak current at a high frequency, a special high-current capacitor is required here. If this capacitor is replaced with a standard-type electrolytic capacitor, *it will explode after a few minutes of operation.* We have found that replacing the original electrolytic type with a standard foil or mica type proves far more reliable. This replacement is physically larger and may not fit in some cases. Remember, the high-voltage situation can be extremely dangerous. *Do not attempt to work on a high-voltage problem until you have learned the proper safety precautions.*

Vertical deflection problems are a dead giveaway. A single horizontal line indicates no vertical sweep. In this case the vertical oscillator is dead or the yoke circuit is open. Most monitors use a push-pull circuit for the vertical output, similar to an audio amplifier. No top or bottom indicates one of the output transistors or its related circuitry is bad. If the picture is distorted, then a wave-shape problem exists, and there is probably a faulty capacitor in the vertical circuit. Small aluminum electrolytic capacitors are notorious for changing value, usually to open. If the problem is no video, simply follow the cathode wire with an oscilloscope back through the video amplifier to the source of video until the failure is found.

Troubleshooting the Display Generator

Carefully observe the picture and try to isolate the failure to a major functional block. Measure the horizontal and vertical synchronization pulses. If the sync pulses are the correct timing values, the master timing must be correct. If the horizontal is good but the vertical is bad, the problem is in the countdown chain. If no sync pulses exist, check the master oscillator. If the picture is synchronized but the displayed image is bad, it will tell a story.

Command the computer to clear the screen. The computer writes all ASCII spaces to the display RAM. The code for a space is hex 20, 00100000 binary. Now let's say, for example, that the screen is full of 0s. The code for a zero is hex 30, 00110000 binary. It becomes obvious that 1 bit is "picked" in memory due to a bad RAM chip or buffer. If the computer displays only the top half of the characters and repeats them twice, the character ROM or an address line to the ROM must be bad.

Here is an experiment to try on the IBM PC with a color graphics card.

1. Type CLS; the screen should clear.
2. Type DEBUG (it must be on your DOS disk).
3. At the '-' prompt, type E B800:0 (enter).
4. Type 41 (enter); an *A* should appear on the top left of the screen.

What we just did was to write the hex code 41, which is an ASCII *A*, at memory address B800:0000, which is the first location of the video RAM. This is a simple way to test the RAM on the display generator.

Troubleshooting Printers

Handle the printer the same way as the video display. Observe the printout sample. Determine if the problem is mechanical or electronic. Printing wrong characters, such as *C* instead of *A,* indicates an electronic failure. Fuzzy, improperly spaced, or missing dots may be mechanical problems. The most common failures are the printheads. The second most common failures are the driver transistors, both printhead and stepper motor drivers. Don't be too hasty about replacing a stepper motor because they rarely fail. To verify the stepper motor is good, slowly rotate the shaft with power off. Each step should be even; jumping or missing indicates a possible shorted winding. If dots are missing, check the coil drive pulses. Look at the printhead dots carefully. The wire dots break easily. Check each coil for an open condition with an ohmmeter.

EXERCISES

8.1　　　Briefly describe a keyboard.

8.2　　　What does the encoder do?

8.3　　　What is the term used when the keys are wired as rows and columns?

8.4　　　What chip is used to encode the IBM keyboard?

8.5　　　What data format will reduce the wire count to a minimum?

8.6　　　What type of display is used on most computers?

8.7　　　What does CRT stand for?

8.8　　　Where does the electron beam originate?

8.9　　　How do we control the beam?

8.10　　What is a raster?

8.11　　The electron beam is ＿＿＿＿＿ during retrace.

8.12　　Show the formula to calculate the maximum number of scan lines.

8.13　　If the horizontal rate is 15,750 and the vertical rate is 60, what is the maximum number of scan lines?

8.14　　Explain why a vacuum is required in the CRT.

8.15　　Name the four basic elements of the CRT.

8.16　　Why do we need the heater?

8.17　　True or false: The anode has a high negative potential on it.

8.18　　How is the electron beam bent in most CRTs?

8.19　　What is painted on the inside face of the CRT?

8.20　　How do we control the brightness?

8.21　　True or false: The screen grid is usually set to a fixed value.

8.22　　What causes the screen to glow?

8.23　　True or false: The high voltage comes from the power transformer.

8.24　　What does the tripler do?

8.25　　A ＿＿＿＿＿ waveform is used to correct the focus nonlinearity.

8.26　　The yoke is made up of ＿＿＿＿＿.

8.27 A _____ waveform is used on the yoke.

8.28 True or false: The horizontal output generates a ramp.

8.29 When is the flyback pulse created?

8.30 The vertical yoke is driven by a _____ waveform.

8.31 What type of circuit is the horizontal oscillator?

8.32 What is the name for the signal that contains the image?

8.33 What is usually applied to the cathode?

8.34 What does the contrast control do?

8.35 Why do color monitors have separate gain controls?

8.36 For what does NTSC stand?

8.37 Draw a typical video waveform.

8.38 What is the color burst for?

8.39 How is composite color modulated?

8.40 What is the high-frequency signal that feeds the shift register called?

8.41 The digital image data is stored in the _____ _____.

8.42 The smallest part of a picture is called a _____.

8.43 What contains the patterns of characters?

8.44 The display RAM in the IBM PC is _____ mapped.

8.45 What is the address of the display RAM in the color graphics adapter?

8.46 What is the maximum horizontal resolution of the IBM color graphics adapter?

8.47 An impact printer uses an _____ _____ on paper.

8.48 Describe a dot-matrix character.

8.49 What is a thermal printer?

8.50 What is on the daisy wheel?

8.51 How does the ink jet printer work?

8.52 What is the photosensitive part of the laser printer?

8.53 The laser printer uses a _____ _____ to scan the drum.

8.54 The most popular parallel interface is the _____.

8.55 Define handshaking.

8.56 Describe one asynchronous data frame.

8.57 What is the typical voltage level for RS232C?

8.58 What is current loop?

8.59 Crossword Puzzle

ACROSS

3. A method of doubling the vertical resolution.

7. The picture information is called _____.

12. If a material will give off light when bombarded by electrons, it must have a _____ characteristic.

14. When the sync and picture information are combined on the same line.

16. Left-to-right deflection.

17. Most monitors use _____ deflection.

18. The print method used when an inked ribbon strikes the paper.

20. The most positive element.

21. When the beam is returning back to the left or top.

22. Converts digital data into audio tones.

23. A sample of the color reference signal.

27. A mechanical device for displaying computer data.
28. The inside face of the CRT is painted with _____.
29. A series of lines.
30. The most popular printer interface standard.

DOWN

1. Clear to send.
2. The high-voltage transformer.
4. The _____ grid will help to make the picture clear.
5. Converting keys into binary is done by the _____.
6. The origination of the electron beam.
8. The elements that control the electron beam.
9. What will gasses do when subjected to high voltage?
10. Top-to-bottom deflection.
11. A simple input device.
13. The electron beam is bent by a means called _____.
14. Cathode ray tube.
15. The shape of the vertical waveform.
16. The _____ will supply the mechanical energy to print a character.
19. Characters made up from a group of dots.
24. An LSI chip that converts data to serial form and back.
25. The serial false level.
26. The component that deflects the electron beam.

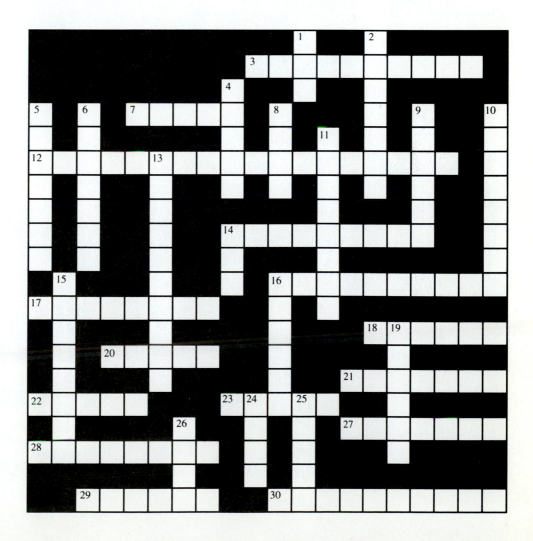

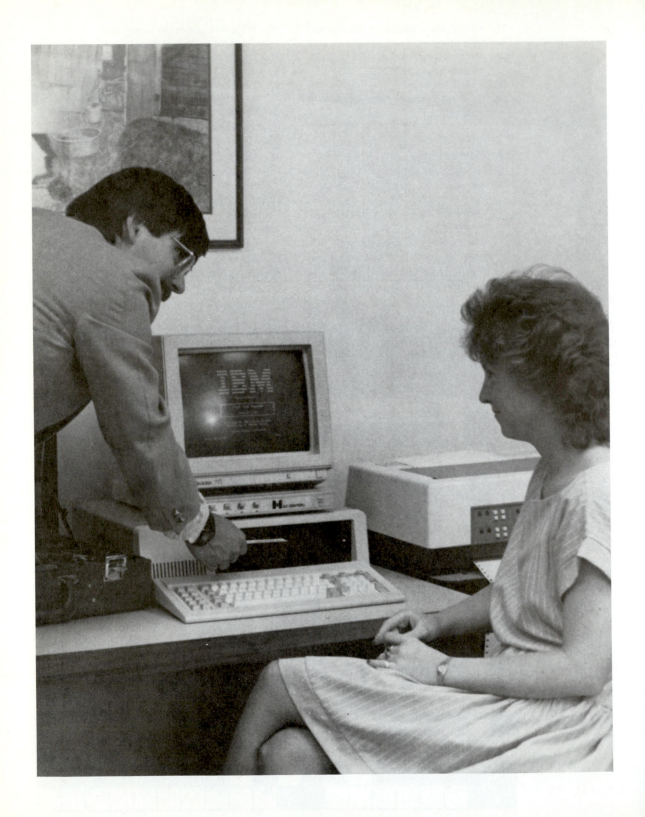

INSTALLATION AND SERVICE

The computer service industry holds an important and unique place in today's business world because it is critical when a business's computer fails. Quick, competent, and reliable servicing and repair are absolute necessities.

Most businesses cannot allow their computers to go down for any period of time. A decade ago, when microcomputers were first introduced into companies, they were used in only a limited fashion; therefore, it wasn't critical if the microcomputer was down for a few days. Today, with the growth of powerful microcomputers in the business world, even 1 day of down time is unacceptable. Imagine what would happen to a business if employee paychecks were not ready on payday, if invoices and billings were sent out late, or if proposals for new business opportunities could not be processed on time.

The traditional computer service process is a straightforward one. A well-trained computer service technician is sent to diagnose a problem on a computer system and to do whatever is necessary to repair the system. In general, this is the way most small business computers are repaired today.

The traditional service call has become increasingly expensive. This is due in part to the substantial and growing salaries of service technicians. While the cost to repair a microcomputer system is rising, the price of these systems keeps falling. These economic pressures have led to the use of a number of new servicing techniques. These techniques take advantage of improved technologies and are designed to lower service costs. The chapters in this section are intended to train the student to become the computer service technician that industry needs.

CHAPTER NINE

SETUP, SERVICING, AND CUSTOMER RELATIONS

KEY TERMS

Appearance

Communication

Configuration Switches

Customer Relations

Directory

DOS

File

File Allocation
Table (FAT)

Initial Program Load
(IPL)

Molex

Path

Post

Product Training

Ribbon Cable

9.0 INTRODUCTION

In this chapter we discuss the initial setup and servicing of the IBM PC. Since in many cases this work will be performed in the field, a good attitude and professional appearance are very important. The customer's opinion of how good your service company is will be based on the customer's impression of you. For this reason a portion of this chapter is dedicated to customer relations.

9.1 CONFIGURATIONS (PC, PC-XT)

There are two basic types of the original IBM PC: the IBM PC, model 5150, and the IBM PC-XT, model 5160. The main difference between the two types is the number of internal I/O slots on the system board and the capacity of the internal power supply. The IBM PC allows five I/O cards on the system board and uses a power supply with a capacity of 65 W. The IBM PC-XT allows 8 I/O cards on the system board and uses a power supply with a capacity of 135 W. Furthermore, the IBM PC has an additional connector mounted next to the keyboard connector, as shown in Figure 9.1. This additional connector is for an audiocassette recorder. The IBM PC allows the use of standard audiocassettes to store data and programs, but this feature is rarely used any more. The audiocassette connector is not implemented on the IBM PC-XT. Two types of system boards are used on the IBM PC, depending on the age of the computer. The original system board used 16,384 by 1-bit RAM chips and allowed for a maximum of 65,536 bytes of RAM. This early-style board is called the 16-64K system board. The later model of the IBM PC uses 65,536 by 1-bit RAM chips and allows 262,144 bytes of

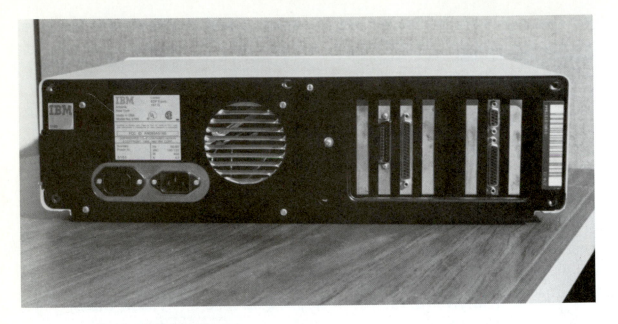

FIGURE 9.1
Rear panel of IBM PC

RAM on the system board. The later-style system board is called the 64-256K system board. A new version of the IBM PC-XT known as the enhanced PC-XT allows a maximum RAM memory of 655,360 (640K) bytes on the system board.

9.2 SWITCH SETTINGS

A common cause of problems in computer hardware is the improper setting of the internal **configuration switches.** The configuration switches in the IBM PC informs the internal device driver programs contained in the BIOS ROM about which devices are installed in the system. It is important to remember that the IBM PC uses two switch blocks, whereas the IBM PC-XT uses only one switch block. The IBM PC requires the two switch blocks because of the different memory chip types used. The older IBM PC used the 16K RAM chips, but the newer IBM PC uses the 64K RAM chips. Since the IBM PC-XT uses only the 64K RAM chips, only one switch block is needed. While switch block 1 is similar on the IBM PC and the IBM PC-XT, some of the switches function differently (see Figure 9.2). A description of the switches of switch block 1 follows.

SW1-1 on the IBM PC indicates if any floppy disk drives are present in the system. Remember that the IBM PC has a cassette interface and can be used without a floppy disk system. If the switch is on, no floppy disk drives are installed. If the switch is off, one or more floppy disk drives are present, and the system will attempt to load the disk operating system (DOS) from disk drive A after the power-on self-test (POST) system

FIGURE 9.2
IBM PC internal configuration switches

check is completed. Switch 1-1 functions differently on the IBM PC-XT. If switch SW1-1 is on, the system will LOOP through the POST forever. This may be helpful if an intermittent problem is suspected. This switch must be off for normal operation of the IBM PC-XT.

SW1-2 indicates if the INTEL 8087 math coprocessor is installed on the system board. This switch must be on if the 8087 chip is not installed.

SW1-3 and SW1-4 indicate how much memory is installed on the system board. Table 9.1 gives the proper settings for both the IBM PC and the IBM PC-XT. In the case of the newer 64-256K IBM PC system board, both switches must always be off. Memory above 64K is set by using switch block 2, which is discussed later.

SW1-5 and SW1-6 indicate the type of display subsystem installed. The settings are the same for both the IBM PC and the IBM PC-XT, as shown in Table 9.2. The BIOS ROM on the system board contains driver programs for both the color graphics and the monochrome display systems. Any display system that does not emulate one of these display systems must contain its own BIOS ROM.

SW1-7 and SW1-8 indicate the number of floppy disk drives installed on the system. Up to four floppy disk drives may be installed on one controller. The switch settings are the same for both the IBM PC and the IBM PC-XT, as shown in Table 9.3.

TABLE 9.1
Memory switch settings

SW1-3	SW1-4	IBM PC	IBM PC-XT
On	On	16K	64K (one row)
Off	On	32K	128K (two rows)
On	Off	48K	192K (three rows)
Off	Off	64K	256K (four rows)

TABLE 9.2
Display switch settings

SW1-5	SW1-6	Display system
On	On	No monitor or EGA system (BIOS on adapter)
Off	On	Color graphics system, 40-column mode
On	Off	Color graphics system, 80-column mode
Off	Off	Monochrome display system

TABLE 9.3
Disk drive switch settings

SW1-7	SW1-8	Number of Disk Drives
On	On	One drive, A
Off	On	Two drives, A, B
On	Off	Three drives, A, B, C
Off	Off	Four drives, A, B, C, D

Floppy disk drives C and D are connected to the rear connector of the controller board and must contain their own power supply.

Switch block 2 indicates the total memory over 64K in 32K byte increments. Switches 6, 7, and 8 of this switch block should always be off. In the case of the later IBM PC, the amount of memory installed on the system board is set by using this switch block, as shown in Table 9.4. Any memory above 640K is installed in the I/O slots and may also contain address switches. Since there are many variations of extended memory boards for the IBM PC, you must also consult the manufacturer's installation manual for that board. Failure to set the address switches on the extended memory board will result in an address contention and may cause erratic operation or total failure of the system. This may be verified by removing the extended memory board and running the system. If the problem clears up, the switches may be set improperly. It should be noted that some clones of the IBM PC and PC-XT may use different switch settings. This information can be found in the documentation that comes with the system.

TABLE 9.4
Additional memory switch locations

SW2-1	SW2-2	SW2-3	SW2-4	SW2-5	Maximum Amount of RAM
On	On	On	On	On	64K (one row, 64–256K SB)
Off	On	On	On	On	96K
On	Off	On	On	On	128K (two rows, 64–256 SB)
Off	Off	On	On	On	160K
On	On	Off	On	On	196K (three rows, 64–256K SB)
Off	On	Off	On	On	224K
On	Off	Off	On	On	256K (four rows, 64–256K SB)
Off	Off	Off	On	On	288K
On	On	On	Off	On	320K
Off	On	On	Off	On	352K
On	Off	On	Off	On	384K
Off	Off	On	Off	On	416K
On	On	Off	Off	On	448K
Off	On	Off	Off	On	480K
On	Off	Off	Off	On	512K
Off	Off	Off	Off	On	544K
On	On	On	On	Off	576K
Off	On	On	On	Off	608K
On	Off	On	On	Off	640K (maximum memory)

9.3 CABLES AND CONNECTORS

Many of the internal components are connected by internal cables (see Figure 9.3). Faulty cables and poor connections are often a source of problems in the IBM PC. It is very important that the cables not be chafed or pinched in any way, or they may short circuit. The cable connectors should be inspected for loose contacts and cracked or broken housings. If the connector housings are damaged, poor contact and pin misalignment may occur, which may lead to component damage. Each pin of the connector should be inspected for damage and misalignment. The pins are very fragile and may become crushed and go unnoticed by a quick inspection. Extreme care must be taken to make sure the cables are not cut by the component leads of adjacent boards. The insulation used on the **ribbon cable** is very thin and is easily cut by the sharp component leads of the I/O boards. If the conductors of the cables should accidentally short to the I/O boards, component damage may occur due to improper voltage levels. Placement and orientation of the internal cables is very important. Careless, improper orientation can cause improper operation or component damage.

The power supply has four power cables coming from it. Two are for the system board power and are marked P_8 and P_9. The other two cables are for the floppy or hard disk power and are marked P_{10} and P_{11}. Some aftermarket upgrade power supplies have two additional cables, which are for additional floppy or hard disk drives, thus allowing four disk drives to be connected to the power supply at the same time. Connector P_8 from the power supply must be connected to P_1 on the system board. Pin 1 of connector P_8 is

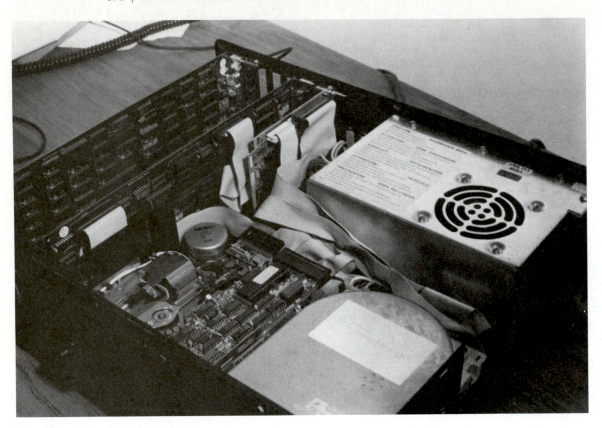

FIGURE 9.3
IBM PC internal cables and connectors

connected to the rearmost pin, closest to the keyboard connector. This may also be identified as the orange wire. Connector P_9 from the power supply must be connected to P_2 on the system board. Pin 1 of connector P_9 is the black wire and is the first pin next to P_1/P_8. The connectors shown in Figure 9.4 are keyed to prevent improper connection; however, the keys may be broken off, allowing for the possibility of an improper connection. If the power supply is improperly connected, serious system damage may occur. The pin definitions are given in Table 9.5.

The disk drive power connectors are the four-pin **molex** type. These connectors are almost impossible to connect backward due to their trapezoidal shape.

The pin definitions of the disk drive power are given in Table 9.6. P_{11} is the same as P_{10}.

The small speaker in the front of the case is connected to the system board P_3 using a four-pin in-line connector. The polarity of this connector does not matter, so it may be connected either way (Figure 9.5).

FIGURE 9.4
Molex power connector

TABLE 9.5
System power

Connector	Pin	Purpose	Wire Color
P_8	1	Power good	Orange
	2	Not used	
	3	$+12$ V	Yellow
	4	-12 V	Blue
	5	Ground	Black
	6	Ground	Black
P_9	1	Ground	Black
	2	Ground	Black
	3	-5 V	White
	4	$+5$ V	Red
	5	$+5$ V	Red
	6	$+5$ V	Red

TABLE 9.6
Disk drive power

P_{10}	1	+12 V	Yellow
	2	Ground	Black
	3	Ground	Black
	4	+5 V	Red

FIGURE 9.5
IBM PC speaker connection

The floppy disk interface cable is a 34-pin ribbon-type cable with three connectors on it. The longest end of the cable is connected to the floppy disk adapter card. The colored stripe is pin 1. The middle connector is for floppy disk drive B. The last connector is connected to floppy disk drive A. It is identified by the strange twist in the cable between the drive A and drive B connectors. Since the disk drive unit-selection jumpers on both disk drives are set the same (for simplicity in the field), the unit selection is done by the twist in the cable. It is important to remember that *all* floppy disk drives are set up as unit 2. Some manufacturers label the first unit as unit 0; in this case the drive is set to respond to unit 1. Just remember to set each floppy disk drive to respond as the second unit. The connectors are usually keyed to prevent improper connection, but the keyways slip out easily. *An obvious sign that the connector is on backward is that the drive-select light is always on.* Connecting the interface cable backward does not cause permanent damage. The disk drive power is also connected to the power supply connector, as discussed earlier, by means of a four-pin molex type connector.

The hard disk drive interface cable is similar to the floppy disk interface cable, with two exceptions. First, the first unit, usually drive C, is connected to the connector *without* the twist. The second drive is connected to the connector *with* the twist. Second, an additional 20-pin ribbon cable is used for the data and clock signals. A separate data cable is required for each hard disk drive. Again, the stripe on the cable indicates the location of pin 1. The adapter board side of the cable uses dual in-line pin headers instead of the card edge connector as in the case of the floppy disk cable. We again emphasize that the cables *must* be dressed neatly to prevent cutting of the insulation on the sharp component leads.

9.4 OPERATION

Once the switches are correctly set and the cables are properly connected, the system may be powered up. The system first runs an internal test and then checks and sizes the memory. When all this is complete, the system attempts to **initial program load (IPL)** the disk operating system from the installed disk drives. The first attempt is to floppy disk drive A. If the system cannot load from floppy disk drive A, it attempts to load from hard disk drive C, if installed. If all disk drive loads fail, the system enters the built-in BASIC interpreter. If a hardware error or disk-read error is encountered during the IPL process, an error message is displayed on the screen along with the message PRESS F1 TO CONTINUE.

9.5 POWER-ON SELF-TEST (POST)

Almost all modern computers and microprocessor-controlled peripheral equipment perform a self-test upon power up. In the IBM PC this self-test is known as **POST.** It differs slightly between the IBM PC and the IBM PC-XT. POST is a series of diagnostic routines, contained in the BIOS ROM on the system board, that are invoked at power up. First, these diagnostic routines check out the various functions on the system board. Any basic system failures are indicated by tones on the speaker. Next, the internal RAM memory is checked, followed by the adapter boards and keyboard. If a failure is detected during this phase, an error code is displayed on the video screen that points out the failing subsystem. A complete list of the failure codes is given in Appendix E. In the IBM PC the screen is cleared, and a small blinking cursor appears in the upper left corner of the screen. This indicates that the early portion of POST has been completed successfully, and the system is checking memory. The system beeps the speaker once upon the successful completion of POST. The IBM PC-XT displays the current memory address under test, during the memory test phase, in the upper left portion of the display screen. The message looks like XXX KB OK, where XXX is a three-digit number indicating the memory address. The IBM PC-XT also beeps the speaker once upon the successful completion of POST. Any deviation—for example, multiple beeps or one long beep tone—is an indication of a POST error.

POST Errors

POST errors may be indicated several different ways, depending upon the type of failure. Early system board failures such as ROM, the first 16K of RAM, DMA, or other basic failures cause POST to halt, and the system appears to be dead. The only way to find the problem is to use a logic analyzer or an LED address bus indicator. Building plans for an address bus indicator called the Universal Microprocessor Tester are given in Chapter 12. The address indicated by the LED display and the IBM BIOS listing points to the failing section.

The IBM PC-XT and the IBM PC-AT added checkpoints to the BIOS diagnostic programs. At the beginning of each test the test number is outputted to a special I/O address. The progress of POST can be monitored visually by simply connecting a decoded LED display to the system bus. If the system halts, the number displayed on the LED display is the diagnostic test that failed. Again, you must refer to the IBM BIOS listing for an explanation of the number. If the system display screen is blank and you hear one long beep tone followed by two short beep tones, POST is indicating that it cannot access the display subsystem. This may be due to a faulty display adapter board, or the system board switches are not set correctly. There is also the possibility that the system board is at fault and cannot access the I/O channel.

Once POST has initialized the display subsystem, all subsequent errors are displayed on the screen. A displayed POST error takes on one of two basic formats: A peripheral or system error is displayed as a single 3- or 4-digit error code. For example, 1701 indicates that the hard disk system is failing. The first or first and second digits indicate the subsystem that failed. The last two digits are the error code. The second format is used for RAM memory errors. A POST memory failure looks like 1002 201. The first 4 digits indicate the failing bit and row of memory chips. The second 3 digits are the error code for a main memory error. This message may also be followed with a message like parity check 1, which indicates that a parity error in main memory has occurred during POST. A complete memory error listing is contained in Appendix E.

9.6 PREVENTIVE MAINTENANCE

The only part of the IBM PC that requires routine preventive maintenance is the floppy disk drive, which requires a periodic head cleaning and an alignment check. The old saying ''don't fix it if it isn't broken'' holds true here. Periodic cleaning of the system, especially of the peripherals (such as the printer) should keep the system functioning for a long time.

Documentation

Before attempting to repair any computer system or peripheral device, it is important to obtain the related documentation. The *IBM Technical Reference Manual* and the *IBM Hardware Maintenance and Service Manual* are excellent sources of information. Many of the disk drive manufacturers also provide excellent maintenance documentation for their products.

9.7 INTRODUCTION TO DOS

The **Disk Operating System (DOS)** is a group of programs that manage the operation of a computer. These programs enable you to communicate with the computer's hardware. They control the operation and uses of the computer's disks, printers, keyboard, monitor, and other devices. DOS also organizes and keeps track of the information that has been stored on computer disks and provides utility programs to copy, delete, edit, move files, etc.

A **file** is a group of related information that is stored in a highly organized manner. All programs, text, and data on a disk reside in files. A file on a disk can be compared to a file folder in a filing cabinet. DOS keeps track of all files using file names, which are kept in **directories** on the disk. Think of a directory as a drawer in the file cabinet. The file cabinet may have many drawers, and a disk may have many directories. These directories contain information about the size of a file, its location on the disk, and the dates that the file was created or updated.

At the beginning of each disk, DOS keeps track of the location of your files in an area called the **file allocation table (FAT).** The file allocation table is a type of index. It also allocates the free space on the disk to new files. Thus, the directories and file allocation table enable DOS to recognize and organize the files on a disk. The name of a file consists of the file name and the file name extension. The file name can be one to eight characters long. The extension can be one to three characters long. The general format for the file name is shown below.

NAME.DTA

Notice that a period is used to separate the file name from the extension. File name extensions can be very useful for organizing your files. You can ask DOS to list all the files with a certain extension. For example, at the DOS prompt, typing DIR will list all of the files in the current directory. Typing DIR *.TXT will list only the files with the extension TXT. These techniques will be illustrated shortly. The asterisk (*) is called a global or wild card character. It indicates that any character can occupy that position or any of the remaining positions on the file name or extension.

The DOS prompt tells you that DOS is operational and ready to accept a command. It also tells you the current or working disk drive. Disk drives are labeled as single letters (beginning with the letter A). The DOS prompt when working with drive A is shown below.

A>

The DOS prompt may also display the current working directory. To work with a different disk drive, simply type the letter of the new drive you want, then type a colon, and press the enter key. For example, at the A> DOS prompt, type B: and press enter. The process is shown below.

A>B: <enter>
B>

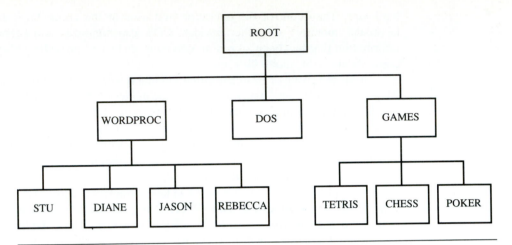

FIGURE 9.6
Directory structure

Directories

Recall that the directory and file allocation table form a type of index on a disk. The directory contains a list of file names, their size and location on the disk, and the dates they were created or updated. However, eventually the index will become cluttered or full. Therefore, DOS allows more than one directory (and even subdirectories) on a disk. Each directory can contain numerous files. Directories themselves are organized in a hierarchical structure as shown in Figure 9.6. The hierarchical directory structure can be thought of as a corporate organization chart. The creators of DOS thought of it as a "tree," except that the tree grows downward. Thus, the "root" is the highest level in the directory structure. The different levels of the subdirectories are the branches of the tree. The files within the directories and subdirectories are the leaves on the branches. The root directory is automatically created when you format a disk. The tree or directory structure grows as you create new directories for groups of files. The DOS TREE command will display the directory structure on the screen or on a printer. The backslash character (\) is used to identify the root directory.

You can create subdirectories using the make directory command (MD). For example, to create the subdirectory WORDPROC in Figure 9.6, type the following at the DOS prompt.

A>MD\WORDPROC

To create the next level subdirectory in Figure 9.6, type the following at the DOS prompt.

A>MD\WORDPROC\STU

You can change from your current working directory to another directory by using the change directory command (CD). For example, to change to the CHESS subdirectory, type the following at the DOS prompt.

A>CD\GAMES\CHESS

You can find out the name of the current directory that you are in by typing CD at the DOS prompt without any options. For example, typing

A>CD   <enter>

will result in

A:\GAMES\CHESS>

Thus, typing CD displays your current drive plus the current working directory.

The directory command (DIR) displays a list of all files in the current directory. A number of useful options exist.

A>DIR	Will respond with a list of all files in the current directory on the A drive.
A>DIR/W	Will respond with a list of files in the current directory on the A drive displayed horizontally. (More files will fit on the screen, but less information is given.)
A>DIR/P	Will cause the screen to pause when the screen is full. Press any key to continue.
A>DIR LETTER1.TXT	Displays all of the directory information (name of file, size of file, date last edited) for the file LETTER1.TXT.
A>DIR *.TXT	Displays all files in the current directory with the extension TXT.

You can access any file in your current directory structure regardless of where you are or where the file is located by typing the **path.** The path is a sequence of directory names followed by a file name. Each name is separated by a backslash (\). For example, referring to Figure 9.6 the path for the file name STUD would be

A:\GAMES\POKER\STUD

The remove directory command (RD) will delete a directory from the tree. The directory to be removed must be empty except for what is referred to as the two hidden files. The hidden files are listed as . and .., which are shorthand notations that represent the working directory and the parent directory (one level up from the working directory). Referring to Figure 9.6, to remove the TETRIS subdirectory, type the following from the root directory.

A>DEL\GAMES\TETRIS*.*

Then from the root directory, type

A>RD\GAMES\TETRIS

In the previous example, the delete command (DEL), the path, and the wild card characters were all used to delete all of the files with any extension from the TETRIS subdirectory. Remember that you cannot be in the directory you want to delete.

Other DOS Commands

The check disk command (CHKDSK) will display a status report for a disk as well as report errors. By including the /F option, CHKDSK will also fix any of the errors it finds. For example, for a status report of the disk in drive B, type

A>CHKDSK B:

or

A>CHKDSK B:/F

Figure 9.7 shows a typical response. The response will vary depending on the version of DOS being used.

Volume DRAWDEMO   created 08-28-1991 2:28p

1457664	bytes total disk space
1439232	bytes in 4 user files
18432	bytes available on disk
512	bytes in each allocation unit
2847	total allocation units on disk
36	available allocation units on disk
655360	total bytes memory
630752	bytes free

FIGURE 9.7
CHKDSK response

If you had used the /F option, you would be asked if you would like to recover any lost data sectors into data files. You would respond with Y or N.

The copy command (copy) is used to copy files from one disk to another or from one directory to another. The general format of the copy command is

> COPY   <source file name>   <destination file name>

The file name should include the complete drive specification and path when necessary. For example,

C>COPY A:FILE1.TXT B:	Copies the file FILE1.TXT from the A drive to the B drive.
C>COPY A:FILE1.TXT B:FILE2.TXT	Copies the file FILE1.TXT from the A drive to the B drive and renames it FILE2.TXT.
C>COPY A:*.* B:	Copies all files from the A drive to the B drive.
C>COPY B:*.* A:	Copies all files from the B drive to the A drive.
C>COPY A:*.TXT B:	Copies all files with the extension TXT from the A drive to the B drive.
A>COPY FILE1.TXT B:	Copies the file FILE1.TXT from the A drive to the B drive.
A>COPY *.* B:	Copies all files from the A drive to the B drive.

The disk copy command (DISKCOPY) can also be used to copy files. The disk copy command copies all files from the source disk to the destination disk. DISKCOPY formats the destination disk as it copies. Therefore, any information on the destination disk will be erased and replaced with the information being copied from the source disk. For example,

A>DISKCOPY A: B:	Copies all data from drive A to drive B.
A>DISKCOPY B: A:	Copies all data from drive B to drive A.
A>DISKCOPY A: A:	Copies all data from drive A into memory, then prompts you to insert the destination disk into drive A and copies the information from memory onto the disk in drive A. (A number of iterations may be required.)

The rename command (REN) can be used to change the name of a file without copying it first. For example,

A>REN FILE1.TXT FILE1.OLD	Changes the name of the file from FILE1.TXT to FILE1.OLD.

TABLE 9.7
Summary of DOS commands

ASSIGN	Changes drive letter assignments.
BACKUP	Backs up fixed-disk files to a floppy diskette.
CD	Changes the current directory.
CHKDSK	Displays disk status and checks and fixes file structures.
COMP	Compares two files.
COPY	Copies files from one disk or directory to another.
DATE	Displays current date.
DEBUG	Assembles programs directly into memory.
DEL	Erases a file.
DIR	Displays disk directory.
DISKCOMP	Compares two diskettes.
DISKCOPY	Copies a diskette and formats the destination diskette if necessary.
EDLIN	Line-oriented text editor.
EDIT	Screen-oriented text editor.
ERASE	Erases a file.
EXE2BIN	Creates a COM file.
FDISK	Creates fixed-disk logical partitions.
FIND	Locates text strings.
FORMAT	Formats or initializes a disk.
GRAPHICS	Enables the print screen key to print graphics.
HELP	Provides information about a DOS command.
JOIN	Joins a disk drive to a directory.
LABEL	Changes the volume label of a diskette.
MD	Creates a subdirectory.
MEM	Displays status of memory usage.
MODE	Sets display, printer, and asynchronous parameters.
MORE	Displays the contents of a file one screen at a time.
PATH	Defines the file search path.
PROMPT	Changes the DOS command prompt.
PRINT	Prints text files.
RECOVER	Recovers data from corrupted or damaged disks.
REN	Renames a file.
RESTORE	Restores backup files.
RD	Removes a subdirectory.
SORT	Sorts lines in alphabetical order.
SUBST	Associates a path with a drive letter.
SYS	Copies system files to a diskette.
TIME	Displays current time.
TREE	Displays a disk's subdirectory structure.
TYPE	Displays an ASCII file on the screen.
VER	Displays the version of DOS.
VERIFY	Controls the verify after write feature.
VOL	Displays the volume label of a diskette.
XCOPY	Copies diskettes from one diskette or subdirectory to another.

A>REN TEXT.TXT NEWTEXT.TXT   Changes the name of the file from
                              TEXT.TXT to NEWTEXT.TXT

The format command (format) initializes a new disk for use. It can also be used to erase all of the contents of a disk. For example,

A>FORMAT A: Prepares the disk in drive A for use.

A>FORMAT B: Prepares the disk in drive B for use.

Table 9.7 is a summary of many of the DOS commands. Not every command is available on every version of DOS. For a complete list of all of the DOS commands, consult the DOS manual for your version of DOS.

9.8   CUSTOMER RELATIONS

Up to this point we have studied the theory and knowledge required to service microcomputers and digital systems. In industry this is known as **product training.** At this time it is appropriate to discuss **customer relations,** or servicing the customer. Product training provides the theory and knowledge of how products operate. Customer service training teaches methods that allow the technician to understand the customer's reaction to a situation. It should also provide the technician with methods to influence the customer and increase sales.

Interfacing With Customers

Effective customer service is difficult because each situation is different. Just as no two people are completely alike, no two customer situations are completely alike. Furthermore, an exact customer situation seldom repeats itself.

The customer service technician is viewed by the customer as a representative of his or her company. To many customers, the customer service technician *is* the company. Just being able to repair the machine is not enough. The customer must be served also. Good *customer perception* of your service is paramount. As anyone who has gone to the movies can attest, truth and reality are not always the same. For example, you can do a great job repairing a machine and leave the customer with a negative impression. Thus you have serviced the machine correctly but not the customer. The customer will perceive your service as poor. Interestingly, though you may do only an adequate job servicing the machine, a properly serviced customer will perceive you and your company as excellent. It is important to understand that while customer service is paramount, we still must repair the machine.

When interfacing with customers, there are two main factors to be considered. These are *appearance* and *communication.*

Appearance   Your **appearance** is made up of several factors. The most important of these factors is a positive attitude. Proper attitude is projected through appropriate dress and clothing, good hygiene and hair care, clear eye contact, and a firm handshake. A great sage once said that you can tell everything you need to know about a person by simply looking at his or her shoes. Look in the mirror and ask yourself, Is this a person you would want to service your valuable computer system? Professional appearance is the first step toward building customer trust.

Communication When interfacing with a customer, it is important to maintain a proper balance of **communication** between you and the customer. In order to maintain a proper balance of communication:

1. Avoid talking too much about yourself.
2. Avoid interrupting the customer when he or she is speaking.
3. Avoid contradictory discussion (don't say, "but . . . !").
4. Avoid inflammatory statements.
5. Use words and phrases that make what you are saying easier for the customer to accept.
6. Use proper language.
7. Make an effort to create a good impression.

Remember, the customer is a human being like yourself. Customers want to be treated with understanding and respect. Furthermore, they are paying for the service. Good communication skills and a proper attitude will help to build a good customer perception of you and your company.

Handling Stressful Conditions

It is important to begin to handle stressful conditions before they occur by creating customer trust and understanding. You should always begin by greeting your customer by name. Learn as much as you can about the customer's business. Understand your customer's position, responsibilities, authority, and limitations. Always be prompt and prepared to work. Be certain to fulfill your promises. If you say you are going to do something (e.g., order a part), make sure you do it. Keep the customer well informed of the situation. Let the customer know what you are doing and how you are doing it. If possible, explain any options the customer might have. Before speaking, think about what you are going to say. Visualize the customer's reactions and tailor your responses to the individual customer. Building customer trust and understanding can temper stressful situations when they do occur.

Handling the Irate Customer When stressful conditions occur, it is important not to lose your composure. Try to defuse the situation and calm the customer. Sometimes, it is not what you say that is important but how you say it. Let the customer relieve some of the pressure by venting some of his or her frustrations. This is the wrong time to argue. When responding, express concern and display confidence. Show the customer that you are going to take charge of the situation. Develop your plan to correct the situation and explain it to the customer. Never blame the problem on a co-worker, supervisor, or other organization in your company. For example, don't complain that your parts department is always out of the part you need. Try to assure the customer that you will do everything necessary to correct the problem as quickly as possible. This is probably the time to overreact in a positive way. Go the extra mile and get extra backup help, parts, and support. Show the customer you care.

Selling the Customer

Selling the customer requires a team approach. Remember that the customer has purchased the services of your entire company. You should always try to sell yourself and your entire company. Without sales, there are no jobs and no growth. Always look for opportunities to help the customer with your services, but be careful to make your suggestions at an appropriate time. Sell the benefit to the customer by letting them know what they will gain by using your company's services. Know your facts and give solid reasons for everything you suggest. Always express a positive attitude about your company's equipment and services. Be sure you pass on all leads about possible equipment purchases to the appropriate person in your company. Do not quote prices on new equipment—that is the function of the salesperson.

Remember that selling the customer starts and ends with good customer relations, which means creating customer trust, knowing the customers and their needs, and working as a team while keeping a positive attitude. Always explain what you are doing and your plan of attack. In one sense, solving a customer relations problem is like solving a digital circuit problem. The most important steps are to look and think. Look at the situation and analyze it first. Then think about your options and choose a plan to rectify the situation. Above all else, always think before you speak. Remember, illusion is as important as reality. The customer's perception of you is as important as your technical competence.

9.9 TECH TIPS AND TROUBLESHOOTING—T³

Good customer perception is very important in field service. The field service technician is viewed by the customer as a representative of the company. For this reason, the field service technician must not only service the equipment but also serve the customer.

Serving the customer requires proper dress, proper attitude, courtesy, and preparation. When you arrive on a service call, you should be prepared to work, which means having the proper tools, test equipment, documentation, and spare parts with you. You should know whom you are going to see and you should have some idea of the problem. It is important not only to dress neatly and be clean but also to work in a neat and clean manner. Don't scatter your tools and parts all over the floor. Be careful in routing and dressing of cables. Secure all connectors properly. Inspect and clean, if necessary, all connector contacts. Always remember to replace all screws and covers properly. Cover all switch settings and adjustments with a piece of tape to prevent accidental mishaps. Clean up your work area when you finish the job. Make sure you discuss the problem and what you did with the customer. If possible, instruct the customer on the preventive maintenance that could have avoided the problem, such as keeping air passages and filters clean, monitoring temperature and humidity settings, and taking general safety precautions. Above all, always be courteous. Consider yourself as a guest in the customer's house and behave accordingly.

EXERCISES

9.1 Discuss the main differences between the IBM PC and the IBM PC-XT personal computers.

9.2 What is a common cause of problems when a computer system is set up?

9.3 Explain the function of switch SW1-1 on the:
    a. IBM PC   b. PC-XT

9.4 Explain how the computer systems knows if the 8087 math coprocessor is installed.

9.5 Define the meaning of setting switches SW1-3 and SW1-4 off.

9.6 How does the computer system know when a monochrome display system is in use?

9.7 Define the switch settings to be used when two floppy disk drives are installed.

9.8 Explain the function of switch block 2 on the PC system.

9.9 Explain what should be done when installing or checking out an extended memory board.

9.10 Discuss what you should look for when inspecting cables.

9.11 The IBM PC power supply usually has four cables. Discuss the purpose of each cable.

9.12 What type of cable is used to interface the floppy disk drive? How is it connected?

9.13 Discuss the meaning of the twist in the cable between drive A: and drive B:.

9.14 What is indicated when the drive-select light is always on?

9.15 Explain the difference between the hard disk interface cable and the floppy disk interface cable.

9.16 Discuss what happens when the system attempts to IPL (initial program load).

9.17 What is POST? Where is it contained?

9.18 Discuss the function of the POST checkpoints.

9.19 Explain the meaning of the error message parity check 1.

9.20 Discuss the two main factors to be considered when interfacing with customers.

9.21 Explain what the technician can do to handle an irate customer.

9.22 Discuss the factors that lead to good customer perception of your company.

9.23 Crossword Puzzle

ACROSS

1. Indicates an error in main memory.
4. Term for manuals used to repair computer equipment.
11. How the customer sees the technician and the service.
12. Above all, when dealing with customers, be _____.
13. Maximum number of floppy disks on one controller.
16. Number of slots on the XT.
18. What you must balance when dealing with customers.

DOWN

1. Theory and knowledge to service equipment.
2. Must also be serviced with the machine.
3. On the PC/XT, if SW1-1 is on, POST will _____.
5. Type of display if SW1-5 is off and SW1-6 is on.
6. Contains diagnostic routines.
7. Type of floppy disk cable.
8. Be careful in the routing and _____ of cables.
9. The way you look.
10. The wrong thing to do with an irate customer.
14. Switch block 2 will indicate.
15. Found on interface cable between drive A and drive B.
17. Number of slots on PC.

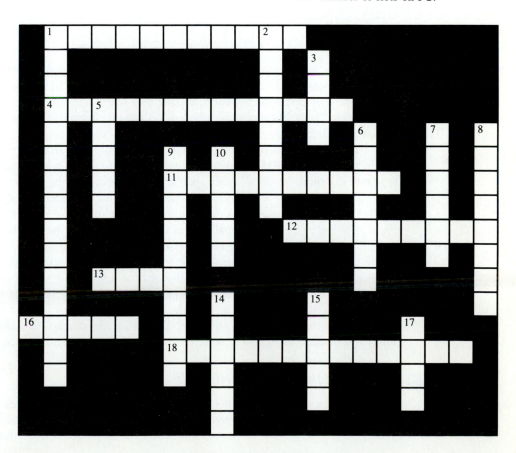

CHAPTER TEN

DIAGNOSTICS AND TROUBLESHOOTING

KEY TERMS

Advanced Diagnostics

Cold Start

Error Code

Headers

Home Menu

Hot Interrupts

Parking the Heads

Shotgun

10.0 INTRODUCTION

In this chapter we discuss diagnostic programs and troubleshooting methods. The first step in diagnosing and troubleshooting any computer system is to run the manufacturer's diagnostics. The diagnostics should also be run when performing routine preventive maintenance. These diagnostics provide a good system checkout and may alert you to an unsuspected problem.

The IBM PC system comes with simple diagnostics. IBM provides **advanced diagnostics** when the *IBM Maintenance and Service Manual* is purchased. The advanced diagnostics should be used when performing repairs on the system. The simple diagnostics are designed as a confidence check for the user. The advanced diagnostics are intended for trained technicians' use only. They include an easy-to-use menu-driven screen. The entire system or small pieces of the system may be checked at the user's discretion. The advanced diagnostics also provide an error logger, which records intermittent errors that may occur while looping the diagnostic tests. If the asynchronous or printer ports are to be tested, you will need the appropriate wrap plugs, which are simply loop-back plugs that connect the output signals back to the input signals and are provided along with the diagnostic diskette. If the floppy disk system is to be tested, you will need some blank formatted diskettes. Do not use the diagnostic diskette during the floppy test because the test will write data on the diskette, destroying the original data.

10.1 STARTING THE ADVANCED DIAGNOSTICS

The diagnostics may be started the same way in which the DOS is started. If the system is off, insert the advanced diagnostics diskette into floppy disk drive A and power the system on. If the system is already on, insert the advanced diagnostics diskette into floppy disk drive A and press the ALT, CONTROL, and DEL keys all at the same time on the keyboard. This will reset the computer and start the diagnostics. The diagnostic supervisor program will take control of the system and prompt you with menu screens.

10.2 THE HOME MENU

When the diagnostic supervisor is loaded and has control of the system, the **home menu** will be displayed on the screen, as shown next.

```
The IBM Personal Computer
ADVANCED DIAGNOSTICS
Version X.YY © Copyright IBM Corp 1981, 1983

SELECT AN OPTION

0 - RUN DIAGNOSTIC ROUTINES
1 - FORMAT DISKETTE
2 - COPY DISKETTE
3 - PREPARE SYSTEM FOR MOVING
9 - EXIT TO SYSTEM DISKETTE

ENTER THE ACTION DESIRED
?
```

The action desired is selected by typing the appropriate number and then pressing enter. Action 0 starts the diagnostic routines. Action 1 formats blank floppy diskettes. Action 2 copies the diagnostic diskette onto a formatted diskette. Action 3 relocates the heads on the hard disk drive to minimize damage if the system is dropped during moving. Action 9 resets the system and reloads DOS.

Run Diagnostics (0)

Selection of option 0 loads and starts the diagnostic program. The first step is a sizing up of the system. During this phase the memory size is checked, and all possible I/O devices are checked to see if they are present in the system. Upon completion of this phase the diagnostic supervisor lists the results of the search. An example of the list is given next.

```
THE INSTALLED DEVICES ARE

 1 - S SYSTEM BOARD
 2 - S 640KB MEMORY
 3 - S KEYBOARD
 5 - S COLOR/GRAPHICS MONITOR ADAPTER
 6 - S 1 DISKETTE DRIVE (S) AND ADAPTER
 9 - S PRINTER ADAPTER
11 - S ASYNC COMMUNICATIONS ADAPTER
```

```
12 - S ALT ASYNC COMMUNICATIONS ADPT
13 - S GAME CONTROL ADAPTER
17 - S 1 FIXED DISK DRIVE(S) & ADAPTER

IS THE LIST CORRECT (Y/N) ?
```

The number corresponds to the subsystem under test. For example, 17-S denotes the hard disk subsystem in the system unit. The letter code following the number indicates if the subsystem is installed in the system unit or the expansion unit. The letter *S* indicates the system unit, whereas the letter *E* indicates the expansion unit. A complete number code listing can be found in Appendix E. Finally, you will be asked if the displayed listing is correct. If the list is not correct and you type N, the current time and the message

```
HH:MM:SS
ERROR-
INSTALLED DEVICE LIST 199 S
```

will be displayed. You will then be asked if you want to add (A) or delete (D) items. If items are missing, you may want to add items. When you type A, a new menu consisting of every possible option supported will be displayed. Type the item or items separated by commas to add to the list and press enter. The diagnostic supervisor will load in the programs for the added devices. If too many devices were displayed after the original list, you may want to delete the excess items by typing D instead of A. When you type D, the original device list will be displayed again along with the message

```
ENTER ITEMS TO DELETE ?
```

Type the undesired item or items separated by commas and press ENTER. Those items are now deleted from the list and are not tested by the diagnostic program. When the list is correct, type Y and press ENTER. After the installed device list is correct, the system checkout menu will be displayed as shown next.

```
SYSTEM CHECKOUT

0 - RUN TESTS ONE TIME
1 - RUN TESTS MULTIPLE TIMES
2 - LOG UTILITIES
9 - EXIT DIAGNOSTIC ROUTINES

ENTER THE ACTION DESIRED
?
```

The system checkout menu is used to control the diagnostic execution and the error logger function.

If action 0 is selected, the installed list is again displayed, along with the message

```
ENTER THE NUMBER (S) OF OPTIONS TO TEST
OR PRESS ENTER TO SELECT ALL OPTIONS
?
```

You may select any one or all the options to test by typing the number(s) separated by commas. If just the ENTER key is pressed without any numbers, *all* listed options will be tested. Some options have submenus associated with the tests; these are discussed later. As soon as the ENTER key is pressed, the diagnostic supervisor will take control and run the tests one at a time. You will be informed of the progress of the tests as they are run, along with the status of each test. If an error is encountered during test execution, the system will beep and a message similar to

```
HH:MM:SS
ERROR -
PRINTER ADAPTER 910 S

PRESS ENTER TO CONTINUE
?
```

will be displayed. The message will differ slightly depending upon the option being tested but will look basically the same.

The first line of all the error messages is the time of the error. The first one or two digits of the error code represent the device that is failing. The second two digits are the **error code** for the failure. For example, the error code 910 indicates that the *printer adapter* has failed. As each option is tested and passes the tests, the code for that device will be followed by the code 00. For example, the message

```
900 - S PRINTER ADAPTER
```

indicates that the printer adapter has passed the diagnostic test. If more than one or all the options are tested, the diagnostic supervisor will automatically run the next test on the list. Upon completion of all the requested tests, the home menu will again be displayed. At this point you may run more tests or exit the diagnostic supervisor at your option.

If action 1 is selected under the system checkout menu, you will get the message

```
ENTER NUMBER OF TIMES TO RUN TESTS
OR PRESS ENTER TO RUN FOREVER
?
```

If you wish to run the diagnostics 10 times, then type the number 10 and enter. If you press ENTER without a number, the diagnostic programs selected earlier will run forever until the system is reset or until you press CONTROL C on the keyboard. You will then be asked if you want the diagnostic program to halt whenever an error is encountered. If you type Y to this question, the diagnostic programs will stop on the first error. If you type N, the diagnostics will list the error and continue on to the next test. If the selected tests have submenus, then the submenu questions must be answered here also, since the tests will most likely be run unattended. Otherwise, the test execution will be the same as for action 0.

If action 2 is selected, the error-logger program will be invoked. The error log utilities menu will be displayed as shown:

```
LOG UTILITIES

0 - START ERROR LOG
1 - STOP ERROR LOG
2 - LIST LOG
3 - SET TIME OF DAY
4 - DISPLAY TIME OF DAY
9 - RETURN FROM UTILITIES

ENTER THE ACTION DESIRED
?
```

Selecting action 0 starts the error logger. This is used when the system is tested for long periods of time unattended or if a record of every system tested is required. You will then be asked where the logged information is to be recorded. You will see the message

```
LOG TO DISK, CASSETTE, OR PRINTER (D C P)?
```

Type the letter of the device on which you wish to record the error log. If the log is to be recorded on the disk, you will be asked to which disk drive the log will go. Enter the disk drive letter. If the floppy disk drive containing the diagnostic diskette is to be used, then you must first make a copy of the diagnostic diskette and use it without the write protect tab installed. The rest of the menu is self-explanatory.

Format Floppy Diskettes (1)

If new unformatted floppy diskettes are to be used during the diagnostic session, they must be formatted first. The formatter program is invoked by typing 1 at the home menu. You will be asked which floppy disk drive contains the floppy diskette to be formatted. Press the letter key for the desired drive. You will then be asked to insert the diskette to be formatted into that drive. *Do not format the diagnostic diskette,* as the formatter program will erase *all* the old data on the diskette. If this is done accidentally, there will be no way of restoring the data unless you have another copy of the diagnostic diskette. Upon completion of the formatter program, the diskette is ready for use. Unlike the DOS formatter, the diagnostic formatter does not allow for any bad spots on the diskette. If the diagnostic formatter cannot successfully format the diskette, an error message similar to

```
FORMAT NOT COMPLETED
CRC ERROR
DRIVE A, TRACK 12, HEAD 1, SECTOR 1
```

is displayed on the screen, and you will be returned to the home menu.

Copy Diagnostic Diskette (2)

Selecting action 2 from the home menu invokes the diskette copy program. This program is intended to make a working copy of the diagnostics diskette only. The target diskette need not be preformatted first, since the copy program will also format the target diskette. Once the copy program is started, you will be asked which disk drive contains the source (original) diskette and which drive contains the target (copy) diskette. Both the source and the target may be the same physical drive. If the source and target are the same drive, you will be asked to switch the diskettes during the copy process.

Prepare System for Relocation (3)

Selecting action 3 under the home menu will relocate the heads of the hard disk drive to the innermost track. This action is often referred to as **parking the heads.** Recall that in an earlier section we discussed the shock sensitivity of the Winchester hard disk drive. When the disk drive is not spinning, the read/write heads *land* on the disk surface. If the disk drive is subjected to excessive forces of gravity, the head may bounce on the surface of the disk platter. This bouncing action may cause a small ''ding,'' or chip in the magnetic coating, which will at least change the recorded pattern. If such damage occurs on the outermost track, track 000, the disk drive will be rendered useless because *no defects* are allowed on track 000. It is a good idea to place the read/write heads on the innermost track, the least-used part of the disk drive, during shipping. Once action 3 is invoked, the system should be shut down *immediately;* otherwise any DOS activity may move the heads back over the usable portion of the disk surface.

Exit to System Diskette (9)

Selecting action 9 causes the system to reset and perform a **cold start.** This has the same effect as powering the system down and back up again.

10.3 DIAGNOSTIC TEST SUBMENUS

Many of the diagnostic tests allow optional testing. These tests will have their own menus associated with them. In the next section we discuss some of the submenus.

Color/Graphics Adapter Test Menu

The color/graphics adapter diagnostic provides one computer diagnostic, nine visual tests, and two external measurement tests. When the diagnostic supervisor runs the color/graphics diagnostic, the color graphics diagnostic menu is displayed as shown:

```
COLOR/GRAPHICS MONITOR ADAPTER TEST

   0 - DISPLAY ADAPTER TEST
   1 - DISPLAY ATTRIBUTES
   2 - CHARACTER SET
   3 - 80X25 DISPLAY
   4 - 40X25 DISPLAY
   5 - 320X200 GRAPHICS
   6 - 640X200 GRAPHICS
   7 - LIGHT PEN TEST
   8 - SCREEN PAGING
   9 - EXIT TO MAIN MENU
```

```
10 - RUN ALL ABOVE TESTS
11 - VIDEO TEST
12 - SYNC TEST
ENTER NUMBER OF DESIRED ACTION
?
```

Action 0 is the only computer-measured diagnostic test of the color/graphics adapter. During this portion of the diagnostic, the display memory, memory addressing, and internal logic are tested. The internal timing is checked during this test by measuring the occurrence of the horizontal interval interrupt. If this test is run on a "turbo" system with a clock rate other than 4.77 MHz, an error will be reported due to the software timing difference. Actions 1 through 8 are visual tests and report an error only if the observer types N to the question

```
IS THE SCREEN CORRECT ?
```

Action 1 displays all possible attributes, including 14 character colors in the 40-by-25 text mode. There will be five character-line attributes displayed, with the first line at normal intensity, the next line intensified, the third line in reverse video, the fourth line blank, and the fifth line blinking. Following this should be seven pairs of colored bars followed by the name of each color.

Action 2 displays all possible characters in the character set for visually checking the internal character generator ROM.

Action 3 displays a shifting, or "barber pole," pattern in the 80-by-25 character mode in inverse video.

Action 4 displays a shifting, or "barber pole," pattern in the 40-by-25 mode with a white border around the text.

Action 5 displays two different graphic patterns of three large different color boxes in the 320-by-200 graphic mode.

Action 6 displays a graphic pattern of three shaded large boxes in the 640-by-200 graphic mode.

Action 7 is the light pen test. You will be asked if you want to skip this test. If you want to test the light pen, a small box will be displayed on the screen. You must place the tip of the light pen onto the box. If you fail to place the light pen in the box or the light pen is faulty, an error message will be displayed.

Action 8 is the screen paging test. During this test all eight text pages of display RAM are displayed on the screen as a screenful of the current page number in the 40-by-25 mode.

Action 9 exits the color/graphics test module. If no other tests were selected, the system checkout menu will be displayed.

Action 10 automatically runs tests 0 through 8.

Action 11 is the video test. In this test *all* possible character colors are displayed over the entire screen, with the name of the color in text in the middle of the screen. Immediately after selecting action (11) and pressing enter, the entire screen will be bright white with the word *white* in the middle of the screen. All available colors may be displayed by pressing any key and observing the screen. With each key depression, the sequence shall be as follows: light white, black, blue, green, cyan, red, magenta, yellow, white, dark gray, light blue, light green, light cyan, light red, light magenta, light yellow. This test is also used as a measurement test.

To perform the IBM measurements test, use the following procedure.

1. Disconnect the color display signal cable.
2. Select action 11 and press ENTER.
3. Measure the voltages with the voltmeter at pins 3, 4, 5, and 6 of the 9-pin connector on the color/graphics board. Use the case screws as the ground. All the measured voltages should read between 2.4 and 5.5 V_{DC}.
4. Measure the voltage on the center conductor of the composite video phono jack. The meter should read between 1.1 and 2.4 V_{DC}.
5. Press ENTER once.
6. Measure the voltage on pins 3, 4, 5, and 6 of the 9-pin connector again. The meter should read between 0.0 and 0.5 V_{DC}.
7. Measure the voltage on the center conductor of the composite video phono jack. The meter should read between 0.0 and 0.9 V_{DC}.

Action 12 is the sync test and is meant to be run with the monitor *disconnected*. In this test voltages are measured at the various pins on the 9-pin connector. If this test is run with the monitor connected, *the monitor may be damaged due to a shift in the horizontal scan frequency!* The measurement procedure is as follows.

1. Select action 12 and press ENTER.
2. Measure the voltage at pin 8 of the 9-pin connector. The meter should read between 0.8 and 1.5 V_{DC}.
3. Measure pin 9 of the connector. The meter should read between 0.3 and 1.0 V_{DC}.
4. Measure the center conductor of the composite video phono jack. The meter should read between 0.2 and 0.6 V_{DC}.

The monochrome/printer adapter test is similar to the color/graphics test, except the printer port is also tested and there are no graphics displays or light pen tests.

Floppy Test Menu

There are five different tests that can be run on the floppy disk drives. When the floppy system test is run, the diagnostic program will test the adapter card first, and if it passes the diskette diagnostic menu is displayed as shown:

```
DISKETTE DIAGNOSTIC MENU

OPTION                   DRIVE
1 - SEQUENTIAL ACCESS    ONE DRIVE
2 - RANDOM SEEK          ONE DRIVE
3 - VERIFY DISKETTE      ONE DRIVE
4 - SPEED TEST           ONE DRIVE
9 - RETURN TO CONTROL PROGRAM
FOR OPTION
9 ENTER ''9'' AND ''ENTER''
FOR OTHER OPTIONS (1 THRU 4)
```

```
ENTER OPTION, DRIVE AND ''ENTER''
?
```

Selecting option 1 writes, reads, and verifies every sector on the diskette one sector at a time. This option should not be run on a diskette that contains valuable data because every sector will be written on. The diskette used should be known to be error free and preformatted.

Selecting option 2 performs 50 random seeks along with write, read, and verify operations. This is a good test to verify the integrity of the disk drive head-position mechanism. The diskette used here should not contain valuable data because random sectors will be written on. Also the diskette should be preformatted and known to be error free.

Selecting option 3 performs a sequential read of every sector on the diskette. No write operations are done, so the data is not altered. This is an excellent test to check for a disk drive compatibility problem or a possible corrupted data diskette. If the system has two disk drives, it might be a good idea to run option 1 on a diskette in drive A and then place the diskette from drive A into drive B and run option 3 on drive B.

Selecting option 4 measures the time period of the occurrence of the index pulse and displays the time on the screen. The diskette rotates at a rate of 300 rev/min, or 5 rev/s. If we use the formula to convert frequency to time,

$$\text{Time} = \frac{1}{\text{frequency}}$$

Then plugging the known values in the formula yields

$$\text{Time} = \frac{1}{5} = 0.200 \text{ s/rev}, \quad \text{or} \quad 200 \text{ ms/rev}$$

The IBM specification calls for a time of 200 ms $\pm$ 2 ms. If the displayed time is less than 198 ms or greater than 202 ms, then an adjustment is required. As discussed in Chapter 12 the speed may be adjusted by means of the potentiometer in the motor control circuit.

Selecting option 9 returns to the system checkout menu or continues on to the next test if more tests were selected.

Fixed Disk Test Menu

The fixed disk test menu contains two diagnostic tests and a fixed disk formatter program. The formatter program is required on a new fixed disk drive before any DOS activity can take place. As in the floppy disk test, the adapter board is tested first and then the fixed disk test menu is displayed. If the diagnostic program cannot access the adapter board or the board is malfunctioning, an error will be displayed instead of the menu. The fixed disk test menu is shown:

```
0 - RUN FIXED DISK TEST
1 - RUN MEASUREMENTS TEST
```

```
2 - FORMAT FIXED DISK
9 - EXIT FIXED DISK TESTS

ENTER THE ACTION DESIRED ?
```

Actions 0 through 2 also display the message

```
ENTER DRIVE ID C/D) ?
```

Action 0 starts the fixed disk drive diagnostic, consisting of four subtests. Action 0 also displays the additional message

```
*** WARNING ***
DATA ON CYLINDER 305 WILL BE
OVERWRITTEN BY FIXED DISK WRITE TESTS

DO YOU WANT TO INCLUDE FIXED DISK
WRITE TEST ON DRIVE x: (Y/N) ?
```

where the x is the selected drive letter. The fixed disk write test attempts to write data using all available read/write heads on the innermost cylinder. On the standard 10-Mb disk drive, there are 4 heads and 306 cylinders. If the disk drive is nearly full, less than 100K free, it is possible that user data may be present on cylinder 305. In this case do not include the write test.

As the subtests are performed, the diagnostic will keep you informed about the progress of the tests. You should observe the following messages:

```
PERFORMING SEEK TEST
PERFORMING WRITE TEST
PERFORMING TRACK ZERO TEST
PERFORMING SURFACE SCAN
PLEASE STAND BY
```

The seek test performs an oscillating seek, which drives the heads from the innermost to the outermost track in a decrementing count pattern, such as, 0–305, 1–304, 2–303, . . . , 153–154. This test checks the integrity to the head servo system.

The write test checks the integrity of the write circuitry and the read/write heads by writing data on all four tracks of the innermost cylinder. If the heads or the circuitry begin failing, the failure will most likely show up on the innermost tracks, where the bit packing is the closest and the read gain is the lowest.

The track zero test will test for any defects on track 000. Since *no* defects are allowed on track 000, the message

```
TRACK 000 BAD - DISK UNUSABLE
```

will be displayed. In this case the disk drive must be replaced.

Drive Saver Trick

In some disk drives the track 000 sensor is adjustable externally. If the disk drive must be scrapped because a replacement drive costs less than a repair, you may wish to try this trick first:

1. Readjust the TRACK 000 flag or sensor inward one or two tracks.
2. *Carefully* rotate the stepper motor (by turning the flag) inward a few tracks.
3. Power up the disk drive. The flag should rotate back to the sensor again when the spindle is up to speed.
4. Readjust the mechanical stop to limit any outward action (if equipped).
5. Run the diagnostic formatter and the track zero test.

If the disk drive passes the diagnostics, the drive should work for DOS. Keep in mind that this is *a last resort* effort before discarding the disk drive.

The surface scan test will read every sector on the disk drive. This is a non-destructive test and may be run on user data. The object of this test is check for any read errors on the disk regardless of the file structure. If errors are found during this phase, the diagnostic formatter must be run. *Before formatting the disk, back up the data.*

Action 1 runs the measurements test. This test is used to take voltage readings at various test points on the disk drive. There are three subtests associated with this test.

Selecting action 2 starts the fixed disk formatter program. This test *destroys* any previously stored data on the entire drive, and the program displays the message

```
ALL OF THE DATA ON FIXED DISK DRIVE x:
WILL BE OVERWRITTEN DURING FORMAT!

ARE YOU SURE YOU WANT TO CONTINUE (Y/N) ?
```

where x is the selected drive letter. A new disk drive requires two levels of formatting. The first level is what we call the brute force formatter. This type of formatting is required on new hard disk drives because there is no information recorded regarding the track and sectors known as the **headers.** The headers are used to identify the location of each sector on the disk drive surface for DOS. In some cases the header information may become corrupted on an existing drive. If the drive fails the surface scan or the track zero test, you should run the formatter again. Once the disk drive has *successfully* been formatted, you *must* run the FDISK program under DOS and the DOS formatter. The DOS formatter builds the root directory and the file allocation table and checks for any bad spots on the entire disk surface. The DOS formatter also checks track zero for any defects before going on.

Selecting action 9 exits the fixed disk test menu and returns to the system checkout menu or goes on to the next test if more tests were selected.

10.4   ERROR CODES

As discussed earlier, any errors encountered during the diagnostic tests will cause the system to beep and display the current time of day and the appropriate error code. The displayed **error code** will vary slightly depending on the subsystem being tested and the type of error. Most error codes are a 3- or 4-digit code. Some test errors will display additional information along with the error code. For example, a memory failure will display the message

```
15:00:55
ERROR -
640KB MEMORY    201 S
FAILING ADDRESS-SPACE/MODULE 10000 20

PRESS ENTER TO CONTINUE
?
```

The first line is the current time of the failure. If the time of day was not set previously, the time displayed will be the elapsed time of the diagnostics. The second line is the message ERROR -. The third line is the test name and the error code. The first digit or first two digits are the code for the device. For example, 2 is for memory. The next two digits are the error code: 01 is memory data failure and 02 and 03 are the codes for a memory address failure. The fourth line is the additional information containing the memory address in 20-bit hexadecimal format and the failing bit(s) in 8-bit hexadecimal format. When you break down this information, you can point to the failing memory IC. Table 10.1 is a list of the address to chip reference. The failing data byte is the result of taking the bad data and EXCLUSIVE ORing the expected data with it. For example, if we write the data pattern 55 hex and we read back 51 hex, then we EXCLUSIVE OR the write data with the read data to get

```
Data bit   7 6 5 4 3 2 1 0
           | | | | | | | |
           0 1 0 1 0 1 0 1   55H      Good data written to memory
    XOR    0 1 0 1 0 0 0 1   51H      Bad data read back from memory
           ─────────────────
           0 0 0 0 0 1 0 0   04H      Result of XOR operation
```

As we can see in this example, the bit that is different will be at the 1 state. All the bits that compare will be at the 0 state.

P	7	6	5	4	3	2	1	0	Memory Bit
☐	☐	☐	☐	☐	☐	☐	☐	☐	First Row
☐	☐	☐	☐	☐	☐	☐	☐	☐	Second Row
☐	☐	☐	☐	☐	☐	☐	☐	☐	Third Row
☐	☐	☐	☐	☐	☐	☐	☐	☐	Fourth Row
00	01	02	04	08	10	20	40	80	Data Error Code

FIGURE 10.1
Memory bit to chip reference

TABLE 10.1
Memory address to chip reference

16K–64K System Board	
00xxx TO 03xxx	1st ROW OF 16K CHIPS
04xxx TO 07xxx	2nd ROW OF 16K CHIPS
08xxx TO 0Bxxx	3rd ROW OF 16K CHIPS
0Cxxx TO 0Fxxx	4th ROW OF 16K CHIPS
64K–256K System Board	
0xxxx	1st ROW OF 64K CHIPS
1xxxx	2nd ROW OF 64K CHIPS
2xxxx	3rd ROW OF 64K CHIPS
3xxxx	4th ROW OF 64K CHIPS
256K–640K System Board with Three Rows of 256K Chips	
0xxxx TO 3xxxx	1st ROW OF 256K CHIPS
4xxxx TO 7xxxx	2nd ROW OF 256K CHIPS
8xxxx TO 9xxxx	3rd ROW OF 256K CHIPS
or Two Rows of 256K Chips and Two Rows OF 64K Chips	
8xxxx	3rd ROW OF 64K CHIPS
9xxxx	4th ROW OF 64K CHIPS

The diagnostics display the failing address in the form of a seven-digit code followed by the number 201. The 201 indicates a memory problem. The first digit in the code indicates the bank that contains the defective memory module. Note that the banks are defined differently on different system boards. Table 10.1 defines the memory bank notation system. For example, if the first character of the memory failure code is a 6 on a 640K system board, the defective memory module resides somewhere in the second row of memory chips.

The last two digits (characters 6 and 7) define the memory bit. For example, if the last two digits are 04, the defective memory module is bit 5. Figure 10.1 illustrates the memory bit to chip relationship.

To illustrate how the memory error code works, consider the following error code for a 640K system board:

$$5C000\ 80\ 201$$

The 5 corresponds to memory bank 2, and the 80 corresponds to memory bit 0.

10.5 THE DEAD MACHINE

Many failures, especially system board failures, may cause the system to appear "dead." This means that when the computer is powered up nothing happens except the fan spins. This type of problem can be very frustrating because there are no symptoms or clues to the source of the problem. Even if the display is dead, listening for beep tones and observing the disk drive lights gives clues to the problem. In this next section we deal with the totally dead system.

Test Equipment

To troubleshoot the dead system effectively you need some additional test equipment. The following list should be considered the minimum setup to troubleshoot the computer:

1. Volt/ohm meter
2. Oscilloscope
3. Spare BIOS ROM
4. Logic probe

If the problem is a bad chip on the system board you may also need more sophisticated test equipment:

5. Logic analyzer
6. The universal microprocessor tester project
7. Microprocessor Emulation Tester (Fluke 9010)

First Things First

Open up the case and check to see if all the cables are plugged in and that nothing *conductive* is lying inside on the boards. There is always the possibility that a child has decided to insert coins into the ventilation slots. These foreign objects will quite effectively short out the power supply and various logic signals. Don't forget to check the line cord to see if it is plugged into a live outlet.

Fan and Power Supply Checks

Never overlook the possibility of a bad power supply. The internal fan is a DC type and runs off $+12$ V. If the fan is spinning, chances are the power supply is good. Power on the system and measure for the presence of $+5$ V on the system board. Pick any 16-pin 74xx series IC and probe pin 16 with the $+$ lead and connect the $-$ lead to the power supply case. The meter should read $+5$ V_{DC}. Next measure the *power good* signal at the rearmost pin on the power connector on the system board. The meter should read at least 2.5 V_{DC}. If either test fails, then replace the power supply. If the power supply is known to be good, then remove *all* of the plug-in boards and the disk drive power connectors. If the power readings are now correct, there is the possibility that one of the boards or the disk drives are loading down the power supply. Power the system down and reinstall the boards one at a time, powering up the system to find which board or disk drive is causing the overload. Replace or repair the faulty board or disk drive. If someone has recently installed a hard disk drive into the model 5150 PC, they should have also replaced the power supply with at least a 130-W unit. The original 65-W unit is not sufficient to run the hard disk drive.

Minimize the System

If the power was good but the system is still dead, power down the system and remove *all* the adapter boards. Power up the system and listen for a beep tone. If you now hear the tone, then one or more of the adapter boards is loading the bus down. Power down the system and replace one board, starting with the display adapter board, and repower the system until you isolate which board is loading the bus. With just the display adapter board installed, you have a minimum usable computer. Any computer system can be cut back to a minimal usable configuration as a starting point from which to work. This is a good practice when working on any type of computer that fails to respond. *Never plug in any adapter boards with the power on or you may damage the boards and the system!*

Faulty System Board

If the system is still dead, then you have a faulty system board. The simplest solution to this problem is to replace the system board. The board is usually an expensive item, but the failure is usually an inexpensive IC. TTL ICs can be purchased through mail order for prices under $1. The trick is to isolate the faulty IC. Some lazy technicians like to **"shotgun"** a defective board, or change every IC until they find the bad IC. Unfortunately this practice usually destroys the board due to static discharge, faulty solder work, or the wrong ICs being installed. If you choose this method you will usually be worse off than when you started to fix the board. The correct solution to repairing the system board is to use an intelligent, logical approach to troubleshooting.

10.6 GETTING IN DEEP

We do not use the term "getting in deep" lightly. If you decide to take on the task of repairing the system board, it is usually quite an undertaking. This task requires a great deal of patience, logical thinking, and careful work. Before beginning you must obtain the proper schematics, a functional block diagram, and at least an oscilloscope. One of the first things we recommend is that you connect a momentary, normally open switch to the reset circuit. This may be achieved by connecting one side of the switch to the *power good* signal at pin 1 of the power supply connector on the system board. Connect the other side of the switch to logic ground or the power supply case. You will need to cause a reset many times while observing the states of various signals during the troubleshooting process.

Using the Oscilloscope

The oscilloscope will prove to be your best friend when you learn how to use it. When properly applied, the oscilloscope enables you to locate the source of any digital problem. You must learn how to use the triggered sweep in the normal mode and stay away from using the automatic mode all the time. If you fail to set the trigger properly, you will miss short duration or single-shot events. It is possible to verify the proper operation of logic gates by triggering on one of the inputs while observing the logic

EXERCISES

10.1   Who should use the advanced diagnostics?

10.2   What three keys will reset the system and start the diagnostics?

10.3   Name the five actions on the home menu.

10.4   What does the installed list tell us?

10.5   What do the *S* and the *E* stand for?

10.6   What do we need to type to select *all* tests?

10.7   What is *always* printed on the first line of the error message?

10.8   What does action 1 allow on the system checkout menu?

10.9   Explain the error logger.

10.10   True or false: A new diskette must be formatted before use during the diskette diagnostic.

10.11   Why should we prepare the system for moving?

10.12   What happens when the system is prepared for moving?

10.13   Which color graphics subtest is tested by the computer alone?

10.14   Should the monitor be connected during the sync test?

10.15   What happens during option (1) of the floppy disk test?

10.16   What option of the floppy disk test should be run to verify user data on a diskette?

10.17   What is the ideal speed number readout of the floppy disk test?

10.18   Name the five subtests of the fixed disk test.

10.19   Is the fixed disk usable if a bad spot exists on track zero?

10.20   Why is the diagnostic formatter different from the DOS formatter?

10.21   If the *last* byte of the error code was 80, what bit is the failing bit? Show your work.

10.22   What is the first thing to check in a dead system?

10.23   True or false: *Never* plug in any adapter boards with the power on.

10.24   What will happen if the *power good* signal is always low?

10.25   Which bus-control line will usually have the most activity?

10.26   What might be an indication that the POST has failed during the bank zero memory test in the dead system?

10.27   Crossword Puzzle

ACROSS

2. There are 40 _____ on the IBM diskette.
4. The test diskette.
7. The utility that records system faults.
9. Read-only memory.
10. The first thing to do to a new disk.
12. Power-on self test.
13. The error code 301 indicates a _____ failure.
14. Disk speed measurement.
19. Portion of a track.
20. The start of a track.
21. Device that detects when the head is at track zero.
23. A copy of an original disk.
24. Power supply–cooling device.
25. Optional light-sensing input device.
27. Lazy technicians do this when troubleshooting.
29. The ROM that contains the POST and the device drivers.
30. Action 1 on the color graphics menu.
31. Track and sector ID.
32. Early POST error will cause the system to _____.

DOWN

1. The main selection screen.
3. Prepare system for moving will _____ the fixed disk heads.
4. A mark or damage on the disk surface.
5. Keyboard reset sequence.
6. Read/write device in the disk.
8. Option (2) of the home menu.
10. This is sensed by the track zero sensor.
11. The error code 910 will indicate the _____ has failed.
15. Some PCs have this high-speed mode.
16. Action (9) on all menus.
17. Row-address strobe.
18. The phono jack of the color graphics card outputs _____ video.
19. Action 1 of the floppy disk menu.
22. The default language on the PC.
23. A row of memory.
26. This must be preformed after the diagnostic formatter on the hard disk.
28. Action 3 on the error log menu will set the _____.
29. Binary digit.

CHAPTER ELEVEN

THE AT CLASS PERSONAL COMPUTER

KEY TERMS

Adaptor Descriptor File

Address Bus Translator

Address Unit

AT Class

Bus Interface Unit

CMOS RAM

Code Prefetch Unit

Descriptor Table

Execution Unit

Extended Industry Standard
* Architecture (EISA) Bus*

Industry Standard Architecture
* (ISA) Bus*

Instruction Unit

Microchannel

Microcode

Paging Unit

Pin Grid Array

Protected Mode

Real Address Mode

Segmentation Unit

Upward Compatible

Virtual Memory

Virtual Mode

Write Through Operation

11.0 INTRODUCTION

The basic design of the IBM personal computer has remained the same since its introduction in the early 1980s. However, there have been many enhancements to the original design. The most significant is the introduction of the AT bus, which was used in the first IBM PC/AT. There have also been enhancements in the display quality with VGA, SUPER VGA, and XGA. The 3.5-in. form factor in floppy drives is a fairly recent introduction with densities of 720kb, 1.44 Mb, and now 2.88 Mb. The hard disk drives have been reduced in size and power requirements, yet they have increased in capacity and reliability and include new interface standards including SCSI, IDE, and ESDI. Today, it is not uncommon to find a 3.5-in. 100–200-Mb hard disk in a desktop computer system. Ten years ago, these disk drives were the size of a household washing machine.

Other improvements include the use of VLSI integration to greatly reduce the size and power requirements of the system board. An entire AT system board may consist of only five or six chips and be only one-third the size of the original PC/AT board. This also has driven down the cost of a computer system.

This chapter will cover the AT class computer including the ISA bus and the Microchannel bus. Section 11.9 Tech Tips and Troubleshooting—T³ describes the complete assembly procedure for AT class systems in detail.

11.1 THE 80X86 PROCESSOR EVOLUTION

Over the past ten years the INTEL microprocessor has undergone many changes and enhancements, including second sourcing from AMD Corporation. All AT class computers use one of the INTEL 80286, 80386-SX, 80386-DX, 80486-SX, or 80486-DX microprocessors. This new line of microprocessors includes:

- 80286 in speeds of 6, 8, 10, 12, and 16 MHz
- 80386-SX in speeds of 16, 20, and 25 MHz
- 80386-DX in speeds of 16, 20, 25, and 33 MHz
- AMD 80386-DX at a speed of 40 MHz
- 80486-SX at a speed of 25 MHz
- 80486-DX in speeds of 25, 33, and 50 MHz.

The IBM PC and PC/XT are centered around the 8088 microprocessor. The **AT class** systems are centered around the 80286, 80386, and 80486 microprocessors. This was done to improve performance, increase processing speed, and increase memory capacity. It is important to note that the processors are all **upward compatible.** That is, anything that will run on an 8088 will run the 8086, 80286, 80386, or 80486. The opposite, of course, is not the case. Programs developed for the 80486 may not work on lower-level processors.

The major differences among the processors revolve around bus size, speed, and memory capacity. For example, the 8088 is an 8-bit processor while the 80286 is a 16-bit processor, and the 80386 and 80486 are 32-bit processors.

11.2 THE 80286 PROCESSOR

The 80286 microprocessor is a high-speed (6, 8, 10, 12, and 16 MHz) 16-bit microprocessor. The 80286 can directly address up to 16 Mb of RAM and up to 1 Gb of virtual memory. The 80286 operates in two modes: real address mode and protected mode. In the **real address mode** the 80286 can execute any programs written for the 8086 and 8088. In the real address mode programs being run on an 8-MHz 80286 will run up to five times faster than on a 5-MHz 8086. In the **protected mode,** the 80286 can still execute 8086 programs but will operate using memory protection and allow virtual memory addressing.

The 80286 microprocessor consists of four basic sections: the instruction unit, execution unit, address unit, and bus interface unit. Figure 11.1 illustrates the interaction of the four basic sections in a block diagram format.

The **bus interface unit** performs all the operations for the MPU that require bus operations. These include generating the command signals for the address and data

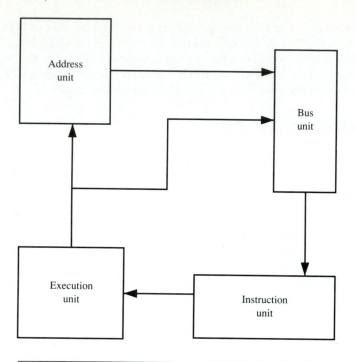

FIGURE 11.1
80286 block diagram

bus. The address and data command signals allow the interfacing of the MPU to external memory or to input and output devices (buffers, flip-flops, keyboards, etc.). The bus unit also controls how the MPU operates with other processors on the same address bus (such as math coprocessors). It also looks ahead and gets the next instruction to be executed from memory. Instructions are stored in the instruction queue to be used by other units in the 80286.

The **instruction unit** gets (fetches) the next instruction to be executed from the instruction queue. The instruction is then decoded into **microcode** (the 1s and 0s used by the MPU) and passed on to the execution unit.

The **execution unit** takes the decoded instruction from the instruction unit queue and performs the action called out by the decoded instruction. The execution unit also uses the bus unit to transfer data into and from memory.

The **address unit** manages and protects the system memory for the MPU. The management that it performs is keeping the sections of memory that are in use by the MPU in consecutive (contiguous) blocks. Protection involves keeping any sections of memory (data) from being erased or corrupted unintentionally.

The 80286 is configured into a 68-pin, high-density package as shown in Figure 11.2. Of the 68 pins two are +5 V (V_{cc}), three are ground (V_{ss}), and six are no connection. The signal lines are as follows:

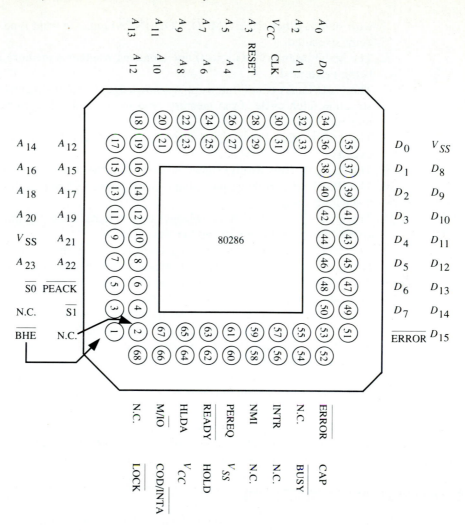

FIGURE 11.2
80286 pinout

1. The CLK (clock) line provides the fundamental timing that is used by the chip.
2. The D_0–D_{15} (data bus) lines provide the bidirectional general purpose path for data signals between the 80286 and other devices.
3. The A_0–A_{23} (address bus) lines provide the connections among the 80286, physical memory, and I/O devices.
4. The $\overline{\text{BHE}}$ (Bus High Enable) line indicates the transfer of data on the upper byte of the data bus (D_8–D_{15}).
5. The $\overline{S}_0$, $\overline{S}_1$ (Bus Cycle Status) lines indicate when the bus cycle starts and along

with several other signals (M/$\overline{\text{IO}}$, COD/$\overline{\text{INTA}}$) indicate what type of bus cycle is being executed.

6. The M/$\overline{\text{IO}}$ (Memory-I/O select) line indicates whether a memory or I/O cycle is being performed.

7. The COD/$\overline{\text{INTA}}$ (Code/Interrupt Acknowledge) signal distinguishes between instruction fetch cycles from memory read cycles and acknowledge signals from interrupt cycles.

8. The $\overline{\text{LOCK}}$ (Bus Lock) signal distinguishes between locked and unlocked bus cycles.

9. The $\overline{\text{READY}}$ (Bus Ready) signal indicates that the bus cycle is complete.

10. The HOLD (Bus Hold Request) input signal indicates a request for bus control by a separate device.

11. The HLDA (Bus Hold Acknowledge) output signal indicates that the 80286 has given control of the bus to another device.

12. The INTR (Interrupt Request) signal requests that the 80286 stop its present operation and service an interrupt, which can be masked by software.

13. The NMI (Non-Maskable Interrupt Request) input signal indicates a request for interrupt service, which cannot be masked by software.

14. The PEREQ (Coprocessor Request) input signal indicates a coprocessor request for a data operand to be transferred to or from the 80286.

15. The $\overline{\text{PEACK}}$ (Coprocessor Acknowledge) signal tells the 80286 when the operand is being transferred.

16. The $\overline{\text{BUSY}}$ (Coprocessor Busy) input signal indicates that the coprocessor is executing and is not able to respond to another request.

17. The $\overline{\text{ERROR}}$ (Coprocessor Error) input signal indicates that the coprocessor has experienced an error in the previous instructions.

18. The RESET (Reset) input signal suspends any operation in progress by placing the 80286 in a known reset state.

11.3   THE 80386 MICROPROCESSOR

The 80386 microprocessor is a high-speed, 32-bit microprocessor. The 80386 consists of 275,000 transistors to perform all the functions of an advanced 32-bit computer. The 80386 can operate software that was written for the 8086 and the 80286, in addition to those programs that were written specifically for the 80386.

The Intel 80386 is a full 32-bit microprocessor, with 32-bit internal registers and a 32-bit data bus. It also has 32 memory address lines. The 80386 can be thought of as two 8086s combined into one package with additional support devices included. With its 32-bit address bus, it can directly access 4 Gb ($2^{32} \approx 4.29 \times 10^9$) of physical memory. To put this into perspective, 4 Gb is more than 4000 times as much memory as the IBM PC with an 8088. This is more than 250 times the maximum memory capability of an 80286-based computer.

The 80386 can operate in three different modes: *real, protected,* and *virtual.* In the **real mode,** the 80386 operates as an 8086 with the same segments and 1 Mb of memory. In this mode, only one program can run at a time. In the protected mode, programs use the same segments and offset registers as in the real mode. In the

protected mode, the segment register is not a *real* address. The base address for each segment is 32 bits wide and can be anywhere within the 4 Gb of addressable memory. The offset addresses are also 32 bits wide. The upper 14 bits of the segment registers are used to look up a base address in a **descriptor table.** A descriptor table is a part of memory containing the physical address. This allows for over 16,000 different segments ($2^{14} = 16,384$), each of which can be 4 Gb long (4 GB = 2^{32}). Thus, the total amount of **virtual memory** is 64×10^{12} or 64 terabytes ($2^{14} \times 2^{32}$). The 80386 also uses on-chip memory management and multitasking. This allows for more than one program to be run at any given time. In the **virtual mode,** the 80386 has an addressing feature that is halfway between the 8086 and the fully protected 80386 mode. In this mode, the 80386 mimics the 1 Mb of addressing space of the 8086. Unlike the real mode, there can be more than one virtual mode operating at one time. Each of these **virtual environments** can have its own DOS application. Figure 11.3 illustrates the layout of the 80386 microprocessor chip. Included are the real estate areas that coincide with the six functional areas of the chip.

The 80386 consists of six sections which perform all the actions of the microprocessor. These sections are the bus interface unit, code prefetch unit, instruction decode unit, execution unit, segmentation unit, and paging unit as shown in Figure 11.4.

The **bus interface unit,** as its name implies, provides the interface between the 80386 and the outside world. It accepts requests for the internal transfer of information (data and addresses) and instructions. The interface unit also assigns levels of priority to these various requests. At the same time the bus interface unit also generates and processes all the information necessary to make up the bus cycles (read and write signals, data acknowledges, address strobes, etc.).

The **code prefetch unit** performs a look-ahead function for the 80386. This means that after the information for the instruction that is presently being executed is loaded and is being processed, the prefetch unit looks ahead to the next instruction and loads it into the 16-bit instruction queue. Because this action is not a direct execution of a program that is currently running, the bus interface unit gives the prefetch requests a low priority. This means that the prefetch unit must wait until the bus interface unit is not busy performing any instructions.

The **instruction decode unit** takes the instructions left in the instruction queue by the prefetch unit and translates them. The instructions written in 80386 operation codes **(op-codes)** are translated down even further by the decode unit from the hexadecimal codes used by the programmer to microcode (1s and 0s that the logic circuits in the microprocessor can understand).

The **execution unit** of the 80386 takes the instructions decoded from the instruction queue and communicates them to all other units that are required to execute the instruction. The execution unit contains three subunits. These units are the **data unit,** which contains the **arithmetic logic unit (ALU),** the **control unit,** and the **protection test unit.** The data unit performs the operations requested by the control unit. The ALU in the data unit performs all the arithmetic operations. The control unit contains the microcode (taken from the instruction decode unit) and the circuitry that performs calculations to locate the proper addresses for the execution of the microcode. The protection unit makes sure that the code being executed does not attempt to violate the movement between segments (blocks) of code.

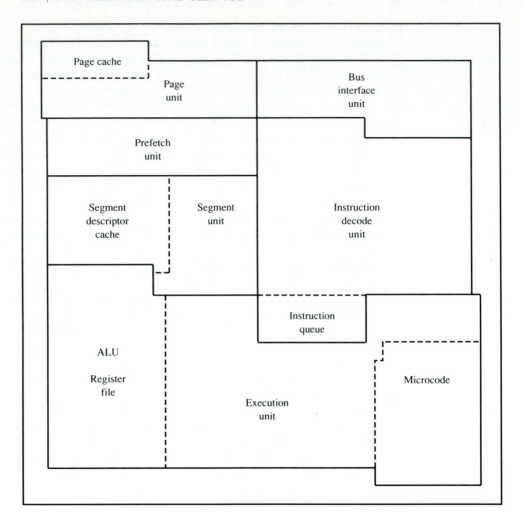

FIGURE 11.3
80386 microprocessor chip

The **segmentation unit** translates the logical addresses in the code being run into addresses that can be used by the execution unit. A segment of memory is a block of memory usually 64 kb long used to store data or addresses separately. This type of memory is referred to as *flat memory*. It provides no protection to the variables in a program because all the information resides in the same block or area of memory.

The **paging unit** in the 80386 translates the addresses generated by the segmentation or prefetch unit into physical addresses. The paging unit also sends these physical addresses to the bus interface unit for use in executing code.

The package of the 80386 is a 132 **pin grid array (PGA)** with a 14 by 14 matrix formed by three rows of pins all around as shown in Figure 16.5. Twenty of these pins are used for power (V_{CC}), 21 are used for ground (V_{SS}), and eight pins are left unused.

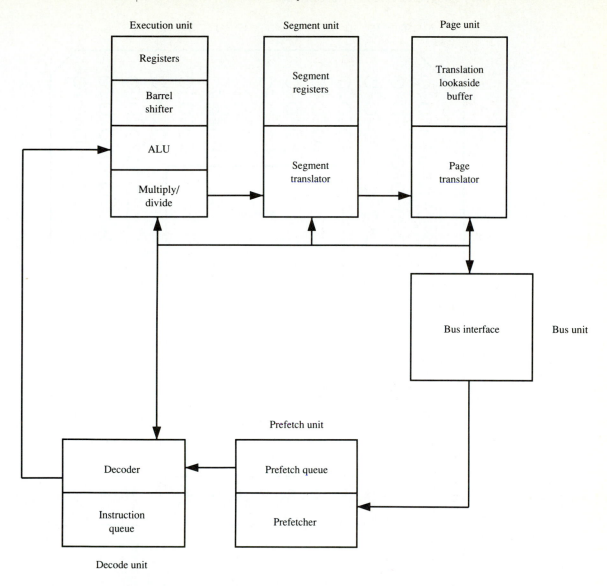

FIGURE 11.4
80386 block diagram

The remaining 83 pins are for carrying information and timing signals. These signals are as follows:

1. The CLK2 (clock) provides fundamental timing that is divided by two for use by the chip.
2. The D_0–D_{31} (Data Bus) lines provide the bidirectional general purpose path for data signals between the 80386 and other devices.

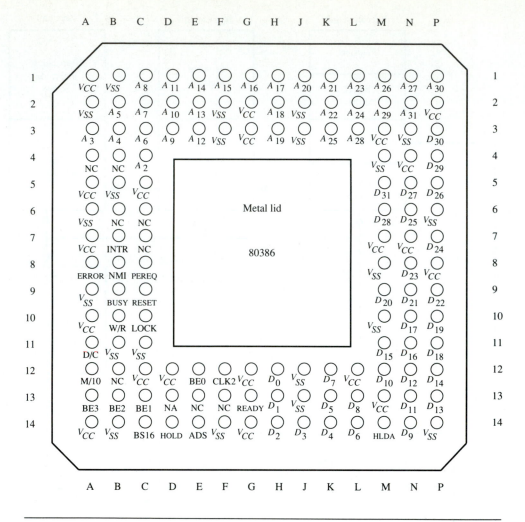

FIGURE 11.5
80386 pinout

3. The A_0–A_{31} (Address Bus) lines provide the tristate path to physical memory and I/O port addresses.

4. The $\overline{BE_0}$–$\overline{BE_3}$ (Byte Enable) outputs indicate which bytes of the 32-bit data bus are being used for the current transfer.

5. W/$\overline{R}$ (Write or Read Indication) is the output signal that distinguishes between write and read cycles.

6. D/$\overline{C}$ (Data-Control Indicator) is the output signal that distinguishes between data and control cycles.

7. M/$\overline{IO}$ (Memory-I/O Indication) is the output signal that distinguishes between memory and I/O cycles.

8. $\overline{\text{LOCK}}$ (Bus Lock Indication) is the output signal that distinguishes between locked and unlocked bus cycles.
9. $\overline{\text{ADS}}$ (Address Status) is the tristate output signal that indicates that a valid address is on the bus.
10. $\overline{\text{READY}}$ (Transfer Acknowledge) is the input signal that indicates a bus cycle is complete.
11. $\overline{\text{NA}}$ (Next Address request) is the input signal used to request the use of address pipelining.
12. $\overline{\text{BS16}}$ (Bus Size 16) is the signal used to indicate if 16- or 32-bit data transfers are to be used.
13. HOLD (Bus Hold Request) is the input signal that indicates a request for bus control for a separate device.
14. HLDA (Bus Hold Acknowledge) is the output signal indicating the 80386 has given control of the bus to another device.
15. PEREQ (Coprocessor Request) is the input signal indicating a coprocessor request for a data operand to be transferred to or from the 80386.
16. $\overline{\text{BUSY}}$ (Coprocessor Busy) is the input signal indicating the coprocessor is executing and is not able to respond to another request.
17. $\overline{\text{ERROR}}$ (Coprocessor Error) is the input signal indicating that the coprocessor has experienced an error in the previous instructions.
18. INTR (Maskable Interrupt Request) is the input signal indicating a request for interrupt service, which can be masked by the Flag register, IF, bit.
19. NMI (Non-Maskable Interrupt) is the input signal indicating a request for interrupt service, which cannot be masked by software.
20. RESET (Reset) is the input signal used to initialize and suspend any operation in progress by placing the 80386 in a known reset state.

The **80386-SX** processor is the same internally as the 80386. It is designed to replace the 80286 although it is *not* pin for pin compatible. The bus lines are designed for a 16-bit bus design like the 80286. In fact there are some clone boards that can accept either the 80286 or 80386-SX processor. Basically, the 80386-SX can run all 80386 applications such as multitasking on Windows 3.1, but without the higher costs of the 80386-DX processor and the 32-bit memory system. Of course the overall speed and performance will not be as good as the 80386-DX processor.

11.4 THE 80486 PROCESSOR

The 80486 is the latest enhancement to the INTEL processor line. The 80486 is functionally the same as the 80386 with the following changes.

1. The numeric coprocessor is included on the chip.
2. An internal 8 kb of CACHE memory is included on the chip. This greatly increases the instruction execution speed.
3. A reduced instruction operation time coding scheme reduces the amount of time required to execute many of the instructions to just one clock cycle.

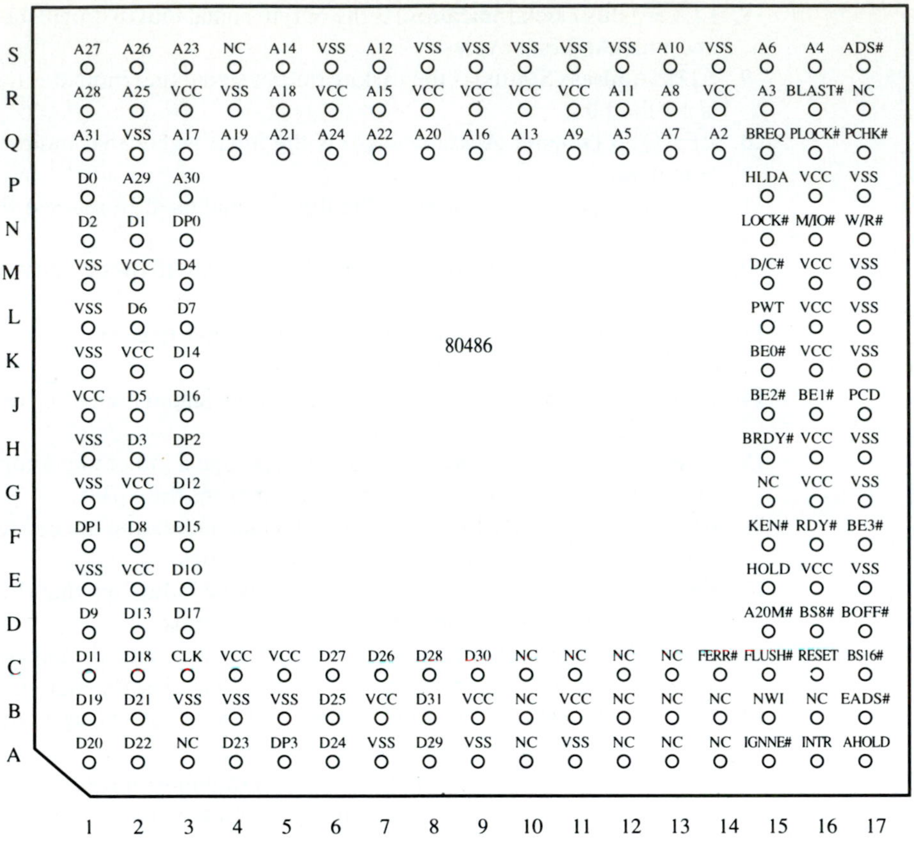

	1	2	3	4	5	6	7	8	9	10	11	12	13	14	15	16	17
S	A27	A26	A23	NC	A14	VSS	A12	VSS	VSS	VSS	VSS	VSS	A10	VSS	A6	A4	ADS#
R	A28	A25	VCC	VSS	A18	VCC	A15	VCC	VCC	VCC	VCC	A11	A8	VCC	A3	BLAST#	NC
Q	A31	VSS	A17	A19	A21	A24	A22	A20	A16	A13	A9	A5	A7	A2	BREQ	PLOCK#	PCHK#
P	D0	A29	A30												HLDA	VCC	VSS
N	D2	D1	DP0												LOCK#	M/IO#	W/R#
M	VSS	VCC	D4												D/C#	VCC	VSS
L	VSS	D6	D7												PWT	VCC	VSS
K	VSS	VCC	D14					80486							BE0#	VCC	VSS
J	VCC	D5	D16												BE2#	BE1#	PCD
H	VSS	D3	DP2												BRDY#	VCC	VSS
G	VSS	VCC	D12												NC	VCC	VSS
F	DP1	D8	D15												KEN#	RDY#	BE3#
E	VSS	VCC	D10												HOLD	VCC	VSS
D	D9	D13	D17												A20M#	BS8#	BOFF#
C	D11	D18	CLK	VCC	VCC	D27	D26	D28	D30	NC	NC	NC	NC	FERR#	FLUSH#	RESET	BS16#
B	D19	D21	VSS	VSS	VSS	D25	VCC	D31	VCC	NC	VCC	NC	NC	NC	NWI	NC	EADS#
A	D20	D22	NC	D23	DP3	D24	VSS	D29	VSS	NC	VSS	NC	NC	NC	IGNNE#	INTR	AHOLD

FIGURE 11.6
80486 pinout

4. A 50-MHz version has been delivered from INTEL, which makes this the fastest single chip CPU to date.

Figure 11.6 shows a diagram of the 80486 pinout. The signals are defined as follows.

1. The CLK (clock) input provides the fundamental timing for the 80486. It is either 25, 33, or 50 MHz, depending on the version of the processor.
2. The D_0–D_{31} (data bus) data lines provide the bidirectional general purpose path for data signals between the 80486 and the other devices.
3. The A_0–A_{31} (address bus) address lines provide the tristate path to physical memory or I/O port addresses.
4. The $\overline{BE_0}$–$\overline{BE_3}$ (byte enable) output signals are used to indicate which bytes of the 32-bit data are being used when fewer than 32 bits of data are being transferred.

5. W/$\overline{R}$ (write or read indicator) is the output signal that distinguishes between write and read cycles.

6. D/$\overline{C}$ (data or control indicator) is the output signal that distinguishes between data and control cycles.

7. M/$\overline{IO}$ (Memory-I/O indication) is the output signal that distinguishes between memory and I/O cycles.

8. $\overline{LOCK}$ (bus lock indicator) is the output signal that distinguishes between locked and unlocked bus cycles.

9. $\overline{PLOCK}$ (pseudo lock) is the output signal that indicates that more than one bus cycle is required to perform the current operation.

10. $\overline{ADS}$ (address status) is the tristate output signal that indicates that a valid address is on the bus.

11. $\overline{READY}$ (transfer acknowledge) is the input signal that indicates that a bus cycle is complete.

12. $\overline{BRDY}$ (burst ready) performs the same function as the $\overline{READY}$ input when a burst cycle is being performed.

13. $\overline{BLAST}$ (last burst) is an output signal that indicates that the next $\overline{BRDY}$ signal will complete the burst bus cycle.

14. DP0–DP3 (data parity generation/detection) is used to generate or detect even parity on the data bus.

15. $\overline{PCHK}$ (parity check) is an output signal used to indicate that a parity error has occurred.

16. RESET (reset) is the input signal used to initialize the processor and suspend any operation.

17. INTR (maskable interrupt request) is an input signal indicating a request for service interrupt, which can be masked by the flag register interrupt enable bit.

18. NMI (nonmaskable interrupt) is the input signal indicating a request for interrupt service, which cannot be masked by software.

19. BREQ (bus request) is an output signal that indicates that an internal bus request has been generated.

20. HOLD (hold) is an input used to request a DMA action that causes all address, data, and control lines to enter the tristate condition.

21. HLDA (hold acknowledge) is an output that indicates the acknowledgment of the hold request.

22. $\overline{BOFF}$ (back off) is an input signal that forces all buses to enter the tristate condition during the next clock cycle.

23. $\overline{AHOLD}$ (address hold) is an input signal that allows another MPU to access the address bus.

24. EADS (external address) is an input signal that indicates that an external address that is on the address bus is to be used to perform an internal cache cycle.

25. $\overline{KEN}$ (cache enable) is an input signal used to indicate whether the current bus cycle is cacheable.

26. $\overline{FLUSH}$ (flush) is an input signal used to erase all of the internal 8 kb of cache memory.

27. PWT (page write) is an output signal that reflects the state of the PWT attribute bit in the page table or page directory entry.

28. PCD (page cache) is an output signal that reflects the state of the PCD attribute bit in the page table or page directory entry.
29. $\overline{\text{A20M}}$ (address bit 20 mark) is a signal used to tell the 80486 to wrap its address around.
30. $\overline{\text{BS8}}$ (bus size 8) is an input signal used to indicate that 8-bit data transfers are being used.
31. $\overline{\text{BS16}}$ (bus size 16) is an input signal used to indicate if 16- or 32-bit data transfers are being used.
32. $\overline{\text{FERR}}$ (floating point error) is an output signal that indicates that the 80387 math coprocessor has detected an error.
33. $\overline{\text{IGNNE}}$ (ignore numeric error) is an input signal that tells the 80486 to ignore a floating point error.

As previously mentioned, the 80486 is almost identical to the 80386 and the 80387 packaged together. There are eight 32-bit general purpose registers, six segment registers that are used to form addresses along with one of the index registers or pointers, an instruction pointer register, and the flag register as shown in Figure 11.7.

The 80486 contains all of the instructions of the 80386 and the 80387 math coprocessor plus six additional new instructions as described in Table 11.1.

TABLE 11.1
80486 New instructions

Instruction	Description
XADD	Swaps low-order and high-order bytes on 16-bit data and also performs addition.
CMPXCHG	Reorders and compares 16-bit data.
BSWAP	Swaps the order of the 4 bytes in a 32-bit register.
INVD	Erases internal cache memory.
WBIVD	Erases internal cache memory after writing to memory.
INVLPG	Invalidates a page table entry.

The 80486 also includes 8 kb of internal cache memory. The cache memory is organized into four 2-kb sections. Whenever data is written to the external bus or memory, it is also written into cache memory. This is known as a **write through operation.** The WBINVD instruction erases data just written into cache memory.

Cache memory significantly improves system performance. This is because it is faster than having to go back to the bus to read the contents of memory through a memory read cycle. Because the 80486 is so fast, it would constantly be waiting for information from memory to be transferred. Figure 11.8 (p. 452) is a block diagram of the 80486 MPU. It is functionally similar to the 80386 with a 80387 math coprocessor.

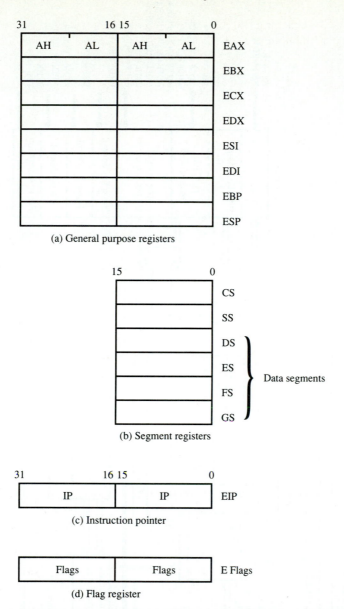

(a) General purpose registers

(b) Segment registers

(c) Instruction pointer

(d) Flag register

FIGURE 11.7
80486 registers

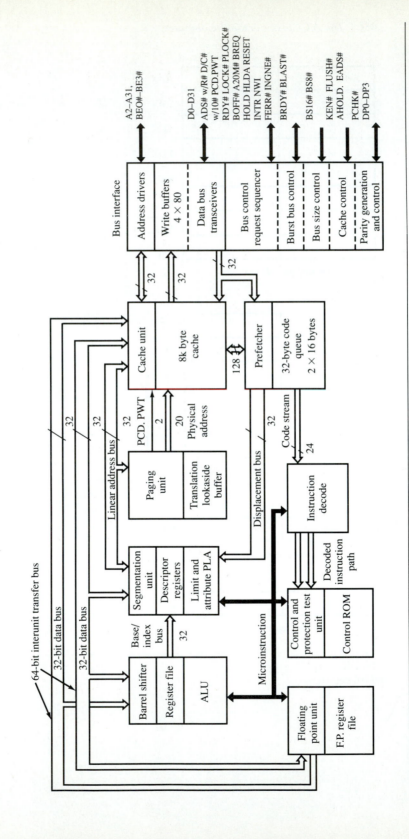

FIGURE 11.8
80486 block diagram

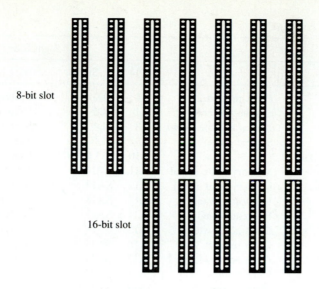

8-bit slot

16-bit slot

FIGURE 11.9
ISA bus connectors

11.5 THE ISA BUS

The 16-bit IBM PC/AT system bus has come to be known as the **Industry Standard Architecture (ISA) bus.** This is by far the most popular bus for MS-DOS computers to date. Almost all adaptor or controller boards designed for the 8-bit bus will work in the 16-bit ISA bus. Any 8-bit board will work in any adaptor slot (8- or 16-bit) as long as the board will physically fit in the chassis. However, 16-bit boards will work only in a 16-bit slot. The ISA bus is easily identified by the second 36-pin connector just in front of the 62-pin PC bus connector, as shown in Figure 11.9.

Many new bus signals have been added along with the additional eight data bits including four new DMA channels, six new interrupt requests, 24-bit addressing, a bus master input, and two 16-bit bus selects. Table 11.2 shows the ISA bus signals with the new AT signals labeled accordingly.

TABLE 11.2
ISA bus connector pins

Left Side			Right Side		
Pin	Signal	Use	Pin	Signal	Use
B1	GROUND		A1	I/O CHCK	Parity errors
B2	RESET DRV	System reset	A2	SD7	System data bit 7
B3	+5V	System power	A3	SD6	System data bit 6
B4	IR9	Interrupt 9 (new)	A4	SD5	System data bit 5
B4	−5V	System power	A5	SD4	System data bit 4

TABLE 11.2, *continued*

	Left Side			Right Side	
Pin	Signal	Use	Pin	Signal	Use
B6	DRQ2	DMA request 2	A6	SD3	System data bit 3
B7	−12V	System power	A7	SD2	System data bit 2
B8	OWS	Zero wait state (new)	A8	SD1	System data bit 1
B9	+12V	System power	A9	SD0	System data bit 0
B10	GROUND		A10	I/O CHRDY	Gen wait state
B11	SMEMW	Memory write signal	A11	AEN	Address enable
B12	SMEMR	Memory read signal	A12	SA19	System address bit 19
B13	IOW	I/O write signal	A13	SA18	System address bit 18
B14	IOR	I/O read signal	A14	SA17	System address bit 17
B15	DACK3	DMA acknowledge 3	A15	SA16	System address bit 16
B16	DRQ3	DMA request 3	A16	SA15	System address bit 15
B17	DACK1	DMA acknowledge 1	A17	SA14	System address bit 14
B18	DRQ1	DMA request 1	A18	SA13	System address bit 13
B19	REFRESH	Memory refresh	A19	SA12	System address bit 12
B20	CLK	System clock	A20	SA11	System address bit 11
B21	IR7	Interrupt request 7	A21	SA10	System address bit 10
B22	IR6	Interrupt request 6	A22	SA9	System address bit 9
B23	IR5	Interrupt request 5	A23	SA8	System address bit 8
B24	IR4	Interrupt request 4	A24	SA7	System address bit 7
B25	IR3	Interrupt request 3	A25	SA6	System address bit 6
B26	DACK2	DMA acknowledge 2	A26	SA5	System address bit 5
B27	T/C	Terminal count	A27	SA4	System address bit 4
B28	BALE	Address latch enable	A28	SA3	System address bit 3
B29	+5V	System power	A29	SA2	System address bit 2
B30	OSC	14.318 color clock	A30	SA1	System address bit 1
B31	GROUND		A31	SA0	System address bit 0

The following are all new to the AT bus.

D1	MEM CS16	16-bit MEM select	C1	SBHE	Bus high enable
D2	I/O CS16	16-bit I/O select	C2	LA23	Address bus bit 23
D3	IRQ10	Interrupt request 10	C3	LA22	Address bus bit 22
D4	IRQ11	Interrupt request 11	C4	LA21	Address bus bit 21
D5	IRQ12	Interrupt request 12	C5	LA20	Address bus bit 20
D6	IRQ15	Interrupt request 15	C6	LA19	Address bus bit 19
D7	IRQ14	Interrupt request 14	C7	LA18	Address bus bit 18
D8	DACK0	DMA acknowledge 0	C8	LA17	Address bus bit 17
D9	DRQ0	DMA request 0	C9	MEMR	Memory read
D10	DACK5	DMA acknowledge 5	C10	MEMW	Memory write
D11	DRQ5	DMA request 5	C11	SD08	System data bit 8
D12	DACK6	DMA acknowledge 6	C12	SD09	System data bit 9
D13	DRQ6	DMA request 6	C13	SD10	System data bit 10
D14	DACK7	DMA acknowledge 7	C14	SD11	System data bit 11
D15	DRQ7	DMA request 7	C15	SD12	System data bit 12
D16	+5V	System power	C16	SD13	System data bit 13
D17	MASTER	Bus master control	C17	SD14	System data bit 14
D18	GROUND		D18	SD15	System data bit 15

DMA channels 5 through 7 are 16-bit transfer channels and can cross the 64-kb boundary to 128 kb. This is possible because the address output lines of the 8237 DMA controller are shifted up 1 bit (BIT 0 is always a 0). Thus, 16-bit transfers are always on an even boundary.

In the PC/AT type computer DMA channel 0 has been freed for 8-bit transfers. In the original 8-bit PC DMA channel 0 was for memory refresh. DMA channel 4 is reserved to cascade the original four DMA channels 0–3.

Seven more Interrupt Request lines have been added. IRQ 8 through IRQ 15 are now cascaded through IRQ2. The hard disk interrupt has been moved to IRQ14. IRQ9 replaces IRQ2 and is redirected to IRQ2's vector, thus resulting in a total of fifteen IRQ lines.

Sixteen-bit transfers are facilitated through the use of the $\overline{\text{MEM CS16}}$ and $\overline{\text{I/O CS16}}$ signals. When these signals are high, normal 8-bit transfers occur in any slot. When these signals go low, 16-bit transfers may be performed as soon as the card is selected. The $\overline{\text{I/O CS16}}$ signal is for I/O operations, and the $\overline{\text{MEM CS16}}$ signal is for external memory operations.

A new signal $\overline{\text{MASTER}}$ is provided to allow an adaptor or second processor to obtain control of the system bus. When this signal is pulled low, the system processor will pause and release control of the system bus.

11.6 ISA BUS SYSTEM SETUP

One vast improvement over the older PC system is the elimination of the system board switches. The setup information is now stored in a battery-powered RAM circuit contained in an on-board real time clock chip. This chip is the Motorola MC 146818 Real Time Clock plus RAM, which contains a clock/calendar circuit and 50 bytes of **CMOS RAM.** By supplying power to the chip with a battery, the time of day and all setup information can be maintained even when the system power is turned off. A block diagram of the MC14618 IC is shown in Figure 11.10.

The system setup information is loaded into the CMOS RAM by running a special program supplied by the computer manufacturer. An example of the PHOENIX BIOS setup program is shown in Figure 11.11 (p. 457).

As can be seen in the above example, much of the guesswork has been eliminated by a user-friendly, menu-driven screen complete with help screens. By pressing the F1 key, help for the selected field is displayed.

In most of the latest computers, this setup program is contained in the BIOS ROM and accessed by pressing the DEL or other key during self-test. One such example of this is the AMI (American Megatrends Inc.) BIOS, which is self-contained and menu-driven for ease of use. Figure 11.12 (p. 458) shows the AMI BIOS setup menu.

11.7 THE MICROCHANNEL

The ISA bus is considered an "open architecture," that is, anyone can use it without paying royalties. The **microchannel bus** is a proprietary bus to IBM Corporation. Anyone wishing to use this bus must pay royalties to IBM. The most popular microchannel bus computers are the IBM PS/2 line of computers. Some companies such as NCR have adopted the microchannel due to the superior performance of the bus.

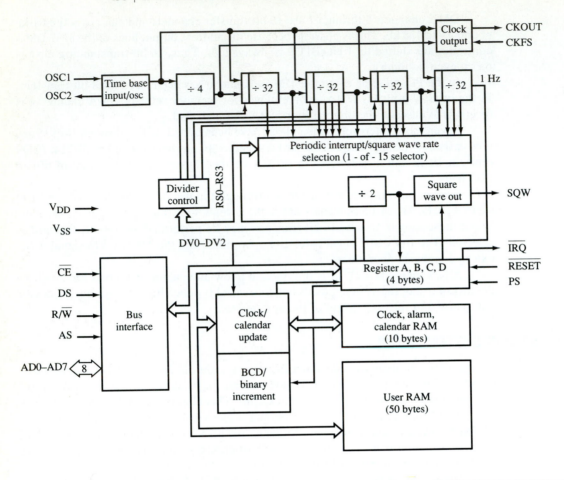

FIGURE 11.10
MC146818 block diagram

The microchannel bus is completely compatible with DOS-based applications but is *not* hardware compatible with ISA controller cards.

The microchannel contains an MPU bus and a system bus. It can handle 32-bits of data and 32 bits of memory addresses in a nonmultiplexed system. That is, there are 32 separate data lines and 32 separate memory address lines. The microchannel bus also contains its own system control and power lines.

The microchannel utilizes a specialized circuit known as the **address bus translator.** This allows 16-bit devices and 32-bit devices to communicate with each other and the MPU. The 16- and 32-bit data transfers require different control signals because the 16-bit 80286 and the 32-bit 80386 address memory differently. The microchannel uses the 80386 data transfer method for 32-bit operation. It uses the 80286 method for 8- and 16-bit operation. Figure 11.13 (p. 459) illustrates the microchannel connectors. Notice that there are three 32-bit connectors (J1, J2, and J4). Also, there are four 16-

```
             Phoenix Technologies Ltd.
             System Configuration Setup V4.0

        Time: 13:14:51
        Date: Sun Feb 02, 1992

        Diskette A:             5.25 Inch, 1.2 MB
        Diskette B:             3.5 Inch, 1.44 MB
        Hard Disk C:            Type 47
        Hard Disk D:            Not Installed
        Base Memory:            640 KB
        Extended Memory:        3072 KB
        Display:                EGA/VGA
        Keyboard:               Installed
        CPU Speed:              LOW

        Coprocessor:            Not Installed

        Up and Down Arrow to select entries
        Left and Right Arrow to change entries
        F1 to get help on current entry
        F10 to exit Setup
        Esc to reboot the system
```

FIGURE 11.11
Phoenix BIOS setup screen

bit connectors (J3, J5, J6, and J7). J6 is slightly larger to accommodate an optional video extension board.

The microchannel is an asynchronous bus that utilizes handshaking. The signal interchange and response control the bus. The $\overline{ADL}$ (Address Decode Latch) and $\overline{CMD}$ (Command) lines are used to define when the address and data are valid. The trailing edges of these signals are used to strobe and latch address and data information. CD CHRDY (Channel Ready) is used to extend the bus cycle. When CD CHRDY goes high, it triggers CMD, which ends the bus cycle. For example, Figure 11.14 (p. 460) illustrates the basic timing diagram for the microchannel basic write cycle.

1. T_1—At time T_1, the cycle begins with address and control line information. $\overline{S_0}$ and $\overline{S_1}$ go low, providing status to the MPU.
2. T_2—$\overline{ADL}$ defines the presence of a stable address.
3. T_3—The addressed card responds with CD16 for 16-bit data or CD32 for 32-bit data

```
    CMOS SETUP  (C)  Copyright 1985-1990, American Megatrends Inc.,

Date (mn/date/year) : Sat, Feb 01 1992     Base memory size  : 640 KB
Time (hour/min/sec) : 11 : 31 : 26         Ext. memory size  : 3072 KB
Floppy drive A:     : 1.2  MB, 5¼"         Numeric processor : Not Installed
Floppy drive B:     : 1.44 MB, 3½"

Hard disk C: type   : 47 = USER TYPE       Cyln   Head  WPcom  LZone  Sect  Size
Hard disk D: type   : Not Installed        980    10    65535  980    17    81 MB
Primary display     : VGA or EGA
Keyboard            : Installed

Scratch RAM option  : 1
                                           Sun  Mon  Tue  Wed  Thu  Fri  Sat
                                                 26   27   28   29   30   31    1
                                             2    3    4    5    6    7    8
                                             9   10   11   12   13   14   15
Month : Jan, Feb,.....Dec                   16   17   18   19   20   21   22
Date  : 01, 02, 03,....31                   23   24   25   26   27   28   29
Year    1901, 1902,.....2099                 1    2    3    4    5    6    7

ESC = Exit,←↓→↑ = Select, PgUp/PgDn = Modify
```

FIGURE 11.12
AMI BIOS setup screen

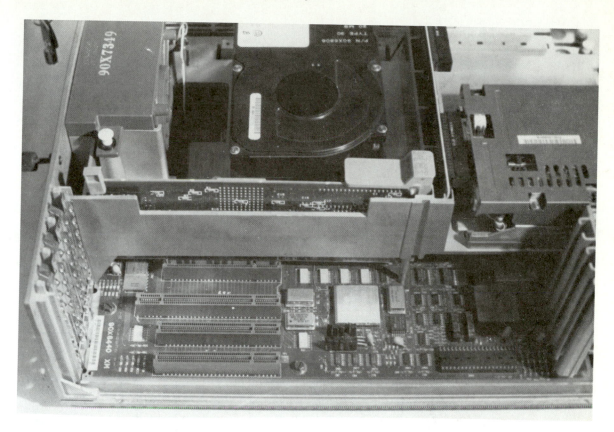

FIGURE 11.13
Microchannel connectors

and $\overline{\text{CD SFDBK}}$ to acknowledge that it is being addressed. Furthermore, CD CHRDY will go low to extend the bus cycle (wait state) if necessary.

4. T_4—Data appears on the bus.
5. T_5—$\overline{\text{CMD}}$ goes low, indicating that the data on the bus is now valid. $\overline{\text{ADL}}$ will go high.
6. T_6—If CD CHRDY was in the wait state, it will now go high to release the wait state.
7. T_7—$\overline{\text{CMD}}$ goes high, ending the bus cycle.

The microchannel defines the direction in which personal computers are heading. That is, a larger bus size with more power, memory, and speed. Clone manufacturers have developed the **Extended Industry Standard Architecture (EISA) bus** to compete with the microchannel bus. This is because the microchannel is proprietary to IBM and cannot be used by anyone without paying royalties. In general, the EISA bus is a high-speed, 32-bit bus with more power than the ISA bus.

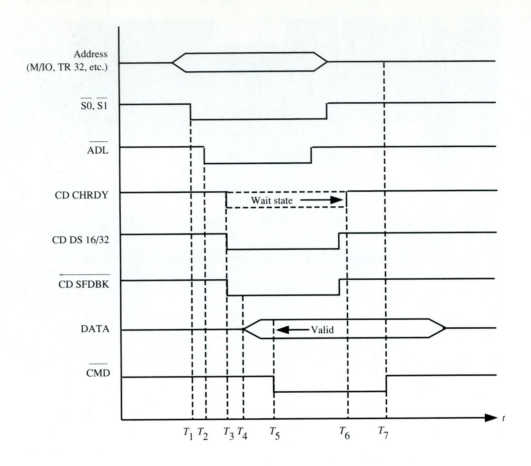

FIGURE 11.14
Bus write cycle for microchannel

11.8 THE MICROCHANNEL SYSTEM SETUP

Setup on a microchannel computer is very different from, and more complicated than, the setup on an ISA-based computer. In the ISA bus system, any card can go in any slot as long as it fits. This is not so in the microchannel system. There is a special slot for the video adaptor card indicated by an additional set of pins as previously shown in Figure 11.13.

Each slot must be programmed for the card that is inserted in that particular slot. Every adaptor card for the microchannel is supplied with an installation diskette. The installation diskette contains an **Adaptor Descriptor File (ADF).** The ADF is a text file describing all possible I/O addresses, memory addresses, interrupt levels, and DMA information. The file name is the @ symbol followed by four hex digits and the dot ADF extension (.ADF), for example, @E7FE.ADF. This file must be installed after

```
┌─────────────────────────────────────────────────────────────┐
│  Main Menu                                                    │
├─────────────────────────────────────────────────────────────┤
│                                                               │
│      1.  Learn about the computer                             │
│      2.  Backup the Reference Diskette                        │
│      3.  Set configuration                                    │
│      4.  Set features                                         │
│      5.  Copy and option diskette                             │
│      6.  Test the computer                                    │
│                                                               │
├─────────────────────────────────────────────────────────────┤
│   Use    or      to select. Press Enter.                      │
│   Esc=Quit       F1=Help                                      │
└─────────────────────────────────────────────────────────────┘
```

FIGURE 11.15
Microchannel setup main menu

the adaptor card is installed by running the manufacturer's setup program. When an adaptor card is inserted without running the setup program, the system will not boot from the hard disk until the setup program is run successfully. It is important to have all the setup information and programs handy before attempting an installation, or you may render the system totally inoperable.

Setting up the IBM PS/2 system involves inserting the reference diskette that came with the computer and powering up the system. It is important to note that you must have the correct reference diskette for the system you are working on. For example, a model 50 diskette will not work on a model 80 system. The IBM logo appears on the screen when you start the setup program. Simply press ENTER and the system will load the rest of the setup program. Upon completion the main menu will be displayed as shown in Figure 11.15. IBM has incorporated a brief tutorial to teach you about your computer. Select 1 from the Main Menu to run the tutorial. The second selection is for making a backup copy of the diskette, which is a good idea since without it you cannot change the configuration of the computer. The third and fourth selections are to actually configure the system. The fifth selection is to copy the ADF file from the option adapter card onto your setup diskette. The sixth selection is to test the system.

Pick your selection by using the arrow keys to highlight the desired selection and pressing the enter key. In this case we will choose the **set configuration** option. After you press the enter key, a second menu will be displayed as shown in Figure 11.16.

From this menu you can view the current system configuration by selecting 1. This allows you to see the current configuration but not change it. This is a good idea the first time through the process in order for you to become familiar with the system configuration. The second selection shows the same information as the first but allows you to change the configuration. You must be very careful to make the correct configuration choices or the system may not boot up normally.

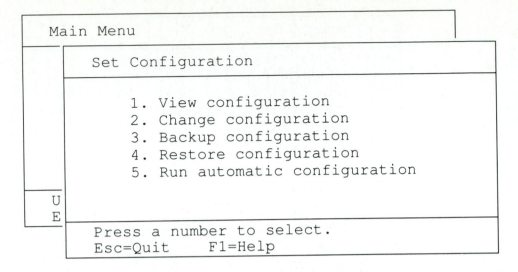

FIGURE 11.16
Microchannel set configuration menu

Once you have configured the system properly you can save the current configuration onto the reference diskette by selecting **backup configuration.** If for any reason the system configuration is improperly changed or is lost, the saved configuration can be restored by selecting **restore configuration.**

An **automatic configuration** can be run on a new system. This method is a good idea if you are not sure of how to configure the system. Automatic configuration will ensure that there are no conflicts and that the system will boot. However, it may not be the optimum configuration for your system. Upon selection of the **change configuration** option, an additional menu labeled change configuration will pop up as shown in Figure 11.17.

You may change the configuration by using the arrow keys to highlight the item to be changed and pressing enter. A list of available choices (if any) will be displayed, and then you may choose the desired parameter. If your choice causes a conflict with another device, a warning message will be displayed. Once you have made all the required changes to the menu you must save the changes by pressing the F10 key. Help is available on all menus and is selected by pressing the F1 key. Figures 11.18 through 11.20 are examples of NCR 486-25 microchannel computer system configuration menus, which are similar to the IBM menus just described.

11.9 TECH TIPS AND TROUBLESHOOTING—T³

The general procedures for assembling or disassembling PC, XT, or AT class computers are very similar. Variations occur due to the type of system and hardware supplied. You can save money by assembling your computer, and it can be an interesting,

```
Change Configuration

Total System Memory
  Installed Memory ..................... 4096kb  (4.0MB)
  Usable Memory ........................ 3968KB  (3.9MB)

Built In Features
  Installed Memory ..................... 7168KB  (7.0MB)
  Diskette Drive A Type ................ [1.44MB 3.5" ]
  Diskette Drive B Type ................ [Not Installed]
  Math Coprocessor ..................... Installed
  Serial Port .......................... [SERIAL_1]
  Parallel Port ........................ [PARALLEL_1]

Slot1 - NCR SCSI Host Adapter Board
  Host Adapter Board Interrupt Level ... [INT LEVEL 9]
  I/O Address Select ................... [240    ]
  DMA Level Select ..................... [DMA Level 3]
  Fairness ............................. [Fairness Enabled]


Esc=Quit   F5=Previous   F10=Save
F1=Help    F6=Next                    End    PageDown
```

FIGURE 11.17
Microchannel change configuration menu

```
┌──────── NCR SETUP UTILITY PC486 ────────
│                 NCR CORPORATION
│                 Version 1.01
│       (c)  Copyright 1988 Phoenix Technologies Ltd.
│                   MAIN MENU
├─────────────────────────────────────────
│ Configuration Utilities
├─────────────────────────────────────────
│ Set the system configuration
├─────────────────────────────────────────
│ Use the <──> keys to move highlight, press ⌐┘ to continue, or Esc to Quit
└─────────────────────────────────────────
```

FIGURE 11.18
NCR setup main menu

```
                    CONFIGURATION MENU

Install  Automatic  View  Change  Backup  Restore

Manually select new settings to resolve conflicts

Internal Options
  SLOT  1:  NCR SCSI Host Adapter Board

  SLOT  2:  NCR VGA Adapter

  SLOT  3:  Plexus AIP2 Card

  SLOT  4:  3Com EtherLink/MC Ethernet Adapter

  SLOT  5:  Cornerstone DualPage Display

  SLOT  6:  EMPTY

  Use ↓ ↑ to move highlight,  press ◀┘ to view the slot,  or Esc to Quit
```

FIGURE 11.19
NCR configuration menu—internal options

```
                          CONFIGURATION MENU

  Install Automatic View Change Backup Restore

  Manually select new settings to resolve conflicts

                                    ┌─Adapter Memory Location─┐
                                    │   Segment C400          │
  Fixed resources                   │ * Segment C800          │
                                    │   Segment CC00          │
  Adapter Memory Location           │ * Segment D000          │
                                    │ * Segment D400          │
  Memory Chip Size                  │ * Segment D800          │
                                    │ * Segment DC00          │
  AIP Card Option                   │   Segment B000          │
                                    │   Segment B400          │
  Daughtercard Board Subtype        │   Segment B800          │
                                    │   Segment BC00          │
  Daughtercard Option 0             │ * Segment C000          │
                                    └─────────────────────────┘
  Daughtercard Option 1


  F1 = help, ↓ ↑ = move highlight, ◄┘ = select,  F10 = save,  Esc = Quit
```

FIGURE 11.20
NCR configuration menu/fixed resources

valuable, and satisfying experience. Furthermore, it is a very important skill to master for anyone wishing to learn to repair or upgrade personal computers. This section outlines the assembly procedure. It can easily be adapted for disassembly.

Motherboard Assembly

1. Always begin by grounding or discharging yourself to protect against damage that may occur because of static electricity. You should do this frequently, especially if you do not have a static electricity wrist strap to stop the buildup of static charge. A simple way to do this is to touch a metal wall outlet or metal appliance that is plugged into an outlet and grounded. Be certain the outlet or appliance is metal (not plastic) and is grounded.

2. Unpack the motherboard and place it on top of the conductive packaging material in order to protect it from static electricity.

3. Install the memory modules in the sockets on the motherboard. If you are using ICs, be certain that pin 1 of the IC is installed in pin 1 of the socket. A dot or a ''U''-shaped notch will indicate the position of pin 1. Be certain not to bend or break any of the pins. Also, be certain that all of the pins make proper connection in the socket. It is easy for pins to get bent under the IC and not enter the socket. If you are installing SIM or SIP modules, again be certain that pin 1 of the module is inserted into pin 1 of the socket. Install the memory starting at bank 0. On AT class machines, each bank will have a high and low byte, for example, BANK0–H and BANK0–L. Memory must be installed one bank at a time. While you do not have to use every memory bank, memory banks cannot be partially filled. Therefore, if you install modules in BANK0–L, you must install modules in BANK0–H. Be certain that all pins make proper connection in the socket. Be careful not to force or break anything. Figure 11.21 illustrates memory modules being installed in a motherboard socket.

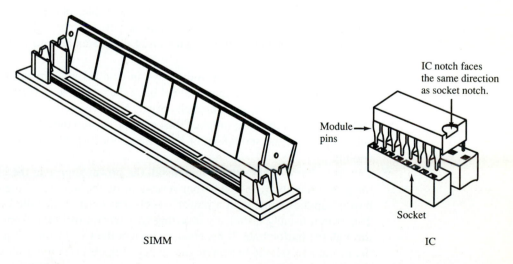

IC notch faces the same direction as socket notch.

Module pins

Socket

SIMM

IC

FIGURE 11.21
Inserting memory

4. Set and/or verify any memory jumpers and switch settings. You may wish to set and/or verify any *other* jumpers and switch settings that are required for your system configuration at this time, for example, monitor type, cache memory, battery backup, etc. The newer generation of machines require very few jumper settings. Many do not have switch settings at all. Almost everything is sensed automatically or configured by software during the CMOS setup. Read your manual and make sure you understand how to set up the motherboard. If you do not understand something, contact your supplier before you go any further. Figure 11.22 illustrates how to set or remove a jumper.

 Jumper off

Jumper on

FIGURE 11.22
Setting jumpers

5. Verify or install the ROMs on the motherboard. Some motherboards have two ROMs. They may be labeled **Odd** and **Even** or **Low** and **High.** Be certain that the ROMs are inserted into the proper socket and that pin 1 is in the correct spot. Also check that all pins make proper connection in the socket. Press down firmly on the ROMs to insure proper seating but be careful not to crack the motherboard or break anything. Again, use care and take precautions against static electricity.
6. Remove the screws that hold the cover onto the chassis. Remove the cover. Figure 11.23 illustrates how to remove the cover.
7. If they are installed, remove all of the connector filler plates from the back of the chassis. Each plate is attached to the chassis with a screw. Save the plates and the screws to be reinstalled later. Figure 11.24 illustrates how to remove or install a filler plate.
8. Place the computer chassis upside down in front of you. Install the four rubber feet on the bottom of the chassis. Peel back the adhesive covering and install the rubber feet about 2 in. in from each corner. Not every chassis comes with rubber feet; however, if they are supplied, be certain to install them. Rubber feet not only help to prevent the scratching of table tops, but they also help to insure proper cooling.
9. Turn the chassis right side up and install the power supply in the chassis. Secure the power supply by inserting four screws through the back of the chassis. Some power supplies come with a power switch that must be installed on the chassis. The switch usually installs by inserting two screws from the front of the chassis through the button hole. If necessary, connect the wires from the power supply to the switch. Install the button on the switch. Figure 11.25 illustrates how to install the power supply.
10. Install the speaker in the plastic holder. Mount the holder with one screw at the top left front of the chassis.

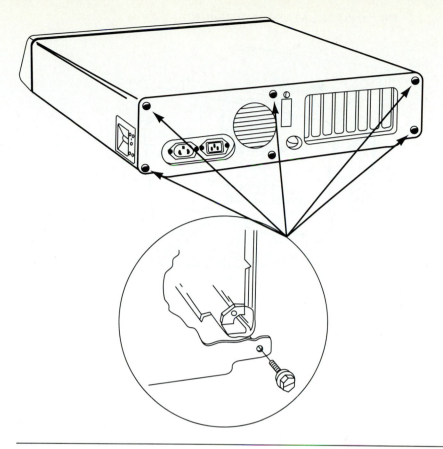

FIGURE 11.23
Cover removal

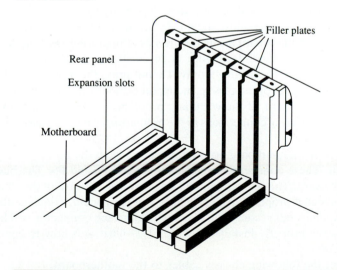

Filler plates

Rear panel

Expansion slots

Motherboard

FIGURE 11.24
Filler plates

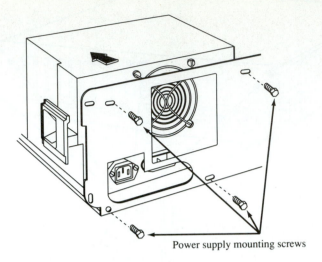

Power supply mounting screws

FIGURE 11.25
Power supply removal

11. Some chassis require that two metal inserts or standoffs be installed on the chassis to secure the motherboard. The exact location of the inserts will vary depending upon your chassis and motherboard. Placing the motherboard inside the chassis temporarily will help to find the correct location for the inserts. Install the inserts if required.

12. Insert four to six plastic standoffs that support the motherboard above the metal chassis. The exact location will vary depending upon your chassis and motherboard. Try to give the most support in the area of the expansion slot connectors. Placing the motherboard inside the chassis temporarily will help to find the correct location for the standoffs. Figure 11.26 illustrates installation of the standoffs.

13. Check the motherboard for fit only. Do not press the motherboard into place yet. Make sure that all of the plastic and metal standoffs align with the mounting holes in the motherboard. If there are any problems, correct them before proceeding. You will be making connections to the motherboard next, so leave the motherboard loose for now.

14. Connect the motherboard power connectors from the power supply to the motherboard. These connectors are usually labeled P8 and P9. The black wire on P8 faces forward. The red wire on P9 faces forward. Be careful that these connectors are connected properly. An error here will permanently damage the board. Note that on almost all systems the black wires on each connector will be next to each other when properly installed. Figure 11.27 illustrates how to connect the power connectors.

15. Connect the following chassis cables to the motherboard:
    - Turbo switch
    - Reset switch

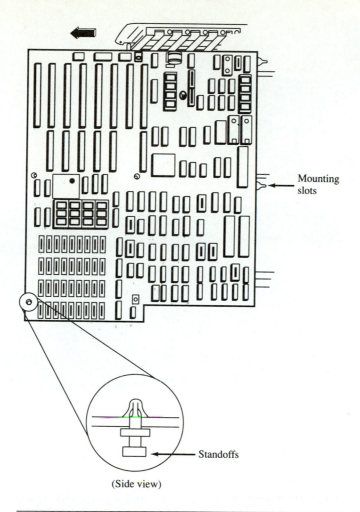

Mounting slots

Standoffs

(Side view)

FIGURE 11.26
Plastic standoff

- Keyboard lock switch
- Turbo LED
- Power LED
- Speaker

Consult your motherboard manual for the proper connection points. The polarity of the switch wires is not important. However, if you install them backward, the switch will work backward. If the switch does not work the way you want it to, simply reverse the wires. The polarity of the speaker wires also does not matter. The polarity of the LEDs *is* important. However, no damage will be done if the LEDs are wired backward. Simply reverse the wires if the LEDs do not light. Often the information supplied by the manufacturers of motherboards is vague and polarity information is omitted.

FIGURE 11.27
Molex power connector

16. Slide the motherboard into the chassis, making sure that the plastic inserts are aligned with the holes in the motherboard. Be certain that the board is oriented correctly. The keyboard connector should be in the rear and should align with the access hole in the rear of the chassis. Press the motherboard onto the standoffs. Do not force anything. Be careful not to crack the motherboard or damage any of the parts on the motherboard. Use care and take precautions to protect against static electricity.

17. Insert the two screws that hold the motherboard onto the chassis. Be careful not to overtighten the screws. Again, use care and take precautions against static electricity.

Disk Drive Installation

18. Unpack the hard drive, being careful to save all of the documentation. You will need to look up information during the hard disk software setup.

19. Check that the drive select jumper, which is usually located on a connector at the rear of the drive, is set at position 0 (factory setting). Position 0 is the first position

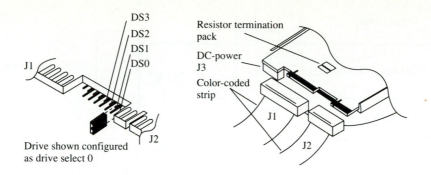

FIGURE 11.28
Drive select jumper

and is usually next to the twenty-pin edge connector. Figure 11.28 illustrates how to set the drive select jumper.

20. Check that the resistor terminator is installed on the bottom of the disk drive. Verify that it has not been jarred loose or lost during shipping. The terminator is illustrated in Figure 11.28.

21. On some systems, it may be necessary to remove the front faceplate from the hard disk so that the drive can be recessed into the chassis. This is accomplished by removing the two screws that hold the faceplate onto the drive. Some chassis also require that rails be attached to the hard drive for mounting. These rails are attached with two screws on each side of the drive.

22. Insert the hard disk into the desired mounting bay. Position the drive so the chassis cover installs properly and that the front faceplate of the drive (if used) is flush with the front of the chassis cover. Secure the hard drive with four screws (two on each side).

23. Unpack the floppy disk drive and verify that the drive select jumper is set for device 1.

24. Insert the floppy disk drive into the desired mounting bay. Position the front faceplate of the floppy disk drive to extend out from the front of the chassis so it will be flush with the front of the cover when the cover is installed. The mounting screws will probably end up approximately in the center of the slotted adjustment. You may need to readjust the position of the disk drive after you install the cover so the disk drive is in its proper position. Secure the floppy disk drive with four screws (two on each side).

25. Install any additional floppy disk drives in the same manner. Be certain that all of the floppy disk drives are set for device 1 as in step 23 above. It is the cable that differentiates drive A from drive B.

Disk Controller Installation

26. Unpack the disk controller PC board. On AT class systems, the controller will support up to two hard disk drives and two floppy disk drives. Use care and take precautions against static electricity.

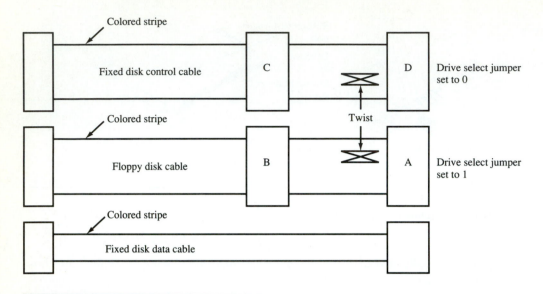

FIGURE 11.29
Disk drive cables

27. Using the disk controller manual, verify that all jumper settings are correct. Unless you are doing something special, you will probably find that the factory settings are what you want.

28. Locate and identify the three disk-drive flat-ribbon cables and lay them on the table with the colored stripe on the top as shown in Figure 11.29.

29. Connect the disk drive cables to the disk controller board connectors. Most disk controller boards are clearly marked. Be certain that pin 1 on the cable corresponds to pin 1 on the connector. Note that the narrow cable is the hard disk data cable. The wide cable with the twist toward the bottom is the hard disk control cable (colored stripe at top). The wide cable with the twist toward the top is the floppy disk cable (colored stripe at top).

30. Insert the disk drive controller PC board into a 16-bit slot (full slot) on the motherboard. It is generally a good idea to select a slot close to the disk drives. This will help to keep the cable routing neat. Insert the hold-down screw from the previously removed filler plates to secure the board. Figure 11.30 illustrates the board insertion process.

31. Connect the hard disk data cable and control cable to the hard disk drive. Be certain to use the middle connector before the twist in the cable. The middle connector corresponds to the jumper setting for device 0, which was previously set. Device 1 would correspond to the end connector after the twist and is used for a second hard disk drive. The connectors are keyed and should only fit one way. Notice that the edge connector on the hard disk drive is slotted or has a space at one side of the connector. The colored stripe will go toward the slotted side of the connector Be certain that pin 1 of the cable corresponds to pin 1 of the connector. Putting the cables on backward should not damage anything, but the disk drives will not work.

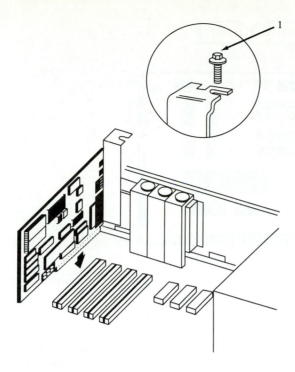

FIGURE 11.30
Controller board installation

32. Connect the floppy disk drive cable to the floppy disk drive. The end connector after the twist in the cable attaches to drive A. The middle connector before the twist attaches to drive B. Be certain that pin 1 on the cable corresponds to pin 1 on the connector. Again, the colored stripe will go toward the slotted side of the connector.

33. Connect a power cable from the power supply to each floppy disk drive and to the hard disk drive. These connectors are keyed so they cannot be inserted backward. There are four connectors coming from the power supply. They are all wired exactly the same way, so you can use any one you wish. The remaining connector is supplied for additional options.

34. Connect the remaining cable from the front of the chassis to the disk controller interface board. This cable is for the hard disk access LED. Generally, the red wire goes toward the front of the connector. Polarity matters. If you put the cable on backward, you probably will not do any damage, but the LED will not light when the hard disk drive is being accessed. Simply reverse the wires.

Multifunction I/O Board Installation

35. The multifunction I/O board controls up to two serial ports called COM ports, a parallel port, and a game port. Installation and jumper settings will vary from one manufacturer to another. Read the instruction manual and identify how to set up

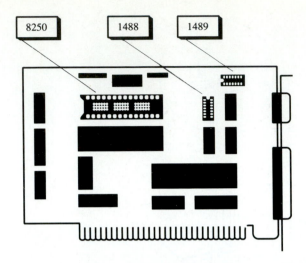

FIGURE 11.31
Installation of a second serial port

the board. If you have any questions or do not understand something, contact your supplier. The following steps outline the general procedure for installation and identify the areas to watch out for.

36. If your board has two COM ports, you may have to install the ICs for the second serial port. This generally involves inserting three ICs (8250, 1488, and 1489) into the multifunction card. Pin 1 on the ICs is identified with a dot on top of the chip. Be careful not to bend or break any of the pins. It is easy for pins to get bent under the IC and not enter the socket. Generally, when the chips are inserted properly, all of the chips on the board will be facing in the same direction. (Notice the placement of pin 1 on each chip.) Use care and take precautions against static electricity. Figure 11.31 illustrates how to add the second serial port to the multi-function board.

37. Verify and set up all of the required jumpers. Be careful if you are going to install a modem. The modem requires a COM port. If your modem is set for COM 1, you cannot set the serial port for COM 1, or a conflict will occur. Simply set the serial ports as COM 2 and COM 3.

38. If supplied, install the 9-pin serial port connector and the 15-pin game port connector to the board.

39. Install the board on the motherboard and insert the serial/game connector into the next filler plate position over. Insert the hold-down screws to secure the board and connectors. Use care and take precautions against static electricity.

Video Board Installation

40. The video board installation will vary with the type of board (CGA, EGA, VGA, monochrome, etc.) and manufacturer. Verify all jumper and switch settings and

install the board on the motherboard. Most video boards come from the factory ''ready to go.'' Insert the hold-down screws to secure the board. Use care and take precautions against static electricity.

Miscellaneous

41. Install the connector filler plates to cover the remaining holes in the back of the chassis. These are the filler plates that were previously removed. Install a hold-down screw for each plate. Operating a system with missing filler plates might cause improper air circulation and cooling. This can shorten the life of a system.
42. Verify that the switch on the bottom of the keyboard is set in the AT position for AT class machines or the XT position for XT class machines. Connect the keyboard cable to the motherboard.
43. Connect the monitor cable to the video board.
44. Connect the AC power cord to the power supply and the monitor.
45. Visually inspect the system, making sure that parts are not touching, all connections are good, no screws or metal scraps are lying on any of the boards, and no tools are lying in the chassis. Turn on the power switch for the monitor and then turn on the system. If everything is working correctly, install the cover on the chassis.

EXERCISES

11.1   Will programs written for the 8-bit PC XT run on a 16-bit AT-class computer?

11.2   How many bits are there on the data bus for the 80486, 80386, 80286, and 8088 microprocessors?

11.3   Identify the four basic sections of the 80286 microprocessor.

11.4   Explain the function of the instruction unit.

11.5   Identify the three memory modes of the 80386 microprocessor.

11.6   Explain the function of the 80386 segmentation unit.

11.7   What is the ISA bus and where is it found?

11.8   Will an 8-bit ISA video card work in a 16-bit slot?

11.9   For what is DMA channel 0 used in the PC XT and the PC AT?

11.10   How many IRQ lines are there in an ISA bus AT class computer system?

11.11   Which IRQ line is used for the hard disk in the ISA bus AT class computer system?

11.12   Describe the function of the master signal.

11.13   What happened to the IRQ2 line in the ISA bus AT class computer?

11.14   If an I/O controller pulls the signal IOCS16 low, what kind of transfer is taking place?

11.15   Where is the setup information saved on an AT class computer system?

11.16   Why isn't the setup information lost when the system power is turned off?

11.17   Discuss the differences between the XT and AT setup procedures.

11.18   List the differences between the ISA bus and the microchannel bus.

11.19   Can the microchannel video card plug into any slot?

11.20   Describe the microchannel setup procedure.

11.21   Crossword Puzzle

ACROSS

1. System board in a PC that contains the microprocessor.
3. High-speed switch on the front of the chassis.
4. Math chip.
8. New 80486 coding scheme.
10. The 1s and 0s that the MPU understands.
11. AT class bus architecture standard.
14. The unit that manages the system memory for the MPU.
16. Memory that saves the system setup information.
17. Unit that translates segmentation addresses into physical addresses.
18. Unit that decodes the operation codes.
19. The 80486 has 64 Tb of _____ memory.
20. The unit that connects the microprocessor to the outside world.

DOWN

1. IBM proprietary bus architecture.
2. Plastic device used to install a system board on a chassis.
5. Manufacturer of BIOS setup programs.
6. Translates logical addresses for the execution unit.
7. Unit that performs a code look-ahead function.
9. An economy version of the 80386 or 80486.
12. AT class 32-bit clone bus architecture standard.
13. High-quality video standard.
15. Unit that decodes instructions and performs commands.
17. IC packaging style.

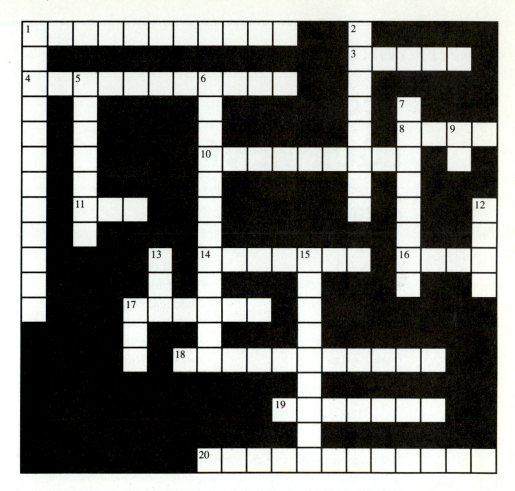

CHAPTER TWELVE

TEST EQUIPMENT

KEY TERMS

Aliasing

Checkpoints

Digital Storage Oscilloscopes

Emulative Tester

Functional Tester

In-circuit Tester

Logic Analyzer

Logic Probe

Logic Pulser

Power Line Monitor

PROM Burner

Undersampling

Universal Microcomputer Tester

Variable Persistence Oscilloscope

Volt Ohm Milliammeter (VOM)

12.0 INTRODUCTION

In this chapter we discuss the various types of test equipment used in the microcomputer repair shop. We begin with the simplest logic probes and meters and work up to the latest in automatic testers. Included in this chapter is a universal microcomputer tester project. This is a project you can build and use to diagnose and repair most types of microcomputer systems in use today.

12.1 LOGIC PROBES AND PULSERS

Logic probes are simple logic level indicators (Figure 12.1). Most logic probes have three lamps, indicating the *high state, low state,* and *pulse*. The pulse indicator flashes whenever the logic level transitions from one valid level to the other valid level. The pulse indicator is required because it may be impossible to see a short or infrequently occurring pulse on the high and low indicators. Some more sophisticated logic probes may also include a separate gate input, which allows you to observe a logic level only when enabled by the gate input.

Using the logic probe is quite simple. Power to the probe is provided from the unit under test by connecting the probe power leads to the board. Be careful to observe the polarity of the power leads. When the probe tip is placed on an IC pin, the indicators

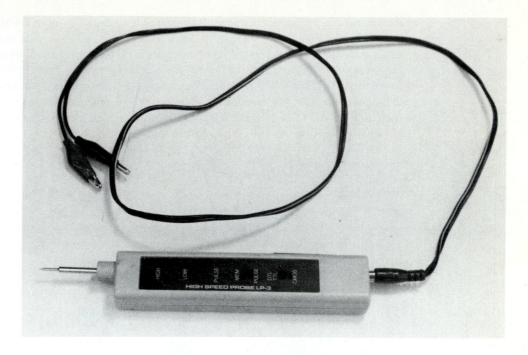

FIGURE 12.1
Digital logic probe

reflect the logic state of that pin. If no indicators are illuminated, an illegal logic state is present. When either the high or the low indicator is illuminated, the pin tested is at a valid stationary logic level. If the high and the pulse indicators are illuminated, the pin is mostly at the high state and pulsing low. If the low and the pulse indicators are illuminated, the pin is mostly at the low state and pulsing high. If all three, high, low, and pulse indicators, are illuminated, the pin is transitioning high and low at a ratio of approximately 50%. It is possible to approximate the high to low ratio, which is called the *duty cycle,* by observing the difference between the intensity of the high and low indicators.

The **logic pulser** is a device that will drive, or force, an IC pin to a desired logic level. This is a handy device when used in conjunction with the logic probe. A logic gate may be checked by driving an input pin with the logic pulser while observing the respective output pin with the logic probe.

12.2 METERS

No electronic repair shop is complete without at least a **volt ohm milliammeter (VOM).** The VOM is required for measuring the power supply output and for finding short and open circuits. If you decide to use a digital volt ohm milliammeter (DVM), the meter should include a diode check range. It is preferable to use a 3½-digit DVM similar to the one shown in Figure 12.2. Recall the input diode anomaly discussed earlier. In many cases static discharge causes the input diodes of TTL gates to short. This short is usually approximately 30 to 200 Ω. This is easily found by using the VOM. A normally functioning TTL input will measure open when the ohmmeter positive lead is placed on the input pin and the negative lead is placed on the ground pin. A low resistance reading, such as 30 to 200 Ω, indicates a possible short. Always check if a resistance to ground or power is present on the suspect pin before replacing the chip.

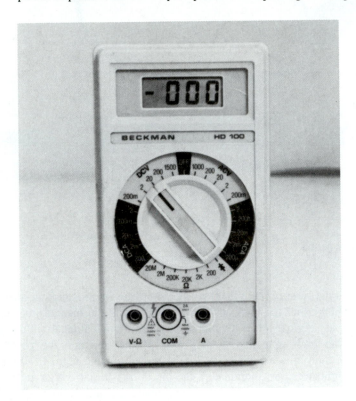

FIGURE 12.2
Beckman digital volt milliammeter

12.3 OSCILLOSCOPES

As discussed throughout this text, an oscilloscope is required whenever waveform measurements are taken. The oscilloscope used should include at least two DC coupled vertical inputs. The horizontal time base should be the triggered sweep type, preferably with a delaying time base. The low-cost TV, service oscilloscope should not be used in this application due to its slow speed and lack of DC inputs.

There are many brands and types of oscilloscopes on the market, with a wide range in price and performance. An oscilloscope with a vertical bandwidth of 50 MHz is acceptable; however, a bandwidth of 100 MHz is preferred. Some manufacturers offer **variable-persistence oscilloscopes** for viewing single-shot events. The latest development in oscilloscopes are the **digital storage oscilloscopes,** which convert the incoming analog waveform into digital data and store the data in RAM. The RAM data is then displayed on the screen as the waveform. These digital scopes offer many advantages over the analog types, with the biggest advantage being the ability to capture single-shot events and store the waveforms for later viewing and comparison. The digital scope is not without a few disadvantages. The first is its relative high price, and the second is that the scope may miss high-frequency noise, or oscillation, which may occur during a single-shot or low-repetition event. If the noise, or oscillation, is at or above the sample rate of the scope, the noise will be missed or digitized improperly. This problem is known as **undersampling,** or **aliasing.**

Using the oscilloscope can be difficult for the novice technician. The first thing you must do is to familiarize yourself with all the controls. Most importantly, learn how to properly use the triggered sweep. As already discussed, many oscilloscopes include an automatic trigger mode. Do not depend on this mode all the time. Learn how to use the oscilloscope in the normal trigger mode. One example of using the oscilloscope to troubleshoot a microcomputer might be to check the BIOS ROM output pins. Since many devices are connected to the data bus, there will be a great deal of activity on the data bus lines. Simply observing the bus waveforms without setting the oscilloscope to trigger on a specific event is not adequate. To check the ROM output pins, connect the oscilloscope vertical input A to the ROM select pin. Set the trigger on the oscilloscope to the internal trigger mode from vertical channel A. Since most ROM select lines are active low, set the trigger slope to (−) or the negative edge. Set the vertical mode to display both channels in the chopped mode. Adjust both the vertical input gains to display 2 V/cm. Position the channel A trace to the upper portion of the display. Adjust the timebase and trigger level to display a stable negative (low) going pulse at least one-half the width of the display, as shown in Figure 12.3 for channel A. Connect vertical input channel B to one of the ROM data output lines. Channel B should display a waveform similar to the waveform shown in Figure 12.3. By observing the voltage levels on channel B, you can determine if the output drivers of the ROM are functioning properly. By observing the time delay from the point where the select line goes active to the point where the data output is at a valid level, you can measure the *access time* of the ROM chip. From this display you cannot determine if the bit is at the correct logic state; you can determine only that the output is at a correct logic voltage level. A voltage level between 0.8 V and 2.4 V indicates a bad ROM or a loaded output circuit. If, for example, some other device on the bus is active at the same time, a bus contention problem may exist. This will show up as an illegal voltage level on one of the data pins during the ROM select. Analyzing the output data patterns requires a multiple-channel display device with enough input channels to accommodate all the address and data lines simultaneously.

Oscilloscope display

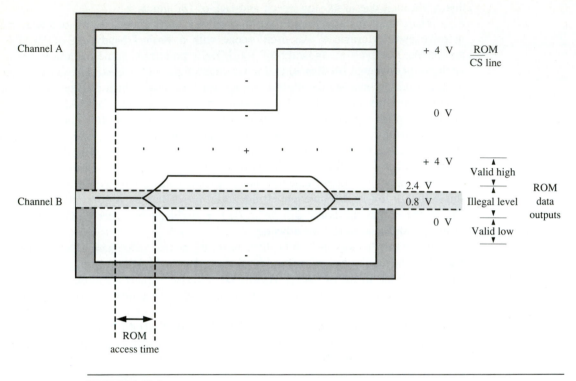

FIGURE 12.3
Oscilloscope

12.4 LOGIC ANALYZERS

The **logic analyzer** is a multichannel digital signal display device. Unlike the oscilloscope, the logic analyzer does not allow analog inputs. Logic analyzers are available with input channel numbers ranging from 8 up to 64, depending on price. Most logic analyzers will display the acquired data as timing waveforms, similar to an oscilloscope display, and as binary data in hexadecimal, octal, or binary format. The logic analyzer is well suited for analyzing bus activity. Using the logic analyzer, you will be able to observe the address bus and the data bus simultaneously. To perform this, connect some of the input channels to the address bus and connect the other input channels to the data bus. Set the logic analyzer to the external clock mode and connect the external clock input to the appropriate bus control line. In this case we will use the memory-select line. Many logic analyzers also include clock qualifier inputs, which allow the clock in only when the signals are valid. You must now set the logic analyzer to trigger on some desired memory address. By observing the bus activity, you will be able to follow the microprocessor instruction fetch sequence. You will also be able to observe RAM writes and reads. Many microprocessors use RAM when performing subroutine calls and returns. If a RAM error should occur during a subroutine, the microprocessor will ''get lost,'' because the value of the calling routine's program counter is stored when the subroutine is run. When the subroutine is finished, the value of the calling routine's program counter is restored to the program counter from RAM. If the value is corrupted, the program counter will return to the wrong address, causing it to be lost. By observing this activity on the logic analyzer, you can determine the cause of the fault to the faulty bit. Consider the following MC6800 example:

```
ADDRESS DATA

     MAIN PROGRAM
0100  BD0200   Jump to subroutine at address 0200
0103  XXXXXX   Next instruction
01XX           Next instruction . . .

     SUBROUTINE
0200  B68002   Load accumulator a from port at 8002
0203  39       Return from subroutine, to caller
```

The logic analyzer should display the address and data, as follows:

```
0100 BD
0101 02
0102 00
XXFF 03    PROGRAM COUNTER LOW BYTE STORED TO STACK RAM
XXFE 01    PROGRAM COUNTER HIGH BYTE STORED TO STACK RAM
0200 B6
0201 80
0202 02
0203 39    RETURN INSTRUCTION
XXFE 01    PROGRAM COUNTER HIGH BYTE FROM STACK RAM
XXFF 03    PROGRAM COUNTER LOW BYTE FROM STACK RAM
0103 XX    NEXT INSTRUCTION IN MAIN PROGRAM
```

Now let's assume that a memory failure exists. In the next example we assume that memory bit 7, the MSB, is stuck high. The logic analyzer might display the following:

```
0100 BD
0101 02
0102 00
XXFF 03    STORED PROGRAM COUNTER LOW BYTE
XXFE 01    STORED PROGRAM COUNTER HIGH BYTE
0200 B6
0201 80
0202 02
0203 39    RETURN INSTRUCTION
XXFE 81    WRONG VALUE DUE TO PICKED BIT
XXFF 83    WRONG VALUE DUE TO PICKED BIT
8183 XX    JUNK INSTRUCTION DUE TO ILLEGAL ADDRESS
XXXX XX    COULD BE ANY ADDRESS DEPENDING UPON JUNK
XXXX XX    INSTRUCTION
           THE MICROPROCESSOR IS NOW LOST
```

As we can see in the preceding example, when the microprocessor executed the RETURN instruction, corrupted data were restored to the program counter (8183 instead of 0103). This is just one example of how the logic analyzer may be used to track down a bus problem.

Most logic analyzers are very flexible and are limited only by the user's imagination. Since the logic analyzer will also display the input channels as timing charts, many or all the bus-control lines may be viewed simultaneously and measured for correct timing. All the timing diagrams in Chapter 6 were obtained by using a logic analyzer connected to the IBM PC. Some of the latest logic analyzers include built-in disassemblers, which will translate the machine code into a format that humans can read. This feature will save the time of looking up the machine codes but will usually add to the cost of the logic analyzer.

12.5 PROM BURNERS

The name **PROM burner** is an acronym for a programmable read-only memory programmer. The PROM burner is usually a compact self-contained device designed to read in and program various types of programmable memory devices. There are many variations of the PROM programmer available on the market, including some in kit form. The newer versions of PROM programmers support various types of programmable logic devices (such as PLD, PAL, and PLA) by using adapter modules (Figure 12.4). Recent

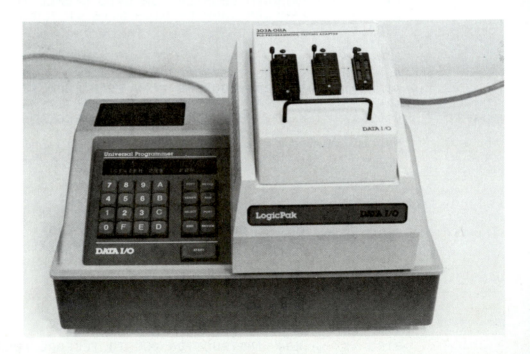

FIGURE 12.4
Data I/O PROM programmer

repair histories have shown that programmable devices have a high failure rate. In the repair shop, the PROM programmer can serve two functions. The first is the ability to program blank parts to use as replacement parts. The second is the ability to check quickly and verify a suspect part from a bad board.

12.6 POWER LINE MONITORS

The **power line monitor** is a recording voltmeter (Figure 12.5). This device is handy when analyzing the incoming AC power over a period of time. On occasion you will hear a complaint about a higher-than-normal failure rate or intermittent system crashes. In cases like this it makes sense to monitor the incoming power for unusual conditions. Excessive voltage drops, called *sags*, may cause the computer system to lock up or reset. Voltage spikes, called *surges,* may damage the power supply or sneak through the power supply and damage the system. Connecting the power line monitor to the supply power over the period of a few days to one week will give a good profile of the incoming

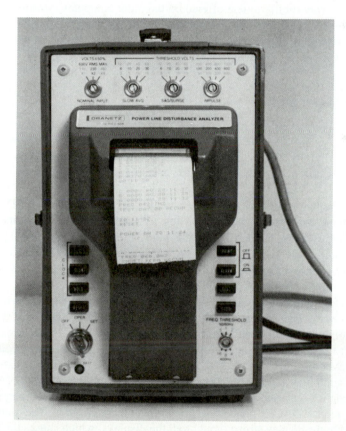

FIGURE 12.5
Dranetz power line monitor

power. If the results show excessive power variations, connect the computer to a different line or add a power line conditioner to the system. The worst offender to power line problems are inductive loads such as air conditioners and refrigerators.

12.7 THE UNIVERSAL MICROCOMPUTER TESTER PROJECT

Almost all the 1970 and earlier vintage minicomputers and large mainframe computers included various display panels. These display panels showed the status of various CPU buses and control lines. The display panels enabled the technician to diagnose the system by single-stepping the computer one instruction at a time and observing the status of the display panels. Even if the system were totally dead, the display panels would give some clue as to the problem. Most modern computers have eliminated these display panels. Today, when the system is dead, you do not have a clue as to the cause of the problem. What we offer here is an inexpensive alternative to the more expensive test equipment. This project was designed by the authors to enable you to observe the address bus and data bus in a way similar to that offered on the older computer systems. You will be able to select the tester to stop and display on I/O read, I/O write, memory read, or memory write operations or any combination thereof. The basic design of this project may be applied to almost any computer system.

Theory of Operation

The universal microprocessor tester project is basically an address and data line status display. We also include a WAIT STATE generator circuit, which performs a HALT FUNCTION. The display will enable you to observe the bus activity visually. The wait state generator will allow you to stop and single-step the computer one instruction at a time.

The display is centered around seven TIL 311 hexadecimal LED display devices manufactured by Texas Instruments, Inc. These display devices include a DATA LATCH, DECODER, and LED DRIVER built in to the display, which greatly simplifies the construction of this project, as shown in Figure 12.6. The DATA inputs of the display are connected directly to the PC bus address and data lines, as shown in Figure 12.7.

The first five displays are for the 20 address bus lines. The last two displays are for the 8 data lines. The address and data bus information is displayed by selecting any one or any combination of read and write control lines. This is accomplished by using switches to connect the 4 inputs of a 4-input NAND gate to the 4 control lines IOR, IOW, MEMR, and MEMW. NAND gate IC2a is actually used as a negative-OR gate and drawn as such (Figure 12.7(b)). The output from IC2a is connected to NAND gate IC2b. NAND gate IC2b is used to block the display of refresh cycles by gating the select signal with the signal DACK0, which is the refresh DMA cycle. The output of IC2b is connected to the display strobe input of all the displays, which causes the bus address and data to be latched on the displays.

The wait circuit consists of a D-type flip-flop, IC 1a, which is clocked by the output of gate IC2a. The wait circuit is armed by flipping the wait enable switch up.

FIGURE 12.6
TIL 311 hexadecimal displays

When the selected display operation occurs, the output of IC2a triggers the flip-flop and causes the microprocessor to wait indefinitely by pulling the line IOCHRDY low.

The single-step circuit consists of a double-pole, single-throw momentary switch connected to flop-flop IC1b used as a set/reset flip-flop. The flip-flop is required to *debounce*, or clean up, the noisy output of the momentary switch. The output of the single-step flip-flop is fed to a resistor-capacitor (*RC*) network, which is used to create a very narrow *low-going pulse*. This pulse is fed to the reset input of the wait flip-flop IC1a, which removes the wait condition when the button is depressed. This action will allow you to step to the next selected function.

Construction

The construction of this project is quite simple and requires no special skills except for some light soldering and wire-wrapping. Before beginning construction, review the physical layout of the pins on the components. Make certain you know the orientation of pin 1 of the display and other ICs. Keep in mind that when you are wiring the sockets,

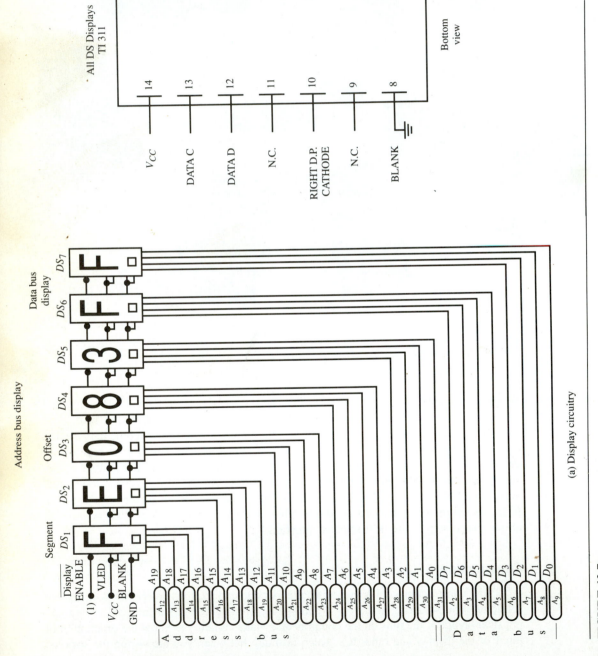

(a) Display circuitry

FIGURE 12.7a
Universal microcomputer tester project

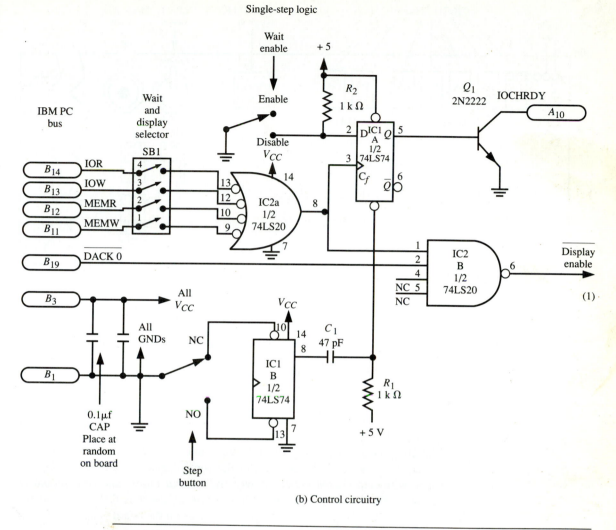

Single-step logic

(b) Control circuitry

FIGURE 12.7b

you will be looking at the pins from the bottom view. Normally, pin 1 is at the top left side of the IC. When you are wiring the sockets, pin 1 will be the top right side of the IC because you are looking at the bottom of the IC. We once observed a student lay out a printed circuit board for a digital clock backward because he did not check the IC orientation. The result was the project had to be scrapped and built over again, so don't let this happen to you. We constructed our prototype on a universal prototype board designed to fit into the IBM PC bus. These prototype boards are commercially available and provide easy access to the PC bus connections. The displays and switches should be mounted on the reverse side of the board, as shown in Figure 12.8. This should be done

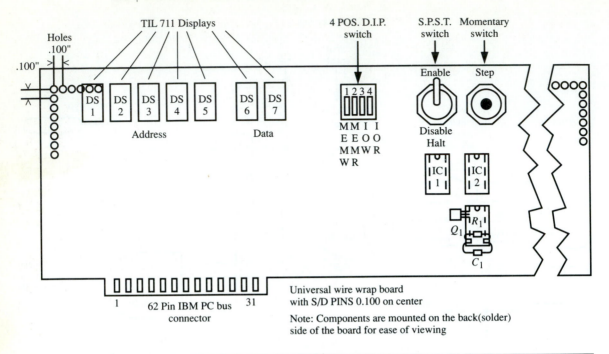

FIGURE 12.8
Universal microcomputer tester layout

so the display and switches are easily accessible when the board is placed in the last slot on the left side of the computer.

All the components, including the transistor and resistors, can be mounted on 14-pin wirewrap IC sockets. The placement of the components is not critical. Many of these universal wirewrap boards include *power* and *ground* buses, and care should be taken not to place the socket pins through these holes unless it is done intentionally. First, put the wirewrap sockets into their respective places on the board. The sockets may be anchored by using cement or by soldering two opposite corner pins of the IC socket to the plated through holes (if equipped). Next, wire up the power and ground pins on all the sockets that require power and ground. Using an ohmmeter, check the wiring on the sockets and check for shorts between power and ground. This power check is an important step and should not be skipped. Next, drill larger holes to mount the switches. Remove the copper traces within ⅛ in. around the drilled holes. If this is not done, a short will exist between power and ground when the switch is installed. Install the switches and again check for any shorts between power and ground. Next, wire up the sockets according to the schematic and check *all* the wiring by using the ohmmeter. Next, install a few 0.1-μF capacitors at random locations on the board between the power and ground buses for signal decoupling. The number and placement of the capacitors are not critical. Install all the components into their respective sockets and verify their orientations. Last, prepare labels for the switches and install them in their proper places. These labels not only make the tester look nice, but they make it easy for you and other people to use the tester as well. The **universal microcomputer tester** is now ready for use.

A complete kit or assembled version of this project is available from:

RMB Associates Ltd.
51 Birchbrook Dr.
Smithtown, NY 11787

Operation

The operation of this tester is quite simple. First, remove the cover of any IBM PC or compatible (*always turn off the power first*). Next, install the tester into the end slot on the left side of the computer. If a board is already in this slot, move it to another slot. Set switch 2 of the switch block on the tester, labeled MEMR, to the on position. Set the wait enable switch to the enable position. What we just did was to set the tester to display and cause the computer to wait on any memory read operation. Power on the computer. The tester display should read

        F F F F 0 E A

Under *no* condition should the display be dark! If the display is dark, *immediately* turn off the computer and check your work. This is an indication of no power to the display or possibly of a misplaced display blanking wire. If the digits appear fuzzy, it indicates the wait circuitry is miswired and the computer has not entered the wait state.

The RESET line, which is active during power up, will cause the 8088 microprocessor to vector, or begin execution, at address FFFF0 hex. Since we set the tester to display and wait on a memory read operation, the display should show the address and data values of the first read from memory. The RESET vector address is FFFF0 hex, and the first instruction should be EA hex, a JUMP instruction. The next two bytes fetched will be the offset value placed into the program counter and the last two bytes are the segment value placed into the code segment register, CS. Recall that the Intel series microprocessors fetch the register values backward. That is, the LSB is fetched first. Each time you depress the step button on the tester, you should observe the next byte fetched along with its address. The sequence for the IBM PC with a BIOS ROM dated 10/27/82 from power on should look as follows,

F	F	F	F	0	E	A	The jump instruction
F	F	F	F	1	5	B	The least significant offset byte
F	F	F	F	2	E	0	The most significant offset byte
F	F	F	F	3	0	0	The least significant segment byte
F	F	F	F	4	F	0	The most significant segment byte
F	F	F	F	5	3	1	Dummy read (execute cycle does prefetch)
F	E	0	5	B	F	A	The first instruction of POST, (CLI)
F	E	0	5	C	B	4	The next instruction
			⋮				Subsequent instructions

You may continue to follow the POST execution by repeatedly depressing the step button. If the preceding sequence is correct, you can safely assume the system data bus is intact. If a bit on the data bus is stuck, the first few instructions will usually show the problem.

Next, power off the computer and set the wait enable switch to the disable position. Power on the computer. The display should appear fuzzy because the address and data lines are changing at a rate of 1 million times per second. The computer should come up normally. By observing the display you may notice some patterns, specifically on the high-order address display, where the changes occur less frequently. Perform the same test sequence for the MEMW, IOR, and IOW switches as we did for the MEMR switch to verify their operation. The displayed address and data values will vary, depending upon the current BIOS ROM revision installed into the computer. To use the tester properly, you must obtain the BIOS listing.

Recall the POST from Chapter 10. If the test fails early on in the sequence, the system will simply halt and give no clue to the problem. By using this tester with the wait enable switch in the disable position and the MEMR switch on, the address value displayed will be the address of the halt instruction plus a few locations. Recall that the 8088 microprocessor contains a prefetch queue and will fetch a few extra instructions while executing the current instruction. By referring to the BIOS listing, you can determine which test has failed by the address of the halt instruction. By analyzing the test that has failed, you will gain clues to accuse the faulty circuitry. The POST in the IBM PC/XT and the PC/AT have added **checkpoints** into the POST test. The checkpoint is the currently executing test number output to an unused I/O port address. The port address on the IBM PC/XT is 60 hex, and on the PC/AT the port address is 80 hex. This may be observed by setting the tester to display IOW functions. If the computer is dead and the tester display shows address 00060 and data 01, the system failed at checkpoint 1.

With the wait enable switch set to disable, observing the display while selecting the various display functions should prove interesting. One example of this is observing the MEMW display function while running the IBM memory diagnostics. You will see the address value incrementing very rapidly while the data display shows a pattern of AA, 55, 01, 00. These are the actual patterns written to RAM during the test. The IOR and IOW displays will prove equally interesting.

If desired, you may add address decoding circuitry to the tester to only detect and display the checkpoint addresses. This feature will allow you to observe the progress of the POST test while the tests are running.

One important note on this tester and the IBM PC: This tester should not be used to single-step program routines in RAM or subroutines in ROM. You may, however, *display* any function at any time. When the tester causes the computer to wait, no RAM refresh cycles will occur. When we cause the system microprocessor to wait, we also cause the DMA and all other bus activity to wait. Any data stored in RAM will be lost, including any data in the stack RAM, which may be the calling routine's program counter. Recall the results when the stack memory is corrupted.

12.8 AUTOMATIC TEST EQUIPMENT

Troubleshooting modern microcomputers and microprocessor-based boards can be a tedious and time-consuming task. So far we have offered many ways of troubleshooting a microcomputer system manually. If you will be involved with production repairs where high volume and quick turnaround are required, then you will need a more efficient method of troubleshooting and repairing faulty boards and computers. Over the past decade a new breed of test equipment known as automatic test equipment has been developed. An automatic tester, put simply, is a collection of driver/sensor pins or wires controlled by a programmable computer. The computer, controlled by a set of instructions, will drive some of the pins while taking measurements on other pins. If we consider testing a two-input AND gate, we would require three pins, two to drive and one to sense. By driving the two inputs through all four possible logic combinations and monitoring the output, we can then compare the results to a software model. If the actual device and the model are the same, the device must be good. Any difference will indicate the device is faulty. Today's automatic testers are an elaboration on this simple principal. Currently there is a wide range of automatic testers with price tags from $5000 to over $500,000. The lower-cost units are designed for the service shop, and the higher-cost units are intended for the large production factory. The test methods and implementation varies, depending upon the user's specific needs. For the remainder of this text we discuss three different types of automatic testers, in-circuit, functional, and emulative automatic testers.

In-Circuit Automatic Testers

The **in-circuit tester** to which we are referring is the "clip the chip" type (see Figure 12.9). This tester uses standard IC test clips and tests the board one chip at a time. There are two basic types of this tester, *software comparison* and *hardware comparison*. Software comparison testers use the *overdrive* method to stimulate the IC under test, which means that the tester can drive the test pins at high currents to force the input pins of the IC under test to the desired state, regardless of the preceding logic. At first, this method may seem dangerous and damaging to other components. But, it has been proven that forcing IC output pins to the opposite logic state for short durations will not harm the IC. The input pins of the IC under test are driven to follow the software model truth table while the output pins are monitored and compared with the software model output truth table. If the output of the IC and the software model do not agree, the test will report a failure. The IC is flagged as faulty or the output pin may be loaded by some other component in the circuit. Recall the two-input AND gate example mentioned earlier. The truth table for this gate, where A and B are the inputs and Y is the output, is as follows:

```
A B Y
0 0 0    NOT A AND NOT B = FALSE
0 1 0    NOT A AND B = FALSE
1 0 0    A AND NOT B = FALSE
1 1 1    A AND B = TRUE
```

The test sequence for this gate, written for a FACTRON/SLUMBERGER 635 tester, looks as follows,

FIGURE 12.9
Factron in-circuit automatic tester

```
.  (pin definitions and parameter block)
.
.
LOW A B    ;A AND B FALSE
TESTL Y    ;Y IS FALSE
HIGH B     ;B TRUE AND A FALSE
TESTL Y    ;Y IS FALSE
LOW B      ;B FALSE
HIGH A     ;AND A TRUE
TESTL Y    ;Y IS STILL FALSE
HIGH B     ;A AND B NOW TRUE
TESTH Y    ;Y IS NOW TRUE
CLEAR      ;END OF TEST
```

An error is reported by the word FAIL on the screen, and the failing statement will appear red when viewed in the debugger. The hardware comparison automatic tester with which we are familiar monitors only the pins of the IC under test. The board must be in the system and in the failing state. The tester contains a hardware library of components for comparison. The input pin signals are fed to the library device input pins inside the tester. The output signals of the device under test are fed to a comparitor circuit along with the output signals from the internal library device. If the IC under test and the library device do not match, the IC under test must be faulty or the output is loaded by the circuitry connected to the output of the IC.

Functional Automatic Testers

The **functional tester** is designed to test the entire board as opposed to testing one chip at a time (see Figure 12.10). Since this test method must emulate the host system,

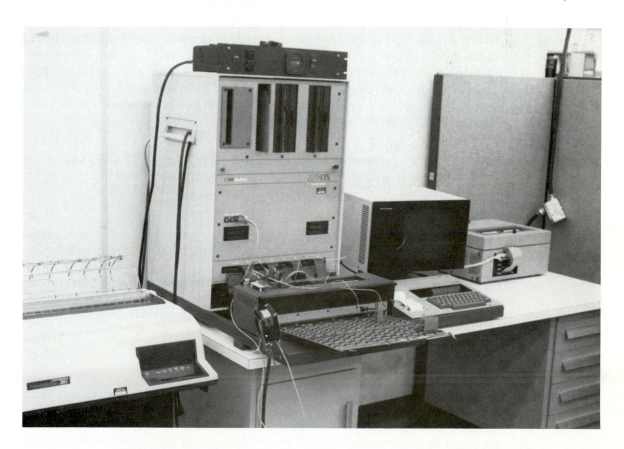

FIGURE 12.10
Gen Rad 2235 functional automatic tester

the entire board, including the artwork, is tested, from the board connectors inward. This is the best test method but requires far more program development time. The logical function of the board under test must be modeled in software along with the component interconnects, called the *node list,* or *image.* The modeling process takes considerable time to create. In some cases this test method cannot match the actual system timing, specifically where high-speed logic is concerned, which may become a major drawback. Using the guided probe fault isolation provided with the functional tester will prove to be the fastest repair method once the programs are developed. We have experienced cases where logic boards were tested and repaired in a matter of minutes.

Emulative Automatic Testers

The **emulative tester** is really a functional tester that uses a different test philosophy. The functional tester tests the board from the outside in. The emulative tester tests the board from the inside out. The tester is connected to the board's microprocessor chip socket. The tester then takes over the function of the microprocessor and controls the board under test. Since this type of tester is designed to test boards that contain off-the-shelf microprocessors, the board under test *must* contain a standard microproces sor to use this tester. This type of tester is ideal for the average microcomputer repair shop. These testers are easy to use and program and some contain built-in, or canned, tests. An example of a simplified test program for the PC system board, written in the language TL/1 for the Fluke 9100, looks as follows:

```
program TEST_PC
   testbus  addr  A0000              Canned CPU bus test
   testrom  addr  FE000 upto FFFFF   Canned ROM test
   testram  addr  0000  upto 3FFFF   Canned RAM test
   ⋮                                 More tests as required
```

The recent versions of this tester also contain external guided probe and guided fault-isolation software. One manufacturer has also included an asynchronous clock module for measuring asynchronous events and up to four 40-pin I/O modules for testing and driving various connectors and points on the board under test. These features greatly increase the flexibility of this tester up to and including in-circuit component testing, where the microprocessor may lack direct visibility to certain nodes. See Figure 12.11.

12.9 TECH TIPS AND TROUBLESHOOTING—T³

When using the oscilloscope to check bus timing, try to find a unique signal from which to trigger the sweep. It is impossible to tell what is happening on the bus by simply using the automatic trigger mode. When checking the RAM RAS and CAS timing, you should not trigger the sweep on the RAS line. Most dynamic RAM ICs are refreshed by causing RAS-only cycles, and the RAS to CAS timing will be difficult to observe. Try to find a signal unique to the RAM read function.

FIGURE 12.11
Fluke 9100 emulative automatic tester

The BIOS ROM chips in the IBM PC are the masked program type. That is, the program code is placed on the ROM during the final metalization process. Most of these masked-type ROMs cannot be copied in the PROM programmer because the chip-select pin must be toggled for every address change. Most PROM programmers do not do this; therefore, the ROMs cannot be read. There is a way in which these ROMs can be copied if your PROM programmer has a serial input port. Connect the serial port of the PC to the serial port of the PROM programmer. Write a small program, in any suitable language, to read the data from memory at address FE000 hex through FFFFF hex and send the data to the serial port. Before starting the program, command the PROM programmer to copy data from the serial port to the internal RAM. Once this is completed, a blank EPROM with the same pinout as the mask ROM may be programmed and installed in the PC under repair.

EXERCISES

12.1 A simple logic level indicating device is known as a _____ _____.

12.2 What three things will the device in Exercise 12.1 show? _____ _____ _____.

12.3 A device that will 'pulse' a circuit is called _____ _____.

12.4 What should every electronic repair shop contain?

12.5 True or false: A DC-coupled scope should be used when checking digital logic.

12.6 What is the minimum band width scope that should be used when testing a microcomputer system?

12.7 Briefly describe the digital storage oscilloscope.

12.8 Briefly describe the logic analyzer.

12.9 True or false: The logic analyzer can be used to analyze bus activity and bus timing.

12.10 What is a PROM burner?

12.11 Crossword Puzzle

ACROSS

4. Multichannel digital display device.
8. Power line recording voltmeter.
9. Light-emitting diode.
10. Voltage rises.
11. Voltage drops.
13. Used to perform waveform measurements.
15. Memory-write signal.
16. I/O read signal.
17. ATE that tests the entire PC board.
19. TIL 311.
21. Digital scope sampling-rate problem.

DOWN

1. Used to inject a signal into a gate.
2. Logic 1.
3. Memory-programming device.
5. Time to read data from a ROM.
6. An oscilloscope sweep control.
7. Clip-the-chip tester.
9. Logic-level-indicating tool.
12. Volt-ohmmeter.
14. ATE that tests from the inside out.
18. Logic gate.
20. Logic state.

BOOLEAN THEOREMS

Basic OR operation

$A + 0 = A$

$A + 1 = 1$

$A + \overline{A} = 1$

Basic AND operation

$A \cdot 0 = 0$

$A \cdot 1 = A$

$A \cdot \overline{A} = 0$

Basic NOT operation

$\overline{\overline{A}} = \overline{A}$

$\overline{\overline{A}} = A$

$\overline{\overline{A}} = \overline{A}$

Identity laws

$A + A = A$

$A \cdot A = A$

Commutative laws

$A + B = B + A$

$A \cdot B = B \cdot A$

Associative laws

$A + (B + C) = (A + B) + C$

$A \cdot (B \cdot C) = (A \cdot B) \cdot C$

Distributive law

$A \cdot (B + C) = (A \cdot B) + (A \cdot C)$

$A + (B \cdot C) = (A + B) \cdot (A + C)$

Redundancy law

$A + (A \cdot B) = A$

$A \cdot (A + B) = A$

Special theorems

$$A + (\overline{A} \cdot B) = A + B$$
$$A \cdot (\overline{A} + B) = A \cdot B$$

} Nashelsky

$$\overline{(A + B)} = \overline{A} \cdot \overline{B}$$
$$\overline{(A \cdot B)} = \overline{A} + \overline{B}$$

} DeMorgan

INTEL 8086/8088 INSTRUCTION SET

Effective address (EA) times.

Address	Component	Clocks
displacement	disp	6
base or index	BX, BP, DI, SI	5
displacement plus base or index	BX + disp, BP + disp, DI + disp, SI + disp	9
base plus index	BP + DI, BX + SI, BP + SI, BX + DI	7 8
displacement plus base plus index	BP + DI + disp, BX + SI + disp, BP + SI + disp, BX + DI + disp	11 12

Intel 8086/8088 Instruction Set (pp. 505–525) reprinted by permission of Intel Corporation, copyright 1985.

The 8086/8088 Instruction set.

AAA
0011   0111
Adjust for ASCII addition

Flags:
O	D	I	T	S	Z	A	P	C
?				?	?	*	?	*

Operand	Clocks	Transfers	Bytes	Example
none	4	none	1	AAA

AAD
1101   0101   0000   1010
ASCII adjust for division

Flags:
O	D	I	T	S	Z	A	P	C
?				*	*	?	*	?

Operand	Clocks	Transfers	Bytes	Example
none	60	none	2	AAD

AAM
1101   0110   0000   1010
ASCII adjust for multiplication

Flags:
O	D	I	T	S	Z	A	P	C
?				*	*	?	*	?

Operand	Clocks	Transfers	Bytes	Example
none	83	none	2	AAM

AAS
0011   1111
ASCII adjust for subtraction

Flags:
O	D	I	T	S	Z	A	P	C
?				?	?	*	?	*

Operand	Clocks	Transfers	Bytes	Example
none	4	none	1	AAS

ADC
0001   00dw   oo   rrr   mmm dp-l   dp-h
1000   00sw   oo   010   mmm da-l   da-h   dp-l   dp-h   (immediate)
0001   010w   da-l   da-h   (acc immediate)
Add with carry

Flags:
O	D	I	T	S	Z	A	P	C
*				*	*	*	*	*

Operand	Clocks	Transfers	Bytes	Example
register, register	3	none	2	ADC AX,DX
register, memory	9(13) + EA	1	2–4	ADC CL,[SI]
memory, register	16(24) + EA	2	2–4	ADC DATA,CX
register, immediate	4	none	3–4	ADC AL,22H
memory, immediate	17(25) + EA	2	3–6	ADC DATA,[BX],3
accumulator, immediate	4	none	2–3	ADC AL,23H

(Continued)

ADD
```
0000  00dw  oo    rrr    mmm  dp-l  dp-h
1000  00sw  oo    000    mmm  da-l  da-h  dp-l  dp-h  (immediate)
0001  010w  da-l         da-h                         (acc immediate)
```
Addition

Flags:
O	D	I	T	S	Z	A	P	C
*				*	*	*	*	*

Operand	Clocks	Transfers	Bytes	Example
register, register	3	none	2	ADD AL,DX
register, memory	9(13) + EA	1	2–4	ADD CX,[SI]
memory, register	16(24) + EA	2	2–4	ADD DATA,CX
register, immediate	4	none	3–4	ADD CL,22H
memory, immediate	17(25) + EA	2	3–6	ADD DATA [BX],3
accumulator, immediate	4	none	2–3	ADD AX,2333H

AND
```
0010  00dw  oo    rrr    mmm  dp-l  dp-h
1000  00sw  oo    100    mmm  da-l  da-h  dp-l  dp-h  (immediate)
0001  010w  da-l         da-h                         (acc immediate)
```
AND logical

Flags:
O	D	I	T	S	Z	A	P	C
0				*	*	?	*	0

Operand	Clocks	Transfers	Bytes	Example
register, register	3	none	2	AND AL,BH
register, memory	9(13) + EA	1	2–4	AND CX,[SI]
memory, register	16(24) + EA	2	2–4	AND DATA,CX
register, immediate	4	none	3–4	AND CL,22H
memory, immediate	17(25) + EA	2	3–6	AND DATA [BX],3
accumulator, immediate	4	none	2–3	AND AX,2333H

CALL
```
1110  1000  dp-l  dp-h                          intrasegment direct
1111  1111  oo    010   mmm                     intrasegment indirect
1001  1010  of-l              of-h  sg-l  sg-h  intersegment direct
1111  1111  oo    011   mmm                     intersegment indirect
```
CALL procedure

Flags: O D I T S Z A P C

Operand	Clocks	Transfers	Bytes	Example
near	19(23)	1	3	CALL NEAR__PROC
far	28(36)	2	5	CALL FAR__PROC
memptr16	21(29) + EA	2	2–4	CALL TABLE[DI]
regptr16	16(24)	1	2	CALL BX
memptr32	37(57) + EA	4	2–4	CALL DATA[BX]

(Continued)

CBW
1001   1000
Convert byte to word   Flags: O D I T S Z A P C

Operand	Clocks	Transfers	Bytes	Example
none	2	none	1	CBW

CLC
1111   1000
Clear carry   Flags: O D I T S Z A P C
                                                                            0

Operand	Clocks	Transfers	Bytes	Example
none	2	none	1	CLC

CLD
1111   1100
Clear direction flag   Flags: O D I T S Z A P C
                                                          0

Operand	Clocks	Transfers	Bytes	Example
none	2	none	1	CLD

CLI
1111   1010
Clear interrupt-enable flag   Flags: O D I T S Z A P C
                                                             0

Operand	Clocks	Transfers	Bytes	Example
none	2	none	1	CLI

CMC
1111   0101
Complement carry flag   Flags: O D I T S Z A P C
                                                                            *

Operand	Clocks	Transfers	Bytes	Example
none	2	none	1	CMC

(Continued)

CMP
```
0011  10dw  oo    rrr    mmm dp-l   dp-h
1000  00sw  oo    111    mmm da-l   da-h   dp-l   dp-h   (immediate)
0011  110w  da-l         da-h                      (acc immediate)
```
Compare   Flags: O   D   I   T   S   Z   A   P   C
                                         *   *   *   *   *   *

Operand	Clocks	Transfers	Bytes	Example
register, register	3	none	2	CMP AX,DI
register, memory	9(13) + EA	none	2–4	CMP CX,[SI]
memory, register	9(13) + EA	none	3–4	CMP DATA,CX
register, immediate	4	none	3–4	CMP CL,22H
memory, immediate	10(14) + EA	none	3–6	CMP DATA,[BX],3
accumulator, immediate	4	none	2–3	CMP AX,2333H

CMPS
```
1010   011w
```
Compare strings   Flags: O   D   I   T   S   Z   A   P   C
                                         *   *   *   *   *   *

Operand	Clocks	Transfers	Bytes	Example
dest,source	22(30)	2	1	CMPS DAT1,DAT2
repeated	9 + 22(30)/rep	2/rep	1	REP COMPS ID,DATA

CWD
```
1001   1001
```
Convert word to double word   Flags: O   D   I   T   S   Z   A   P   C

Operand	Clocks	Transfers	Bytes	Example
none	5	none	1	CWD

DAA
```
0010   0111
```
Decimal adjust for addition   Flags: O   D   I   T   S   Z   A   P   C
                                         ?   *   *   *   *   *

Operand	Clocks	Transfers	Bytes	Example
none	4	none	1	DAA

(Continued)

DAS
0010   1111
Decimal adjust for subtraction Flags: O   D   I   T   S   Z   A   P   C
                                         ?   *   *   *   *

Operand	Clocks	Transfers	Bytes	Example
none	4	none	1	DAS

DEC
1111   111w   oo   001   mmm   dp-l   dp-h
0100   1rrr
Decrement Flags: O   D   I   T   S   Z   A   P   C
                    *   *   *   *   *

Operand	Clocks	Transfers	Bytes	Example
reg16	2	none	1	DEC CX
reg8	3	none	2	DEC DH
memory	15(23) + EA	2	2–4	DEC DATA[BP]

DIV
1111   011w   oo   001   mmm   dp-l   dp-h
Divide Flags: O   D   I   T   S   Z   A   P   C
                 ?   ?   ?   ?   ?   ?

Operand	Clocks	Transfers	Bytes	Example
reg8	80–90	none	2	DIV BH
reg16	144–162	none	2	DIV BP
mem8	(86–96) + EA	1	2–4	DIV DATA
mem16	(154–172) + EA	1	2–4	DIV NUMBER[DI]

ESC
1101   1xxx   oo   xxx   mmm   dp-l   dp-h
Escape Flags: O   D   I   T   S   Z   A   P   C

Operand	Clocks	Transfers	Bytes	Example
memory	8(12) + EA	1	2–4	FADD DATA
register	2	none	2	ESC 4,BL

HLT
1111   0100
Halt Flags: O   D   I   T   S   Z   A   P   C

Operand	Clocks	Transfers	Bytes	Example
none	2	none	1	HLT

(Continued)

IDIV
1111 011w oo 111 mmm dp-l dp-h
Integer division   Flags: O D I T S Z A P C
                                                ?   ? ? ? ? ?

Operand	Clocks	Transfers	Bytes	Example
reg8	101–112	none	2	IDIV CL
reg16	165–184	none	2	IDIV SI
mem8	(107–118) + EA	1	2–4	IDIV INFO
mem16	(175–194) + EA	1	2–4	INDIV MEM__DAT

IMUL
1111 011w oo 101 mmm dp-l dp-h
Integer multiplication   Flags: O D I T S Z A P C
                                                *   ? ? ? ? *

Operand	Clocks	Transfers	Bytes	Example
reg8	80–98	none	2	IMUL AL
reg16	128–154	none	2	IMUL AX
mem8	(86–104) + EA	1	2–4	IMUL BYTE__NUMB
mem16	(138–164) + EA	1	2–4	IMUL WORD__DATA

IN
1110 010w port fixed
1110 110w   variable
Input byte or word   Flags: O D I T S Z A P C

Operand	Clocks	Transfers	Bytes	Example
acc,imm8	10(14)	1	2	IN AL,0FDH
acc,DX	8(12)	1	1	IN AL,DX

INC
1111 111w oo 000 mmm dp-l dp-h
0100 0rrr
Increment   Flags: O D I T S Z A P C
                                                *   * * * *

Operand	Clocks	Transfers	Bytes	Example
reg8	3	none	2	INC CL
reg16	2	none	1	INC DI
memory	15(23) + EA	2	2–4	INC DATA[BX]

(Continued)

INT
1100   1100   INT 3
1100   1101   type x   INT x
Interrupt   Flags: O   D   I   T   S   Z   A   P   C

Operand	Clocks	Transfers	Bytes	Example
type 3	52(72)	5	1	INT 3
not type 3	51(71)	5	2	INT 55

INTO
1100   1110
Interrupt on overflow   Flags: O   D   I   T   S   Z   A   P   C

Operand	Clocks	Transfers	Bytes	Example
none	73 or 4	5 or 0	1	INTO

IRET
1100   1111
Interrupt return   Flags: O   D   I   T   S   Z   A   P   C
                                       *   *   *   *   *   *   *   *   *

Operand	Clocks	Transfers	Bytes	Example
none	32(44)	3	1	IRET

JA/JNBE
0111   0111   disp
Jump above/not below or equal to   Flags: O   D   I   T   S   Z   A   P   C

Operand	Clocks	Transfers	Bytes	Example
short label	16/4	none	2	JA NEXT JNBE NEXT

JAE/JNB
0111   0011   disp
Jump above or equal to/not below   Flags: O   D   I   T   S   Z   A   P   C

Operand	Clocks	Transfers	Bytes	Example
short label	16/4	none	2	JAE DOWN JNB DOWN

(Continued)

JB/JNAE
0111 0010 disp
Jump below/not above or equal to   Flags: O D I T S Z A P C

Operand	Clocks	Transfers	Bytes	Example
short label	16/4	none	2	JB BELOW
				JNAE WHERE

JBE/JNA
0111 0110 disp
Jump below or equal to/not above   Flags: O D I T S Z A P C

Operand	Clocks	Transfers	Bytes	Example
short label	16/4	none	2	JBE LOOP
				JNA LABEL

JC
0111 0010 disp
Jump on carry   Flags: O D I T S Z A P C

Operand	Clocks	Transfers	Bytes	Example
short label	16/4	none	2	JC OUT

JCXZ
1110 0011 disp
Jump if CX is 0   Flags: O D I T S Z A P C

Operand	Clocks	Transfers	Bytes	Example
short label	18/6	none	2	JCXZ FINISHED

JE/JZ
0111 0100 disp
Jump equal to/zero   Flags: O D I T S Z A P C

Operand	Clocks	Transfers	Bytes	Example
short label	16/4	none	2	JE END__IT
				JZ ONCE

(Continued)

JG/JNLE
0111 1111   disp
Jump greater/not less than or equal to   Flags: O D I T S Z A P C

Operand	Clocks	Transfers	Bytes	Example
short label	16/4	none	2	JG BIG
				JNLE NOT__SMALL

JGE/JNL
0111 1101   disp
Jump greater than or equal to/not less than   Flags: O D I T S Z A P C

Operand	Clocks	Transfers	Bytes	Example
short label	16/4	none	2	JGE UPWARD
				JNL LEFT

JL/JNGE
0111 1100   disp
Jump less than/not greater than or equal to   Flags: O D I T S Z A P C

Operand	Clocks	Transfers	Bytes	Example
short label	16/4	none	2	JL NEXT
				JNGE AGAIN

JLE/JNG
0111 1110   disp
Jump less than or equal to/not greater than   Flags: O D I T S Z A P C

Operand	Clocks	Transfers	Bytes	Example
short label	16/4	none	2	JLE NEXT

JMP
1110 1001   dp-l   dp-h   intrasegment direct
1110 1011   disp   intrasegment short
1111 1111   oo   100   mmm   dp-l   dp-h   intrasegment indirect
1110 1010   of-l   of-h   sg-l   sg-h   intersegment direct
1111 1111   oo   101   mmm   intersegment indirect
Jump unconditional   Flags: O D I T S Z A P C

(Continued)

Operand	Clocks	Transfers	Bytes	Example
short label	15	none	2	JMP SHORT NUMB
near label	15	none	3	JMP NEAR__PLACE
far label	15	none	5	JMP FAR__WAY
memptr16	18 + EA	none	2–4	JMP TABLE[BX]
regptr16	11	none	2	JMP DX
memptr32	24 + EA	none	2–4	JMP FAR__SEG[DI]

JNC
0111 0011 disp
Jump no carry   Flags: O D I T S Z A P C

Operand	Clocks	Transfers	Bytes	Example
short label	16/4	none	2	JNC BACK

JNE/JNZ
0111 0101 disp
Jump not equal to/not 0   Flags: O D I T S Z A P C

Operand	Clocks	Transfers	Bytes	Example
short label	16/4	none	2	JNE OVER
				JNZ INNER

JNO
0111 0001 disp
Jump not overflow   Flags: O D I T S Z A P C

Operand	Clocks	Transfers	Bytes	Example
short label	16/4	none	2	JNO GOOD

JNS
0111 1001 disp
Jump not sign   Flags: O D I T S Z A P C

Operand	Clocks	Transfers	Bytes	Example
short label	16/4	none	2	JNS POSITIVE

(Continued)

JNP/JPO
0111 1011 disp
Jump no parity/parity odd   Flags: O D I T S Z A P C

Operand	Clocks	Transfers	Bytes	Example
short label	16/4	none	2	JNP NO
				JPO ODD

JO
0111 0000 disp
Jump on overflow   Flags: O D I T S Z A P C

Operand	Clocks	Transfers	Bytes	Example
short label	16/4	none	2	JO OVER__FLOW

JP/JPE
0111 1010 disp
Jump parity/parity even   Flags: O D I T S Z A P C

Operand	Clocks	Transfers	Bytes	Example
short label	16/4	none	2	JO PAIR
				JPE EVEN

JS
0111 1000 disp
Jump on sign   Flags: O D I T S Z A P C

Operand	Clocks	Transfers	Bytes	Example
short label	16/4	none	2	JS MINUS

LAHF
1001 1111
Load AH from flags   Flags: O D I T S Z A P C

Operand	Clocks	Transfers	Bytes	Example
none	4	none	1	LAHF

(Continued)

LDS
1100 0101 oo rrr mmm dp-1 dp-h
Load pointer and DS   Flags: O D I T S Z A P C

Operand	Clocks	Transfers	Bytes	Example
reg16,mem32	24 + EA	2	2–4	LDS DI,DATA

LEA
1000 1101 oo rrr mmm dp-1 dp-h
Load effective address   Flags: O D I T S Z A P C

Operand	Clocks	Transfers	Bytes	Example
reg16,mem16	2 + EA	none	2–4	LEA DI,[BP + SI]

LES
1100 0100 oo rrr mmm dp-1 dp-h
Load pointer and ES   Flags: O D I T S Z A P C

Operand	Clocks	Transfers	Bytes	Example
reg16,mem32	24 + EA	2	2–4	LES SI,MESS

LOCK
1111 0000
Lock the bus   Flags: O D I T S Z A P C

Operand	Clocks	Transfers	Bytes	Example
none	2	none	1	LOCK ADD AX,BX

LODS
1010 110w
Load string   Flags: O D I T S Z A P C

Operand	Clocks	Transfers	Bytes	Example
source string	12(16)	1	1	LODS WOOD
repeat	9 + 13(17)/rep	1/rep	1	REP LODS DATA

(Continued)

LOOP
1110 0010 disp
Loop while CX is not 0   Flags: O D I T S Z A P C

Operand	Clocks	Transfers	Bytes	Example
short label	17/5	none	2	LOOP BACK

LOOPE/LOOPZ
1110 0001 disp
Loop while equal to/while 0   Flags: O D I T S Z A P C

Operand	Clocks	Transfers	Bytes	Example
short label	18/6	none	2	LOOPE AGAIN

LOOPNZ/LOOPNE
1110 0000 disp
Loop while not 0/not equal to   Flags: O D I T S Z A P C

Operand	Clocks	Transfers	Bytes	Example
short label	19/5	none	2	LOOPNE TOP

MOV

1000	10dw	oo	rrr	mmm	dp-l	dp-h	
1100	011w	oo	000	mmm	da-l da-h dp-l dp-h	(immediate)
1011	wrrr	da-l			da-h	(reg immediate)
1010	000w	adr-l			adr-h	(mem to acc)
1010	001w	adr-l			adr-h	(acc to mem)
1000	1110	oo	0rr	mmm	dp-l dp-h	(to segment)
1000	1100	oo	0rr	mmm	dp-l dp-h	(from segment)

Move   Flags: O D I T S Z A P C

Operand	Clocks	Transfers	Bytes	Example
mem,acc	10(14)	1	3	MOV ARRAY,AL
acc,mem	10(14)	1	3	MOV AL,DATA
reg,reg	2	none	2	MOV AX,BX
reg,mem	8(12) + EA	1	2–4	MOV DI,DATA
mem,reg	9(13) + EA	1	2–4	MOV MEM,BL
reg,imm	4	none	2–3	MOV BH,33
mem,imm	10(14) + EA	1	3–6	MOV DATA[BX + DI],1
seg,reg	2	none	2	MOV ES,AX
seg,mem	8(12) + EA	1	2–4	MOV DS,MEMORY
reg,seg	2	none	2	MOV AX,DS
mem,seg	9(13) + EA	1	2–4	MOV SAVE,DS

(Continued)

MOVS
1001   010w
Move string   Flags: O   D   I   T   S   Z   A   P   C

Operand	Clocks	Transfers	Bytes	Example
string	18(26)	2	1	MOVSB
repeat	9 + 17(25)/rep	2/rep	1	REP MOVSW

MUL
1111   011w   oo   100   mmm   dp-l   dp-h
Multiply   Flags: O   D   I   T   S   Z   A   P   C

Operand	Clocks	Transfers	Bytes	Example
reg8	70–77	none	2	MUL CL
reg16	118–123	none	2	MUL AX
mem8	(76–83) + EA	1	2–4	MUL DATA[BP]
mem16	(128–143) + EA	1	2–4	MUL RATE

NEG
1111   011w   oo   011   mmm   dp-l   dp-h
Negate   Flags: O   D   I   T   S   Z   A   P   C

Operand	Clocks	Transfers	Bytes	Example
reg	3	none	2	NEG AL
mem	16(24) + EA	2	2–4	NEG DATA

NOP
1001   0000
No operation   Flags: O   D   I   T   S   Z   A   P   C

Operand	Clocks	Transfers	Bytes	Example
none	3	none	1	NOP

NOT
1111   011w   oo   010   mmm   dp-l   dp-h
Logical inversion(not)   Flags: O   D   I   T   S   Z   A   P   C

Operand	Clocks	Transfers	Bytes	Example
reg	3	none	2	NOT BX
mem	16(24) + EA	2	2–4	NOT DATA[BX]

(Continued)

OR

0000	10dw	oo	rrr	mmm	dp-l	dp-h		
1000	00sw	oo	001	mmm	da-l	da-h	dp-l	dp-h	(immediate)
0000	110w	da-l			da-h			(acc immediate)

Logical OR

Flags:

O	D	I	T	S	Z	A	P	C
0				*	*	?	*	0

Operand	Clocks	Transfers	Bytes	Example
reg,reg	3	none	2	OR AH,AL
reg,mem	9(13) + EA	1	2–4	OR AX,DATA
mem,reg	16(24) + EA	2	2–4	OR [BX + 4],AL
acc,imm	4	none	2–3	OR AX,345
reg,imm	4	none	3–4	OR BL,12H
mem,imm	17(25) + EA	2	3–6	OR DATA,1234H

OUT

1110	011w	port	fixed
1110	111w		variable

Output a byte or word

Flags: O D I T S Z A P C

Operand	Clocks	Transfers	Bytes	Example
port,acc	10(14)	1	2	OUT 44H,AL
DX,acc	8(12)	1	1	OUT DX,AX

POP

1000	1111	oo	000	mmm	dp-l	dp-h
0101	1rrr	(register)				
000r	r111	(segment)				

Pop

Flags: O D I T S Z A P C

Operand	Clocks	Transfers	Bytes	Example
reg	12	1	1	POP CX
seg	12	1	1	POP SS
mem	25 + EA	2	2–4	POP MEMORY

POPF

1001	1100

Pop flags

Flags:

O	D	I	T	S	Z	A	P	C
*	*	*	*	*	*	*	*	*

Operand	Clocks	Transfers	Bytes	Example
none	12	1	1	POPF

(Continued)

PUSH

1111	1111	oo	110	mmm	dp-l	dp-h
0101	0rrr	(register)
000r	r110	(segment)

Push   Flags: O   D   I   T   S   Z   A   P   C

Operand	Clocks	Transfers	Bytes	Example
reg	15	1	1	PUSH BP
seg	14	1	1	PUSH DS
mem	24 + EA	2	2–4	PUSH DATA

PUSHF

1001   1101

Push flags   Flags: O   D   I   T   S   Z   A   P   C

Operand	Clocks	Transfers	Bytes	Example
none	14	1	1	PUSHF

RCL

1101   00vw   oo   010   mmm   dp-l   dp-h

Rotate left through carry   Flags: O   D   I   T   S   Z   A   P   C
                                                *   *

Operand	Clocks	Transfers	Bytes	Example
reg	2	none	2	RCL AX
reg,CL	8 + 4/bit	none	2	RCL BL,CL
mem	15(23) + EA	2	2–4	RCL DATA[DI]
mem,CL	20(2) + EA + 4/bit	2	2–4	RCL DATA,CL

RCR

1101   00vw   oo   011   mmm   dp-l   dp-h

Rotate right through carry   Flags: O   D   I   T   S   Z   A   P   C
                                                *   *

Operand	Clocks	Transfers	Bytes	Example
reg	2	none	2	RCR AX
reg,CL	8 + 4/bit	none	2	RCR BL,CL
mem	15(23) + EA	2	2–4	RCR DATA[DI]
mem,CL	20(2) + EA + 4/bit	2	2–4	RCR DATA,CL

(Continued)

REP (conditional)
1111   001z
Repeat conditional   Flags: O D I T S Z A P C

Operand	Clocks	Transfers	Bytes	Example
REPE/REPZ	2	none	1	REPE CMPSB
REPNE/REPNZ	2	none	1	REPNE SCASW

RET
1100   0011   intrasegment
1100   0010   da-l   da-h   intrasegment with add
1100   1011   intersegment
1100   1010   da-l   da-h   intersegment with add
Return   Flags: O D I T S Z A P C

Operand	Clocks	Transfers	Bytes	Example
intra, no add	20	1	1	RET
intra, add	24	1	3	RET 6
inter, no add	32	2	1	RET
inter, add	31	2	3	RET 2

ROL
1101   00vw   oo 000 mmm   dp-l dp-h
Rotate left   Flags: O D I T S Z A P C
                                                        *   *

Operand	Clocks	Transfers	Bytes	Example
reg	2	none	2	ROL CL
reg,CL	8 + 4/bit	none	2	ROL BX,CL
mem	15(23) + EA	2	2–4	ROL DATA[DI]
mem,CL	20(28) + EA + 4/bit	2	2–4	ROL MEM,CL

ROR
1101   00vw   oo 001 mmm   dp-l dp-h
Rotate right   Flags: O D I T S Z A P C
                                                        *   *

Operand	Clocks	Transfers	Bytes	Example
reg	2	none	2	ROR AX
reg,CL	8 + 4/bit	none	2	ROR AX,CL
mem	15(23) + EA	2	2–4	ROR LIST
mem,CL	20(28) + EA + 4/bit	2	2–4	ROR LIST,CL

(Continued)

SAHF
1001 1110
Store AH into flags   Flags: O D I T S Z A P C
                                                                 * * * * *

Operand	Clocks	Transfers	Bytes	Example
none	4	none	1	SAHF

SAL/SHL
1101 00vw   oo 100   mmm   dp-l dp-h
Shif left arithmetic/logic   Flags: O D I T S Z A P C
                                                     *   * * ? * *

Operand	Clocks	Transfers	Bytes	Example
reg	2	none	2	SHL AX
reg,CL	8 + 4/bit	none	2	SHL AX,CL
mem	15(23) + EA	2	2–4	SHL LIST
mem,CL	20(28) + EA + 4/bit	2	2–4	SHL LIST,CL

SAR
1101 00vw   oo 100   mmm   dp-l dp-h
Shift right arithmetic/logic   Flags: O D I T S Z A P C
                                                     *   * * ? * *

Operand	Clocks	Transfers	Bytes	Example
reg	2	none	2	SAR AX
reg,CL	8 + 4/bit	none	2	SAR AX,CL
mem	15(23) + EA	2	2–4	SAR LIST
mem,CL	20(28) + EA + 4/bit	2	2–4	SAR LIST,CL

SBB
0001 10dw   oo rrr   mmm   dp-l dp-h
1000 00sw   oo 011   mmm   da-l da-h da-l dp-h   (immediate)
0001 110w   da-l   da-h   (acc immediate)
Subtract with borrow   Flags: O D I T S Z A P C
                                                     *   * * * * *

Operand	Clocks	Transfers	Bytes	Example
reg,reg	3	none	2	SBB AL,BL
reg,mem	9(13) + EA	1	2–4	SBB BX,DATA
mem,reg	16(24) + EA	2	2–4	SBB DATA,BX
acc,imm	4	none	2–3	SBB AH,12
reg,imm	4	none	3–4	SBB DI,1000H
mem,imm	17(25) + EA	2	3–6	SBB DATA,33

(Continued)

SCAS
1010   111w
Scan for byte or word   Flags: O D I T S Z A P C
                                                  *   * * * * *

Operand	Clocks	Transfers	Bytes	Example
string	15(19)	1	1	SCASB
repeat	9 + 15(19)/rep	1/rep	1	REPE SCASW

SHR
1101   00vw   oo   101   mmm   dp-l   dp-h
Shift right   Flags: O D I T S Z A P C
                                                  *   * * ? * *

Operand	Clocks	Transfers	Bytes	Example
reg	2	none	2	SHR AX
reg,CL	8 + 4/bit	none	2	SHR AX,CL
mem	15(23) + EA	2	2–4	SHR LIST
mem,CL	20(28) + EA + 4/bit	2	2–4	SHR LIST,CL

STC
1111   1001
Set carry   Flags: O D I T S Z A P C
                                                                           1

Operand	Clocks	Transfers	Bytes	Example
none	2	none	1	STC

STD
1111   1101
Set direction   Flags: O D I T S Z A P C
                                                     1

Operand	Clocks	Transfers	Bytes	Example
none	2	none	1	STD

STI
1111   1011
Set interrupt-enable flag   Flags: O D I T S Z A P C
                                                        1

Operand	Clocks	Transfers	Bytes	Example
none	2	none	1	STI

(Continued)

STOS
1010 101w
Store byte or word   Flags: O D I T S Z A P C

Operand	Clocks	Transfers	Bytes	Example
string	11(15)	1	1	STOSB
repeat	9 + 10(14)/rep	1/rep	1	REP STOSW

SUB
0010 10dw oo rrr mmm dp-l dp-h
1000 00sw oo 101 mmm da-l da-h dp-l dp-h   (immediate)
0010 110w da-l   da-h   (acc immediate)
Subtract   Flags: O D I T S Z A P C
                                                  *   * * * * *

Operand	Clocks	Transfers	Bytes	Example
reg,reg	3	none	2	SUB AL,BL
reg,mem	9(13) + EA	1	2–4	SUB BX,DATA
mem,reg	16(24) + EA	2	2–4	SUB DATA,BX
acc,imm	4	none	2–3	SUB AH,12
reg,imm	4	none	3–4	SUB DI,1000H
mem,imm	17(25) + EA	2	3–6	SUB DATA,33

TEST
1000 01dw oo rrr mmm dp-l dp-h
1111 011w oo 000 mmm da-l da-h dp-l dp-h   (immediate)
1010 100w da-l   da-h   (acc immediate)
Test   Flags: O D I T S Z A P C
                                                  0   * * ? * 0

Operand	Clocks	Transfers	Bytes	Example
reg,reg	3	none	2	TEST DI,BP
reg,mem	9(13) + EA	1	2–4	TEST BX,NUMB
acc,imm	4	none	2–3	TEST AX,2
reg,imm	5	none	3–4	TEST CL,10H
mem,imm	11 + EA	none	3–6	TEST MOM,01H

(Continued)

WAIT
1001   1001
Wait   Flags: O   D   I   T   S   Z   A   P   C

Operand	Clocks	Transfers	Bytes	Example
none	3 + 5n	none	1	WAIT

XCHG
1000   011w   oo   rrr   mmm   dp-l   dp-h
1001   0rrr
Exchange   Flags: O   D   I   T   S   Z   A   P   C

Operand	Clocks	Transfers	Bytes	Example
acc,reg	3	none	1	XCHG AX,BX
mem,reg	17(25) + EA	2	2–4	XCHG DATA,AL
reg,reg	4	none	2	XCHG AL,AH

XLAT
1101   0111
Translate   Flags: O   D   I   T   S   Z   A   P   C

Operand	Clocks	Transfers	Bytes	Example
none	11	1	1	XLAT

XOR
0011   00dw   oo   rrr   mmm   dp-l   dp-h
1000   00sw   oo   110   mmm   da-l   da-h   dp-l   dp-h   (immediate)
0011   010w   da-l   da-h   (acc immediate)
Exclusive-OR   Flags: O   D   I   T   S   Z   A   P   C
                                                                 0   *   *   ?   *   0

Operand	Clocks	Transfers	Bytes	Example
reg,reg	3	none	2	XOR AL,BL
reg,mem	9(13) + EA	1	2–4	XOR BX,DATA
mem,reg	16(24) + EA	2	2–4	XOR DATA,BX
acc,imm	4	none	2–3	XOR AH,12
reg,imm	4	none	3–4	XOR DI,1000H
mem,imm	17(25) + EA	2	3–6	XOR DATA,33

Notes: oo = modifier bits, rrr = register, mmm = R/M, w = word, d = direction, v = CL if 1, s = sign-extend immediate data, z = repeat loop while 0 if set, dp-l = displacement-low, dp-h = displacement-high, da-l = data-low, da-h = data high, adr-l = address-low, and adr-h = address-high

DATA SHEETS

Texas Instruments Data Sheets (pp. 527–556) reprinted by permission of Texas Instruments Inc.

Intel Data Sheets (pp. 557–561) reprinted by permission of Intel Corporation, copyright 1981.

SN54ALS00A, SN54AS00, SN74ALS00A, SN74AS00
QUADRUPLE 2-INPUT POSITIVE-NAND GATES

D2661, APRIL 1982–REVISED MAY 1986

- Package Options Include Plastic ''Small Outline'' Packages, Ceramic Chip Carriers, and Standard Plastic and Ceramic 300-mil DIPs

- Dependable Texas Instruments Quality and Reliability

description

These devices contain four independent 2-input NAND gates. They perform the Boolean functions $Y = \overline{A \cdot B}$ or $Y = \overline{A} + \overline{B}$ in positive logic.

The SN54ALS00A and SN54AS00 are characterized for operation over the full military temperature range of −55°C to 125°C. The SN74ALS00A and SN74AS00 are characterized for operation from 0°C to 70°C.

FUNCTION TABLE (each gate)

INPUTS		OUTPUT
A	B	Y
H	H	L
L	X	H
X	L	H

logic symbol[†]

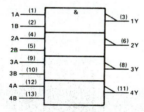

[†]This symbol is in accordance with ANSI/IEEE Std 91-1984 and IEC Publication 617-12.

Pin numbers shown are for D, J, and N packages.

SN54ALS00A, SN54AS00 . . . J PACKAGE
SN74ALS00A, SN74AS00 . . . D OR N PACKAGE
(TOP VIEW)

SN54ALS00A, SN54AS00 . . . FK PACKAGE
(TOP VIEW)

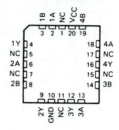

NC—No internal connection

logic diagram (positive logic)

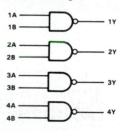

TEXAS INSTRUMENTS

POST OFFICE BOX 655012 • DALLAS, TEXAS 75265

2-3

ALS and AS Circuits

2

SN54ALS00A, SN74ALS00A
QUADRUPLE 2-INPUT POSITIVE-NAND GATES

absolute maximum ratings over operating free-air temperature range (unless otherwise noted)

Supply voltage, V_{CC} . . . . 7 V
Input voltage . . . . 7 V
Operating free-air temperature range: SN54ALS00A . . . . −55°C to 125°C
                                                 SN74ALS00A . . . . 0°C to 70°C
Storage temperature range . . . . −65°C to 150°C

recommended operating conditions

		SN54ALS00A			SN74ALS00A			UNIT
		MIN	NOM	MAX	MIN	NOM	MAX	
V_{CC}	Supply voltage	4.5	5	5.5	4.5	5	5.5	V
V_{IH}	High-level input voltage	2			2			V
V_{IL}	Low-level input voltage			0.7			0.8	V
I_{OH}	High-level output current			−0.4			−0.4	mA
I_{OL}	Low-level output current			4			8	mA
T_A	Operating free-air temperature	−55		125	0		70	°C

electrical characteristics over recommended operating free-air temperature range (unless otherwise noted)

PARAMETER	TEST CONDITIONS		SN54ALS00A			SN74ALS00A			UNIT
			MIN	TYP[†]	MAX	MIN	TYP[†]	MAX	
V_{IK}	V_{CC} = 4.5 V,	I_I = −18 mA			−1.5			−1.5	V
V_{OH}	V_{CC} = 4.5 V to 5.5 V,	I_{OH} = −0.4 mA	V_{CC}−2			V_{CC}−2			V
V_{OL}	V_{CC} = 4.5 V,	I_{OL} = 4 mA		0.25	0.4		0.25	0.4	V
	V_{CC} = 4.5 V,	I_{OL} = 8 mA					0.35	0.5	
I_I	V_{CC} = 5.5 V,	V_I = 7 V			0.1			0.1	mA
I_{IH}	V_{CC} = 5.5 V,	V_I = 2.7 V			20			20	μA
I_{IL}	V_{CC} = 5.5 V,	V_I = 0.4 V			−0.1			−0.1	mA
I_O[‡]	V_{CC} = 5.5 V,	V_O = 2.25 V	−30		−112	−30		−112	mA
I_{CCH}	V_{CC} = 5.5 V,	V_I = 0 V		0.5	0.85		0.5	0.85	mA
I_{CCL}	V_{CC} = 5.5 V,	V_I = 4.5 V		1.5	3		1.5	3	mA

[†]All typical values are at V_{CC} = 5 V, T_A = 25°C.
[‡]The output conditions have been chosen to produce a current that closely approximates one half of the true short-circuit output current, I_{OS}.

switching characteristics (see Note 1)

PARAMETER	FROM (INPUT)	TO (OUTPUT)	V_{CC} = 5 V, C_L = 50 pF, R_L = 500 Ω, T_A = 25°C	V_{CC} = 4.5 V to 5.5 V, C_L = 50 pF, R_L = 500 Ω, T_A = MIN to MAX				UNIT
			'ALS00A	SN54ALS00A		SN74ALS00A		
			TYP	MIN	MAX	MIN	MAX	
t_{PLH}	A or B	Y	7	3	16	3	11	ns
t_{PHL}	A or B	Y	5	2	13	2	8	

NOTE 1: Load circuit and voltage waveforms are shown in Section 1.

TEXAS
INSTRUMENTS

POST OFFICE BOX 655012 • DALLAS, TEXAS 75265

2

ALS and AS Circuits

**HIGH-SPEED
CMOS LOGIC**

**TYPES SN54HC00, SN74HC00
QUADRUPLE 2-INPUT POSITIVE-NAND GATES**

D2684, DECEMBER 1982—REVISED MARCH 1984

- **Package Options Include Both Plastic and Ceramic Chip Carriers in Addition to Plastic and Ceramic DIPs**

- **Dependable Texas Instruments Quality and Reliability**

description

These devices contain four independent 2-input NAND gates. They perform the Boolean functions $Y = \overline{A \cdot B}$ or $Y = \overline{A} + \overline{B}$ in positive logic.

The SN54HC00 is characterized for operation over the full military temperature range of $-55\,°C$ to $125\,°C$. The SN74HC00 is characterized for operation from $-40\,°C$ to $85\,°C$.

**SN54HC00 . . . J PACKAGE
SN74HC00 . . . J OR N PACKAGE
(TOP VIEW)**

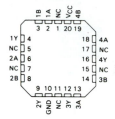

**SN54HC00 . . . FH OR FK PACKAGE
SN74HC00 . . . FH OR FN PACKAGE
(TOP VIEW)**

NC—No internal connection

FUNCTION TABLE (each gate)

INPUTS		OUTPUT
A	**B**	**Y**
H	H	L
L	X	H
X	L	H

logic symbol

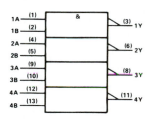

Pin numbers shown are for J and N packages.

maximum ratings, recommended operating conditions, and electrical characteristics
See Table I, page 2-4.

3

HCMOS DEVICES

**TEXAS
INSTRUMENTS**
POST OFFICE BOX 225012 • DALLAS, TEXAS 75265

TYPES SN54HC00, SN74HC00
QUADRUPLE 2-INPUT POSITIVE-NAND GATES

switching characteristics over recommended operating free-air temperature range (unless otherwise noted), C_L = 50 pF (see Note 1)

PARAMETER	FROM (INPUT)	TO (OUTPUT)	V_{CC}	T_A = 25°C			SN54HC00		SN74HC00		UNIT
				MIN	TYP	MAX	MIN	MAX	MIN	MAX	
t_{pd}	A or B	Y	2 V		45	90		135		115	ns
			4.5 V		9	18		27		23	
			6 V		8	15		23		20	
t_t		Y	2 V		38	75		110		95	ns
			4.5 V		8	15		22		19	
			6 V		6	13		19		16	

C_{pd}	Power dissipation capacitance per gate	No load, T_A = 25°C	20 pF typ

NOTE 1: For load circuit and voltage waveforms, see page 1-14.

3

HCMOS DEVICES

TEXAS INSTRUMENTS

POST OFFICE BOX 225012 ● DALLAS, TEXAS 75265

TYPES SN5476, SN54H76, SN54LS76A, SN7476, SN74H76, SN74LS76A
DUAL J-K FLIP-FLOPS WITH PRESET AND CLEAR
REVISED DECEMBER 1983

- **Package Options Include Plastic and Ceramic DIPs**

- **Dependable Texas Instruments Quality and Reliability**

description

The '76 and 'H76 contain two independent J-K flip-flops with individual J-K, clock, preset, and clear inputs. The '76 and 'H76 are positive-edge-triggered flip-flops. J-K input is loaded into the master while the clock is high and transferred to the slave on the high-to-low transition. For these devices the J and K inputs must be stable while the clock is high.

The 'LS76A contain two independent negative-edge-triggered flip-flops. The J and K inputs must be stable one setup time prior to the high-to-low clock transition for predictable operation. The preset and clear are asynchronous active low inputs. When low they override the clock and data inputs forcing the outputs to the steady state levels as shown in the function table.

The SN5476, SN54H76, and the SN54LS76A are characterized for operation over the full military temperature range of −55 °C to 125 °C. The SN7476, SN74H76, and the SN74LS76A are characterized for operation from 0 °C to 70 °C.

SN5476, SN54H76, SN54LS76A . . . J OR W PACKAGE
SN7476, SN74H76 . . . J OR N PACKAGE
SN74LS76A . . . D, J OR N PACKAGE
(TOP VIEW)

1CLK	1	16 1K
1 $\overline{PRE}$	2	15 1Q
1 $\overline{CLR}$	3	14 1$\overline{Q}$
1 J	4	13 GND
V_{CC}	5	12 2K
2CLK	6	11 2Q
2 $\overline{PRE}$	7	10 2$\overline{Q}$
2 $\overline{CLR}$	8	9 2J

'76, 'H76 FUNCTION TABLE

INPUTS					OUTPUTS	
PRE	CLR	CLK	J	K	Q	$\overline{Q}$
L	H	X	X	X	H	L
H	L	X	X	X	L	H
L	L	X	X	X	H†	H†
H	H	⊓	L	L	Q_0	$\overline{Q}_0$
H	H	⊓	H	L	H	L
H	H	⊓	L	H	L	H
H	H	⊓	H	H	TOGGLE	

'LS76A FUNCTION TABLE

INPUTS					OUTPUTS	
PRE	CLR	CLK	J	K	Q	$\overline{Q}$
L	H	X	X	X	H	L
H	L	X	X	X	L	H
L	L	X	X	X	H†	H†
H	H	↓	L	L	Q_0	$\overline{Q}_0$
H	H	↓	H	L	H	L
H	H	↓	L	H	L	H
H	H	↓	H	H	TOGGLE	
H	H	H	X	X	Q_0	$\overline{Q}_0$

† This configuration is nonstable; that is, it will not persist when either preset or clear returns to its inactive (high) level.

FOR CHIP CARRIER INFORMATION,
CONTACT THE FACTORY

3

TTL DEVICES

Texas
INSTRUMENTS
POST OFFICE BOX 225012 • DALLAS, TEXAS 75265

**TYPES SN5476, SN54H76,
SN7476, SN74H76
DUAL J-K FLIP-FLOPS WITH PRESET AND CLEAR**

logic diagrams

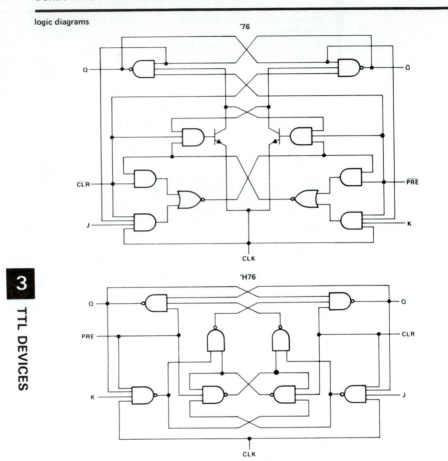

**TEXAS
INSTRUMENTS**
POST OFFICE BOX 225012 ● DALLAS, TEXAS 75265

**TYPES SN5476, SN54H76, SN54LS76A,
SN7476, SN74H76, SN74LS76A
DUAL J-K FLIP-FLOPS WITH PRESET AND CLEAR**

logic diagrams (continued)

'LS76A

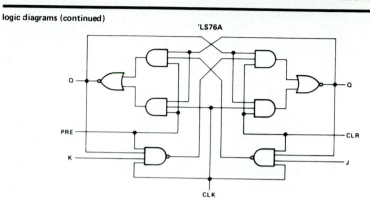

logic symbols

'76, 'H76

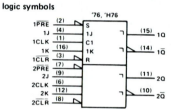

'LS76A

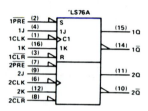

Pin numbers shown on logic notation are for D, J or N packages.

schematics of inputs and outputs

'76

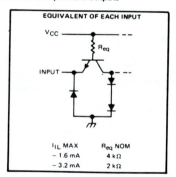

EQUIVALENT OF EACH INPUT

I_IL MAX	R_eq NOM
− 1.6 mA	4 kΩ
− 3.2 mA	2 kΩ

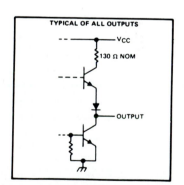

TYPICAL OF ALL OUTPUTS

TEXAS INSTRUMENTS
POST OFFICE BOX 225012 ● DALLAS, TEXAS 75265

3 TTL DEVICES

TYPES SN54LS76A, SN74LS76A
DUAL J-K FLIP-FLOPS WITH PRESET AND CLEAR

recommended operating conditions

			SN54LS76A			SN74LS76A			UNIT
			MIN	NOM	MAX	MIN	NOM	MAX	
V_{CC}	Supply voltage		4.5	5	5.5	4.75	5	5.75	V
V_{IH}	High-level input voltage		2			2			V
V_{IL}	Low-level input voltage				0.7			0.8	V
I_{OH}	High-level output current				− 0.4			− 0.4	mA
I_{OL}	Low-level output current				4			8	mA
f_{clock}	Clock frequency		0		30	0		30	MHz
t_w	Pulse duration	CLK high	20			20			ns
		$\overline{PRE}$ or $\overline{CLR}$ low	25			25			
t_{su}	Setup time before CLK↓	data high or low	20			20			ns
		$\overline{CLR}$ inactive	20			20			
		$\overline{PRE}$ inactive	25			25			
t_h	Hold time-data after CLK↓		0			0			ns
T_A	Operating free-air temperature		− 55		125	0		70	°C

electrical characteristics over recommended operating free-air temperature range (unless otherwise noted)

PARAMETER		TEST CONDITIONS[†]			SN54LS76A			SN74LS76A			UNIT
					MIN	TYP[‡]	MAX	MIN	TYP[‡]	MAX	
V_{IK}		V_{CC} = MIN,	I_I = − 18 mA				− 1.5			− 1.5	V
V_{OH}		V_{CC} = MIN,	V_{IH} = 2 V,	V_{IL} = MAX,	2.5	3.4		2.7	3.4		V
		I_{OH} = − 0.4 mA									
V_{OL}		V_{CC} = MIN,	V_{IL} = MAX,	V_{IH} = 2 V,		0.25	0.4		0.25	0.4	V
		I_{OL} = 4 mA									
		V_{CC} = MIN,	V_{IL} = MAX,	V_{IH} = 2 V,					0.35	0.5	
		I_{OL} = 8 mA									
I_I	J or K	V_{CC} = MAX,	V_I = 7 V				0.1			0.1	mA
	$\overline{CLR}$ or $\overline{PRE}$						0.3			0.3	
	CLK						0.4			0.4	
I_{IH}	J or K	V_{CC} = MAX,	V_I = 2.7 V				20			20	μA
	$\overline{CLR}$ or $\overline{PRE}$						60			60	
	CLK						80			80	
I_{IL}	J or K	V_{CC} = MAX,	V_I = 0.4 V				− 0.4			− 0.4	mA
	All other						− 0.8			− 0.8	
I_{OS}§		V_{CC} = MAX,	See Note 4		− 20		− 100	− 20		− 100	mA
I_{CC}		V_{CC} = MAX,	See Note 2			4	6		4	6	mA

† For conditions shown as MIN or MAX, use the appropriate value specified under recommended operating conditions.
‡ All typical values are at V_{CC} = 5 V, T_A = 25°C.
§Not more than one output should be shorted at a time, and the duration of the short circuit should not exceed one second.
NOTE 2: With all outputs open, I_{CC} is measured with the Q and $\overline{Q}$ outputs high in turn. At the time of measurement, the clock input is grounded.
NOTE 4: For certain devices where state commutation can be caused by shorting an output to ground, an equivalent test may be performed with V_O = 2.25 V and 2.125 V for the 54 family and the 74 family, respectively, with the minimum and maximum limits reduced to one half of their stated values.

switching characteristics, V_{CC} = 5 V, T_A = 25°C (see note 3)

PARAMETER	FROM (INPUT)	TO (OUTPUT)	TEST CONDITIONS		MIN	TYP	MAX	UNIT
f_{max}			R_L = 2 kΩ,	C_L = 15 pF	30	45		MHz
t_{PLH}	$\overline{PRE}$, $\overline{CLR}$ or CLK	Q or $\overline{Q}$				15	20	ns
t_{PHL}						15	20	ns

NOTE 3: See General Information Section for load circuits and voltage waveforms.

TEXAS
INSTRUMENTS
POST OFFICE BOX 225012 ● DALLAS, TEXAS 75265

3-317

TTL DEVICES

3

**HIGH-SPEED
CMOS LOGIC**

**TYPES SN54HC76, SN74HC76
DUAL J-K FLIP-FLOPS WITH CLEAR AND PRESET**

D2684, DECEMBER 1982 – REVISED MARCH 1984

- **Package Options Include Both Plastic and Ceramic Chip Carriers in Addition to Plastic and Ceramic DIPs**

- **Dependable Texas Instruments Quality and Reliability**

description

These devices contain two independent J-K negative-edge-triggered flip-flops. A low level at the Preset or Clear input sets or resets the outputs regardless of the levels of the other inputs. When Preset and Clear are inactive (high), data at the J and K inputs meeting the setup time requirements are transferred to the outputs on the negative-going edge of the clock pulse. Clock triggering occurs at a voltage level and is not directly related to the rise time of the clock pulse. Following the hold time interval, data at the J and K inputs may be changed without affecting the levels at the outputs. These versatile flip-flops can also perform as toggle flip-flops by tying J and K high.

SN54HC76 . . . J PACKAGE
SN74HC76 . . . J OR N PACKAGE
(TOP VIEW)

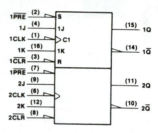

1CLK [1	16] 1K
1$\overline{PRE}$ [2	15] 1Q
1$\overline{CLR}$ [3	14] 1$\overline{Q}$
1J [4	13] GND
V$_{CC}$ [5	12] 2K
2CLK [6	11] 2Q
2$\overline{PRE}$ [7	10] 2$\overline{Q}$
2$\overline{CLR}$ [8	9] 2J

For functionally and electrically identical parts in chip carrier packages, see SN54HC112 and SN74HC112.

logic symbol

1$\overline{PRE}$ (2) — S
1J (4) — 1J
1CLK (1) — C1
1K (16) — 1K
1$\overline{CLR}$ (3) — R
1$\overline{PRE}$ (7)
2J (9)
2CLK (6)
2K (12)
2$\overline{CLR}$ (8)

(15) 1Q
(14) 1$\overline{Q}$
(11) 2Q
(10) 2$\overline{Q}$

Pin numbers shown are for J and N packages.

**FUNCTION TABLE
(EACH FLIP-FLOP)**

INPUTS					OUTPUTS	
$\overline{PRE}$	$\overline{CLR}$	CLK	J	K	Q	$\overline{Q}$
L	H	X	X	X	H	L
H	L	X	X	X	L	H
L	L	X	X	X	H*	H*
H	H	↓	L	L	Q$_0$	$\overline{Q}_0$
H	H	↓	H	L	H	L
H	H	↓	L	H	L	H
H	H	↓	H	H	TOGGLE	
H	H	H	X	X	Q$_0$	$\overline{Q}_0$

*This configuration is nonstable; that is, it will not persist when either Preset or Clear returns to its inactive (high) level.

logic diagram, each flip-flop (positive logic)

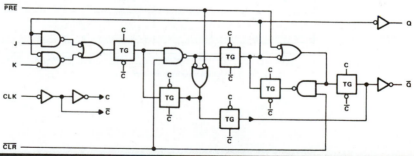

**TEXAS
INSTRUMENTS**
POST OFFICE BOX 225012 ● DALLAS, TEXAS 75265

3

HCMOS DEVICES

TYPES SN54HC76, SN74HC76
DUAL J-K FLIP-FLOPS WITH CLEAR AND PRESET

maximum ratings, recommended operating conditions, and electrical characteristics

See Table II, page 2-6.

timing requirements over recommended operating free-air temperature range (unless otherwise noted)

		V_{CC}	$T_A = 25°C$ MIN	MAX	SN54HC76 MIN	MAX	SN74HC76 MIN	MAX	UNIT
f_{clock} Clock frequency		2 V	0	6	0	4.2	0	5	
		4.5 V	0	31	0	21	0	25	MHz
		6 V	0	36	0	25	0	29	
t_w Pulse duration	$\overline{PRE}$ or $\overline{CLR}$ low	2 V	100		150		125		
		4.5 V	20		30		25		
		6 V	17		25		21		ns
	CLK high or low	2 V	80		120		100		
		4.5 V	16		24		20		
		6 V	14		20		17		
t_{su} Setup time before CLK↓	Data	2 V	150		225		190		
		4.5 V	30		45		38		
		6 V	25		38		32		ns
	$\overline{PRE}$ or $\overline{CLR}$ inactive	2 V	100		150		125		
		4.5 V	20		30		25		
		6 V	17		25		21		
t_h Hold time after CLK↓		2 V	0		0		0		
		4.5 V	0		0		0		ns
		6 V	0		0		0		

switching characteristics over recommended operating free-air temperature range (unless otherwise noted), $C_L = 50$ pF (see Note 1)

PARAMETER	FROM (INPUT)	TO (OUTPUT)	V_{CC}	$T_A = 25°C$ MIN	TYP	MAX	SN54HC76 MIN	MAX	SN74HC76 MIN	MAX	UNIT
f_{max}			2 V	6	9		4.2		5		
			4.5 V	31	41		21		25		MHz
			6 V	36	50		25		29		
t_{pd}	$\overline{PRE}$ or $\overline{CLR}$	Q or $\overline{Q}$	2 V		65	155		250		190	
			4.5 V		16	31		47		39	ns
			6 V		15	26		40		33	
t_{pd}	CLK	Q or $\overline{Q}$	2 V		70	145		220		180	
			4.5 V		19	29		44		36	ns
			6 V		16	25		37		31	
t_t		Q or $\overline{Q}$	2 V		38	75		110		95	
			4.5 V		8	15		22		19	ns
			6 V		6	13		19		16	

C_{pd}	Power dissipation capacitance per flip-flop	No load, $T_A = 25°C$	36 pF typ

NOTE 1: For load circuit and voltage waveforms, see page 1-14.

TEXAS INSTRUMENTS
POST OFFICE BOX 225012 • DALLAS, TEXAS 75265

3

HCMOS DEVICES

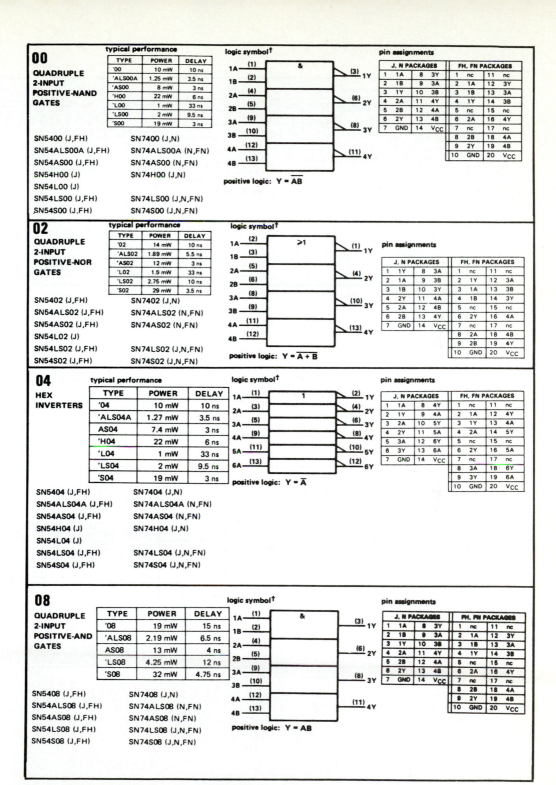

00 — QUADRUPLE 2-INPUT POSITIVE-NAND GATES

typical performance

TYPE	POWER	DELAY
'00	10 mW	10 ns
'ALS00A	1.25 mW	3.5 ns
'AS00	8 mW	3 ns
'H00	22 mW	6 ns
'L00	1 mW	33 ns
'LS00	2 mW	9.5 ns
'S00	19 mW	3 ns

SN5400 (J,FH)   SN7400 (J,N)
SN54ALS00A (J,FH)   SN74ALS00A (N,FN)
SN54AS00 (J,FH)   SN74AS00 (N,FN)
SN54H00 (J)   SN74H00 (J,N)
SN54L00 (J)
SN54LS00 (J,FH)   SN74LS00 (J,N,FN)
SN54S00 (J,FH)   SN74S00 (J,N,FN)

logic symbol†

positive logic: $Y = \overline{AB}$

pin assignments

J, N PACKAGES				FH, FN PACKAGES			
1	1A	8	3Y	1	nc	11	nc
2	1B	9	3A	2	1A	12	3Y
3	1Y	10	3B	3	1B	13	3A
4	2A	11	4Y	4	1Y	14	3B
5	2B	12	4A	5	nc	15	nc
6	2Y	13	4B	6	2A	16	4Y
7	GND	14	Vcc	7	nc	17	nc
				8	2B	18	4A
				9	2Y	19	4B
				10	GND	20	Vcc

02 — QUADRUPLE 2-INPUT POSITIVE-NOR GATES

typical performance

TYPE	POWER	DELAY
'02	14 mW	10 ns
'ALS02	1.89 mW	5.5 ns
'AS02	12 mW	3 ns
'L02	1.5 mW	33 ns
'LS02	2.75 mW	10 ns
'S02	29 mW	3.5 ns

SN5402 (J,FH)   SN7402 (J,N)
SN54ALS02 (J,FH)   SN74ALS02 (N,FN)
SN54AS02 (J,FH)   SN74AS02 (N,FN)
SN54L02 (J)
SN54LS02 (J,FH)   SN74LS02 (J,N,FN)
SN54S02 (J,FH)   SN74S02 (J,N,FN)

logic symbol†

positive logic: $Y = \overline{A + B}$

pin assignments

J, N PACKAGES				FH, FN PACKAGES			
1	1Y	8	3A	1	nc	11	nc
2	1A	9	3B	2	1Y	12	3A
3	1B	10	3Y	3	1A	13	3B
4	2Y	11	4A	4	1B	14	3Y
5	2A	12	4B	5	nc	15	nc
6	2B	13	4Y	6	2Y	16	4A
7	GND	14	Vcc	7	nc	17	nc
				8	2A	18	4B
				9	2B	19	4Y
				10	GND	20	Vcc

04 — HEX INVERTERS

typical performance

TYPE	POWER	DELAY
'04	10 mW	10 ns
'ALS04A	1.27 mW	3.5 ns
AS04	7.4 mW	3 ns
'H04	22 mW	6 ns
'L04	1 mW	33 ns
'LS04	2 mW	9.5 ns
'S04	19 mW	3 ns

SN5404 (J,FH)   SN7404 (J,N)
SN54ALS04A (J,FH)   SN74ALS04A (N,FN)
SN54AS04 (J,FH)   SN74AS04 (N,FN)
SN54H04 (J)   SN74H04 (J,N)
SN54L04 (J)
SN54LS04 (J,FH)   SN74LS04 (J,N,FN)
SN54S04 (J,FH)   SN74S04 (J,N,FN)

logic symbol†

positive logic: $Y = \overline{A}$

pin assignments

J, N PACKAGES				FH, FN PACKAGES			
1	1A	8	4Y	1	nc	11	nc
2	1Y	9	4A	2	1A	12	4Y
3	2A	10	5Y	3	1Y	13	4A
4	2Y	11	5A	4	2A	14	5Y
5	3A	12	6Y	5	nc	15	nc
6	3Y	13	6A	6	2Y	16	5A
7	GND	14	Vcc	7	nc	17	nc
				8	3A	18	6Y
				9	3Y	19	6A
				10	GND	20	Vcc

08 — QUADRUPLE 2-INPUT POSITIVE-AND GATES

typical performance

TYPE	POWER	DELAY
'08	19 mW	15 ns
'ALS08	2.19 mW	6.5 ns
AS08	13 mW	4 ns
'LS08	4.25 mW	12 ns
'S08	32 mW	4.75 ns

SN5408 (J,FH)   SN7408 (J,N)
SN54ALS08 (J,FH)   SN74ALS08 (N,FN)
SN54AS08 (J,FH)   SN74AS08 (N,FN)
SN54LS08 (J,FH)   SN74LS08 (J,N,FN)
SN54S08 (J,FH)   SN74S08 (J,N,FN)

logic symbol†

positive logic: $Y = AB$

pin assignments

J, N PACKAGES				FH, FN PACKAGES			
1	1A	8	3Y	1	nc	11	nc
2	1B	9	3A	2	1A	12	3Y
3	1Y	10	3B	3	1B	13	3A
4	2A	11	4Y	4	1Y	14	3B
5	2B	12	4A	5	nc	15	nc
6	2Y	13	4B	6	2A	16	4Y
7	GND	14	Vcc	7	nc	17	nc
				8	2B	18	4A
				9	2Y	19	4B
				10	GND	20	Vcc

† Pin numbers shown on logic symbols are for J and N packages only.
nc — no internal connection.

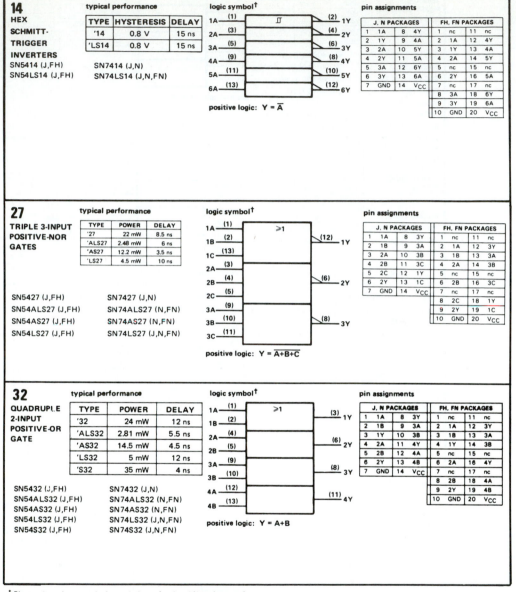

14
HEX SCHMITT-TRIGGER INVERTERS

SN5414 (J,FH)
SN54LS14 (J,FH)

SN7414 (J,N)
SN74LS14 (J,N,FN)

typical performance

TYPE	HYSTERESIS	DELAY
'14	0.8 V	15 ns
'LS14	0.8 V	15 ns

logic symbol†

1A (1) — 1Y (2)
2A (3) — 2Y (4)
3A (5) — 3Y (6)
4A (9) — 4Y (8)
5A (11) — 5Y (10)
6A (13) — 6Y (12)

positive logic: $Y = \overline{A}$

pin assignments

	J, N PACKAGES				FH, FN PACKAGES		
1	1A	8	4Y	1	nc	11	nc
2	1Y	9	4A	2	1A	12	4Y
3	2A	10	5Y	3	1Y	13	4A
4	2Y	11	5A	4	2A	14	5Y
5	3A	12	6Y	5	nc	15	nc
6	3Y	13	6A	6	2Y	16	5A
7	GND	14	V_{CC}	7	nc	17	nc
				8	3A	18	6Y
				9	3Y	19	6A
				10	GND	20	V_{CC}

27
TRIPLE 3-INPUT POSITIVE-NOR GATES

SN5427 (J,FH)
SN54ALS27 (J,FH)
SN54AS27 (J,FH)
SN54LS27 (J,FH)

SN7427 (J,N)
SN74ALS27 (N,FN)
SN74AS27 (N,FN)
SN74LS27 (J,N,FN)

typical performance

TYPE	POWER	DELAY
'27	22 mW	8.5 ns
'ALS27	2.48 mW	6 ns
'AS27	12.2 mW	3.5 ns
'LS27	4.5 mW	10 ns

logic symbol†

1A (1), 1B (2), 1C (13) — ≥1 — (12) 1Y
2A (3), 2B (4), 2C (5) — (6) 2Y
3A (9), 3B (10), 3C (11) — (8) 3Y

positive logic: $Y = \overline{A+B+C}$

pin assignments

	J, N PACKAGES				FH, FN PACKAGES		
1	1A	8	3Y	1	nc	11	nc
2	1B	9	3A	2	1A	12	3Y
3	2A	10	3B	3	1B	13	3A
4	2B	11	3C	4	2A	14	3B
5	2C	12	1Y	5	nc	15	nc
6	2Y	13	1C	6	2B	16	3C
7	GND	14	V_{CC}	7	nc	17	nc
				8	2C	18	1Y
				9	2Y	19	1C
				10	GND	20	V_{CC}

32
QUADRUPLE 2-INPUT POSITIVE-OR GATE

SN5432 (J,FH)
SN54ALS32 (J,FH)
SN54AS32 (J,FH)
SN54LS32 (J,FH)
SN54S32 (J,FH)

SN7432 (J,N)
SN74ALS32 (N,FN)
SN74AS32 (N,FN)
SN74LS32 (J,N,FN)
SN74S32 (J,N,FN)

typical performance

TYPE	POWER	DELAY
'32	24 mW	12 ns
'ALS32	2.81 mW	5.5 ns
'AS32	14.5 mW	4.5 ns
'LS32	5 mW	12 ns
'S32	35 mW	4 ns

logic symbol†

1A (1), 1B (2) — ≥1 — (3) 1Y
2A (4), 2B (5) — (6) 2Y
3A (9), 3B (10) — (8) 3Y
4A (12), 4B (13) — (11) 4Y

positive logic: $Y = A+B$

pin assignments

	J, N PACKAGES				FH, FN PACKAGES		
1	1A	8	3Y	1	nc	11	nc
2	1B	9	3A	2	1A	12	3Y
3	1Y	10	3B	3	1B	13	3A
4	2A	11	4Y	4	1Y	14	3B
5	2B	12	4A	5	nc	15	nc
6	2Y	13	4B	6	2A	16	4Y
7	GND	14	V_{CC}	7	nc	17	nc
				8	2B	18	4A
				9	2Y	19	4B
				10	GND	20	V_{CC}

† Pin numbers shown on logic symbols are for J and N packages only.

nc — no internal connection.

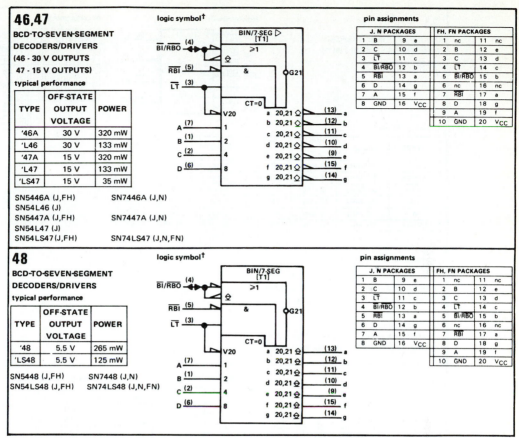

46,47

BCD-TO-SEVEN-SEGMENT DECODERS/DRIVERS
(46 - 30 V OUTPUTS
47 - 15 V OUTPUTS)

typical performance

TYPE	OFF-STATE OUTPUT VOLTAGE	POWER
'46A	30 V	320 mW
'L46	30 V	133 mW
'47A	15 V	320 mW
'L47	15 V	133 mW
'LS47	15 V	35 mW

SN5446A (J,FH)   SN7446A (J,N)
SN54L46 (J)
SN5447A (J,FH)   SN7447A (J,N)
SN54L47 (J)
SN54LS47 (J,FH)   SN74LS47 (J,N,FN)

logic symbol†

pin assignments

J, N PACKAGES				FH, FN PACKAGES			
1	B	9	e	1	nc	11	nc
2	C	10	d	2	B	12	e
3	LT	11	c	3	C	13	d
4	BI/RBO	12	b	4	LT	14	c
5	RBI	13	a	5	BI/RBO	15	b
6	D	14	g	6	nc	16	nc
7	A	15	f	7	RBI	17	a
8	GND	16	VCC	8	D	18	g
				9	A	19	f
				10	GND	20	VCC

48

BCD-TO-SEVEN-SEGMENT DECODERS/DRIVERS

typical performance

TYPE	OFF-STATE OUTPUT VOLTAGE	POWER
'48	5.5 V	265 mW
'LS48	5.5 V	125 mW

SN5448 (J,FH)   SN7448 (J,N)
SN54LS48 (J,FH)   SN74LS48 (J,N,FN)

logic symbol†

pin assignments

J, N PACKAGES				FH, FN PACKAGES			
1	B	9	e	1	nc	11	nc
2	C	10	d	2	B	12	e
3	LT	11	c	3	C	13	d
4	BI/RBO	12	b	4	LT	14	c
5	RBI	13	a	5	BI/RBO	15	b
6	D	14	g	6	nc	16	nc
7	A	15	f	7	RBI	17	a
8	GND	16	VCC	8	D	18	g
				9	A	19	f
				10	GND	20	VCC

† Pin numbers shown on logic symbols
  are for J and N packages only.
nc – no internal connection.

FONT TABLE T1 -- FOR '46, '47, '48, '49

74

DUAL D-TYPE POSITIVE-EDGE-TRIGGERED FLIP-FLOPS WITH PRESET AND CLEAR

logic symbol†

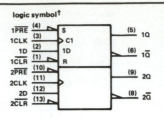

pin assignments

J, N PACKAGES				FH, FN PACKAGES			
1	1CLR	8	2Q̄	1	nc	11	nc
2	1D	9	2Q	2	1CLR	12	2Q̄
3	1CLK	10	2PRE	3	1D	13	2Q
4	1PRE	11	2CLK	4	1CLK	14	2PRE
5	1Q	12	2D	5	nc	15	nc
6	1Q̄	13	2CLR	6	1PRE	16	2CLK
7	GND	14	V_CC	7	nc	17	nc
				8	1Q	18	2D
				9	1Q̄	19	2CLR
				10	GND	20	V_CC

typical performance

TYPE	f_{max}	PWR/F-F	SET-UP	HOLD
'74	25 MHz	43 mW	20 ns↑	5 ns↑
'ALS74	50 MHz	6 mW	15 ns↑	0 ns↑
'AS74	125 MHz	26 mW	4.5 ns↑	0 ns ↑
'H74	43 MHz	75 mW	15 ns↑	5 ns↑
'L74	3 MHz	4 mW	50 ns↑	15 ns↑
'LS74A	33 MHz	10 mW	20 ns↑	5 ns↑
'S74	110 MHz	75 mW	3 ns↑	2 ns↑

↑ Rising edge of clock pulse.

SN5474 (J,FH)	SN7474 (J,N)
SN54ALS74 (J,FH)	SN74ALS74 (N,FN)
SN54AS74 (J,FH)	SN74AS74 (N,FN)
SN54H74 (J)	SN74H74 (J,N)
SN54L74 (J)	
SN54LS74A (J,FH)	SN74LS74A (J,N,FN)
SN54S74 (J,FH)	SN74S74 (J,N,FN)

76

DUAL J-K FLIP-FLOPS WITH PRESET AND CLEAR

typical performance

TYPE	f_{max}	PWR/F-F	SET-UP	HOLD
'76	20 MHz	50 mW	0 ns↑	0 ns↓
'H76	30 MHz	80 mW	0 ns↑	0 ns↓
'LS76A	45 MHz	10 mW	20 ns↓	0 ns↓

↑ Rising edge of clock pulse.
↓ Falling edge of clock pulse.

SN5476 (J)	SN7476 (J,N)
SN54H76 (J)	SN74H76 (J,N)
SN54LS76A (J)	SN74LS76A (J,N)

logic symbol, '76, 'H76†

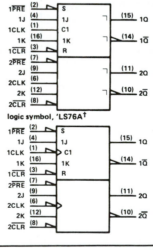

logic symbol, 'LS76A†

pin assignments

J, N PACKAGES			
1	1CLK	9	2J
2	1PRE	10	2Q̄
3	1CLR	11	2Q
4	1J	12	2K
5	V_CC	13	GND
6	2CLK	14	1Q̄
7	2PRE	15	1Q
8	2CLR	16	1K

For chip carrier information, contact the factory.

† Pin numbers shown on logic symbols are for J and N packages only.

nc − no internal connection.

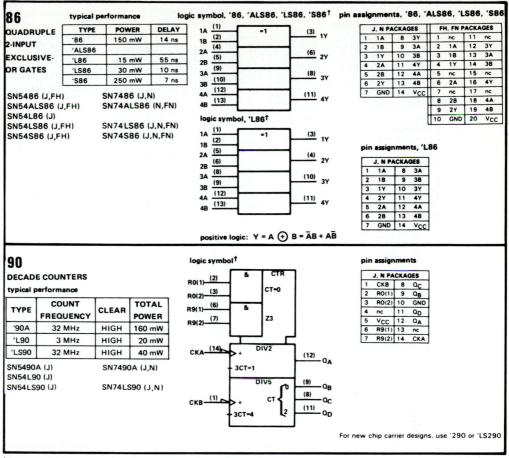

86

QUADRUPLE 2-INPUT EXCLUSIVE- OR GATES

typical performance

TYPE	POWER	DELAY
'86	150 mW	14 ns
'ALS86		
'L86	15 mW	55 ns
'LS86	30 mW	10 ns
'S86	250 mW	7 ns

SN5486 (J,FH)   SN7486 (J,N)
SN54ALS86 (J,FH)   SN74ALS86 (N,FN)
SN54L86 (J)
SN54LS86 (J,FH)   SN74LS86 (J,N,FN)
SN54S86 (J,FH)   SN74S86 (J,N,FN)

logic symbol, '86, 'ALS86, 'LS86, 'S86[†]

pin assignments, '86, 'ALS86, 'LS86, 'S86

J, N PACKAGES				FH, FN PACKAGES			
1	1A	8	3Y	1	nc	11	nc
2	1B	9	3A	2	1A	12	3Y
3	1Y	10	3B	3	1B	13	3A
4	2A	11	4Y	4	1Y	14	3B
5	2B	12	4A	5	nc	15	nc
6	2Y	13	4B	6	2A	16	4Y
7	GND	14	V_CC	7	nc	17	nc
				8	2B	18	4A
				9	2Y	19	4B
				10	GND	20	V_CC

logic symbol, 'L86[†]

pin assignments, 'L86

J, N PACKAGES			
1	1A	8	3A
2	1B	9	3B
3	1Y	10	3Y
4	2Y	11	4Y
5	2A	12	4A
6	2B	13	4B
7	GND	14	V_CC

positive logic: $Y = A \oplus B = \bar{A}B + A\bar{B}$

90

DECADE COUNTERS

typical performance

TYPE	COUNT FREQUENCY	CLEAR	TOTAL POWER
'90A	32 MHz	HIGH	160 mW
'L90	3 MHz	HIGH	20 mW
'LS90	32 MHz	HIGH	40 mW

SN5490A (J)   SN7490A (J,N)
SN54L90 (J)
SN54LS90 (J)   SN74LS90 (J,N)

logic symbol[†]

pin assignments

J, N PACKAGES			
1	CKB	8	Q_C
2	R0(1)	9	Q_B
3	R0(2)	10	GND
4	nc	11	Q_D
5	V_CC	12	Q_A
6	R9(1)	13	nc
7	R9(2)	14	CKA

For new chip carrier designs, use '290 or 'LS290

[†] Pin numbers shown on logic symbols are for J and N packages only.

nc — no internal connection.

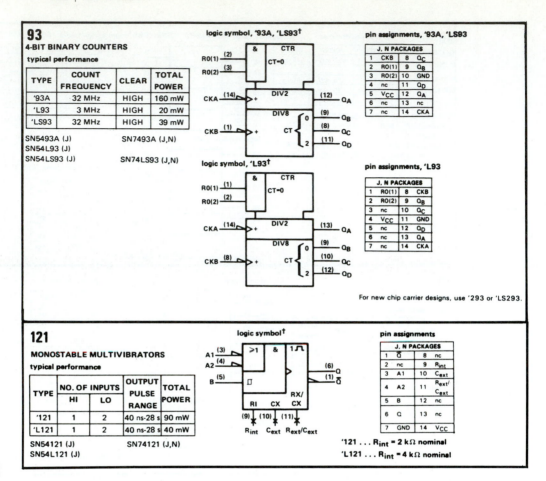

93

4-BIT BINARY COUNTERS

typical performance

TYPE	COUNT FREQUENCY	CLEAR	TOTAL POWER
'93A	32 MHz	HIGH	160 mW
'L93	3 MHz	HIGH	20 mW
'LS93	32 MHz	HIGH	39 mW

SN5493A (J)　　　　SN7493A (J,N)
SN54L93 (J)
SN54LS93 (J)　　　SN74LS93 (J,N)

logic symbol, '93A, 'LS93†

pin assignments, '93A, 'LS93

J, N PACKAGES			
1	CKB	8	Q_C
2	RO(1)	9	Q_B
3	RO(2)	10	GND
4	nc	11	Q_D
5	V_{CC}	12	Q_A
6	nc	13	nc
7	nc	14	CKA

logic symbol, 'L93†

pin assignments, 'L93

J, N PACKAGES			
1	RO(1)	8	CKB
2	RO(2)	9	Q_B
3	nc	10	Q_C
4	V_{CC}	11	GND
5	nc	12	Q_D
6	nc	13	Q_A
7	nc	14	CKA

For new chip carrier designs, use '293 or 'LS293.

121

MONOSTABLE MULTIVIBRATORS

typical performance

TYPE	NO. OF INPUTS		OUTPUT PULSE RANGE	TOTAL POWER
	HI	LO		
'121	1	2	40 ns-28 s	90 mW
'L121	1	2	40 ns-28 s	40 mW

SN54121 (J)　　　　SN74121 (J,N)
SN54L121 (J)

logic symbol†

pin assignments

J, N PACKAGES			
1	$\overline{Q}$	8	nc
2	nc	9	R_{int}
3	A1	10	C_{ext}
4	A2	11	R_{ext}/C_{ext}
5	B	12	nc
6	Q	13	nc
7	GND	14	V_{CC}

'121 . . . R_{int} = 2 kΩ nominal
'L121 . . . R_{int} = 4 kΩ nominal

† Pin numbers shown on logic symbols are for J and N packages only.

nc − no internal connection.

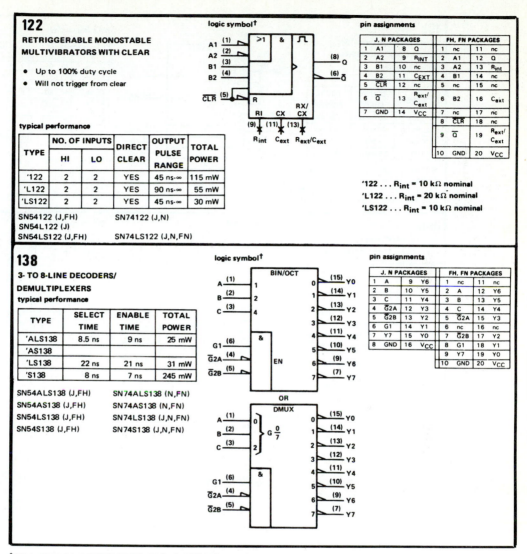

122

RETRIGGERABLE MONOSTABLE MULTIVIBRATORS WITH CLEAR

- Up to 100% duty cycle
- Will not trigger from clear

logic symbol†

pin assignments

	J, N PACKAGES				FH, FN PACKAGES		
1	A1	8	Q	1	nc	11	nc
2	A2	9	R_{INT}	2	A1	12	Q
3	B1	10	nc	3	A2	13	R_{int}
4	B2	11	C_{EXT}	4	B1	14	nc
5	$\overline{CLR}$	12	nc	5	nc	15	nc
6	$\overline{Q}$	13	R_{ext}/C_{ext}	6	B2	16	C_{ext}
7	GND	14	V_{CC}	7	nc	17	nc
				8	$\overline{CLR}$	18	nc
				9	$\overline{Q}$	19	R_{ext}/C_{ext}
				10	GND	20	V_{CC}

typical performance

TYPE	NO. OF INPUTS		DIRECT CLEAR	OUTPUT PULSE RANGE	TOTAL POWER
	HI	LO			
'122	2	2	YES	45 ns-∞	115 mW
'L122	2	2	YES	90 ns-∞	55 mW
'LS122	2	2	YES	45 ns-∞	30 mW

SN54122 (J,FH)   SN74122 (J,N)
SN54L122 (J)
SN54LS122 (J,FH)   SN74LS122 (J,N,FN)

'122 . . . R_{int} = 10 kΩ nominal
'L122 . . . R_{int} = 20 kΩ nominal
'LS122 . . . R_{int} = 10 kΩ nominal

138

3- TO 8-LINE DECODERS/ DEMULTIPLEXERS

typical performance

TYPE	SELECT TIME	ENABLE TIME	TOTAL POWER
'ALS138	8.5 ns	9 ns	25 mW
'AS138			
'LS138	22 ns	21 ns	31 mW
'S138	8 ns	7 ns	245 mW

SN54ALS138 (J,FH)   SN74ALS138 (N,FN)
SN54AS138 (J,FH)   SN74AS138 (N,FN)
SN54LS138 (J,FH)   SN74LS138 (J,N,FN)
SN54S138 (J,FH)   SN74S138 (J,N,FN)

logic symbol†

pin assignments

	J, N PACKAGES				FH, FN PACKAGES		
1	A	9	Y6	1	nc	11	nc
2	B	10	Y5	2	A	12	Y6
3	C	11	Y4	3	B	13	Y5
4	$\overline{G2A}$	12	Y3	4	C	14	Y4
5	$\overline{G2B}$	13	Y2	5	$\overline{G2A}$	15	Y3
6	G1	14	Y1	6	nc	16	nc
7	Y7	15	Y0	7	$\overline{G2B}$	17	Y2
8	GND	16	V_{CC}	8	G1	18	Y1
				9	Y7	19	Y0
				10	GND	20	V_{CC}

† Pin numbers shown on logic symbols are for J and N packages only.

nc — no internal connection.

193

SYNCHRONOUS UP/DOWN
DUAL CLOCK COUNTERS
(binary with clear)

typical performance

TYPE	COUNT FREQ	TOTAL POWER
'193	25 MHz	325 mW
'ALS193	40 MHz	50 mW
'L193	3 MHz	42 mW
'LS193	25 MHz	85 mW

SN54193 (J,FH)   SN74193 (J,N)
SN54L193 (J)
SN54LS193 (J,FH)   SN74LS193 (J,N,FN)
SN54ALS193 (J,FH)   SN74ALS193 (N,FN)

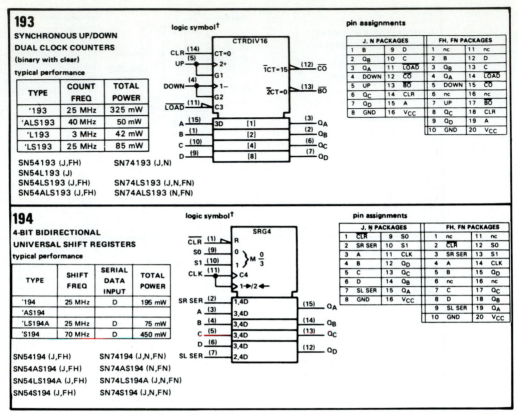

logic symbol†

pin assignments

J, N PACKAGES

1	B	9	D
2	Q_B	10	C
3	Q_A	11	LOAD
4	DOWN	12	CO
5	UP	13	BO
6	Q_C	14	CLR
7	Q_D	15	A
8	GND	16	V_CC

FH, FN PACKAGES

1	nc	11	nc
2	B	12	D
3	Q_B	13	C
4	Q_A	14	LOAD
5	DOWN	15	CO
6	nc	16	nc
7	UP	17	BO
8	Q_C	18	CLR
9	Q_D	19	A
10	GND	20	V_CC

194

4-BIT BIDIRECTIONAL
UNIVERSAL SHIFT REGISTERS

typical performance

TYPE	SHIFT FREQ	SERIAL DATA INPUT	TOTAL POWER
'194	25 MHz	D	195 mW
'AS194			
'LS194A	25 MHz	D	75 mW
'S194	70 MHz	D	450 mW

SN54194 (J,FH)   SN74194 (J,N,FN)
SN54AS194 (J,FH)   SN74AS194 (N,FN)
SN54LS194A (J,FH)   SN74LS194A (J,N,FN)
SN54S194 (J,FH)   SN74S194 (J,N,FN)

logic symbol†

pin assignments

J, N PACKAGES

1	CLR	9	S0
2	SR SER	10	S1
3	A	11	CLK
4	B	12	Q_D
5	C	13	Q_C
6	D	14	Q_B
7	SL SER	15	Q_A
8	GND	16	V_CC

FH, FN PACKAGES

1	nc	11	nc
2	CLR	12	S0
3	SR SER	13	S1
4	A	14	CLK
5	B	15	Q_D
6	nc	16	nc
7	C	17	Q_C
8	D	18	Q_B
9	SL SER	19	Q_A
10	GND	20	V_CC

† Pin numbers shown on logic symbols are for J and N packages only.

nc — no internal connection.

244

**OCTAL BUFFERS/LINE
DRIVERS/LINE RECEIVERS**
(non-inverted three-state outputs)
typical performance

TYPE	DELAY	MAX SOURCE CURRENT	MAX SINK CURRENT	POWER DISSI-PATION
SN54ALS244A	7 ns	− 12 mA	12 mA	
SN74ALS244A	7 ns	− 15 mA	24 mA	68 mW
SN74ALS244A-1	7 ns	− 15 mA	48 mA	
SN54AS244	4.5 ns	− 12 mA	48 mA	
SN74AS244	4.5 ns	− 15 mA	64 mA	235 mW
SN54LS244	12 ns	− 12 mA	12 mA	
SN74LS244	12 ns	− 15 mA	24 mA	127 mW
SN54S244	6 ns	− 12 mA	48 mA	
SN74S244	6 ns	− 15 mA	64 mA	558 mW

SN54ALS244A (J,FH)   SN74ALS244A (N,FN)
                            SNALS244A-1 (N,FN)
SN54AS244 (J,FH)   SN74AS244 (N,FN)
SN54LS244 (J,FH)   SN74LS244 (J,N,FN)
SN54S244 (J,FH)   SN74S244 (J,N,FN)

logic symbol†

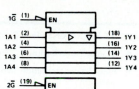

pin assignments

J, N PACKAGES

1	1G̅	11	2A1
2	1A1	12	1Y4
3	2Y4	13	2A2
4	1A2	14	1Y3
5	2Y3	15	2A3
6	1A3	16	1Y2
7	2Y2	17	2A4
8	1A4	18	1Y1
9	2Y1	19	2G̅
10	GND	20	V_CC

FH, FN PACKAGES

1	1G̅	11	2A1
2	1A1	12	1Y4
3	2Y4	13	2A2
4	1A2	14	1Y3
5	2Y3	15	2A3
6	1A3	16	1Y2
7	2Y2	17	2A4
8	1A4	18	1Y1
9	2Y1	19	2G̅
10	GND	20	V_CC

245

OCTAL BUS TRANSCEIVERS
(non-inverted three-state outputs)
typical performance

TYPE	DELAY	MAX SOURCE CURRENT	MAX SINK CURRENT	POWER DISSI-PATION
SN54ALS245A	6 ns	− 12 mA	12 mA	
SN74ALS245A	6 ns	− 15 mA	24 mA	173 mW
SN74ALS245A-1	6 ns	− 15 mA	48 mA	
SN54AS245	6 ns	− 12 mA	32 mA	
SN74AS245	6 ns	− 15 mA	48 mA	310 mW
SN54LS245	8 ns	− 12 mA	12 mA	
SN74LS245	8 ns	− 15 mA	24 mA	290 mW

SN54ALS245A (J,FH)   SN74ALS245A (N,FN)
                            SN74ALS245A-1 (N,FN)
SN54AS245 (J,FH)   SN74AS245 (N,FN)
SN54LS245 (J,FH)   SN74LS245 (J,N,FN)

logic symbol†

pin assignments

J, N PACKAGES

1	DIR	11	B8
2	A1	12	B7
3	A2	13	B6
4	A3	14	B5
5	A4	15	B4
6	A5	16	B3
7	A6	17	B2
8	A7	18	B1
9	A8	19	G̅
10	GND	20	V_CC

FH, FN PACKAGES

1	DIR	11	B8
2	A1	12	B7
3	A2	13	B6
4	A3	14	B5
5	A4	15	B4
6	A5	16	B3
7	A6	17	B2
8	A7	18	B1
9	A8	19	G
10	GND	20	V_CC

† Pin numbers shown on logic symbols are for J and N packages only.

nc − no internal connection.

MOS
LSI

TMS4016
2048-WORD BY 8-BIT STATIC RAM

FEBRUARY 1981   REVISED AUGUST 1983

- 2K X 8 Organization, Common I/O
- Single +5-V Supply
- Fully Static Operation (No Clocks, No Refresh)
- JEDEC Standard Pinout
- 24-Pin 600 Mil (15.2 mm) Package Configuration
- Plug-in Compatible with 16K 5 V EPROMs
- 8-Bit Output for Use in Microprocessor-Based Systems
- 3-State Outputs with $\overline{S}$ for OR-ties
- $\overline{G}$ Eliminates Need for External Bus Buffers
- All Inputs and Outputs Fully TTL Compatible
- Fanout to Series 74, Series 74S or Series 74LS TTL Loads
- N-Channel Silicon-Gate Technology
- Power Dissipation Under 385 mW Max
- Guaranteed dc Noise Immunity of 400 mV with Standard TTL Loads
- 4 Performance Ranges:

	ACCESS TIME (MAX)
TMS4016-12	120 ns
TMS4016-15	150 ns
TMS4016-20	200 ns
TMS4016-25	250 ns

TMS4016 . . . NL PACKAGE
(TOP VIEW)

A7	1	24	V_CC
A6	2	23	A8
A5	3	22	A9
A4	4	21	$\overline{W}$
A3	5	20	$\overline{G}$
A2	6	19	A10
A1	7	18	$\overline{S}$
A0	8	17	DQ8
DQ1	9	16	DQ7
DQ2	10	15	DQ6
DQ3	11	14	DQ5
V_SS	12	13	DQ4

PIN NOMENCLATURE	
A0 - A10	Addresses
DQ1 - DQ8	Data In Data Out
$\overline{G}$	Output Enable
$\overline{S}$	Chip Select
V_CC	-5-V Supply
V_SS	Ground
$\overline{W}$	Write Enable

description

The TMS4016 static random-access memory is organized as 2048 words of 8 bits each. Fabricated using proven N-channel, silicon-gate MOS technology, the TMS4016 operates at high speeds and draws less power per bit than 4K static RAMs. It is fully compatible with Series 74, 74S, or 74LS TTL. Its static design means that no refresh clocking circuitry is needed and timing requirements are simplified. Access time is equal to cycle time. A chip select control is provided for controlling the flow of data-in and data-out and an output enable function is included in order to eliminate the need for external bus buffers.

Of special importance is that the TMS4016 static RAM has the same standardized pinout as TI's compatible EPROM family. This, along with other compatible features, makes the TMS4016 plug-in compatible with the TMS2516 (or other 16K 5 V EPROMs). Minimal, if any modifications are needed. This allows the microprocessor system designer complete flexibility in partitioning his memory board between read write and non-volatile storage.

The TMS4016 is offered in the plastic (NL suffix) 24-pin dual-in-line package designed for insertion in mounting hole rows on 600-mil (15.2 mm) centers. It is guaranteed for operation from 0°C to 70°C.

(Courtesy of Texas Instruments Inc.)

TMS4016
2048-WORD BY 8-BIT STATIC RAM

operation

addresses (A0 – A10)

The eleven address inputs select one of the 2048 8-bit words in the RAM. The address-inputs must be stable for the duration of a write cycle. The address inputs can be driven directly from standard Series 54/74 TTL with no external pull-up resistors.

output enable ($\overline{G}$)

The output enable terminal, which can be driven directly from standard TTL circuits, affects only the data-out terminals. When output enable is at a logic high level, the output terminals are disabled to the high-impedance state. Output enable provides greater output control flexibility, simplifying data bus design.

chip select ($\overline{S}$)

The chip-select terminal, which can be driven directly from standard TTL circuits, affects the data-in/data-out terminals. When chip select and output enable are at a logic low level, the D/Q terminals are enabled. When chip select is high, the D/Q terminals are in the floating or high-impedance state and the input is inhibited.

write enable ($\overline{W}$)

The read or write mode is selected through the write enable terminal. A logic high selects the read mode; a logic low selects the write mode. $\overline{W}$ must be high when changing addresses to prevent erroneously writing data into a memory location. The $\overline{W}$ input can be driven directly from standard TTL circuits.

data-in/data-out (DQ1 – DQ8)

Data can be written into a selected device when the write enable input is low. The D/Q terminal can be driven directly from standard TTL circuits. The three-state output buffer provides direct TTL compatibility with a fan-out of one Series 74 TTL gate, one Series 74S TTL gate, or five Series 74LS TTL gates. The D/Q terminals are in the high impedance state when chip select ($\overline{S}$) is high, output enable ($\overline{G}$) is high, or whenever a write operation is being performed. Data-out is the same polarity as data-in.

(Courtesy of Texas Instruments Inc.)

logic symbol†

A0	(8)		RAM 2048x8

```
A0 ──(8)──      RAM 2048x8
A1 ──(7)──    0
A2 ──(6)──
A3 ──(5)──
A4 ──(4)──
A5 ──(3)──    A  0
A6 ──(2)──      ────
A7 ──(1)──       2047
A8 ──(23)──
A9 ──(22)──
A10 ──(19)──  10
S̄ ──(18)──   G1
Ḡ ──(20)──   G2
W̄ ──(21)──   1,2 EN (READ)
             1C3 (WRITE)

DQ1 ──(9)──  A,3D      A,Z4
             ▽ 4
DQ2 ──(10)──
DQ3 ──(11)──
DQ4 ──(13)──
DQ5 ──(14)──
DQ6 ──(15)──
DQ7 ──(16)──
DQ8 ──(17)──
```

FUNCTION TABLE

W̄	S̄	Ḡ	DQ1-DQ8	MODE
L	L	X	VALID DATA	WRITE
H	L	L	DATA OUTPUT	READ
X	H	X	HI-Z	DEVICE DISABLED
H	L	H	HI-Z	OUTPUT DISABLED

† This symbol is in accordance with IEEE Std 91/ANSI Y32.14 and recent decisions by IEEE and IEC. See explanation on page 10-1.

absolute maximum ratings over operating free-air temperature range (unless otherwise noted)†

Supply voltage, V_{CC} (see Note 1)	−0.5 V to 7 V
Input voltage (any input) (see Note 1)	−1 V to 7 V
Continuous power dissipation	1 W
Operating free-air temperature range	0°C to 70°C
Storage temperature range	−55°C to 150°C

† Stresses beyond those listed under "Absolute Maximum Ratings" may cause permanent damage to the device. This is a stress rating only and functional operation of the device at these or any other conditions beyond those indicated in the "Recommended Operating Conditions" section of this specification is not implied. Exposure to absolute-maximum-rated conditions for extended periods may affect device reliability.

NOTE 1: Voltage values are with respect to the V_{SS} terminal.

recommended operating conditions

PARAMETER	MIN	NOM	MAX	UNIT
Supply voltage, V_{CC}	4.5	5	5.5	V
Supply voltage, V_{SS}		0		V
High-level input voltage, V_{IH}	2		5.5	V
Low-level input voltage, V_{IL} (see Note 2)	−1		0.8	V
Operating free-air temperature, T_A	0		70	°C

NOTE 2: The algebraic convention, where the more negative (less positive) limit is designated as minimum, is used in this data sheet for logic voltage levels only.

(Courtesy of Texas Instruments Inc.)

TMS4016
2048-WORD BY 8-BIT STATIC RAM

electrical characteristics over recommended operating free-air temperature range (unless otherwise noted)

	PARAMETER	TEST CONDITIONS		MIN	TYP[†]	MAX	UNIT
V_{OH}	High level voltage	$I_{OH} = -1$ mA,	$V_{CC} = 4.5$ V	2.4			V
V_{OL}	Low level voltage	$I_{OL} = 2.1$ mA,	$V_{CC} = 4.5$ V			0.4	V
I_I	Input current	$V_I = 0$ V to 5.5 V				10	μA
I_{OZ}	Off-state output current	$\overline{S}$ or $\overline{G}$ at 2 V or $\overline{W}$ at 0.8 V, $V_O = 0$ V to 5.5 V				10	μA
I_{CC}	Supply current from V_{CC}	$I_O = 0$ mA, $V_{CC} = 5.5$ V, $T_A = 0\,^\circ$C (worst case)			40	70	mA
C_i	Input capacitance	$V_I = 0$ V,	$f = 1$ MHz			8	pF
C_o	Output capacitance	$V_O = 0$ V,	$f = 1$ MHz			12	pF

[†]All typical values are at $V_{CC} = 5$ V, $T_A = 25\,^\circ$C.

timing requirements over recommended supply voltage range and operating free-air temperature range

	PARAMETER	TMS4016-12		TMS4016-15		TMS4016-20		TMS4016-25		UNIT
		MIN	MAX	MIN	MAX	MIN	MAX	MIN	MAX	
$t_{c(rd)}$	Read cycle time	120		150		200		250		ns
$t_{c(wr)}$	Write cycle time	120		150		200		250		ns
$t_{w(W)}$	Write pulse width	60		80		100		120		ns
$t_{su(A)}$	Address setup time	20		20		20		20		ns
$t_{su(S)}$	Chip select setup time	60		80		100		120		ns
$t_{su(D)}$	Data setup time	50		60		80		100		ns
$t_{h(A)}$	Address hold time	0		0		0		0		ns
$t_{h(D)}$	Data hold time	5		10		10		10		ns

switching characteristics over recommended voltage range, $T_A = 0\,^\circ$C to $70\,^\circ$C with output loading of Figure 1 (see notes 3 and 4)

	PARAMETER	TMS4016-12		TMS4016-15		TMS4016-20		TMS4016-25		UNIT
		MIN	MAX	MIN	MAX	MIN	MAX	MIN	MAX	
$t_{a(A)}$	Access time from address		120		150		200		250	ns
$t_{a(S)}$	Access time from chip select low		60		75		100		120	ns
$t_{a(G)}$	Access time from output enable low		50		60		80		100	ns
$t_{v(A)}$	Output data valid after address change	10		15		15		15		ns
$t_{dis(S)}$	Output disable time after chip select high		40		50		60		80	ns
$t_{dis(G)}$	Output disable time after output enable high		40		50		60		80	ns
$t_{dis(W)}$	Output disable time after write enable low		50		60		60		80	ns
$t_{en(S)}$	Output enable time after chip select low	5		5		10		10		ns
$t_{en(G)}$	Output enable time after output enable low	5		5		10		10		ns
$t_{en(W)}$	Output enable time after write enable high	5		5		10		10		ns

NOTES: 3. $C_L = 100$ pF for all measurements except $t_{dis(W)}$ and $t_{en(W)}$.
$C_L = 5$ pF for $t_{dis(W)}$ and $t_{en(W)}$.
4. t_{dis} and t_{en} parameters are sampled and not 100% tested.

(Courtesy of Texas Instruments Inc.)

TMS4164
65,536-BIT DYNAMIC RANDOM-ACCESS MEMORY

MAY 1985–REVISED NOVEMBER 1985

This Data Sheet Is Applicable to All TMS4164s Symbolized with Code ''A'' as Described on Page 4-57.

- **65,536 X 1 Organization**
- **Single 5-V Supply (10% Tolerance)**
- **JEDEC Standardized Pinout in Dual-in-Line Package**
- **Performance Ranges:**

	ACCESS TIME ROW ADDRESS (MAX)	ACCESS TIME COLUMN ADDRESS (MAX)	READ OR WRITE CYCLE (MIN)	READ-MODIFY-WRITE CYCLE (MIN)
'4164-12	120 ns	70 ns	230 ns	255 ns
'4164-15	150 ns	85 ns	260 ns	290 ns
'4164-20	200 ns	135 ns	330 ns	345 ns

- **Upward Pin Compatible with TMS4116 (16K Dynamic RAM)**
- **First Military Version of 64K DRAM**
- **Also Available with MIL-STD-883B Processing and L(0 °C to 70 °C), E(−40 °C to 85 °C), S(−55 °C to 100 °C), or M(−55 °C to 125 °C) Temperature Ranges**
- **Operations of the TMS4164 Can Be Controlled by TI's TMS4500A and/or THCT4501 Dynamic RAM Controllers**
- **Long Refresh Period . . . 4 ms**
- **Low Refresh Overhead Time . . . As Low As 1.8% of Total Refresh Period**
- **All Inputs, Outputs, Clocks Fully TTL Compatible**
- **3-State Unlatched Output**
- **Common I/O Capability with Early Write Feature**
- **Page-Mode Operation for Faster Access**
- **Low Power Dissipation**
  - **Operating . . . 135 mW (Typ)**
  - **Standby . . . 17.5 mW (Typ)**
- **SMOS (Scaled-MOS) N-Channel Technology**

N PACKAGE
(TOP VIEW)

NC	1	16	V_SS
D	2	15	$\overline{CAS}$
$\overline{W}$	3	14	Q
$\overline{RAS}$	4	13	A6
A0	5	12	A3
A2	6	11	A4
A1	7	10	A5
V_DD	8	9	A7

FP PACKAGE
(TOP VIEW)

4

Dynamic RAMs

PIN NOMENCLATURE	
A0-A7	Address Inputs
$\overline{CAS}$	Column-Address Strobe
D	Data In
NC	No Connection
Q	Data Out
$\overline{RAS}$	Row-Address Strobe
V_DD	5-V Supply
V_SS	Ground
$\overline{W}$	Write Enable

description

The TMS4164 is a high-speed, 65,536-bit, dynamic random-access memory, organized as 65,536 words of one bit each. It employs state-of-the-art SMOS (scaled MOS) N-channel double-level polysilicon gate technology for very high performance combined with low cost and improved reliability.

TEXAS
INSTRUMENTS

POST OFFICE BOX 1443 ● HOUSTON, TEXAS 77001

4-41

TMS4164
65,536-BIT DYNAMIC RANDOM-ACCESS MEMORY

The TMS4164 features $\overline{\text{RAS}}$ access times of 120 ns, 150 ns, and 200 ns maximum. Power dissipation is 135 mW typical operating and 17.5 mW typical standby.

Refresh period is extended to 4 milliseconds, and during this period each of the 256 rows must be strobed with $\overline{\text{RAS}}$ in order to retain data. $\overline{\text{CAS}}$ can remain high during the refresh sequence to conserve power.

All inputs and outputs, including clocks, are compatible with Series 74 TTL. All address lines and data in are latched on chip to simplify system design. Data out is unlatched to allow greater system flexibility. Pin 1 has no internal connection to allow compatibility with other 64K RAMs that use this pin for an additional function.

The TMS4164 is offered in 16-pin dual-in-line plastic (N suffix) and 18-lead plastic chip carrier (FP suffix) packages. The dual-in-line plastic package is designed for insertion in mounting-hole rows on 7,62-mm (300-mil) centers. The TMS4164 is guaranteed for operation from 0°C to 70°C.

4

Dynamic RAMs

operation

address (A0 through A7)

Sixteen address bits are required to decode 1 of 65,536 storage cell locations. Eight row-address bits are set up on pins A0 through A7 and latched onto the chip by the row-address strobe ($\overline{\text{RAS}}$). Then the eight column-address bits are set up on pins A0 through A7 and latched onto the chip by the column-address strobe ($\overline{\text{CAS}}$). All addresses must be stable on or before the falling edges of $\overline{\text{RAS}}$ and $\overline{\text{CAS}}$. $\overline{\text{RAS}}$ is similar to a chip enable in that it activates the sense amplifiers as well as the row decoder. $\overline{\text{CAS}}$ is used as a chip select activating the column decoder and the input and output buffers.

write enable ($\overline{\text{W}}$)

The read or write mode is selected through the write-enable ($\overline{\text{W}}$) input. A logic high on the $\overline{\text{W}}$ input selects the read mode and a logic low selects the write mode. The write-enable terminal can be driven from standard TTL circuits without a pull-up resistor. The data input is disabled when the read mode is selected. When $\overline{\text{W}}$ goes low prior to $\overline{\text{CAS}}$, data out will remain in the high-impedance state for the entire cycle permitting common I/O operation.

data in (D)

Data is written during a write or read-modify-write cycle. Depending on the mode of operation, the falling edge of $\overline{\text{CAS}}$ or $\overline{\text{W}}$ strobes data into the on-chip data latch. This latch can be driven from standard TTL circuits without a pull-up resistor. In an early write cycle, $\overline{\text{W}}$ is brought low prior to $\overline{\text{CAS}}$ and the data is strobed in by $\overline{\text{CAS}}$ with setup and hold times referenced to this signal. In a delayed-write or read-modify-write cycle, $\overline{\text{CAS}}$ will already be low, thus the data will be strobed in by $\overline{\text{W}}$ with setup and hold times referenced to this signal.

data out (Q)

The three-state output buffer provides direct TTL compatibility (no pull-up resistor required) with a fan out of two Series 74 TTL loads. Data out is the same polarity as data in. The output is in the high-impedance (floating) state until $\overline{\text{CAS}}$ is brought low. In a read cycle the output goes active after the access time interval $t_{a(C)}$ that begins with the negative transition of $\overline{\text{CAS}}$ as long as $t_{a(R)}$ is satisfied. The output becomes valid after the access time has elapsed and remains valid while $\overline{\text{CAS}}$ is low; $\overline{\text{CAS}}$ going high returns it to a high-impedance state. In an early write cycle, the output is always in the high-impedance state. In a delayed-write or read-modify-write cycle, the output will follow the sequence for the read cycle.

refresh

A refresh operation must be performed at least every four milliseconds to retain data. Since the ouput buffer is in the high-impedance state unless $\overline{\text{CAS}}$ is applied, The $\overline{\text{RAS}}$-only refresh sequence avoids any output during refresh. Strobing each of the 256 row addresses (A0 through A7) with $\overline{\text{RAS}}$ causes all bits in each row to be refreshed. $\overline{\text{CAS}}$ can remain high (inactive) for this refresh sequence to conserve power.

TEXAS
INSTRUMENTS
POST OFFICE BOX 1443 ● HOUSTON, TEXAS 77001

page mode

Page-mode operation allows effectively faster memory access by keeping the same row address and strobing random column addresses onto the chip. Thus, the time required to setup and strobe sequential row addresses for the same page is eliminated. To extend beyond the 256 column locations on a single RAM, the row address and $\overline{RAS}$ are applied to multiple 64K RAMs. $\overline{CAS}$ is then decoded to select the proper RAM.

power up

After power up, the power supply must remain at its steady-state value for 1 ms. In addition, $\overline{RAS}$ must remain high for 100 μs immediately prior to initialization. Initialization consists of performing eight $\overline{RAS}$ cycles before proper device operation is achieved.

logic symbol[†]

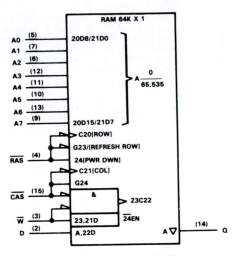

[†]This symbol is in accordance with ANSI/IEEE Std 91-1984 and IEC Publication 617-12.
Pin numbers shown are for the dual-in-line package.

TEXAS
INSTRUMENTS
POST OFFICE BOX 1443 ● HOUSTON, TEXAS 77001

Dynamic RAMs

4

TMS4164
65,536-BIT DYNAMIC RANDOM-ACCESS MEMORY

functional block diagram

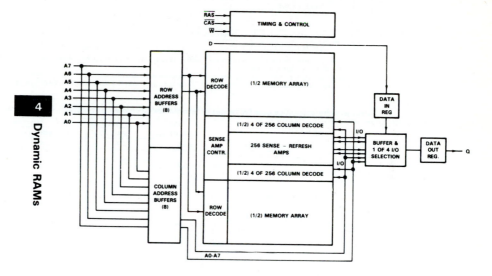

4

Dynamic RAMs

absolute maximum ratings over operating free-air temperature range (unless otherwise noted) †

Voltage on any pin except V_{DD} and data out (see Note 1)	−1.5 V to 10 V
Voltage on V_{DD} supply and data out with respect to V_{SS}	−1 V to 6 V
Short circuit output current	50 mA
Power dissipation	1 W
Operating free-air temperature range	0°C to 70°C
Storage temperature range	−65°C to 150°C

† Stresses beyond those listed under ''Absolute Maximum Ratings'' may cause permanent damage to the device. This is a stress rating only and functional operation of the device at these or any other conditions beyond those indicated in the ''Recommended Operating Conditions'' section of this specification is not implied. Exposure to absolute-maximum-rated conditions for extended periods may affect device reliability.

NOTES: 1. All voltage values in this data sheet are with respect to V_{SS}.
2. Additional information concerning the handling of ESD sensitive devices is available in a document entitled ''*Guidelines for Handling Electrostatic-Discharge-Sensitive (ESDS) Devices and Assemblies*'' in Section 12.

TEXAS INSTRUMENTS
POST OFFICE BOX 1443 ● HOUSTON, TEXAS 77001

TMS4164
65,536-BIT DYNAMIC RANDOM-ACCESS MEMORY

recommended operating conditions

			MIN	NOM	MAX	UNIT
V_{DD}	Supply voltage		4.5	5	5.5	V
V_{SS}	Supply voltage			0		V
V_{IH}		$V_{DD} = 4.5$ V	2.4		4.8	V
		$V_{DD} = 5.5$ V	2.4		6	
V_{IL}	Low-level input voltage (see Notes 3 and 4)		−0.6		0.8	V
T_A	Operating free-air temperature		0		70	°C

NOTES: 3. The algebraic convention, where the more negative (less positive) limit is designated as minimum, is used in this data sheet for logic voltage levels only.
4. Due to input protection circuitry, the applied voltage may begin to clamp at −0.6 V. Test conditions must comprehend this occurrence. See application report entitled "TMS4164A and TMS4416 Input Protection Diode" on page 9-5.

electrical characteristics over full ranges of recommended operating conditions (unless otherwise noted)

	PARAMETER	TEST CONDITIONS	TMS4164-12			TMS4164-15			UNIT
			MIN	TYP[†]	MAX	MIN	TYP[†]	MAX	
V_{OH}	High-level output voltage	$I_{OH} = -5$ mA	2.4			2.4			V
V_{OL}	Low-level output voltage	$I_{OL} = 4.2$ mA			0.4			0.4	V
I_I	Input current (leakage)	$V_I = 0$ V to 5.8 V, $V_{DD} = 5$ V, All other pins = 0 V			±10			±10	µA
I_O	Output current (leakage)	$V_O = 0.4$ to 5.5 V, $V_{DD} = 5$ V, $\overline{CAS}$ high			±10			±10	µA
I_{DD1}[‡]	Average operating current during read or write cycle	t_c = minimum cycle, All outputs open		40	48		35	45	mA
I_{DD2}[§]	Standby current	After 1 memory cycle, $\overline{RAS}$ and $\overline{CAS}$ high, All outputs open		3.5	5		3.5	5	mA
I_{DD3}[‡]	Average refresh current	t_c = minimum cycle, $\overline{CAS}$ high and $\overline{RAS}$ cycling, All outputs open		28	40		25	37	mA
I_{DD4}	Average page-mode current	$t_{c(P)}$ = minimum cycle, $\overline{RAS}$ low and $\overline{CAS}$ cycling, All outputs open		28	40		25	37	mA

[†] All typical values are at $T_A = 25$ °C and nominal supply voltages.
[‡] Additional information on page 4-58.
[§] $V_{IL} > -0.6$V. See application report entitled "TMS4164A and TMS4416 Input Protection Diode" on page 9-5.

4

Dynamic RAMs

TEXAS
INSTRUMENTS
POST OFFICE BOX 1443 ● HOUSTON, TEXAS 77001

TMS4164
65,536-BIT DYNAMIC RANDOM-ACCESS MEMORY

electrical characteristics over full ranges of recommended operating conditions (unless otherwise noted)

	PARAMETER	TEST CONDITIONS	TMS4164-20 MIN	TYP[†]	MAX	UNIT
V_{OH}	High-level output voltage	$I_{OH} = -5$ mA	2.4			V
V_{OL}	Low-level output voltage	$I_{OL} = 4.2$ mA			0.4	V
I_I	Input current (leakage)	$V_I = 0$ V to 5.8 V, $V_{DD} = 5$ V, All other pins = 0 V			±10	µA
I_O	Output current (leakage)	$V_O = 0.4$ to 5.5 V, $V_{DD} = 5$ V, $\overline{CAS}$ high			±10	µA
I_{DD1}[‡]	Average operating current during read or write cycle	t_c = minimum cycle All outputs open		27	37	mA
I_{DD2}[§]	Standby current	After 1 memory cycle, $\overline{RAS}$ and $\overline{CAS}$ high, All outputs open		3.5	5	mA
I_{DD3}[‡]	Average refresh current	t_c = minimum cycle, $\overline{CAS}$ high and $\overline{RAS}$ cycling, All outputs open		20	32	mA
I_{DD4}	Average page-mode current	$t_{c(P)}$ = minimum cycle, $\overline{RAS}$ low and $\overline{CAS}$ cycling, All outputs open		20	32	mA

[†] All typical values are at $T_A = 25$ °C and nominal supply voltages.
[‡] Additional information on page 4-58.
[§] $V_{IL} > -0.6$V. See application report entitled ''TMS4164A and TMS4416 Input Protection Diode'' on page 9-5.

capacitance over recommended supply voltage range and operating free-air temperature range, f = 1 MHz

	PARAMETER	TYP[†]	MAX	UNIT
$C_{i(A)}$	Input capacitance, address inputs	4	5	pF
$C_{i(D)}$	Input capacitance, data input	4	5	pF
$C_{i(RC)}$	Input capacitance strobe inputs	6	8	pF
$C_{i(W)}$	Input capacitance, write enable input	6	8	pF
C_o	Output capacitance	5	6	pF

[†] All typical values are at $T_A = 25$ °C and nominal supply voltages.

switching characteristics over recommended supply voltage range and operating free-air temperature range

PARAMETER		TEST CONDITIONS	ALT. SYMBOL	TMS4164-12 MIN	MAX	TMS4164-15 MIN	MAX	UNIT
$t_{A(C)}$	Access time from $\overline{CAS}$	$C_L = 100$ pF, Load = 2 Series 74 TTL gates	t_{CAC}		70		85	ns
$t_{a(R)}$	Access time from $\overline{RAS}$	$C_L = 100$ pF, $t_{RLCL} = $ MAX, Load = 2 Series 74 TTL gates	t_{RAC}		120		150	ns
$t_{dis(CH)}$	Output disable time after $\overline{CAS}$ high	$C_L = 100$ pF, Load = 2 Series 74 TTL gates	t_{OFF}	0	40	0	40	ns

TMS4164
65,536-BIT DYNAMIC RANDOM-ACCESS MEMORY

switching characteristics over recommended supply voltage range and operating free-air temperature range

PARAMETER		TEST CONDITIONS	ALT. SYMBOL	TMS4164-20		UNIT
				MIN	MAX	
$t_{a(C)}$	Access time from $\overline{CAS}$	$C_L = 100$ pF, Load = 2 Series 74 TTL gates	t_{CAC}		135	ns
$t_{a(R)}$	Access time from $\overline{RAS}$	$C_L = 100$ pF, t_{RLCL} = MAX, Load = 2 Series 74 TTL gates	t_{RAC}		200	ns
$t_{dis(CH)}$	Output disable time after $\overline{CAS}$ high	$C_L = 100$ pF, Load = 2 Series 74 TTL gates	t_{OFF}	0	50	ns

4

Dynamic RAMs

TEXAS
INSTRUMENTS
POST OFFICE BOX 1443 ● HOUSTON, TEXAS 77001

2716*
16K (2K x 8) UV ERASABLE PROM

- **Fast Access Time**
  - **— 2716-1: 350 ns Max.**
  - **— 2716-2: 390 ns Max.**
  - **— 2716:   450 ns Max.**
  - **— 2716-5: 490 ns Max.**
  - **— 2716-6: 650 ns Max.**
- **Single +5V Power Supply**
- **Low Power Dissipation**
  - **— Active Power: 525 mW Max.**
  - **— Standby Power: 132 mW Max.**

- **Pin Compatible to Intel 2732A EPROM**
- **Simple Programming Requirements**
  - **— Single Location Programming**
  - **— Programs with One 50 ms Pulse**
- **Inputs and Outputs TTL Compatible During Read and Program**
- **Completely Static**

The Intel® 2716 is a 16,384-bit ultraviolet erasable and electrically programmable read-only memory (EPROM). The 2716 operates from a single 5-volt power supply, has a static standby mode, and features fast single-address location programming. It makes designing with EPROMs faster, easier and more economical.

The 2716, with its single 5-volt supply and with an access time up to 350 ns, is ideal for use with the newer high-performance +5V microprocessors such as Intel's 8085 and 8086. A selected 2716-5 and a 2716-6 are available for slower speed applications. The 2716 is also the first EPROM with a static standby mode which reduces the power dissipation without increasing access time. The maximum active power dissipation is 525 mW while the maximum standby power dissipation is only 132 mW, a 75% savings.

The 2716 has the simplest and fastest method yet devised for programming EPROMs—single-pulse, TTL-level programming. No need for high voltage pulsing because all programming controls are handled by TTL signals. Program any location at any time—either individually, sequentially or at random, with the 2716's single-address location programming. Total programming time for all 16,384 bits is only 100 seconds.

*Part(s) also available in extended temperature range for Military and Industrial grade applications.

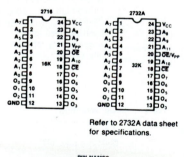

Refer to 2732A data sheet for specifications.

PIN NAMES	
A_0–A_{10}	ADDRESSES
$\overline{CE}$/PGM	CHIP ENABLE/PROGRAM
$\overline{OE}$	OUTPUT ENABLE
O_0–O_7	OUTPUTS

Figure 1. Pin Configuration

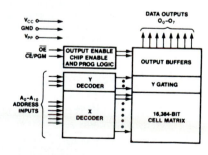

Figure 2. Block Diagram

SEPTEMBER 1981
AFN-00811B

intel

DEVICE OPERATION

The five modes of operation of the 2716 are listed in Table 1. It should be noted that all inputs for the five modes are at TTL levels. The power supplies required are a +5V V_{CC} and a V_{PP}. The V_{PP} power supply must be at 25V during the three programming modes, and must be at 5V in the other two modes.

Read Mode

The 2716 has two control functions, both of which must be logically satisfied in order to obtain data at the outputs. Chip Enable ($\overline{CE}$) is the power control and should be used for device selection. Output Enable ($\overline{OE}$) is the output control and should be used to gate data to the output pins, independent of device selection. Assuming that addresses are stable, address access time (t_{ACC}) is equal to the delay from $\overline{CE}$ to output (t_{CE}). Data is available at the outputs t_{OE} after the falling edge of $\overline{OE}$, assuming that $\overline{CE}$ has been low and addresses have been stable for at least $t_{ACC}-t_{OE}$.

Standby Mode

The 2716 has a standby mode which reduces the active power dissipation by 75%, from 525 mW to 132 mW. The 2716 is placed in the standby mode by applying a TTL high signal to the $\overline{CE}$ input. When in standby mode, the outputs are in a high impedance state, independent of the $\overline{OE}$ input.

Output OR-Tieing

Because 2716s are usually used in larger memory arrays, Intel has provided a 2-line control function that accomodates this use of multiple memory connections. The two-line control function allows for:

a) the lowest possible memory power dissipation, and

b) complete assurance that output bus contention will not occur.

To most efficiently use these two control lines, it is recommended that $\overline{CE}$ (pin 18) be decoded and used as the primary device selecting function, while $\overline{OE}$ (pin 20) be made a common connection to all devices in the array and connected to the READ line from the system control bus. This assures that all deselected memory devices are in their low-power standby modes and that the output pins are only active when data is desired from a particular memory device.

Programming

Initially, and after each erasure, all bits of the 2716 are in the "1" state. Data is introduced by selectively programming "0's" into the desired bit locations. Although only "0's" will be programmed, both "1's" and "0's" can be presented in the data word. The only way to change a "0" to a "1" is by ultraviolet light erasure.

The 2716 is in the programming mode when the V_{PP} power supply is at 25V and $\overline{OE}$ is at V_{IH}. The data to be programmed is applied 8 bits in parallel to the data output pins. The levels required for the address and data inputs are TTL.

When the address and data are stable, a 50 msec, active-high, TTL program pulse is applied to the $\overline{CE}$/PGM input. A program pulse must be applied at each address location to be programmed. You can program any location at any time—either individually, sequentially, or at random. The program pulse

Table 1. Mode Selection

Pins Mode	$\overline{CE}$/PGM (18)	$\overline{OE}$ (20)	V_{PP} (21)	V_{CC} (24)	Outputs (9–11, 13–17)
Read	V_{IL}	V_{IL}	+5	+5	D_{OUT}
Standby	V_{IH}	Don't Care	+5	+5	High Z
Program	Pulsed V_{IL} to V_{IH}	V_{IH}	+25	+5	D_{IN}
Program Verify	V_{IL}	V_{IL}	+25	+5	D_{OUT}
Program Inhibit	V_{IL}	V_{IH}	+25	+5	High Z

AFN-00811B

has a maximum width of 55 msec. The 2716 must not be programmed with a DC signal applied to the $\overline{CE}$/PGM input.

Programming of multiple 2716s in parallel with the same data can be easily accomplished due to the simplicity of the programming requirements. Like inputs of the paralleled 2716s may be connected together when they are programmed with the same data. A high-level TTL pulse applied to the $\overline{CE}$/PGM input programs the paralleled 2716s.

Program Inhibit

Programming of multiple 2716s in parallel with different data is also easily accomplished. Except for $\overline{CE}$/PGM, all like inputs (including $\overline{OE}$) of the parallel 2716s may be common. A TTL-level program pulse applied to a 2716's $\overline{CE}$/PGM input with V_{PP} at 25V will program that 2716. A low-level $\overline{CE}$/PGM input inhibits the other 2716 from being programmed.

Program Verify

A verify should be performed on the programmed bits to determine that they were correctly programmed. The verify may be performed with V_{PP} at 25V. Except during programming and program verify, V_{PP} must be at 5V.

ERASURE CHARACTERISTICS

The erasure characteristics of the 2716 are such that erasure begins to occur when exposed to light with wavelengths shorter than approximately 4000 Angstroms (Å). It should be noted that sunlight and certain types of fluorescent lamps have wavelengths in the 3000–4000 Å range. Data show that constant exposure to room-level fluorescent lighting could erase the typical 2716 in approximately 3 years, while it would take approximately 1 week to cause erasure when exposed to direct sunlight. If the 2716 is to be exposed to these types of lighting conditions for extended periods of time, opaque labels are available from Intel which should be placed over the 2716 window to prevent unintentional erasure.

The recommended erasure procedure (see Data Catalog PROM/ROM Programming Instruction Section) for the 2716 is exposure to shortwave ultraviolet light which has a wavelength of 2537 Angstroms (Å). The integrated dose (i.e., UV intensity X exposure time) for erasure should be a minimum of 15 W-sec/cm^2. The erasure time with this dosage is approximately 15 to 20 minutes using an ultraviolet lamp with a 1200 μW/cm^2 power rating. The 2716 should be placed within 1 inch of the lamp tubes during erasure. Some lamps have a filter on their tubes which should be removed before erasure.

2716

ABSOLUTE MAXIMUM RATINGS*

Temperature Under Bias .... −10°C to +80°C
Storage Temperature .... −65°C to +125°C
All Input or Output Voltages with
  Respect to Ground .... +6V to −0.3V
V_{PP} Supply Voltage with Respect
  to Ground During Program .... +26.5V to −0.3V

NOTICE: Stresses above those listed under "Absolute Maximum Ratings" may cause permanent damage to the device. This is a stress rating only and functional operation of the device at these or any other conditions above those indicated in the operational sections of this specification is not implied. Exposure to absolute maximum rating conditions for extended periods may affect device reliability.

DC AND AC OPERATING CONDITIONS DURING READ

	2716	2716-1	2716-2	2716-5	2716-6
Temperature Range	0°C–70°C	0°C–70°C	0°C–70°C	0°C–70°C	0°C–70°C
V_{CC} Power Supply[1,2]	5V ±5%	5V ±10%	5V ±5%	5V ±5%	5V ±5%
V_{PP} Power Supply[2]	V_{CC}	V_{CC}	V_{CC}	V_{CC}	V_{CC}

READ OPERATION
D.C. AND OPERATING CHARACTERISTICS

Symbol	Parameter	Limits			Units	Test Conditions
		Min.	Typ.[3]	Max.		
I_{LI}	Input Load Current			10	μA	V_{IN} = 5.25V
I_{LO}	Output Leakage Current			10	μA	V_{OUT} = 5.25V
I_{PP1}[2]	V_{PP} Current			5	mA	V_{PP} = 5.25V
I_{CC1}[2]	V_{CC} Current (Standby)		10	25	mA	$\overline{CE}$ = V_{IH}, $\overline{OE}$ = V_{IL}
I_{CC2}[2]	V_{CC} Current (Active)		57	100	mA	$\overline{OE}$ = $\overline{CE}$ = V_{IL}
V_{IL}	Input Low Voltage	−0.1		0.8	V	
V_{IH}	Input High Voltage	2.0		V_{CC}+1	V	
V_{OL}	Output Low Voltage			0.45	V	I_{OL} = 2.1 mA
V_{OH}	Output High Voltage	2.4			V	I_{OH} = −400 μA

AFN-00811B

2716

TYPICAL CHARACTERISTICS

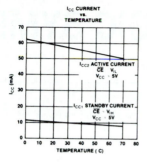
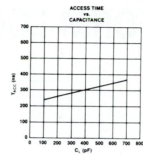
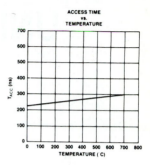

A.C. CHARACTERISTICS

Symbol	Parameter	Limits (ns)										Test Conditions
		2716		2716-1		2716-2		2716-5		2716-6		
		Min.	Max.	Min.	Max.	Min.	Max.	Min.	Max.	Min.	Max.	
t_{ACC}	Address to Output Delay		450		350		390		450		450	$\overline{CE} = \overline{OE} = V_{IL}$
t_{CE}	$\overline{CE}$ to Output Delay		450		350		390		490		650	$\overline{OE} = V_{IL}$
t_{OE} [4]	Output Enable to Output Delay		120		120		120		160		200	$\overline{CE} = V_{IL}$
t_{DF} [4]	Output Enable High to Output Float	0	100	0	100	0	100	0	100	0	100	$\overline{CE} = V_{IL}$
t_{OH}	Output Hold from Addresses, $\overline{CE}$ or $\overline{OE}$ Whichever Occurred First	0		0		0		0		0		$\overline{CE} = \overline{OE} = V_{IL}$

CAPACITANCE[4] (T_A = 25°C, f = 1 MHz)

Symbol	Parameter	Typ.	Max.	Units	Test Conditions
C_{IN}	Input Capacitance	4	6	pF	V_{IN} = 0V
C_{OUT}	Output Capacitance	8	12	pF	V_{OUT} = 0V

A.C. TEST CONDITIONS

Output Load . . . . 1 TTL gate and
C_L = 100 pF
Input Rise and Fall Times . . . . ≤20 ns
Input Pulse Levels . . . . 0.8V to 2.2V
Timing Measurement Reference Level:
  Inputs . . . . 1V and 2V
  Outputs . . . . 0.8V and 2V

AFN-00811B

UNIFORM LOGIC SYMBOLS

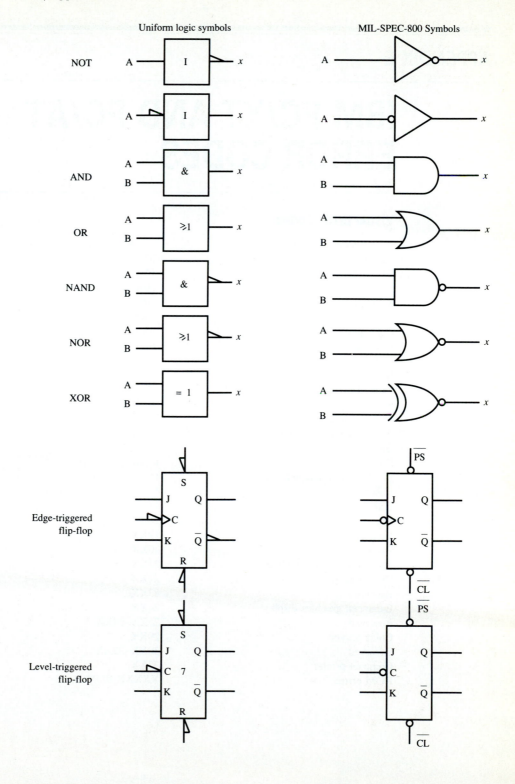

IBM PC/XT AND PC/AT ERROR CODES

Visual Error Codes

Major Subsystem	Error Code
Power	02X
System board	1XX
Memory	20X XXXX XXX20X
Keyboard	30X or XX30X
Monochrome display	4XX
Color graphics display	5XX
Diskette	6XX
Math coprocessor	7XX
Reserved	8XX
Parallel printer adapter	9XX
Reserved	10XX
Asynchronous comm. adapter	11XX
Alt. asynchronous comm. adapter	12XX
Game control adapter	13XX
Printer	14XX
SDLC comm. adapter	15XX
Reserved	16XX
Fixed disk	17XX
Expansion unit	18XX
Reserved	19XX
Bisync comm. adapter	20XX
Alt bysync comm. adapter	21XX
Cluster adapter	22XX
Reserved	23XX
Enhanced graphics display	24XX
Reserved	25XX–28XX
Color printer	29XX
Reserved	30XX–32XX
Compact printer	33XX
ROM errors	XXXXX ROM

Audible Error Codes

Indication	Possible cause
No beeps or continuous tone	System board or power supply
One long and one short beep	System board
One long and two short beeps	Display
One short beep and blank display	Display or switches incorrect

Detailed Error Codes

1XX System Board Failures

101   Interrupt failure, 8259 chip and associated logic.
102   Timer failure, 8253 chip and associated logic.
103   Timer interrupt failure, 8253 or 8259 chip failure.
104   Protected mode failure (PC/AT only).
105   8042 MCU chip failure (PC/AT only).
106   Converting logic failure.
107   Hot NMI failure (NMI stuck active).
108   Timer bus test failure.
109   Direct memory access failure, 8237 chip and logic.
121   Unexpected interrupts, 8259 chip or stuck input (short).
131   Cassette interface failure, PC only.

The following are for the PC/AT only:

161   System option error, MC146818 chip or battery.
162   System options not set correctly, adapter board failure.
163   Time and date not set, MC146818 or battery failure.
164   Memory size error, memory failure or changed.

2XX RAM Memory Errors

201   Memory test data failure, see text.
202   Memory address test failure, check for shorts.
203   Memory address test failure, check for shorts.

3XX Keyboard Errors

301   Keyboard did not respond to software reset command correctly or stuck key detected. If a stuck key was detected, the hex keycode for the stuck key is displayed.
302   User-indicated failure or PC/AT keylock is locked.
303   Keyboard or system board error, check cable.
304   Keyboard error—CMOS (MC146818) does not match system.

4XX Monochrome Display Errors

401   Monochrome display adapter failed, adapter memory, horizontal frequency, or video failure.
408   User-indicated display attributes are incorrect.
416   User-indicated character set incorrect.
424   User 80X25 mode incorrect.
432   Parallel port failure, missing loop-back plug.

5XX Color Graphics Display Errors

501   Color graphics display adapter failed, adapter memory horizontal frequency, or video failure.

508 User-indicated display attributes are incorrect.
516 User-indicated character set is incorrect.
524 User-indicated 80X25 mode is incorrect.
532 User-indicated 40X25 mode is incorrect.
540 User-indicated 320X200 graphics mode is incorrect.
548 User-indicated 640X200 graphics mode is incorrect.

6XX Diskette Errors

601 Diskette post failed.
602 Unable to read boot record.
606 Diskette-verify function failed.
607 Write-protected diskette or sensor failure.
608 Illegal diskette command, status returned.
610 Diskette initialization failed.
611 System timeout, status returned.
612 Bad NEC, floppy disk controller chip bad.
613 Diskette DMA failure, no data transferred.
621 Seek error, status returned.
622 Read error, bad CRC.
623 Read error, record not found (could not find header).
624 Read error, bad address mark (AM) or not found.
625 Bad NEC seek, status returned.
626 Diskette data-compare error.

7XX Math Coprocessor Errors

7XX 8087 or 80287 math coprocessor chip failure.

9XX Parallel Printer Adapter Errors

901 Parallel printer adapter failed, requires test plug.

11XX Asynchronous Communications Adapter Errors

1101 Asynchronous adapter failed, requires test plug.

12XX Alternate Asynchronous Communications Adapter Errors

1201 Alternate asynchronous communications adapter failed.

13XX Game-Control Adapter Errors

1301 Game-control adapter failed.
1302 Joystick test failed.

14XX Printer Errors

1401 Printer test failed.
1404 Matrix printer failed.

15XX Synchronous data link (SDLC) Communications Adapter

1510 8255 PPI chip port A failure.
1511 8255 PPI chip port B failure.
1512 8255 PPI chip port C failure.
1513 8253 timer 1 did not reach terminal count.
1514 8253 timer 1 stuck on.
1515 8235 timer 0 did not reach terminal count.
1516 8253 timer 0 stuck on.
1517 8253 timer 2 did not reach terminal count.
1518 8253 timer 2 stuck on.

1519 8273 port B error.
1520 8273 port A error.
1521 8273 command/read timeout.
1522 Interrupt level 4 failure.
1523 Ring indicate stuck on.
1524 Receive clock stuck on.
1525 Transmit clock stuck on.
1526 Test indicate stuck on.
1527 Ring indicate not on.
1528 Receive clock not on.
1529 Transmit clock not on.
1530 Test indicate not on.
1531 Data set ready not on.
1532 Carrier detect not on.
1533 Clear to send not on.
1534 Data set ready stuck on.
1536 Clear to send stuck on.
1537 Level 3 interrupt failure.
1538 Receive interrupt results failure.
1539 Wrap data miscompare.
1540 DMA channel 1 failure.
1541 DMA channel 1 failure.
1542 Error in 8273 error checking or status reporting.
1547 Stray interrupt level 4.
1548 Stray interrupt level 3.
1549 Interrupt presentation sequence timeout.

16XX Display Emulation Errors (327X, 5520, 525X)

No codes available at this time.

17XX Fixed Disk Errors

1701 Fixed disk POST error.
1702 Fixed disk adapter error.
1703 Fixed disk drive error.
1704 Fixed disk drive or adapter error.
1780 Fixed disk drive 0 error.
1781 Fixed disk drive 1 error.
1782 Fixed disk adapter failure.
1790 Fixed disk drive 0 error.
1791 Fixed disk drive 1 error.

18XX I/O Expansion Unit Errors

1801 I/O expansion unit POST error.
1810 Enable/disable failure.
1811 Extender card wrap test failed.
1812 High order address lines failed.
1813 Wait state failure.
1814 Enable/disable could not be set on.
1815 Wait state failure.
1816 Extender card wrap test failed (enabled).

1817 High-order address lines failure (enabled).
1818 Disable not functioning.
1819 Wait request switch not set correctly.
1820 Receiver card wrap test failure.
1821 Receiver high-order address lines failure.

19XX 3270 PC Attachment Card Error

No codes available at this time

20XX Binary Synchronous Communications (BSC) Adapter Errors

2010 8255 port A failure.
2011 8255 port B failure.
2012 8255 port C failure.
2013 8253 timer 1 did not reach terminal count.
2014 8253 timer 1 stuck on.
2016 8235 timer 2 did not reach terminal count or stuck on.
2017 8251 data set ready failed to come on.
2018 8251 clear to send not sensed.
2019 8251 data set ready stuck on.
2020 8251 clear to send stuck on.
2021 8251 hardware reset failed.
2022 8251 software reset failed.
2023 8251 software error reset failed.
2024 8251 transmit ready did not come on.
2025 8251 receive ready did not come on.
2026 8251 could not force overrun status to come on.
2027 Interrupt failure—on timer interrupt.
2028 Interrupt failure—transmit.
2029 Interrupt failure—transmit.
2030 Interrupt failure—receive.
2031 Interrupt failure—receive.
2033 Ring indicate stuck on.
2034 Receive clock stuck on.
2035 Transmit clock stuck on.
2036 Test indicate stuck on.
2037 Ring indicate not on.
2038 Receive clock not on.
2039 Transmit clock not on.
2040 Test indicate not on.
2041 Data set ready not on.
2042 Carrier detect not on.
2043 Clear to send not on.
2044 Data set ready stuck on.
2046 Clear to send stuck on.
2047 Unexpected transmit interrupt.
2048 Unexpected receive interrupt.
2049 Transmit data did not equal receive data.
2050 8251 detected overrun error.
2051 Lost data set ready during wrap.
2052 Receive timeout during wrap.

22XX Cluster Adapter Errors

24XX Enhanced Graphics Adapter Errors

29XX Color Matrix Printer Errors

33XX Compact Printer Errors

ANSWERS TO SELECTED ODD-NUMBERED EXERCISES

Chapter 1

1.1 a. 113   b. 17   c. 245   d. 47

1.3 a. 1101101   b. 10000000   c. 11111010   d. 100000001

1.5 a. 27   b. 4E c. 100   d. 3E8

1.7 a. 1010101110001101   b. 1111111000010101   c. 1111000000001110
d. 00000100000001010001

1.9 a. 7E b. 21D c. 10D d. FDC87

1.11 a. 0   b. 0   c. Z   d. A

1.13 a. Dual-in-line package   b. See Figure 1.6.

1.15 CMOS

1.17 Logic 1

1.21 Using a logic probe on the source and destination of a connection.

1.23 a. See Figure 1.10(c).   b. See Figure 1.8(c).

1.25 a. Setup time: Minimum time that the input data must be stable before the clock transition.
b. Propagation delay time: The time it takes for the output of a flip-flop actually to change state.
c. Asynchronous inputs: Inputs that act directly on a flip-flop without the clock.
d. Race condition: When the data changes at the same time that the clock pulse occurs.

1.27 See Figure 1.22, which must be modified.

1.29 Plastic chip carrier, ceramic chip carrier, plastic DIP, and ceramic DIP (see Figure 1.25).

1.31 a. $V_{cc(max)} = 7$ V   b. $V_{in(max)} = 7$ V   c. Storage temp (max) = 150°C

1.33 a. $V_{cc(min)} = 4.75$ V   b. $V_{IH(min)} = 2$ V   c. $V_{OH(min)} = 2.7$ V

1.35 a. $V_{NMH} = 0.5$ V, $V_{NML} = 0.3$ V   b. $V_{NMH} = 0.7$ V, $V_{NML} = 0.3$ V

1.37 Connect them to V_{CC} or ground. (See Tech Tips and Troubleshooting.)

1.39 a. This occurs when the input diode is blown, resulting in a high resistance short to ground.
b. With a DMM on the diode test scale.

Chapter 2

2.1   a. A flip-flop that represents a single storage bit is called a memory cell.

b. A memory address is a unique location in memory. The address tells the computer where to find the memory cell.

c. The process by which a computer retrieves data from memory is called a memory-read cycle.

d. A memory-write cycle is a process in which a computer stores or writes data into memory.

2.3   Nonvolatile memory is memory that does not lose its data when the power is turned off, such as ROM memory. Volatile memory is memory that loses data whenever the power is switched off, such as RAM memory.

2.5   See equation (2.1). It would have 16 memory locations, each of which could store one word of data.

2.7   ROMs are used in applications where data is of a permanent nature, such as code converters, character generators, and data tables.

2.9   Redraw Figure 2.4(a) so that the first two bipolar cells have their fuses intact (store logic 1) and the last two bipolar cells have their fuses open (store logic 0). Thus, the data stored will be 1100.

2.11   Static RAM (SRAM) will hold its data as long as the power is applied to the device. It is essentially an array of flip-flops in which each flip-flop represents one bit or memory cell.

Dynamic RAM (DRAM) is a type of RAM in which the data must be periodically recharged or refreshed. Refreshing is accomplished by performing a repetitive read or write operation or a special refresh operation.

The added cost and complexity of DRAMs as compared to SRAMs are more than offset by the higher cell density, which lowers the per-bit cost for DRAM devices.

2.13   a. See Figure 2.7 and modify. All data inputs (pins 9 to 11 and 13 to 17) are wired to a logic 1 ($+5$ V_{DC}). All address inputs (pins 1 to 8 and 19, 22, 23) are wired to logic 0 (0 V_{DC}), and $\overline{W} = 0$ V, $\overline{S} = 0$ V, $\overline{G} = 0$ V (control lines).

b. All data pins are now used as outputs (not wired to $+5$ V), and $\overline{W} = +5$ V, $\overline{S} = 0$ V, $\overline{G} = 0$ V.

2.15   In order to save address lines and reduce the number of pins required on the IC, this device uses address multiplexing. During read or write operations the seven address lines first contain the row information and then the column information. This is controlled by the $\overline{RAS}$ and $\overline{CAS}$ control lines.

2.17   Modify Figure 2.11 by using only four devices (4116). For data D_0 to D_3 use the first four DRAMs.

2.19 U_4 must be activated to select the upper bank $(1800\text{-}1FFF)_{16}$. Therefore, $A_{11} = 1$, $A_{12} = 1$, and A_0 to A_{10} are all logic 1s. $\overline{G}_4$ must be a logic 0 in order to read U_4.

2.21   A PLD can be used to replace a large number of logic devices. The PLD is programmed to perform the same logic function as the individual logic gates.

2.23   Product line 1 would have $\overline{X}$ and Z connected.

Product line 2 would have $\overline{Y}$ and Z connected.

Product line 3 would have X, Y, and Z connected, and one of the sum lines (O_1) would be connected to the outputs of AND gates 1, 2, and 3.

2.25   Modify Figure 2.19 by changing the product lines as follows: Product line 1: All fuses are blown, producing a logic 1.

Product line 2: $\overline{I}_1$, I_2, and $\overline{I}_3$ are left connected by the fuses.

Product line 3: All the fuses are left connected, producing a logic 0.

2.27 A 2-to-1 multiplexer uses only two input lines, I_0 and I_1 and one select line, S_0.
Out $= I_0 = (\overline{S}_0 \cdot I_0)$
Out $= I_1 = (S_0 \cdot I_1)$
Modify Figure 2.23.

2.29 In word parity or parity word, a parity bit is added to each data word (row) and also to each vertical data position (column). The parity word is calculated by determining the odd or even parity for each vertical position (column). If a single bit error occurs, it can be detected and corrected.

Chapter 3

3.1 General-purpose computing, automobile applications, calculators, digital clocks, appliances, robotics

3.3 AX (accumulator), BX (base), CX (count), DX (data)

3.5

Data Bus	Instruction Queue
8088 | 8-bit	4-byte (2-word)
8086 | 16-bit	6-byte (3-word)

3.7 Execution unit: arithmetic logic unit, flag register, general register, and pointer and index registers.
Bus interface unit: address generator, address-control unit, bus-control unit, instruction queue, instruction pointer, and segment registers.

3.9 Address and data lines 0 through 7; address and data line 15; address line 16 and status line 3; address line 17 and status line 4; address line 18 and status line 5; address line 19 and status line 6;

3.11

Address lines	Memory size
8	256
16	65,536
20	1,048,576

3.13 a. $\overline{WR} = 0$, $DT/\overline{R} = 1$ b. $DT/\overline{R}$ c. $10/\overline{M}$ d. $ALE = 1$ e. $\overline{INTA}$
f. $\overline{RD} = O$ g. $MN/\overline{MX} = 0$

3.15 The flag register is used to store information about the conditions of the operation of the ALU.

3.17 Data registers AX (accumulator); BX (base); CX (count); DX (data). These data registers are used for arithmetic and logic operations. They can temporarily hold the accumulated results.
Pointer and index registers: SP (stack); BP (base); SI (source); DI (destination). These registers are used to point to or index to a specific location in memory.

3.19 CS is a code segment register.

3.21 Static RAM is memory that keeps information until power is removed. Dynamic RAM is memory that needs constant refreshing to keep information.

3.23 Modify Figure 3.14.

3.25 See Figure 3.18.

3.27 The 8088/8086 microprocessor is faster than older MPUs because it is divided into two independent fetch and execute units (BIU and EU).

3.29 *F*1200

3.31 221*F*

Chapter 4

4.1 Fortran, Pascal, BASIC, COBOL

4.3 a. Determine what the program should do.

b. Develop a flow chart.

c. Translate the flow chart into program form.

d. Enter the program and edit, assemble, and link it.

e. Run the program and verify the results.

4.5 The contents in the DX register will be moved to the CS register, so both registers will have the same contents.

4.7 BX contains the address where the content is to be moved into the AX.

4.9 MOV destination, source

4.11 LEA, PUSH, POP, MOV

4.13 ADD, SUB, MUL, DIV

4.15 AX = 0000*H*

4.17 OR destination, source

4.19 The loop instruction is a special form of the jump instruction with a built-in count capability.

4.21

MOV	AX, 0004H	;load 4H into AX register
MOV	BX, 0003H	;load 3H into BX register
ADD	AX, BX	;add BX to AX, result in AX = 7H
MOV	SUM, AX	;move result into memory address ;labeled SUM

Chapter 5

5.1 a. MPU   b. Input/output   c. Bus system   d. Memory

5.3 Input/output

5.5

8088	8086
8-bit data bus	16-bit data bus
4-byte instruction queue	6-byte instruction queue
I-O/$\overline{\text{M}}$	M/$\overline{\text{I-O}}$
$\overline{\text{SS0}}$	$\overline{\text{BHE}}$/S7

5.7 The QS_0 and QS_1 provide status information about the instruction queue.

5.9 The 8284A chip is a clock generator providing the basic timing for the microprocessor.

5.11 This is used to control the bus control signals when the system is used with the MPU in maximum mode.

5.13 DT/$\overline{\text{R}}$, DEN, MCE/PDEN, ALE

5.15 The 74LS245 transceiver is used to buffer and control the direction of data flow on the data bus.

5.17 Refer to Figure 5.11.

5.19 See Figure 5.14.

5.21 Idle and active cycles

5.23 a. Load command register

b. Load internal registers

c. Enable DMA channel request

5.25 The I/O subsystem is responsible for the movement of data between the basic microcomputer system and the peripheral or external devices connected to it.

5.27   AX, AL

5.29   Read/write ($\overline{RD}$, $\overline{WR}$)

5.31   Instruction pointer and the affected registers

5.33   PIC (programmable interrupt control)

5.35   Data bus buffer, read/write logic, cascade buffer, control logic, inservice register (ISR), priority resolver (PR), interrupt request register (IRR), interrupt mask register (IMR)

5.37   See Figure 5.23.

5.39   Mode 1: programmable one-shot
Mode 2: rate generator
Mode 3:square-wave rate generator
Mode 4: software-triggered strobe
Mode 5: hardware-triggered strobe

5.41   By using the DEBUG input/output instructions for controlling devices

Chapter 6

6.1   Central processing unit, disk drives, keyboard, printer, display

6.3   Television or composite monitor, RGB monitor, RGBI TTL monitor

6.5   The Winchester disk spins at a rate of 3600 rev/min, which is over 10 times faster than the floppy disk, resulting in faster data rates and shorter latency times. Also, the head flies over the surface of a rigid disk, in contrast to the head in the floppy, or flexible, disk, which contacts the disk, resulting in mechanical wear.

6.7   Linear-pass and switching regulator types.

6.9   See Figure 6.9(a).

6.11   Yes

6.13   The microprocessor, RAM, BIOS ROM, DMA, interrupt and control logic.

6.15   The processor bus, the system bus, the internal I/O bus

6.17   Main system timing, CPU, ROMs, RAM, DMA, interrupts, internal I/O

6.19   4.77 MHz

6.21   This signal is used by I/O devices to cause the processor to wait.

6.23   See Figure 6.19.

6.25   This is the interrupt-controller chip.

6.27   The BIOS ROM contains the POST and the basic I/O program code.

6.29 U_{33}

6.31   See Figure 6.21.

6.33   *00000H* to *3FFFFH*

6.35   By decoding address lines A_{16} and A_{17} through IC U_{65}.

6.37   One parity bit per byte or row of memory chips

6.39   See Figure 6.28.

6.41   The refresh is required in the IBM PC because dynamic RAMS are used. Since the memory cells are simply capacitors, they must be recharged or refreshed periodically.

6.43   DMA is a fast data-transfer method that does not require the CPU.

6.45   The IBM PC DMA circuit is centered around the Intel 8237A chip. There are four DMA channels, but channel 0 is dedicated for memory refresh. The other three channels may be used to transfer a maximum of 65,536 bytes.

6.47   An interrupt-driven system is more efficient than polled I/O. Using this method the processor can start many tasks and continue processing until a device requires attention rather than having to poll each device.

6.49   Triple timer, triple parallel I/O port, keyboard interface, speaker driver

6.51 Port A is all inputs used for reading the configuration settings. Port B is all output and used to control the internal I/O devices. Port C bits 0–3 are used to determine the source of an NMI. Bits 4–7 are used to read switch bank 2.

6.53 000–01*F* DMA controller select, 020–03*F* interrupt controller select, 040–05*F* triple timer select, 060–075 internal I/O port (8255) select, 080–09*F* DMA page RAM, 0A0–0B*F* NMI mask flip-flop

Chapter 7

7.1 Paper tape
7.3 Retentivity
7.5 Iron (ferric) oxide
7.7 Electromagnet
7.9 No
7.11 Droop
7.13 Frequency shift keying
7.15 Twice the density of FM encoding
7.17 False
7.19 Track
7.21 Directory
7.23 512 in the IBM DOS format
7.25 During the preamble time
7.27 03*F*2 hex
7.29 Index; track zero; write protect
7.31 True
7.33 Trim the edges of a recorded track.
7.35 Band-driven; lead screw; grooved disk
7.37 Head switching is accomplished by biasing a diode matrix.
7.39 A special prerecorded diskette for alignment purposes
7.41 Cat's-eye pattern
7.43 Both the negative and positive indications will be the same.
7.45 200 μs plus or minus 100 μs
7.47 Amplitude modulation in the constant frequency pattern
7.49 Low-frequency output compared with the high-frequency output
7.51 Bent load spring resulting in insufficient load tension
7.53 No
7.55 Yes

Chapter 8

8.1 A simple computer input device consisting of switches
8.3 MATRIX (ED)
8.5 Serial
8.7 Cathode-ray tube
8.9 Voltage changes between cathode and grid 1
8.11 Blanked
8.13 262.5
8.15 Filament; cathode; grids; anode
8.17 False

8.19 Phosphor

8.21 True

8.23 False

8.25 Parabolic

8.27 Ramp (sawtooth)

8.29 During retrace

8.31 Phase-locked loop

8.33 Video information

8.35 Due to the difference in the gain of the electron guns

8.37 See Figure 8.29(a).

8.39 Phase modulation

8.41 Screen RAM

8.43 Character generator (ROM)

8.45 *B*8000 hex

8.47 Inked ribbon

8.49 A matrix printer that uses the heat-transfer method

8.51 By firing electrically charged ink droplets onto the paper

8.53 Laser beam

8.55 Status checking between two devices that communicate data

8.57 Plus and minus 12

Chapter 9

9.1 The main difference is the number of I/O slots on the system board and the capacity of the power supply. The PC has five I/O slots, the PC/XT has eight I/O slots. The PC has a 65-W power supply. The PC/XT has a 135-W power supply. The PC also has a connector for an audiocassette recorder.

9.3 a. On the PC, SW1-1
　　　　If ON = NO DISK DRIVE
　　　　If OFF = DISK DRIVE
　　　b. On the PC/XT, SW1-1
　　　　If ON = LOOP POST FOR TESTING
　　　　If OFF = USE FOR NORMAL OPERATION

9.5 If SW1-3 and SW1-4 are OFF, then the PC has 64K on the system board. The PC/XT has 256K on the system board.

9.7 If two floppy disks are installed on the PC or PC/XT, then SW1-7 = OFF and SW1-8 = ON

9.9 You must consult the manufacturer's installation manual and check the address switch settings on the board.

9.11 There are four cables on the PC's power supply. P_8 and P_9 supply power to the system board; P_{10} and P_{11} supply power to the disk drives.

9.13 The twist is used to identify the connector used for disk drive A.

9.15 The hard disk cable is similar to the floppy disk cable except that (1) the first hard disk unit (drive C) is connected to the connector without the twist and (2) a separate 20-pin ribbon cable is used for the data and clock signals for each hard disk.

9.17 POST stands for power-on self-test. POST is contained in the BIOS ROM on the PC and PC/XT.

9.19 The error message, parity check 1, indicates that a parity error has occurred during POST.

9.21 (1) Don't lose your composure.
(2) Show the customer that you will take charge of the situation.
(3) Develop and explain your plan of action.
(4) Don't blame and complain.
(5) Assure the customer.
(6) Go the extra mile.
(7) Show you care.

Chapter 10

10.1 The service technician
10.3 Run diagnostic routines; format diskette; copy diskette; prepare system for relocation; exit to system diskette
10.5 S for system unit; E for expansion unit
10.7 The time of the failure
10.9 Keeps a list of any errors in a file or printer
10.11 To protect the hard disk from shock
10.13 The adapter test
10.15 Sequential access
10.17 200 ms
10.19 No
10.21 The most significant bit, bit 7.
80 40 20 10 8 4 2 1
1 0 0 0 0 0 0 0 = 80 hex
10.23 True
10.25 Memory read

Chapter 11

11.1 Yes
11.3 Instruction unit, Execution unit, Address unit, Bus interface unit
11.5 Real, Protected, Virtual
11.7 Industry Standard Architecture Bus. It is found on 16-bit IBM PC/AT class and compatible (clones) computer systems.
11.9 PC/XT—DMA channel 0 is used for memory refresh. PC/AT—DMA channel 0 is used for 8-bit transfers.
11.11 IRQ14
11.13 IRQ2 is used to cascade IRQ8 through IRQ15 on the PC/AT.
11.15 CMOS RAM
11.17 The PC/XT uses switches for its setup. The PC/AT uses a battery-powered CMOS RAM chip to hold the setup information.
11.19 No

Chapter 12

12.1 Logic probe
12.3 Logic pulser
12.5 True
12.7 The digital storage oscilloscope converts the incoming analog waveform into digital data and stores the data in RAM. The data can then be displayed on the screen as a waveform.
12.9 True

GLOSSARY

access time   The time delay between the instant data is requested from the memory device and the instant data is received.

accumulator   An MPU register used for data operations.

accuracy   The percentage of error between the expected and actual measurement.

active high   The description of a signal that indicates that it is true (active) when the level of that signal is at a high voltage level (usually $+5$ V).

active low   The description of a signal that indicates that it is true (active) when the level of that signal is at a low voltage level (usually 0 volts).

adapter   A device used to expand the operation of a system (e.g., memory boards, modems, display drivers, etc.).

ADC   Analog-to-digital converter.

address   A value defining a memory location.

address bus   The multiple lines which carry the binary coded address from the MPU throughout the system.

alphanumeric   The character set that contains both letters (alpha) and numbers (numeric).

ALU   Arithmetic logic unit.

analog   Signals that are constantly variable over a range of levels and physical quantities (as opposed to digital).

AND gate   A logic circuit which produces a 1-output only when all inputs are 1.

ASCII (American Standard Code for Information Interchange)   The standard 7-bit code used for exchanging information between data processing systems, data communication systems, and any associated equipment. The ASCII character set consists of control characters, graphic characters, and alphanumeric characters.

assembler   A program which converts a symbolic code (ADD) to binary machine code (1s and 0s).

astable multivibrator   A circuit with no stable state. An oscillator or clock.

asynchronous   Not clocked or occurring at the same time.

BASIC   A high-level computer programming language.

baud   A unit of measure used for serial data communication. The unit baud represents 1 bit of data per second (e.g., 1200 baud is the same as 1200 bits per second.).

BCD (Binary Coded Decimal)   A 4-bit coding of decimal numbers.

Binary   A numbering sequence with 2 as the base. Only 2 digits are valid 0 or 1. This is used in digital computers where the values are similar to the *off* or *on* level of the electrical switches.

BIOS (Basic Input/Output System)   The machine-level program that interfaces the computer hardware with higher-level programs (e.g., DOS, BASIC, etc.).

Bit (Binary digit)   A single binary character (either a 1 or a 0).

Boolean algebra   The mathematics of digital logic.

buffer   A device used for temporary storage of information. This can be either a section of system memory or an integrated circuit used in combination with a data or address bus. Also used to supply additional current drive.

bus   A group of signals with similar purposes such as address or data lines.

byte   A binary word made up of a group of 8 bits.

CAS (Column Address Strobe)   A signal used to enable a column address in a memory device.

CGA (Color Graphics Adapter)   The format used for the display of low resolution color graphics. The resolution is 640 by 200 pixels with four colors or 640 by 350 pixels with four colors.

character generator   A unit (usually a programmable memory device) which converts character codes into displayable characters.

check sum   An error detection scheme used in ROMs.

clear   An asynchronous input used to reset or clear a flip-flop. ($Q = 0$, $\overline{Q} = 1$)

clock   An input to a digital circuit used for timing. Also an astable multivibrator or oscillator.

CMOS (Complimentary Metal Oxide Semiconductor)   A type of material used in the manufacture of semiconductor devices. Devices made with CMOS usually have lower power requirements compared with similar devices manufactured using standard semiconductor materials.

combinational logic   A digital logic circuit containing only gates (no flip-flops).

complement   The opposite, or inverse.

computer   A machine designed to solve problems using a systematic program of instructions.

configuration   The arrangement of a computer system that is defined by the nature of the work to be performed and the type of components used.

contiguous   Touching or joining at the edge or boundary; adjacent as in memory systems.

CPU (Central Processing Unit)   The main processor of a computer system. Also known as the MPU in a microcomputer.

CRC (Cyclic Redundancy Check)   A method used to test the accuracy of data stored using a combination of shift registers and exclusive-OR gates.

(CRT) Cathode-ray Tube   A vacuum tube similar to a television tube used as a display device for computers.

current sinking   The drawing of current by a device from a load.

current sourcing   The driving current from a device to a load.

cylinder   The tracks of a disk (floppy or hard) that are used for storing data.

DAC (Digital-to-Analog Converter)   A device or circuit which converts digital signals to analog signals.

data   Information used by a system.

debounce   The method used to eliminate the make/break bouncing of keyboard switches.

decade counter   A counter with ten states.

decoupling capacitor   A capacitor used to provide a low-impedance path to ground to prevent interference between circuits.

DeMorgan's Theorem   A Boolean algebra principle used to define the complementing of a function.

demultiplexer   A switch connecting one input to one of many outputs (selector).

DIP (Dual In-Line Package)   A container used on printed circuit boards for integrated circuits, resistor packages, and switches. DIPs have connection pins in two parallel rows which are generally spaced 1/10th of an inch apart.

DIP switch   A small set of switches which are mounted in a dual-in-line package.

disable   To stop the operation of a circuit or device.

diskette   A recording medium used for storage of information on a computer system.

diskette drive   A device which magnetically stores information from the computer system onto a diskette.

display   A device used with a computer to present temporary information to the operator visually.

DMA (Direct Memory Access)   A method used to transfer information stored in memory to I/O devices that does not require the processor for control.

DOS (Disk Operating System)   A computer program to control the operation of the disk subsystem.

dot matrix   A pattern of dots used to create alphanumeric or graphic characters on a printer.

dynamic memory   Random-access memory (RAM) that uses transistors and capacitors as storage elements. This type of memory requires a recharging cycle (refresh) every few milliseconds.

EEPROM (Electrically Erasable Programmable Read-only Memory)   A programmable memory device which can be erased or reprogrammed.

EMI (Electromagnetic Interference)   Electrical noise.

enable   To activate the operation of a circuit or device.

EOF (End of File)   A label used by programs to indicate the file being used has ended.

EPROM (Erasable Programmable Read-only Memory)   A programmable memory device that can be erased and reprogrammed.

EXCLUSIVE-NOR   A logic gate whose output is 1 when the inputs are the same (comparator).

EXCLUSIVE-OR   A logic gate whose output is 1 when the inputs are different.

falling edge   Synonym for negative-going edge of a logic signal.

fan out   The number of inputs that can be driven from a gate output.

FIFO (First In, First Out)   A method used for the sequential storage and retrieval of data. As the name implies the first information stored is the first retrieved.

fixed disk drive   A unit consisting of nonremovable magnetic disks, which is used for storing and retrieving data from the disks.

flag   A bit in a register that is used to indicate the occurrence of a specific condition.

flip-flop   A bistable multivibrator that can store one binary digit.

floppy diskette   A synonym for a diskette.

FM (Frequency Modulation)   A modulation technique used to encode data.

font   A family or assortment of characters that share a common style.

formatting   The process of writing identification information on each track and sector of a diskette.

FSK (Frequency Shift Keying)   A modulation technique which encodes digital information into two different frequencies.

gate   A digital logic circuit that performs one of the basic Boolean functions.

glitch   An electrical spike or pulse of a very short duration.

hard disk   See *fixed disk drive*.

hardware   Physical equipment used in data processing, as opposed to programs.

head   The portion of the floppy or hard disk drive that reads and writes the data onto the magnetic disk.

Hertz (Hz)   A unit measuring the number of cycles per second; pertaining to frequency.

hexadecimal   The base sixteen number system used on personal computers pertaining to a 16-bit base, which uses the digits 0 through 9 and *A* through *F,* as follows: 0, 1, 2, 3, 4, 5, 6, 7, 8, 9, *A, B, C, D, E, F.*

high-impedance state   A state when the output of a device is isolated from the circuit (e.g., Tristate buffer).

IC (Integrated Circuit)   A device that incorporates many electrical components on a single semiconductor material.

index   The point on a diskette at which a track begins.

inhibit   To prevent the operation of a circuit or device.

initialize   To set system or device variables to a known state from which to begin operation.

instruction set   The set of instructions in a computer or of a programming language.

interface   A circuit used to connect devices together in a compatible way.

interrupt   A command that pauses the processing of the current set of instructions and calls attention to a condition which requires processor intervention.

inverter   A logic circuit whose output is the opposite of its input.

I/O (Input/Output)   Referring to a device or devices that perform the function of receiving or transmitting information to or from a processor or controller.

JK flip-flop   A type of flip-flop with *J* and *K* inputs, which can be set, reset or toggled.

Johnson counter   A type of counter in which the inverted output of the last flip-flop is fed back to the input of the first flip-flop.

k (kilo)   Prefix with a value of 1000.

K   Used when referring to memory or storage capacity and equal to 1024 (1024 is 2^{10}).

Karnaugh map   A graphical method of representing a truth table. Used to minimize Boolean expressions.

LED (Light-emitting Diode)   A semiconductor that gives off visible or infrared light when activated.

LSI (Large-scale Integration)   An IC that contains thousands of electronic gates.

machine code   The machine language used for entering program instructions onto the recording medium or into storage.

machine language   A language used directly by a processor or computer.

main storage   Addressable storage from which instructions and other data can be loaded directly into registers in the MPU for processing.

mask   A pattern of characters used to control if a specific character or characters are to be saved or eliminated (ignored).

MCGA (Multi Color Graphics Array)   A display format used by the models 25 and 30 of the new IBM PS/2 line. These displays output an analog signal to the monitors, which can display up to 16 colors at a resolution of 640 pixels by 200 pixels. The MCGA is also a subset of the video graphics array (VGA).

megahertz (MHz)   Abbreviation for 1 million hz.

MFM (Modified Frequency Modulation)   A modulation technique used to encode data.

microcode   A code that represents a machine instruction when broken down into logic ones and zeros for use by the processor hardware.

microprocessor   A large-scale integrated circuit that can carry out programmed instructions. The instructions can be programmed externally or stored internally.

mnemonic   A symbol used to assist the programmer in remembering instructions, such as ''LD'' for the command ''load.''

mode   A method of operation; for example, binary mode, alphanumeric mode.

modulus   The number of unique states in a sequential circuit or counter.

monitor   A synonym for cathode-ray tube display.

monostable multivibrator   A device whose output will become active for a predetermined amount of time after it is triggered. Also known as a one-shot.

MSI (Medium-scale Integration)   An IC containing hundreds of electronic gates.

multiplexer   A device capable of interleaving the events of two or more activities without affecting either of them (e.g., address and data).

NAND gate   A logic gate whose output is a 1 whenever any input is a 0.

nibble   Half of a byte; usually 4 bits.

noise immunity   The difference between input and output logic voltage levels. The ability to resist electrical noise.

noise margin   See *noise immunity*.

NOR gate   A logic circuit that produces a 1 output only when all inputs are 0.

Op-code   A binary, octal, or hex number that indicates the operation a computer system is to perform.

one   The high logic level.

operating system   Software that controls the execution of programs.

OR gate   A logic circuit that produces a 1 output whenever any input is a 1.

PAL (Programmable Array Logic)   A semicustom logic device that performs Boolean logic functions.

parity   Error detection technique that counts the number of 1s in a data word.

Pixel (Picture element)   The smallest displayable unit on a monitor. Controlled by the resolution of the display adapter.

polling   A method of examining the electrical state of a device to determine the operational status.

port   An access point for data or information entry or exit.

POS (Product of the Sums)   A form of a Boolean expression that AND's together all ORed terms.

positive-going   The edge of a signal that is changing in a positive direction. Synonymous with rising edge.

priority   A rank assigned to a task that determines the order in which the tasks will be carried out.

processor   Synonymous with microprocessor.

program   A sequential set of instructions stored in a computer system's memory.

PROM (Programmable Read-only Memory)   A read-only memory that can be erased and changed by the user.

propagation delay   The time necessary for a signal to travel from one point on a circuit to another; also the time delay between a signal change at an input and the corresponding change at an output of a device.

protocol   The set of rules governing the operation of functional units of a communication system.

queue A line of instructions or items waiting to be serviced by a computer system.

RAM (Random-access Memory) Memory which can be written to and read from many times.

race A logic condition where signals arrive at the same time.

radix The base of a number system.

RAS (Row Address Strobe) In memories using dynamic RAMs, the row address strobe is used to refresh the stored data.

refresh The process of rewriting data periodically into a dynamic RAM.

register A digital circuit capable of storing binary data.

ring counter A type of shift register in which the output of the last flip-flop is fed back or recirculated to the first flip-flop.

ripple counter A counter in which each flip-flop is toggled from the output of the previous flip-flop. See also *asynchronous*.

rise time The time required to go from 10% to 90% of the value of the positive-going edge of a pulse.

ROM (Read-only Memory) A storage device whose contents cannot be modified. The memory is retained when the power is removed.

RS-232C A standard by the EIA (Electronic Industry Association) for communication between computers and external equipment over a serial data path.

Schmitt trigger A wave-shaping circuit that operates on switching threshhold voltages.

sector A part of a track or band on a magnetic storage disk that can be accessed by the read/write head.

sequential logic A logic circuit whose output depends on the present state of its input and previous memory condition. Logic circuits which involve flip flops.

shift register A register used to move data either left or right.

SOP (Sum of the Products) A form of a Boolean expression that OR's together all ANDed terms.

SSI (Small-scale Integration) ICs containing less than a hundred electronic gates.

static memory RAM using flip-flops as storage elements. Data are retained as long as power is applied to the storage device without recharging (refreshing).

strobe A pulse used for timing and synchronization.

synchronous Occurring at the same time.

three-state logic A type of logic circuit with three unique logic states: high, low and hi-Z. Also known as tristate logic.

track A band of magnetic data created on the surface of a diskette.

trigger A pulse or signal used to initiate an action.

truth table A table that defines all possible output and input conditions for a digital circuit.

TTL (Transistor Transistor Logic) The 7400 logic family of digital devices.

UART (Universal Asynchronous Receiver/Transmitter) A device used in digital communications systems.

unit load The loading effect of one gate's input to the output of another gate.

VDT (Video Display Terminal) The CRT terminal used to display computer data.

VGA (Video Graphics Adapter) A display format used by models 50, 60, and 80 of the IBM PS/2 computers. These adapters are capable of displaying 256 colors at a resolution of 640 by 480 pixels. The output is in an analog format.

VLSI (Very Large Scale Integration) An IC containing tens of thousands of electronic gates.

volatile memory   A type of memory that loses its data when power is removed.

Winchester drive   A type of disk drive in which the read/write heads do not contact the disk surface. Also known as a hard disk drive.

XNOR   See *EXCLUSIVE-NOR*.
XOR   See *EXCLUSIVE-OR*.

yolk   A set of coils on the neck of a CRT used to deflect the electron beam horizontally and vertically.

zero   The low logic level.

INDEX

ISBN 0-02-304241-9

90000>